Y0-CAS-578

HISTORICAL DICTIONARIES OF LITERATURE AND THE ARTS

Jon Woronoff, Series Editor

1. *Science Fiction Literature*, by Brian Stableford, 2004.
2. *Hong Kong Cinema*, by Lisa Odham Stokes, 2007.
3. *American Radio Soap Operas*, by Jim Cox, 2005.
4. *Japanese Traditional Theatre*, by Samuel L. Leiter, 2006.
5. *Fantasy Literature*, by Brian Stableford, 2005.
6. *Australian and New Zealand Cinema*, by Albert Moran and Errol Vieth, 2006.
7. *African-American Television*, by Kathleen Fearn-Banks, 2006.
8. *Lesbian Literature*, by Meredith Miller, 2006.
9. *Scandinavian Literature and Theater*, by Jan Sjåvik, 2006.
10. *British Radio*, by Seán Street, 2006.
11. *German Theater*, by William Grange, 2006.
12. *African American Cinema*, by S. Torriano Berry and Venise Berry, 2006.
13. *Sacred Music*, by Joseph P. Swain, 2006.
14. *Russian Theater,* by Laurence Senelick, 2007.

Historical Dictionary of Hong Kong Cinema

Lisa Odham Stokes

with contributions by
Jean Lukitsh
Michael Hoover
Tyler Stokes

Historical Dictionaries of Literature and the Arts, No. 2

The Scarecrow Press, Inc.
Lanham, Maryland • Toronto • Plymouth, UK
2007

SCARECROW PRESS, INC.

Published in the United States of America
by Scarecrow Press, Inc.
A wholly owned subsidiary of
The Rowman & Littlefield Publishing Group, Inc.
4501 Forbes Boulevard, Suite 200, Lanham, Maryland 20706
www.scarecrowpress.com

PO Box 317
Oxford
OX2 9RU, UK

British Library Cataloguing in Publication Information Available

Library of Congress Cataloging-in-Publication Data

Stokes, Lisa Odham.
Historical dictionary of Hong Kong cinema / Lisa Odham Stokes ; with contributions by Jean Lukitsh, Michael Hoover, Tyler Stokes.
p. cm. — (Historical dictionaries of literature and the arts ; no. 2)
Includes bibliographical references.
ISBN-13: 978-0-8108-5520-5 (hardcover : alk. paper)
ISBN-10: 0-8108-5520-8 (hardcover : alk. paper)
1. Motion pictures–China–Hong Kong–History–Dictionaries. I. Lukitsh, Jean. II. Hoover, Michael. III. Stokes, Tyler. IV. Title.
PN1993.5.C4S885 2007
791.43'095125–dc22 2006019322

∞™ The paper used in this publication meets the minimum requirements of American National Standard for Information Sciences—Permanence of Paper for Printed Library Materials, ANSI/NISO Z39.48-1992.
Manufactured in the United States of America.

For Nana, in Loving Memory

Contents

Editor's Foreword (Jon Woronoff)	ix
Preface	xi
Acknowledgments	xv
Reader's Note	xvii
Acronyms and Abbreviations	xix
Chronology	xxi
Introduction	xxix
THE DICTIONARY	1
Bibliography	573
About the Author and Contributors	589

Editor's Foreword

It is quite amazing that, despite its small size and population, Hong Kong has become so big in the field of cinema, exceeding the production of both Taiwan and the People's Republic of China, and ranking just after giants Hollywood and Bollywood. Admittedly, in earlier years, it was more notable for quantity than quality, but that is rapidly changing with increasingly sophisticated directors, producers, writers, and actors, and remarkable films that have won numerous awards at home and abroad. On top of this, rather than being restricted to their home market, Hong Kong films have gained a worldwide audience and contributed such genres as martial arts cinema to the broader public. This is an enviable record, and how it was achieved is an intriguing story.

That is the background for this *Historical Dictionary of Hong Kong Cinema*, which tells the story in the usual format of these reference works, starting with a chronology charting about a century of cinema history. The introduction then describes the progression, which was anything but slow and steady and included some serious setbacks, all of which were overcome while awaiting the next challenge. The dictionary section, however, is the most interesting, with hundreds of entries on significant actors, writers, producers, and directors, as well as businessmen, the more outstanding films and notable categories (martial arts, Chinese opera, and others), path-breaking cinema companies, and some of the Chinese terminology. The book concludes with a brief but useful bibliography.

This volume in the cinema subseries was written by Lisa Odham Stokes, who has been a professor of Humanities at Seminole Community College, Sanford, Florida, for more than two decades. Her strongest interest—and this should be obvious to any reader—is Hong Kong cinema, on which she has written extensively, including many scholarly articles but also film reviews, and is coauthor of the book *City on Fire: Hong Kong Cinema*. A historical dictionary packages the information in another manner, and one which should be relatively bland for a reference work, yet this one not only provides the essential facts, it also gives a feeling for the local scene and a taste for the passion for cinema that reigns in Hong Kong and among its numerous fans.

Jon Woronoff
Series Editor

Preface

To cover more than a century of cinema is a major undertaking. This book includes as much information as feasible, considering its length restriction. For those individuals, topics, and films omitted, apologies. At present, this book gives a comprehensive and detailed overview of the immense contribution of Hong Kong to film culture. Its artistry, intensity, excitement, and speed deserve attention.

Time and again, Hong Kong cinema has reinvented itself across the sweep of history and economics. The pattern set by two world wars and Hong Kong film's survival despite the industry twice being shut down remains. Its pioneer days and early film production were halted by World War I, but revitalized through investment following. Similarly, during World War II, as Japanese occupiers destroyed film stock for its silver nitrate, the industry again remade itself with localized product. Later, it faced the derogatory and dismissive labeling of its martial arts action imports as "chopsocky," a form and style later appropriated by Hollywood itself. More recently, the impetus of a crisis cinema impacted by events such as the Tiananmen Square massacre and the impending return of Hong Kong to the Mainland emerged, putting Hong Kong on the international film map as it experienced a heyday in the 1980s and early 1990s, only to suffer setbacks with the Asian economic crisis in the late 1990s and the severe acute respiratory syndrome (SARS) epidemic in 2002. The industry's uncanny ability to remake itself continues in a global context as the movies of the Special Administrative Region (SAR) have been accepted on the Mainland as local product and as Hong Kong stories are refashioned by Hollywood.

Compared to Hollywood product, Hong Kong films have always, with few exceptions, operated on shoestring budgets. Rather than serve as a deterrent, this obstacle has been turned to an advantage with an inventiveness and resourcefulness for practical problem solving that has created an original and refreshing cinema. Furthermore, Hong Kong films, like Shakespeare's plays, have something for everyone. Unbound by genre, a single film will include elements from all the classical genres, with something to offer the viewer wanting action, emotion, sentiment, comedy, suspense, you name it. As a popular art form, film is democratic rather than elitist; Hong Kong film is democratic to the nth degree.

Like many other film lovers, I grew up going to the movies with adult family members, seeing the films they wanted to see, films that were beyond me at the time, such as Alfred Hitchcock's *Psycho* and John Huston's *The Misfits* (1961), or being parked with an older child at the Saturday all-day kiddie matinee, where children ruled the theater and we were thrilled by creature features, mad scientists, insane comedies, and Sidney Furie's *The Snake Woman*. Those were heady times for an impressionable child, as was the resurgence of American cinema in the late 1960s and early 1970s to young people. Like many others, for me, college film courses and film festivals opened my world to international cinema, because where I came from, the closest we got to seeing international cinema was Claude Lelouch's *A Man and a Woman* when it played at the local porno theater. Beginning in the 1980s, however, I noticed my interest waning in Hollywood product, and by that time my hometown had its own established art house and independent cinema.

My interest in Hong Kong cinema among international cinemas began as I turned away from overproduced, formulaic, audience-tested Hollywood product and away from overintellectualized international and independent cinema to discover a cinema of heart. And tangible joy. The movies bring back the pleasures of that Saturday matinee, whether it's the eponymous Chow Yun-fat as a heroic gangster in John Woo's *A Better Tomorrow* series or as a likeable and lackadaisical immigrant taking a bite out of the Big Apple in Cheung Yuen-ting's *An Autumn's Tale*, Donnie Yen as a villain using a wet cloth as a weapon opposite Jet Li in Tsui Hark's *Once upon a Time in China 2*, or Faye Wong's pixie dreaming in Wong Kar-wai's *Chungking Express*; there remains the beauty of Stanley Kwan's meticulous recreations of 1930s Shanghai atmosphere, Peter Chan's sense of humor and irony in urban dramedies, Ronny Yu's flights of fantasy and horror, and Yonfan's sensuality. The thrill may be gone from Hollywood, but with the recent release of the old Cathay and Shaw Brothers libraries, it's back, as audiences can now experience the masculine ethos of a bare-chested youthful Ti Lung in Chang Cheh's *The Heroic Ones*, and Ge Lan's joyful rendition of "Ja-Jambo" in Wang Tianlin's *The Wild, Wild Rose*. Everyone can now share in what was previously otherwise pirated, passed around, or discovered in the United States in Chinatowns and the now disappeared Chinatown theaters.

The author and editor is responsible for the bulk of the writing of this book, but a trio of talented contributors, who took on entries according to their own expertise, assisted greatly; namely Jean Lukitsh, with a specialty in martial arts; Michael Hoover, with a knowledge of politics and history; and emerging scholar Tyler Stokes, with a comprehension of Chinese music and literature.

Acknowledgments

Many people deserve recognition for this book, considering film is a collaborative art, including not only those in this creative industry, but the critics, scholars, and audiences who respond to its contributions. First, we would like to offer heartfelt thanks to Mr. Law Kar, associated with the Hong Kong International Film Festival and the Hong Kong Film Archive for many years, for his rewarding scholarship, his input, and his willingness to closely read the manuscript and provide valuable insight and information. Second, the same to producer Terence Chang, for his encouragement, perceptiveness, and generosity. Third, Roberta Chin, for her kind assistance in providing up to date information. We would also like to thank Serene Lai and Angus Choi at the Hong Kong Film Archive for their assistance. Many thanks to those individuals and their assistants who generously provided interviews and illustrations, including (alphabetically): Peter Chan (Tairy Chan), Stanley Kwan (James Tsim), Tony Leung Ka-fai (Tom Chan), Karen Mok (Mrs. Eleanor Morris), Tsui Hark (Janet Ma), Anthony Wong (Doris Luey), John Woo (Brittany Philon), Yonfan (Joyce Yang), Herman Yau, Donnie Yen (Kenji Tanagaki), and Ronny Yu. Thanks also to Carson Lau for his input. Too, thanks are due to those who checked Cantonese and Mandarin throughout the text, specifically Jamie Wong Hei-kwan, Chan Yeit-hoo, and Qiping Shen, and Bess Lin for translation. And thanks to Ryan Law at the Hong Kong Movie Database and to Gere La Due for sharing information. And last, much appreciation to those who took on the daunting task of proofreading the text, Karen Longtin and Louise Tyler Odham.

Reader's Note

In order to simplify the text, individuals are listed according to their English names (if chosen) and the Romanized name they are best known by in Hong Kong, which may be in Cantonese, or may be in Mandarin (parenthetically, other names are listed) or Japanese or Korean, as the case may be. Names follow the cultural practice of last name followed by first name. For example, actress Li Lihua or actor Kaneshiro Takeshi, both surnames first. Actress Ge Lan is listed by her Mandarin name, followed by her English name, Grace Chang, parenthetically, and then as Zhang Yufang (her real name). John Woo is better known by his English name, John Woo, and appears first as WOO, JOHN (NgYu-sum, Wu Yusen), followed by his Cantonese name then his name in Mandarin. Sometimes individuals are listed by their English and best-known Chinese name simultaneously, as with actor Leslie Cheung, who appears as CHEUNG, LESLIE KWOK-WING, with his surname followed by his chosen English name followed by his first and middle name in Cantonese.

Regarding film titles, English titles and Chinese titles frequently have no relation to each other, so, considering such circumstances, the English title is followed by a parenthetical literal Chinese title in English, or an alternate title; then Cantonese and Mandarin titles follow, in that order throughout. For example, Woo's *A Better Tomorrow* (1986) appears as *A Better Tomorrow (True Colors of a Hero)/Ying hung boon sik/Yingxiong bense*, listing its English title, followed by the parenthetical Chinese title in English, then in Cantonese, followed by Mandarin. In most cases, the Yale system has been used for transliteration of Cantonese titles in English, and Pinyin for Mandarin. In most, but not all cases, both Cantonese and Mandarin titles appear (exceptions include Mainland films mentioned, and films noted elsewhere, secondary to the entry at hand).

Acronyms and Abbreviations

AFP — French Press Agency
ATV — Asia Television Limited
BOB — Best of the Best
CEO — chief executive officer
CEPA — Closer Economic Partnership Agreement
CGI — computer-generated imagery
CID — Divisional Investigation Team (formerly Criminal Investigation Department)
CTV — Commercial Television
DTS — Digital Theater System
EEG — Emperor Entertainment Group
FIAF — International Federation of Film Archives
FIPRESCI — The International Film Critics Federation Award
FPSEA — Federation of Motion Picture Producers of Southeast Asia
FSO — Film Services Office
HKADC — Hong Kong Arts Development Council
HKFA — Hong Kong Film Archive
HKFA — Hong Kong Film Awards
HKFAA — Hong Kong Film Awards Association
HKFCA — Hong Kong Film Critics Association
HKGIS — Hong Kong Government Information Services
HKIFF — Hong Kong International Film Festival
ICAC — Independent Commission against Police Corruption
MP&GI — Motion Pictures and General Investment Film Company
NYU — New York University
OBE — Officer of the Order of the British Empire
PRC — People's Republic of China

PTU	Police Tactical Unit
RTHK	Radio Television Hong Kong
RTV	Radio Television
RTV	Rediffusion Television
TELA	Television and Entertainment Licensing Authority
TVB	Hong Kong Television Broadcasts Limited
UFO	United Filmmakers Organization

Chronology

1841 British occupation of Hong Kong.

1842 China cedes Hong Kong Island's commercial and territorial rights to Britain. Treaty of Nanjing ends first Opium War. Unfettered access to the Mainland for the British.

1843 British declare Hong Kong a colony.

1850s Taiping Rebellion, many Chinese flee to Hong Kong.

1860 Treaty of Peking. British wrest Kowloon from China.

1898 British acquire the New Territories from the Mainland under terms of a 99-year lease.

1909 Asia Film Company (Shanghai) makes silent short *Stealing the Roast Duck* by producer/cinematographer Benjamin Brodsky (and starring Liang Shaopo and Li Beihai).

1912 Chinese Republic created, many Mainland Chinese immigrate to Hong Kong.

1913 Huamei (Wah Mei, Chinese American) Film Company established and produces *Zhuangzi Tests His Wife*, first Hong Kong wholly produced short.

1917 China enters World War I, film industry halted.

1922 Seaman's strike. Mingxing (Star) Film Company founded.

1923 Minxin (China Sun) Studios established, Hong Kong's first studio.

1924–1925 10 movies produced in Hong Kong.

1925 Minxin produces first feature-length drama, *Rouge (Lipstick)/Yanzhi*, starring Lin Chuchu (Lam Cho-cho, 1904–1979), Hong Kong's first movie star. Runje Shaw creates Tianyi (Unique) Studios in Shanghai; it produces the first martial arts movie, *Swordswoman Li Feifei/Nuxia Li Feifei*.

1925–1926: General strike and boycott of British goods; movie theaters closed.

1926: Hong Kong's first (and short-lived) movie magazine, *Yinguang (Silver Light)* published.

1927 Li Minwei's *Romance of the West Chamber/Xi Xiang Ji*, a martial arts fantasy, released in Shanghai.

1928 Hong Kong Film Company founded by Li Bei-hai; it revives the industry.

1930 Minxin merges with several other companies to create Lianhua Film Company (United Photoplay Service).

1933 Cantonese talking pictures born; the first film is *White Gold Dragon* (director Tang Xiaodan), made with Shanghai's Tianyi Studio. The movie is successful in Hong Kong, Guangzhou, Singapore, and Malaysia.

1934 Shaw Brothers, owner of Tianyi Studio, locate a branch studio in Hong Kong. They shut down their studio in Shanghai, and rename the company Nanyang (South Seas). A second Cantonese talkie, *Romance of the Songsters*, produced by Grandview (Daguan) Film Company, United States.

1934 Grandview reestablished in Hong Kong.

1935 Cai Chusheng becomes the first Chinese filmmaker to win an international film award, for *Song of the Fisherman* (1934) at the 1935 Moscow International Film Festival. Tianyi releases Siu Chui-yung's two-part Cantonese opera adaptation, *The Butterfly Lovers/Leung San Bok Chuk Ying Toi/Liang Shanba Zhu Yingtai*.

1935, 1938, 1949 A series of "clean-up" movements occur, aiming to improve the quality of Cantonese movies (as opposed to the more highly regarded Mandarin competition).

Mid-1930s–Early 1940s 500 Hong Kong features produced. Also, Kwan Man-ching's *Lifeline/Sang meng geng/Sheng ming jin* is the first patriotic Hong Kong movie released.

1937 Outbreak of the Sino-Japanese War. **August 13:** The Japanese invade Shanghai and occupy all sections of the city except for the foreign concessions. Three of the largest Shanghai studios close. Tianyi moves permanently to Hong Kong. Many Shanghai filmmakers flee to Hong Kong.

1938 Xinhua (Hsin Hwa, New China) makes Hong Kong's first Mandarin-language movie, *Sable Cicada*. Mandarin dialect films first made in Hong Kong. *Adorned Pavilion*, the first Cantonese martial arts movie, is produced by Jin Cheng Film Company in Hong Kong in Cantonese dialect, marking the start of Cantonese *wuxia pian* (martial chivalry films). By 1970, there were 514 of these movies, with strong regional and cultural elements.

1939–1941 Anti-Japanese films are made on the fly across China. Leftist filmmakers move to Hong Kong, including Cai Chusheng.

1941 The Japanese occupy foreign concessions in Shanghai. **December:** Hong Kong falls to the Japanese, who occupy the colony for the next three years, eight months. No Hong Kong films are made, and the Japanese burn film stock for the silver nitrate.

1946 Theater impresario Jiang Boying and others establish Dazhonghua (Great China) Film Company in Hong Kong, which makes more than 40 films and closes down within two years' time. Runde Shaw returns to Hong Kong and resumes ownership of Nanyang Studios.

1946–1949 With Civil War in China, Chinese film people migrate to Hong Kong.

1946–1950 Hong Kong becomes the regional center for Mandarin and Cantonese film production, remaining the center for Chinese film for two decades.

1947 Li Zuyong (Lee Ysu-yung) and Zhang Shankun (S. K. Chang) found Yonghua Studios.

1948 Many left-wing filmmakers return to China.

1949 Great Wall (Changcheng) Film Production Company established. First Wong Fei-hung film made, Wu Pang's *The True Story of Wong Fei-hung,* starring Kwan Tak-hing. **October 1:** People's Republic of China founded.

1951 Mainland border closed. Loke Wan Tho creates a Cathay branch in Hong Kong.

1952 Leftist filmmakers in Hong Kong instigate a crippling studio strike. Many are deported while restricted franchise is granted for elections to an advisory Urban Council in Hong Kong.

1954 Asian Film Festival begins.

1955 Cathay takes over Yonghua in 1955

1957 Cathay restructured and renamed MP&GI; Shaw Brothers Studio established in Hong Kong.

1962 Mao's Great Leap Forward, begun in 1958, leads to famine in China and results in 100,000 immigrants crossing into Hong Kong.

1963 Li Hang-hsiang's *huangmei diao* (plum blossom) opera movie *The Love Eterne* becomes highest grossing Hong Kong film of the era. The Taipei Golden Horse Film Festival (Taiwan), which screens international features, documentaries, shorts, and animation, but singles out Chinese-language films, begins and establishes the Golden Horse Awards, recognizing outstanding figures in Chinese-language cinema.

1965 MP&GI renamed Cathay Organization HK.

1966 Great Proletarian Cultural Revolution.

1967 Cultural Revolution creates a flood of refugees from the Mainland that continues into the early 1970s. Local labor demonstrations and student confrontations with Royal Hong Kong Police.

1970 Raymond Chow creates Golden Harvest Studios.

1973 Bruce Lee's *Enter the Dragon*, a Hong Kong–United States co-production, released posthumously, defines the kung fu genre internationally.

1975 Producer-director Ng See-yuen establishes Seasonal Films.

1976 King Hu recognized at the Cannes Film Festival for *A Touch of Zen*, given a special award for superior technique.

1977 The Hong Kong International Film Festival begins, screening Hong Kong and international movies.

1979 The emergence of Hong Kong's New Wave.

1981 The Hong Kong Film Awards Association (HKFAA) establishes the Hong Kong Film Awards, Hong Kong's equivalent of Hollywood's Oscars.

1982–1997 Six *Aces Go Places* action comedy series released.

1983 Tsui Hark's *Zu: Warriors from the Magic Mountain* released using locally made special effects with assistance from Hollywood technological effects.

1984 Sino–British Joint Declaration establishes a "one country, two systems" arrangement by which Britain will return Hong Kong to the Mainland, but Hong Kong will remain unchanged for 50 years. Tsui Hark and Nansun Shi create Film Workshop.

1986 John Woo's *A Better Tomorrow* released, starts heroic bloodshed trend.

1989 Tiananmen Square tragedy results in 1.5 million Hong Kongers demonstrating against the Beijing government's human rights abuses.

1990 Peter Chan and partners create United Filmmakers Organization (UFO).

Early 1990s Two hundred Hong Kong films made a year.

1992 Patten Reform provides for elected members to the Legislative Council. After completing *Hard-Boiled*, director John Woo moves to Hollywood.

1993 The Hong Kong Film Archive (HKFA) is established, to collect and preserve Hong Kong movies, program series, publish informative studies, and provide research facilities.

1995 154 Hong Kong films made. Centro Digital Pictures (digital effects technology) founded by John Chu.

1996 116 Hong Kong films made. The Hong Kong Film Critics Association (HKFCA) establishes the Golden Bauhinia Awards (Hong Kong's equivalent of the Golden Globe Awards in the United States.

1996–2000 Six *Young and Dangerous* films released, set Triad-boyz trend.

1997 The Hong Kong International Film Festival adds "The Age of Independents: New Asian Film and Video," including the screening of more independent film and digital production, and establishes the FIPRESCI (the International Federation of Film Critics) award for young Asian cinema, another way of recognizing a newer generation of filmmakers. **July 1:** Return of Hong Kong to the Mainland; Hong Kong is renamed the Special Administrative Region (SAR). **October:** Asian economic crisis hits.

1997–1999 Three of the planet's 10 wealthiest inhabitants live in Hong Kong. One hundred Hong Kong films are made. Box office receipts decline for the fifth year in a row. For the first time, a Hollywood product (*Jurassic Park: The Lost World*) beats local product (including Jackie Chan's *Mr. Nice Guy*) at the box office.

1998 Hong Kong experiences negative growth for the first time since Hong Kong films have been made. The Film Services Office (FSO) is established under the Television and Entertainment Licensing Authority to implement the policy initiatives announced by the chief executive in his 1997 policy address to promote the Hong Kong film industry. **August:** Second wave of Asian economic crisis.

2000 Ang Lee's Hong Kong-influenced *Crouching Tiger, Hidden Dragon* wins four Oscars at the Academy Awards, including Best Foreign Picture and Best Cinematography.

2001 Toe Yuen's *My Life as McDull/Mak dau goo si/Maidou gushi* reanimates Hong Kong animation style with local flavor.

2002 Andrew Lau/Alan Mak's *Infernal Affairs/Mo gaan do/Wu jian dao*, *Infernal Affairs 2/Mo gaan do 2/Wu jian dao 2*, and *Infernal Affairs 3/Mo gaan do chung gik miu gaan/Wu jian dao zhong ji wu jian* reinvigorate Hong Kong cinema, with good writing, acting, directing, and camerawork; *Infernal Affairs 3* opens on 111 screens, the largest number ever allotted to one film in Hong Kong.

2003 40 Hong Kong films made. **April 1:** Superstar Leslie Cheung (affectionately called "Gor Gor," Big Brother) commits suicide, having suffered from depression for 20 years, shocking fans and the film community alike. **December:** Superstar Anita Mui (the Hong Kong Madonna, a "sour beauty" of the film world) passes away shortly before year's end of cervical cancer.

2004 64 Hong Kong films made. Stephen Chiau's *Kung Fu Hustle* becomes Hong Kong's all-time grosser and is released in the United States the following year. **January:** The Closer Economic Partnership Agreement (CEPA) goes into effect, allowing Hong Kong films to be considered Mainland product.

2005 **Spring:** Hong Kong holds the Entertainment Expo, bringing together eight creative events, including the Hong Kong International Film Festival, the Hong Kong Film Awards, Hong Kong Filmart (a forum for industry professionals to network and make deals), and the Hong Kong-Film Asia Film Financing Forum (a way for Asian filmmakers to present production-ready projects to industry professionals).

Introduction

The *Tao Te Ching* advises: "In work, do what you enjoy," and Hong Kong filmmakers, from actors, to directors, to crews have all taken a cue from this advice. On-screen there is an enjoyment to be had by audiences, not despite but because of the filmmakers' hard work. And there is much hard work. Actor Leslie Cheung once remarked to *The Boston Globe*'s Betsy Sherman, "That's the attitude of the Chinese crowd. Even if you're sick, or maybe seriously ill, if you've not died, you still have to work." And if there is a common factor to Hong Kong filmmaking through its close to first century, it is that palpable enjoyment.

Hong Kong cinema began attracting international attention in the 1980s. By the early 1990s, Hong Kong had become "Hollywood East" as its film industry rose to first in the world in per capita production, was ranked second to the United States in the number of films it exported, and stood third in the world in the number of films produced per year behind the United States and India. The initial years of Hong Kong cinema, however, were characterized by instability that prevented the film industry from coming into its own, with problems ranging from limited investment capital and restrictive social conditions stemming from Hong Kong's status as a British colony to perennial water shortages that limited processing work to labor unrest. Hong Kong filmmakers during the "silent era" generally produced low budget movies for Shanghai companies, the latter city having emerged as the first "Asian Hollywood." The Hong Kong output was considered of lesser quality, although knowledge of its early movie history is negligible because few prints, scripts, and magazines from that time have survived. One account suggests that only four of more than 500 pre–World War II Hong Kong films still exist, the result of wartime Japanese occupiers melting prints to extract silver, Hong Kong locals discarding older prints, and the toll that Hong Kong's heat and humidity has taken on early prints.

Hong Kong's first motion picture, *Stealing the Roasted Duck*, was produced in 1909; financed by Russian émigré and U.S. businessman Benjamin Brodsky, the movie starred and was directed by stage veteran Leung Siu-bo. Brodsky and theater director Lai Man-wai would establish Hong Kong's first film studio, Chinese–American Film, in 1913. Lai scripted, and his brother Lai Buk-hoi directed, the studio's only production, *Zhuangzi Tests His Wife/Chuang Tsi Tests His Wife* (1913). Lai Man-wai was also featured in the role of the wife as women actors were forbidden in Hong Kong until the 1920s. Brodsky took the only print with him upon his return to the United States; thus, the film was never screened in Hong Kong. The Lai brothers would be the driving force behind Hong Kong's first film company owned and controlled entirely by Chinese, **China Sun (Minxin)**, founded in 1923. However, the colonial government's refusal to grant China Sun a permit to build a set stage led the brothers to move the company to Guangzhou, where *Rouge* (also known as *Love Is Dangerous*, 1925), considered Hong Kong's first feature film, was made. Meanwhile, cinematographer Pang Nin started Daihan Film Production Company in 1924, making films such as its initial feature, *Calamity of Money* (1924), on commission. When Hong Kong's 1925 general strike brought local movie production to a halt, Daihan ceased operations and Lai Man-wai moved China Sun to Shanghai. Not until 1928, when Lai Buk-hoi returned to cofound the Hong Kong Film Company, did Hong Kong filmmaking resume. In the same year, Tong Wing-yiu and Lee Wing-gun established the Hong Kong Film Studio, with Pang Nin at the helm.

Hong Kong's film industry received a shot in the arm when Renji Shaw (Shao Zuiweng, eldest of the now-celebrated Shaw Brothers, also known as C. W. Shaw) decided to relocate his Shanghai-based **Tianyi Studios** (also known as the Unique Film Production Company and forerunner of Hong Kong's renowned **Shaw Brothers** Studio) in 1934. Shaw's success with the first Cantonese-dialect talking picture, the opera film *White Gold Dragon* (1933), coupled with the Chinese government's opposition to certain issues and topics, made Hong Kong attractive to him. On the one hand, he saw potential markets for his films in the Cantonese communities of Southeast Asia and U.S. Chinatowns. On the other, he wished to escape Chinese government censors who frowned upon the studio's staple of martial arts fantasy films. Several film companies followed Shaw to Hong Kong, most notably **Grand-**

view Film, a company headed by Chinese-Americans Moon Kwan (**Kwan Man-ching**) and Joseph Chiu (Chiu Shu-sun), who moved their San Francisco operation to Hong Kong in 1935. Grandview broke new ground with *Lifeline* (1935), the first "national defense" film produced in Hong Kong, which set local box office records.

The number of Hong Kong productions increased dramatically during the 1930s; more than 400 movies were made between 1933 when sound was introduced and 1941 when the Japanese occupation began. "Talkies" offered the industry an opportunity to compete with opera for audiences long in love with stage performers and performances. No surprise, therefore, that the majority of movies were in Cantonese, the language of the vast majority of Hong Kong's Chinese population. An influx of Mainlanders in the decade's latter years, however, impacted the Hong Kong film industry, as most émigrés were Mandarin speakers who made Mandarin-dialect motion pictures. Fueled by a desire to stir anti-Japanese feelings, Mainland film veterans brought social concerns to bear upon the movies that they produced; perhaps the most outstanding of these individuals was **Cai Chusheng**, the first Chinese director to win an international film prize, for *Song of the Fisherman* (1934). Cai's film set a then-Shanghai box office record for receipts during an unprecedented 84-day run.

The Japanese occupation of World War II brought Hong Kong film production to a halt for the second time in two decades. Upon resumption in the postwar period, both Cantonese- and Mandarin-dialect films were successful with Hong Kong moviegoers. Cantonese filmmakers thrived by returning to popular martial arts and opera genres that critics ridiculed for their lack of quality and inattention to important social issues. Characteristically lacking direction, relying upon minimal sets, and utilizing prerecorded sound, Cantonese-dialect movies were often completed in a week and scheduled for one week-runs in theaters. About 200 of these "seven day wonders" were released each year from the late 1940s through the mid-1960s. The few familiar stars, such as Chow Kwun-ling, or the duo of **Yam Kim-fai** and **Pak Suet-sin**, appeared in numerous films, establishing patterns of work that continue to the present day in Hong Kong's film industry. Meanwhile, Mandarin filmmakers, many of whom were among the stream of refugees who arrived in Hong Kong from the Mainland between 1946 and 1952, offered Hong Kong audiences "***wenyi***" (literature and art). Generally more costly to produce, Mandarin films with superior performance and technical value, appealed to Cantonese-speakers even though they could not understand the dialogue. Most arrivals from the Mainland expected their exile to be temporary; thus, both financial backers and film artists viewed Hong Kong as a production site for Shanghai-like films intended for Mainland audiences.

Artistic quality and dialect were not the only issues dividing Hong Kong's film industry, as Cantonese and Mandarin blocs split ideologically as well. Before 1949, directors such as **Zhu Shilin** could make films like the comedy *Where Is My Darling* (1948), with its themes of gender and class oppression, for the Great China studio, as well as late-19th-century period pieces such as ***Sorrows of the Forbidden City*** (1948), with its narrative of preserving the past, for the **Yonghua Film Company**. Crossover of this kind became almost impossible, however, following the Chinese Revolution as Hong Kong studios polarized along political lines. Some filmmakers returned to the Mainland following the Communist victory, including Cai Chusheng, who assumed the reins of the People's Republic of China's (PRC) film ministry. Significantly, so-called message movies found an audience among Hong Kong moviegoers during this time of political flux and turmoil as local companies such as **Southern Film**, **Great Wall**, Phoenix, **Longma**, and **Asia Film Company** scored box office successes with the release of meaningful quality productions, among them **Wang Weiyi's** seminal Cantonese ***Tears of the Pearl River*** (1950), Li Pingqian's *The Awful Truth* (1950), Yue Feng's *Modern Red Chamber Dream* (1952), Zhu Shilin's *Between Fire and Water* (1955), **Tu Guangqi's** *Half Way Down* (1955), and **Tang Huang's** *Life with Grandma* (1955).

Postwar revitalization of Hong Kong's film industry would eventually depend upon the financing of individuals such as **Run Run Shaw** (the youngest of six Shaw Brothers) and **Loke Wan-tho** (who died in a 1964 airplane accident). Rivals for a decade, the Shaw studio and Loke's Cathay company (whose formal name was the **Motion Pictures and General Investment, MP&GI**, until 1965), controlled production, distribution, and exhibition of their films. The two companies operated similarly, signing actors, directors, stagehands, and technicians to long-term contracts and providing crews with modern equipment and sophisticated production techniques. Both owned theaters throughout Southeast Asia. Shaw Brothers even built a 46-acre facility housing multiple studios, permanent outdoor sets, dubbing and processing departments, and staff living quarters. At its peak, the studio had 1,500 performers and 2,000 other personnel under contract, conducted its own acting school, maintained a wardrobe of 80,000 costumes, and worked three eight-hour shifts daily.

Competition between the two studios stimulated industry growth and production quality. MP&GI's most productive period was from the late 1950s to the mid-1960s (between 1956 and 1965, over 100 films were released). The studio produced primarily high-quality Mandarin-language films, specializing in comedy, musicals, and melodrama, including box office record breakers and award winners. Melodramas and musicals borrowed from Hollywood but added distinctive Chinese sensibilities. Tang Huang's ***Her Tender Heart*** (1959) created a human drama characteristic of the best Mandarin melodramatic films of the era, while **Wang Tianlin's** Mandarin musical ***The Wild, Wild Rose*** (1960) is a musical *film noir*, with a femme fatale, tangible sexuality, and a cynical attitude. **Ge Lan** shone as a doomed songstress, and the film alludes to Georges Bizet's *Carmen*, Giacomo Puccini's *Madame Butterfly*, and Joseph von Sternberg's *Blue Angel* (1930). Director **Evan Yang's** *Sun, Moon, and Star* (1961) is a romantic and historical epic in two parts, set just prior to, during, and following the Sino-Japanese War, and based on a popular novel. Even in nonmusicals, musical interludes highlighted films of the 1950s and 1960s.

Mandarin-dialect Shaw and Cathay films were dominant in the Hong Kong culture of Cantonese speakers by the end of the 1960s; production of Cantonese movies fell precipitously over the course of the decade, falling from 211 releases in 1961 to one in 1971. Hong Kong moviegoers rejected hackneyed Cantonese cinema in favor of fare directed by the likes of the Shaws' celebrated **Li Han-hsiang**, whose ***The Love Eterne*** (1963) was the highest grossing Hong Kong film of the era. Efforts by committed Cantonese filmmakers to improve the quality of their low-budget films paled beside the Shaw Brothers' epics and romances and Cathay's comedies and musicals that dominated both local and export box offices. By the early 1970s, kung fu swordplay movies and imported Taiwanese romantic "weepies" dominated Hong Kong movie screens. Shaw Brothers, which had bested Cathay, faced a new challenge from its own former production chief, **Raymond Chow**, who opened **Golden Harvest** studio in 1970. Chow deviated from the Shaw studio model in decentralizing the production aspects of his firm through semi-independent "satellite companies" identified with well-known actors and directors. Golden Harvest did maintain control of distribution and presentation of its films through both theater ownership and exhibition agreements with other companies.

Golden Harvest had quick box office success with several films starring martial arts master **Bruce Lee**. Lee's films—*Big Boss* (entitled *Fists of Fury* for U.S. release, 1971), *Fists of Fury* (called *Chinese Connection* in the United States, 1972), and ***Enter the Dragon*** (1973)—released posthumously and widely considered the greatest martial arts film of all time—came to define the genre. *Enter the Dragon* was the first-ever co-production between the United States (Warner Brothers) and Hong Kong (Golden Harvest); it was the second highest U.S. box office draw in 1973 and set the stage for future Golden Harvest–Hollywood co-ventures, including the hits *Cannonball Run* (1981) and *Teenage Mutant Ninja Turtles* (1990). More importantly, Chow's films performed consistently well in Asia, spawning a distribution network of more than 500 theaters that produced 70 percent of the top earning films in the region by the mid-1980s. While Hong Kong's film industry, led by Golden Harvest, thrived for much of the 1970s on kung fu films, comedic talents and social satire offered moviegoers relief from a steady diet of martial arts heroes. In films produced for and distributed by Golden Harvest, **Michael Hui**, and his brothers Sam and Ricky, caricatured Hong Kongers' obsession with "getting rich" in *Games Gamblers Play* (1974) and *The Last Message* (1975), and made fun of the television industry in *The Contract* (1978). Moreover, hundreds of martial arts productions apparently left Hong Kong film audiences hungering for change, evidenced by the emergence of hybrid "kung-fu comedies" and the popularity of **Jackie Chan**'s slapstick rendering of legendary Chinese nationalist-patriot **Wong Fei-hung** in *Drunken Master* (1978), while Chan's meteoric rise to stardom led to a deal with Raymond Chow, allowing the actor opportunities to "make it" in Hollywood.

Golden Harvest's coming to prominence in the 1970s was only one of a number of Hong Kong film industry features during the decade. For one thing, film production increased as the number of Hong Kong moviegoers exploded; in particular, an emerging middle class, with relatively few entertainment and leisure options, flocked to theaters. In addition, Mandarin productions disappeared by 1980 as Cantonese-dialect films benefited from the crossover appeal of popular Cantopop singers and the box office clout of young stars such as Jackie Chan. Finally, a "**New Wave**" of young directors, many of whom had been raised in Hong Kong and later educated in overseas film schools, graduated from television to film as the decade waned. Technically proficient, socially conscious, and aesthetically multicultural, this group, including among others, **Ann Hui**, **Tsui Hark**, **Allen Fong**, and **Yim Ho**, foreshadowed both the creative explosion in 1980s Hong Kong cinema and the population's quest for self-identity in the face of the imminent handover of the British colony to China in 1997. Although genre classification remains a useful label for categorizing film, during the heyday of the 1980s–1990s, genre to some extent became meaningless since no matter what the genre, elements of all the others would be included in the same film. Hong Kong is a small and crowded place; people wanted to get out of their tiny apartments and socialize, seeing movies and dining out. Like Shakespeare's audience, viewers of all persuasions attended the movies, and the films needed to satisfy all tastes, so that people felt they got their money's worth—some action, some drama, some comedy, and some horror.

Director **John Woo** would receive international acclaim for his 1980s action films such as ***A Better Tomorrow*** (1986), in the process putting Hong Kong on the filmmaking map. Woo, in effect, reinvented the gangster genre (which came to be known as "heroic bloodshed") by combining elements from Hollywood Westerns and Chinese swordplay movies, the former revolving around opposites continually confronting one another and the latter involving the use of martial arts choreography. Meanwhile, Tsui Hark, called Hong Kong's "Steven Spielberg." because of his fondness for special effects, has mixed and matched almost every genre imaginable. Tsui's wire-worked, martial arts spectacle-fantasy *Zu Warriors from the Magic Mountain* (1983) and his gender-bending *Peking (Beijing) Opera Blues* (1986), weaving together ballet, pomp, satire, stunts, and tragedy, solidified his reputation as an adventurous and visionary filmmaker. While spectacle and speed, both in camera and footwork, became the cinema's trademark in the West, contemporary Hong Kong films have covered a broad spectrum, from gangster films and martial arts costumers, to lightweight comedies and meditative dramas. In fact, by the end of the decade, a second "new wave" of filmmakers had emerged, a group including **Stanley Kwan**, the team of **Cheung Yuen-ting** and **Alex Law**, and partners **Clara Law** and **Eddie Fong**.

Box office success and artistic growth notwithstanding, budget matters and fiscal concerns went largely unchanged during the "anything goes" years of the 1980s. Half of the Hong Kong movie companies operating in the early 1970s were out of business 10 years later. Therefore, name stars remained crucial for the Hong Kong movie business; companies would guarantee success by lining up a big star or a combination of them, say, **Andy Lau** (**Lau Tak-wah**, not to be confused with director/cinematographer **Andrew Lau Wai-keung**) and **Leslie Cheung** in *Shanghai Grand* (1996) based on a successful **Chow Yun-fat** television series. They would then presell the as yet nonexistent film based on the lineup to movie distributors around the Asian market. Getting the film onto as many screens as possible was important, since release would be in a set number of theaters and run as long as the movie made money. Without Asian presales, movies usually played for three weeks domestically and most did not produce a profit. Thus, Hong Kong movie companies toed the bottom line; films had to be delivered on time and be cost effective.

By the end of the decade, rising costs led the Shaw Brothers studio to stop film production in favor of television. Hong Kong filmmakers made some of the most imaginative films in the history of cinema itself in the 1980s. But neither they, nor the success of the **Cinema City Company**, whose six-film *Aces Go Places* series running from 1982 to 1990 broke then-existing Hong Kong box office records, could alter the basic financial and production structures of the industry. Hong Kong's movie industry contrasted greatly with Hollywood in such matters, with budgets ranging from US$100,000 to US $1 million, and production times shortened to seven or eight weeks from contract-signing to theater screening. Postproduction was generally out of the question; films were generally edited as they were shot and, even into the 1990s, were without synchronized sound as shooting without sound made simultaneous release in Cantonese and Mandarin easier. Subtitles, work for which very little was paid, could result in unintentionally amusing mistranslations. Stunts were filmed using harnesses, wires, and sandbags; absent were blue screens, second camera units, and computer technology. While Tsui Hark's innovative *Zu: Warriors from the Magic Mountain* gave birth to local special effects production, small budgets and quick production schedules generally precluded high-tech filmmaking in Hong Kong.

Hong Kong film credits could be approximate at best as actual production often reflected the work of a small number of individuals performing a variety of tasks. Producers involved themselves in direction, cinematographers and the occasional second unit directors were charged with handling outside shoots, and several directors might work on the same project. *Swordsman* (1990) offers an example of the potential confusion, with **Ching Siu-tung**, Tsui Hark, and **Raymond Lee** receiving director credits, and both King Hu, who quit the project before filming began, and Ann Hui, whose work was minimal, receiving codirector credits. **Stanley Tong**'s experience with his first film, *Stone Age Warriors* (1989), included work as production manager, screenwriter, choreographer, set builder, stunt double, special effects coordinator, props person, and makeup artist. Meanwhile, screenwriting in Hong Kong was considered to be of little importance; some films were shot unscripted. Directors shooting without synch sound would simply have actors count to 20 before the cameras and add dialogue later. Other movies were released without recognizing the screenwriter; **Wong Karwai**, for example, is said to have written more than 60 scripts but is credited for only 10 in the days before he turned to film directing.

Hong Kong film industry working conditions, even for the handful of Hong Kong film stars, would likely have been unacceptable for the lowliest of Hollywood actors. Working on several movies at the same time in different locations and going without sleep a few days at a time were the norm in the heady days of the 1980s and early 1990s. Superstar Chow Yun-fat completed most of his 70 Hong Kong films in 10 years, an average of seven movies per year. Illegal shoots were common as filmmakers worked without obtaining the necessary permits. In addition, shoots could be dangerous and dirty, as the hot, overcrowded, and unsanitary premises to which those working on **Ringo Lam's** *Prison on Fire* (1987) were subjected attest. Ann Hui's *Ah Kam* (1996) provides a disturbing visual example of the risks involved; a scene outtake shown as the closing credits roll reveals that **Michelle Yeoh** was seriously injured during a stunt in which she was pushed from a highway overpass onto a moving truck.

Historically, the portrayal of women on-screen as well as the few women offscreen in Hong Kong cinema bore a striking similarity to

Hollywood. In front of the camera, actresses functioned primarily as set decorations. Behind the camera, Esther Eng (Ng Kam-ha) was the only woman to make films in Hong Kong for many years, making four films between 1937 and 1939. Several decades later, director **Tang Shuxuan** made two films, ***The Arch*** (1970) and *China Behind* (1974), that are considered precursors to Hong Kong's cinematic "New Wave" of the early 1980s. Some changes were, in fact, evident by the 1980s as women moved into creative and decision-making capacities in the Hong Kong film industry. In addition, actresses such as **Maggie Cheung**, **Brigitte Lin**, and **Anita Mui** began receiving more substantial roles. Shifting gender attitudes even became apparent in the work of certain male directors such as Stanley Kwan, Ching Siu-tung, and Tsui Hark, as assertive female characters become one marker distinguishing Hong Kong and Hollywood film sensibilities. Towards this end, a small group of notable women directors emerged during these years as well, including Ann Hui, Cheung Yuen-ting, Clara Law (who would later move to Australia), and **Sylvia Chang**.

The business of Hong Kong cinema in the late 1980s and early 1990s was shrouded in mystery; it included the likes of a multimillionaire like Dickson Poon, owner of a chain of upscale jewelries and boutiques, who cofounded **D&B Films**, as well as Jimmy and Charles Heung, sons of a Triad organization crime boss, who established the **Win's Entertainment Group** (**Win's Movie Production**) that was second only to Golden Harvest in prominence in the early 1990s. For a time, some in the Hong Kong film industry set aside their concerns about the networks of money and people because it meant increased film output even as reported Triad activities ranged from face-offs, intimidation, payoffs, and extortion to death threats, armed robbery, and contract killings. Those affected by the state of affairs included actor Andy Lau, who was allegedly pressured to appear in Triad-financed productions, and popular comedian **Stephen Chiau**, ostensibly denied Canadian citizenship for alleged Triad connections. The deaths of movie producers Jimmy Choi Chin-ming (also martial artist **Jet Li's** manager) and Wong Long-wai were linked to organized crime. Director **Wong Jing** supposedly had his teeth bashed in for saying the wrong thing publicly. Meanwhile, producer Chan Chi-ming was connected to several episodes, including a foiled attempt to destroy the negative print of *All's Well Ends Well* (1992), when Mandarin Films refused to release star Leslie Cheung for

Chan's next project. Furthermore, Cantopop star and actor Anita Mui apparently underwent a self-imposed temporary exile due to an incident in a karaoke bar with a movie producer/Triad who slapped her across the face.

The industry's "on the fly" approach to filmmaking has, at its best, brought an exuberant energy and fresh inventiveness long absent from Hollywood, and, at its worst, led to unabashedly commercial gimmicks and uninspired cheap product. On the one hand, formulas of successful films are replicated, like the ***Once Upon a Time in China*s**, *Chinese Ghost Stories*, and *A Better Tomorrows*. Additionally, films feed upon themselves as when Wong Kar-wai's arty *Days of Being Wild* (1991) was remade as the parody *Days of Being Dumb* (1992). Copycats and knockoffs have been common; for example, a spate of gambling movies followed the success of the comedy-drama *God of Gamblers* (1989) starring Chow Yun-fat. Hong Kong filmmakers have also appropriated plots and concepts from Hollywood commercial successes, such as when *Back to the Future* was re-made as **Peter Chan's** *He Ain't Heavy, He's My Father* (1993). On the other hand, the best of Hong Kong cinema has crafted evocative stories rooted in character, exploiting nuts and bolts filmmaking through rapidly changing camera angles, employing collision editing for action sequences, and changing film speeds to visualize narratives.

Amidst frequent complaints of theater audiences and film critics alike that too many Hong Kong films are poor-quality productions with lackluster story lines, cloying dialogue, and second-rate performances, Hong Kong filmmakers have interpreted the idiom of film uniquely, often utilizing dislocation and displacement as well as irony and metaphor. Films have considered the former colony's triadic past, the axis by which Hong Kong, China, and Great Britain are linked, as a way to look for and understand an identifiable present. The oft-noted penchant that both the Hong Kong movie business and Hong Kong movie fans have for escapism notwithstanding, Hong Kong directors have tackled sociocultural topics both directly and indirectly, interpolating economic development and international trade, gender role and social class, East–West and Hong Kong–China themes in various ways. In the process, 1980s and 1990s Hong Kong cinema revealed itself to be a "crisis cinema" situated at a historic juncture where new patterns of language, time and space, place and identity, and meaning itself were emerging.

The anxiety of the return of Hong Kong to the Mainland stimulated filmmaking during those 20 years, in all kinds of allusions to the handover, both direct and as subtexts. The idea of time running out and change on the horizon provided the impetus for creativity as well as the commercial push to make money fast. However, the Asian economic crisis that hit almost immediately following the return has had a tremendous impact since. While Hong Kong missed the devastating experience of Indonesia, Malaysia, and Thailand, its markets were hard hit in October 1997 and August 1998 by speculation, driving down currencies and stock markets. Audiences became more choosy in spending their dollars, financing became scarce, films were shot on shoestring budgets and tight schedules, and the number of films produced declined. Video piracy began to run rampant, cutting out studio profits; Hollywood films battled local product at the box office, reaching 69 percent of exhibited films in late 1997 and far exceeding Hong Kong revenues from that point onward. *Titanic* remains the top box office grosser to date. Furthermore, the SARS (severe acute respiratory syndrome) epidemic on the Mainland in 2003 exacerbated Hong Kong's problems. The suicide of much-loved actor and Cantopop superstar **Leslie Cheung** on April Fool's Day and the death of the "Asian Madonna" Anita Mui at year's end further dispirited not only the entertainment community, but Hong Kong at large.

In the last several years, however, glimmers of a Hong Kong cinema resurgence have begun to appear. Three factors help explain the phenomenon. One, the PRC lifted restrictions on Hong Kong films in January 2004 through the enactment of the Closer Economic Partnership Agreement (CEPA). Prior to this date, Hong Kong films were not considered domestic productions and subject to restrictions that limited the entry of foreign films into the Mainland to 20 per year. Two, Hong Kong's participation in coproductions on the Mainland, pioneered in the 1980s and 1990s, has increased; in 2003, there were 40 films (out of the 91 Hong Kong films made); in 2004, more than half of the 64 Hong Kong films made were coproductions. Furthermore, U.S. companies still hope to use their economic clout in co-ventures with Hong Kong partners who have working relations on the Mainland. And three, the flexibility of the Hong Kong industry, both local and cosmopolitan, positions it to pursue the global marketplace through its distinctive style and outlook (genre blending and commercial interests); through production and distribution deals, including films on-screen as well as the selling of film concepts; and through the DVD medium (due to technological advance and the opening up of classic Shaw Brothers and Cathay Studios film libraries).

For example, distinctive Hong Kong style and outlook as well as an eye to the global market is evident in Stephen Chiau's *Kung Fu Hustle* (2004), a Hong Kong–China–United States coproduction in which the director/actor/writer/producer incorporated elements of the Hollywood musical bent into his expected Hong Kong flavor, leading film critic Stuart Klawans to describe the film as "tak[ing] its peculiar place in a now venerable line of Asian films that have reminded us of the simple, kinetic joys that American movies have lost." Despite references to *Spiderman* and *The Matrix*, the film is unmistakably Hong Kong in its sensibility, a love letter to films of old like *The House of 72 Tenants* (1963, remade 1973) to mention one, as well as Chiau's youth, growing up poor, and the locale, Pigsty Alley, characteristically Chinese, plays an important role in developing the flavor of the film. *Kung Fu Hustle* is the current all-time local grosser in Hong Kong to date, and a wide U.S. release played respectably in theaters stateside.

Furthermore, remaking Asian films stateside is a current trend. Martin Scorsese is directing an adaptation of a recent Hong Kong blockbuster, the Andrew Lau–Alan Mak codirected *Infernal Affairs* (2002), the first in a trilogy. Scorsese's Hollywood adaptation for Warner Brothers, titled *The Departed,* starring Matt Damon and Leonardo DiCaprio, will shift the landscape from Hong Kong to Boston and tell a tale of Irish gangsters and undercover cops.

Following the bounce back from the Asian economic crisis, Hong Kong has been confronted by the SARS epidemic as well as failed businesses, investment pullouts, and a paucity of good script writing. In a recent effort to lead Asian entertainment, in the Spring of 2005, Hong Kong held the Entertainment Expo, tying together eight creative entertainment events, including the 29-year-old **Hong Kong International Film Festival** as well as Hong Kong Filmart (a forum for industry professionals to network and make deals), the Hong Kong-Film Asia Film Financing Forum (a way for Asian filmmakers to present production-ready projects to industry professionals), and the **Hong Kong Film Awards**, among others.

The Dictionary

– A –

ACTION MOVIES. Hong Kong cinema is known internationally for its action, with films emphasizing fighting (whether martial arts, swordplay, or gunplay), and including physical stunts, whether including acrobatics, violence, and bloodshed or car chases and special effects. **Martial arts films** define Hong Kong cinema for most of the world, and hundreds of this genre have been made, from the fantasy films into the 1960s, to the **Bruce Lee** kung fu films of the 1970s, the **Jackie Chan** comedies of the 1980s, and the ***wuxia pian*** that reigned in the 1960s–1970s, including women warriors (***nuxia***). Throughout the 1980s, comedies with zany car chases and technology thrived, such as the **Karl Maka** series *Aces Go Places/Chui gai pak dong/Zui jia pai dang* (1982–1989), but from the mid-1980s, gangsters (Triads, Hong Kong's equivalent to the Mafia) usurped the screen. **John Woo** put "heroic bloodshed" on the map with **Chow Yun-fat** in ***A Better Tomorrow****/Ying hung boon sik/Yingxiong bense*, with a charismatic romantic hero with a code of honor. **Ringo Lam's** *City on Fire/Lung foo fung wan/Long hu feng yun* (1987) also starred Chow (Quentin Tarantino would cannibalize the plot for *Reservoir Dogs*). Lam's work, compared to Woo's aesthetic violence and code of honor, would be grittier and feature the dead end of the working class, and Lam has featured more car chase action throughout his career. **Kirk Wong's** *Organized Crime and Triad Bureau/Chung ngon sat luk gei/Chong an shi lu ji* (1994)**,** starring **Anthony Wong** and **Danny Lee**, would flip the attention to abuses in law enforcement, but deliver mixed messages, with a paradoxical repulsive and sympathetic gangster and cop pairing. True crime dramas have found a niche as well, often bordering on the horrific, as in **Herman Yau's** *The Untold Story/Baat sin* *faan dim jim yan yuk cha shiu baau/Ba xian fan dian zhi ren rou cha shao bao* (1993, also starring Anthony Wong). At the same time, **Tsui Hark** reinvented the martial arts period piece with his ***Once upon a Time in China/Wong Fei-hung/Huang Feihong* series** (1991–1997), based on the folk hero **Wong Fei-hung**. In the late 1990s, **Andrew Lau's** Triad Boyz films appeared on the scene, updating heroic bloodshed with lots of knives and slashing, as opposed to the martial arts with automatic weapons of Woo and company. **Johnnie To** also contributed with stylish postmodern character ensembles, such as *The Mission*, an action film with little physical action but lots of waiting (except for a few set pieces). Lau also used state of the art special effects and computer-generated imagery (CGI) in *Storm Riders/Fung wan hung ba tin ha/Feng yun xiong ba tian xia* (1998), a mythic fantasy period piece. Hong Kong action remains the way most people think of the culture's film production, probably due to the expertise of its stuntmen, action directors, and **wirework**, and their impact on Hollywood at present, in films such as *The Matrix* and *The Transporter*, courtesy of action directors **Yuen Wo-ping** and **Corey Yuen**.

***AH CHAN* CHARACTER.** Taken from the name of a clownish character, Cheng Can, in a TV series called *The Good, The Bad, and The Ugly* (1979), the pejorative term "Ah Chan" (pronounced Ah Tsahn) came to refer to country bumpkin Mainlanders, characterized by everything Hong Kongers are not—unsophisticated, naïve, awkward, lacking in taste and style, and falling into telling habits of the countryside. Portrayals on film can be humorous, as in **Chow Yun-fat's** performance in **Clarence Ford's** *The Greatest Lover/Gung ji doh ching/Gong zi duo qing* (1988) or **Michael Hui's** portrayal in **Clifton Ko's** *Mr. Coconut/Gap ga foon/He gu huan* (1989); brutal, as in the "Big Circle" thugs portrayed in **Johnny Mak's** *Long Arm of the Law/Saang gong kei bing/Sheng gang qi bing* (1984); or heartbreaking, as in the bewildered family of **Alfred Cheung's** *Family Light Affair/Shing shut ji gwong/Cheng shi zhi guang*, or **Maggie Cheung** and **Leon Lai** trying to sell Teresa Tang tapes in **Peter Chan's** *Comrades, Almost a Love Story/Tim mat mat/Tian mi mi* (1996).

***AH FEI* CHARACTER.** "*Ah fei*" literally means "those who fly free as birds," i.e., without family connections; the Cantonese term applies to rebellious, disaffected, alienated, and errant youth, and was first used to describe characterizations by actors and actresses such as **Chan Po-chu**, **Lydia Shum**, **Josephine Siao**, **Kenneth Tsang Kong**, and **Paul Chun Pui** in the late 1960s youth movies *Waste Not Our Youth/Mok foo ching chun/Mofu qingchun* (1967), *Joys of Sorrow and Youth* (1969), *Teddy Girls/Fei liu jing chuen/Feinu zhengzhuan* (1969), and *Social Characters/Fei laam fei lui/Fei nan fei nu* (1969). The movies came in the wake of the 1967 riots in Hong Kong and borrow elements from Hollywood movies such as *The Wild One*, *Rebel without a Cause*, and *West Side Story*, from knife fights and drag racing, to leather jackets and the wrong side of the tracks. For example, in writer and director **Chan Wan's** *Social Characters,* Peter Ko (**Alan Tang Kwong-wing**) is the leader of a high school biker gang called the Seven Bandits. Lisa is his girlfriend and the daughter of a police detective. After a gang fight, the father puts his own daughter in jail. The daughter submits and Peter vows to live up to his rebel reputation. The Cantonese title (male and female equivalents of "*ah fei*") implies the adult view of these youth, while the English title suggests the youth perspective and the movie's approach. All the kids come from good homes and the story points out parental neglect and lack of understanding. The story demonstrates the pull between duty and a less restrictive lifestyle. *Social Characters* was one of the last 1960s Cantonese youth films to show the betrayal of the younger generation by their elders and from the point of view of youth.

Ah fei characters disappeared in the productive 1970s, but were revived by **Patrick Tam** with *Nomad* (1982) and reinvented by **Wong Kar-wai** in *Days of Being Wild* (*The True Story of Ah Fei*, 1990) and **Lawrence Ah-mon** with *Arrest the Restless* (1992). All three of these films starred **Leslie Cheung** as the *ah fei*. In *Days of Being Wild*, Cheung plays a misogynistic albeit charming womanizer who is a damaged soul so emotionally needy that his fundamental motivation is to be loved, yet he does everything to escape loving someone himself. Wong sets his story of "wild days" in 1960s Hong Kong, and uses Cheung's voice-over, more like a voice-off resonating as onscreen absence, to set tone and story. Cheung's voice-over interior narrative describes, "I've heard there's a kind of bird on earth without legs that can fly and fly and sleep in the wind when it's tired. The bird lands only once in its life. That's when it dies." The bird, a play on the "to fly" of *ah fei*, both alludes to the genre and foreshadows the evocative mood piece Wong's film is and the updated approach to the genre. The film won five awards at the 1991 **Hong Kong Film Awards** (including Best Actor, Picture, and Director).

***AN ALL-CONSUMING LOVE* (1947). He Zhaozhang's** Mandarin musical *An All-Consuming Love/Chang Xiangsi* (1947) starred **Zhou Xuan**. Made immediately following the war, it is close to the Shanghai films that preceded it. It also comes the closest of the genre to approving of an extramarital affair. When her secret agent husband disappears after being called off to war, a wife (Zhou Xuan) is forced into the life of a disreputable lounge singer; meantime, in the husband's absence, his best friend can express his long-suffering love for the wife, to which she responds. Although the husband's eventual return is never doubted, the suspense lies in how the romance will be consummated. Though set in Shanghai, the film is also notable for using Hong Kong as a framing device and recording the dynamics of the city at the time. This tale of two cities also finds a parallel in real life. Interestingly, **Zhang Shankun** started as the film's director, but left halfway through the production, with He taking over to finish the film. Zhang had been charged with treason and was forced to return to the Mainland to defend himself.

ANIMATION. Hong Kong's animation begins with Tan Xin-feng's *Prince of the Big Tree* (1948), a puppet animation film using traditional string puppets (now lost). The twin **Wan Brothers** (Wan Guchan and Wan Laiming), who came to Hong Kong from Shanghai in 1949 and remained until 1954, working as art directors for **Great Wall**, mostly created backgrounds for live-action movies, and their story reflects Hong Kong's animation history, namely, animation as peripheral to mainstream live action features, and, for the most part, lacking an original local style. Animation was used mostly for special effects and it is only recently, in a now rapidly changing and technologically enhanced industry, that animation is reanimated. Hong Kong's second animation was also puppet animation, Huang Yu's *Princess Hibiscus/Foo yung sin ji/Fu rong xian zi* (1957). Puppet theater was popular in Guangdong province, and its story came from a popular folktale concerning the love story of a Sung dynasty scholar and a flower spirit. Also produced by Great Wall, more than 100 puppeteers were involved.

In the 1960s and 1970s, Radio Television Hong Kong (RTHK) advanced animation, and independent animation has been around since the 1970s, when the Phoenix Cine Club organized its first Hong Kong Independent Short Festival. Club participants involved many from Hong Kong Baptist University's School of Communications and Hong Kong Polytechnic University's Swire School of Design. Independent animation in Hong Kong has gathered strength since 1993 when the Hong Kong Urban Council (renamed in 2000 as Leisure and Cultural Services Department) revived independent shorts as part of the **Hong Kong International Film Festival** (HKIFF) and the Hong Kong Arts Center organized the first Hong Kong Independent Short Film and Video Awards simultaneously, both including animations.

In terms of feature films, Wu Sau-yee's *Older Master Cute/Liu foo ji/Lao fu zi* series (1981–1983) was based on a popular Hong Kong comic strip *Old Master Cute*, which was influenced by a popular comic strip character, "Mr. Wang," from 1930s Shanghai; the Hong Kong strip and the feature updated the character to contemporary Hong Kong. While the sequels were not popular, recycling backgrounds and repeating actions and plot devices, the first film was a commercial success with which audiences identified; it showed an everyman coping with daily life in urban Hong Kong and even introduced **Bruce Lee** as a **martial arts** teacher. The film won the 18th **Golden Horse Award** for animation. Almost two decades later, producer **Tsui Hark** drew on another source, **Pu Songling's** *Strange Stories from Liu Jai (Strange Tales from a Chinese Studio)* in *A Chinese Ghost Story: The Tsui Hark Animation/Siu sin/Xiao qian* (1997), which captured the Hong Kong spirit in the aftermath of Hong Kong's return to the Mainland. Four years in the making, the production involved numerous Hong Kong animators and showcased special 3-D animation effects. Tsui, since his *Zu: Warriors from the Magic Mountain/ Suk san sun suk san geen hap/Zuo shan shen zuo shan jian xia* (1983), has been fascinated by and proved innovative with state-of-the-art technology available. The animation also employed the stylistic effects that are signature Tsui, ushered in with **New Wave** experimentation. Although nominated for a Golden Horse animation award, the animated feature did not fare well commercially.

So it is not surprising that in 1995, when John Chu founded Centro Digital Pictures, a company specializing in digital effects technology, Hong Kong animation history began repeating itself. Like the Wan Brothers, Chu has worked mostly creating 3-D special effects for live action features as disparate as **Cheung Yuen-ting's** epic historical drama *Soong Sisters/Sung ga wong chiu/Song gu huang chao* (1997) to **Andrew Lau's** mythic fantasy *Storm Riders/Fung wan hung ba tin ha/Feng yun xiong ba tian xia* (1998), based on a martial arts action comic series by Ma Wing-shing.

The relationship between **television** and independent animation continues. Director **Toe Yuen**, writer Brian Tse, and art director Alice Mak animated an early-1990s series of comic books (cowritten by Tse and Mak) for television, the "McMug" series. Its success led to two feature animated films, *My Life as McDull/Mak dau goo si/Maidou gushi* (2001) and *McDull, Prince de la Bun/Mak dau boh loh yau wong ji/Mai dou bo luo you wang zi* (2004). The former won the International Film Critics Federation Award (FIPRESCI) at the 26th Hong Kong International Film Festival. In 1999 the festival added a program called "The Age of Independents: New Asian Film and Video," which included the screening of independent features and shorts, animation, and digital production. That same year, the festival had established the FIPRESCI award for young Asian cinema, another way of recognizing a newer generation of filmmakers.

Although there is a superficial whimsical cuteness factor in the *McDull* features (a young piglet and his pudgy animal friends interacting with humans), the satirical tone of the story has bite, and the stories incorporate puns, Cantonese slang, songs, and in-jokes. Like the Older Master Cute before him, the naïve and inexperienced McDull attempts to understand the urban Hong Kong experience, trying to make sense of a nonstop city with ambitious and often pushy people. Hong Kongers responded to recognizable Hong Kong personalities and could laugh at themselves. Furthermore, from the swooping 3-D crane shots of *Prince* to the small-scale detailed drawings of *McDull*, sense of place and accurate depiction of locale captured a unique Hong Kong style and sensibility. Such productions suggest a brighter future for Hong Kong animation.

APPLAUSE PICTURES. Director **Peter Chan** returned to Hong Kong from Hollywood (where he directed *The Love Letter* for

Dreamworks) in 2000 and formed Applause Pictures with Teddy Chen and Allen Fung, successfully producing the horror suspense film *The Eye*, an international hit, by the **Pang Brothers**. The studio is a collective of filmmakers dedicated to a Pan-Asian approach to filmmaking, and one of its purposes is to strengthen ties between Asian-Pacific filmmakers and the film industry by securing financing, promoting coproductions, exchanging talent, and expanding distribution possibilities both regional and global for Pan-Asian filmmakers. Based in Hong Kong, the company has associates in South Korea, Thailand, Japan, and Singapore. Applause also produced *Three* (2002) and *Three . . . Extremes* (2004), omnibus horror films (for which Chan himself directed an episode, *Going Home*, in the first). *Three . . . Extremes* includes **Fruit Chan's** *Dumplings*, Japanese director Takeshi Miike's *Box*, and Korean director Park Chan-wook's *Cut*. The company has also produced *Golden Chicken 1* and *2* (2002, 2003), and *The Eye 2* (2004).

***THE ARCH* (1970). Tang Shuxuan** directed, wrote, and produced *The Arch/Dung foo yan/Dong fu ren*, and it remains an overlooked experiment in **gender** politics and experimental film. A Ming dynasty period piece, the film stars **Lisa Lu** as a village widow who has undertaken an expected and traditional vow of chastity since her husband's demise; she raises a daughter and works as a teacher and doctor to the locals. When soldiers are billeted in the village, she falls in love with the officer (**Roy Chiao**), but cannot declare her love, much less act upon it. Instead, she arranges for her daughter to marry him, and the daughter leaves with him when the soldiers depart. The arch of the title is resurrected in the village in the mother's honor for her celibate propriety.

Lu Zhenyuan was responsible for the musical soundtrack and Satyajit Ray's cameraman, Subrata Mitra, served as cinematographer on the movie, and the musical interludes as well as the visual language represent the psychological states of the characters in a way unknown to commercial Hong Kong cinema of the time. Furthermore, Tang neither follows a dogmatic feminist line criticizing the widow's choice nor approves of the traditional ethical code to which she adheres. With the widow left alone, the viewer must decide, and the director allows the art to speak for itself. *The Arch* is a precursor of **New Wave** and independent Hong Kong cinema that followed.

ASHES OF TIME* (1994).** Generally regarded as **Wong Kar-wai's** most complex and difficult film, *Ashes of Time/Dung chea sai duk/Dong xie xi du* is loosely based on the **Louis Cha** novel *The Legend of the Condor Heroes*. However, Wong, in his characteristic style, takes the characters out of the context of the novel and makes the film his own. Shot by **Christopher Doyle**, the film won high acclaim in Venice for its stunning visuals. While the art house crowd was thrilled, those in Hong Kong who had come expecting to see a beautiful adaptation of their favorite ***wuxia novel were apoplectic. Complaints ranged from the plot to characterizations and the music. The film especially paled to general audiences when compared to the Hong Kong Television Broadcasts Limited (TVB) version of the book, which had all the plot details, dramatic characterizations, and a very Chinese sounding soundtrack with songs like "Blood of Iron, Heart of Loyalty," and "Great Wall Ballad," sung by top Cantonese singers **Roman Tam** and **Jenny Tseng**. Wong's soundtrack for the film was gritty, and gone in the film were all the characteristics of Chinese culture that stand out so much in Cha's novels.

Though the film had an all-star cast including **Brigitte Lin**, **Tony Leung Ka-fai**, **Tony Leung Chiu-wai**, **Leslie Cheung**, and **Carina Lau**, it was not a box office success in Hong Kong, nor was it a favorite among many of the local critics. The film has become the darling of many foreign film lovers, mostly those among the art house crowd. The action was directed by **Samo Hung**; however, most audiences found this did not matter since, due to Doyle's blurred camera work, it was nearly impossible to tell what was happening anyway. As the title implies, Wong's opus has a sense of timelessness and the plot is very unclear, divided into vignettes.

Ou Yangfeng (Leslie Cheung) ties the plot together as the other characters pass through his inn in the desert and recount their tales to him, including the drunken swordsman Huang Yaoshi (Tony Leung Ka-fai) and the ambiguously gendered Mu Rongyin/Mu Rongyang (Brigitte Lin). The film won numerous awards, including the Golden Osella for Best Cinematography at the Venice Film Festival, as well as Best Art Direction, Best Cinematography, and Best Costume and Make-Up Design at the **Hong Kong Film Awards**. It also won two **Golden Horse Awards** for Best Cinematography and Best Editing.

ASIA FILM COMPANY (Yazhou). Asia Film Company was founded with financial backing from the United States and operated from 1953 to 1956. Its manager, Zhang Guozing, had worked as Far-East correspondent for United Press International. At first, the company used the **Grandview** studio, but built its own next to **Yonghua** on Fu Shan Road in Kowloon. Tu Ongqian managed the new studio. The company's first film was **Tang Huang's** *Tradition/Chuantong* (1955), followed by **Hong Shuyun** and **Evan Yang's** *The Story of Yang E/Yang E* (1955) and others. Zhang Guoxing discovered actress Mai Ling, and starred her with **King Hu** in an Italian neorealist-styled film, *Shoeshine Boy*, which was never released.

ASIAN FILM FESTIVAL. The Asian Film Festival started in 1954, following the international recognition of the Japanese film *Rashomon* (1951) by Kurosawa Akira, as the Southeast Asia Film Festival, with the name change in 1957. It was organized by the Federation of Motion Picture Producers of Southeast Asia (FPSEA). After later restructuring (the federation changed its name to the Federation of Motion Picture Producers of Asia-Pacific) the name was again changed to the Asia-Pacific Film Festival, with that name currently in use. Member countries include Australia, Hong Kong, Indonesia, Japan, Kuwait, Malaysia, New Zealand, the Philippines, the Republic of Korea, Singapore, Taiwan, Thailand, and Vietnam. Between 1954 and 2002, 47 festivals were held.

AU, TONY TING-PING (1954–). Director and art director Tony Au was born in Guangdong province, brought up in Hong Kong, and educated at the London Film School. He worked as a fashion designer in Hong Kong. Director **Dennis Yu** brought him into the film industry as an art director on his film *See-Bar (Godfather)/Shi ba* (1980), and Au's association with **New Wave** directors was in the field of production design. He worked closely with **Ann Hui**, **Tsui Hark**, and **Stanley Kwan**. His directorial debut was *The Last Affair (Flower City)/Fa sing/Hua cheng* (1983), with striking cinematography by **Bill Wong**, a psychological drama and woman's story starring **Chow Yun-fat** and **Carol Cheng**. Cheng's character is traumatized when she discovers her lover (Chow) is a womanizer. Au's films have art house sensuality, explore relationships between men and women, and usually involve sad love stories and sexual content. Chow also starred (with **Brigitte Lin**) in Au's *Dream Lovers (Dream People)/ Mung cheung yan/Meng zhong ren* (1986), a doomed love story of reincarnated lovers. *I Am Sorry/Shuohuang de nuren* (1989), shot by cinematographer **Christopher Doyle**, starred **Carina Lau** as a kept woman struggling with guilt and self-pity as well as coming to terms with her lover's disloyalty.

Au Revoir, Mon Amour (Will Mr. Sun Come Back?, Till We Meet Again)/Hoh yat gwan joi loi/ He ri jun zai lai (1991) paired **Tony Leung Ka-fai** and **Anita Mui** as doomed lovers in a Shanghai-set Japanese occupation story, with Mui paying homage to the doomed songstress character with a strong and touching portrayal of her own. Au again directed Tony Leung Ka-fai alongside **Veronica Yip** in the romantic comedy *A Roof with a View (The Moonlight from Heaven's Windowsill,* aka *Love on the Roof)/Tin toi dik yuet gwong/Tian tai de yue guang* (1993), and again paired with Leung (the actor playing Japanese this time) and costarring with Tomita Yasuko in the dramatic *Christ of Nanjing (The Christ of Nanjing)/Laam ging dik gei duk/Nan jing de ji du* (1995), based on the memoirs of Japanese journalist Okagawa Ryuichiro's fascination with China. Beautifully lensed by Bill Wong, highly sensual and painterly, the film examines acceptable social practices and taboos, love and sexuality, and their costs. It also demonstrates why Au's work as a director is generally overshadowed by his work as an art director—the visual beauty of the film is so breathtaking that for some viewers it eclipses its story.

– B –

BAI, GUANG. Mandarin actress Bai Guang was known for her sultry and sensual presence on-screen and had a large male following. She got her start in Shanghai during the Japanese occupation singing the title song for *Peaches and Pears Fighting for Spring*. Her thick singing voice earned her the name "Standard Alto."

Bai was typically cast as the femme fatale, the bad but charismatic woman who causes suffering for her man and others, but sometimes her actions were not without reason. She was often shot in reclining positions and has been compared to Marlene Dietrich. In **Yue Feng's** *An Unfaithful Woman/Dong foo sam/Dang fu xin*

(1949), she starred as a downtrodden prostitute with a good heart; the story was adapted by **Tao Qin** from Leo Tolstoy's novel *Resurrection*. That same year, with the same director and writer, she starred in one of her classic roles in *Blood-Stained Begonia/Huet yim hoi tong hung/Xie ran hai tang gong*. The title refers to the husband (**Yan Jun**), a petty thief, forced into crime by his conniving wife (Bai) who lives lavishly, frames her husband, abandons her child, seduces men, pimps and hits women, and blackmails the family caring for her daughter. When she is not sexily singing, she has a cigarette dangling from her painted lips. In Jack **Li Pingqian's** *A Strange Woman (The Bewitching Woman of All Ages)/Yat doi yiu gei/Yi dai yao ji* (1950), adapted from Giacomo Puccini's *Tosca*, she played a Chinese opera singer who offers her body to a corrupt official to spare her lover, then plots revenge. Because of Bai's extraordinary performance, the Chinese title "The Bewitching Woman of All Ages" became her nickname.

Bai was often paired with actor Yan Jun, in the three films above, as well as in *Lexicon of Love/Fung lau bo gaam/Feng liu bao jian* (1949) and *The Joy of Spring/Ying chun lok/Yin chun le* (1951). She established Guoguang through **Cathay** in 1956, and produced *Fresh Peony/Sin maau daan/Xian mu dan* (1956), which she cowrote and codirected with Lo Chen, and in which she starred and sang. Bai had read Sima Sangdun's story *Lady by the Waterfront*, and liked the character Lin Baoru (Fresh Peony), an opera diva pursued by her warlord brother-in-law. She remarked that the personality and environment were similar to her own. Many stories circulated about the actress' exploits and carefree lifestyle.

BAI, LUMING (Christine Pai Lu-ming) (1936–). Actress Bai Luming (real name Xu Liqiong), a native of Guangdong province, attended the Tack Ching Girls' Middle School in Hong Kong. Interested in acting from an early age, she trained under famous opera actor **Sit Kok-sin** (Xue Juexian) and his wife Tong Suet-hing (Tang Xueqing) and performed opera onstage. Encouraged by her godmother, celebrated opera actress **Yam Kim-fai** (Ren Jianhui), she joined Tai Seng (Dacheng) film company in 1953. Her first starring role was *Now That I've Got a Daughter, Everything's Okay (Everything's Okay When You Have a Daughter)/Yau lui maan si chuk/You nu wan shi ju* (1955), director-writer Chiang Wai-kwong's Cantonese comedy that takes its cue from a well-known saying that favors males over females in families. Yam Kim-fai played a young woman who also disguises herself as her lost twin brother, and Bai played the brother's fiancée, with a lover on the side; Yam's husband also becomes infatuated with the fiancée, and the humor comes from the bizarre relationships. Other films included *The Wise Guys Who Fool Around/Chat lut laap fook/Zha ma na fu* (1956) and *Mother's Heart Is Broken (Mother's Broken Heart)/Ngai sam sui miu sam/Er xin sui mu xin* (1958).

Bai joined **Motion Pictures and General Investment (MP&GI)** in 1957 and starred in *Memories of Love (A Lovely Girl's Lovely Dreams)/Mei yan chun mung/Mei ren chun meng* (1958); she made 14 Cantonese films at MP&GI. In **Tso Kea's** *Memories of Love*, she starred opposite **Ng Cho-fan** as a smitten songstress who falls for him, despite their age differences. Since he is married, her mother defies the match, and she takes ill. A rich heir (**Cheung Ying**) proposes to no avail, so he shoots the lover. The movie was an adaptation of a Hollywood movie, Richard Fleischer's *The Girl in the Red Velvet Swing* (1955), starring Ray Milland and Joan Collins. *Bitter Lotus/Foo sam lin/Ku xin lian* (1960) broke box office records from the previous 10 years. Bai appeared in Mandarin features as well, including *Four Brave Ones/Dip hoi sei chong si/Die hai si zhuang shi* (1963), which won at the third **Golden Horse Awards**; the comedy *The Greatest Civil War on Earth/Naam bak who seung fung/Nan bei he xiang feng* (1961); part of the **North–South trilogy**; the melodrama *Father and Son/Yan ji choh/Ren zhi chu* (1963); and the costume drama *The Magic Lamp* (1964). Bai's last film was *Mistaken Lover* (1966). She retired in 1965 to marry a lawyer.

BAI, YING (Pai Ying, Baak Ying) (1940–). Actor Bai Ying (real name Wang Jingchun) was born in Sichuan province, performed his national service in the Taiwanese army, and began actor training in Taiwan at Union Film Company. His film debut was **King Hu's** classic **martial arts film** *Dragon Gate Inn/Lung moon haak chan/Long men ke zhan* (1967), in which he played the powerful villainous eunuch, copied by many others in many other films to follow. He also appeared in Hu's *A Touch of Zen (The Gallant Lady)/Hap lui/Xia nu* (1971) as the general being tracked down by evil eunuchs usurping power over the secretive palace guard and operating as a power unto themselves. The film includes a breathtaking bamboo forest fight, acknowledged in **Ang Lee's** *Crouching Tiger, Hidden Dragon* (2000).

Bai came to Hong Kong in 1970 and joined **Shaw Brothers**. He starred in the title role in *The Eunuch/Gwai taai gaam/Gui tai jian* (1971), as well as in **Huang Feng's** *The Angry River/Gwai liu chuen/Gui nu chuan* (1971), **Golden Harvest's** first feature, and **Lo Wei's** *The Invincible Eight/Tin lung baat cheung/Tian long ba jiang* (1971). By 1977, the actor had appeared in 20 features, primarily martial arts films, and had become known for his cold stare. He was prominent in other King Hu films, especially *The Fate of Lee Khan/Ying chun gok ji fung boh/Ying chun ge zhi feng bo* (1973) and *The Valiant Ones/Chung lit tiu/Zhong lie tu* (1975). In the former, Bai played the scholar-swordsman and spy-rebel working against the Mongol Lee Khan and his sister, intent on intercepting a map with rebel troop whereabouts, to assist the five heroines. In the latter, set during the Ming dynasty in the 16th century, he played a resistance swordfighter, half of a taciturn couple, his knight-lady played by **Hsu Feng**, who assists an unorthodox soldier (**Roy Chiao**) in defeating Japanese pirates.

The actor starred in Taiwan's first 3-D feature, *Dynasty* (1977), for which he won the best supporting actor award at the **Golden Horse Awards**. He appeared in another Taiwan production, *Waiting for the East Wind* (1978), and returned to Hong Kong for Peter Yung's *The System/Hang kwai/Hang gui* (1979), in which he played an incorruptible policeman whose inflexibility leads to tragedy. Bai also was cast as a gang leader in **Dennis Yu's** contemporary action film *See Bar/Shi ba* (1980), opposite **Chow Yun-fat**.

BAO, FANG (Baau Fong) (1922–). Actor and director Bao Fang was born in Nanchang and was a student of engineering and law at Guangxi University, where he performed in many plays, including Cao Yu's *Sunrise*. He joined **Yonghua** in 1948, and his film debut was in **Bu Wancang's** Mandarin period history *The Soul of China/Guohun* (1948). The epic film was the studio's first production, made with a large budget and cast, intent on transplanting the Mainland's style to Hong Kong. Set in the Sung dynasty, the story celebrates the loyalty of imperial secretary and prime minister Wen Tianxing, a martyr who fought against treachery and the Mongols.

Over the next 30 years, Bao appeared in more than 50 films at Yonghua, **Great Wall**, and **Feng Huang**, including **Zhu Shilin's** period history ***Sorrows of the Forbidden City**/Qinggong mishi* (1948) and his family dramas *Year In, Year Out* (1955) and *A Widow's Tears* (1956). *Sorrows of the Forbidden City* was shown in major Chinese cities in 1950, and was condemned by Mao Zedong as reactionary; in 1976, that label was lifted. Although the film was criticized by some for its distortion of history, it was also praised for its acting, art direction, and camerawork. In *Year In, Year Out/Yat nin jin gai/Yi nian zhi ji* Bao played one of two brothers who share the same home with their mother and respective families; the brothers' financial situations differ, and they constantly quarrel over money. The film won one of the excellence of film awards presented by China's Ministry of Culture.

With actor **Chen Jingbo**, Bao codirected the Mandarin drama *Girl, Age 15 (A Teenage Girl)/Yau lui choh cheung shing/You nu chu chang cheng* (1960) and the mystery *Qu Yuan (Chu Yuan)/Wat Yuen/Qu Yuan* (1977). He directed 18 films for Feng Huang, including the comedy *The Reluctant Bridegroom/Ga sai shing lung/Jia xu cheng long* (1964). He appeared as one of the elders in **Ann Hui's** ***Summer Snow**/Nui Yan Sei Sap /Nu ren si shi* (1995). He also acted in **television** and dubbed more than 100 movies.

BEE, KENNY (Chung Chun-to) (1953–). Born in Hong Kong, actor and singer Kenny Bee began in the entertainment industry in the mid-1970s when he formed a rock group with singer/actor **Alan Tam** and producer/actor Anthony Chan Yau and others. They entered the All Hong Kong Singing Contest as "The Losers," won first place, and changed their name to "The Wynners." Their lyrics mixed Cantonese and English and they became very popular, making several teen movies. The band broke up in the early 1980s, with both Bee and Tam pursuing solo careers as singers and actors, and Bee making films in Taiwan and Hong Kong.

Bee appeared in close to 80 movies, most of them made in the 1980s–1990s. Bee's casual style and pleasant looks led him to being cast as romantic leads. He stands out in **Ann Hui's** ghost story *The Spooky Bunch/Chong do jing/Zhuang dao zheng* (1980), in which he costarred with **Josephine Siao**, and in **Tsui Hark's** bittersweet romance *Shanghai Blues* (1984), in which he costarred with **Sylvia**

Chang and **Sally Yeh**. Equally at home in drama and comedy, Bee directed and costarred (with **Chow Yun-fat**) in the battle of the sexes comedy *100 Ways to Murder Your Wife/Sat chai yee yan cho/Sha qi er ren zu* (1986), in which he played **Anita Mui's** henpecked husband. He also appeared as an alcoholic chef who has lost his sense of taste in Tsui's *The Chinese Feast/Gam yuk moon tong/Jin yu man tang* (1995).

More recently, Bee has participated in Wynner reunion concerts, appeared in television serials, and acted in a handful of films.

BEIJING (PEKING) OPERA FILMS. *See* CHINESE OPERA FILMS.

***A BETTER TOMORROW* SERIES.** A trilogy of films that established the "heroic bloodshed" genre in Hong Kong, the "better tomorrow" films (literally, "True Colors of a Hero") were a collaborative effort between **John Woo** and **Tsui Hark** (Woo directed the first two and produced the third; Tsui produced the first two and directed the third). The series reinvigorated the careers of John Woo and the films' star, **Chow Yun-fat**, and the first film will indelibly be linked to director and actor. All three movies share the following characteristics: a romanticized hero and male bonding, that hero being flawed but with a strong moral code; an underworld (Triad) element; and over-the-top action and gunplay. Director Stanley Tong explains: "In Chinese there are four main things that we have to know: *Zhong* is loyalty; *xiao* is being very good to your parents; and *ren* is being good to people, forgiving them even when they're trying to harm you. The last thing Woo always puts into his movies. . . . It's *yi*. *Yi* means when you are a friend, you can give up your life for a friend." [Tong quotation from *Premiere* magazine, interviewed by Andy Webster.] Woo's characters draw upon these basic ideals, and the code of honor by which they live and die, and which dignifies them, is based on Confucian values of mutual dependence and nonacquisitiveness, the Christian values of compassion and self-sacrifice, and chivalric swordsman values of courage and loyalty.

Woo used the bare bones plot of **Patrick Lung Gong's** *The Story of a Discharged Prisoner* (1967) as a basis for the story of *A Better Tomorrow (True Colors of a Hero) Ying hung boon sik/Yingxiong bense* (1986), which allowed him to explore values among his characters and enrich the characterizations. He also borrowed the look of Alain Delon's Jeff from Jean-Pierre Melville's *Le Samourai*; Chow Yun-fat's character Mark wears a similar trench coat and Delon sunglasses (his character John, aka Jeff, in *The Killer* [1989] appears stylishly clothed in Armani). This film drew on Woo's previous experience in **martial arts** actioners, becoming the model for the martial arts with automatic weapons genre, as well as establishing for Woo a code of honor that provides a morality for his film world and inventing his films as urban morality plays. His characters, whether hit men, Triad muscle, undercover cops, or detectives, serve as romanticized figures who lament the loss of traditional values, and consequently their own place, in the world.

In *A Better Tomorrow*, Chow plays Mark Gor, a Triad hit man with heart injured on the job and betrayed by the new company man. He remains loyal to the old boss and his "blood brother" Ho (**Ti Lung**), who in turn has a brother Kit (**Leslie Cheung**) who is a detective fighting the Triads. Although Ti Lung's character was supposed to be the lead (and the actor delivered a powerful and nuanced performance), Chow's warmth and humor as well as dignity and cool mesmerized audiences, and Chow stole the show. The influence of the film on Hong Kong youth and the exposure of Hong Kong film internationally due to this movie and *The Killer* that followed should not be underestimated. The film broke box office records in Hong Kong and throughout Asia and led to male teens taking to the humid streets of Hong Kong in dusters and shades, dressed like Mark Gor.

The popularity of the first film demanded a second, and since Chow Yun-fat's character sacrificed himself in the first, in the sequel, *A Better Tomorrow 2* (1987), he was reintroduced as Ken, twin brother to the deceased character. Ti Lung and Leslie Cheung reappeared as well; **Dean Shek Ten** was introduced as a retired Triad boss needing Chow's help. Even Mark's trademark duster and arsenal was reintroduced into the plot. The third film, *A Better Tomorrow 3: Love and Death in Saigon* (1989), is a prequel to the first. Set in Hong Kong and Vietnam, the story narrates how Mark became the heroic gangster whose masculine image audiences idolized. Tsui added **Tony Leung Ka-fai** and **Anita Mui** to the cast, the former as Mark's cousin and the latter as the woman who will teach Mark his trade. All of the signatures of the character, from his distinctive shades and duster, to shooting with two guns and facing off with the villains, come from her character. The film allowed Tsui to introduce a strong female protagonist and play around with **gender**, a favorite of the director; it also allowed him not only to explore issues of the Vietnam War (from his childhood) but to relate those issues to the impending return of Hong Kong to the Mainland. The following year, Woo would direct his Vietnam saga, *Bullet in the Head* (1990).

***THE BLACK ROSE* (1965).** Directed by **Chor Yuen** (among his best **action**) and starring **Nam Hung** and **Chan Po-chu**, *The Black Rose/Hak mui gwai/Hei mei gui* started a brief mid-1960s phenomenon of fantasy entertainment with spies, secret weapons, and gadgetry. The movie and its sequel *Who Is That Rose?* (1966) were Hong Kong's answer to the James Bond movies, with Alfred Hitchcock's *To Catch a Thief* (1955) thrown in. The plot of the first combined insurance fraud, spies, an amoral drug dealer (Li Pengfei), a jewel thief, an acrobatic swordsman, and a stoical inspector (**Patrick Tse Yin**). Its comic book quality derived from its source material, Oriole, the Flying Heroine, a popular pulp fiction series. Loosely connected action, set pieces with choreographed fights, car chases, and games of cat and mouse were linked by verbal repartee, an enjoyable lifestyle, and pairing with a bimbo male love interest, the inspector. The fad disappeared in the early 1970s, but was revived with homage pastiches *92 Legendary la Rose Noire/92 Hak mooi gwai dui hak mooi gwai/92 Hei mei gui dui hei mei gui*, directed and written by **Jeff Lau**; *Rose, Rose I Love You* (1993), directed by Jacky Pang and produced by Jeff Lau; and *Black Rose 2 (Black Rose Befriends Golden Tulip)/Hak muigwai yi git gam laan/Hei mei gui yi jie jin lan* (1997), directed by Jeff Lau and **Corey Yuen Kwai**. The approach also had an influence on movies like **Johnnie To's** *Heroic Trio/Dung fong saam hap/Dong fang san xia* and *Executioners/Yin doi ho hap chuen/Xian dai hao xia chuan* (both 1993). **Donnie Yen's** giddy action spoof *Protégé de la Rose Noire/Gin chap hak moooi gwai/Jian xi hei mei gui* (2004) combined Lau's approach with action filmmaking and capitalized on the popularity of the **Twins** (Gillian Chung and Charlene Choi); in this latest version **Teresa Mo** plays "Black Rose." The opening credits are both a throwback to the days of Chan Po-cho with an update to the *Powerpuff Girls* and *Charlie's Angels* (the movies and the TV series).

***BLOOD IN THE SNOW* (1956).** *Blood in the Snow (Red Bloom in the Snow)/Suet lee hung/Xue lihong* is director **Li Han-hsiang's** directorial debut (he was also the writer). A behind-the-scenes story of a small-time folk opera troupe and other performers in Northern China in the 1930s, the movie is a melodrama that helped set the pace for songs integrated into the story as the characters stage their performances. **Li Lihua** plays Xue Lihong, a fiery folk-opera singer and jealous lover trying to win back her former lover, Jin Hu, a strongman (**Lo Wei**) by setting up her rival, Hehua (**Ge Lan**), with a rich man. She is thwarted by the troupe owner (**Wang Yuanlong**), another jealous lover who has lived off her for years. Reforming at the last minute, she nonetheless meets the fate of many doomed songstresses of this genre. The movie is well crafted, with all major characters introduced in a chain of intersecting actions. A background of authentic street life, markets, and courtyards, along with lively renditions of Beijing folk songs, capture the shades of Northern Chinese folk culture, further enhanced by a strong ensemble supporting cast of Mandarin actors of Northern origin, including the young **King Hu**.

***THE BLUE AND THE BLACK* (1966). Tao Qin's** *The Blue and the Black/Lan yu hei, shang ji (1); Lan yu hei, xia ji (2),* starred **Lin Dai** and **Kwan Shan**, and it won Best Picture at the 13th **Asian Film Festival** and Best Supporting Actress for Angela Yu Chien at the fifth **Golden Horse Awards** (also an honorable mention for dramatic feature there). A romantic epic in two parts, the movie had to be completed with a stand-in after Lin Dai committed suicide before the second was finished. She played a victimized woman caught in star-crossed romances. Part one was set in Tianjin during the Sino–Japanese War, dramatizing the romance between two orphans (Lin Dai and Kwan Shan) brought up by foster families who naturally oppose their union. In part two, she played the misunderstood and self-sacrificing songstress who warms up to the Japanese while her lover (Kwan Shan) is away at war.

BLUE BIRD FILM COMPANY. Although short-lived, only existing from 1982 to 1984, Blue Bird Film, founded by Xia Meng and other filmmakers, made three films, two of which won the Best Film Award at the **Hong Kong Film Awards**. Those films, made by **New Wave**

filmmakers **Ann Hui** and **Yim Ho**, are, respectively, *Boat People/Touben nuhai* (1982) and *Homecoming (The Years Flow by Like Water)/Si shui liu nian* (1984).

BO HO FILMS PRODUCTION COMPANY LTD. Martial arts actor and director **Samo Hung** founded Bo Ho, a subsidiary of **Golden Harvest**, in 1980. Primarily active during the 1980s, the company produced more than 40 films and became known for its ensemble cast filmmaking, as evidenced in its first film, the supernatural **kung fu** comedy *Encounter of the Spooky Kind (Ghost Strikes Ghost)/Gui da gui* (1980), which Hung wrote and in which he action directed, directed, and acted. The film also starred **Wu Ma**, **Lam Ching-ying**, **Tai Bo**, and a host of others. *The Dead and the Deadly/Yan haak yan/Ren he ren* (1982) followed, spurring the **vampire movie** fad that followed, with the Bo Ho–produced *Mr. Vampire* series, starting with Ricky Lau's *Mr. Vampire (Mr. Stiff Corpse)/Geung shi sin sang/Jiangshi xiansheng* (1985).

Other notable productions of various genres include **Johnny Mak's** vérité-style Mainland thug actioner *Long Arm of the Law/Sheng gang qi bing* (1984); **Leong Po-chih's** Japanese occupation drama *Hong Kong 1941 (Waiting for Dawn)/Dang doi lai ming/Deng gai li ming* (1984), starring **Chow Yun-fat**; *Heart of the Dragon (Dragon's Heart)/Long de xin* (1985), in which Hung directed and costarred with **Jackie Chan**, playing Chan's retarded brother; and, **Alfred Cheung's** Hong Konger/Mainlander conflict comedy *Her Fatal Ways/Biu che le ho yeh/Biao jie ni hao ye* (1990), starring Carol Cheng, which spawned several sequels. The company's last release was **David Lai's** period action thriller *Operation Scorpio/Xie zi zhan shi* (1992).

BOB & PARTNERS. Directors **Andrew Lau** and **Wong Jing**, along with writer Manfred Wong, formed BOB (Best of the Best) Film Production in the late 1990s. The company is known for its production of the *Young and Dangerous* series (1996–2000), as well as *Storm Riders* (1998).

BU, WANCANG (1903–1974). A native of Anhui province, director and writer Bu Wancang (aka Richard Poh) grew up in Yangzhou. He started in the film industry at 18, and was working as a cinematographer by 1924. His directorial debut was a silent film in 1925. Early major works include *Love and Duty/Lianai yu yiwu* (1930) and *A Spray of Plum Blossoms* (1931), both for **Lianhua** Studios. He worked in the left-wing literary movement collaborating with dramatist and director Tian Han at the outbreak of the Sino–Japanese War; *Maiden of Armor/Mulan congjun* (1939) was a version of the Hua Mulan story, made in **Orphan Island** Shanghai during the occupation and serving as a thinly veiled patriotic response against the Japanese.

Bu came to Hong Kong in 1948, directing two films for **Yonghua**, including *The Soul of China/Gwok wan/Guohun* (1948), the studio's first production, a story concerning Song dynasty imperial secretary and prime minister Wen Tianxiang, who fights against the Mongols. The director described the movie as a story about justice and taking a stand against authoritarianism, with a warning for the present. Bu's *Sins of Our Father/Daai leung saan yan chau gei/Daliangshan enchou ji* (1949) was a contemporary melodrama about ethnic conflict.

Bu formed **Taishan** Film Company in 1951, discovering new talents like **Ge Lan**, Shi Hui, **Lee Ching**, and **Zhong Qing**. His *Portrait of a Lady/Suk lui tiu/Diao jinqui* (1953), featuring Shi Hui, who plays the youngest and most promising daughter of a father disappointed by her elder sisters, features an antipatriarchal theme as the daughter rejects her father's authoritarianism. It also demonstrates the director's ability to guide actresses, as he would throughout his career. Ge Lan starred in the company's realist melodrama *The Seven Maidens* (1953) and in the melodrama *It Blossoms Again (The Moon That Breaks Free from the Clouds)/Jou chun fa/Zai chun hua* (1954) as a blind girl. *Blood-Stained Flowers (The 72 Martyrs of Canton)/Bik huet wong dut/ Bixue hua* (director, among eight others, 1953), produced by **Zhang Shankun's Xinhua** Company, that celebrated the revolutionaries who in 1911 rose against the Qing dynasty in Guangzhou, alluded to current Nationalists fighting against leftists and Communists, serving as Kuomintang propaganda, but also shows the growing sophistication of Mainland films made in Hong Kong. *Three Winning Smiles (Story of Tang Bohu and Qiuxiang, The Ingenious Seduction)/Tangba Hu yu Qiuxiang* (codirector, writer, 1956), codirected with Li Ying, was based on a folktale about famed scholar Tang Bohu, smitten by the smiles of a maidservant in the household of the Grand Tutor; the film was remade by **Yue Feng** as one of the last ***huangmei diao***, *The Three Smiles* (1969).

Although Bu's forte was the realistic melodrama, he made his share of Mandarin comedies with songs, including *Bean Curd Queen (Queen of the Folk Songs)/Dau foo sai si/Doufu Xishi* (1959), starring **Jeanette Lin Tsui**. The tender story *Nobody's Child (The Wanderings of a Poor Child)/Kuer liulang ji* (1960), made during the last phase of this veteran filmmaker's career, is among his best. An adolescent **Josephine Siao** starred as an orphan taken in by a street entertainer (another Orphan Island figure, actor **Wang Yin**). Touring the countryside with a monkey and three dogs, the mismatched companions bond. When the old man is imprisoned, the child is taken in by a barge mistress (played by another Shanghai expatriate, **Butterfly Wu**) as a companion to her bedridden daughter. With few close-ups and naturalistic acting, the film recaptures the glory of Shanghai style at its best.

– C –

CAI, CHUSHENG (1906–1968). Self-taught Shanghai-born Cantonese director Cai Chusheng formed a theater troupe in Guangdong. In 1929 he entered the Shanghai film industry as an extra, continuity person, and stagehand. Director Zheng Zhenqiu gave him a job as assistant director at 23 and taught him directing and writing. By the 1930s, he was a leading director in the Shanghai film industry; he worked on nine films at Mingxing (Star), then China's largest film company, then moved to **Lianhua** Studios in 1931, where many left-wing filmmakers had gathered. Cai directed *Share the Burden of the National Crisis/Gong fu guo nan* (1932), *Down over the Metropolis/Duhui de Zaochen* (1933), *Song of the Fisherman/Yuguang Qu* (1934), *The New Women/Xin nuxing* (1934), and *The Lost Kids/Mitu de gaoyang* (1936). *Song of the Fisherman* was the first Chinese film to win an international prize, at the 1935 Moscow International Film Festival; *The New Women* was a prescient film defining the "new **woman**" as a liberated and independent spirit, an educated good thinker with high morals, financially resourceful, living in urban settings undergoing change and confusion. The film starred **Ruan**

Lingyu (who committed suicide shortly after the film's release), and Cai based his story on her circumstances as well as those of screenwriter Ai Xia (whose last film, *A Modern Woman*, also shared many similarities with her circumstances and suicide as a "modern woman"). Cai knew both women intimately, and as such his film stands as an indictment of not only the tabloid press but the society that supports it. **Stanley Kwan's** *Actress* (*Centre Stage*, 1992), an homage to Ruan Lingyu and an examination of the past and present film industry, features Cai Chusheng as a character (portrayed by **Tony Leung Ka-fai**).

When Shanghai fell to the Japanese, Cai temporarily moved to Hong Kong in 1937, where he made anti-Japanese films and cowrote several scripts with **Situ Huimin**, such as *Blood Splashes on Baoshan Fortress (Blood-Stained Baoshan Fortress)/Huet chin bo saan shing/Xie jian bao shan cheng* (1938, awarded a prize of excellence by the Guangzhou Film Jury Committee) and *March of the Guerillas (Song of Righteousness)/Youji jingxing qu (Zhenqi ge)* (writer, 1938, released 1941). The latter, directed by Situ Huimin, was banned in Hong Kong because of its intent to rally Mainlanders in the war effort; the British at the time wished to remain neutral. The ban was lifted in 1941, and finally the Cantonese-speaking cast was seen on-screen, many for the first time. Set in a village overrun by Japanese soldiers (there are some who question their government's intervention), a young man tries to organize a local resistance movement but is injured. Following his recovery, he joins mountain guerillas to resist. He discovers his girlfriend has been captured by the Japanese, and the couple is briefly reunited as the rebels attack the Japanese camp. *Orphan Island Paradise/Goo do tin tong/Gudao tiantang* (director, writer, 1939) was one of the first Mandarin films made in Hong Kong, and serves as an example of Cai's cinematic aesthetics. Set in Shanghai, the story (adapted from Zhao Yingcai) follows a group of patriotic youth who fight local traitors, becoming resistance guerillas in the process. One scene features a New Year's Eve party invaded by assassins who gun down their victims; the gunshots are crosscut with popping balloons. The film played for 12 days in Hong Kong, setting a box-office record of 50,000 tickets sold.

Cai's politics appeared on- and offscreen. He wrote an article for the *Commercial Daily Newspaper/Hwa Shiang Pao/Huashang Bao*

(May 10, 1941) entitled "The Film Industry at the Crossroads of Man or Beast—Exposing the Enemy's Conspiracy against the South China Film Industry." He wrote, "We are at the crucial juncture where we will be sorely tested as to whether we should be humans or animals. There is hardly a hair's breath in between. I hope we will hold out our national and artistic conscience and struggle to become humans—that we will stand up and wipe out the poisonous conspiracy that the Japanese have plotted against out film industry." ***Ten Thousand Li Ahead*** *(Boundless Future)/Chin ching maan lee/Qian cheng wan li* (1941), which Cai wrote and directed, was released a few months earlier than the article. The film depicts Mainlanders living under hardships in exile in Hong Kong, and portrays the city as coarse and unforgiving in its capitalism, with some Hong Kongers as materialistic and indifferent to their plight as well as to the Sino–Japanese War effort on the Mainland. Working-class people are characterized as willing to become men, according to a similar line in the film, when they find themselves "at the crossroads of man and ghost." The film ends with the Mainlanders marching into China to fight.

As a leftist filmmaker, Cai emphasized social issues and themes, with didactic purpose, stressing character and content, with an eye to making films for the common person. He believed films should be both socially and politically conscious. Truth, goodness, and beauty were defining goals for Cai. As Shanghai talent, he brought a generally perceived higher quality to Cantonese-language films of the era. Cai returned to the Mainland when Hong Kong fell to the Japanese in 1941, and briefly went back to Hong Kong following the war to work with progressive filmmakers under the Nanguo (Nam Kwok, Southern) Film Company. He produced **Wang Weiyi's** ***Tears of the Pearl River*** *(Dawn Must Come)/ Zhujiang lei* (1950), a hard-hitting tragic drama of social conscience with high production values for its time. Cai returned to the Mainland in 1949, where he assumed the reins of the People's Republic of China's (PRC) film ministry and wrote and directed *Waves of the Southern Sea* (1958). He did not join the Chinese Communist Party until 1956, and died during the Cultural Revolution.

CANTONESE OPERA FILMS. *See* CHINESE OPERA FILMS.

CANTOPOP. Shanghai-style pop songs were favored in Hong Kong until the late 1960s when Mandarin ballads from Taiwan superseded them. Then Hong Kong Television Broadcasts Limited (TVB) began hiring songwriters to write Cantonese-language songs for its serials, among them **Joseph Koo** and **Sam Hui**. Hui emerged in the 1970s as the Father of Cantopop, introducing a new style that was based on Cantonese-language songs about everyday life with Western melodies and instrumentation. The music took off, and Hui sang the theme song for *Games Gamblers Play*, a film in which he costarred. It became the first Cantopop hit. The Cantopop singers who emerged in the 1970s included the Chopstick Sisters' Debora (Dik Bo-lai, ex-wife of **Patrick Tse** and mother of Nicolas Tse), **Alan Tam**, **Kenny Bee**, **George Lam**, and **Roman Tam**. Imitators followed, but by the end of the 1970s, Hong Kong audiences favored Japanese pop, yet that fad soon faded. In the 1980s, singers Danny Chan Pah-keung and **Leslie Cheung** appeared on the scene; Chan died from a drug overdose at 35, but Cheung went on to develop a large Asian following, singing romantic ballads of desire and loss, themes not unlike those that would resonate in his best film work. Fan clubs, fanzines, souvenirs, and an entire industry developed. **Peter Chan's** comedy ***He's a Woman, She's a Man*** (starring Cheung) examines the phenomenon.

Following in Cheung's footsteps, four singers, supported by opinionated fans, claimed the limelight. Called the Four Great Heavenly Kings (or Four Sky Kings), the singers are **Jacky Cheung**, **Leon Lai**, **Andy Lau**, and **Aaron Kwok**. Their concerts are like Las Vegas stage shows, a style originated by Roman Tam. Commonplace in Hong Kong is that singers also become actors. All the aforementioned have.

CATHAY. *See* MOTION PICTURES AND GENERAL INVESTMENT, LTD. (MP&GI).

CEN, FAN (Sam Faan) (1926–). Director Cen Fan (real name Cen Lifan), a native of Guangxi province, was born in Shanghai; at school in Nanjing, he wanted to be an athlete but his interests turned to film and theater. Inspired by **Zhu Shilin's** films like *Rendezvous in the Late Afternoon* (1942), Cen wrote and sent a screenplay, *Brother-*

hood, to the director, who encouraged him, beginning a correspondence and friendship. In 1945, Cen joined a professional acting company and appeared in many plays. In 1946, when Zhu was invited to Hong Kong to direct for Dazhonghua, he in turn invited Cen to accompany him as assistant director. There, Cen also studied film production under Zhu and worked as an actor.

Cen was Zhu's assistant director on the historical drama ***Sorrows of the Forbidden City****/Ching gung bei shut/Qinggong mishi* (1948), and his first produced script, *Life and Death* (1953), was directed by Zhu. The former was adapted from Yao Ke's play, and depicts the struggle between conservatives and reformists during the late Qing dynasty, with an eye to contemporary politics. The latter film was delayed from 1948 because of negatives being destroyed in a fire; the story, of a suicidal wife criticized by her in-laws and not supported by her husband, emphasized the determination to live, and starred Wang Xichun.

Cen was an actor in **Li Pingqian's** Mandarin dramas *A Bachelor Is Born/Fong mo ji/Fang mao zi* (1952) and *Marriage Affair/Moon/Men* (1953). In the former, a son is sent to a 1930s Shanghai University by his ambitious father, but does not share his father's aspirations and becomes a revolutionary. In the latter, **Hsai Moon** starred as a married woman believing in free love, who finds herself confined by marriage and seeking independence.

In 1951, Cen returned to the Mainland, working for Beijing, August First, and Shanghai film studios. Numerous films he appeared in were Chinese operas. He codirected (with Zheng Junli) the war-themed film *The Opium War/A pin chin chang/Ya pian zhan zheng* (1959), and he directed the comedy ***The True Story of Ah Q****/A Q Jing Chuen/A Q Zhengzhuan* 1983), which played the Cannes Film Festival.

CENSORSHIP. Hong Kong film censorship officially began in 1953, when all movies for public release had to be submitted to a censor's office. Beginning in 1977, both film and television were required to submit to the Television and Entertainment Licensing Authority (TELA) under the proviso of the regulatory code known as the Film Censorship Regulations according to the Places of Public Entertainment Ordinance, in existence until 1987. Regulations especially noted corrupt morals; an effect of deep shock and disgust; anything provoking hatred between races, classes, and nationality; or anything encouraging public disorder. Hence, sex and violence were allowed, whereas politically sensitive issues were not, from the 1960s on. Full frontal female nudity was allowed by 1977, and full frontal male nudity in 1988. Regarding politics, a chilling effect seems to have been ever present, with filmmakers examining politics mostly indirectly, especially in regard to the return of Hong Kong to the Mainland, in films such as **Leong Po-chi's** *Hong Kong 1941/Dang doi lai ming/Deng dai li ming* (1984) or **Ann Hui's** *Love in a Fallen City/King sing zi luen/Qingcheng zhi lian* (1984), both released the year of the signing of the Joint Declaration Agreement and both of which use the Japanese invasion as a metaphor for 1997, or **John Woo's** *Bullet in the Head/Dip huet gaai tau/Die xue jie tou* (1990) and **Tsui Hark's** *A Better Tomorrow 3/Ying hung boon sik 3 chik yeung ji goh/ Yingxiong bense 3* (1989), both of which use Vietnam as the metaphor. Consider **Tang Shuxuan's** *China Behind (Goodbye China)/Joi gin chung gwok/Zaijian zhongguo* (1974), the first Hong Kong film to critically examine the Cultural Revolution, which was banned and not released locally until 1987, or Tsui's *Dangerous Encounters of the First Kind/Dai yat lui ying aau him/Di yi lei xing wei xian* (1980). In the latter, bomb-happy teens raised memories of the 1967 riots, and the film only passed the censors following recutting and reshooting.

While Deng Xiao-ping promised that Hong Kong would remain the same for 50 years following the return, the effect on filmmakers cannot be delineated at present; the Asian economic crisis of 1997–1998 and the SARS epidemic of 2003 have overshadowed any way to estimate how filmmakers have been affected. A chilling effect seems present. Even **Jackie Chan** obtained an Australian passport just in case of problems with the return, illustrating the psychological effect on many. *See also* RATINGS SYSTEM.

CENTURY FILM COMPANY. Directors Dennis Yu and **Jeff Lau** founded Century Film in 1980, supported by Philippine investors. Its first production was **Alex Cheung's** drama *Man on the Brink/Bian yuan ren* (1981). The company was designed to encourage and support **New Wave** directors and also produced films with actor Eddie Yip and actress **Cecilia Yip**. Over a three-year span, the company produced seven films, including Yu's horror heavy *The Imp/Xiong bang* (1981), Cheuk Pak-tong's thriller *Marianna (Filipina Girl)/Bin mei* (1982), **Terry Tong's** dark hit man–themed *Coolie Killer/Saai chut sai ying poon/Shachu xiying pan* (1982), **Patrick Tam's** arty and angst-ridden youth genre *Nomad/(Flaming Youth) Lit foh ching chu/Lie huo qing chun* (1982), and Tony Hope's romance *My Darling, My Goddess/Ai ren nu shen* (1982). The company's last production was Wong Ching's crime movie *Sketch/Xie zhong xie* (1983).

CHA, LOUIS LEUNG YUNG (Jin Yong/Kam Yung) (1924–). Novelist Louis Cha was born in Zhejiang province. After studying at the Zhejiang Province Jiaxing High School, he became a faculty member at Chunking Central University in the Department of Foreign Languages, and later a member of the faculty at Dong Wu University in the Law Department. Cha began working for a Shanghai newspaper in 1947 and was transferred to the paper's Hong Kong branch in 1948. In 1955, Cha wrote the first of his eight ***wuxia*** novels, *The Legend of Book and Sword*. Two years later, he worked from 1957 to 1959 as a screenwriter for **Great Wall** Movie Enterprises Ltd. In total, Cha wrote 14 novels and one short story. These novels are often the basis for many **martial arts** films, and perhaps even more importantly, **television** series. Cha cofounded *Ming Pao* newspaper in Hong Kong in 1959.

The last of the novels, *The Deer and the Cauldron,* was written in 1972. Cha participated in Hong Kong politics beginning in the late 1970s, helping to write the Hong Kong Basic Law, but he resigned in 1989 after the Tiananmen incident. In 1993, Cha retired from *Ming Pao*, which by then had come to be regarded as the best and most accurate Hong Kong newspaper and had launched other ventures including *Ming Pao Weekly*, a magazine, as well.

The author's novels would go on to have an effect that at the time would have been unimaginable. To date, Cha has sold over 300 million copies of his books, though this number would be much higher if the people in Mainland China had not been forced to read illegal copies due to government restriction (the ban has since been lifted). Hong Kong stars like **Adam Cheng**, who got his big break in Hong Kong Television Broadcasts Limited's (TVB) adaptation of *The Legend of Book and Sword*, and **Tony Leung Chiu-wai**, who starred in the TVB adaptation of *The Deer and the Cauldron*, not to mention **Jet Li** in ***Swordsman** 2/Siu ngo gong woo ji Dung Fong Bat Baai/Xiao ao jianhu zhi Dongfang Bubai* (1992), an adaptation of Cha's *The Smiling, Proud Wanderer*, appeared in adaptions of Cha's works. One of TVB's most popular series ever, *The Legend of the Condor Heroes* (1982), was based on the Cha novel, and helped cement television careers as well as give a top-selling album to **Roman Tam** and **Jenny Tseng**, which, along with the series itself, is still in demand today.

Cha has received numerous honors for his contributions to literary culture, including an Officer of the Order of the British Empire (OBE) in 1981, an Ordre des Arts et des Lettres, and a Chevalier de la Légion d'Honneur. Cha's work has been the subject of many academic conferences, and he is an honorary professor at many Chinese universities as well as an honorary doctor at the University of Cambridge, as well as being an honorary fellow at different colleges at both Oxford and Cambridge.

CHAN, BENNY MUK-SING (1961–). Director Benny Chan was born in Hong Kong and joined the **television** industry at Hong Kong Television Broadcasts Limited (TVB) in 1983, where he worked for four years as assistant director to **Johnnie To** and as writer-director. He directed the movie *Goodbye Darling/Hap cho dai cheung foo/Xia cu da zhang fu* (1987) under **Raymond Wong Pak-ming's** supervision and his directorial debut was romance actioner *A Moment of Romance (If Heaven Has Love)/Tin yeuk yau ching/Tian ruo you qing* (1990, starring **Andy Lau**), which led to another, *A Moment of Romance 2 (If Heaven Has Love 2: Enduring Loyalty)/Tin yeuk yau ching 2 ji tin cheung dei gau/Tian ruo you qing 2 zhi tian chang di jiu* (1993, starring **Aaron Kwok**). Chan has directed 14 movies to date and is known for revving up the action and camerawork. He wrote and directed *Gen-X Cops/Dak ging san yau lui/Te jing xin ren lei* (1999), which put a handful of younger actors, known as **Gen-X**, on the Hong Kong film map, followed by *Gen-Y Cops/Dak ging san yan lui 2/Te jing xin ren lei 2* (2000).

CHAN, CONNIE PO-CHU (1947–). A native of Guangdong Province and the daughter of two Beijing opera stars, Chan Fei-nung and Kung Fan-hung, actress Chan Po-chu was trained in Southern and Northern **martial arts** styles. She made her screen debut with the Mandarin movie *The Scout Master/Tung gwan gaau lin/Tong jin jiao lian* (1959). She acted in a series of martial arts movies, among them *The Six-Fingered Lord of the Lute/Loke chi kam moh/Liu zhi qin mo* (1965), a sword and sorcery adventure and the first screen adaptation of Ngai Hong's (Ni Kuang) novels. Her first lead role was in *You Do Me Wrong/Yuk lui ham yuen/Yu nu han yuan* (1966), and the peak of her career was 1966–1969. She was one of the two most popular female stars of the 1960s, the other being **Josephine Siao** (with whom she often costarred.) Together, they virtually launched the contemporary youth genre movie. Besides martial arts movies, Chan starred in musicals, melodramas, comedies, and action spy films. Chan's nickname was "Movie Princess." She immigrated to Canada in 1970, but returned to Hong Kong to film **Chor Yuen's** *The Lizard/Bek foo/Bi hu* (1972). All told, she made 90 films.

In **Lee Tit's** ***Eternal Love****/Chat choi woo bat gwai/Qicai hu bugui* (1966), Chan plays a traveling male scholar who falls in love with and marries the dutiful Josephine Siao. Based on the **Cantonese opera** *Hu Bugui (Why Not Return?)*, the movie includes singing performances by Chan and Siao (both trained in Cantonese opera) and is one of the decade's best opera films. At the wife's grave, the grief-stricken husband performs the famous aria *Hu Bugui* ("Why do you not return? The broken hearted cries like the cuckoo in mourning. . . .") and is on the verge of committing suicide when the couple is reunited.

The musical ***Girls Are Flowers****/Goo leung sap baat yat tiong fah/Guniang shiba yiduo hua* (1966) essentially launched the youth genre movie, and starred Chan as Ng Hoi-yin, a bubbly teen orphan who is also a talented singer and a martial artist defending her honor.

Chan Wan's *The Dutiful Daughter (The Dutiful Daughter Zhu Zhu)/Haau liu Chu Chu /Xiaonu Zhuzhu* (1966) is one of Chan Po-chu's most representative roles. She plays acrobat-showgirl Chu-chu in this backstage melodrama. Defying all odds, she resolves to be a Cantonese opera star (the film was designed to show off Chan's opera talents). In the story, she plays the filial daughter who looks after her mentally ill mother. This movie reflects the 1960s transition from male to female superstars in Cantonese movies. She also starred in *Waste Not Our Youth/Mok foo ching chun/Mofu qingchun* (1967), another problem youth movie, as an upper middle-class rich girl who develops mental problems. Only shock therapy saves her. Chan stands out going mad in a hospital lobby as she battles hospital orderlies like a martial arts heroine; later, she experiences a surreal go-go party where her parents and other household elders dance to the beat in a failed attempt to bring her back from madness.

Two of her roles for director Chor Yuen demonstrate the range of the actress. In *The Black Rose/Hak mui gwai/Hei mei gui* (1965) and its sequel, she starred along with **Nam Hung**. The movie was Hong Kong's answer to the James Bond movies, with *To Catch a Thief* thrown in, combining spies, a lone-wolf jewel thief, Cantonese acrobatic swordsman, and stoical inspector. This fantasy entertainment had a comic book quality, and Oriole, the Flying Heroine, from popular pulp fiction series, was an influence. The heroine was paired with a bimbo male love interest (**Patrick Tse Yin**), and besides the secret weapons, gadgetry, and action set pieces with choreographed fights and car chases, there was verbal repartee and an enjoyable lifestyle. In Chor's screwball comedy *Young, Pregnant and Unmarried/Yuk lui tim ding/Yunu tianding* (1968), Chan starred as the younger daughter of a status-conscious father. As the favored daughter, she feigns pregnancy, blaming next-door neighbor **Lui Kei**, while it is her older sister who finds herself in an out of wedlock pregnancy.

CHAN, EVANS YIU-SHING. Born in Hong Kong, director Evans Chan grew up in Hong Kong and Macau, graduated from Hong Kong Baptist College in 1981, and received his master's degree from the New School for Social Research in New York in 1991. He had worked at the *Hong Kong Standard* as its staff film critic in the 1980s, and when he returned to Hong Kong in the 1990s, he directed his first film, *To Liv(e) (Love Song from a Floating World)/Fau sai luen kuk/Fu shi lian qu* (1992), an exploration of Hong Kong socially and politically in light of the deportation of Vietnamese boat people and the Tiananmen Square massacre. Inspired by Swedish actress Liv Ullman's criticism of Hong Kong as well as memories of a girl reading her autobiography, Chan cast the film as an older woman–younger man love story. In the more mainstream *Crossings (Wrong Love)/Cho oi/Cuo ai* (1994), starring **Anita Yuen** and **Simon Yam**, the former plays an innocent and the latter a drug smuggler who uses her. Chan was inspired by an actual New York subway killing, and underlying the seemingly doomed romance/gangster genre, the film navigates between New York and Hong Kong to examine issues of identity, illegal immigration, and the international drug trade and directly addresses the then-impending handover. Chan currently lives in the United States. With *The Map of Sex and Love/Ching sik dei tiu/Qingse ditu* (2001), an expatriate Chinese filmmaker living in New York (not unlike the director himself) returns to Hong Kong to make a film and encounters two others with whom he has a month-long involvement. Loose in its structure, and raising more questions than providing answers, the film reflects the newly burgeoning spirit of independent Hong Kong film.

CHAN, FRUIT KUO (GOH) (1959–). Born in Guangzhou, Fruit Chan moved to Hong Kong in 1969. He studied scriptwriting and directing at the Hong Kong Film Cultural Center and became its assistant administration manager. He started working in film in the mid-1980s as an actor and assistant director. His directorial debut was with the psychological horror film *Finale in Blood/Daai laan gong cheong lung/Da nao guang chang long* (1991). He established himself as an independent in 1994 and wrote the screenplay for the gay film *Bugis Street/Yiu gaai wong hau/Yao jie huang hou* (1995).

Chan gained widespread attention with the independent-styled *Made in Hong Kong/Heung Gong jai jo/Xiang Gang zhi zao* (1997), which Chan made on a shoestring budget (US$80,000) with film stock he saved from other shoots, an ensemble of amateur actors, and a five-member crew. A gritty depiction of disaffected Hong Kong youth, the movie was inspired by Hong Kong's return to the Mainland and the ending of a historical era. It charted a territory for Chan's future projects of a changing city and the disenfranchised. *The Longest Summer/Hui nin yin dut dak bit doh/Qunian yanhua tebie duo* (1998) explores the impact of the return of Hong Kong to China by focusing on random characters and everyday life. His films are known for their edginess and unpredictability. The road movie *Public Toilet/Yan man gong chi/Renmin gongche* (2002) was shot on digital video with deliberately shaky effects and features characters of different nationalities and is set in different countries. The story concerns an orphan abandoned in a Beijing public toilet, and uses bodily functions and water as metaphors for life and death. It played numerous international film festivals, including Toronto, Venice, Vancouver, and Pusan.

Three . . . Extremes/Saam gang/San geng (2004), an omnibus film and product of **Applause Pictures**, a company recently founded by director **Peter Chan**, was made with an avowed Pan-Asian market in mind, and included Fruit Chan's *Dumplings/Gaau ji/Jiao zi*, which was also released in an extended version. Shot by cinematographer **Chris Doyle**, the film artfully displays a Hong Kong that worships youth culture and the new, set against tradition and reverence for ancestors and the elderly. **Leung Ka-fai** plays a philandering husband, consumed by virility and youth, with a wife who wants to remain young to please her husband. Tellingly, Hong Kong entrepreneurialism (the wife, portrayed by Miriam Yeung) wins out over Mainlander smarts (Bai Ling as a Hong Kong outsider who sells eternal youth), the latter being reduced to the lowest social class (carrying buckets over her shoulder in the old fashion), following her fall from stardom, the medical profession, and as a sought-after unusual secretive herbalist. The film provides an apt metaphor for Hong Kong's intervention in the Mainland market.

CHAN, GAM-TONG (Chen Jintang) (1906–1981). Cantonese opera actor and **martial artist** Chan Gam-tong was born in Guangdong province. A follower of Cantonese opera actor Xin Bei, he studied with **Sit Kok-sin** as well. He performed as a *xiaosheng* (a handsome young man, either a scholar or military general) and a *wusheng* (those specializing in fighting). He was successful with the Juenxiansheng Opera Troupe's *Sweet Girl*. He played opposite actress Hongxian Nu in many famous operas.

Chan's screen debut was *The Righteous Thief, Jin Maoshu*. Many of the 60 films in which Chan appeared were Cantonese opera movies, including *Bodyguard Huang Tian Ba 1 and 2/Gam biu wong tin ba/Jin biao hunag tian ba* (1948), *The Story of Dong Xiaowan/ Dung siu yuen/ Dong Xiaowan* (1950), and *Woman General Hua Mulan/Dut Muk Laan/Hua Mulan* (1961). The actor was called "martial arts champion" for his formidable performances. He founded one of the longest-lasting opera troupes, Jintianhua, in the 1940s, and his students Xiao Zhongkun and Su Shaotang continued his artistic legacy.

The actor also starred in some contemporary films, including Chan Pei's romantic tragedy *Silk Factory Girl/Siu shut lui/Sao si nu* (1955), in which Chan played a sacrificing lover who marries his cousin in order to save his true love, played by **Tang Pak-wan**, as the disillusioned title character, from an arranged marriage. Chan's last film was the Cantonese historical drama *Valiant Pan An* (1963).

CHAN, GORDON KAR-SEUNG (1960–). Born in Hong Kong, director and screenwriter Gordon Chan was educated in Hong Kong and in Canada at Toronto University. He returned to Hong Kong in 1981 and worked in amateur theater and then for **Shaw Brothers** in the special effects unit on films such as *Twinkle, Twinkle Little Star/Sing chai dun toi/Xing ji dun tai* (1983) and *The Boxer's Omen (Demon)/Moh/Mo* (1983). He began writing the same year, beginning with **Taylor Wong's** *Behind the Yellow Line/Yuen ban/Yuan fen* (1983) that starred **Leslie Cheung**, **Maggie Cheung**, and **Anita Mui**, and contributing to *No Regret/Ching mooi jing chuen/Jing mei zheng chuasn* (1987), *Hearts to Hearts/Saam yan sai gaai/San ren shi jie* (1988), and **Jackie Chan's** *Dragons Forever* (1988), starring Chan, **Samo Hung**, and **Yuen Biao**. He contributed to the direction of *Hearts to Hearts* and made his directorial debut with *The Yuppie Fantasia/Siu laam yan chow gei/Xiao nan ren zhou ji* (1989) and its sequel (1990). His work has run the gamut from urban young people's stories, as in *The Long and Winding Road (Bright Future)/Gam sau chin ching/Jin xiu qian cheng* (1994), also starring Cheung and **Tony Leung Ka-fai**, to comedy like *Inspector Pink Dragon/San taam ma yue long/Shen tan ma ru long* (1991) and hard-hitting action, such as *The Final Option* (1994), a tense cop thriller starring **Michael Wong**, and *Fist of Legend (The Hero of Jing Wu Society)/Cheng miu ying hung/Jing wu ying xiong* (1994), a **Jet Li** vehicle paying homage to **Bruce Lee** and *Fist of Fury* (1972).

Chan directed **Stephen Chiau** in *Fight Back to School, 1* and *2 (Escape from School Mighty Dragon)/To hok wai lung/Tao xue wei long* (1991, 1992), in which Chiau played an undercover cop who infiltrates a high school, and *King of Beggars (Top Martial Scholar: Beggar So)/Mo jong yuen: So hat yi/Wu zhuang yuan: Su qi er* (1992), a comic retelling of the Beggar So story. He also directed Jackie Chan in *Thunderbolt (Thunderbolt Fire)/Pik lik feng/Pi li huo*

(1995) and *Highbinders (The Medallion)/Fei lung joi sang/Fei long zai sheng* (2003). He made the curious *Armageddon/Tin dei hung sam/Tian di xiong xin* (1997), starring **Andy Lau** and **Anthony Wong**, a supernatural and apocalyptic tale released shortly before the return of Hong Kong to China. *Beast Cops/Yau sau ying ging/Ye shou xing jing* (1998) cast Anthony Wong opposite Michael Wong, and their on-screen chemistry, as well as the addition of **Roy Cheung's** sympathetic gangster, contributed to a memorable character-driven, local story of cops and Triads. *Cat and Mouse/Low sue oi seung mau/Lao shu ai shang mao* (2003) is a period costume comedy pairing Andy Lau and **Cecilia Cheung** in the title roles and costarring Anthony Wong as Judge Pao; the movie was loosely based on popular Chinese novel *Qi Xia Wu Yi*, set in the Song dynasty, featuring exploits of the harsh but fair judge and his followers who bring criminals to justice. Gordon Chan is well known for writing strong scripts and directing action sequences with a sure hand. He wrote the tragic romance *Au Revoir, Mon Amour* (directed by **Tony Au**, 1991), in which Anita Mui shone as the love-torn songstress caught in the turmoil of the Japanese occupation. Chan also has consistently worked with the same group of actors in very different types of movies.

CHAN, JACKIE SING-LUNG (1954–). Jackie Chan was born as Chan Kong-sang (Chen Gangsheng, meaning "born in Hong Kong") to a poor family. His father worked as a cook for the French consulate and his mother as a cleaning woman, and they almost sold their son at birth because they feared not being able to afford to keep him. His father, Charles Chan, was skilled in **martial arts** and began training and encouraging his young son to become an athlete. (**Cheung Yuen-ting's** 2003 documentary, *Traces of a Dragon: Jackie Chan and His Lost Family*, reveals Chan's father's and mother's pre– and post–World War II experiences, his father's real name Fang Daolong, and the existence of Jackie Chan's two half-brothers [by his father] and two half-sisters [by his mother] on the Mainland). In 1961, Chan's parents had the opportunity to immigrate to Australia with the U.S. consul, and the young Chan entered Master Yu Jim-yuen's Beijing Opera School at age seven, where he remained a student until 1971. The school, Zhongguo Xiji Xueyuan (Chinese Opera Research Institute), was located in Tsimshatsui, and the site serves as the current location of Chan's offices.

Chan learned acrobatics, martial arts, singing, dancing, and stage makeup. With fellow students **Samo Hung** and **Yuen Biao**, he became one of the **Seven Little Fortunes**. (In his autobiography, *I Am Jackie Chan*, Chan remembers his early years at the school and the arduous training he underwent; another source is **Alex Law's** film *Painted Faces*, which stars Samo Hung.) As the opera died out, many performers picked up work in the burgeoning film business; Yu Jim-yuen found work for his students as stuntmen and extras in numerous movies.

Chan's film debut was in 1962 in a Cantonese melodrama *Big and Little Wong Tin Bar*. After leaving opera school, Chan worked as a stuntman, martial actor, and film extra for **Shaw Brothers**. He also became an action choreographer and appeared in a number of 1970s **Golden Harvest** movies, including two **Bruce Lee** films, *Fist of Fury (Chinese Connection)/Jing mou moon/Jing wu men* (1972) and ***Enter the Dragon****/Lung chang foo dau/Loong zheng hu dou* (1973); in the former, Lee kicked Chan through a wall, and in the latter, he snapped Chan's neck. Chan played the lead in the formulaic **kung fu** *Cub Tiger of Canton/Gong dung siu liu foo/Guangdong xiao lao hu* (also known as *Young Tiger of Canton*, 1973, reedited and released as *Master with Cracked Fingers*, 1979) and a major role in **John Woo's** *Hand of Death (Countdown in Kung Fu)/Siu lam moon/Shaolin men* (1976). Ironically, after Bruce Lee's premature death, the studios groomed Chan and others to become the next Bruce Lee. **Lo Wei** miscast Chan as the new Bruce Lee in *New Fist of Fury/San jing mou moon/Xin jing wu men* (1976), a sequel to Lee's *Fist of Fury/Chinese Connection*. The movie proved a box office flop but a lesson for Chan. (However, for this movie Chan adopted the Chinese name Sing-lung, meaning "becoming dragon," in honor of Bruce Lee, whose Chinese name is Lee Siu-lung, meaning "little dragon." Chan still uses "Sing-lung" today.)

Jackie Chan invented himself, in effect, as the anti-Bruce Lee. Where Lee kicked high, Chan kicks low; when Lee breaks through a wall with a single punch, Chan cracks the wall but hurts his hand. The former was serious and grimaced, the latter was comic and smiled. The persona moviegoers would embrace first appeared on-screen in the **Ng See-yuen**–produced **Yuen Wo-ping**–directed period piece *Snake in the Eagle's Shadow (Snake Form Trick Hand)/Sau ying diu san/She xing diao shou* (1978), as a provincial rebellious idler bullied both by the villain (Hung Cheng-li) and his wayward teacher (**Yuen Siu-tin**, the director's father); the role allowed for physical and verbal comedy as Chan's character is punched, kicked, and joked about through much of the film, but his resilience and determination allow him to prevail. Ng See-yuen's **Seasonal Films** continued Chan's period pieces with *Drunken Master (Drunken Monkey in the Tiger's Eye)/Chui kuen/Zui quan* (1978) and *Fearless Hyena/Siu kuen gwaai chiu/Xiao quan guai zhao* (1979) recycling the impetuous student and eccentric teacher and assuring Chan's popularity, ranking him among Hong Kong's most famous and highest paid actors. His movies of this period in part contributed to the reemergence of Cantonese-language action movies in Hong Kong.

In 1980, Chan signed with **Raymond Chow's Golden Harvest**, starring in *The Young Master (Little Brother's Turn to Shine)/Si dai chut ma/Shi di chu ma*, another period piece in which Chan played folk hero **Wong Fei-hung**; this is the first film in which Chan sang while the credits rolled. Through Golden Harvest, Chan became a film producer, through a subsidiary, **Golden Way** (1980–). Through Golden Harvest, Chan also set his sights on Hollywood. He starred in *The Big Brawl* (1980) and *The Protector* (1985) and appeared in *Cannonball Run* (1981) and *Cannonball Run 2* (1984). The experience proved dissatisfying and was short-lived as Chan was denied the creative control he was used to having on his films. He continued making Hong Kong movies for Golden Harvest, many with two of the Seven Little Fortunes of his youth, Samo Hung and Yuen Biao (they are known as the "Three Brothers").

Chan participated in part of the series known as the *Lucky Stars* movies with his two brothers, a series spanning more than a decade and consisting of 13 **action** comedies to date. He appeared with them in *Winners and Sinners (Strange Plan Brilliant Idea of the Five Lucky Stars)/Kei man miu gai ng fook sing/Qi mou miao ji wu fu xing* (1983), *My Lucky Stars (Lucky Stars Glorious Glow)/Fook sing go chiu/Fu xing gao zhao* (1985), and *Twinkle Twinkle Lucky Stars (Summer Sun Lucky Stars)/Ha yat fook sing/Jia ki fu xing* (1985), all directed by Samo Hung, with simple plots and dependent upon the chemistry of the actors. Each features a different female love interest pursued by all the fellows (among them, **Richard Ng**, **Charlie Chin Cheung-lam**, and **John Shum**). Hung also directed himself, Chan, and Biao in *Wheels on Meals (Fast Food Car)/Faai chaan che/Kuai can che* (1984) and *Dragons Forever (Flying Dragon Fierce Challenge)/Fei lung maang cheung/Fei long meng jiang* (1988), the latter being the last film the three have appeared in together.

Chan, meantime, himself began directing: *Project A/A gai waak/A jihua* (1983), *Police Story/Ging chaat goo si/Jing cha gu shi* (1985), *Armor of God (Dragon Elder Brother, Tiger Younger Brother)/Lung hing foo dai/Long xiong hu di* (1987), *Project A 2 (Project A Sequel)/A gai waak chuk chap/A ji haa xu ji* (1987), *Police Story 2 (Police Story Sequel)/Ging chaat goo si juk jaap* (1988), *Mr. Canton and Lady Rose* (aka *Miracles)/Gei jik/Qi ji* (1989), *Operation Condor (Armor of God 2; Flying Eagle Plan)/Fei ying gai waak/Fei ying ji hua* (1990), and *Who Am I?/Ngo shut sui/Wo shi shui* (1998). With the exception of *Project A 2*, he also served as writer for these movies, and action director and producer for several of them. He began his own team of stuntmen for his movies, Jackie Chan's Stuntmen Association, that work not only as stuntmen and extras, but on action choreography as well. With the exception of the *Armor of God* films (in which Chan played an Indiana Jones-type adventurer), in these films Chan's persona, despite the physical talent, is easily identifiable as an ordinary man caught in unusual circumstances, who acts extraordinarily. Mistreated through much of each story, he emerges victorious. Villains are killed or jailed, and good triumphs over evil.

Stanley Tong Gwai-lai directed Chan in three films, *Police Story 3: Supercop* (known as *Supercop* in the United States)*/Ging chat goo si 3 chiu kap ging chat/Jing cha gu shi 3 chao ji jing cha* (1992), *Rumble in the Bronx (Red Indian Territory)/Hung faan kui/Hong fan qu* (1995), and *First Strike (Police Story 4: A Simple Mission)/Ging chaat goo si ji gaan daan yam mou/Jing cha gu shi zhi jian chan ren wu* (1996), maintaining the screen persona but adding stronger female characters. **Michelle Yeoh's** jump from a racing motorcycle onto a rapidly moving train in *Supercop*, for instance, was topped only by Chan's jumping from a building onto a hovering helicopter rope ladder high above Kuala Lumpur. *Supercop* and *Rumble in the Bronx*, with another breathtaking action scene in which Chan helms a hovercraft chasing villains through the streets of New York (actually Vancouver), served as Chan's calling card to Hollywood. (The actor and director reunited for *The Myth/San wa/Shen hua* [2005].) Thereafter several other Chan Hong Kong films have been distributed nationwide, and Chan was invited a second time to make movies in Hollywood. This time around, Chan has retained more creative control and used his own action team; the movies so far have proved commercially successful and popular. Chan has remade his kung fu clowning Hollywood style, with larger budgets and greater production values. In each film, he has been paired with a sidekick (Chris Tucker in *Rush Hour* and *Rush Hour 2*; Owen Wilson in *Shanghai Noon* and *Shanghai Knights*; and Jennifer Love Hewitt in *The Tuxedo*). Chan continues filming in Hong Kong.

Chan's fame at home and internationally rests upon his persona and audiences' expectations being fulfilled when they go to see a Jackie Chan movie. Chan has made a career out of performing his own action and stunts, creating a physical comedy closer to silent films stars like Buster Keaton, Harold Lloyd, and Charlie Chaplin, mentors Chan readily acknowledges. His action stunts are large and jaw-dropping (in *Police Story* he slides down a 30-something foot string of light bulbs; in *Project A* he falls from a clock tower some 40 feet, his fall broken by canvas awning only; in *Armor of God*, he jumps from a mountaintop onto a hot air balloon; in *Drunken Master 2 [Drunken Fist 2]/Jui kuen 2/Zui quan 2*, he moves through a bed of hot coals; and in *First Strike* he swims with a shark). The fight scenes involve much hand-to-hand combat one-on-one, incorporating everyday objects found in the setting, from furniture to refrigerators, skateboards, bottles, and ladders. Climactic fight scenes can last as long as 20 minutes, certainly so in the period pieces. Chan has experienced serious injury, damaging every part of his body at one time or another. A simple jump from a wall to a tree branch in *Armor of God* almost killed him when he fell 45 feet to the ground, landing on his head. Chan's end credits are well known for the outtakes and behind-the-scene shots of the dangers involved. Chan began the practice to warn children and admirers from imitating him.

Chan won Taiwan's **Golden Horse Award** for Best Actor in 1992 for *Police Story 3 (Supercop)* and in 1993 for *Crime Story (Serious Crime Unit)/Chung ngon cho/Zhonganzu*. He has also recorded numerous musical recordings (and sings a famous version of the Wong Fei-hung theme song). He founded and is an officer of the **Hong Kong Directors Guild**, Performing Artists Guild, and Society of

Cinematographers. He also is involved in several business operations, including a modeling agency, a store selling Chan souvenirs, and a high-tech gym. In 2000, the U.S.-syndicated *Jackie Chan Adventures* animated TV series premiered on the WB station.

CHAN, JORDAN SIU-CHUN (1967–). Actor Chan joined Hong Kong Television Broadcasts Limited's (TVB) dancer training classes in 1985 and was a TVB dancer, dancing backup for popular singers like **Anita Mui**. With fellow dancers Jason Chu Wing-tong and Michael Tse Tin-wah, he formed the musical group Wind, Fire, and Sea in 1992. His manager, Clarence Hui Yuen, introduced him to Chan Tak-sum at a Sandy Lam Yak-lien concert in 1993; this led to his film debut in 1994 in Chan's *Twenty Something/Man chiu/Wan chao* (1994), as he was looking for new actors. The same year, he appeared as **Anita Yuen's** roommate in **Peter Chan's** ***He's a Woman, She's a Man*** *(Golden Branch, Jade Leaf)/Gam chi yuk yip/Jin qi yu ye*, in a memorable role. An intuitive actor and an astute observer, Chan learned on the job without any training. He became identified with Chicken, the character he played in the *Young and Dangerous* series (1996–2000), by observing the attitudes and behavior of young Triad gangs. Memorable roles include Sonny, the younger man in a gay relationship, in **Shu Kei's** *A Queer Story (Gay Man at 40)/Gei liu 40/Ji lao 40* (1997), and the sensitive Louie in **Yim Ho's** *Kitchen (I Love Kitchen)/Ngoh oi chui fong/Wo ai chu fang* (1997, adapted from the novel by Banana Yoshimoto). For the latter, he tried to imagine the feelings of loneliness and helplessness of a character losing his family. Chan was scheduled to appear in **Jackie Chan's** *Rush Hour*, but due to last-minute scheduling problems, had to cancel. He continues to sing (having released solo Cantonese and Mandarin recordings) and act in films (over 50 to date) and **television** (including *The Duke of Mount Deer*) in Hong Kong. His English name, Jordan, was chosen because of his admiration of basketball player Michael Jordan.

CHAN, KELLY WAI-LAM (1973–). Born in Hong Kong, actress Kelly Chan was sent to Japan for her high school education, where she won the art award. After leaving Japan, she attended Parsons School of Design in New York City. According to Chan she wanted to go to New York ever since she saw **Cheung Yuen-ting's** *An*

Autumn's Tale (1987), a fairy-tale love story starring charismatic **Chow Yun-fat** and **Cherie Chung** and filmed on location in the city. After graduating with a degree in graphic design, Chan returned to Hong Kong for the summer and was cast in a **Jacky Cheung** music video. After that Chan filmed a commercial in Shanghai. Chan signed on as a singer with Go! East Entertainment and as an actress with **United Filmmakers Organization (UFO)**. Her first role came opposite **Aaron Kwok** in **Jacob Cheung's** *Whenever Will Be, Will Be/Sin lok piu piu/Xian le piao piao* (1995). Simultaneously Chan's career in the music industry took off at an even more rapid pace.

Since her feature debut, Chan has been paired with some of Hong Kong's leading younger actors, generally in charming smaller love stories about loss and overcoming it. Chan was the lead female role in **Lee Chi-Ngai's** *Lost and Found (Edge of the World)/Tin aai hoi gok/Tian ya hai jiao* (1996) alongside art house regular **Kaneshiro Takeshi** and tough cop movie star **Michael Wong**. She starred in another UFO production, **Yee Chung-man's** *Anna Magdalena/On na ma tak lin na/An na ma de lian na* (1998), working again with Kaneshiro, as well as Heavenly King Aaron Kwok and **Cantopop** legend **Leslie Cheung**. Chan also starred alongside **Ekin Cheng** and **Jordan Chan** that same year in **Jingle Ma's** *Hot War/Waan ying dak gung/Huan ying te gong* (1998). Chan played one of the leads in the hugely successful Lunar New Year comedy *Tokyo Raiders/Dung ging gung leuk/Dong jing gong lu* (2000). In **Yip Kam-hung's** tender *Lavender/Fan dut cho/Xun yi cao* (2000), costarring Kaneshiro Takeshi, she played a lonely aromatherapist mourning her boyfriend's death to Kaneshiro's angel sent to console her. She was matched again with Aaron Kwok in **Hai Chung-man's** comedy *And I Hate You So/Siu chan chan/Xiao qin qin* (2000). Chan is also very popular in Japan and starred in the Japanese romance *Calmi Couri Apassionati* (2001). She was one of two actresses (the other being **Carina Lau**) featured in the first and third installments of the **Andrew Lau–Alan Mak** *Infernal Affairs/Mou gaan dou/Wu jian dao* trilogy. In addition to her screen activities, Chan is also a wildly successful singer.

CHAN, LIT-BUN (Chen Liepin) (1923–). Martial arts director Chan Lit-bun joined the **Nanyang** Film Company, the predecessor of **Shaw Brothers**, in 1947. He became a director in residence for the Hong

Kong Film Company (Sin-hok Kong-luen, Xianhe **Ganglian**), specializing in ***wuxia*** novels adapted to film. His directorial debut was *The Golden Hairpin/Bik huet gam chaai/Bixie jinchai* (1963), a serial in four parts based on a popular newspaper serial. The film starred **Cheung Ying-tsoi**, **Chan Po-chu**, **Suet Nei**, and Chan Ho-kau, all at the beginning of their careers. Cheung plays a rebellious loner swordsman seeking revenge for his father's death, who gains martial arts powers and encounters three women during his adventures, all with their own dilemmas and problematic for him too. *The Six-Fingered Lord of the Lute/Loke chi kam moh/Liu zhi qin mo* (1965), in three parts, was based on Ni Kuang's (Ngai Hong) novel, the author who became **Chang Cheh's** scriptwriting partner. Chan Po-chu starred in a cross-dressing role as the son whose parents argue over his martial arts education. The protagonists, all from different martial arts schools, brandish various weaponry, travel, fight, and undertake numerous adventures in search of the six-fingered lute that guarantees invincibility. The story was remade as *Deadful Melody* (1994) starring **Brigitte Lin** and **Yuen Biao**.

Green-Eyed Demoness/Biyan monu (1967) draws from the horror thriller and starred Suet Nei as "the green-eyed lady monster from the Snow Mountain" and **Tsang Kong** as "the golden hand scholar from the South Sea" who join forces to defeat the princess of Taishan Fortress, where the villains of the ***jiang hu***, representing various martial arts schools, reside. Chan specialized in handcrafted special effects, inventive action sequences, and rebellious characterizations that spilled suspense, violence, and the supernatural across the screen. He made *The One-Armed Magic Nun/Dubi shen ni* (1969) for the Kei Lun (Qilin) Film Company, concerning a one-armed nun who loses her mind. He retired from film in the early 1970s to focus on business.

CHAN, PETER HO-SUN (1962–). Born in Hong Kong, Chan moved with his parents to Thailand at 12, where he studied in an American high school. He came to the United States at 18 and studied film at the University of California at Los Angeles, leaving at 21 to work as a translator for **John Woo** in Thailand on the shoot of *Heroes Shed No Tears*. He also worked as production manager and assistant director on several **Jackie Chan** projects, including *Wheels on Meals* and *Armor of God*. In 1987, he worked in distribution and sales at the production company Alan & Eric (singer/actor **Alan Tam** and actor/director **Eric Tsang**), which closed after the Asian stock market crash later that year. In 1989, he worked at Impact Film, producing the buddy-cop story *Curry and Pepper*. Through these business experiences, Chan went on to cofound **United Filmmakers Organization (UFO)** in 1990 with partners Tsang, Claudie Chung, and directors **Jacob Cheung** and **Lee Chi-ngai** (Chi Lee), who wanted to make movies outside the action genre. Writer/director **James Yuen** later came onboard. The company wished to fill in the gap between very commercial and extremely noncommercial films, producing high-quality but commercial films. In 1996, UFO, in need of a major studio, merged with **Golden Harvest**. The group has always functioned in a collaborative spirit, encouraging creative freedom, nurturing first-time directors, sharing credits for writing and directing, and so on.

Chan's directorial debut was with *Alan and Eric: Between Hello and Goodbye/Seung shing goo si/Shuang cheng gu shi* (1991), which starred Alan Tam, Eric Tsang, and **Maggie Cheung**, but Chan has been active as a writer and just as prolific a producer as director, including *Days of Being Dumb* (1992), *Twenty Something* (1994), and *Twelve Nights* (2003). Chan's film territory has been middle-class twenty-somethings in search of self and examination of relationships that are not working. He creates urban "dramedies" (combinations of comedy and drama), such as 1993's *Tom, Dick and Hairy (Three World-Weary Heroes)/Fung chan saam hap/Feng chen san xia* (codirector, 1993) and *He Ain't Heavy, He's My Father (New Two of a Kind)/San naam hing naan dai/Xin nan xiong nan di* (1993). He credits Woody Allen's work as an influential style and believes in the globalization of filmmaking. He has often worked with an ensemble cast including Tsang, **Tony Leung Ka-fai**, **Tony Leung Chiu-wai**, **Leslie Cheung**, **Anita Yuen**, Maggie Cheung, and **Jordan Chan**. His gender-bending hit ***He's a Woman, She's a Man*** *(Gold Branch, Jade Leaf)/Gam chi yuk yip/Jin qi yu sye* (1994) was a local box office and international critical success. The film starred Leslie Cheung as a homophobic music producer, tired of the singing star (and girlfriend) he has promoted (**Carina Lau**), who falls for an androgynous new singer (actually female but whom he believes to be male, played by Anita Yuen). A comedy that nailed Hong Kong's fascination with celebrity, the film was pure fairy tale, capped by a kiss between the heterosexual couple. Reality set in with its sequel, inspired by Stanley Donen's *Two for the Road*, and the producer and new star try to live together. **Anita Mui** was added to the cast as a famous star not unlike the Hong Kong Madonna herself; a passionate kiss between Yuen and Mui not only disturbed Cheung's character but Hong Kong audiences, as did a tame lesbian sex scene. The sequel disappointed audiences and was not as successful at the box office, but again demonstrated Chan's exploration of **gender** identity.

While Chan considers himself Hong Kong Chinese, he believes his films appeal to international urban audiences and that contemporary city life is similar everywhere except for the language. Hollywood offered him many Asian-themed scripts, but he did not want to be pigeonholed as a Chinese director, so he accepted the Dreamworks invitation to direct *The Love Letter* (1999), with Tom Selleck and Kate Capshaw. He returned to Hong Kong in 2000 and formed **Applause Pictures**, producing the horror suspense film *The Eye/Gin gwai/Jian gui*, an international hit, by the **Pang Brothers**. Applause also produced *Three/Saam gang/San geng* (2002), an omnibus horror film for which he directed the episode *Going Home*; *Golden Chicken 1* and *2 Gam gai/Jin ji* (2002, 2003); and *The Eye 2/Gin gwai 2/Jian gui 2* (2004). A second omnibus horror film, *Three . . . Extremes* (2004) with Chan producing, included **Fruit Chan's** *Dumplings*, Japanese director Takeshi Miike's *Box*, and Korean director Park Chan-wook's *Cut*. Chan's latest project, a musical, *Perhaps Love/Yu guo aoi/ Ruoguo ai* (2005), was the closing film at the Venice Film Festival and was Hong Kong's official entry for the 2006 Academy Awards.

CHAN, PHILIP YAN-KIN (1945–). Born in Hong Kong, actor, director, and screenwriter Philip Chan graduated from La Salle College, became a police inspector in 1965, and was promoted to the Criminal Investigation Department (CID, the official name is now Divisional Investigation Team) superintendent in 1974. He left the force to join the entertainment industry, working on the Rediffusion Television (RTV) (now Asia Television Limited [ATV]) crime show *Operation Manhunt* for producer Johnny Mak and on Hong Kong Television Broadcasts Limited's (TVB) series *New CID*. He served as cowriter on **Leong Po-chih's** *Foxbat/Woo fook/Hu fu* (1979) and as production supervisor on **Yim Ho's** *The Extras/Ga law fau/Jia li fei* (1978). He codirected (with **Ronny Yu**) *The Servant/Cheung laap cheung ngoi/Qiang nei qiang wai* (1979), starring **Paul Chu Kong**, and his directorial debut was the drama *Charlie Bubbles/Man chai dik fei cho pau/Wen zai de fei zao pao* (1980). Chan has acted in close to 50 films, among them the Richard Ng–**John Shum** series of Pom Pom films (which he also directed) such as *Return of Pom Pom (Double Dragons Come from the Sea)/Seung lung chut hoi/Shuang long chu hai* (1984) and **John Woo's** *Hard-Boiled/Sau san taam/Lashou shentan* (1992), and written and directed close to a dozen each. Other directed films include the **Hui Brothers** vehicle *Inspector Chocolate (Godly Inspector Chocolate)/San taam ju goo lik/Shen tan zhu gu li* and *Tongs, A Chinatown Story (Tong Story)/Tong hau gu si/Tang kou gushi* (both 1986). Chan is currently CEO of **Mandarin Films**.

CHAN, WAN (Chun Man-to) (1921–). Director and screenwriter Chan Wan (real name Chan Lo-man) started as an uncredited screenwriter in the 1950s. He worked in **Shaw Brothers'** Cantonese division and the division head, Chow Sze-luk, gave him the opportunity to direct. His first film was *The Pursuers/Yuk lui chui chung/Yu nu zhui zong* (1959), starring **Lam Fung**, one of Chan's discoveries. In 1962, he joined Kwong Ngai studio, where his breakthrough film was *My Friend's Wife/Siu foo yan/Sou furen* (1962), starring **Patrick Tse Yin** and Nam Hung, which he adapted from his future wife's radio play. He wrote and directed under the pseudonyms Yu Ho and Chun Man-to. His wife, Ngai Man, wrote the screenplays for several of his movies, including *Love of a Pedicab Man/Sau che foo ji luen/Shou che fu zhi lian* (1965), *The Young Love (Youth's Love)/Ching chun ji luen/Qingchun zhi lian* (1967), and *Romance of a Teenage Girl* (1966). He worked with two of the leading stars of Cantonese cinema of the 1960s, **Josephine Siao** and **Connie Chan Po-chu**, directing them in youth musicals, and their work together signaled the transformation of prominence from male to female stars in Cantonese cinema.

Colorful Youth (1966) starred Siao and Chan in a youth musical that was a great box office success. *Romance of a Teenage Girl/Shaonu xin* was tailor-made to Josephine Siao's talents and she played three parts, in one scene all together. *The Dutiful Daughter (The Dutiful Daughter) Zhu Zhu/Haau liu Chu Chu/Xiaonu Zhuzhu* (1966) starred Chan Po-chu as Chu-chu (Pearl), a talented variety performer with aspirations to be an opera star. She is conflicted between caring for her mentally ill mother and the demands of her stern teacher (**Cantonese opera** master Liang Tsi-pak). The story emphasized duty to her father-figure teacher over that owed her mother.

Social Characters/Fei laam fei lui/Fei nan fei nu (1969) is one of the last 1960s Cantonese youth films to show the betrayal of the younger generation by their elders and from the point-of-view of youth. The Cantonese title (male and female equivalents of ***ah fei***) implies the adult view of these youth, while the English title suggests the youth perspective and the movie's approach. The film may have been influenced by **Chor Yuen's** earlier release the same year, ***Joys and Sorrows of Youth****/Lengnuan Qingchun*.

Chan continued his career in television in the 1970s and retired in 1985.

CHANG, CHEH (Zhang Che) (1923–2002). Born in Zhejiang Province, Mainland China, filmmaker Chang Cheh was educated at Chungking University. During the Sino–Japanese War, he formed a social education team focusing on cultural and dramatic work with other exiled students. At war's end, he went to Shanghai, where he became manager of the Wenhua Huitang (Cultural Hall) and staged plays and **Peking (Beijing) opera** and showed movies. He started in the film industry when he scripted the Shanghainese film *The False Faced Woman* (1947). He wrote and codirected *Storm Cloud over Alishan/Alishan Fengyun* (1949), the first Mandarin film produced in Taiwan. Made when he was only 26, the movie exhibited predilections that would become his signature, a romantic sensibility in an action film featuring largely male casts. He remained in Taiwan, directing plays and writing. He wrote a suspense script that became *The Cruel Heart of My Man* (1956), starring **Li Mei**. He came to Hong Kong, invited by that actress to direct her in *Wild Fire/ Ye huo* (1958). Although the film was not a great success, he remained as a screenwriter for **MP&GI**, then moving on to **Shaw Brothers**. His Hong Kong directorial debut was *Tiger Boy* (1966), his first ***wuxia*** action movie, starring **Jimmy Wang Yu** and **Lo Lieh**. His first blockbuster came the next year with *The One-Armed Swordsman/Duk bei diy/Du bi dao*, which made his name in Hong Kong, grossed over one million Hong Kong dollars, and made a star of Wang Yu.

Chang remains one of the most prolific and highly influential figures of Hong Kong action filmmaking, specializing in masculine-themed **martial arts** action celebrating *yanggang* (staunch masculinity), pioneering a new style with realistic violence and invigorating bare-chested heroes. His heroes are symbols of strength and power, embodying martial values of loyalty, integrity, righteousness, and filial piety. They often die but there is meaning in their deaths. In the early 1970s, he turned attention to another aspect of martial arts action filmmaking, focusing on various authentic training techniques and styles, in films like *Five Deadly Venoms/Yan je mo dik/Ren zhe wu di* (1978). In all, he has directed more than 90 films. Among his classics are *The One-Armed Swordsman* (1967), *Golden Swallow (The Girl with the Thunderbolt Kick)/Gam yin ji/Jin yan zi* (1968), *The Water Margin (Outlaws of the Marsh, Seven Blows of the Dragon)/Shui hui chuen/Shui hu zhuan*(1972), *The Blood Brothers/Chi ma/Ci ma* (1973), *The Boxer from Shantung (Killer from Shantung)/Ma wing ching/Ma yong zhen* (1972), *Shaolin Temple/Siu lam chi/Shaolin si* (1976), *Na Cha the Great/Na Cha/Na Zha* (1974), *Five Deadly Venoms,* and *Vengeance!/Bou sau/Bao chou* (1970). He discovered and developed new talent in front of and behind the camera, including actors like Wang, Lo, **Alexander Fu Sheng**, **Ti Lung**, and **David Chiang**, and directors like **Wu Ma** and **John Woo**, the latter Chang's assistant director on a number of films and Woo's acknowledged mentor. Chang received a Lifetime Achievement Award at the 2000 **Hong Kong Film Awards**. He is the godfather of Hong Kong **action** cinema (both martial arts and heroic bloodshed). If not for him, its film history would have written a different story.

CHANG, EILEEN (Zhang Ailing) (1920–1995). From Hebei province, writer Eileen Chang (real name Cheung Ying) wrote short stories and screenplays. Her grandfather Zhang Peilun was an important court official in the Qing dynasty. Her grandmother was the daughter of Li Hongzhang (Hunghang), who played a significant and powerful role in Chinese history as prime minister. Chang was educated in Shanghai at St. Mary's Hall Girls' School and entered the University of Hong Kong in 1939; she was unable to pursue studies at the University of London because of the war. With Hong Kong occupied by the Japanese, she returned to Shanghai in 1942 where she began publishing short stories and gained international literary attention; there she also wrote the screenplays *Love without End/Bu liao qing* and *Long Live the Wife/Taitai Wansui* (1947), produced by **Wenhua Studio** and directed by Sang Hu. She published stories and novellas, including *Love in a Fallen City/King sing zi Luen/ Qingcheng zhi lian,* which deals with Hong Kong shortly before and into the occupation. Her first anthology of stories, *Chuanqi (Romance)*, was published in 1942.

She returned to Hong Kong in 1952, where she met **Stephen Soong** (Song Qi) and in 1955 joined the script committee of the International Motion Picture Company (later **Motion Pictures and General Investment Company** [**MP&GI**], Cathay). That same year, she embarked for the United States and was given permanent citizenship status. She wrote screenplays for the company from 1957 to 1964, published her English-language novel *The Naked Earth* (1968), and moved to an artists' colony in Peterborough, New Hampshire, where she met and married U.S. writer Ferdinand Reyher.

Chang's first two screenplays for MP&GI were *The Battle of Love/Ching cheung yue chin cheung/ Qingchang Ru Zhangchang* and *A Tale of Two Wives/Yan choi leung dak/Ren cai liang de* (released 1957, 1958), directed by **Yue Feng**, with the former, MP&GI's first comedy, starring **Lin Dai**, **Chang Yang**, **Chen Ho**, and **Liu Enjia**, and the latter starring Kitty Ting Hao and Chen Ho. In *The Battle of Love*, the rich ingénue (Lin Dai) toys with men and attempts to seduce her cousin (Chang Yang), who loves her but won't commit; she pursues a white-collar worker (Chen Ho) and a lecturer (Liu Enjia), to make her cousin jealous, even though her sister (Qin Yu) is in love with the worker. Eventually the right couples are matched. Typical of Chang's screenwriting, the dialogue is witty, the setting is Chinese society, the tone is light, and the characters are middle-class Chinese straddling East and West, old and new.

In the 1960s, she wrote the comedy *June Bride/Luk yuet san leung/Liuyue xinniang* (1960, directed by **Tang Huang**), a film that marked Mandarin cinema's shift from Shanghai nostalgia to Hong Kong integration. She also wrote two of a **North–South trilogy** directed by **Wang Tianlin,** including *The Greatest Wedding on Earth/Nam bak yut ga chan/Nan bei yijia qin* (1962) and *The Greatest Love Affair on Earth/Naam bak hei seung fung/Nan bei xi xiang feng* (1964). (The first film, *The Greatest Civil War on Earth/Naam bak who/Nan be he* [1961], was written by Stephen Soong.) Leung Sing-po and Liu Enjia starred in all three as Cantonese and Northern Chinese whose clash of language and culture leads to comedy; by story's end, the animosity between the characters dissolves into mutual but grudging respect, better understanding, and cooperation. Chang's only tragic Hong Kong screenplay was *Please Remember Me/Yat kuk laan mong/Yi qu nan wang* (1964), adapted from Mervyn LeRoy's *Waterloo Bridge* (1940, U.S.).

When the head of MP&GI, **Loke Wan Tho**, was unexpectedly killed in a plane crash and Stephen Soong left the company shortly thereafter, Chang lost connection with the company. She worked for the Voice of America in Washington, adapting famous novels into broadcast plays. Her serialized novels were published in newspapers between 1966 and 1967, and she began as a writer-in-residence at Miami University (Oxford, Ohio) and then Radcliffe College (Cambridge, Massachusetts), where she reworked her novel *Eighteen Springs* into *Destiny Unfulfilled/Bansheng Yuan* (1968) for Taipei's Crown Publishers. Between 1969 and 1971, she was a researcher for Professor Chen Shijun at the University of California, Berkeley, moving to Los Angeles in 1972, where she wrote articles for Hong Kong and Taiwan newspapers. More novels were published in the 1970s.

Chang's novels and stories explore the relationships between **women** and men, raise gender issues, and relate to women's daily lives and tell their stories. Penetrating observation of characterization and the expression of a variety of women's contradictory feelings and desires create depth and insight. Chang's women are often caught between the old and new, and in moments of conflict and crisis discover themselves. Several Hong Kong films have been based on her fiction, including **Ann Hui's** *Love in a Fallen City/King Sing zi Luen/Qingcheng Zhi Lian* (1984) and *Eighteen Springs/Boon sang yuen/Ban seng yuen* (1997), and **Stanley Kwan's** *Red Rose, White Rose/Hung mooi gwai baak mooi gwai/Hong mei gui bai mei gui*

(1994). *Love in a Fallen City* starred **Chow Yun-fat** and Cora Miao. Chow played a wealthy playboy drawn to a Shanghai divorcee (Miao); with a sexist attitude toward women, he commits to marriage only after she leaves him and he is afraid of losing her. Their love truly blossoms only after she finds herself and he loses his fortune during Hong Kong's Japanese occupation. Kwan's *Red Rose, White Rose* stars **Joan Chen** as a passionate married lover (the "red rose") and **Veronica Yip** as the repressed wife (the "white rose") of Winston Chao in the 1920s. Chang's fiction (and the film adaptations) speaks to women today as much as when it was originally written.

CHANG, SYLVIA NGAI-GA (Cheung Ai-chia) (1953–). Born in Taiwan, multitalented actress, director, and writer Sylvia Chang began as a singer on variety **television** (by 1997, she had earned seven platinum recordings), joined **Golden Harvest** in the early 1970s to make movies, but quickly returned to Taiwan, appearing on television and in films. After marrying in 1979, she moved permanently to Hong Kong, and joining with Selina Chow, produced **Ann Hui's** *The Secret/Fung gip/Feng jie* (in which she costarred with Alex Man). Her acting debut was the **kung fu** flick *Flying Tigers/Fei foo siu ba wong/Fei hu xiao ba wang* (1971) and her directorial debut, after apprenticing under **King Hu** on *Legend of the Mountain/Saan chung chuen kei/ Shanzhong chuanqi* 1979), was *A Certain Day/Mou nian mou yue yi tian* (1980), replacing director Tu Zhongxun, who died unexpectedly, for Golden Harvest. She played (albeit underused) in numerous *Aces Go Places/Chui gai pak dong/Zui jia pai dang* movies (1982–1989), but one moving performance includes her role in **Cheung Yuen-ting's** third film in her immigrant trilogy, *Eight Taels of Gold/Baat a gam/Ba ya jin* (1989), in which she plays cousin to **Samo Hung**, who, after getting his green card, returns home to China to visit his parents and travels with his cousin (Chang). At first they do not get along, but grow to love each other. His family encourages him to find a wife and return to the United States while her American fiancé comes to marry her. Bai gives Wu all he has, namely, eight taels of gold. In 1990, she appeared in films as diverse as **Johnnie To's Lunar New Year's comedy** *The Fun, the Luck and the Tycoon (Lucky Star Join Hands and Shine)/Gat sing gung jiu/Ji xing gong zhao* (in which she costarred opposite **Chow Yun-fat**) and

Stanley Kwan's drama *Full Moon in New York (People in New York)/Yan joi nau yeuk/Ren zai niu yue* (1989), among a three-**women** ensemble. She also costarred with Chow in To's Hong Kong tearjerker version of *The Champ*, *All about Ah-Long/A Long dik goo si/A Lang de gu shi* (1989, which she wrote), also sharing similarities to *Kramer vs. Kramer*. Chang has appeared in Hollywood movies as disparate as the actioner *Slaughter in San Francisco* (1973, opposite Chuck Norris) and the art house pleaser *The Red Violin* (1998, starring Samuel L. Jackson).

Chang began managing **Cinema City's** Taiwan branch in 1983; the year prior she directed **Gong Li** in *Mary from Beijing (Awaken from Dream Time)/Mung seng shut fan/Meng xing shi fen*, which she also wrote. She sang the concluding song for Yonfan's *Bishonen (Love of a Beautiful Boy)/Me siu nin ji luen/Mei shao nian zhi lian* (1998). Her latest directed film, the romantic comedy *20:30:40*, casts her as one of three women at various stages in their lives, and all of the films she has directed (10 to date) reflect women's issues and honestly address their sexuality.

Chang has won numerous awards for acting, directing, and writing, including Taiwanese **Golden Horse** Best Actress awards for *My Grandfather/Ngo dik yau yau/Wo de ye ye* (1982) and *Passion/Chui oi/Zui ai* (1986) and **Hong Kong Film Awards'** Best Actress winner for *Passion* and *Forever and Forever/Dei gau tin cheung/Di jiu tian chang* (2001) and Best Screenplay for *Tempting Heart/Sam dung/Xin dong* (1999).

CHANG, TERENCE JIA-TSUN (Zhang Jiacun) (1949–). Born in Hong Kong, producer and manager Chang is known in film circles for his business savvy and artistic acumen. Chang studied architecture at the University of Oregon before studying film at New York University. He returned to Hong Kong in 1978 and was production manager on two films before joining Rediffusion Television (RTV, now ATV) in 1979 as administration officer of the Production Department, where he supervised operation of all **television** productions for two years. He joined **Johnny Mak** Productions in 1981, producing *Lonely 15*, *Dragon Force*, and *Everlasting Love* (starring **Andy Lau** and chosen for the 1984 Cannes Director's Fortnight). From 1986 to 1988, he was in charge of distribution at **D&B Films**, successfully launching the careers of **Michelle Yeoh** (he later became her manager) and Brandon Lee. In 1988, he joined **Film Workshop** as general manager; he was executive in charge of *The Killer*, *Swordsman*, *Spy Games*, *Love and Death in Saigon*, *A Chinese Ghost Story 2*, and *Gunmen*. He first met **John Woo** in 1978, and they met again during this time and became business partners. In 1990, with Linda Kuk, they formed Milestone Pictures, producing *Now You See Love . . . Now You Don't*, *Once a Thief*, and *Hard-Boiled*; he also became manager of **Chow Yun-fat** and internationally regarded novelist Lillian Lee (*Farewell, My Concubine* and *The Last Princess of Manchuria*, both published in English by William Morrow).

Chang was instrumental in guiding Woo to Hollywood, first taking *The Killer* to Cannes. In 1993, he coproduced Woo's U.S. film debut, *Hard Target*; in 1994 they formed WCG Entertainment (also with Christopher Godsick), producing *Broken Arrow*, *Face/Off*, *The Replacement Killers*, and *Mission: Impossible 2*. In 2000, Chang and Woo formed **Lion Rock Productions**, producing Woo's *Windtalkers*, *The Big Hit*, *Bulletproof Monk*, and *Paycheck*. Chang and Woo currently have several international projects in development, including a remake of Jean-Pierre Melville's *Le Cercle Rouge* and a remake of Franklin J. Schaffner's *Papillon*, and two Chinese language films, an homage to Woo's *Bullet in the Head* called *Blood Brothers* (directed by Asian American Alexi Tan and shifted to 1930s Shanghai), and the epic *Red Cliff* (directed by Woo and starring Chow Yun-fat). *The Divide*, which will reunite Chow Yun-fat and Woo for their first Hollywood movie, is the movie most anticipated by Western Hong Kong movie fans. The 19th-century story concerns the Chinese and Irish immigrants who built the railroad across the United States.

Chang also directed a film, *Escape from Coral Cove/Tow chut saan woo hoi/Tao chu shan hu hai* (1986), starring **Alex Fong**, and he appears in a cameo for *Now You See Love . . . Now You Don't*. A modest and behind-the-scenes man, Chang is nonetheless articulate, insightful, and prominent in the industry.

CHANG, WILLIAM SUK-PING (1953–). Art director William Chang was born and educated in Hong Kong. He worked as a fabric designer before he befriended director **Tang Shuxuan** (Tong Shushuen) and became her assistant director on *Sup Sap Bup Dup/Sap saam bat daap/Shisan buda* (1975) and *The Hong Kong Tycoon/Biu* *faat woo/Bao fa hu* (1979). In the late 1970s, he studied at the Vancouver School of Arts, returning to Hong Kong to work as a designer. He served as art director on **Patrick Tam's** *Love Massacre/Ai sha* (1981) and *Nomad (Flaming Youth)/Lit foh ching chun Lit foh ching chun /Lie huo qing chun* (1982), the start of a working relationship with numerous **New Wave** directors such as **Tsui Hark** (*All the Wrong Clues [for the Right Solution]/Gwai ma ji doh sing/Gui ma zhi duo xing* [1981]), **Tony Au** (*The Last Affair/Fa sing/Hua cheng* [1983]), **Yim Ho** (*Homecoming/Chi shui lau nin/Si shui liu nian* (1984), and **Stanley Kwan** (*Love unto Waste [Underground Love]/Dei ha ching/Di xia qing* [1986]).

Chang's collaborations with director **Wong Kar-wai** began in 1988 with *As Tears Go By (Mongkok Carmen, Carmen of the Streets)/Wong kok Ka Moon/Wang jiao Ka Men* (1988). Along with cinematographer **Christopher Doyle**, the three (known as the "holy trinity") began a productive relationship over numerous films, including *Chungking Express (Chungking Forest)/Chung Hing sam lam/Zong qing sen lin* (1994), *Happy Together (A Sudden Leak of Spring Light)/Chun gwong ja sit/Chun guang zha xie* (1997), and *In the Mood for Love/Fa yeung nin wa/Hua yang nian hua* (2000). Working with Wong, Chang also became creatively involved in other ways, as costume designer, editor, and producer. Chang's distinctive look for films involves color symbolism, subtle design, and a look true to the world of the film, whether realistic or over the top. Besides Wong, he has continued to work with Tsui, Kwan, and Yim, among others, and served as costume designer on **Ronny Yu's** *The Phantom Lover (Midnight Song)/Ye boon goh sing/Ye ban ge sheng* (1995), **Chen Kaige's** *Temptress Moon/Fung yuet/Feng yue* (1996), and **Carol Lai's** *The Floating Landscape/Luen ji fung ging/Lian zhi feng jing* (2003). Since the 1980s, Chang has expanded into other media, working in interior design, the recording industry, and on the stage.

CHANG, YANG (Cheung Yeung, Zhang Yang) (1930–). A native of Guangdong province, actor Chang Yang was educated in Tianjin and Beijing and enrolled at Furen University. He came to Hong Kong in 1951 and joined **Shaw Brothers** in 1953. His film debut was the drama *Black Gloves/Hak sau tow/Hei shou tao* (1953), costarring **You Min**. He joined the **Motion Pictures and General Investment**

Ltd. (MP&GI, Cathay) in 1956, and his first film for the company was **Evan Yang**'s Chinese opera *Gloomy Sunday/Chun sik liu yan/ Chun se nao ren* (1956). **Yue Feng's** *Scarlet Doll/Hung wa/Hong wa* (1958), costarring **Lin Dai** and **Wang Yin**, made him a star.

As a leading man, Chang worked with directors **Tao Qin**, Yue Feng, **Tang Huang**, and **Wang Tianlin**; he was often paired with the most popular and leading actresses of the day, including **Ge Lan**, Lin Dai, **Li Mei**, You Min, **Lin Cui**, and **Ye Feng**, in romantic dramas, musicals, and comedies. For the most part, he was the embodiment of gentleness, the model son of a traditional Chinese family, playing the husband, boyfriend, or target of very strong women. For example, his collaborations with Ge Lan include the musical *Girl with a Thousand Guises/Chin min lui long/ Qianmian nulang* (1959) and the tragic ***The Wild, Wild Rose****/Yau mooi gwai ji luen/Yemeigui zhi lian* (1960) and the comedies *Our Dream Car/Heung che mei yan/Xiang che mei ren* (1959) and *June Bride/Luk yuet san leung/Liuyue xinniang* (1960, written by **Eileen Chang**). Chang's films include Yue Feng's comedies *The Battle of Love/Ching cheung yue chin cheung/ Qingchang Ru Zhangchang* (1957, with Lin Dai and Qin Yu) and *Bachelors Beware/Wan yau hing/Wen rou qing* (1960, with Lin Dai), and his drama *For Better, for Worse/Yue goh tin ching/Yu guo tian qing* (1959, with Li Mei), in the latter as a widower making a new life with Li's widow. He appeared with You Min in her first film for MP&GI, Tang Huang's drama ***Her Tender Heart****/Yuk lui shut ching/ Yunu siqing* (1959), and with Lin Cui and Ye Feng in Evan Yang's comedy *Too Young for Love/Yee baat gaai yan/Er ba jia ren* (1959). Evan Yang's ***Sun, Moon, and Star*** *1* and *2/Sing sing yuet leung taai yeung/Xingxing, Yueliang, Taiyang* brought together three of the actresses, Ye Feng, Ge Lan, and You Min. Based on a popular novel, the title is based on the three female leads as representative types of women, with Chang as the love interest of all three.

Chang could play the light tone in Eileen Chang's screenplays for *The Battle of Love* and *June Bride* (in the latter he is the prospective groom of a Shanghai bride as they accept Hong Kong as home). In Wang Tianlin's *Darling Stay at Home/Taai taai maan sui/Tai tai wan sui* (1968), he played a chauvinistic husband whose wife (**Le Di**) disguises herself, gets a job in the hotel where he works, and is promoted to become his boss. But Chang could also play the sensitive companion of a confused girl in *Her Tender Heart*, a torn tragic figure in *Sun, Moon and Star*, or the downwardly spiraling lover of a songstress in *The Wild, Wild Rose*.

Chang was married to actress Ye Feng from 1961 to 1965, when they divorced. He remarried and moved to Taiwan to continue his career. He appeared in **Chang Cheh's** *The Water Margin (Outlaws of the Marsh, Seven Blows of the Dragon)/Shui hui chuen/Shui hu zhuan* (1972) and took part in directing a short-lived series of "Bumpkin" themed films in the mid-1970s (*Crazy Bumpkins/A ang yap shing gei/A niu ru cheng ji*, *Return of the Crazy Bumpkin/A ang chut yut gei/A iu chu yu ji*, and *The Lucky Bumpkin/A fook bei guai mai/A fu bei gui mi,* 1974, 1975, and 1976 respectively). He retired from film in 1975, moved to the United States, and went into business.

CHEN, DIEYI (Dik Yee) (1909–). Movie film score and song lyricist and screenwriter Chen Dieyi was born in Jiangsu province. His father was a scholar and his home had a large library, so Chen was encouraged to study classical Chinese literature. In 1924, he moved to Shanghai, trained in a newspaper office, and was a reporter and newspaper and magazine editor. He became a leading writer of the romantic school, and was approached by director **Fang Peilin** to write song lyrics for *Two Phoenixes Fly Together* (1942), thus beginning his career as a lyricist. His more than five thousand songs include popular ones such as "Shangri-la," "You Are Spring Breeze," "Kiss of Spring," and "Lovers' Tears."

Chen wrote lyrics under several pseudonyms, using the names Di Yi, Chen Shi, Fang Da, Xin Yi, and Fang Bian. He wrote in the language of ordinary people. His preference for working was to write freely and turn over his words to the musicians to set them to music, but when required he also would take existing scores and write the lyrics to fit the meter. His most memorable work was in musicals and comedies.

The lyricist was also a screenwriter, writing more than 50 screenplays. His first, *Little Phoenix/Siu fung sin/Xiao fengxian* (1953), starred **Li Lihua**, as did his new version of *Dream of the Red Chamber/San hung lau mung/Xin hong lou meng* (1978).

CHEN, JINGBO (Chan Jing-boh) (1924–1995). Producer, director, and actor Chen Jingbo, a native of Fujian province, was born and educated in Shanghai. At 16, he joined the Yilin Amateurs' Acting Group and enrolled in the Tianfeng Drama Troupe training course. He immigrated to Hong Kong in 1946, making his screen debut in the Companion Company's war-themed *Lady in Distress/Mung laan foo yan/Meng nan fu ren* (1947). Chen also appeared in the contemporary Mandarin realist drama *Peasant's Tragedy/Shan he lei* (1949); **Zhu Shilin's** satirical Mandarin comedy *Map of 100 Treasures/Bak bo tiu/Bai bao tu* (1953, for which Chen was also the makeup artist), in which a swindler is swindled; and **Great Wall's** romantic tragedy *A Torn Lily/Niehai hua* (1953).

Chen began working as assistant director to Zhu Shilin beginning with *Festival Moon/Zhon qiu yue* (1953). He codirected *Troubles with Bachelors (Troubles of the Bachelors)/Laam daai dong fan/Nan da dang hun* (1957) with Law Kwun-hung, and between 1957 and 1976, collaborated with others on 25 films, including *Love's Miracle/Ching dau choh hoi/Qing dou chu kai* (1958, codirector Luo Junwei) and *The Precious Little Moon/Siu yuet leung/Xiao yue liang* (1959, codirectors Zhu Shilin and **Ren Yizhi**). He directed *Mutual Hearts/Tung sam git/Tong xin jie* (1959), *Let's Get Married/Ngo moon yiu git fan/Wo men yao jie hun* (1962), and the first Hong Kong million-dollar hit at the box office, *Golden Eagle/Gam ying/Jin ying* (1964). *Mutual Hearts*, a contemporary family melodrama, concerns the trials of a husband (Lee Ching) and wife (Chen Juanjuan) with a son; the husband is fired from his job because of an eye disease and the pregnant wife miscarries fending off a gangster. The husband considers working as a coolie to pay for his wife's medical expenses, but relatives come up with the money.

Chen also was a screenwriter, writing *Love's Miracle* and *The Precious Little Moon*, among others. Considered to be one of Feng Huang's best comedies and featuring a strong cast (**Fu Che**, Zhu Hong, Sek Lui, and Gong Qiuxia), *Love's Miracle* concerns two neighboring middle-aged couples that squabble over minor issues; the humor hinges on their children falling in love and concocting numerous ways to reconcile the feuding parents. Chen became manager of **Feng Huang** Film Company in 1978, producing **Allen Fong's** *Father and Son* (1981) and *Ah Ying* (1983). He became assistant general manager when **Sil-Metropole** was established in 1982.

CHEN, JOAN CHUNG (1961–). Actress Joan Chen was born in Shanghai to physician parents. She was enrolled in the actors' training program at the Shanghai Film Studio where she was discovered by director Xie Jin, and she won the Best Actress award in China for her performance in his *Little Flower/Siu dut/Xiao hua* (1980). She left China in 1981 to study filmmaking and graduated with honors from California State University, Northridge. Her Hollywood acting debut was in Daryl Duke's *Tai-Pan* (1986), and she appeared in numerous Western films, from action to drama, including the internationally well-regarded *The Last Emperor* (1987), directed by Bernardo Bertolucci, and the first Western production to be allowed to shoot in the Forbidden City. Chen, known for her beauty and sensuality onscreen, played the wife of the titular Pu Yi, and her performance reflected the tragedy of her character, who falls from an elevated position into dementia, as well as the tumultuous political change of a nation. Although Chen became well known in the United States for her performance as Josie Packard in David Lynch's surreal TV series *Twin Peaks* (1990), she is also recognized in Hong Kong for her dual performance in expatriate director **Clara Law's** erotic *Temptation of a Monk/Yau jang/You seng* (1993) and her performance as the life-affirming Red Rose in art house director **Stanley Kwan's** *Red Rose White Rose/Hung mooi gwai baak mooi gwai/Hong mei gui bai mei gui* (1994), for which she won Taiwan's **Golden Horse Award** and the Hong Kong Film Critics Award for Best Actress.

Chen turned to directing with *Xiao Xiao: The Sent-Down Girl/Tian Yu* (1997), based on the story "Heavenly Bath" by Yan Geling, set during the Cultural Revolution when a generation of urban youth was sent to the countryside and narrating the unusual love story that develops between a Tibetan horseman and a young, innocent girl. Her Hollywood directorial debut was *Autumn in New York* (2000), starring Richard Gere and Winona Ryder. Although Chen stars in Mainland director Zhang Yang's *Sunflower* (2005), she also has recently turned toward independent film, exhibiting a flair for comedy in Chinese American Alice Wu's *Saving Face* (2004) and in Eric Byler's *Americanese* (2006), the latter based on the Shawn Wong novel *American Knees*.

CHEN, JUANJUAN (Chan Guen-guen) (1928?/29?/31?–1976). Actress Chen Juanjuan (real name Chen Sujuan), a native of Sichuan province, was born in Malaya, came to Shanghai at age three, traveled China and Southeast Asia at 10 as a member of a song and dance troupe, and by 12 had appeared in a dozen films, including **Zhu Shilin's** *Song of a Mother* (1937). Shot on location in rural Zhejiang and Jiangsu, the story revolves around a peasant mother with a lazy husband and four sons, the eldest of which abuses her and the third who protects her.

Following the war, Chen worked for several film companies in Hong Kong, including **Great Wall**, **Dazhonghua**, and **Feng Huang**, and appeared in movies such as *Witch, Devil, Gambler* (1952) and Zhu Shilin's comedy *To Marry or Not to Marry/Hung cheuk bing/Kong que ping* (1954). The actress starred in the latter as an eligible middle-class high school graduate whose parents attempt to arrange her marriage; three prospective suitors are exposed for their hypocrisy, and the young woman is allowed to continue her studies. Chen had earlier appeared in Zhu's romance tragedy *A Dream of Spring/Chun ji mung/Chun zhi meng* (1947), playing stepdaughter to **Butterfly Wu**. Chen acted chiefly in Mandarin dramas.

Chen worked as an assistant director on several films and codirected the Mandarin war movie *The Heroic New Generation/Ying hung hau doi/Ying xiong hou dai* (1969) and romance *Three Seventeens/Saam goh sap chat sui/San ge shi qi sui* (1972). She died in Hong Kong.

CHEN, KAIGE (1952–). Director Chen Kaige was born in Beijing; his father, Chen Huaiai, was a famous film director whose work spanned two decades, from the 1950s to the 1970s. As a teenager, he joined the Red Guard, and, as many youth were, was sent down during the late 1960s, where he worked in Yunnan province defoliating land on a rubber plantation, later joining the army. Returning to Beijing in the mid-1970s, Chen began studying film at the Beijing Film Academy, graduating in 1982. *Yellow Earth* (1984), Chen's first film, won international attention, telling its story primarily through imagery, not dialogue, and visual truth remains the acid test of his work, although numerous political subtexts have been analyzed. Chen's comrade and classmate **Zhang Yimou** worked as the cameraman on the film. Both are a part of the Fifth Generation filmmakers who were among the first graduating class of the Beijing Film Academy following the school's reopening after the Cultural Revolution; although their styles differed, they revitalized Chinese cinema in the mid-1980s. In the late 1980s Chen served as a visiting scholar at New York University Film School. Chen's early films are small in scale and stark by comparison to later films that include the epic *The Emperor and the Assassin* (1999).

Although not a Hong Kong director, Chen worked with Hong Kong actor **Leslie Cheung** on two important films, *Farewell My Concubine* (1993) and *Temptress Moon/Fung yuet/Feng yue* (1996). The former is epic in scope. Adapted from a Lillian Lee novel that tracks cultural and political change in 20th-century China, the film explores love, betrayal, and fate among three characters (Cheung, Zhang Fengyi, and **Gong Li**), two male opera singers and the woman who comes between them, set against the background of tumultuous history; it won the Palme d'Or at the Cannes Film Festival. Brooding and beguiling, Cheung played the **Peking (Beijing) opera** singer of the title, whose real-life experience he conflates with the doomed concubine he plays. Actors Cheung and Li and the director collaborated again on *Temptress Moon*, another story of love and betrayal, set in 1920s Shanghai. Sumptuously lit and shot by **Christopher Doyle**, with numerous sensual close-ups of Cheung as a sympathetic wounded but cruel gigolo, the movie is not only a visual lament for the glamour of a bygone era, but also an insightful examination of corruption at many levels.

CHEN, KUAN-TAI (Chen Guantai) (1945–). A martial artist originally from Guangdong, actor Chen Kuan-tai specializes in monkey-style **kung fu**, a type of fighting art that requires speed and agility. His first teacher was his grandfather, also a monkey stylist. He excelled in the art, winning a championship tournament in 1969 against fighters from all over Southeast Asia. At around the same period, he joined the **Shaw Brothers** studio, just in time for the boom in kung fu movies sparked by the success of **Bruce Lee** and Shaw director **Chang Cheh**.

After giving him bit parts in a few films, Chang cast Chen Kuan-tai as the lead in *Boxer from Shantung/Ma wing ching/Ma yong zhen* (1972), and he really tore up the screen in his big fight scene. The Shaw studio was quick to capitalize on the film's success, positioning Chen as the "blood brother" of popular kung fu actors **David**

Chiang and **Ti Lung**. In Chang Cheh–directed films, such as *Blood Brothers/Chi ma/Ci ma* (1973) and *Heroes Two/Fong Sai-yuk yue Hung Hei-goon /Fang Shiyu yu Hong Xiguan* (1974), Chen's presence contributed a down-to-earth, good-humored quality to the tales of masculine camaraderie. After making a couple of socially aware contemporary films, *The Teahouse/Shing gei cha lau/Cheng ji cha lou* (1974) and *Big Brother Cheng/Da ge Cheng* (1975), he came to embody the ideal *da ge* (big brother): generous, fond of a joke or a drink, and always protective of those who are weak or in trouble.

Chen had worked with choreographer **Lau Kar-leung** on classic kung fu films like *Heroes Two* and *Men from the Monastery/Siu lam ji dei/Shaolin zi di* (1974); in them, he frequently played *hung gar* kung fu founder Hung Hsi Kwan. Lau naturally turned to Chen when he began to direct the series of *hung gar* films that were to about to make the international audience sit up and take notice. *Challenge of the Masters/Wong Fei-hung yue Luk a Choi/Huang Fei-hong yu Liu a Cai* (1976) was Lau's take on another *hung gar* story cycle about the life of Wong Fei-hung, a legendary master. Chen Kuan-tai played Wong's own teacher. And in *Executioners from Shaolin/Hung Hei-goon/Hung He kuan Hung Hei-kwun/Hong Xiguan*(1977), he once again was cast as lineage founder Hung.

In 1977, Chen stepped out of the Shaw studio to direct and act the title role in a well-regarded independent kung fu film, *Iron Monkey/Tit ma lau/Tie ma liu*. There was a contract dispute as a result, and Chen went back to Shaw for a few more productions. His most memorable film from this time is **martial arts action** film *Killer Constable/Maan yan jarm/Wan jen chan* (1981). He continued to work in the Hong Kong film and television industry through the 1980s and 1990s.

CHEN, LIPIN (Chan Laap-ban) (1911–?). Actress Chen Lipin (real name Chen Huifang), a native of Guangdong province, was born in Guangzhou, where she finished secondary education. She began learning **Cantonese opera** at age 12 and started performing with a professional opera troupe at 16. She was a supporting actress with Longfeng Cantonese Opera Troupe when she left to marry at 24.

Chen's screen debut was in the Cantonese family melodrama *A Happy Marriage Means Wealth/Jiahe wanshi xing* (1950). The next year she appeared in the Cantonese contemporary comedy *This Glamorous Life/Chi chui gam mai/Zhi zui jin mi* (1951), set in the Chinese opera world. Chen starred as the shrewish woman in numerous films. She has appeared in over 700 features, including the Ba Jin-based trilogy *Family/Ga/Jia* (1953), *Spring/Chun/Chun* (1953), and *Autumn/Chau/Qiu* (1954); the parents' love for their children–themed movies ***Parents' Hearts****/Foo miu sam/ Fumu Xin* (1955, directed by **Chun Kim**) and *The Great Devotion/Hoh lin tin gwong foo miu sam/Ke lian tian xia fu mu xin* (1960, directed by **Chor Yuen**); and others as disparate as Chor Yuen's martial arts brothel-set *Intimate Confessions of a Chinese Courtesan/Oi No/Ai Nu* (1972) and **Michael Hui's** comedic *Games Gamblers Play/Gwai ma seung sing/Gui ma shuang xing* (1974). In **John Woo's** *From Riches to Rags/ Chin jok gwaai /Qian zuo guai* (1980), she played Ricky Hui's grandmother, and in **Wong Jing's** *God of Gamblers/Do san/Du shen* (1989), she played **Andy Lau's** mother.

Selina Chow encouraged Chen to sign on with **television** in the 1970s. She started with the *Hui Brothers Show* (1970), and many soap operas followed, including *The Bund* (1979), starring **Chow Yun-fat**. She played a poor grandmother in the award-winning television drama *Wild Child* (1977).

CHEN, MELINDA MANLING (1947–). Actress Chen Manling was born in Fujian province and joined Cathay **(Motion Pictures and General Investment)** in 1965, working first as a continuity assistant on *Gunfight in Lo Ma Lake* (1966) as she trained in the studio's actor's course. Her screen debut was *Operation Macau* (1967) and she appeared in a Japanese Toho production, *Soccer Star* (1967).

The actress's first lead role was in **Evan Yang's** melodrama *Boat Girl* (1968). Chen played a fisherman's daughter who falls in love with a college student, and her performance earned her the title the "gem of Cathay Studio."

Chen starred in 25 films, the majority of them **martial arts** movies. They include **Tu Guangqi's** *The First Sword/Dai yat kim/Di yi jian* (1967) and *Invisible Saber/Aan ling dou/Yan ling dao* (1968), **Wang Tianlin's** *Stealing the Imperial Seal (The Royal Seal)/Dou saai/Dao xi* (1968), and **Chor Yuen's** *Cold Blade/Lung muk heung/Long mu xiang* (1970). In *The First Sword*, Chen played the assistant to the chief of the Golden Dragon clan (**Zhao Lei**), and they seek the help of elders who specialize in poisons to save the clan. The film was the actress's first swordplay film. In *Cold Blade*, the director's first martial arts movie, she starred as a Mongolian princess vying for possession of a treasure map with Song patriots and caught in a love–hate relationship with an enemy swordsman. She also appeared in Chor Yuen's Mandarin drama *Violet Clove and Firebird/Feng diu dai yat hou/Huo niao di yi hao* (1970) and romance *The Lost Spring/Yuk lau chun mung/Yu lou chun meng* (1970).

The actress was borrowed by the Taiwan studio Wu Zhou for a film, and returned to Cathay with *Inn of the Goddess/Guanyin kezhan* (1971), which remained unfinished. Following that film, she withdrew from the film industry, except for a cameo as the pregnant prostitute in **Patrick Lung Gong's** *Call Girls/Ying chiu lui long/Yingzhao nulang* (1973).

CHEN, PETER HO (1929–1970). Actor Peter Chen Ho (real name Chen Shanghou) was the closest Mandarin musicals ever got to a male star, functioning as the inconspicuous lead; he worked at both **Motion Pictures and General Investment** (Cathay) and **Shaw Brothers**. A Shanghaiese who came to Hong Kong with his family in 1950, he started working with Shaw in 1953, but director **Tu Guangqi** recommended him to Hsin Hwa, where he signed and made his debut in the director's *Qiu Jin, the Revolutionary Heroine/Chau Gan/Qin Jin* (1953). He appeared in **Wang Tianlin's** Mandarin musical ***Songs of the Peach Blossom River****/Tou Fa Kong/Taohua jiang* (1956) as a tone-deaf country boy who cannot sing, but his first leading role was in **Evan Yang's** musical *Holiday Express/Dak bit faai che/Te bie kuai che* (1957). He held his own against **Ge Lan** in Yi's ***Mambo Girl****/Maan boh lui long/Manbo nulang* (1957), as an uptight and innocent admiring dance student, considering the film was tailor-made for her talents and epitomized the Mandarin musical.

He costarred in a series of Mandarin comedies, including **Yue Feng's** extravagant production *The Battle of Love/Ching cheung yue chin cheung/Qingchang ru zhanchang* (1957), a battle of the sexes story based on **Eileen Chang's** witty screenplay. Chen falls for **Lin Dai's** flirtatious beauty; she loves her cousin (Chang Yang), while her sister (Qin Yu) secretly loves Chen. He also starred as the romantic interest for **Li Mei** and Zhang Zhongwen in **Tao Qin's** musical comedy *Calendar Girl/Lung cheung fung mo/ Longxiang fengwu* (1959), MP&GI's first color film, as well as one of the boyfriends in Tao's musical melodrama ***Our Sister Hedy****/Se chin gam/Si qianjin* (1957). He costarred with Lin Dai in **Tang Huang's** Mandarin musical comedy *Cinderella and Her Little Angels/Wan seung yim hau/Yunchang yanhou* (1959), delivering an outstanding comic performance that earned him the name "Holy Hand of Comedy." In a plot involving a big show to benefit orphans, the movie combined the integrated and backstage musical. At one point Chen sings to dolls. A very different comedy was Evan Yang's *The Loving Couple/Sam Sam Seung Yan/ Xin Xin Xiang Yin* (1960) for Cathay, in which a husband (Chen) and wife (Ge Lan) quarrel because of the husband's inattentiveness due to business. Ever experimental, Yang used split screens, point-of-view sequences, and a *Rashomon*-like telling from each spouse's perspective, to the befuddlement of the brother called in to moderate.

Tao Qin's *Love Parade/Fa tuen gam chuk/Hua tan jin cu* (1963) was another battle of the sexes comedy, a big budget Shaw musical with attention-getting art design and lavish sets and fashions. Chen plays a fashion designer opposite the single, and old-fashioned, obstetrician Lin Dai; the story follows their falling in love, marrying, and wedding night, which is constantly interrupted to humorous effects. Some of Chen's musicals were also dramatic. He starred in two of the musicals made by the Japanese director at Shaw, **Inoue Umetsugu**, *Hong Kong Nocturne/Heung Kong fa yuet yeh/ Xiangjiang huayue ye* (1967) and *Hong Kong Rhapsody/Fa yuet leung siu/Hua yue liang xiao* (1968). In the former, he played husband to **Cheng Pei-pei**, who dies in a plane crash. In the latter, he played a womanizing magician who becomes foster father to a beautiful orphan girl (**Li Ching**, disguised as a boy).

Chen's dramas featured strong musical elements, as in **Chun Kim's** *Till the End of Time/Hoh yat gwan joi loi/He ri jun zai lai* (1966) for Shaw. An update of the tragic songstress story, with elaborate art design, the film stars Chen as a rich man's son who falls for a nightclub singer (Hu Yanni, in her screen debut); disowned by his father for choosing an unacceptable woman, Chen works to support the couple, losing his eyesight. When the wife returns to singing to care for him, he makes the ultimate sacrifice for her out of love. The film won Honorable Mention for Dramatic Feature and Best Score for a Nonmusical at the fifth **Golden Horse Awards**.

Chen was married for a time to actress **Le Di** (Betty Lo Tieh), but they divorced. He died of colon cancer at age 40 while living in the United States.

CHEN, SISI (Chen Sze-sze) (1937–). Actress Chen Sisi (real name Chen Limei) was born in Zhejiang province. She joined **Great Wall** in 1956 and her film debut was *Ming Phoon/Ming Fung/Ming Feng* (1957). The romance *The Brigands/Hung dang lung/Hong denglong* (1957) was her first leading role. Chen played Seventh Sister, sister to a bandit who rescues a shipwrecked boatman (**Ping Fan**). The boatman falls in love with her, and joins the bandit, but after a falling out, they flee. About to rob a young man, the boatman discovers the dupe is his son. Seventh Sister leaves so the family can be reunited.

Over the next decade, Chen made 32 films with Great Wall. Chen, together with actresses **Hsia Moon** and **Shek Hwei**, were called the "Three Princesses of Great Wall." Chen's Great Wall movies include **Li Pingqian's** *Girl on the Front Page/San man yan mat/Xin wen ren wu* (1960), his ***huangmei diao*** opera film *Three Charming Smiles/Saam siu/San xiao* (1964), and two swordplay movies, **Zhang Xinyan's** *The Jade Bow/Wan hoi yuk gung yuen/Yun hai yu gong yuan* (1966) and *Ying Ku/Seung cheong wong Ying Goo/Shuang qiang huang Ying Gu* (1967). The actress starred in *Three Charming Smiles* as the maid whose smile attracts a suitor; the movie is one of several versions of the legend *Huang Bo Hu's Seduction of Qiu Xiang* (*The Ingenious Seduction*).

In 1968, the actress signed with Wing Kin and starred in four films, including the **martial arts** movie *Filial Girl at the Icy Valley/Bing guk moh lui/Bing gu mo nu* (1970) and **Chor Yuen's** drama *I Don't Want a Divorce/Ngo bat yiu lee fan/Wo bu yao li hun* (1970). She left the industry for 10 years, reemerging with the swordplay film *The Warrant of Assassination* (1980).

CHEN, YANYAN (1915–1999). A Mandarin actress, born of Manchu origins and of a noble family, Chen Yanyan grew up in Beijing. In 1930, she signed a five-year contract with **Lianhua** and appeared in

Love and Duty (1930), *Spring in the South* (1932), *Three Modern Ladies* (1933), *Maternal Love* (1933), *The Big Road* (1934), *Family Happiness* (1935), and *Song of a Mother* (1937). She acted and sang, and her singing talent earned her the name "The Little Bird." She was a favorite of students and one of the most popular among Chinese actresses of her day.

Chen joined **Xinhua** in 1938, starring in *The Beggar and the Rich Girl* (1938) and playing in many tragedies, earning her another name, the "Queen of Tragedy." After Shanghai fell, she stayed to continue her film career, working for the Japanese Huaying, and she appeared onstage in roles in *Madame Butterfly* (1943) and *Youth Slipping By* (1943) and in Chinese opera. She returned to film with *Never Ending Love* (1947).

Chen immigrated to Hong Kong in 1949, and with actor **Wang Hao** founded Haiyan Film Company. She played supporting roles during most of her Hong Kong career, and some of her roles were in **Yue Feng's** Mandarin dramas *Bitter Sweet/Wai sui san foo wai sui mong/Wei shui xinku wei shui mang* (1963) and *Sons and Daughters/Chin maan yan ga/Qian wan renjia* (1971), **Yan Jun's** *The* ***Grand Substitution*** (1965), **Tao Qin's** romantic epic *The Blue and the Black, Part 1/Laam yue hak/Lan yu hei, Xia ji* (1966), and Ching Gong's **martial arts** movie *The Fourteen Amazons/Sap sei lui ying ho/Shi si nu ying hao* (1972). In *Bitter Sweet*, Chen played a mother in a story about the parents' generation's disappointment with the young; the actress also played the mother role in a remake, *Sons and Daughters*. She appeared in **Stanley Kwan's** homage to early Chinese filmmaking and **Ruan Lingyu**, *Centre Stage (Actress)/Yuen Ling-yuk/Ruan Lingyu* (1992), as herself.

Chen moved to Taiwan, where she appeared on **television**.

CHENG, ADAM SIU-CHOW (1947–). Actor and singer Adam Cheng made his big screen debut in *The Black Killer/Hak sat sing/Hei sha xing* (1967) alongside **Connie Chan Po-chu** and **Shek Kin**. Cheng would continue to make films up until the late 1970s, though he went through a slump, appearing in no films in 1970–1972. During this time, Cheng's father died and he had to help his family, but his salary as an actor was not very high, about US$250 per month, so after a failed clothing business, Cheng became a lounge singer, making around US$1500 per month. While singing he met some Hong Kong Television Broadcasts Limited (TVB) actors who gave him an opening at the station. After hosting a musical program, he won praise for his role in the 1971 TV drama *Freezing Point*. Also returning to film, he went back to **television** in 1976 to star in *The Legend of Book and Sword*, which helped make Cheng a household name. In 1979, he starred in the series *Chor Lau Heung*, in which he played the lead role, Swordsman Chu, a sort of period piece Chinese James Bond, cementing Cheng's fame. It earned him the nickname "Chow Goon," "*goon*" being in reference to the Cantonese "*goon jai*," a young, handsome, polite, and knowledgeable man.

At the same time, Cheng had launched a successful singing career, often singing the theme songs for the series in which he was acting. Cheng also studied with a Chinese opera master to perform songs in that style. In addition, he performed in a Chinese musical of *Cyrano de Bergerac*. He also made films during the period, including **Lau Kar-leung's** *Cat vs. Rat/Nga maau saam fai gam mo sue/Yu mao san hu jin mao shu* (1982) and **Tsui Hark's** *Zu: Warriors From the Magic Mountain/ Suk san sun suk san geen hap/Zuo shan shen zuo shan jian xia* (1983). Other significant films include *Gunmen/Tin law dei mong/Tian luo di wang* (1988), *Fong Sai Yuk/Fong Sai Yuk/Fang Shi Yu* (1993), and the **King Hu**–helmed *Painted Skin/Wa pei ji yam ye-ung faat wong/Hua pi zhi yinyang fawang* (1993). Cheng made his last film in 1994. However, he has continued to work on recent TV series, including the super hit *Greed of Man*, as well as *Divine Retribution*, both with **Lau Ching-wan**. The singer gave another series of concerts in the summer of 2005.

CHENG, BUGAO (Ching Bo-go) (1894–1966). Director Cheng Bugao, a native of Zhejiang province, graduated from a university in Shanghai and studied in France. He briefly worked as a film critic for Shanghai newspapers and as editor of a film magazine. A great influence on Cheng was Nikolai Ekk's Russian allegorical drama *Road to Life* (1931), which he and other critics believed was the right direction for Chinese cinema.

Cheng created Dalu Film Company in 1924, where he directed his first silent film, and was the assistant director on the first sound film (on disc) *Singsong Girl Red Peony* (1930). He directed a number of films for Mingxing (Star), including classics like *Wild Torrent* (1933), *Spring Silkworms* (1933), *A Bible for Girls* (1934), and *Xiao*

Lingzi (1936). *Wild Torrent*, written by Xia Yan, dramatized the 1931 Wuhan floods. *Spring Silkworms*, adapted by Xia Yan from a novel by Mao Dun, was shot in a neorealistic style and set in 1930s Zhejiang.

In 1947, Cheng came to Hong Kong and directed films for **Yonghua** and **Great Wall**, including the Mandarin dramas *Songs of Warfare/Luen sai ngai lui/Luan shi er nu* (1947), *Virtue in the Dust/Chun shing dut laai/Chuncheng hualuo* (1949), and *A Fisherman's Honor/Hoi sai/Ha shi* (1949); the Mandarin fantasy *Fairy Dove/Siu gaap ji goo leung/Xiao ge zi gu niang* (1957); and the Mandarin comedies *Merry Go Round/Foon choi yuen ga/Huanxi yuanjia* (1954) and *The Nature of Spring/Yau lui waai chun/You nu huai chun* (1958). The Yonghua production *Virtue in the Dust* follows the lives of two orphan sisters doomed to poverty by fate. *A Fisherman's Honor* explored the consequences of exploitation by a boss and his son on fishermen. In the former films, Cheng's social consciousness was apparent. In both *Merry Go Round* and *The Nature of Spring*, Cheng played with the battle of the sexes, in the former between a husband and wife, and in the latter, between five eligible daughters in one family and their love interests and entanglements.

Cheng's last feature was the Mandarin comedy *The Lady Racketeer/Mei yan gai/Mei ren ji* (1961). He died in Hong Kong.

CHENG, CAROL (DODO) YU-LING (1957–). Actress Carol Cheng has appeared in more than 50 films. She began in 1976 at the now defunct Commercial Television (CTV) in the series *This Generation* and in 1978 moved to Hong Kong Television Broadcasts Limited (TVB), where she costarred with **Chow Yun-fat** in the series *The Good, The Bad, and The Ugly* and *Brothers*. Her film debut was with Chow in **Tony Au's** *The Last Affair/Dut shing/Hua cheng* (1983), and they were paired in a trio of other films, including the **Lunar New Year's comedy** *Eighth Happiness (Eight Stars Greetings)/Bat sing bo hei/Ba xing bao xi* (1988) as well as *Now You See Love . . . Now You Don't (I Love Nau Man-chai [Rogue Meets Warrior])/Ngoh oi Nau Man-chai (lau man yue do bing)/Wo ai Niu Wenchai (liu mang yu dao bing)* (1992). In the latter romantic comedy, directed by **Alex Law**, Cheng played Firefly Kwok, a country girl grown up in the city after spending time in England and returning to her village. Chow played the country headman who must woo her back, and the charming and humorous story played loose with battle of the sexes and country mouse–city mouse fairy tales. Cheng won a **Golden Horse** Best Supporting Actress award for her portrayal of an alcoholic, downtrodden club girl in ***Moon, Star, Sun***/*Yuet leung sing sing taai yeung/Yue liang xing xing tai yan* (1988), during a time when she made nine movies in nine months. She was the lead Mainland cop/fish out of water sent to Hong Kong in **Alfred Cheung's** *Her Fatal Ways/Biu che lei ho yeh/Biao jie ni hao ye* series (1990–1993), and she won Best Actress for the third film at the **Hong Kong Film Awards**. She joined ensemble casts in the comedies *Boys Are Easy (Chasing Boys)/Chui lam chai/Zhui nan zai* (1993) and *It's a Wonderful Life/Big Rich Family/Daai foo ji ga/Da fu zhi jia* (1994). In recent years, she has abandoned films for television work.

CHENG, EKIN YEE-KIN (Dior Cheng, Noodle Cheng) (1967–). Actor and singer Ekin Cheng joined the Hong Kong Television Broadcasts Limited's (TVB) actors' training program and appeared in several **television** dramas and a children's show, *Shuttle 430*, before his film debut, *Girls without Tomorrow/Yin doi ying chiu lui long/Xian dai ying shao nu lang* (1992). He appeared in light entertainments, such as **Wong Jing's** ensemble comedy *Boys Are Easy/Chui lam chai/Zhui nan zai* (1993) and Norman Lau Man's *Mermaid Got Married (Mermaid Legend)/Yan yue chuen suet/Ren yu chuan shui* (1994), a Hong Kong version of Ron Howard's *Splash*. With pretty boy good looks, he appealed primarily to a teenage audience.

Cheng's roles changed with **Andrew Lau's** *Young and Dangerous* series, in which he played a sympathetic and stylish Triad-boyz gang leader through a series of films, including *Young and Dangerous (Young Rascals: Man of the World)/Goo wak jai ji yan joi gong woo/Gu huo zi zhi ren zai jiang hu*, *Young and Dangerous 2 (Young Rascals 2: Mighty Dragon Crosses River)/Goo wak jai 2 ji mang lung gwoh gong/Gu huo zi 2 zhi meng long guo jiang*, *Young and Dangerous 3 (Young Rascals 3: Single Hand Covers the Sky)/Goo wak jai 3 ji jek sau je tin/Gu huo zi 3 zhi shou zhe tian* (all 1996), *Young and Dangerous 4 (97 Young Rascals: Have Battle, Will Win)/97 goo wak jai jin mo bat sing/97 gu huo zi zhan wu bu sheng*, *Young and Dangerous 5/98 Goo wak chai ji lung chang foo dau/98 Gu huo zai zhi* *long zheng hu dou* (both 1997), and *Born to Be King/Sing chea wai wong/Sheng zhe wei wang* (2000). Lau also cast him in his *Storm Riders (Wind Cloud: Heroic Tyrant Heaven Earth)/Fung wan hung ba tin ha/Feng yun xiong ba tian xia* (1998), one of the first Hong Kong films to make extensive use of computer-generated images (CGI).

CHENG, GANG (Ching Gong) (1924–). Director and writer Cheng Gang was born in Anhui, received three years of primary education, and left home at an early age, gaining a wide variety of life experiences that served him well in his later writing. During the Sino–Japanese War, while working as a library doorman, Cheng learned about theater and film and began working with an acting troupe. In Chongqing in 1942, he began writing, and during the 1950s, Cheng contributed to Cantonese cinema, writing many scripts for **Ng Wui** films.

Cheng directed more than 30 films in the Amoy dialect. In 1962, the director signed with **Shaw Brothers** and began making **martial arts** movies. *The Fourteen Amazons/Sap sei lui ying ho/Shi si nu ying hao* (1972), which Cheng wrote and directed, won best direction and screenplay at the 1973 **Asian Film Festival**. The women warriors of the Yang family included actresses **Lisa Lu**, **Lily Ho**, **Ivy Ling Bo**, and Betty Ting Pei.

Conflict is a theme running through Cheng's films. He has made films in Amoy, Cantonese, and Mandarin, and besides writing and directing, he has acted in a handful of films, including *The House of the 72 Tenants/Chat sap yee ga fong hak/Qi shi er gu fang ke* (1973), and worked as a production manager. He is the father of action director **Tony Ching Siu-tung**.

CHENG, KENT JAK-SI (1951–). Portly actor Kent Cheng is a veteran of both film and **television**, debuting on television in Hong Kong's first soap opera, *Hotel* (1976), and acting in over 100 movies. He is usually cast as a working-class slob, but his characters vary in levels of intelligence and humanity. He has played stupid cops, smart criminals, kindly fathers, scheming buddies, mentally challenged relatives, and frustrated romantics. He was the murderous cop paired with **Jackie Chan** in *Crime Story (Serious Crime Unit)/Chung ngon cho/Zhonganzu* (1993) and he has won Best Actor at the **Hong Kong**

Film Awards twice, for his portrayal of a mentally challenged adult in *Why Me?/Hoh bit yau ngoh/He bi you wo* (1985, which he also directed and wrote) and as an on-edge veteran cop in *The Log (3 Injured Policemen)/3 goh sau seung dik ging chaat/3 go shou shang de jing cha* (1996). He has directed eight films and currently focuses on work in television.

CHENG, PEI-PEI (Zheng Pei-Pei) (1946–). Shanghai-born Cheng Pei-Pei, the "Queen of ***wuxia*** movies," already had undergone extensive training as a dancer when the **Shaw Brothers** Studio hired her from their own performing arts program in 1963 and cast her in a number of musicals and romantic dramas. Her ethereal loveliness drew favorable attention and a Golden Knight Award for Best New Actress from the International Independent Producers' Association for *The Rock (Lover's Rock)/Ching yan sek/Qing ren shi* (1964). Then director **King Hu** cast her as swordswoman Golden Swallow in his groundbreaking ***wuxia*** epic *Come Drink with Me/Daai chui hap/Da zui xia* (1966) despite her lack of training in **martial arts**. She later recalled that Hu was impressed by her energy and also by her expressive eyes, which he felt were necessary for a woman playing a heroic role. Cheng incorporated the jazzy rhythms of her modern dance background into the fight choreography, and the resulting film was so popular that she went on to star in over a dozen *wuxia* films for the Shaw studio over the next five years, including *Golden Swallow/Gam yin ji/Jin yan zi* (1968), *The Lady Hermit /Chung kwai leung ji/Zhong kui niang zi* (1971), and *The Shadow Whip/Ying ji san bin/ Yingzi shen bian*(1971).

Her most successful films in this period were the ones that allowed her to show a measure of ruthlessness and strength, in stark contrast to the sweetness of her expression. Cheng preferred to do her own stunts, and had a well-publicized dust-up with director **Chang Cheh** during the filming of *Golden Swallow*, when he opined that women should not be so physically aggressive. The veteran directors **Lo Wei** and **He Menghua**, on the other hand, had no problem working with the feisty leading lady, frequently pairing her with actors **Yueh Hua**, **Lo Lieh**, and **Ku Feng**, in films that worked a number of variations on the theme of martial heroine.

Cheng married in 1970, and left Hong Kong soon after to settle in the United States, where she founded a dance school and performance troupe. She continued to make periodic returns to the film world, starring in a couple of **action** films in the 1970s. She made *None but the Brave/Tit wa/Tie wa* (1973) for Lo Wei, and *Whiplash/Foo bin ji/Hu bian zi* (1974) and contributed cameos to films like **Samo Hung's** *Painted Faces/Chat siu fuk/Qi qiao fu* (1988) and **Yuen Wo-ping's** *Wing Chun/Wing Chun/Yong Chun* (1994).

It was **Ang Lee's** determination to cast her in the role of Jade Fox, the wily villainess of *Crouching Tiger, Hidden Dragon/Ngo foo chong lung/Wo hu cang long* (2000), that once again brought Cheng to an international audience. Her performance in the part, with her jade-white mask of simple dignity eroding into fury as the desire for vengeance consumes her, was electrifying, and has made her once again in demand for *wuxia* and kung fu roles. Her daughters, Marsha and Eugenia Yuen, have also made their careers in film, following in the footsteps of one of the greatest heroines of the Hong Kong screen.

CHEUNG, ALFRED KIN-TING (1955–). Born in Guangzhou, director, screenwriter, and actor Alfred Cheung studied at Hong Kong's Baptist College and at Columbia University in New York. He began working in film, however, right after high school, first as a dubbing artist at Radio Television Hong Kong (RTHK) and as a **television** researcher, writer, and anchorperson, working at all the television stations in the 1970s. He wrote for the drama series *Under (Below) the Lion Rock* at RTHK in 1977.

Cheung wrote his first film script for **Ronny Yu's** *The Savior/Gau sai che/Jiu shi zhe* (1980), a movie in which he also acted. He contributed to the writing of many scripts, notable among them **Allen Fong's** *Father and Son/Foo ji ching/Fu zi qing* (1981) and **Ann Hui's** *The Story of Woo-Viet/Woo Yuet dik goo si/ Huyue de gu shi* (1981). His directorial debut was *Monkey Business/Ma lau goh hoi/Ma liu guo hai* (1982), starring **Kenny Bee**, and his breakthrough success was *Let's Make Laugh/Biu cho chat yat ching/Biao cu qi ri qing* (1983), also starring Kenny Bee (and leading to a sequel two years later). The action comedy *Paper Marriage/Goh fow san leung/Guo fu xin niang* (1988) starred **Samo Hung** as a Chinese boxer Canadian emigrant and **Maggie Cheung** as the woman who needs a "paper marriage" to remain. Alfred Cheung is known for directing and acting in the popular comedy series *Her Fatal Ways*, consisting of four films beginning with *Her Fatal Ways* (*Cousin, You're Great!*)/*Biu che lei ho yeh/Biao jie ni hao ye* (1990), three of which he also wrote. The films star **Carol Cheng** as a Mainland cop who comes to Hong Kong, and the director plays her loyal assistant. In the first film, **Tony Leung Ka-fai** starred as her Hong Kong cop counterpart. A culture clash comedy, the film also suggested mutual respect between the two Chinese and a message of cooperation. Cheung also directed the **Lunar New Year's comedy** *All's Well, Ends Well 1997 (97 Family Has Happy Affairs)/97 Gar yau hei si/97 Jia you xi si* (1997), written by **Raymond Wong**, which united some of the cast of previous incarnations (Raymond Wong, **Stephen Chiau**), and the quirky *The Group/Chuen chik daai dou/Quan zhi da dao* (1998), featuring an ensemble cast including **Francis Ng** and **Anthony Wong**, the story of a group of orphans indebted to a priest who become modern-day Robin Hoods.

Alfred Cheung has directed 20 films, written 30, produced a dozen, and acted in over 60, including **Herman Yau's** *Master Q 2001/Low foo ji 2001/Lao fu zi* 2001 and *Shark Busters/Faan sau so dak hin dui /Fan shou shu te qian dui* (2002). His *Manhattan Midnight/Ng yau maan gwong duk/Wu ye man ka dun* (2001), starring Richard Grieco and **Michael Wong**, was filmed in New York and shot with high-definition video, thus becoming one of the very first digital movies made by a Hong Kong filmmaker.

CHEUNG, CECILIA PAK-CHI (1980–). Actress Cecilia Cheung, who has a natural on-screen presence, came to the Hong Kong entertainment scene from Australia, appearing in a lemon tea commercial and attracting the attention of **Stephen Chiau**, who cast her in her film debut, *King of Comedy/Hei kek ji wong/Xi ju zhi wang* (1999), as a tough club girl with a heart of gold. She was cast in the melodrama *Fly Me to Polaris/Sing yuen/Xing yuan* (1999), for which she won Best Newcomer Award, and her theme song won Best Song at the **Hong Kong Film Awards**. In *Cat and Mouse/Low sue oi seung mau/Lao shu ai shang mao* (2003), a costume comedy, she was paired with **Andy Lau**, costarring with **Anthony Wong** as Judge Pao, and loosely based on the popular Chinese novel Q*i Xia Wu Yi*, set in the Soong dynasty, featuring exploits of the harsh but fair judge and his followers who bring criminals to justice.

Cheung has appeared in 25 films, over the course of which she has further developed her acting talent; she is becoming more and more popular on the Mainland. The **Hong Kong Film Critics Society** (HKFCS) awarded her its Best Actress Award for her role opposite Andy Lau in **Johnnie To/Wai Ka-fai's** *Running on Karma/Daai chek liu/Da zhi lao* (2003). She also won Best Actress at the 2004 Hong Kong Film Awards and the **Golden Bauhinia** for her portrayal of a young woman who loses her fiancé and struggles to survive with his young son (by another woman) in **Derek Yee's** *Lost in Time/Mong bat liu/Wang bu le* (2003). More and more of her best roles are character-driven stories. She will play **Brigitte Lin** in **Tsui Hark's** forthcoming documentary about the actress.

CHEUNG, CHING (Zhang Qing) (1935–2005). Actor Cheung Ching (real name Zhang Kunyang), a native of Shandong province, was born and educated in Hong Kong. He graduated from **Motion Pictures and General Investment's** first actors' training course, was signed, and appeared in *Green Are the Hills* (1956), becoming one of the studio's major actors. Cheung appeared in numerous Mandarin features, including **Tso Kea's** *My Eligible Son-in-Law/Dong chong gaai sai/Dong chuang jia* xu (1959) and **Wang Tianlin's** *The Greatest Civil War on Earth/Naam bak who/Nan bei he* (1961). In the former, a contemporary satirical comedy, Cheung played the title character, sought after and soaked by a heavily in-debt mother in search of a wealthy son-in-law for her daughter. The prospective son-in-law and his father live frugally, so when the woman's demands for money are unrelenting, her daughter leaves her and marries him, for better or worse. The latter was a part of the **North–South trilogy** in which Cheung played one of the undesirable (at least according to the prejudiced father) suitors for a daughter.

In 1965, Cheung began appearing in the Cantonese cinema, and made many popular films, among them *One Queen and Three Kings/Yau hau saam wong/Yi hou san wang* (1963), *Master Cute/Liu foo ji/Lao fu zi* (1965), and **Chor Yuen's** mystery thriller *I Love Violet (Violet Girl)/Ngo oi chi law laan/Wo ai zi luo lan* (1966). In **Chan Lit-bun's** urban *comedy One Queen and Three Kings*, Cheung played one of three bachelors caught in a love trap devised by **Ha Ping** and carried out convincingly by Xue Ni to even the score in the battle of the sexes. This fast-paced comedy criticizes male chauvinism. *In I Love Violet*, Cheung played best friend to Lu Qi, a telephone operator receiving calls from a strange woman (Man Lan). As an avid reader of detective novels, Cheung's character attempts to help solve the mystery, and they get more than they bargained for, including an amnesiac, a drowning, and psychiatric breakdown.

Cheung was usually cast as the handsome bachelor or the honest, shy intellectual. He excelled in comedy. One of his last screen roles was *The Motherless Man (A Child in Need of a Mother's Love)/Sat hui miu oi dik yan/Shi qu mu ai de ren* (1969). He also made commercial radio broadcasts in the 1950s and later worked at Rediffusion Television (RTV) as a director and coordinator of television soap operas. He and his family immigrated to the United States in the mid-1970s.

CHEUNG, JACKY HOK-YAU (1961–). First and foremost a singer, Jacky Cheung has also become a respected actor. He has proven adept at comedy, drama, and legends (Hong Kong's "swordsman" genre, set anywhere in the past two thousand years of Chinese history, comprised of fact, fable, or fantasy; legend films require a different acting style than contemporary genres). Cheung was an airline reservations clerk when he came in first out of 10,000 male vocalists to win a recording contract in the 1985 All Hong Kong Singing Contest. His career took off, and he was soon put in teen romance comedies, which gave him an opportunity to learn acting and related skills (martial arts, swordplay, horseback riding, wirework, etc.). A publicity ploy that named him and three other singer/actors (**Aaron Kwok**, **Andy Lau**, and **Leon Lai**) as the "Sei Tai Tien Wang" or "Four Big Heavenly Kings" of Cantopop was hugely successful, and so was Cheung, becoming by 1993 the best-selling singer in not only the Chinese market, but all of Asia. He was given a World Music Award (the only Chinese singer to have that distinction) in 1996. Cheung put out two CDs a year, did two months of concerts, often around the world, made six to eight music videos per CD and acted in several films each year between 1990 and 1996.

This period represents his best work as an actor. He costarred in three **Wong Kar-wai** films. He received the **Hong Kong Film Award** for Best Supporting Actor for his portrayal of a hot-tempered small-timer always in trouble in Wong's *As Tears Go By (Mongkok Carmen,*

Carmen of the Streets)/Wong kok Ka Moon/Wang jiao Ka Men (1988); he was the working-class dreamer and best friend of **Leslie Cheung** in Wong's *Days of Being Wild (The True Story of Ah Fei)//Ah Fei ching chuen/A Fei zhengzhuan* (1990); and he provided the balance of simple practicality and conscience for Wong's Eastern–Western ***Ashes of Time*** *(Evil East, Malicious West)/Dung chea sai duk/Dong xie xi du* (1994). In **John Woo's** autobiographical *Bullet in the Head (Bloodshed on the Streets)/Dip huet gaai tau/Die xue jie tou* (1990), Cheung played the titular character who suffers from a lodged bullet inflicted by a former friend crazed by greed. The goodness and innocence his character projects before the horror of the incident is offset by the pain, suffering, and despair that event causes him. Woo called him "innocent and pure" in both his performance and personality, and remarked he reminded him of his younger brother. In **Andrew Lau's** *To Live and Die in Tsimshatsui (New Edge Man)/San bin yuen yan/Xin bian yuan ren* (1994), Cheung portrayed an undercover cop who has infiltrated a Triad gang and is torn between his duty and his underworld friends. The former standout dramatic performances were equally matched by many other delightful and silly characters in a host of comedies and romances, and Cheung has appeared in more than 50 films. Cheung has the ability to play different facets of a character's personality just by the way an angle or side of the face is lit and photographed; he can appear goofy, slow-witted, sophisticated, intense, clever, kindly, vicious, strikingly handsome, or endearingly ugly.

Cheung's true life story (a grindingly poor sailor's son has meteoric rise, crashes, makes a comeback with the help of the woman he loves but his family despises, becomes an Asian music star, marries his 10-year love in the face of family and fan reaction, wins world notice, keeps fans, reconciles family, and produces a daughter) would not only make a great movie, but has given him an understanding of numerous segments of Chinese society. He has convincingly played everything from rich businessman (which he now is) to down-and-out Triad wannabe (which he came close to in his teens). Cheung is known for taking his work, but not himself, seriously. He has donated or raised millions of Hong Kong dollars for charities and closed membership to his fan club when it reached a level to which he felt he could not "personally respond."

Cheung's most outstanding personal trait appears to be loyalty; he actually "schooled" close friend **Tony Leung Chiu-wai** in the demands of loyalty, enabling Leung to heal a lifelong breach with his father. That trait is the one feature the many varied characters Cheung has played have in common; whether cops or killers, all are either intensely loyal (which usually lands them in trouble) or lack loyalty until they are taught by another character—either way, loyalty is an issue, and he has never played a character where loyalty did not factor in some way.

In 1997, Cheung took on the musical *Snow Wolf Lake*, a simple tale of ill-fated lovers presented in grand style, as artistic director and lead in one of several Cantonese-language musicals ever presented in Hong Kong (others include performances by **Roman Tam** in the 1980s and **Sam Hui** in the 1990s). Common wisdom had always been that a Hong Kong audience would not be big enough to support the expense of a musical that did not play to the English-speaking residents of the colony. The production was designed for the Hong Kong Civic Auditorium, using the back quarter for a stage and allowing audience seating of about 15,000. The play was set to run nightly for six weeks; ultimately, it was twice extended for a total run of 12 weeks, all sold out.

Cheung stopped appearing in films after 1996, stating that he had not seen a quality project to tempt him back. His voice returned to film as the lead character in the Chinese version of Disney's *Dinosaur* (2000), and he also recorded the theme song in Cantonese, Mandarin, and English. He remains active in the music industry, and when his label, Polygram, was sold in 1998, he fulfilled his contract and then formed his own production company. In 2000, he released his first English CD, which included a duet with American country star Reba McEntire. Cheung returned to film in **Ann Hui's** *July Rhapsody/Laam yan sei sap/Nan ren si shi* (2002) and Wong Ching-po's *Jiang Hu/Kong woo/Jiang hu* (2004). He also costars in **Peter Chan's** musical *Perhaps Love/Yu guo aoi/Ruoguo ai* (2005).

Cheung recently became the official spokesperson for the Hong Kong Disneyland theme park.

CHEUNG, JACOB CHI-LEUNG (1959–). Born in Hong Kong, director Jacob Cheung, after graduating from high school, entered a Hong Kong Television Broadcasts Limited (TVB) training course and became an assistant director-writer. He joined **Cinema City** two years later, becoming an assistant producer, then full producer on *The*

Happy Ghost (1984), *Aces Go Places 3* (1984), *Our Man in Bond Street* (1984), and *Merry Christmas* (1985). He left Cinema City and joined **Boho Films** as production supervisor on *Mr. Vampire* (1985) and *The Final Test* (1987). His directorial debut was *Lai Shi, China's Last Eunuch (Last Eunuch in China)/Chung gwok chui hau yat goh taai gaam/Zhong guo zui hou yi ge tai jian* (1988), which details the end of the empire and beginnings of republicanism, as seen through the eyes of a eunuch with no place. *Beyond the Sunset* (1989), a story about growing older, starring **Richard Ng** and **Fung Bo-bo**, won Best Picture at the ninth **Hong Kong Film Awards**.

In 1988, Cheung established Filmagica, whose first production was *Goodbye Hero/Waan meng seung hung/Wan ming shuang xiong* (1990), which Cheung wrote and directed, starring **Derek Yee** as a stuntman. *Cageman (Cage People)/Lung man/Long min* (1992) tackled the social housing problem of approximately 3,200 "cage people" in Hong Kong, and although the film won the Hong Kong Film Award for Best Picture, audiences stayed away. In 1993, Cheung founded Simpson Productions to produce independent works with Mainland and Taiwanese directors, such as *Back to Back, Face to Face* (1994). Cheung directed *Intimates (Self-Combed)/ Ji soh/Zi shu* (1997), based on stories of the "self-combed" women who vowed chastity and female solidarity, and starring **Carina Lau** and Charlie Yeung. He also remade the tearjearker *The Kid/Lau sing yue/Liu zing yu* (1999), drawing on the **Bruce Lee** movie of 1950, starring **Leslie Cheung**, **Ti Lung** (who won a Best Supporting Actor Award at the Hong Kong Film Awards), and **Carrie Ng**. He directed the art house gender film *Midnight Fly/Fong sam ga gei/Huang xin jia ji* (2001), starring **Anita Mui**. Throughout his career, Jacob Cheung consistently has directed his attention to subjects of everyday life involving working-class people as well as a sensitivity to **women**, and he has avoided following the whims of the marketplace.

CHEUNG, LESLIE KWOK-WING (1956–2003). Born in Hong Kong, the youngest (and loneliest, he stated) of 10 children, actor/singer Leslie Cheung shook the Asian world when he committed suicide on April Fool's Day, 2003, by leaping from the roof, overlooking Victoria Harbor, of the Mandarin Oriental Hotel in Central, the city's financial district. He seemed to have it all. His father was an esteemed tailor to the stars, including William Holden and Alfred Hitchcock. Cheung was sent to England for his education, attending boarding school at the Norwich School in Suffolk and the University of Leeds to study textile management, but he began singing in clubs while a college student. He returned to Hong Kong and began in the entertainment industry in 1977 by entering the Asian Amateur Singing Contest and winning first runner-up (his selection, Don McLean's "American Pie"), was signed up at Rediffusion Television (now ATV, Asia Television), and began recording at Polygram Records. Cheung became known as the Hong Kong Elvis, turning the heads of Asian teens. Singing love ballads as well as dance tunes, Cheung became the **Cantopop** icon of the 1980s, wearing numerous costume changes of sequined shiny suits and boas onstage in spectacular theatrical shows, accompanied by a full orchestra and dancers, and singing with sensitivity and intimacy to sold-out coliseums. He retired from music in late 1989 (after more than 30 consecutive Hong Kong concerts), only to return seven years later (signing with Rock Records and first recording movie theme songs that sold out in Asia) with more flamboyant performances, during one of which, held on New Year's 1997, he acknowledged both his mother and his longtime male companion. For his 2000 concerts, Jean Paul Gaultier designed the costumes and Cheung appeared wearing long hair and skirts. He took the name "Leslie" in homage to his favorite film star, Leslie Howard in *Gone with the Wind*. He was working on his 88th recording at his death.

Cheung also appeared in numerous Hong Kong Television Broadcasts Limited (TVB) serials with **Teresa Mo**. He made his film debut at 21 with *Dream of the Erotic Chamber (Erotic Dream of the Red Chamber)/Hung lau chun seung chun/Hong lou chun shang chun* (1978) and appeared in a series of teen-angst features, such as *Teenage Dreamers (Lemon Cola)/Ling mung hoh lok/Ning meng ke le* and *Energetic 21/Chung gik 21/Chong ji 21* (both 1982) and including **Patrick Tam's** groundbreaking **New Wave** *Nomad (Flaming Youth)/Lit foh ching chun/Lie huo qing chun* (also 1982), but his turning point was in **John Woo's** *A Better Tomorrow (True Colors of a Hero)/Ying hung boon sik/Yingxiong bense* (1986), in the role of a youthful, hopeful, and impulsive cop who becomes torn between his job and his Triad brother. Cheung also appeared in the sequel and Woo's crime caper *Once a Thief (Criss Cross Over Four Seas)/Jung* *waang sei hoi/Zhong heng si hai*, and he worked consistently with most of Hong Kong's best directors.

Tsui Hark cast Cheung for two of the *Chinese Ghost Story (Sien, the Female Ghost)/Sin nui yau wan/Qian nu you hun* (1987, 1990) movies as an innocent; **Stanley Kwan** chose him for the part of a spoiled son who betrays his lover in *Rouge (Rouge Hook* ["hook" means a Chinese knot or buckle])/*Yin chi kau/Yan zhi kou* (1988); **Ronny Yu** collaborated with him on both *Bride with White Hair (The Evil White-Haired Lady)/Baak faat moh nui/Bai fa mo nu* (1993, in which Cheung plays a mischievous swordsman and sings the theme song, which won him a Taiwanese **Golden Horse Award**) and *Phantom Lover (Midnight Song)/Ye boon goh sing/Ye ban ge sheng* (1995, in which he plays a sensitive artist in a cross between *Romeo and Juliet* and *Phantom of the Opera*, and for which he wrote and sang the music. **Peter Chan** also worked with him for ***He's a Woman, She's a Man*** *(Golden Branch, Jade Leaf)/Gam chi yuk yip/Jin qi yu ye* (1994) and *Who's the Woman, Who's the Man (Golden Branch, Jade Leaf 2)/Gam chi yuk sip 2/Jin qi yu ye 2* (1996), in which he played a homophobic music producer who falls for a woman he believes to be a man (and in which he sings, and for which he won a **Hong Kong Film Award** for Best Song). A versatile actor, Cheung could play light comedy and did so in numerous **Lunar New Year's** movies, such as *It's a Wonderful Life (Big Rich Family)/Daai foo ji ga/Da fu zhi jia* (1994), *The Chinese Feast (Gold Jade Full Hall)/Gam yuk moon tong/Jin yu man tang* (1995), and *Ninth Happiness/Gau sing biu hei/Jiu xing bao xi* (1998).

Art house director **Wong Kar-wai** cast Cheung as an ***ah fei*** character (disaffected and rebellious youth) in *Days of Being Wild (The True Story of Ah Fei)/ Ah Fei ching chuen/Ah Fei zhengzhuan* (1990). The film became his big hit and Cheung won both the Best Actor Award at the Hong Kong Film Awards and the Taiwanese Golden Horse for his performance as a wounded heartbreaker who was also a cad. With his androgynous appeal and boyish good looks, Cheung would be compared to James Dean and Johnny Depp and he became known for his characterization of elusive charmers who bring people close but keep them at a distance. He would also costar in Wong's Eastern–Western ***Ashes of Time*** *(Evil East, Malicious West)/Dung chea sai duk/Dong xie xi du* (1994) and cause a scandal with the sexual scenes in *Happy Together (A Sudden Leak of Spring Light)/Chun gwong ja sit/Chun guang zha xie* (1997), in which he costarred with **Tony Leung Chiu-wai** as a pair of gay lovers for whom it is impossible to be happy together. He played gay in another film, Mainland director Chen Kaige's *Farewell My Concubine*, costarring as one of a Beijing Opera duo who plays the female roles but can't distinguish real life from the stage. His nuanced performance, appropriate use of the movements and gestures of Beijing opera, and speech in the dialect earned him international attention. The film was also Oscar-nominated and won the Grand Prize at the Cannes Film Festival in 1993. Cheung reunited with Chen for *Temptress Moon/Fung yuet/Feng yue* (1996, costarring **Gong Li** and shot by cinematographer **Christopher Doyle**) as a wounded youth, a character not unlike the one he played in *Days of Being Wild*, but set in another era and locale, in which he plays a victim of the social system. Cheung also won the **Hong Kong Film Critics' Society** Award for Best Actor Year Round Performance in 1995.

Cheung's last role was in Law Chi-leung's *Inner Senses/Yee diy hung gaan/Yidu kongjian* (2002) as a psychiatrist almost lured to death off a rooftop by his deceased girlfriend's spirit. Some Chinese speculated that Cheung's suicide was sparked by him being haunted by an evil spirit during and after film production, although Cheung suffered from depression for 20 years. Throughout his career, Cheung made more than 50 films, receiving numerous music awards and nominations at the Hong Kong Film and Golden Horse Awards. He worked hard and was nicknamed "one-take Leslie" as he usually nailed the scene on the first take. Both on-screen and with his suicide, his youth and beauty are immortalized. He never forgot his salad days and was deeply involved in two charities, the Children's Cancer Foundation and The End Child Sexual Abuse Foundation. Ten thousand mourners attended a memorial viewing held for the public, and they lined the streets to see the casket leave for cremation at the height of the SARS outbreak. Gay organizations in Hong Kong and Taiwan have declared April first "Leslie Day" in honor of Cheung, Madame Tussaud's in Hong Kong recently unveiled a wax figure of Cheung from his role in *Farewell My Concubine* (he is one of 16 Asians represented), and the 2004 Hong Kong Film Awards posthumously recognized him with a lifetime achievement award.

CHEUNG, MAGGIE MAN-YUK (Zhang Manyu) (1964–). Born in Hong Kong, prolific actress Maggie Cheung moved with her parents to England when she was eight years old. After completing her secondary education, Cheung returned to Hong Kong in 1983. That same year, she entered the Miss Hong Kong beauty pageant, where she was crowned first runner-up, as well as being named Miss Photogenic. After signing contracts with Hong Kong Television Broadcasts Limited (TVB) and **Shaw Brothers**, Cheung began to appear in **television** and film. Her film debut was the **Wong Jing**–written and directed *Prince Charming/Ching wa wong ji/ Qing wa wang zhi* (1984) which costarred several other up-and-comers including **Rosamund Kwan**, **Cherie Chung**, and **Kenny Bee**. That same year she starred alongside **Cantopop** legends **Leslie Cheung** and **Anita Mui** in *Behind the Yellow Line/Yuen ban*, for which she received a **Hong Kong Film Award** nomination. Cheung went on to star opposite **Jackie Chan** and **Brigitte Lin** in *Police Story/Ging chaat goo si/Jing cha gu shi* (1985) as May, Chan's ditzy girlfriend, a role that she would reprise in two sequels. She appeared in several films with **Chow Yun-fat** in the mid- to late 1980s, including **Yonfan's** *Rose (Lost Romance, Story of Rose)/Mooi gwai dik goo si/Mei gui de gu shi* (1986), where Chow Yun-fat plays her brother, dies, and returns as her boyfriend. She also worked with Chan in *Project A 2/A gai waak chuk chap/A ji haa xu ji* (1987).

Cheung's first serious performance came in **Wong Kar-wai's** *As Tears Go By (Mongkok Carmen, Carmen of the Streets)/Wong kok Ka Moon/Wang jiao Ka Men* (1988) alongside **Andy Lau** and **Jacky Cheung**. This garnered Cheung another Hong Kong Film Award Nomination. From 1988 to 1993, Cheung starred in over 50 Hong Kong productions. While she was in many run-of-the-mill films, she also starred in many significant ones as well. She was cast as the female lead in **Anthony Chan's** *A Fishy Story/Bat tuet maat dik yan/Bu tuo wa de ren* (1989), with Kenny Bee, for which she won her first Hong Kong Film Award. That same year, she won a **Golden Horse Award** for her work in **Stanley Kwan's** *Full Moon in New York (People in New York) Yan joi nau yeuk/Ren zai niu yue* (1989). Cheung was nominated twice the next year at the Hong Kong Film Awards for both **Clara Law's** *Farewell China (Demon Love Painting)/Moh wah ching/Mo hua qing* (1990), in which she played a victim of the diaspora who becomes schizophrenic opposite **Tony**

Leung Ka-fai, and for **Yim Ho's** *Red Dust (Swirling Red Dust)/ Gwan gwan hung chan/Gun gun hong chen* (1990). Both Cheung and *Red Dust*'s main star, **Brigitte Lin**, received Golden Horse awards for their work in this female-bonding film.

At the same time, Cheung was also seen on the screen in two other art house productions. The first was Wong Kar-wai's *Days of Being Wild (The True Story of Ah Fei)/ Ah Fei ching chuen/A Fei zhengzhuan* (1990), a story about an ***ah fei*** character played by Leslie Cheung with a supporting cast including Jacky Cheung, Andy Lau, **Carina Lau**, and **Rebecca Pan**. The other was **Ann Hui's** ***Song of the Exile*** *(Exile and Autumn Sorrow)/Haak to chau han/Ketu qiuhen* (1990), Hui's autobiographical film with Cheung playing her, remembering her Japanese mother, who is treated as only half-human by her in-laws. The movie is a self-discovery about class, nationality, and womanhood for the character. Cheung also made other significant movies outside the art house scene during this period, including the **Tsui Hark**–produced, **Raymond Lee**–directed remake of **King Hu's** classic *Dragon Gate Inn/Lung moon haak chan/Long men ke zhan Longmen kezhan* (1967), *Dragon Inn (New Dragon Gate Inn)/ San lung moon haak chan/Xin Longmen kezhan* (1992), in which she starred alongside Brigitte Lin, Tony Leung Ka-fai, and **Donnie Yen**, earning her another Hong Kong Film Award nomination.

Re-teaming with director Stanley Kwan and actor Tony Leung Ka-fai, Cheung starred in *Centre Stage (Actress)/Yuen Ling-yuk/Ruan Lingyu* (1992), a postmodern docudrama based on the life of famous Chinese actress **Ruan Lingyu**. Cheung's subtle and spot-on portrayal received both a Hong Kong Film Award and the prestigious Silver Bear Award from the Berlin International Film Festival for her work in this film. Cheung made a flurry of films the next year, including Tsui Hark's *Green Snake/Ching se/Qing she* (1993), a film known for its eye-candy and its two female leads, Cheung and **Joey Wang**. Cheung was also in many comedies during the early 1990s, including the Wong Kar-wai–produced, **Jeff Lau**–directed *The Eagle Shooting Heroes/Seh diu ying hung chuen ji dung shing sai jau/Shediao yingxiong zhi dongcheng xijui* (1993) a zany postmodern comedy with a superstar cast including Brigitte Lin, Leslie Cheung, Jacky Cheung, **Veronica Yip**, Joey Wang, and both **Tony Leungs**. That same year, Cheung starred in the cult favorite *The Heroic Trio (The Three Asian Heroes)/Dung fong saam hap/Dong fang san xia* (1993) with Anita Mui and **Michelle Yeoh**. Directed by **Johnnie To**, the film portrays a world in the near future where a dark city is protected by three comic book female superheroes. Cheung also made her last goofy Wong Jing–related movie that year with *Boys Are Easy (Chasing Boys)/Chui lam chai/Zhui nan zai* (1993), an ensemble piece with Brigitte Lin, Tony Leung Ka-fai, Jacky Cheung, **Chingmy Yau**, **Ekin Cheng**, **Richard Ng**, and **Sandra Ng**. The next year, Cheung was part of an all-star cast including Brigitte Lin, Leslie Cheung, both Tony Leungs, Jacky Cheung, Carina Lau, and **Charlie Yeung** in Wong Kar-Wai's epic ***Ashes of Time*** *(Evil East, Malicious West)/Dung chea sai duk/Dong xie xi du* (1994), based on the **Louis Cha** (Jin Yong) novel *The Eagle Shooting Hero*.

Slowing down from her frantic filming pace, Cheung became much more selective in her projects after 1993, and she serves as an example of a beauty pageant winner who became a serious actress. Her next film did not come until several years later. Costarring with Hong Kong pop idol **Leon Lai** in **Peter Chan's** *Comrades, Almost a Love Story (Honeysweet)/Tim mat mat/Tian mi mi* (1996), a film about two mainlanders who meet in Hong Kong, Cheung took home another Hong Kong Film Award and another Golden Horse Award for her touching and nuanced performance, as well as a **Golden Bauhinia** Award and a **Hong Kong Film Critics Society** Award. That same year, she traveled to France and made *Irma Vep* (1996), a film in which she plays herself playing a part, with French director Olivier Assayas, whom she married in 1998. She returned to Hong Kong to make **Cheung Yuen-ting's** *The Soong Sisters/Sung ga wong chiu/Song gu huang chao* (1997), a docudrama about the lives of the three daughters of the famous and powerful Soong family chronicled in Sterling Seagrave's *The Soong Dynasty*, for which she received another Hong Kong Film Award. She also played a facially disfigured character in **Wayne Wang's** *Chinese Box*, set during the 1997 return of Hong Kong to the Mainland, costarring **Michael Hui**, Jeremy Irons, and **Gong Li**.

Cheung spent the next several years in France with Assayas, making one movie, a comedy, Anne Fontaine's *Augustin, King of Kung-Fu* (1999). Returning to Hong Kong filmmaking soon after, Cheung starred in **Andrew Lau's** *Sausalito/Yat gin chung ching/Yi jian zhong qinq* (2000), a tender drama shot in the United States, once again acting alongside Leon Lai. That same year, Cheung re-teamed with Wong Kar-wai to make *In The Mood for Love/Fa yeung nin wa/Hua yang nian hua* (2000), a fragile mood poem, art house evocation of romance and longing set in 1960s Hong Kong. Cheung is best known today by international audiences for her work in this film. She won both a Golden Horse award and another Hong Kong Film Award. In 2001, Cheung divorced her husband Assayas.

For her next film, the actress signed on to do a period piece with Mainland director **Zhang Yimou**, *Hero/Ying hung/Ying xiong* (2002), his first attempt at a period piece **action** film. Costarring **Jet Li**, **Chen Daoming**, Donnie Yen, and **Tony Leung Chiu-wai**, the film detailed the quest of Qin Shi-huang, the first sovereign emperor of China, and his mission to unite the country. Cheung was nominated for a Hong Kong Film Award for her performance. Most recently Cheung won the Best Actress Award at the Cannes Film Festival for her performance in the Olivier Assayas–directed *Clean* (2004) with Nick Nolte, and she is also part of the ensemble cast in Wong Kar-wai's latest film, *2046* (2004) with Tony Leung Chiu-wai, Gong Li, and **Faye Wong**. Cheung continues to fascinate with the nuances of her acting skills and her beauty on-screen.

CHEUNG, PETER YIU-TSUNG (Cheung Yiu-chung) (1945–). Born in Shanghai, editor Cheung Yiu-tsung was educated in Hong Kong and began his career at **Motion Pictures and General Investment** (Cathay) in 1963. When **Golden Harvest** took over the studio lot, he signed on with the new company. He has edited more than a hundred films over his career, matching his technique to the film's aesthetics, working with many respected directors, including **John Woo**, **Stanley Kwan**, **Alfred Cheung**, **Jacob Cheung**, **Stanley Tong**, **Gordon Chan**, **Kirk Wong**, **Corey Yuen**, and **Benny Chan**, among others, and actors like **Chow Yun-fat**, **Anita Mui**, **Leslie Cheung**, **Jackie Chan**, and **Samo Hung**. He began working with **Lo Wei** and **Bruce Lee**, and has since edited numerous action films, including many **Jackie Chan** vehicles. He has also edited thrillers, horror movies, and comedies, as well as quiet dramas like those for Stanley Kwan, including *Rouge/Yin chi kan/Yan zhi kou* (1988), winning the best editing award at the **Hong Kong Film Awards**, and *Centre Stage (Actress)/Yuen Ling-yuk/Ruan Lingyu* (1992).

Cheung has won numerous awards for editing, including **Golden Horse Awards** for best editing of the films *Fist of Fury/Jing mou moon/Jing wu men* (1972), *The Way of the Dragon/Maang lung goh kong/Meng long guo jiang* (1972), *The Himalayan/Mat chung sing sau/Mi zong sheng shou* (1976), *The Contract/ Maai san kai/Mai shep qi* (1978), *Long Arm of the Law/Saang gong kei bing/Sheng gang qi bing* (1984), *Police Story 3 Supercop/Ging chaat goo si 3: Chiu kap ging chaat/Jing cha gu shi 3: Chao ji jing cha* (1992), *Fong Sai-yuk/Fong Sai Yuk/ Fang Shiyu* (1993), and *The Big Bullet/Chung fung dui liu feng gaai tau/Chong feng dui nu huo jie tou* (1996). He has also won other Hong Kong Film Awards for best editing, including *Mr. Canton and Lady Rose (Miracles, Canton Godfather)/Gei jik/Qi ji* (1989), *Crime Story/Chung ngon cho/Zonganzu* (1993), *Drunken Master 2/Chiu kuen 2/Zui quan 2* (1994), *Rumble in the Bronx/Hung faan kui/Hong fan qu* (1995), and *The Big Bullet* (1996).

CHEUNG, ROY YIU-YEUNG (1963–). Actor Roy Cheung was born in Hong Kong and has become famous for his supporting roles and villains. He was a fashion model before becoming an actor in 1986, when his modeling agent sent him to **Cinema City** for an audition for a role in **Ringo Lam's** *City on Fire (Dragon Tiger Turbulence)/Lung foo fung wan/Long hu feng yun* (1987). He continued making films with Lam, including *Prison on Fire (Prison Turbulence)/Gaam yuk fung wan/Jian yu feng yun* (1987), *School on Fire (School Turbulence)/Hok gaau fung wan/Xiao jiao feng yun* (1988), and *Wild Search (Let's Face the World Together)/Boon ngoh chong tin ngaai/Ban wu chuang tian ya* (1989); he gained attention for his portrayal of a sadistic prison guard in *Prison on Fire*. While early on he preferred action to drama, Cheung came to like drama over action because of its challenge. A case in point is Samson Chiu's *Rose (White Rose, Blue Valentine)/Baak mui gwai/Bai mei gui* (1992), in which Cheung plays a conflicted Triad trying to start anew and falling for a sensitive **Maggie Cheung**. He also appeared in three of the *Young and Dangerous* series as various Triad villains, as well as in the artier send-up of those movies, *Once upon a Time in a Triad Society 2 (Let's Go! Man in Charge Brigade)/Hui ba! Ja FIT yan bing tuen/Qu ba! Zha FIT ren bing tuan* (1996). With *Beast Cops/Yau sau ying ging/Ye shou xing jing* (1998) and *The Mission (Gunfire)/Cheong for/Qiang ho* (1999), he added a subtle dramatic edge to his Triad characterizations, winning the **Golden Bauhinia Award** (from the **Hong**

Kong Film Critics' Association) for Best Supporting Actor for his role in the former. In **Andrew Lau's** *Infernal Affairs 2/Mou gaan dou 2/Wu jian dao 2* (2003), his character is mostly reticent but his performance speaks loudly. Cheung has made 60 films to date.

CHEUNG, WOOD-YAU (Zhang Huoyou) (1910–1982). Actor and producer Cheung Wood-yau (real name Zhang Ganyu) was a native of Guangdong province and a theater ticket salesperson before joining the Opera Actors Training Class of the Chinese Artists' Association of Guangzhou, from which he graduated in 1936. Invited by renowned opera actor Pak Yuk-tong (Bai Yutang), he became lead actor of the Xingzhonghua Opera Troupe and performed alongside some of the best, including **Sit Kok-sin** and **Ma Sze-tsang**.

Cheung's screen debut was *Shattering the Copper Net Array (Breaking through the Bronze Net)/Daai poh tung mong chan/Da po tong wang zhen* (1939), and he appeared in numerous prewar films. One of his most popular films was **Hong Shuyun's** (Hung Suk-wan) *A Girl Named Lengyan/Leung Laang-yim/Liang Lengyan* (1950), in which he played a nonjudgmental savior to **Fong Yim-fan**, in the title role, as a young woman who flees from the Mainland to Hong Kong with her grandfather, only to be raped and impregnated by a blackguard office manager who schemes with the second wife in the wealthy household where the girl works.

Cheung cofounded **Zhonglian** with **Pak Yin**, **Ng Cho-fan**, and others in 1952, and he starred in many of its classics, like *Family/Ga/Jia*, *Spring/Chun/Chun*, and *Autumn/Chau/Qiu* (1953, 1953, 1954, respectively, based on the Ba Jin trilogy) and *Broken Spring Dreams/Chun chaan mung duen/Chun can meng duan* (1955). In Lee Sun-fung's *Broken Spring Dreams*, he starred as the lover opposite Pak Yin's married woman (the film was adapted from Leo Tolstoy's *Anna Karenina*). Director **Ng Wui**, Cheung, and Pak Yin (whom he was often paired with on-screen) founded **Shanlian** in 1954, producing *Madame Yun/Wan Leung/Yun Niang*, *Parents' Love (Great Devotion)/Hoh lin ting gwong foo miu sam/Ke lian tian xia fu mu xin*, and *A Mad Woman/Fung foo/Feng fu* (1954, 1960, 1964, and featuring Zhang and Bai). He was also one of the founders of the South China Artists' Association.

Cheung appeared in 400 films and retired in 1982. He died of heart disease.

CHEUNG, YING (Zhang Ying) (1919–). Actor and director Cheung Ying (real name Zhang Yisheng) was born in Hong Kong; he graduated from Wah Yan College and joined the film industry, appearing in *Night Pearl* (1937). He gained fame following his performance in *Tears for the Society (Rouge Tears)/Yin chi lui/Yan zhi lei* (1940, starring **Butterfly Wu**), a remake of the Shanghai classic *The Goddess*, starring **Ruan Lingyu**.

Cheung has appeared in 400 movies, working primarily in drama, historical drama, and romance. He often starred opposite actress **Pak Yin** and worked with directors **Wong Toi**, **Ng Wui**, **Lo Dun**, **Lee Sun-fung**, **Tso Kea**, and **Chun Kim** and in several comedies with director **Mok Hong-si**, including *Broker La (Broker Lai)/Ging gei Laai/Jing ji La* (1950). In Tso Kea's *Many Aspects of Love/Laai ha goo miu/Luo xia gu mu* (1961), he costarred with Pak Yin and **Ha Ping** in a love triangle complicated by the friendship between the two women involved; adapted from **Mandarin Duck and Butterfly** author Zhang Henshui's novel, the story also depends upon the women's various sacrifices and the visual symbolism, a trademark of Zuo's films. Zuo credited Cheung with working very hard to get into the scripts and characters of his films, also including *Salvation/Tsz miu sam/Ci mu xin* (1960), in which the actor played two roles, father and son, and *Sunset on the River/Moon kong hung/Man jiang hong* (1962), another Zhang Henshui adaptation, in which he again starred opposite Pak Yin, Cheung playing an intellectual who falls in love with a tea house singer (Bai), and produced by Cheung's Hua Qiao Film Company.

Cheung's directorial debut was the drama *A Peaceful Family Will Prosper/Ga who maan si hing/Jia he wan shi xing* (1956, starring Pak Yin), and he directed more than a dozen films, including the drama *Driver No. 7/Dai chat hiu shut gei/Di qi hao si ji* (1958, starring **Ng Cho-fan**), the horror movies *The Night the Spirit Returns/Wooi wan yau/Hui hun ye* (1962) and *Conjuring Spirit at Midnight/Ng yau chiu wan/Wu ye zhao hun* (1964), and the Mandarin drama *The Sword Mates/Yin leung/Yan niang* (1969).

Cheung established two film companies, Hua Qiao in 1957, and Hao Hua in 1962, and he was one of the founders of **Zhonglian** (Union). He turned to **television** in 1969, and has appeared in the soap operas *Crocodile Tears, Reincarnated*, *Chameleon*, and *Rainbow Connection*.

CHEUNG, YUEN-TING. Born and raised in Hong Kong, director Cheung Yuen-ting graduated from the University of Hong Kong with a double major in English and psychology and completed graduate work in drama and creative writing at Bristol University (England). In 1978, she returned to Hong Kong as chief writer at Hong Kong Radio Television (RTV). She worked as a production assistant on a BBC documentary called *The World around Us*, and found filmmaking fascinating. Because of this experience, she enrolled in film school and in 1983 completed a master's degree in Film at New York University (NYU). While at NYU she met writer and director **Alex Law**, and the two began a fruitful partnership in film (and married). Generally, Law is the writer and Cheung the director, but they collaborate in the best sense of the word, throughout production.

Cheung's first feature film, *The Illegal Immigrant/Fai faat yee man/ Feifa yimin* (1985), was her thesis film at NYU and shot on location in New York. She used classmates for her crew and nonprofessionals from Chinatown for her actors, but received sponsorship from **Shaw Brothers** to make it a 35mm feature. The film became the first of her *Immigrant Trilogy*. In the film, a newly arrived illegal immigrant desperately tries to find work and legal status. He arranges a paper marriage with an ABC (American-born Chinese) woman who wants money for a nose job. The story ends tragically. The film won a Special Jury Award at the 30th Asia Pacific Film Festival in Tokyo in 1985.

Cheung's second film, also second in the trilogy, was *An Autumn's Tale (An Autumn's Fairy Tale)/Chau tin dik tung wa/Qiu tian de tong huo* (1987), starring **Chow Yun-fat**, who had committed to the project shortly before the success of ***A Better Tomorrow*** *(True Colors of a Hero) Ying hung boon sik/Yingxiong bense* (1986). Despite having since signed for 10 features in Hong Kong, Chow came to New York for the six-week shoot. Chow played a Chinese immigrant who had escaped to New York during the Cultural Revolution and reestablished himself in Chinatown without assimilating. Falling for a visiting distant cousin (**Cherie Chung**) who outclasses him, he remakes himself, and the film has a fairy-tale ending. In 1987, the film won five **Hong Kong Film Awards**, including Best Picture and Best Screenplay, and six **Hong Kong Film Directors' Choice Awards**, including Best Picture and Best Screenplay.

Third in the trilogy was the episode *Eight Taels of Gold/Baat a gam/Ba ya jin* (1989), starring **Samo Hung** as Bai, an immigrant who succeeds in getting his green card, only to return home to China to find a world he no longer understands and a China that considers him a stranger. **Sylvia Chang** costarred as a distant cousin, Wu. While Bai's family encourages him to find a wife and return to the United States, Wu's fiancé from the United States comes to marry her. Bai gives Wu all he has—eight taels of gold.

Cheung's films emphasize characterization and human emotion, but also examine identity and cultural politics and reunification. In 1989, she set foot on the Mainland for the first time, in her own words "to discover a country and a people I did not understand. . . . I tried to reestablish a link with the past, to study the history of China as we stepped towards the unknown future, and to find out who I really am." Her research led to *The Soong Sisters (The Sung Family Dynasty)/ Sung ga wong chiu/Song gu huang chao* (1997), a historical drama and epic based on the lives of three important and unusual **women**, Soon Qing-ling (the future Madame Sun Yat-sen, played by **Maggie Cheung**), Soong Ai-ling (the future Mrs. H. H. Kung, China's finance minister, played by **Michelle Yeoh**), and Soong Mei-ling (the future Madame Chiang Kai-shek, played by Vivian Wu). The saga shows the women poised to create a new China, and confronting the forces of political power; problems with Mainland censors resulted in release delays as well as 18 minutes of the film being cut. Still, the film won six awards at the 17th **Hong Kong Film Awards**.

City of Glass/Boh lee je shing/Bo li zhi cheng (1998) a drama of two romances, past and present, also metaphorically addresses the reunification issue, and *Beijing Rocks/Bakging lok yu lo/Beijing le yu le* (2001), set in Beijing's underground rock music scene, a love-triangle relationship story, describes the contradictions of the new China in a global marketplace. Cowritten by Cheung and partner Alex Law, and shot by cinematographer **Peter Pau**, the project grew out of Cheung's listening to underground rock bands while arguing with Chinese censors over *The Soong Sisters*. Her latest film, *Traces of the Dragon: Jackie Chan and His Lost Family/Longde shenchu: shiluode pin tu* (2003), is a documentary concerning **Jackie Chan's** discovery of his parents' other families left behind on the Mainland, and continues Cheung's interests in cultural differences among Mainlanders and Hong Kongers.

Cheung's films straddle mainstream and art house films, and as such she occupies a unique position in the Hong Kong film industry. She has never attempted to cross over too far in either direction, maintaining her integrity of vision. She reveals telling aspects of human nature and behavior throughout her films.

CHIANG, DAVID WEI-NIEN (Keung Dai-wei, Jiang Dawei) (1947–). Born in Suzhou, China, to the actors Yim Fa and Hon Wei, David Chiang has been a professional performer since the age of four. In 1965, he began to train with the upcoming action director **Lau Kar-leung**, and then was recruited by the **Shaw Brothers** studio as a stuntman. He soon caught the eye of **Chang Cheh**, director of the successful early movies of **Jimmy Wang Yu**. Chiang contributed stunt work and small fighting roles to *The One-Armed Swordsman/Duk bi diy/Du bei dao* (1967) and *Golden Swallow/Gam yin ji/Jin yan zi* (1968). His agility in the action sequences won him the nickname "The Elastic Double." His first starring role was in *The Wandering Swordsman/You xia er/Yau hap ngai* (1970). Over the next half decade, Chiang and his "Blood Brothers" **Ti Lung** and **Chen Kuan-tai** starred in over 40 **action** films for Chang Cheh and the Shaw Brothers studio.

Small-framed and rail-thin, David Chiang might seem an unlikely martial hero, but his agility, combined with the intelligence he projected, made him a formidable adversary. He played a range of characters in his Shaw studio films, from ***wuxia*** swordsmen to classic kung fu fighters and contemporary gangsters, but he was at his best in the roles that allowed his natural intensity to edge into obsession and fury. In *Vengeance!/Bou sau/Bao chou* (1970), Chiang single-mindedly tracks down and eliminates his brother's killers with a display of cold-blooded mayhem that won him the Best Actor Award at the 1970 **Asian Film Festival**. In *The New One-Armed Swordsman/San duk bei do/Xin du bi dao* (1971), he perfectly embodies the Chang Cheh ideal of tortured, depressive hero. In *The Heroic Ones/Sap saam taai biu/Shi san tai bao* (1970), he makes the ultimate sacrifice to his clan, being drawn and quartered. Chiang's performances in films such as *Blood Brothers/Chi ma/Ci ma* (1973), *The Boxer from Shantung/Ma wing ching/Ma yong zhen* (1971), and *Generation Gap/Boon ngaak/Pan ni* (1973), for which he picked up a second Best Actor Award, etch variations on the theme of frustrated idealist turned doomed cynic.

Before leaving the Shaw Brothers studio in the late 1970s for independent work, Chiang starred in one of Lau Kar-leung's early **kung fu** films, the underappreciated *Shaolin Mantis/Tong long/Tang lang* (1978). As a Qing dynasty agent trapped in a web of deception, Chiang once again plots to decimate his enemies, but this time he carries the knowledge that right and wrong are not so easily discerned. After *Shaolin Mantis*, his career followed a more erratic path, including forays into comedy and eventually a specialization in character parts, as seen in his portrayal of a revolutionary agent in **Tsui Hark's** *Once upon a Time in China 2/Wong Fei-hung 2/Huang Feihong 2* (1992). Chiang's older half brother, **Paul Chun**, is also a character actor, and his younger half brother, **Derek Yee Tung-sing**, is a well-known actor and director.

CHIAO, ROY (Kiu Wang, Qiao Hong) (1927–1999). Born in Shanghai and a native of Shanxi province, actor Roy Chiao attended schools in Chongqing and Shanghai. His father participated in the Chinese Revolution as a supporter of Sun Yat-sen. The younger Chiao went to Taiwan during the Korean War; fluent in languages (Mandarin, Cantonese, Shanhainese, Japanese, and English), he worked as a radio broadcaster and interpreter for the United States Army before becoming an actor. He went to Japan in 1955 and began his career with the help of **Bai Guang**, the Mandarin actress he met there. She cast him in his screen debut, *Red Peony (Fresh Peony)/Sin maau daan/Xian mu dan* (1956), produced by her new company, Guoguang (financed by **Motion Pictures and General Investment**). Before her retirement in 1957, she recommended Chiao to MP&GI and he signed with the company that year. With an athletic physique, he became one of its important actors, starring in many of its features, including the musical *Spring Song/Ching chun ngai lui/Qing chun ernu* (1959, starring **Ge Lan** and **Jeanette Lin Cui**), *Air Hostess/Hung chung siu che/Kongzhong xiaojie* (1959), and the comedy *Sister Long Legs/Cheung tiu che che/Chang tui jiejie* (1960), and for its later incarnation Cathay, in the family war-torn drama *A Debt of Blood/Luen sai ngai lui/Luan shi er nu* (1966); the melodrama ***The Story of Three Loves****/Tai siu yan yuen/Ti xiao yin yuan* (1964), in which he played the villainous warlord; and the swordplay *Escorts over Tiger Hills/Foo saan hang/Hushan hang* (1969), Cathay's first

wuxia film, in which Chiao played a conflicted swordsman who renounces his violent life and becomes a monk, but is torn between his vows, his soldierly duty, and his feelings for a woman.

In the early 1970s, Chiao's career entered a new phase as he starred in many period dramas and *wuxia* films. In **Tang Shuxuan's** *The Arch/Dung foo yan/Dong fu ren* (1970), Chiao played a soldier with whom a widow (**Lisa Lu**) falls in love; but social mores prohibit her proclaiming her love, much less marrying him, so she arranges a marriage with her daughter. Chiao became a prominent actor in classic **King Hu** productions, atmospheric, elegant, and lyrical *wuxia* treatments that involve intrigue, suspense, and tested loyalties; Chiao appeared in *A Touch of Zen (Gallant Lady)/Hap lui/Xia nu* (1971), *The Fate of Lee Khan (Incident at Spring Inn)/Ying chun gok ji fung boh/Ying chun ge zhi feng bo* (1973), and *The Valiant Ones/Chung lit tiu/Zhong lie tu* (1975). In *A Touch of Zen*, he played the virtuous and benevolent Zen master. In *The Fate of Lee Khan*, Chiao not only holds his own against five female heroines and a female villain, but plays the Mongol leader's military officer who is really a rebel ally, working to overthrow the Mongols. In *The Valiant Ones*, Chiao stars as the sacrificing hero in a story of devotion to duty; he plays a soldier known for his unorthodox style who recruits a group of fighters to eliminate pirates working with corrupt Ming officials. He also appeared in **Bruce Lee's** ***Enter the Dragon****/Lung chang foo dau/Loong zheng hu dou* (1973), *Game of Death/Sei miu yau fai/Si wang you hu* (1978), and *Tower of Death/Sei miu taap/Si wang ta* (1981) and **Michael Hui's** comedies *The Last Message/Tin choi yue baak chi/ Tian cai yu bai chi* (1975) and *Inspector Chocolate/San taam ju goo lik/Shen tan zhu gu li* (1986).

Chiao continued making a variety of genres, including Karl Maka's *The Good, the Bad, and the Loser/Yat chi gwong gwan chow tin aai/Yi qi guang gun zou tian ya* (1976), **John Woo's** *Follow the Star/Daai saat sing yue siu mooi tau/Da sha xing yu xiao mei tou* (1978), **Samo Hung's** *Enter the Fat Dragon/Fei lung goh kong/Fei loong guo jiang* and *Dragons Forever/Fei lung maang cheung/Fei long meng jiang* (1978 and 1988, respectively), **Leong Po-chih's** *Itchy Fingers/San tau miu taam doh doh/Shen tou miao tan shou duo duo* (1979), **Yuen Biao's** *A Kid from Tibet/Sai chong siu ji/Xi cang xiao zi* (1992), and **Alfred Cheung's Lunar New Year's comedy**

All's Well Ends Well 1997 (97 Family Has Happy Affairs)/97 Fung yau hei si/97 Gu you xi shi (1997). Talented in action and comedy, Chiao was equally talented in drama, which he demonstrated more forcefully as he aged. His turn in **Jacob Cheung's** *Cageman (Cage People)/Lung man/Long min* (1992) as the manager of a poor men's hostel provided a point of view for the film as well as showing Chiao in a talented ensemble cast that humanized a social problem and portrayed a strong sense of community. In **Jeff Lau's** *Treasure Hunt/Dut kei siu lam/ Hua qi shaolin* 1994), he played an advice-giving uncle to **Chow Yun-fat**. In **Peter Chan's** touching *Age of Miracles/Lut lut faan faan/Ma ma fan fan* (1996), he played a friendly Death in a white suit handing out ice cream cones and carrying balloons. Chiao will be remembered for his portrayal of an Alzheimer's victim in **Ann Hui's** ***Summer Snow*** *(Woman, Forty)/Nui yan Sei sap/Nuren sishu* (1995), for which he won the Best Actor Award at the **Hong Kong Film Awards**. Chiao's elderly patriarch ran the gamut from tyranny and confusion to warmth, humor, and fear, and his chemistry with **Josephine Siao** as the daughter-in-law who comes to understand him is as true to human relationships as a mid- and late life story can be.

Chiao also appeared in Hollywood productions including Lewis Gilbert's *Ferry to Hong Kong* (1959, starring Orson Welles), Steven Spielberg's *Indiana Jones and the Temple of Doom* (1984), and James Glickenhaus's **Jackie Chan** vehicle *The Protector* (1985). He began television roles in 1979, starting with Hong Kong Television Broadcasts Limited's (TVB) drama *Guardian Angel*, and including Rediffusion Television's (RTV) *Blowing in the Wind* (1980), and Radio Television Hong Kong's (RTHK) *Amazing Bubble* (1983–1984). He also dubbed films and TV shows into Mandarin, beginning in the 1950s.

A devout Christian from his early twenties (when he married disc jockey Siu Kam-chi, also a Christian), Chiao became actively involved in missionary work after immigrating to Seattle, Washington, with his wife in 1964. He died of a heart attack there. His last film, *Sometimes, Miracles Do Happen (City of Angels)/Tin sai ji shing/ Tian shi zhi cheng* (1999), in which he played an angel in a hospital ward, was made in Hong Kong, for the church. Chiao's career spanned almost 50 years and he made close to 90 films.

CHIAU, STEPHEN SING-CHI (Stephen Chow) (1962–). Born in Hong Kong, director/actor Stephen Chiau grew up in a working-class neighborhood in Kowloon (his offices are there). He graduated from Hong Kong Television Broadcasts Limited's (TVB)'s training course in 1983, and he began cohosting a successful children's program with **Tony Leung Chiu-wai** that lasted six years and led to other **television** roles; he had become a TV star by 1987. He started acting in movies with **Danny Lee's** *Final Justice (Thunderbolt Vanguard)/Pik lik sin fung/Pi li xian feng* (1988), for which he won Best Supporting Actor at Taiwan's **Golden Horse Awards**; half a dozen of his films have broken local box office records, among them *Justice My Foot!/Sam sei goon/shen si guan* (1992), *Royal Tramp (The Legend of Mountain Deer)/Luk ting kei/Lu ding ji* (1992), and *Shaolin Soccer/Siu lam chuk kau/Shaolin zuqiu* (2001). His codirecting debut was in the James Bond parody *From Beijing (China) with Love (Country Made 007)/Gwok chaan Ling Ling-chat/Guo chan Ling Lingqi* (1994). Heir to popular comedian **Michael Hui**, Chiau received the mantle when a changing of the guard was signaled in *The Banquet (Powerful Family Midnight Banquet)/Ho moon ye yan/Hao men ye yan* (1991) during a dueling chopsticks scene between the two comedians. Chiau frequently teams with older actor **Ng Man-tat**, who plays sidekick and straight man to Chiau's zany portrayals.

Called the "Chinese Jim Carrey," Chiau is known for slapstick, pratfalls, **kung fu**, and wit in both period parodies and urban comedies in the 50 films he has made to date. His screwball farces include goofball characterizations and nonsense, mismatched word play called ***mo-lei-tau***. These Cantonese puns, drawn from contemporary (and fast-changing) Hong Kong slang, play better to a local and younger audience than most. Early on, even among locals, Chiau was considered a brazen upstart, both crude and impolite. That changed when his characterizations, arrogant and self-serving, expanded to include not only Hong Kong disaffected youth, but an everyman character trying to survive hard times. Although he has been the top Hong Kong film star for more than a decade, a handful of his films following *God of Cookery (The Eating God)/Jeung san/Shi shen* (1996) tanked at the box office. With *Shaolin Soccer*, however, Chiau once more returned to top form, playing a Shaolin monk with extraordinary **martial arts** skills and a "leg of steel," who organizes a soccer team of has-beens. *Shaolin Soccer* combines Chiau's brand of humor with kung fu and state-of-the-art special effects. This film not only broke box office records in Hong Kong (raking in HK$60 million locally), but to date it is Hong Kong's highest grossing movie of all time, earning US$46 million across Asia. It also won seven awards at the 2002 **Hong Kong Film Awards** (including Best Picture, Best Director, and Best Actor). Sony Picture Classics Studios spent two million dollars to secure North American distribution rights, but delayed release in the United States, undermining the film. *Kung Fu Hustle/Gung foo/Gong fu* (2004) not only paid homage to *The House of 72 Tenants*, but retained Hong Kong flavor with an eye to the global market; the film broke Hong Kong box office records and Miramax finally found its footing, releasing the film widely in the United States to box office and critical success.

CHIN, HAN (Sun Siangchong) (1946–). Born in Shanghai, actor Chin Han is the son of a nationalist hero, General Sun Yuen-ling, who fought during World War II. His film debut was *Sister's Lover/Cheo cheu dik ching yan/Jie jie de qing ren* (1976), and he became a leading male actor in Taiwan in the 1970s. His frequent pairing with **Brigitte Lin Ching-hsia** on-screen led to a scandalous romantic involvement, with the actor leaving his wife and two children. (Lin eventually married the owner of the San Francisco-based clothing company, Esprit.) Their on-screen pairing in **Yim Ho's** *Red Dust/Gwan gwan hung chan/Gun gung hong chen* (1990) visualized a desperate and passionate couple, while Chin's appearance in **Stanley Kwan's** *Centre Stage/Yuen Ling-yuk/Ruan Lingyu* (1992), opposite **Maggie Cheung** as **Ruan Lingyu**, was a dramatic coup. The actor has appeared in close to 60 films, and also starred in the anti-Japanese historical drama *Don't Cry, Nanking/Naam ging 1937/Nanjing 1937*.

Following in his painter-mother's footsteps, he is known in Taiwan for his paintings, in oils and watercolors.

CHIN, NELLIE YU (Qin Yu, Chun Yue) (1929–). Writer Nellie Chin Yu (also known as Qin Yifu), a native of Zhejiang province, came from an old and scholarly Beijing family, performed onstage during her university days, and graduated with a degree in literature from the University of Hong Kong. Chin joined the film industry in 1954 as an actress, and her screen debut was *The 72 Martyrs of Canton*

(1954). She subsequently appeared in **Yue Feng's** contemporary battle of the sexes comedy *The Battle of Love/Ching cheung yue chin cheung/ Qingchang Ru Zhangchang* (1957), written by **Eileen Chang** and starring **Linda Lin Dai**, who plays off several suitors (**Peter Chen Ho** and **Liu Enjia**) to win the man (**Chang Yang**) she loves. Chin played Lin Dai's dutiful sister.

During the early 1950s, she wrote essays and translated English plays and novels. In 1956, the actress became a screenwriter supervisor for **Motion Pictures and General Investment**. Chin's first screenplay, for Yue Feng's *Scarlet Doll/Hung wa/Hong wa* (1958), was written for Dianmao and its first color feature. She wrote almost 20 screenplays and excelled at drama featuring **women**, whether innocent young girls or experienced women, always endearing. She won best screenplay at the **Golden Horse Awards** for ***The Wild, Wild Rose****/Yau mooi gwai ji luen/Yemeigui zhi lian* (1960), ***Sun, Moon and Star****/Sing sing Yuet leung Tai leung/Xing xing Yue liang Tai yang* (1961), and ***The Story of Three Loves****/Tai siu yan yuen/Ti xiao yin yuan* (1964). For the widescreen ***huangmei diao*** *Wife of a Romantic Scholar (Young Miss Su)/So siu mooi/Su xiao mei* (1967), an adaptation of Feng Menglong's popular novel *How Su Xiaomei Thrice Tested His Bride*, Chin won the best screenplay award at the **Asian Film Festival**.

For **Tang Huang's** ***Her Tender Heart****/Yuk lui shut ching/Yunu siqing* (1959), Chin wrote the story of an innocent, young, and talented girl (the film was **Lucilla You Min's** first film for MP&GI) who has been raised by a single father (**Wang Yin**). When her admired aunt (**Wang Lai**) visits from Italy, a series of shocks come the girl's way. First, she learns that the aunt is her mother, and she accepts her only at the insistence of her father. Next, her father's leg is amputated following an accident. Then, she is told her father is not her natural father, her mother and her husband want to take her to Italy to study music, and the father who has raised her rejects her and disappears. The screenplay builds each additional jolt in a believable and devastating fashion.

The Wild, Wild Rose, one of **Wang Tianlin's** best-known Mandarin musicals, starred **Ge Lan** as a doomed songstress with spitfire spirit and heart in a fatalistic drama that integrated the symbolic content of the songs as a commentary on the action and characters. Ge Lan costarred in both of the epics *Sun, Moon and Star* and *The Story of Three Loves*, in the former, directed by **Evan Yang**, as the city cousin and traditional Chinese woman in love with the weak hero (**Chang Yang**) and in the latter, directed by Wang, as the likeable traditional street performer violated by an evil warlord. Chin adapted *Sun, Moon and Star* from Xu Su's lengthy novel and she adapted *The Story of Three Loves* from a **Mandarin Duck and Butterfly** novel by Zhang Henshui. In the latter, set during the early days of the Republic, the forced transformation of the heroine is all the more dramatic because of the sense of tragic fate and loss conveyed.

Chin continued working at MP&GI following her marriage to a physician. She cochaired the company's scriptwriting committee with **Yao Ke**, giving the studio's movies a distinctive and recognizable style. She retired in 1967 and immigrated to Canada.

CHINESE OPERA FILMS. Chinese Opera began circa 720 C.E. during the Tang dynasty under Emperor Xuanzong, who founded the first opera troupe in China, called Pear Garden, performing for the emperor's pleasure. During the following years, opera troupes with various distinctive styles emerged, and today there are close to 400 identifiable styles throughout numerous Chinese districts. Northern styles, including Peking (Beijing) Opera, which came into its own during the Qing dynasty (1644–1910), were considered the most prestigious. Northern styles relied more heavily on sound, Southern, including Shanghai, on sight. There are more than a thousand Peking (Beijing) operas; they use traditional stringed and percussion instruments, the music provides rhythm for the acting, and spoken dialogue and singing are used. During the Cultural Revolution, opera troupes were disbanded as reactionary. **Chen Kaige's** *Farewell, My Concubine/Ba wong bit gei/Ba wang bie ji* (1993), based on the Lillian Lee novel, records its 20th-century history.

Traditionally, as in Shakespeare, audiences were familiar with the stories being dramatized, and males played the female parts (in China, when females began acting, males and females were not allowed onstage together at the same time). Generally, Chinese operas include music, singing, acting, acrobatics, and **martial arts**, drawing especially on the art of refined footwork, precise hand gestures, and codified body language. Stories draw from history, myth, and classical literature. Often moral messages are conveyed. Performances include standardized plots, with the sequence of incidents varying from performance to performance, depending on the actors. Specialized roles, such as *sheng* (male), *dan* (female), and *chou* (clown) developed, and elaborate face painting is used to indicate recognizable characters. Actors became famous for the types they played.

The Southern, Cantonese Opera style probably migrated south from the north, emerging in Guangdong during the late Southern Song dynasty. It eventually became popular in Guangdong, Guangxi, and Hong Kong, among other places. Two types of plays developed, *mun* (highly educated), emphasizing poetry and refinement, featuring scholar characters, and *mo* (martial arts), emphasizing warfare, with weapons and action, featuring generals. Six roles predominate: *wen wu sheng* (a learned man who can also fight); *xiao sheng* (a young scholar); *hua dan* (a young female); *er hua* (a supporting female); *chou sheng* (a clown); and *wu sheng* (an acrobatic performer).

Some of the well-known performers who moved from stage to screen include (alphabetically) **Fong Yim-fan**, **Fung Wong Nui**, **Hong Sin-nui**, **Lam Ka-sing**, **Ma Sze-tsang**, **Mak Bing-wing**, **Pak Suet-sin**, **Sit Kok-sin**, and **Yam Kim-fai**. In the 1950s, the *ling-xing* controversy erupted, that is, *ling* meaning opera stars and *xing* movie stars, as opera stars moved into film from the stage. Opera stars worried that films would not encourage opera's further development as an art form, while film stars complained opera films were not well-made and the opera performers were usurping their medium. Nevertheless, opera films were immensely popular, with over 500 opera films produced during the decade, roughly one-third of Cantonese cinema's output over the period.

Beloved operas include **Lee Tit's** ***The Purple Hairpin*****/*Chi chaai gei/ Zichai ji*** (1959), considered by many to be a masterpiece of the genre, and based on well-known Ming dynasty opera, and *Why Not Return?/Woo bat gwai/Hu bugui* (1958). The latter, based on an original script and libretto written during prewar times by Feng Zhifen, is considered to be one of the most artistically complete opera stories. It includes the famous aria *Hu Bugui* ("Why do you not return? The broken hearted cries like the cuckoo in mourning. . . ."), which a distraught husband sings at his wife's grave. Filmed often, the story basically narrates the conflict between a mother-in-law and daughter-in-law over a son/husband. Malicious and jealous lovers play their part by spreading rumors that the wife suffers from tuberculosis. The

doomed spirit. Although not a martial arts film per se, *A Chinese Ghost Story* soars on Ching's **wirework** expertise.

"I just know how to adjust the angle, adapt the filmmaking to the actors, to make them look good. I have always held the camera myself. I work the camera so I have complete control," he has stated. This control also extends to editing the action sequences himself, and often includes involvement in story development. Despite his unmistakable action style, Ching is able to seamlessly weave from high drama to pratfalls, from edgy eroticism to refined spirituality. His astonishing versatility has been recognized by numerous awards, including Best Action Choreography at the **Hong Kong Film Awards** in 2003, for his work on **Zhang Yimou's** *Hero*. His resume as action director includes approximately 1,500 **television** shows in Hong Kong, and at least 100 movies, including the recent *House of Flying Daggers/Shimian maifu* (2004). He also has directed a number of highly regarded feature films.

CHIU, KANG-CHIEN (Qiu Gangjian) (1940–). Screenwriter Chiu Kang-chien was born on Gu Lang Island in Fujian province. In 1949, he immigrated to Taiwan, later earning a degree in screenwriting from Taiwan State College and studying in the theater program at the East-West Center of the University of Hawaii. In 1964, he returned to Taiwan and, with others, began a serious film periodical, *Theater Quarterly*.

Chiu began working in Hong Kong in 1966 as a **Shaw Brothers** screenwriter, under **Stephen Soong** and his successors. His first script, directed by **Yue Feng**, was *Bells of Death/Duet wan ling/Duo hun ling* (1966), adapted from the Hollywood vehicle for Steve McQueen, Henry Hathaway's *Nevada Smith* (1966). *Twin Blades of Doom/Aau yeung diy/Yin yang dao* (1968) followed, **Tao Qin's** only swordplay movie.

Chiu wrote several **Chang Cheh** movies, including *The Singing Detective/Daai diy goh wong/Da dao ge wang* (1969, rewritten from a **Ni Kuang** script), *Dead End/Sei gok/Si jiao* (1969), *The Singing Killer/Siu saat sing/Xiao sha xing* (1970), and *The Duel/Daai kuet dau/Da jue dou* (1971). He also wrote scripts for **Chor Yuen**, including *Intimate Confessions of a Chinese Courtesan (Ai Nu)/Oi No/Ai Nu* (1972) and *The Bastard/Siu chap chung/Xiao za zhong* (1973).

Although Chiu directed a film in 1973, it was never completed. A year later, he resigned from Shaw. The writer rewrote and directed a Singapore production of *Dream of the Red Chamber* (1977), a project originally offered and declined by Yue Feng. Chiu continued working in Taiwan, primarily rewriting scripts for director Cai Yangming, including *Thou Shalt Not Kill but Once/Siu lam saai gaai/Shaolin sha jie* (1977), among others.

Chiu has written more than 35 scripts, and is well-known in Hong Kong and Taiwan, especially for his **martial arts** screenplays that have strong narratives and focus on the conflict between sexual desires and the heroic code.

The writer ventured into **New Wave** and independent cinema, serving as script advisor for **Ann Hui's** *The Story of Woo-Viet/Woo Yuet dik goo si/Hu yue de gu shi* (1981), starring **Chow Yun-fat**, and *Boat People/Tau ban liu hoi/Touben nuhai* (1982). He also cowrote other Chow Yun-fat movies, **Stanley Kwan's** *Love unto Waste/(Underground Love)/Dei ha ching/Di xia qing* (1986), and the actor's only martial arts film prior to *Crouching Tiger, Hidden Dragon*, director **Ronny Yu's** *The Postman Strikes Back/Chun sing ma/Xun cheng ma* (1982). Others include **Patrick Tam's** *Nomad/Lit foh ching chun/Lie huo qing chun*, starring **Leslie Cheung**, **Eddie Fong's** *Amorous Woman of the Tang Dynasty/Tong chiu ho fong lui/Tang chao hao fang nu* (1984), and Kwan's *Rouge/Yin chi kau/Yan zhi kou* (1988) and *Full Moon in New York/ Yan joi nau yeuk/Ren zai niu yue* (1989).

Chiu was awarded Best Screenplays at the second, sixth, and eighth **Hong Kong Film Awards** and at the 26th **Golden Horse Awards**.

CHOR, YUEN (Chu Yuan) (1934–). Director and screenwriter Chor Yuen was born Cheung Bo-kin/Zhang Baojian in Guangzhou. He studied chemistry at Sun Yat-sen University in China. His father, **Cheung Wood-yau/**Zhang Huoyou, was a famous Cantonese cinema actor, and under his influence Chor began work as a Cantonese cinema screenwriter under the penname Chun Yu/Qin Yu. He found a mentor in director **Chun Kim** and worked as assistant director (1957–1958) on several of his films before his directorial debut with *The Natural Son (Grass by the Lake)/Woo boon cho/Hupan Cao*

(1959). The next year he drew public attention with *The Great Devotion (A Parent's Devotion for Their Children Is Greatest)/Hoh lin tin har foo mo sam/Kelian tianxia fumu xin*, a movie about a parent's love for children and focusing on Hong Kong's underclass, featuring **Fung Bo-bo**.

Chor directed films from many genres, including love stories, thrillers, and comedy farces. Best known among his work are the love stories *Tear-Laden Rose/Yan lui dik mooi gwai/Han lei de meigui* (1963) and *Winter Love (Be My Love)/Dung luen/Dong lian* (1968), the spy thriller *Black Rose/Hak mui gwai/Hei mei gui* (1965), and the farcical *Young, Pregnant and Unmarried/Yuk lui tim ding/Yunu tianding* (1968). *Black Rose*, Hong Kong's answer to James Bond movies, with *To Catch a Thief* thrown in, became an overnight success. **Chan Po-chu** starred in the title role along with **Patrick Tse Yin** as her love interest. A fantasy entertainment, with spies, gadgetry, a jewel thief, acrobatic swordsmen, action set pieces with choreographed fights, and car chases, the movie was part of a brief mid-1960s Cantonese phenomenon that disappeared in the early 1970s, but was revived in the 1990s with movies like **Jeff Lau's** pastiches *Rose, Rose I Love You* and *Black Rose 2* and comic book fantasy like Johnnie To's *Heroic Trio* and *Executioners*.

Young, Pregnant and Unmarried is one of the funniest Hong Kong screwball comedies made, also starring Chan Po-chu. She plays the younger and favored daughter of a status-conscious father and feigns pregnancy, while it is her older sister who finds herself in an out of wedlock pregnancy. Satire abounds as traditional values of marriage and family are upended. Both pessimistic and fatalistic, *Winter Love* is an exceptional film made when Cantonese melodrama was in its decline and possesses all of Chor's characteristic signatures—symbolism, Western influences, elevated dialogue, and unabashed emotionalism. The framing device presents a once popular novelist (Xie Xian) sitting in a coffee shop on Christmas Eve recalling the woman he loved. The movie dramatizes, when they met in the coffee shop four years earlier. She agrees to marry him but jilts him; he later learns she's married to a drug addict (his former classmate). The frame closes a year later, when the writer's sister appears to tell him the woman is dying. Both pessimistic and fatalistic, the plot circles around to suggest the woman's sister (Wang Aiming) will repeat the tragedy.

Chor directed more than 80 Cantonese movies, but when Cantonese cinema fell into decline, Chor joined **Cathay** at the end of 1969 and began making ***wuxia*** Mandarin films, specializing in adaptations of **Gu Long** novels. Complex plots with unexpected twists and dreamy atmospheres characterized his style. He moved to **Shaw Brothers** in 1971 and made *Intimate Confessions of a Chinese Courtesan (Ai Nu)/Oi No/Ai Nu*, an unconventional *wuxia* picture in which the female protagonist of the title (**Lily Ho**) breaks the weak female/lady knight stereotype by using sex and seduction to trap male and female tormentors. Chor made 20 *wuxia* films during the next five years, adapting many from novelist Gu Long, but he broke box office records with *The House of 72 Tenants/Chat sap yee ga fong hak/Qi shi er gu fang ke* (1973), a warm and hilarious Cantonese satire reflecting life in contemporary Hong Kong. It has the makings of comedy that became mainstream in the 1980s. In 1985, Chor formed his own company, Ligao Film, and directed several more movies, spanning 120 over his career. He was active in **television** until his recent retirement.

CHOW, CHI-SING (Zhou Zhicheng) (1909–1956). Actor Chow Chi-sing, a native of Zhejiang province, grew up in Guangdong province and before becoming an actor was a civil servant in Guangzhou. He joined the music department of Feisheng Drama Group as an amateur because he was a music enthusiast; there he met actor Kuang Shanxiao. Together the two appeared in the movie *Hero of Guangdong* (1933). Kuang started Ziwei Film Company in 1933, and invited Zhou to appear in *The Invincible Love Devil* (1933). Meantime, Chow worked as a prompter at the rooftop theater of the Sincere Department Store, where he suffered an injury that resulted in his slightly inclined head.

Chow came to Hong Kong in 1934 and found work at the Astor Theater as a prompter. At Kuang's recommendation, he signed with Daguan and resumed acting. Over a career spanning 25 years, he appeared in over 100 films, including *Bloodshed in Baoshan City (The Blood-Stained Baoshan Fortress)/Huet chin bo saan shing/Xie jian bao shan cheng* (1938), **Wang Weiyi's** ***Tears of the Pearl River*** *(Dawn Must Come)/Chu kong lui/Zhujiang lei* (1950), *Kaleidoscope* (1950), **Lee Tit's** *In the Face of Demolition/Aau lau chun hiu/ Weilou* *chunxiao* (1953), and **Ng Wui's** *Father and Son/Foo yue ji/Fu yu zi* (1954). The characters he played were often fawning and contemptible subordinates, and his portrayals were so successful that he had to deal with public belligerence. In the realist melodrama *The Kid (My Son a Chang)/Sai liu Cheung/ Xilu Xiang* (1950), for example, Chow played Short-sighted Tsui, who, with the owner's eldest son, runs an illegal racket selling factory products. **Bruce Lee** starred in the title role as Kid Cheung, a street orphan and delinquent who reforms.

Chow's last screen appearance was *The Story of Wong Fei-hung, Part 2/Chuk Wong Fei-hung chuen/Xu Huang Feihong chuan* (1955). He died poverty-stricken of encephalemia and heart disease.

CHOW, RAYMOND (Zou Wenhuai) (1927–). Born in Hong Kong, producer Raymond Chow graduated from Shanghai's St. John's University with a bachelor of arts in journalism in 1949, returning to Hong Kong, where he worked as a reporter for the English newspaper, the *Hong Kong Standard*, then in 1951 for the *Voice of America*. In 1959, he entered the film industry at **Shaw Brothers** as a publicity manager, becoming head of production; he worked at Shaw for 10 years. In 1970, he left Shaw to set up his own studio, **Golden Harvest**, using the former **Cathay** Studios premises; in its first year, Golden Harvest produced eight features and set up distribution throughout Hong Kong and across Asia. Chow gave superstar **Bruce Lee** his breakthrough after Lee rejected low offers from Shaw Brothers and signed with Golden Harvest, which produced *The Big Boss/ Tong saan daai hing/Tang shan da xiong* (1971), *Fist of Fury/Jing mou moon/Jing wu men* (1972), and *The Way of the Dragon/Maang lung goh kong/Meng long guo jiang* (1972), creating a new **kung fu** genre, denigrated in the West as "chopsocky," but popular among many Western audiences despite the racism. A later Lee film, ***Enter the Dragon****/Lung chang foo dau/Loong zheng hu dou* (1973), proved the negative element wrong, becoming one of the top-50 box-office successes of all time.

Chow has always been an innovator, ahead of his time, not only signing Bruce Lee, but pursuing the international market and working within Hollywood. He pursued international productions, including *The Boys in Company C* (1978); *Cannonball Run 1* and *2* (1981,

1984), which included Burt Reynolds and **Jackie Chan** in an ensemble cast and grossed an international box office surpassing US$160 million; and *Teenage Mutant Ninja Turtles* (1990).

Locally, Chow also promoted stars such as **Michael Hui**, Jackie Chan, and **Samo Hung** in numerous films. He was the first recipient of the Showman of the Year award by the National Association of Theater Owners in 1980 and Most Outstanding Producer the same year at the **Golden Horse Awards**. In 1987, the Order of the British Empire was bestowed upon him. In 1996, he was awarded a Lifetime Achievement Award by CineAsia (the Asian film industry convention) and the Order of the Sacred Treasure, Gold Rays with Rosette, from the emperor of Japan; in 1998 he received the Gold Bauhinia Star, from the government of the Hong Kong Special Administrative Region.

Although Golden Harvest is a publicly listed company, currently Chow, at 78, still comes into the office daily.

CHOW, STEPHEN. *See* CHIAU, STEPHEN CHI-SING.

CHOW, YUN-FAT (1955–). Born on Lama Island, actor Chow Yun-fat, the third of four children, grew up in the Hong Kong countryside in a poor family. His father was away at sea much of the time, and Chow assisted his mother as a vegetable farmer, selling dim sum in the streets. From childhood he earned the nickname "Gao Tsai" (Little Dog), which he retains to this day. He worked many jobs before entering the film industry; he still visits the market to shop, cooks for his mother, and enjoys cooking. His childhood experiences probably contributed to his acting persona; part of his charisma derives from his work ethic, humor, and modesty; he clearly enjoys acting and sharing his joy with others, on-screen and off. Chow dropped out of high school to help support his family; when he saw an advertisement for Hong Kong Television Broadcasts Limited (TVB) acting classes, he signed up, completing the course in 1974, the same year his father died. He played a variety of roles on television, most notably for the serials *The Bund* and *Hotel*, both romantic parts that earned him a following across Asia. He swept Asia by storm with his performance in *The Bund* as romantic gangster Hui Man-keung. He remains, other than **Jackie Chan** and **Bruce Lee**, the most famous and best loved Chinese actor across Asia and internationally.

Chow crossed over to the big screen beginning in 1976, in a variety of roles. Most notable was his work with director **Ann Hui** in *The Story of Woo Viet (Woo Yuet's Story)/Woo Yuet dik goo si/Hu Yue de gu shi* (1981), a horrific nightmare of a Vietnamese refugee stranded in Manila; and with director **Leong Po-chi** in *Hong Kong 1941 (Waiting for Dawn)/Dang doi lai ming/Deng dai li ming* (1984), an occupation story during the Sino–Japanese War in which Chow's Mainlander befriends a Hong Kong couple and sacrifices his love for their survival. He won Best Actor awards at both the Taiwanese **Golden Horse Awards** and the Asian Pacific Film Festival for his performance. He worked with directors **Stanley Kwan** and **Ronny Yu** as well, but Chow was not as successful crossing over to the big screen as his television success had anticipated.

John Woo changed that when he selected Chow for his breakthrough success ***A Better Tomorrow*** *(True Colors of a Hero)/Ying hung boon sik/Yingxiong bense* (1986). He had read about Chow's generosity and charity work in orphanages in the papers and sought him out for the part of gangster Mark Gor. Woo was also in the doldrums with his film career, and for both the movie served as a turning point. They discovered that the friendship, loyalty, trust, sacrifice, and empathy they shared translated well as themes on-screen. For Woo, Chow Yun-fat became emblematic of the chivalric knight on which he modeled his heroic bloodshed gangster. For both, the film was an opportunity for second chances, either make or break. The movie broke all previous Hong Kong box office records, as Hong Kong youth took to the streets in the emblematic sunshades and black duster Chow Yun-fat wore in the movie. Chow won Best Actor for his portrayal at the **Hong Kong Film Awards**.

Chow continued working with Woo on four more of the director's films; during the three-year period following, Chow starred in 31 movies. The *Los Angeles Times* described him as "the coolest actor in the world," and his screen power comes from a talent usually associated with character actors able to submerge themselves in their roles. Chow, however, as a leading man, acts on the edge, conveying a humanness drawing the viewer to him, never forgetting his roots or identification with the common person. He has sharp instincts and his playfulness is infectious. His good looks, warmth, and intelligence have drawn comparisons with actors as varied as Cary Grant for his suaveness, Montgomery Clift for his wounded sensibility, and Clint Eastwood for his masculinity. Others often mentioned include Paul Newman, Clark Gable, Jack Lemmon, Steve McQueen, and Robert Duvall. Chow himself cites Alain Delon and Jean-Paul Belmondo as influences, once admitted Robert De Niro was his hero, and introduced a special screening of *One Flew over the Cuckoo's Nest* (1975) at the Toronto Film Festival, declaring that Jack Nicholson's acting had had a major impact on his life. Whatever the comparisons, Chow Yun-fat's imprint on film is unique because of his talent and heart. Chow knows how to act to a camera and he is one of those on-screen rarities who comes along once in a generation; he communicates with an audience with a grin and wink as if we are all in this together.

Chow's character was so admired in *A Better Tomorrow* that for the sequel, *A Better Tomorrow 2 (True Colors of a Hero 2)/Ying hung boon sik 2/Yingxiong bense 2* (1987), Chow returned as his deceased brother's twin. The duo followed that up with *The Killer (A Pair of Blood-Splattering Heroes)/Dip huet seung hung/Die xie shuang xiong* (1989), a stylish bullet ballet in which Chow played a hit man with heart, modeled after Alain Delon's professional killer in Jean-Pierre Melville's *Le Samourai* (1967). The film played numerous international film festivals and became a darling of international critics, precipitating Woo's (and later Chow's) move to Hollywood. Woo and Chow continued to work together on the crime caper *Once a Thief (Criss Cross Over Four Seas)/Jung waang sei hoi/Zhong heng si hai* (1991) and Woo's Hong Kong swan song, *Hard-Boiled (Hot-handed God of Cops)/Lat sau san taam/Lashou shentan* (1992), in which Chow played honest detective Tequila, a model Woo considered more appropriate for Hong Kong youth.

Meantime Chow also worked with Hong Kong's best directors, including **Ringo Lam**, starring in his *City on Fire (Dragon Tiger Turbulence)/Lung foo fung wan/Long hu feng yun* (1987) as an exploited undercover cop, for which he also won Best Actor at the Hong Kong Film Awards; *Prison on Fire* 1 *(Prison Turbulence) /Gaam yuk fung wan/Jian yu feng yun* and 2 *(Escaped Criminals: Prison Turbulence Sequel)/To faan gaam yuk fung wan juknjaap/Tao fan jian yu feng yun xu ji* (1987, 1991) as a sympathetic convict; *Wild Search (Let's Face the World Together)/Boon ngoh chong tin ngaai/Ban wu chuang tian ya* (1989) as a driven detective attempting to rescue a child abducted by vicious killers; and *Full Contact (Chivalrous Thief Ko Fei)/Haap dou Ko Fei/Xia dao Gao Fei* (1992) as a rough, motorcycle riding gangster with a no-nonsense buzz cut. Director **Johnnie To** directed him in the tearjerker drama *All about Ah-long (Ah Long's Story)/Ah Long dik goo si/A Lang de gu shi* (1989), in which Chow played a single father sacrificing himself for the good of his son (winning Chow another Best Actor at the Hong Kong Film Awards), as well as To's **Lunar New Year's comedies** *Eighth Happiness (Eight Stars Greetings)/Bat sing bo hei/Ba xing bao xi* (1988) and *The Fun, the Luck, and the Tycoon (Lucky Star Join Hands and Shine)/Gat sing gung jiu/Ji xing gong zhao* (1990). He reprised Mark Gor's character in **Tsui Hark's** *A Better Tomorrow 3: Love and Death in Saigon (True Colors of a Hero 3: Sunset Song)/Ying hung boon sik 3/ Yingxiong bense 3* (1989), the prequel and third film in the ***Better Tomorrow*** **series**. Chow made numerous gangster films as well as comedies during the 1980s, demonstrating his versatility as an actor. He also ushered in a new trend in gambling movies, starring in **Wong Jing's** *God of Gamblers/Do san/Du shen* (1989) and *God of Gamblers' Return (God of Gamblers 2)/Do san 2/Du shen 2* (1994) as Kochun, a talented gambling god and chocolate lover. Despite his success, he agreed to star in **Cheung Yuen-ting's** small-budget tender dramedy *An Autumn's Tale (An Autumn's Fairy Tale)/Chau tin dik tung wa/Qiu tian de tong huo* (1987), the second film in her immigrant trilogy, shot on location in New York, and a happy time for Chow as he wed his wife, Jasmine Chow, also his business manager. Cheung's (and partner **Alex Law's**) *Now You See Love . . . Now You Don't Love . . . Now You See It, Now You Don't (I Love Nau Man-chai)/Ngoh oi Nau Man-chai/Wo ai Niu Wenchai* (1992) is perhaps as close to Chow's roots as any of his movies; Chow plays the headman of an island fishing village, a country boy who goes to the city to find love and happiness.

Chow's manager and friend **Terence Chang** (John Woo's producing partner) was instrumental in bringing both to Hollywood. The actor moved to Los Angeles with his wife to study English, and made his Hollywood debut in Antoine Fuqua's *The Replacement Killers* (1998), a slick gangster film trading on Chow's action image and costarring Mira Sorvino, followed by *Anna and the King* (1999), a readdressing of the story of *Anna and the King of Siam*, best known in its musical version *The King and I*. Epic in scope, the film costarred Jodie Foster and proved Chow's appeal to an older audience of more serious and mature filmgoers. He followed with a psychological thriller, James Foley's *The Corruptor* (1999), costarring Mark Wahlberg.

Chow returned to Asia to work with **Ang Lee** on *Crouching Tiger, Hidden Dragon*, a lyrical **martial arts** action period piece. (Chow's only other martial arts film [discounting the martial arts-with-automatic-weapons style in Woo's movies] had been **Ronny Yu's** *The Postman Strikes Back [City Patrol Horse]/Chun sing ma/Xun cheng ma* [1982].) *Crouching Tiger* received the most nominations ever (10) for a foreign-language film at the Academy Awards and won Oscars for Best Foreign-Language Film, Best Cinematography, Best Art Direction, and Best Score. Recently Chow starred in the action comedy *Bulletproof Monk* (2003), costarring Sean William Scott and appealing to a teen audience. Chow reunited with Ann Hui for *The Aunt's Postmodern Life* (2005) and worked with **Zhang Yimou** on *Curse of the Golden Flower* (2006). He is set to reunite with Woo for *The Battle of Red Cliff* and *The Divide* in the near future, the former a period Chinese battle epic and the latter their first Hollywood movie together, perhaps the movie most anticipated by Western aficionados. This 19th-century story concerns the Chinese and Irish immigrants who built the railroad across the United States.

CHU, KEI (Zhu Ji) (1921–1987). Director Chu Kei (real name Zhu Richuan) was born in Guangdong province and informally educated. Throughout his life, he learned on the job. At 13, he apprenticed at the Hong Kong division of Shanghai's Tianyi Studio, where he learned photography and film processing. He served as assistant director of photography on *The Afang Palace on Fire* (1935), one of the early Hong Kong–produced movies. That same year, he appeared onscreen in *The Butterfly Lovers* (1935), and joined Nanyue Studio as an editor, writer, and, eventually, director. He directed *An Unfaithful Wife/Chut cheung hung hang/Chu qiang gong xing* (1941), and over a career spanning 30 years, he directed 233 films.

Many of the director's films were adaptations of **Cantonese operas**, including *Swallows Come Home (The Swallow's Message)/Yat nin yat diy yin gwai loi/Yi nian yi du yan gui lai* (1958), *How Third Madam Educated Her Son/Saam leung gaau ji/San niang jiao zi*

(1958), *The Dream Meeting (Encounter) between Emperor Wu of Han and Lady Wai/Han Wudi Menghui Wei Furen* (1959), *How Madame Zhao Went Far and Wide in Search of Her Husband/Chiu ng leung maan lee cham foo/Zhao wuniang wanly xunfu* (1959), *Determination/Bat cham lau laan sai/Bu zhan lou lan shi bu hai* (1963), and *Twelve Beauties/Sap yee laan gon sap yee chaai/Shi er lan gan shi er chai* (1964). *How Madame Zhao Went Far and Wide in Search of Her Husband* was adapted from a Yuan opera called *The Lute Song/Pipa ji*. A husband leaves his faithful wife to care for his parents while he sits for the imperial exams; he is forced into marriage with a prime minister's daughter and cannot return. His parents die in a famine, and his faithful wife, armed only with a pipa and portrait of the elders, sets out to retrieve her husband.

Chu also directed adaptations of "airwave novels" (radio serials), such as *The Hypocritical Heart/Leung chung sam/Liang chong xin* (1955); many melodramas, including *A Hymn to Mother/Tsz miu chung/Ci mu song* (1956), *Mother Love/Miu oi/Mu ai* (1961), and *The Search of Loved Ones/Maan lee cham chan gei/Wan li xin qin ji* (1961); and contemporary films like *Madam Yun/Wan Leung/Yun Niang* (1960), starring **Yam Kim-fai** and **Pak Suet-sin**, and *Filial Piety/Haau diy/Kao dao* (1960). *Mother Love* and *Filial Piety* starred **Josephine Siao Fong-fong** and **Butterfly Wu**.

Chu was one of the founding members of **Zhonglian**, and he directed some of his best works there, including *An Orphan's Tragedy/Goo sing huet lui/Gu xing xie lei* (1955) and *Myriad Homes/Chin maan yan ga/Qian wan ren gu* (1955), both starring **Ng Cho-fan** and the young **Bruce Lee**. In the former, Ng played a doctor, framed and falsely imprisoned, who escapes and manages to provide for the education of his young son (Lee); the grown son (**Cheung Wood-yau**) is a country doctor who defends his father against his tormentor. The director also started his own company, Haiyang, which produced *Xi Shi, the Eternal Beauty/Sai Si/Xi Shi* (1960), also starring the Pak–Yam duo. Chu's final direction was for *The Smart Master and the Rich Girl* (1969), after which he retired. He died in Hong Kong. *See also* CHINESE OPERA FILMS.

CHU, PAUL KONG (Zhu Jiang) (1945–). Growing up in Hong Kong, actor Chu Kong, a native of Guangdong province, began acting in *Ten Schoolgirls/Sap dai che/Shi da jie* (1960), followed by *The Elevator Murder Case/Din tai ching sat ngon/Dian ti qing sha ang* (1960), in which he was the male lead. He has appeared in 40 films and delivered a poignant performance as a former hit man, friend, and Triad brother of **Chow Yun-fat** in **John Woo's** *The Killer/Dip huet seung hung/Die xie shuang xiong* (1989). Since 1975, he has played in numerous **television** dramas and is a dubbing artist for both television and film.

CHUN, KIM (Qin Jian) (1926–1969). Born in Guangdong, director and screenwriter Chun Kim was a Hong Kong middle school graduate, where he worked as a teacher. In 1944, he began in the film industry as an assistant director to Hu Peng. His first screenplay was *Two Dragons Fighting for a Pearl* (1948), followed by a codirection with **Ng Wui**. His directorial debut was *Red Brimmed River* (1949), a commercial debacle. *Infancy* (1952), about childhood education, was also a disappointment. *Following the Gentle Light* (1953), a serious consideration of youth problems, was a commercial success. He was known for his melodramas, including *Sweet Seventeen* (1954).

The director explored family relationships, in both traditional settings and tragic melodramas as well as in contemporary romances and urban comedies. His most popular films included *A Melancholy Melody (The Song of Love's Regret; The Melancholy Shadow Falls on My Lover)/Goh sing lui ying/Gesheng leihing (Gesheng re qinghen; Leiying zhao langxin)* (in two parts, 1952), *Autumn/Chau/Qiu* (1954), *Neighbors All/Ga ga woo woo/Jia jia hu hu* (1954), *We Owe It to Our Children (The More the Merrier)/Ngai lui chai/Er nu zhai* (1955), ***Parents' Hearts**/Foo miu sam/Fumu xin* (1955), *Autumn Comes to the Purple Rose Garden (Crepe Myrtle) Garden/Chi mei yuen dik chau tin/Ziwei yuan de qiutian* (1958), *Intimate Partners (My Intimate Partner)/Laan fong laan dai/Nan xiongnan di* (1960), and *How to Get a Wife/Chui chai gei/Zhui qi ji* (1961). All of the above were Cantonese-language films. *Autumn* was an adaptation of the third Ba Jin novel in a trilogy and is a nostalgic and painful look back at the expense of the feudalistic system on the lives of families and individuals. The film concludes with the disintegration of a family and their scattering like the leaves in an autumn wind, under an atmospheric seasonal sky. Perhaps Chun's masterpiece is *Neighbors*

All, which treated the mother-in-law and wife conflict in a complex manner to unearth generational differences and get at the different ideas between the older and younger generation. The film was shot in an economical style, with the family apartment serving as the location, by cinematographer **Luo Junxiong**, who carefully composed the rich detail of the mise-en-scène and effectively exploited deep focus shots.

Parents' Hearts is an enduring classic of Cantonese melodrama and one of **Zhonglian** production company's undeniable masterpieces. Chun parallels the decline of **Cantonese opera's** popularity with the economic and social misfortunes of an opera troupe family, similar to the director's own career.

Chun was adept at comedy. *Intimate Partners*, a classic comedy produced during the transitional period of Cantonese film, used off-screen narration to comic effect. A story of two on-the-outs bachelors trying to make ends meet and simultaneously chase girls, the feature emphasized overcoming obstacles through group efforts; it was remade under the same title in 1968 by Chen Wen, and again at **Cinema City** as *It Takes Two* (1982).

In 1965, Chun joined **Shaw Brothers** and began directing Mandarin-language features, among them *Pink Tears/Chi ching lui/Chi qing lei* (1965), *Till the End of Time/Hoh yat gwan joi loi/He ri jun zai lai* (1966), *Four Sisters* (1967), and *Unfinished Melody/Bik hoi ching tin yau yau sam/Bi hai qing tian ye ye xin* (1969). *Till the End of Time* is a contemporary update of the songstress story, here introducing actress Hu Yanni, with **Chen Hou** playing a rich man's son who falls for the nightclub singer and goes blind after working 16-hour days.

The director established several film companies, including Ling Feng in 1950, Hong Mian in 1953, Xing Yi in 1954, Guang Yi in 1955, Xin Yi in 1963, and Guo Yi in 1964. Chun promoted numerous actors and actresses, including **Patrick Tse Yin**, Jia Ling, and Hu Yanni. He influenced directors **Patrick Lung** and **Chor Yun**, among others. He was married to actress **Helen Lin Cui** in 1959, although they divorced in 1967. Chun committed suicide by hanging himself in 1969.

CHUN, PAUL PUI (1945–). The prolific supporting actor Chun Pui has appeared in close to 125 movies playing characters of all types in all genres, although he is often cast as a loathsome villain or a bombastic policeman. He began acting in the 1960s, in movies like the Cantonese drama *Three Young Girls/Yuk lau saam fung/Yu lou san feng* (1968) with **Connie Chan Po-chu**, and was uncredited in Robert Wise's *The Sand Pebbles* (1966), starring Steve McQueen, and he appeared in the ***wuxia pian*** *The Water Margin/Shui hui chuen/Shui hu zhuan* (1972) among other **martial arts** actioners. Memorable roles include **Peking (Beijing) opera** diva Fa, in **Tsui Hark's** *Peking (Beijing) Opera Blues/Diy ma dan/Dao ma dan* (1986, opposite **Wu Ma** playing **Sally Yeh's** father, for which he was nominated as Best Supporting Actor at the Hong Kong Film Awards) and as the sympathetic uncle in **Derek Yee's** melodrama *C'est la Vie, Mon Cheri (New Not End Love, New Endless Love)/San bat liu ching/Xin bu liao qing* (1993), for which he won Best Supporting Actor at the Hong Kong Film Awards. A memorable villain is the one in **Ringo Lam's** *Wild Search (Let's Face the World Together)/Boon ngoh chong tin ngaai/Ban wu chuang tian ya* (1989), who is intent on murdering a child witness, while a typical policeman is the blundering captain in **Johnnie To's** superhero fantasy *The Heroic Trio (The Three Asian Heroines)/Dung fong saam hap/Dong fang san xia* (1993).

Director Derek Yee is the actor's brother and actor **David Chiang** is his half brother.

CHUNG, CHERIE CHO-HUNG (1960–). Born in Hong Kong, actress Cherie Chung, like many others, entered the Miss Hong Kong contest (but was not a winner). Her film debut was **Johnnie To's** **martial arts** actioner *The Enigmatic Case/Bik shui hon saan duet meng gam/Bi shui han shan duo ming jin* (1980), also his directorial debut. She made a handful of films with **Chow Yun-fat**, and they had an on-screen chemistry in **Ann Hui's** *The Story of Woo-Viet/Woo Yuet dik goo si/Huyue de gu shi* (1981), **Ronny Yu's** *The Postman Strikes Back/Chun sing ma/Xun cheng ma* (1982), **Cheung Yuen-ting's** *An Autumn's Tale (An Autumn's Fairy Tale)/Chau tin dik tung wa/Qiu tian de tong huo* (1987), To's *Eighth Happiness (Eight Stars Greetings)/Bat sing bo hei/Ba xing bao xi* (1988), **Ringo Lam's** *Wild Search/Boon ngo chong tin ngaai/Ban wo chuang tian ya* (1989), and **John Woo's** *Once a Thief (Criss Cross Over Four Seas)/Jung waang sei hoi/Zhong heng si hai* (1991), among others. An attractive girl next door type character, she made 50 films before retiring in 1991 and marrying.

CHUNG, ROBERT KAI-MAN (Zhong Qiwen) (1919–1993). A Cantonese native, Chung Kai-man graduated from the University of Hong Kong. Film mogul Li Zuyong chose him to head **Yonghua Film Studios**. He subsequently studied color film and processing in the United States. In 1957, when **Loke Wan Tho** reorganized International Films into **Motion Pictures and General Investment**, he appointed Chung general manager, which he served as for seven years, during the studio's most productive period.

Besides affecting broader company decisions, Chung also turned to directing. His debut was the tender and sentimental *The Education of Love/Oi dik gaau yuk/Ai de jiao yu* (1961). Based on Italian novelist Edmondo de Amici's *Cuore*, the story pays homage to the selfless devotion of elementary school teachers. **Jeanette Lin Cui** (called "Student Darling" by her fans) starred as the daughter who replaces her bedridden father as an elementary school teacher. At first reluctant because she detests children, as she learns more about their situations and realizes the influence her father has played in their lives, she not only comes to a better understanding of her father, but decides to follow her father's career path. Veteran Shanghai director **Wang Yin** played the ailing and dedicated father with dignity, and **Kelly Lai Chen** played the daughter's sympathetic boyfriend. A young **Samo Hung** played one of the needy students, a shy, quiet boy from a single-parent home where his despairing father has turned to alcohol. Chung also directed Wang Yin the following year in *A Fine Romance/Yat duen ching/Yi duan qing* (1962, starring **Chang Yang**), and Chang Yang and **Julie Ye Feng** the next year in **Eileen Chang's** tragic script *Please Remember Me/Yat kuk laan mong/Yi qu nan wang* (1964).

Chung joined Rediffusion Television as the director of its Chinese channel. He immigrated to the United States in 1979 and worked in color film processing.

CHUTE, DAVID. Film specialist David Chute earned his BA from St. Johns College, Annapolis, Maryland. He works under Hungry Ghost Productions in Los Angeles and has participated in various capacities on films as well as writing film analysis for magazines like *Film Comment*. His special interest is Hong Kong cinema and he is currently writing *Tigers and Dragons: Rediscovering Chinese Martial Arts Movies*.

CINEMA CITY. Actors, director, and producers **Karl Maka**, **Raymond Wong**, and **Dean Shek** founded Cinema City in 1980. The company became famous in the 1980s for its action comedies with Hollywood production values that were both commercial and critical successes. The comedies featured stunts, slapstick, stars, and cameos, and required a laugh quotient, that is, an eye to so many laughs per reel. A brainstorm committee oversaw film production, and as the company grew, filmmakers like **Tsui Hark** and **Eric Tsang** came onboard. Cinema City's first production was **John Woo's** *Laughing Times/Gu ji shi dai* (1980), in which the three founders appeared. *Aces Go Places/Chui gai pak dong/Zui jia pai dang* (1982) was one of Hong Kong's highest grossing films and led to a popular five-film series.

Not all of Cinema City's films were comedies. Significant productions and contributions to the development of film include John Woo's groundbreaking ***A Better Tomorrow****/(True Colors of a Hero)/Ying hung boon sik/Yingxiong bense* (1986), which began the "heroic bloodshed" action genre, and its two sequels, as well as **Ringo Lam's** gritty gangster grind *City on Fire (Dragon Tiger Turbulence)/Long hu feng yun* (1987), all starring **Chow Yun-fat**. The company's final production was *In the Lap of God/Man huang de tong hua* (1991), starring **Roy Cheung**.

CLEARWATER BAY FILM STUDIO. Located at Clearwater Bay, the Clearwater Bay Studio was founded in 1959 and developed from overseas Chinese investments; it includes three sound stages, exterior sets, and a staff dormitory. Studio chiefs have been Lu Yuanliang and Liu Huanyi, among others. **Great Wall**, **Feng Huang**, **Xinliang**, and **Hualian** have used the facilities, making films such as **Ng Wui's** *The Prodigal Son/Baijia zai* (1952) and *Family/Jia* (1953), Yuen Yan-an's ***The True Story of Ah Q****/A Q zhengzhuan* (1958), **Chen Jingbo's** *The Golden Eagle/Jin ying* (1964), and **Lee Sung-fung's** *Tragedy of a Poet King* (1968). Since the 1970s, the studio has been increasingly used for producing **television** series and commercials.

CORDERO, MARIA (Ma Lei-a). Primarily a deep-in-your-gut blues singer (a la Janis Joplin), Filipina actress Maria Cordero has appeared in close to 40 Hong Kong films, mostly in small roles. Her film debut was in **Ringo Lam's** *City on Fire (Dragon Tiger Turbulence)/ Lung foo fung wan/Long hu feng yun* (1987), in which she is seen and heard in a red-tinged nightclub performing the gritty theme song of the film, reinforcing the hellish life of the working-class deep cover played by **Chow Yun-fat**. Another memorable performance is as the seemingly tough but loving mother of a disfigured daughter; it is revealed that she literally carries her daughter on her back in **Lee Chi-ngai's** *Lost and Found/Tin aai hoi gok/Tian ya hai jiao* (1996).

– D –

D&B FILMS COMPANY LTD. D&B was founded in 1984 by businessman Dickson Poon (ex-husband of **Michelle Yeoh**) and actor **John Shum**. Its first production was **Philip Chan's** cop actioner *The Return of Pom Pom/Shuang long chu hai* (1984), in which Shum costarred. Over its eight years in production, the company made 60 films. Production ranged from **Corey Yuen's** crime actioner *Yes, Madam!/Huang gu shi jie* (1985), a vehicle for Michelle Yeoh that spawned a series of four films without her; **Tony Au's** *Dream Lovers/Meng zhong ren* (1986, coproduced with **Pearl City**), starring **Chow Yun-fat** and **Brigitte Lin**; Clifton Ko's zany comedy *It's a Mad, Mad World/Fu gui bi ren* (1987), with Bill Tung and **Lydia Shum**; **Cheung Yuen-ting's** *An Autumn's Tale (An Autumn's Fairy Tale)/Qiu tian de tong huo* (1987), starring **Chow Yun-fat** and **Cherie Chung**; and **Stephen Shin's** romantic comedy *Heart to Hearts/San ren shi jie* (1988), starring **George Lam** and **Carol Cheng**.

In 1985, the company began a distribution chain that distributed over 200 movies. The company's final production was Shin's *Black Cat 2/Hei mao 2 ci sha she li qin* (1992), with Jade Leung and Robin Shou, before it ceased operations.

DACHENG FILM COMPANY LTD. Founded in 1957 by brothers Kwan Chi-kin and Kwan Chi-sing (Kwan Ka-pak and Kwan Ka-yu), Dacheng's first production was *Misguided Jealousy* (1951). Over 15 years of filmmaking, the company produced 130 films. Its Cantonese opera films include *Princess Cheung Ping (Tragedy of the Emperor's Daughter)/ Dinu hua* (1959), *Snow Storm in June/Liu yue xue* (1959), and *The Nymph of the River Lo/Luo shen* (1957). Others are *Do unto Others as They Do unto You/Ren ren wei wo, wo wei ren ren* (1954), *River of Mandarin Duck/Yuan yang jiang wei hen* (1960), *Mother Love/Mu ai* (1961), and *The Big Revenge/Li jiang he pan xie hai chou* (1963). Dacheng's last film was *The Ambitious Prince/Xiong xin tai zi* (1965), after which it reorganized and became **Kin Sing**. *See also* CHINESE OPERA FILMS.

DENG, JICHEN (1912–199?). Comic actor Deng Jichen, a native of Guangdong province, joined Yangcheng Music Society after graduating from secondary school; after the war, he worked as a radio broadcaster in Guangzhou. He was recruited by Hong Kong's Rediffusion Broadcasting Company, where he created eight different voices for various radio plays, earning him the name "King of Comedy."

Deng's film debut was *The Great Idler/Sau wong/She wang* (1950), and the same year he made *The Blundering Couple/Woo lung foo chai/Wulong fuqi*. Over a career spanning more than 30 years, he made over 100 films, mostly comedies, including *A Star of Mischief Is Born (A Star of Mischief)/Faan dau/Fan dou* (1951), *Daddy and Sonny/Leung chai yau/Liang zai ye* (1951), *The Scatterbrain/Sat wan yue/Shi hun yu* (1951), and *Crossroads/Sap chi gaai tau/Shi zi jie tou* (1955). In **Zhou Shilu's** *Daddy and Sonny*, Deng played a runaway son rebelling against his father who is unable to survive independently. In **Mok Hong-si's** *Crossroads*, Deng played part of an honest and industrious couple (Zheng Biying played the woman) set against another couple (**Cheung Ying** and **Fong Yim-fan**) who mistake each other to be well off but are not, and struggle to keep up the pretense, although they are neighbors in the same apartment. The situation comedy used the honest couple as foil to the other's vanity. Deng also appeared in numerous **Wong Hok-sing** movies, including the **Chinese opera** comedy Wong directed that costarred famous opera singer **Sun Ma Sze-tsang**, *The Feuds between Huang Tangjing and Chen Mengji/Fong tong geng ng dau chan mung gat/Huang Tangjing wu dou Chen Mengji* (1958). Deng also costarred with Sun Ma in numerous Chinese opera comedies, Deng playing the indecisive dummy and Sun Ma, the confident figure who criticizes and corrects him. The two paired as the foolish duo in the *Two Fools* series (*Two Fools in Hell/Leung she yau dei yuk/Liang sha you di yu* and *Two Fools in Paradise/Leung soh yau tin tong/Liang sha you tian tang*, 1958, *Two Fools Capture the Criminal [Two Fools Capture the Murderer]/Leung soh kam hung gei/Liang sha qin xiong ji*, and *Two Fools Capture a Ghost/Liang sha zhuo gui ji*, 1959).

Besides being a popular singer, Deng wrote the screenplays for *A Star of Mischief Is Born*, *The Scatterbrain*, *Crossroads*, and *The Feuds between Huang Tangjing and Chen Mengji*. He immigrated to Canada in 1975, lecturing at the University of Toronto on traditional Chinese opera, music, and film. He returned to Hong Kong in 1981, and has since appeared in films like **Tsui Hark's** *All the Wrong Clues/Gwai ma ji doh sing/Gui ma zhi duo xing* (1981) and **Karl Maka's** *Chasing Girls/Chui lui chai/Zhui nu zai* (1981).

DIASPORA FILMS. The Chinese diaspora goes back to the mid-19th century; with people looking for a better life, many men traveled to the United States to work on the railroads. Chinese emigration to Hong Kong begins with the thousands of people who fled the Mainland during the 1850s Taiping Rebellion. Hong Kong has always been a refuge for Mainland Chinese; when times were bad in China, border crossers left, expecting to return when circumstances improved. In 1851, 31,463 Chinese lived in Hong Kong; in 1931, 859,425. After 1912, numbers swelled following the establishment of the Chinese Republic, and again following the Sino–Japanese War in the 1930s. Over a million fled during the Japanese Occupation during World War II, returning at a rate of about 1,000 a month after the war. In 1948, following the Communist revolution, a mass exodus of approximately 750,000 occurred, which continued until borders were closed in 1951. In 1962, due to famine during the Great Leap Forward, an estimated 100,000 immigrants made the trek, and between 1976 and 1981, about 500,000 legal and illegals fled. More recently, with the 1997 return of Hong Kong to the Mainland looming, Hong Kongers began leaving home not to return to the real and imagined homeland, but to countries like Australia, Canada, and the United States.

Hong Kong's film industry development is indelibly linked to overseas Chinese, with many early Mainland filmmakers producing movies in Hong Kong. During the Japanese occupation, filmmakers such as **Cai Chusheng** left Shanghai temporarily for the then colony, and likewise today filmmakers like **Clara Law**, **Ann Hui**, and **Ronny Yu** film in Australia. Even **Jackie Chan** held an Australian passport just in case of need following the handover. **John Woo** left Hong Kong for Hollywood in 1992.

On-screen, numerous films since the emergence of the **New Wave** have tackled the Chinese diaspora. Several films have used New York settings: **Stanley Kwan's** *Full Moon in New York/Yannjoi lau yeuk Yan joi nau yeuk /Ren zai niu yue* (1989) dramatizes the friendship between three very different women; **Clara Law's** hard-hitting *Farewell, China/Oi joi bit heung dik gwai chit/Ai zai bie xiang de ji jie* (1990), a story in which sacrifices are endured in hopes of a better life, leads to madness and tragedy; **Cheung Yuen-ting's** tender immigrant trilogy includes the fairy tale *An Autumn's Tale/Chau tin dik tung wa/Qiu tian de tong hua* (1987), in which obstacles are overcome; **Evans Chan's** *Crossings/Cho oi/Cu ai* (1994) was based on an actual New York City subway killing and addresses illegal immigration and drug trafficking; and **Peter Chan's** *Comrades/Tim mat mat/Tian mi mi* (1996), partly set in New York, reveals loneliness, yearning, and nostalgia. Generally these films reflect the difficulty of assimilation, the establishment of tight-knit ethnic communities and networking, and the ache for home. In some instances, people do return home, although not always to the expected, as in **Yim Ho's** *Homecoming/Chi shui lau nin/Si shui liu nian* (1984).

Other filmmakers, such as **John Woo** and **Tsui Hark**, used Vietnam settings in *Bullet in the Head/(Blood-Splattered Streets)/Dip huet gaai tau/Die xue jie tou* (1990) and *A Better Tomorrow 3/ Ying hung boon sik 2/Yingxiong bense 3* (1989) to examine characters' resilience in extreme circumstances. **Wong Kar-wai's** *Happy Together/Chun gwong a sit/Chun guang zha xie* (1997) was set in Buenos Aires and used a gay couple on the outs and disconnected to emote the tone of yearning and emptiness, while his love letter to Shanghai's exile community in Hong Kong appeared in *In the Mood for Love/Fa yeung nin wa/Hua yang nian hua* (2000). Mainland director Zheng Xiaolong's *The Gua Sha Treatment/Gwaat Qui/Gua Sha* (2002), starring Hong Kong actor **Tony Leung Ka-fai**, was filmed in St. Louis and used cultural misunderstanding as the linchpin for drama. A traditional

Chinese treatment used on an ill child leads to his father (Leung) being charged with child abuse and losing his son. Filmmakers continue to examine the Chinese diaspora in a variety of ways.

DOCUMENTARY. Although the documentary began strong in Hong Kong, it has not fared well overall. Filmmaker and producer **Li Minwei** coordinated and photographed Hong Kong's first documentary, *Chinese Competitors at the Sixth Far East Sports Games in Japan* (1923), and he was also known for the footage he shot of early Chinese Republic leader Dr. Sun Yat-sen. Li followed Sun from 1926 to 1927 on the Northern Expedition to destroy the warlords and unify the country, and Li's footage of Sun and other Republicans remains a landmark historical record as well as reflecting the filmmaker's belief in the power of film to affect the world. It was produced by Li's **Minxin** Film Company. **Lianhua** Film Company also produced documentaries at its Hong Kong branch. However, documentaries were not among popular movies in Hong Kong, dominated by mainstream 35mm commercial features, other than newsreels during the Sino–Japanese War (1937–1945) and during Hong Kong's occupation by Japan, definitely pro-Japanese as to what was screened in theaters. Following the war, and the Communist revolution, Hong Kongers seemed to avoid politics and reality on-screen, a preference that continues to this day. Newsreels, government information and propaganda films, trailers, and commercials prevailed in regard to the documentary. Documentaries by now-deceased Hugh Baker on the rituals of Southern China stand out.

Socially engaged documentaries followed from Action Films, including Lo King-wah's *Solidarity with El Salvador*, shot when he was a student at Canada's York University in the early 1980s, as well as the fleshed-out feature *The Incident* (1984), based on interactions between idealistic political young people and industrial abuses with workers. Action Films, a socially engaged documentary group, produced a number of films and videos in tandem with Hong Kong's Christian Industrial Committee, an organization fighting against abuses and for workers' rights (especially in sweatshops) during the latter colonial period. It also produced a feature, *War of Positions*, exposing Hong Kong's first attempts at democracy during the transitional period.

Intermittent and significant documentaries have been made, from **Fu Che's** *Sports Scenes in China* (1976) to **Ann Hui's** *Prodigal's Return/Gui qu lai xi* (1992). The latter follows singer, political dissident, and writer Hou De Jian, arrested following Beijing's June Fourth incident, and was shot on video. Other documentaries of note include **Stanley Kwan's** *Yang and Yin: Gender in Chinese Cinema* (1996), a study of Chinese cinema in which gay filmmaker Kwan publicly came out of the closet; Choi Kai-kwong's *Lai Man-wai: Father of Hong Kong Cinema* (2001), which covers the period from 1900 to 1953 in Chinese cultural history through a significant contributing person; and **Clara Law's** *Letters to Ali* (2004), which concerns an Afghan boy seeking Australian asylum, in a situation similar to Chinese emigrants, exploring the diasporic experience in Australia and associating the emptiness of the landscape with the lack of wholeness in characters' lives.

Actually, Hong Kong documentary is best seen on the smaller screen. **New Wave** directors such as Hui worked on 1970s series like *ICAC*, *CID*, and *Under (Below) the Lion Rock* that, although dramatized, drew from real life. Indelibly, these popular shows affected the Hong Kong mind-set and help explain the lack of documentary feature films in Hong Kong to this day (Hong Kong averages a feature a year). There is a limited market for documentaries in Hong Kong because of a memory of propaganda films, docudramas, and investigative, educational program-like documentary such as *Hong Kong Connection*, all available free on television.

More recently, however, the Hong Kong Arts Development Council (HKADC), originated in 1995, has provided funding for documentarians. Government-affiliated Radio and Television Hong Kong (RTHK) provides broadcasting for in-house productions, and the Internet and digital/DVD technology is opening avenues. Still, the majority of documentaries made in Hong Kong are shorts, not features, such as Lam Chi-hang's *Homesick* (2003), a less than half hour documentary shot on digital video about the way in which SARS has affected a neighborhood. Most documentaries remain political, in the broadest sense of the word, which remains problematic in Hong Kong.

DONG, KEYI (Wong Dek, Huang Di) (1906–1973). Cinematographer Dong Keyi, a native of Zhejiang province, joined Mingxing

(Star) Film Company at 18 as an apprentice cameraman. Because of his interest in the art of cinematography, Dong traveled to Hollywood in the 1930s to meet Chinese American director of photography **James Wong Howe**, a master of lighting and knowledgeable judge of film quality, traits also ascribable to Dong as his career flourished.

Dong's career spanned 40 years and he collaborated with many of the major Chinese directors, including **Cai Chusheng**, **Cheng Bugao**, **Zhu Shilin**, **Li Pingqian**, and **Tao Qin**. Skilled in production technique and having an immense knowledge of filmmaking, Dong was one of the foremost cinematographers of his time.

For Mingxing studio, Dong developed a range of special effects for the 18-part ***wuxia pian*** epic *Burning of the Red Lotus Monastery* (1928–1931). For *Singsong Girl Red Peony* (1930), the first sound-on-disc film, he experimented with synchronized sound, and within six months, he and the sound recordist succeeded. Dong's other Mingxing films include *Wild Torrent* (1933), *Salty Tide* (1933), and *New Year Coin* (1937).

The cameraman also shot movies for Guohua, Huamei, and **Zhonglian** studios. Following the war, he worked in Hong Kong for **Great Wall**. He filmed Tao Qin's *Aren't the Kids Lovely?/Ngai lui ging/Er nu jing* (1953) and *Loves of the Youngsters/Daai ngai lui ging/Da emu jing* (1955). For **Evan Yang's *Mambo Girl/Maan boh lui long/Manbo nulang*** (1957), produced by Dianmao, he captured the youthful exuberance of **Ge Lan's** title character, and the black-and-white checkered patterns of the opening dance sequence, created through the art direction and cinematography, set the tone for the film.

Dong died in Hong Kong but left behind two sons who became successful cinematographers.

DOYLE, CHRISTOPHER (1952–). Born in Sydney, Australia, autodidact cinematographer Christopher Doyle joined the Norwegian Merchant Marines at 17. He traveled widely, working various jobs, and settled in Taiwan, where he worked with the Lanling Theater Workshop, Taiwan's first professional (and unconventional) modern drama group, in 1978. He began shooting **documentaries** with an 8mm camera and shot the series *Travelling Images* for Taiwan TV. Taiwanese director Edward Yang chose him to shoot his first feature, *That Day on the Beach/Haitan de yitian* (1983), and Doyle has since shot more than 20 features. He has worked with Taiwanese directors **Sylvia Chang** (*Mary from Beijing [Awakening])/Mung seng shut fan/Meng xing shi fen* [1992]), Stan Lai (*Peach Blossom Land/Aau luen tiu dut yuen/An lian tao hua yuan* [1992] and *Red Lotus Society/ Feixia Ahda* [1994]), and Chen Kuo-fu (*Peony Pavilion/Ngo dik mei lai yue ngoi sau/Wo de mei li yu ai chou* [1995]). He has also worked with some of the best Hong Kong directors, including **Shu Kei** (*Soul/Liu leung gau siu/Lao niang gou sao* [1986]), **Patrick Tam** (*Burning Snow/Suet joi shiu/Xue zai shao* and *My Heart Is That Eternal Rose/Saai san woo dip mung/Sha shou hu die meng* [both 1988]), **Tony Au** (*I Am Sorry/Suet fong dik lui yan/Shui huang de nuren* [1989]), **Stanley Kwan** (*Red Rose White Rose/Hung mooi gwai baak mooi gwai/Hong mei gui bai mei gui* [1994] and *Yang and Yin: Gender in Chinese Cinema* [1996]), **Jan Lam** (*Out of the Blue/Tin hung siu suet/Tiankong xiaoshuo* [1995]), **Eric Kot** (*First Love: The Litter on the Breeze/Choh chin luen hau dik yee yan sai gaai/Chu chan lian hon de er ren shi jie* [1997]), as **Peter Chan** (the episode *Going Home* in *Three/Saam gang/san geng* [2002] and co-cinematographer on the musical *Perhaps Love/Yu guo aoi/Ruoguo ai* [2005]), and **Fruit Chan** (*Dumplings/Gaau ji/Jiao zi* [2004]).

Doyle has shot films with Mainlander directors **Chen Kaige** (*Temptress Moon/Fung yuet/Feng yue* [1996]), **Zhang Yimou** (*Hero/Ying hung/Ying xiong* [2002]), and **Yuan Zhang** (*Green Tea/Lu cha* [2003]). For *Temptress Moon*, his camera made love to both stars, **Gong Li** and **Leslie Cheung**. With *Hero*, Doyle was instrumental in devising the symbolic color schemes that represented various characters and thematic approaches. He made two films for Australian director Philip Noyce (*Rabbit-Proof Fence* and *The Quiet American*, both 2001) and for American directors Gus Van Sant (*Psycho*, 1998), Barry Levinson (*Liberty Heights*, 1999), and Jon Favreau (*Made*, 2001). Van Sant's remake was a shot-by-shot reinvention in color. His work demonstrates a great range, adaptability, talent, and intuitive visual style, emphasizing imagery over content.

Doyle is best known for his collaborations with Hong Kong arthouse director **Wong Kar-wai**, a partnership that has served as a critical breakthrough for him, developing a freestyle aesthetic. Together they have made seven films, beginning with *Days of Being Wild (The True Story of Ah Fei)/ Ah Fei ching chuen/A Fei zhengzhuan* (1990), and including *Chungking Express (Chungking Forest)/Chung Hing sam lam/Zong qing sen lin* (1994), ***Ashes of Time*** *(Evil East, Malicious West)/Dung chea sai duk/Dong xie xi du* (1994), *Fallen Angels/ Doh lok tin si/Duoluo tianshi* (1995), *In the Mood for Love/Fa yeung nin wa/Hua yang nian hua* (with Mark Pang, 2000), and *2046* (2004). For *Happy Together (A Sudden Leak of Spring Light)/Chun gwong ja sit/Chun guang zha xie* (1997), Doyle trekked to Argentina and confronted numerous problems, including placing the camera undetected in small rooms with low ceilings with mirrors. He is known for mixing artificial and natural light, using high-contrast film and deeply saturated colors, and working with handheld and Steadicam cameras.

Doyle wrote and directed *Away with Words/Saam tiu yan/San tiao ren* (1999), a personal and visual collage in the style of Andy Warhol, in which Doyle used various lenses and filters, creating the effect of looking at life through a beer bottle. Starring Japanese actor Asano Tadanobu, the film premiered at the Cannes Film Festival. Besides his calling as a director of photography, Doyle works as a still photographer, and has published several books, such as *Backlit by the Moon* (1996) and *A Cloud in Trousers* (1998), based on his on-set photography. He also creates photo collages and installations, and a retrospective of his films was shown at the University of California at Los Angeles (UCLA) in 1994, while his collages were exhibited in several galleries there. He has shot music videos for Leslie Cheung and **Leon Lai**. A documentary about Doyle was made by Australian director Rick Farquharson called *Orientations—Christopher Doyle: Stirred Not Shaken* (2000). Doyle enjoys drinking, even at work. Doyle goes by the Chinese name Du Ke-feng ("Gentleman of the Sea"), a name given him by his first Cantonese language teacher.

DUNN, PETER (Deng Xiaoyu) (1951–). Child actor Peter Dunn, a native of Guizhou province, was born in Hong Kong. His father sent him to a **Motion Pictures and General Investment (MP&GI)** audition at seven, and director **Yue Feng** cast him in *Our Beloved Son/ Ngo moon dik ji lui/Wo men de zi nu* (1959). He played a seven-year-old boy reunited with a businessman father, but when his mother gives birth to another child, the little boy feels neglected and runs away. The parents (**Kelly Lai Chen** and **Helen Li Mei**) realize they need to be better parents.

Following, Dunn appeared in other MP&GI family melodramas, including Yue's *For Better, For Worse/Yue goh tin ching/Yu guo tian qing* (1959) and **Wang Tianlin's *Father Takes a Bride*/***Siu ngai lui/Xiao er nu* (1963). In the former, he played the son of a widower (**Chang Yang**) who remarries; the new wife (Helen Li Mei) has a superstitious daughter (**Connie Chan Po-chu**), and when the father loses his job and the child becomes ill, she convinces him the mother is bringing bad luck to the household. He regrets his decision and returns, "for better or worse." In the latter movie, Dunn played the middle child of a widower (Wang Yin); his older sister (**Lucilla You Min**) is contemplating marriage but feels duty bound to raise her two little brothers, and his father takes up with a younger colleague (**Wang Lai**), leaving the children feeling abandoned by the older sister and afraid of abuse by a new stepmother. Dunn's part was pivotal, expressing anger, fear, helplessness, and finally, acceptance.

Dunn ceased acting when he entered secondary school. He graduated from American universities, the University of Georgia and Temple University. In 1976, he cofounded the local cultural *City Magazine*, which he left in 1983 to work in his father's business.

– E –

***ENTER THE DRAGON* (1973). Bruce Lee** was at the peak of his career when he made the justly famous *Enter the Dragon/ Lung chang foo dau/Loong zheng hu dou*, the movie that would establish him as the preeminent **martial artist** on film. The U.S.–Hong Kong coproduction entailed an unprecedented degree of collaboration between the Hollywood production team and the mostly Asian crew. Director Robert Clouse, working from a script by Michael Allin, in tandem with **Raymond Chow's Golden Harvest** studio and U.S. producers Fred Weintraub and Paul Heller, packed every scene with macho style and eye-popping exotica. American martial arts actors John Saxon and Jim Kelly (making his film debut), in a nod to international solidarity, were cast as Lee's pals, while Bolo Yeung and Bob Wall played heavies. Popular Golden Harvest stars **Samo Hung** and **Angela Mao** appear in cameos. The main villain was none other than longtime Hong Kong film bad guy **Shek Kin** (Shih Kien). Shek's portrayal of the psychopathic drug lord who augments his **kung fu** with a lethally clawed artificial hand is chilling. But it is Lee's performance as the revenge-driven secret agent that remains one of the most widely known, and frequently imitated, screen characterizations of all time. His action scenes, self-choreographed, display a speed and muscular tension that appear almost superhuman. He was a flexible and versatile fighter, but in this film he emphasized the power and "emotional content" of his Jeet Kune Do style, ripping through armies of opponents and delivering blows like lightening strikes. The film went on to make over US$200 million worldwide, but Bruce Lee was dead at the age of 32 before the premiere. *Enter the Dragon* remains his masterpiece.

***ETERNAL LOVE* (1955).** *Eternal Love (Everlasting Love)/Tin cheung dei gau/Tianchang dijiu* is an innovative **Zhonglian** production company melodrama, the first to come to terms with a changing Hong Kong and its individualistic-oriented growing and affluent middle class. Director **Lee Tit's** movie sets up the dialectic between new Western and traditional Chinese values, and the protagonist's nostalgia for the past in a changing world. It draws on Theodore Dreiser's *Sister Carrie* as well as **Cai Chusheng**/Zheng Junli's 1940s Shanghai classic *Spring River Flows East* in both theme and frame composition. A humiliated hotel manager (**Ng Cho-fan**) steals from work to get the money to elope to Macau with a peasant girl (**Hong Sinnui**) on staff; after encountering numerous obstacles, including a miscarriage, she abandons him to pursue a career as an opera singer. Following her success, she recognizes him in the audience, now homeless and suffering from tuberculosis.

***ETERNAL LOVE* (1966).** Director **Lee Tit's** *Eternal Love/Qicai hu bugui* marks the swansong for Cantonese opera films. A remake of Chiang Wai-kwong's Cantonese opera *Why Not Return?/Hu bugui* (1958), the story was adapted from **Sit Kok-sin's** opera of the same title. In Lee's updated version, Western instrumentation and a revised libretto with *xiaoqu* (popular tunes), courtesy of the team of **Lee Yuen-man** and **Pong Chau-wa**, the result is less genuine opera and more modern movie musical.

Connie Chan Po-chu and **Josephine Siao Fong-fong** starred as the male and female leads, respectively. Chan plays a male scholar on a winter journey who falls ill and is nursed by a retired widower and his daughter (Siao). The couple fall in love and marry, but when they return to the scholar's home and to his widowed and domineering mother (**Tam Lanqing**), the new wife falls ill and the mother-in-law forces husband and wife to live apart, using the wife's supposedly infectious illness as an excuse. When the husband is called away to the army, the mother-in-law continues to abuse her daughter-in-law, testing her many times, but eventually forcing Siao to leave, and telling her son, upon his return, that his wife is gone. A distraught son, searching for his wife, is told she is dead. At the wife's grave, the grief-stricken husband performs the famous aria *Hu Bugui* ("Why do you not return? The broken hearted cries like the cuckoo in mourning. . . .") and is on the verge of committing suicide when Siao returns. The reunited couple and now-accepting mother-in-law bring the movie to a happy ending.

Both Chan and Siao were trained in Cantonese opera. The singing performances are outstanding, and the costume picture emphasizes filial duty, demonstrating children as dutiful and obedient to their parents, winning them over through duty and devotion, not rebellion. With two female leads, the film also transferred the theme of filial piety from filial sons to dutiful daughters. The movie remains one of the best opera films of the decade. *See also* CHINESE OPERA FILMS.

***THE ETERNAL LOVE* (1960).** Director and writer **Zhu Shilin's** *The Eternal Love/Tung meng tut yeung/Tong ming yuan yang* was adapted from a classic Poxian opera (traditional in Fujian province) *After the Reunion* (also called *The Remorse of Father and Son*). The tragic story follows scholar Shi Yisheng (**Fu Che**), who performs first at the imperial exams, and returns home to deliver the good news to his mother, Madame Ye (**Gong Qiuxia**) and uncle, Zheng Sicheng (**Bao Fang**). He also announces his nuptials and discovers that his wish that his long-widowed mother be honored has come true; the emperor has presented her with a tablet for her chastity. Shi's wife (**Hsia Moon**) discovers that Madame Ye and the uncle have been secret lovers for years, that the mother was expelled from her husband's family when he died three days after the wedding, and that Shi is Zheng's son. Madame Ye commits suicide and Shi fears execution for misrepresenting his mother to the court. Father and son are reconciled before their deaths by poisoned wine, and the wife joins them. The film serves as a critique of the costs of upholding traditional feudal structure and examines family and moral values.

– F –

FANG, PEILIN (Fong Pooi-lam) (?– 1949). Fang Peilin worked as a set decorator in the Shanghai film industry in the 1930s. His directorial debut was *Girl in Disguise* (1936). He remained in Shanghai (**Orphan Island**) during the Japanese occupation, making several films, including *Moon Flanked by Three Stars* (1937) and two sequels to *Girl in Disguise*. He gained the reputation of "master of musicals," with movies like *Orioles Soar on Earth/Ying fei renjian* (1947), a postwar Mandarin musical starring Ouyang Fei'an, a singer with formal voice training. Dancing was minimal, because of the **Peking (Beijing) opera** tradition, with more emphasis on singing. This movie featured a dozen songs and leftist politics.

Fang came to Hong Kong in 1947 to make musicals, the first being ***Orioles Banished from the Flowers****/Dut ngoi lau aau/Huawei liuying* (1948). Starring **Zhou Xuan**, this Mandarin musical situation comedy tells the story of two feuding neighbors who eventually fall in love. The musical interludes steal the show.

Song of a Songstress*/Goh lui ji goh/Genu zhi ge* (1948) also starred Zhou Xuan, the epitome of the songstress as a tragic figure in 1930s and 1940s films, who gave audiences hope despite difficult times. In this story, the chanteuse starts out with everything—beauty, talent, a satisfying family life as a loving mother, and romance with a sensitive painter—only to be ruined by a heartless playboy (**Wang Hao**). In a flashback sequence, Zhou and Wang play her mother and father as well. The climactic musical number echoes heartbreak and fascination. The story eerily paralleled Zhou Xuan's own life and sad end. Fang's career was short-lived due to a plane crash in 1949 that caused his death.

***FATHER TAKES A BRIDE* (1963).** *Father Takes a Bride/Siu ngai lui/Xiao er nu*, director **Wang Tianlin's** family drama, is based on a script by **Eileen Chang**, and features a Northern immigrant family confronting change. A daughter (**Lucilla You Min**) of a widower (the veteran actor **Wang Yin**) worships her deceased mother and must deal with her own yearnings for marriage to a former schoolmate (**Kelly Lai Chen**), take care of her little brothers (the elder is **Peter Dunn**), and understand her father's prospective marriage to a sympathetic and moral colleague (**Wang Lai**). Her fear of a wicked stepmother is reinforced by a neighbor who abuses her stepdaughter. The eventual understanding between the women is what turns the tide. The popular song about mother love that appears throughout reinforces the theme for the deceased mother, the new mother, and the next generation mother-to-be.

FENG HUANG FILM COMPANY. Feng Huang, meaning "phoenix," formerly the **Longma Film Company**, was modeled on the **Fifties Film Company**. It was a leftist film studio founded by director **Zhu Shilin** and other filmmakers (some former members of the defunct Fifties Film Company) in 1953 as a cooperative company that nurtured and groomed emergent talent. Among its members were **Wen Yimin**, **Chen Jingbo**, and **Ren Yizhi**. The company received some support from the Chinese government. Its first film, directed by Zhu, was *Festival Moon* (1953). When the company reorganized in 1955, Zhu served as a director and member of its artistic committee. Productions were often codirected, with Zhu as the primary director and his students executing the direction. The company, over its 30-year history, produced 110 films.

Feng Huang was known for its comedies, among them Chen Jingbo's *Troubles of the Bachelors/Nan da dang hun* (1957) and *Love's Miracle/Qing dou chu kai* (1958), and Zhu Shilin's *Husband Hunters/Qiang xin lang* (1958). The company also produced award-winning pictures, including **Bao Fang's** *Year In, Year Out/Yi nian zhi ji* (1955), Zhu Shilin's ***Garden of Repose**/Guyuan meng* (1964), and **Allen Fong's** *Father and Son/Foo ji ching/Fuzi qing* (1981) and *Ah Ying/Ban bian ren* (1983, shared with **Sil-Metropole**). Among its commercial successes are Chen Jingbo's *The Golden Eagle/Jin ying* (1964), the first Hong Kong feature to break the local box office with

HK$1 million, and the opera film *Dream of the Red Chamber/ Hong lou meng* (1962). In 1982, the company was incorporated into Sil-Metropole.

FENG, YINGXIANG (Fung Ying-seung) (1909–1955). Actor Feng Yingxiang, a native of Guangdong province, was born in the United States but returned to Hong Kong for his education. He studied at Pui Ching Middle School and Queen's College and was working in an office when he met director **Yang Gongliang**, who recommended him to the film industry. He appeared in *Lady Lan, the Thief* (1936) and his first starring role was *The Cave of the Silken Spider Web* (1938), although throughout his career he was mostly a supporting actor.

Feng's career spanned only seven years, but he appeared in over 100 films and usually played the bad guy, but not as malicious as some others. He was typecast as the swinging playboy or ostentatious young man. Among his memorable films are *Kaleidoscope/Yan hoi maan dut tung/Ren hai wan hua tong* (1950), *Five Sisters/Ng che mooi/Wu jie mei* (1951), *Sweepstake Madness/Mai piu kwong/Ma piao kuang* (1952), **Lee Tit's** *In the Face of Demolition/Aau lau chun hiu/ Weilou chunxiao* (1953), and **Ng Wui's** *The Postponed Wedding/ Goi gei git fan/Gai qi jie hun* (1954). In **Chun Kim's** family melodrama *Five Sisters*, he played a philandering husband who pushes his pregnant wife downstairs.

Feng was a sportsman, talented in martial arts and gymnastics. In 1929, he was a member of the Hong Kong baseball team. His last film was *This Wonderful Land* (1955). He died of appendicitis.

FIFTIES FILM COMPANY (50th Year Motion Pictures, Wushiniandai). The Fifties Film Company was founded in 1949, the first film cooperative of its kind, and grew out of the Southern China Film Movement of the late 1940s–early 1950s. Director **Cai Chusheng**, who had come to Hong Kong from Shanghai, envisioned a workers' cooperative from which the company emerged. Directors, writers, actors, and technicians participated and salaries were determined democratically depending on an evaluation of workload. Members received expenses during production (not exceeding half their salaries) with the remainder going into shares. Production capital came from private funding sources, and after film distribution and repayment of loans, the remainder was put into a reserve fund for member welfare or paid out on a percentage basis.

Consequently, serious and active participation resulted from the members. Emerging following the lull of the Japanese occupation of 44 months, during a difficult time for film workers as they attempted to reestablish themselves, the company provided a livelihood as well as united film workers, providing fertile ground for the free exchange of ideas and techniques and the growth of the film industry.

Two of the company's productions were extremely successful, **Wang Weiyi's** *The Fiery Phoenix* (1951) and *Witch, Devil, Gambler/Shen, gui, ren* (1952, codirected by Gu Eryi, Bai Shen, and **Shu Shi**), encouraging the establishment of another film cooperative, **Zhonglian**. At the end of 1951, as filmmakers who had migrated from China began returning, those remaining joined **Longma Film Company**, which later reorganized, renaming the company **Feng Huang**, under the management of director **Zhu Shilin**, and it became sole producer of more mainstream comedies.

FILM WORKSHOP. Filmmaker **Tsui Hark** founded Film Workshop in Hong Kong in 1984 with his wife and partner Nansun Shi. Tsui manages his production company like a Chinese family business; Tsui and his wife are partners, with Shi managing the business side of affairs while Tsui oversees the creative aspects; an organization of apprenticeship exists, and apprentices and crew develop close relationships. Idealistic Tsui wanted to round up the best Hong Kong directors and create an environment where all of them, under his leadership, would have the opportunity and encouragement to make artistic and commercial movies. Exploiting the aesthetics of cinematic techniques and style, developing involved stories of substance and depth, and using state-of-the-art special effects were encouraged. Film Workshop at the time of its inception gained a group of exclusive contract players, including **Chow Yun-fat** (shared with **Cinema City**), **Sally Yeh**, **Tony Leung Ka-fai**, **Waise Lee**, and **Joey Wang**, among others.

Film Workshop counts among its successes Tsui's *Shanghai Blues/Seung hoi ji yau/Shanghai zhiye* (1984) and *Peking (Beijing) Opera Blues (Knife, Horse, Dawn [name of Beijing Opera character])/Do ma dan/Dao ma dan* (1986), **John Woo's** *A Better Tomorrow (True*

Colors of a Hero) Ying hung boon sik/Yingxiong bense (1986, coproduced with **Cinema City**), **Ching Siu-tung's** *A Chinese Ghost Story (Sien, the Female Ghost)/Sin nui yau wan/Qiannu you hun* (1987), *Once upon a Time in China/Huang Feihong* series (1991–1997, largely directed by Tsui), Tsui's *The Legend of Zu/Shu shan chuan* (2001), and **Herman Yau's** *Master Q 2001/Low foo ji 2001/Lao fu zi 2001* (2001).

FIVE VENOMS (Five Deadly Venoms). During the later years of noted **kung fu** director **Chang Cheh's** tenure at the **Shaw Brothers** studio, his films showcased the work of a crew of former stuntmen who came to be known as the Venoms, or Five Venoms, after their most famous movie. There were actually more than five members of this elite troupe, although Kuo Chui, Chiang Sheng, Lo Meng, Lu Feng, and Sun Chien are the best known. In the original *Five Venoms/Ng duk/Wu du* (1978), Chiang played a student, and Wei Pei was the fifth Venom. Other actors associated with the so-called Venom films were Chin Siu-hou, Yu Tai-ping, Lung Tien-sheng (or Tien-hsiang), Wang Li, and Chu Ke. These gifted **martial artists** formed a repertory company that Chang drew upon in casting the films he made between 1976 and 1982. Many of the young performers were recruited in Taiwan when Chang created his own production unit there in 1973. Kuo, Chiang, Lu, and Yu were all veterans of opera training programs. At first they were used as stunt performers and given minor acting roles in films like *Chinatown Kid/Tong yan gaai siu ji/Tang ren jie xiao zi* (1977) and the *Brave Archer/Sau diu ying hung chuen/She diao ying xiong chuan* series (1977–1982). Eventually they moved up to leading roles, and Venoms played both heroes and villains in films like *Invincible Shaolin/Naam siulam yue bak siu lam/Nan shaolin yu bei shaolin* (1978), *Crippled Avengers/Chaan kuet/Can que* (1978), *The Magnificent Ruffians/Maai meng siu ji/Mai ming xiao zi* (1979), and *Kid with the Golden Arm/Gam bei tung/Jin bei tong* (1979). Altogether, members of the Venom crew appeared in at least two dozen of Chang Cheh's films.

The most successful of the Venom veterans is Kuo Chui, now known internationally as **Philip Kwok**, fight choreographer on **John Woo's** *Hard-Boiled/Kwong sau san taam/ Lashou shentan* (1992, also one of the villains), the James Bond film *Tomorrow Never Dies*

(1997), and the French cult hit *Brotherhood of the Wolf/Le pacte des loups* (2001). Chin Siu-hou had a successful run as a leading man at the **Shaw** studio and later at **Golden Harvest**, working with **Lam Ching-ying** and **Yuen Wo-ping**. Wei Pei left the crew in the late 1970s to work with **Jackie Chan** and **Samo Hung**, and both Lo Meng and Lu Feng went on to work in **television** in Hong Kong and Taiwan. Lo has also continued to make films and can be seen in a cameo in *Protégé de la Rose Noire/Gin chap hak mooi gwai/Jian xi hei mei gui* (2004). Chiang Sheng died in 1991, and the others have apparently retired.

FONG, ALEX CHUNG-SUN (1963–). Born in Hong Kong, actor Alex Fong graduated from Yuet Wah College in Macao and was a model before his film debut in **Terence Chang's** (**John Woo's** producer and partner) underwater thriller *Escape from Coral Cove/Tit chut saan woo hoi/Tao chu shan hu hai* (1986). He appeared in several female **action** films such as *Angel/Tin sai hang dung/Tian shi hang dong* (1987) and some Category 3 movies in the early 1990s and appeared in Asia Television Limited (ATV) and Hong Kong Television Broadcasts Limited (TVB) **television** serials, but he also turned in respectable and interesting performances in several more mature roles, namely in **Johnnie To's** version of *Backdraft, Lifeline/Sap maan feng gap/Shi wan huo ji* (1997); Raymond Yip's gang film *Portland Street Blues/Goo waak chai ching yee pin ji hung hing sap saam mooi/Gu huo zai qing yi pian zhi hong xing shi san mei* (1998), as one of **Sandra Ng's** love interests; and Law Chi-leung's *Double Tap/Cheong wong/Qiang wang* (2000), opposite **Leslie Cheung**, as a determined cop. Fong has played in close to 60 films to date.

FONG, ALLEN YUK-PING (1947–). Born in Hong Kong, director Allen Fong graduated in communications from Hong Kong Baptist University; broadcasting, film, and **television** at The University of Georgia in Athens, Georgia, in the United States; and film at the University of Southern California. He returned to Hong Kong and worked in television at Radio Television Hong Kong (RTHK), where he directed drama series, including *Wild Child* and *The Song of Yuen Chau-chai* (both 1977).

Fong's film and directorial debut was *Father and Son (Father Son Love)/Foo ji ching/Fuzi qing* (1981), a semiautobiographical film that won Best Director and Film at the first **Hong Kong Film Awards**. An aging father dies of a heart attack after learning that his son, an aspiring filmmaker, has graduated from an American college. Through flashbacks, the son remembers his father and their tempestuous relationship, first in the 1950s, when the family lived as squatters, and then in the 1960s, when his father forced his two daughters to sacrifice careers for their reluctant brother's education. Fong adopts a counterpoint between social realist film and fantasy, refusing melodramatic conventions while drawing upon their themes and narratives. The film takes its title and themes from director **Ng Wui's** *Father and Son* (*Foo yue ji/Fu yu zi*, 1954), made at **Zhonglian** studios. Fong's film looks at the problems of the 1950s from the perspective of the 1980s and ensured his stature as part of Hong Kong's **New Wave**. Fong himself defines New Wave as "when a group of young people begins to take part in film production, they bring a sense of freshness to the film industry. They are different from the older generation of filmmakers" (*Hong Kong New Wave Twenty Years Later*, 132).

Ah Ying/Boon bin yan/Ban bian ren (1983) followed a director trying to realize a film project who is lecturing on film at a local college. *Just Like Weather/Mei gwok sam/Mei guo xin* (1986), which parallels the travails of a Hong Kong couple in the United States, along with a road trip to San Francisco, won Fong another Best Director Award at the seventh **Hong Kong Film Festival**. Fong shot on 16mm, documentary style, and he narrated the story. The drama *Dancing Bull (Wu Niu)/Miu Ang/Wu Niu* (1990) costarred **Cora Miao** and **Anthony Wong**, but also focused on Fong's adjustments after a divorce, and examined ideas of love and career. Throughout Fong's noncommercial filmmaking there is a strain of autobiography and an objective journalistic approach as the conscience of society, as well as the general theme of understanding the past to direct oneself in the present and toward the future.

Fong has also directed for the stage and worked occasionally in television. He appeared on-screen in **Ann Hui's** ***Summer Snow****/Nui yan sei sap/Nuren Sishi* (1995), among some others. Hui also produced Fong's documentary-style *A Little Life-Opera/Yat sang yat toi fai/Yi sheng yi tai xi* (1997), starring Winston Chao Wen-hsuan.

FONG, EDDIE LING-CHING (1954–). Born in Hong Kong, writer/director Eddie Fong collaborated with **New Wave** directors **Terry Tong** on *Coolie Killer/Saai chut sai ying poon/Shachi xiying pan* (1982), a movie that foreshadowed **John Woo's** hero movies, and **Patrick Tam** on *Nomad/Lit foh ching chun/Lie huo qing chun* (1982), a story of discontented youth that precursed **Wong Kar-wai's** disaffected youth pictures. His most famous collaboration, however, has been with his wife/second wave director **Clara Law**, on movies including *The Other ½ & the Other ½ (I Love Astronaut)/Ngoh oi taai hung yan/Wo ai tai kong ren* (1988), *Farewell China (Demon Love Painting)/Moh wah ching/Mo hua qing* (1990), *Fruit Punch/Yes Yat Chuk/Yes Yi Zu* (1991), *Autumn Moon/Qiuyue* (1992), and *Temptation of a Monk (Seduction of a Monk)/Yau jang/You seng* (1993). Fong's directorial debut was *An Amorous Woman of the Tang Dynasty/Tong chiu ho fong lui/Tang chao hao fang nu* (1984) in which Pat Ha Man-jik starred as the titular character, Yu Xuanji, a Taoist priestess who falls in love with a ***jiang hu*** swordsman and defies a patriarchal society; the film was later awarded a Category 3 rating, when the ratings system went into effect, for its explicit sexuality, and there are at least three versions of the film in existence. Fong also directed **Anita Mui** in *Kawashima Yoshiko/Chuen do fong ji/Chuan dao fang zi* (1990) as the titular character, a Manchurian princess who collaborated with the Japanese during wartime. As do Clara Law's films, Fong's explore gender issues from a feminist perspective, present strong female characters, and investigate sexual liberation and passion.

FONG, YIM-FAN (Fang Yanfen) (1929–). Actress Fong Yim-fan (real name Liang Yanfang), a native of Guangdong province, was performing **Cantonese opera** by 13. Musician Yi Jianquan gave Fong her stage name, and by the 1950s she was known as the "Queen of Cantonese Opera." Her singing and acting talents resulted in the use of the term *fanqiang*, meaning "sweet-voiced."

Fong costarred with some of the most accomplished Cantonese opera actors, including **Ma Sze-tsang**, Pak Yuk-tong, and **Sit Kok-sin**. In 1953, when the Chinese Artists' Association of Hong Kong was founded, she donated her home to the organization. Fong's film debut was in **Ng Wui's** historical drama *Flowers Fallen in a Red House (Flower Drops by the Red Chamber)/Dut laai hung lau/Hua* *la gong lou* (1950), and by decade's end she had appeared in more than 100 films, largely Cantonese operas, like **Lee Tit's** *The Tragic Story of Liang Shanbo and Zhu Yingtai/Leung Chuk Han Shut/Liang Zhu Henshi Henshi* (1958) and **Tso Kea's** *The Story of Wang Baochuan/Wong Bo Chuen/Wang Baochuan* (1959). The former, based on the story of the Butterfly Lovers, was adapted from Fong's Sun Yim Yeung Opera Troupe production. Fong played the male scholar role, Liang Shanbo, who falls in love with Zhu Yingtai (**Yam Kim-fai**), a female disguised as a male to study and sit for exams; an arranged marriage forces the lovers apart, and Liang dies of grief while Zhu ends her life. The lovers are transformed into butterflies.

Fong also acted in dramas like *A Girl Named Liang Lengyan 1* and *2/Leung Laang Yim/Liang Lengyan* (1950) and *A Buddhist Recluse for 14 Years/Feng mong faan gung sap sei nin/Huowang fangong shisi nian* (1953) and in urban comedies such as Cheung Wai-gwong's *She Says No to Marriage/Lu ga/Wu jia* (1951) and **Mok Hong-si's** comic opera *The Sweepstakes Marriage (The Sweepstakes Seller)/Ma piu lui long/Ma piao nu lang* (1959). In Mok Hong-si's *Crossroads/Sap chi gaai tau/Shi zi jie tou* (1955), she played part of a couple that both mistakenly believe the other to be well-to-do, when in actuality, they are neighbors in the same apartment. The comedy comes from them trying to keep up the pretense. Her final screen performance was Tso Kea's Cantonese opera *Sad Music at the Frontier (Moonlight and Pipa of the Borderland)/Maan lee pei ong gwaan ngoi yuet/Wan li pi ba guan wai yue* (1959).

Fong formed Zhili Film Company in 1953, producing movies in which she starred like Lee Tit's *Pretty Girl from Kuala Lumpur* (1954), Mok Hong-si's *The Rich Girl and Her Double* (1955), and **Wong Hok-sing's** *Misguided Love/Yuen wong seung si/Yuan wang xiang si* (1959).

FORD, CLARENCE (Fok Yiu-leung) (1960–). Director Clarence Ford was born in Hong Kong and graduated from Hong Kong Polytechnic, starting at age 15 as a part-time scriptwriter for Hong Kong Television Broadcasts Limited (TVB) and later directing series there such as *The Good, the Bad, and The Ugly*. One of his first feature films was *The Graduate/Sat yip sang/Shi ye sheng* (1991); in *Iceman Cometh (Deep Freeze Strange Knight)/Gap dung gei hap/Ji dong ji* *xia* (1989), Ford united **Yuen Biao** and **Yuen Wah** in a sci-fi ***wuxia*** fantasy. Although Ford has directed close to 25 films and is known for his visual style in action drama and action comedy, he gained notoriety with *Naked Killer (Bare Naked Lamb Cake)/Chik loh go yeung/Chi luo gao yang* (1992), a Category 3 female revenge sex and violence thriller starring **Chingmy Yau**, **Carrie Ng**, and **Simon Yam**.

***FOREVER YOURS* (1960).** **Ge Lan** and **Kelly Lai Chen** star in **Evan Yang's** romantic melodrama *Forever Yours/Ching sam chi hoi/Qing shen si hai*, a tender love story of two simple people attempting to defy fate. He plays a sheltered tubercular, and she works as a clerk in a Pepsi bottling plant. They meet "by chance" at the beach, and Yang uses the seascape symbolically throughout the film, which opens with Ge pondering the point where sky and sea meet as the end point of the ocean and the starting point of life. The couple find their dream house ("a little heaven") alongside the sea, they are like the ocean waves, eternal, and their love is deeper than the ocean. Through love and effort, he conquers his disease only to be killed in an auto accident; she vows to keep the house and raise their son, in whom her husband lives on, as a single mother. Yang uses parallel shots, foreshadowing, and plenty of close-ups of Ge Lan, here resembling **Gong Li**, to heighten the emotional effect.

FU, ALEXANDER SHENG (1954–1983). A native of Hong Kong, actor Fu Sheng was born into a large (he was the ninth of 11 siblings), wealthy, and socially prominent family. Despite this auspicious background, he showed little interest in schoolwork or preparing for a business career, preferring to practice martial arts. In 1971, he enrolled in the **Shaw Brothers** studio training program and was tapped by director **Chang Cheh** to star in a series of **action** films. Chang's earlier films with **Jimmy Wang Yu**, **David Chiang**, **Ti Lung**, and **Chen Kuan-tai** had all been enormously successful, and Fu Sheng was to become one of his biggest stars, and one of Hong Kong's most popular leading men of the 1970s.

When Chang Cheh set up his own production company in Taiwan in 1973, he took choreographer **Lau Kar-leung** (Liu Jialiang) and Fu Sheng with him as the nucleus of his independent unit. The first two projects by Chang's Film Company, *Heroes Two/Fong Sai-yuk yue*

Hung Hei-goon/Fang Shiyu yu Hong Xiguan (1974) and *Na Cha the Great/Na Cha/Na Zha* (1974), starred Fu Sheng, and, released under the Shaw studio umbrella, enjoyed international success. Fu learned *hung gar* style **kung fu** from **martial arts** expert Lau in preparation for his role as Fang Shiyu (Fong Sai-yuk) in *Heroes Two*. The *hung gar* system, made famous by the midcentury **Wong Fei-hung** films, traces its lineage back to the Shaolin Temple, and *Heroes Two* was based on stories of the earliest masters of this style. Fu's energetic performance as young Fang confirmed Chang Cheh's eye for the best new talent, and started a trend for Shaolin Temple movies. Fu went on to play Fang Shiyu in at least three more films for Chang.

Although Fu Sheng was a dynamic presence in straight martial roles, he really shone in parts that allowed him to demonstrate a fine sense of physical comedy. In films as diverse as *New Shaolin Boxers/Choi lee fat siu ji/Cai li fo xiao zi* (1976), *The Deadly Breaking Sword/Fung lau duen kim siu siu diy /Feng liu duan jian xiao xiao dao* (1979), and *Treasure Hunters/Lung ho siu ying hung/Long hu shao ying xiong* (1981), he played the cocky young daredevil, a precursor to the type of role later made famous by **Jackie Chan**. He was a fast and agile fighter, and the kung fu and ***wuxia*** movies he made for Chang Cheh, and later for directors **Chor Yuen** and Lau Kar-leung, remain popular. Two of the movies he made for Lau, *18 Legendary Weapons of China/ Sap baat boon saam ngai/Shi ba ban san yi* (1982) and *Eight Diagram Pole Fighter/Ng long baat gwa gwan/ Wu lang ba gua gun* (1983), are favorites with martial arts film fans everywhere.

But the years of action work had taken a toll in injuries. A severe fracture on the set of *Heroes Shed No Tears/Ying hung miu lui/Ying xiong wei lei* (1981) temporarily sidelined Fu for the first time in his career. He had married a singer named **Jenny Tseng** in 1976. They worked together in *The Chinatown Kid/Tong yan gai siu ji/Tang ren jie xiao zi* (1977), and by all accounts were devoted to each other. But in his professional life, Fu was ready for a change. His younger brother, Chang Chanpeng, had followed him into an acting career at the Shaw studio, and was taking on the kind of roles he used to play. So Fu tried his hand at a lighthearted contemporary comedy, *Hong Kong Playboys/Faa sam daai siu/Hua xin da shao* (1983). By the time the film was in international release, however, Fu Sheng had died in a car accident in Hong Kong. He was only 28 years old. The entire Hong Kong film community attended his funeral in July 1983.

FU, CHE (Fu Qi) (1929–). Actor and director Fu Che (real name Fu Guoliang) was born in Zhejiang province and graduated from St. John's College in Shanghai. His film debut was **Li Pingqian's** romantic comedy *Honeymoon* (1952) for **Great Wall**. In *Honeymoon/Mat yuet/Mi yue* (1952), Fu starred alongside actress **Shek Hwei** as a couple preparing to wed, pressed by others to make their ceremony an occasion beyond their means.

The actor starred in 58 films, 40 of them for Great Wall and 11 for **Feng Huang**. Best known for his comic portrayals, Fu starred in the comedies *Rendezvous/Gaai yan yau yeuk/Jiaren youyue* (1960, directed by Li Pingqian), *Let's Get Married/Ngo moon yiu git fan/Wo men yao jie hun* (1961, directed by **Chen Jingbo**), and Hu Xiaofeng's *A Gentleman Who Steals/Leung seung gwan ji/Liang shang jun zi* (1963) and *The Gold Diggers/Wong gam maan a/Huang jin wan Liang* (1965). *Rendezvous*, a satirical comedy, featured an array of crooks and thieves with sophisticated tastes, embraced Hong Kong, and foreshadowed **gambling** comedies to come. Fu costarred with **Hsia Moon** as professional thieves attracted to each other. Fu also costarred with actress **Chen Sisi** in the **martial arts** movies *The Jade Bow/Wan hoi yuk gung yuen/Yun hai yu gong yuan* (1966) and *Ying Ku Seung cheong wong Ying Goo/Shuang qiang huang Ying Gu* (1967). *The Jade Bow* was adapted from a popular martial arts novel by Liang Yusheng. Fu played a righteous knight who comes to the aid of the Minshan school to fight a palm power villain.

Beginning in 1957, Fu turned his attention to larger film aspects besides leading roles, cowriting **Zhu Shilin's** *Love's Miracle/Ching dau choh hoi/Qing dou chu kai* (1958) and *A Girl in Disguise/Chan ga chin gam/Zhen jia qian ji* (1959), and codirecting *Treasure Island/Ng foo cheung/Wu hu jiang* (1964) and *The Jade Bow* (1966). Fu collaborated with director Jin Sha (Gam Qui) on *My Darling Daughter/Yuk lui fong chung/Yu nu fang zong* (1969), starring actress Shek Hwei.

The actor also turned his hand to directing, with *Rebirth of a Deaf Mute/Tit shu hoi dut/Tie shu kai hua* (1973, also writer), *Sports Scenes in China* (1976), and *Life and Death/Sang sei bok dau/Sheng *si bo dou* (1977), the first a drama, the second a **documentary**, and the third a thriller.

Fu starred in **Stephen Shin's** (Xian Qiran) *Affairs* (1979) as a middle-aged absent-minded husband. He became manager-director of Great Wall. He is married to actress Shek Hwei.

FUNG, CHI-KONG (Feng Zhigang) (1911–1988). Director and writer Fung Chi-kong was born in Guangzhou, attended the Politics and Journalism College there, and took a job working at the Guangdong Radio Station in Shanghai. In 1930, Fung joined Shanghai's Dachangcheng Film Studio to write scripts; at Jinan Studio, he directed a part sound movie in Xia dialect called *Madame Chen* (1933).

Fung came to Hong Kong in 1934 to work for **Feng Huang** as a writer and director. His first film was the antiwar movie *Battle on Burnt Ground (Scorched Land)/Chiu diy kong chin/Jiaotu kangzhan* (1937), starring **Ng Cho-fan** as part of a group of patriotic citizens who resort to a "scorched earth" policy to fight the Japanese and save their country. Before wartime in Hong Kong, he made the opera films *Why Not Return?* (1940), starring **Sit Kok-sin**, and *The Red Bean Ballad (Song of the Red Bean)/Hung dau kuk/Gong dou qu* (1941).

The prolific director made 182 films between 1933 and 1968, writing more than one-third of them himself; among these are *The Impeachment of Yim Sung (Yan Song)/Sap chau yim sung/Shizou yansong* (1952), *Liang Hong Yu's Victory at Huang Tiantang (Leung Hung Yuk's Victory at Wong Tin Tong)/Leung Hung Yuk huet chin Wong Tin Dong/Liang Gong Yu xie zhan Huang Tiandang* (1961), and *The Romantic Pipa Tune (Emperor Han Lured by the Romantic Tune)/Yat kuk pei ong dung Hon wong/Yi qu pi ba dong Han huang* (1962). His modern dress movies include *Life Debt of Our Children/Yat sang ngai lui chai/Yi sheng er nu zhai* (1949) and *A Nagging Wife Meets Her Fierce Mother-in-Law/Lau man san pau nyn ga goo/Niuwen Xinbao e Jiagu* (1956). In the contemporary family tragedy *Life Debt of Our Children*, the miseries of an extended family are blamed on a rigid social system favoring men and depicting **women** as baby makers.

Fung was also responsible for the popular "Fang Shiyu" (Fong Saiyuk) series starring **Sek Yin-ji**, popular in the late 1940s and early 1950s, one of Hong Kong cinema's early **kung fu** series. He founded several film companies, but was one of the 10 prominent Hong Kong directors accounting for one-third of its film in the 1940s–1950s. One of Fung's last films before retiring was *Fan Lihua, the Woman General/Fann Lee Dut/Fan Lihua* (1968), starring **Connie Chan Po-chu**. He died in Hong Kong.

FUNG, FUNG (Feng Feng) (1916–2000). Cantonese opera and **martial arts** actor, writer, director, and producer Fung Fung (real name Feng Rusheng) was born in Guangdong province, educated in Macau, and early on became interested in acting, studying under opera actor Zihou Qi. Fung joined Hong Kong's **Lianhua** at 17 as an apprentice and moved on to Daguan. His film debut was *We Owe It to Our Children* (1936), which drew the attention of actress Tsi Lo-lan (Zi Luolan), who recommended him for the contemporary musical *Spring Flower and Autumn Moon/Chunhua qiuyue* (1937), which her company, Ganlu, produced, and in which she starred, singing eight musical numbers.

Fung became one of the most popular prewar actors, appearing in features such as *Go Back to Our Nation* (1937) and *Homeland in War* (1941). During wartime, he performed Cantonese opera, and at war's end he returned to the cinema in films like the family melodrama *Wife in the Morning, Sister-in-Law at Night/San chai miu siu/Chenqi Musao* (1947), **Tso Kea's** romantic comedy *Four Phoenixes Take Flight/Sei fung chaai fei/Si feng qi fei* (1948), and **Lee Tit's** *The Villain/Dut goon kam sau/Yi guan qin shou* (1948).

In the Sino–Japanese War–set *Wife in the Morning, Sister-in-Law at Night*, Fung played one of two brothers in love with their cousin. He unknowingly impregnates her, but is believed dead at the front, so the other brother intends to marry her; when he reappears, crippled, the couple, after overcoming obstacles, is eventually reunited.

Fung's career changed when he was accidentally injured in the face, resulting in permanent deformity, in 1949. He continued acting, as in Lau Fong's *Laughter and Tears/Gei ga foon siu gei ga/Jijia huanxiao jijia chou* (1950), in which he played a sympathetic country silk farmer betrayed by his eldest son and exploited by a syndicate, but Fung began taking on the roles of heavies or funnymen. Examples include his characters in ***The Kid****/Sai -liu cheung/Xilu xiang* (1950), and **Jackie Chan's** *The Young Master* (1980). In the realist melodrama, *The Kid*, which he also directed, Fung played Flash Knife Lee, a gangster who becomes mentor to **Bruce Lee's** Cheung, the "kid" of the title.

Fung began directing, with *The Girl and the Chivalrous Bandit (Miss Lau and the Arrogant Chiu)/Hap diy ching dut/Xia dao qing hua* (1950), but stopped to pursue stage performance across Southeast Asia. He returned to directing five years later, making 40 features. In 1961, he founded Baofeng Film Company, producing, writing, and directing a number of films, including *Little Artists/Jeung sang siu aau yan/Zi sheng xiao yi ren* (1962), *My Darling Grandchild/Gwaai suen/Guai sun* (1964), *Moonlight/Yuet gwong gwong/Yue guang guang* (1965), and *The Invincible Fang Shiyu/Miu dik san tung Fong Sai Yuk/Wu di shen tong Fang Shiyu* (1965), featuring Fung's small daughter, **Petrina Fung Bo-bo**, called the "Oriental Shirley Temple" and the most popular child star of the 1960s. In *Little Artists*, for example, she played young twins who care for a poverty-stricken Cantonese opera troupe manager; in return, he teaches them singing and acting, and they perform in celebration of a dying art. (His son, Fung Hak-on, became an actor/action director, playing villains in 1970s–mid-1980s martial arts actioners, appearing in close to 150 movies and action directing almost 40, including films for **Jackie Chan** and **John Woo**.)

Fung's last production was *The Invincible Fang Shiyu*. In the 1980s, he starred in several **television** series and made cameo screen appearances. He died in Hong Kong.

FUNG, PETRINA BO-BO (Feng Baobao). Actress Fung Bo-bo began as a child star in Cantonese films and was called the "Shirley Temple of Hong Kong" for performances in movies such as *The Little Prime Minister/Siu gam law baai seung/Xiao gan luo bai xiang* (1961) and *Little Artists/Jeung sang siu aau yan/Zi sheng xiao yi ren* (1962), both directed by her father **Fung Fung**, who was also a character actor. Her godmother was **Lin Dai** and her brother Fung Hak-on is an actor/action director (he played villains in 1970s–mid-1980s **martial arts** actioners, appearing in close to 150 movies and action directing almost 40, including films for **Jackie Chan** and **John Woo**). In her adolescence, she and others, including **Josephine Siao** and **Nancy Sit**, were referred to as the "Seven Princesses," for films such as martial arts *Temple of the Red Lotus/Kong woo kei hap/*

Jianghu qi xia (1965) and drama *Four Darling Daughters/Sei fung kau wong/Si feng qiu huang* (1969). She turned in a comic performance in the **Lunar New Year comedy** *Eighth Happiness (Eight Stars Greetings)/Bat sing bo hei/Ba xing bao xi* (1988) and earned Best Supporting Actress awards at the **Hong Kong Film Awards** for the homage parody *92 Legendary La Rose Noire (92 Black Rose vs. Black Rose)/92 Hak muigwai dui hak mooi gwai/92 Hei mei gui dui hei mei gui* (1992) and the drama *C'est la Vie, Mon Cheri (New Endless Love)/San bat liu ching/Xin bu liao qing* (1993). She played leading roles in several **television** drama series at Hong Kong Television Broadcasts Limited (TVB) and Asia Television Limited (ATV) during the 1980s–1990s.

FUNG, WONG-NUI (Fenghuang Nu) (1925–1992). Cantonese opera actress Fung Wong-nui (real name Guo Ruizhen) was born in Guangdong province and attended Jiefang Girls' Middle School in Guangzhou. She began a professional opera career at 13, studying under actress Zilan Nu, and playing basic parts and progressing to *huadan* (young women and maidens, vivacious or shrewish, with an emphasis on recitation and acting). After she partnered with **Sun Ma Sze-tsang** in *Lust Is the Worst Vice/Maan nyn yan wais au/Wan e yi wei shou* (1963), she became known for her villainesses, earning her the title "queen of second *huadans*."

Fung became principal *huadan* for the Feng Huang Troupe and then for the Dalongfeng (Great Dragon Phoenix) Troupe, where she developed a long-lasting partnership with male lead **Mak Bing-wing**. When he died in 1984, she retired from the stage.

The actress's film debut was in Wong Toi's *Monk in Love/Ching chang/Qing zheng* (1950), starring **Pak Yin**. Early successful films were the Cantonese comedy *A Bachelor's Love Affair/Gwong gwan yan yuen/Guang gun yin yuan*, in which she played a swindler and sang the popular theme song with **Leung Sing-po**, and the musical comedy *The Humiliated Rickshaw Puller (Driver)/Laai che bei yuk/Xin mazai lache bei ru*, in which she played the wise wife of Sun Ma Sze-tsang's title character, and which included nine song numbers (both 1953).

Fung appeared in more than 250 films, many of which were adaptations of famous operas such as *The Orphan Saved Her Adoptive*

Mother/Foo ngai gau miu/Ku er jiu mu (1960), *Hypocrite/Seung gin foon/Xiang jian huan* (1961), *A Ten-Year Dream (Dreams for the Past Events)/Sap nin yat gaam yeung chow mung/Shinian yijue Yangzhou meng* (1961), *Woman General Hua Mulan/Dut Muk Laan/Hua Mulan* (1961), *Romance of the Phoenix Chamber/Fung gok yan chau cing mei liu/Feng ge en chou qing wei le* (1962), and *I Want My Country and My Wife Back/Suen ngo saan hiu suen ngo chai/Hai wo shan he hai wo qi* (1963). In *A Ten-Year Dream*, the actress and Mak Bing-wing played a pair of blind lovers who are separated and have their sight restored; when they are reunited at their old rendezvous, they recognize each other through touching each other's faces; the complication is that they are now enemies. Director **Fung Fung** includes lengthy musical interludes highlighted by the couple's duets.

In the 1970s, Fung appeared on the **television** series *Police Woman* and hosted the show *Ladies and Gentlemen, Miss Fung Wong Nui*. She died in Hong Kong. *See also* CHINESE OPERA FILMS.

– G –

GAMBLING FILMS. Many Hong Kongers like to gamble, from betting on the horses and making junkets to Macau, to playing mahjong and speculating in the stock market and gold. Although the phenomenon has rarely been seriously addressed on-screen, the black-and-white Cantonese movies of the 1950s–1960s portrayed gambling as a vice and evil of society, an attitude that spilled over into **television** in series such as Hong Kong Television Broadcasts Limited's (TVB) *The Good, The Bad, and The Ugly* (1980). Gambling was even alluded to in the two-part swordplay *Sacred Fire, Heroic Wind/Sing feng hung fung/Shenghuo Xiongfeng, 1 (Shang Ji)* and *2 (Xia Ji)* (1966), a **martial arts** adventure serial in which **Josephine Siao** and **Chan Po-chu** star as heroine and hero respectively. Disciples of the Sacred Power Order, they have the power to send fiery missiles that emanate from their palms, and they are committed to using their power only for the good of the people. Eccentric villains from the Persian Sacred Fire sect set out to steal the secret of the power and dominate the martial arts world, in part one, and in part two, conflict erupts between the heroes who possess a mysterious weapon, fighters from the Sacred Fire Sect, and the 36 disciples of the Red Lotus Society. The number 36 alluded to a popular but illegal 1960s gambling game.

By the 1970s, the stigma of gambling was lifted on-screen, and gamblers were depicted as likeable and sometimes heroic; gambling became a source of humor in **Michael Hui's** *Games Gamblers Play/Gwai ma seung sing/Gui ma shuang xing* (1974), in which Hui played a con man and cheat. Tang Shuxuan's comedic *Sup Sap Bup Dup/Sap saam bat daap/Shisan buda* (1976) also depicted, in a series of vignettes, the power of mahjong on its players; the title is a double pun, referring to the sound of scrambling mahjong tiles as well as to what a hand is called when the 13 tiles do not match, and a guaranteed win, alluding to the lifestyle of Hong Kong people.

Gambling films were reinvigorated by **Wong Jing** with *God of Gamblers/Do san/Du shen* (1989), starring **Chow Yun-fat** as a likeable hero. The movie began a trend, and Chow's memorable charming and chocolate-loving gambler had style and morals. Besides its sequel, *God of Gamblers' Return (God of Gamblers 2)/Do san 2/Du shen 2* (1994), also starring Chow, numerous others followed the trend in the 1990s. Although mahjong (mostly in comedies and dramas) and betting (mostly in gangster movies) continue to be elements in numerous films, with the Asian economic crisis in 1997, gambling became related to those who gambled with others' money and livelihood, as in **Jacob Cheung's** remake *The Kid/Lau sing yue/Liu zing yu* (1999), starring **Leslie Cheung** and **Ti Lung**, in which Cheung's speculator character is devastated by the crash and changes his lifestyle for the better.

GANGLIAN FILM COMPANY. In 1956, director **Liu Fang** and Chan Kam-yuen founded Ganglian (also called Pine Tree Ganglian) with productions such as *Thinking the Wrong Way* (1956), although the company was not officially established until 1962. Its inaugural film was **Huang Tang's** *Revenge of the Twin Phoenixes/Shuang feng chou* (1962). Over five more years, the company made nine films, among them **Lee Tit's** *The Millionaire's Daughter/Qian jin zhi nu* (1963), *The Unbearable Sorrow* (1963), *A Loving Couple/Qiao yuan gu* (1964), *Something to Live For/Nie zhai qin qing* (1964), and **Tso Kea's** *Tears of Pearl/Zhen zhu lei* (1965) and ***The Story between Hong Kong and***

Macau/Yat sui goak tin aai/*Yi shui ge tian ya* (1966). The company's biggest star and spokesperson was actress Miu Kam-fung.

GAO, LUQUAN (Ko Lo-chuen, Go Liu-chuen) (1909–). Actor Gao Luquan (real name Wu Juquan), a native of Fujian province, was born in Tianjin but grew up and was educated in Hong Kong. He was a teacher and primary school principal as well as a reporter for Guangzhou newspapers before turning to acting. Encouraged by his brother, actor **Ng Cho-fan**, he started in the film industry in 1935, working in continuity. His acting debut was *Blossoming Roses* (1935). A tall man, Gao was nicknamed "Gao Luquan" which means "tall fellow Quan," and, with his height and a slight stoop, he was cast as an insincere trickster character.

Between 1935 and 1968, Gao appeared in supporting roles in hundreds of movies. Early in his career he played bad guy roles (drug addicts, sycophants, unscrupulous characters) but later switched to aged Confucian moralists and comic characters. He was known for his gestures, especially when he played misers and would greedily rub his hands when he accepted money. He appeared in **Lee Sun-fung's** *The Orphan/Yan hoi goo hung/ Renhai guhong*, 1960), **Chor Yuen's** *Young, Pregnant and Unmarried/Yuk lui tim ding/Yunu tianding* (1968), and the title role in **Chan Lit-bun's** *Master Cute* movies (*Master Cute/Liu foo ji/Lao fu zi*, *Master Cute and Da Fanshu/Liu foo ji yue daai faan sue/Lao fu zi yu da fanshu*, and *How Master Cute Thrice Saved the Idiot Ming/Liu foo ji saam gau soh chai ming/Lao fu zi san jiu sha zai ming*, all 1966). In *Young, Pregnant and Unmarried* he played a Japanese martial arts fan and the hapless father who believes his favorite daughter (**Connie Chan Po-chu**) is pregnant, rather than her elder sister.

Gao was founder of the Hong Kong Actors' Association and served as its president for 13 terms. He retired from the industry in 1972 after suffering a stroke that left him partially paralyzed.

***GARDEN OF REPOSE* (1964).** Director and writer **Zhu Shilin's** *Garden of Repose/Goo yuen mung/Guyuan meng*, adapted by the uncredited Xia Yan, then China's Deputy Minister of Culture in charge of cinema, from the Ba Jin 1947 novel of the same title, was Zhu's final film and shot in Eastmancolor. Set in Chengdu during the

Sino–Japanese War, the story is a critique of feudalism and dramatizes its costs on family and individuals. Zhu's script parallels the lives of two characters, Yang Mengchi, a drug addict from a rich family forced to sell his family home to a businessman, and the businessman's son, Yao Xiaohu, a spoiled and rude boy. Yang lives in an abandoned temple and is beaten to death in the streets; the boy falls down a well in the garden and drowns. Money without virtue corrupts, according to the drama. The boy's mother suffers on-screen and serves as narrator. Zhu uses narrow tracking shots to visualize the oppression of feudalistic attitudes and greed, contrasted with wide shots to suggest openness to change through education and the importance of the individual and nuclear family.

GAY FILMS. One of the landmarks in Hong Kong as regards gay-themed film is not even a Hong Kong film, and the screening of Ron Peck's *Nighthawks* (1980) at the fourth **Hong Kong International Film Festival** to a full house gay gathering when antihomosexual laws were still in effect. Hong Kong falls short in addressing both gays and lesbians on-screen, although cross-dressing and identity changing is a long-standing convention in Chinese culture, portrayed in opera, myth, and martial arts fantasy, both in literature and on-screen. Gays have appeared as comical figures or stereotypical confidants at best and as the butt of homophobic jokes at worst (and still do). However, a handful of films take gender identity seriously and portray it dramatically.

Lawrence Cheng Tan-shui's comedic *He and She/Che mooi ching sam/Jie mei qing shen* (1994) starred **Tony Leung Ka-fai** as a film makeup artist and costumer who is gay, but becomes husband to the unwed and pregnant **Anita Yuen**; his preference is explained as a childhood trauma involving his piano teacher and the end result is he turned gay but is really straight. The story reaffirms heterosexuality and explains away gayness, not atypical of mainstream Hong Kong film in dealing with the issue. The same year, **Peter Chan's** comedy ***He's a Woman, She's a Man***/*Gam chi yuk yip/Jin qi yu ye* indirectly challenged the stereotypes with cross-dressing and a widely known gay actor, **Leslie Cheung**, playing a homophobic character who thinks he has fallen in love with a man (also Yuen, dressed as a man). The movie's sequel, *Who's the Woman, Who's the Man?/Gam chi yuk* *yip?/Jin qi yu ye?* (1996) introduced a lesbian character and included a lesbian kiss between Yuen and **Anita Mui**. While the first film was a box office success, the second was not; both, however, forced audiences to examine gender preferences. In both films, straight actor **Eric Tsang** played gay with exaggerated mannerisms as Cheung's confidant Auntie.

The year of Hong Kong's return to the Mainland, 1997, spurred creativity among filmmakers, and can be seen in three very different gay films produced. **Shu Kei's** *A Queer Story (Gay Man, 40)/Gei lo 40/Ji lao 40* depicted the story of a 40-year-old closeted and conservative gay man (**George Lam**) and his younger, more "open" and liberal lover (**Jordan Chan**), using two straight and popular actors to portray the relationship in a nonthreatening way to unaccepting audiences. **Wong Kar-wai's** *Happy Together/Chun gwong ja sit/Chun guang zha xie* cast **Tony Leung Chi-wai** and Leslie Cheung, in a story of loss, filmed in Buenos Aires, with Wong claiming that the film was not a gay love story, but could be any couple; still, for Hong Kongers, the film was a shocker, opening with a black-and-white lovemaking scene between the two stars, one straight (who made homophobic comments to the press after filming). **Jacob Cheung's** *Intimates/Ji soh/Zi shu*, starring **Carina Lau** and Charlie Yeung, used the historical fact of "self-combed" **women** to explore companionship, female solidarity, and sexual desire in an "intimate" and lesbian love story.

There have been some significant gay films since, as the society, like the world, opens itself to alternatives. **Stanley Kwan** remains the single outspoken gay film director, who acknowledges and embraces his sexual orientation; he examines gender in Chinese cinema and discusses his homosexuality with his mother on film in the **documentary** *Yang and Yin: Gender in Chinese Cinema* (1996) and explored a gay love story in *Lan Yu/Laam Yu/Lan Yu* (2001), the latter not well-received at the box office but receiving international critical recognition. *Lan Yu*, with a budget of only US$900,000, was nominated for 10 Taiwanese **Golden Horse Awards** and won three, including best director for Kwan and actor for Liu Ye. Based on a mid-1990s anonymous Internet novel posted from the Mainland, the film tackled Chinese taboos, including gay relationships and the Tiananmen Square massacre. Director **Yonfan** has also explored gay themes in several visually striking films, including *Bugis Street/Yiu gaai wong hau/Yao jie huang hou* (1995), cowritten with **Fruit Chan**, *Bishonen/Mei siu nin ji luen/Mei shao nian zhi lian* (1998, the title means "Love of a Beautiful Boy"), and *Peony Pavilion/Yau yuen geng mung/You yuan jing meng* (2001). Even the gang genre tackled gender identity in *Portland Street Blues/Goo waak chai ching yee pin ji hung hing sap saam mooi/Gu huo zai qing yi pian zhi hong xing shi san mei* (1998), which featured **Sandra Ng** as the bisexual Sister 13 (a spin-off from her character in *Young and Dangerous 4*), a no-nonsense "butch" gang leader (Triad grrrl as opposed to Triad boy), who dresses and acts manly but responds to both women and men. Ng won Best Actress for her portrayal at the **Hong Kong Film Awards**.

Independent filmmakers continue to push the envelope regarding gay themes. Cinematographer **Chris Doyle's** indulgent and experimental *Away with Words/Saam tiu yan/San tiao ren* (1999) featured nonprofessional Kevin Sherlock as a gay, alcoholic bar owner and borrows from Warhol's underground style. And **Evans Chan's** *The Map of Sex and Love/Ching sik dei tiu/Qingse ditu* (2001) is told from the perspective of its lead and semiautobiographical gay character. Since 1989, Hong Kong has hosted the nonprofit Lesbian and Gay Film and Video Festival, becoming Asia's largest and strongest queer film and video festival.

GE, LAN (Grace Chang) (1934–). Actress Ge Lan (real name Zhang Yufang) was born in Nanjing and grew up in Shanghai. She came to Hong Kong in 1949 and was spotted by director **Bu Wancang**. She enrolled in his Taishan Acting Class and upon graduating debuted in his film *Sisters (Seven Sisters)/Chat che mooi/ Qi zimei* (1953). A versatile actress, she appeared in **Li Han-hsiang's *Blood in the Snow*** *(Red Bloom in the Snow)/Suet lee hung/Xue lihong* (1956), in which she played a rival to **Li Lihua**, but she became identified with the musical. In 1955, she signed with International Films (predecessor of **Motion Pictures and General Investment**). The Mandarin musical was in full bloom with her titular performance in ***Mambo Girl****/Maan boh lui long/Manbo nulang* (1957). The film not only established her as a star of song and dance and major box office draw, but as the face of the musical genre's golden age.

MP&GI (Cathay) Studios chose to make its first color film a musical on the profession of stewardess, then considered glamorous. **Evan Yang** directed *Air Hostess/Hung chung siu che/Kongzhong xiaojie* (1959), with Ge Lan leading a cast of air hostesses through their training and trips to exotic places like Taiwan, Singapore, and Bangkok, where they encounter eligible and handsome men while on the job. The hitch, of course, was that the hostesses were forced to quit their jobs if they married. Examining the predicament of **women** caught between careers and romance, the movie provides an example of attitudes toward women in the late 1950s. Ge Lan sings "A Taiwan Tune," which was later recorded several times in Cantonese and also used as the theme song of *92 Legendary La Rose Noire*. Several years after making the film, she retired after settling into married life, providing another example of life imitating art. She also starred in *Girl with a Thousand Guises/Chin min lui long/Qianmian nulang* (1959), playing two roles as mother and daughter, the long-lost mother, a former songstress (homage to **Zhou Xuan's** iconic figure), and the daughter, an aspiring actress and lively mambo girl. Both this film and *Mambo Girl* related to Ge's life, with scenes such as auditions behind her parents' back, her desire to perform, and her family's objections, etc.

In **Wang Tianlin's** classic Mandarin musical ***The Wild, Wild Rose**/Yau mooi gwai ji luen/Yemeigui zhi lian* (1960), Ge Lan played a good-hearted seductress, who exudes a healthy sexuality as she sashays and shimmies into the life of a naïve pianist (**Chang Yang**), but captures his heart through her selflessness and generosity. Still, as the songstress figure, she ultimately suffers. The film, a combination of Georges Bizet's *Carmen*, Giacomo Puccini's *Madame Butterfly*, Marlene Dietrich in Joseph von Sternberg's *Blue Angel* (1930, Germany), and American noir classics, includes a half dozen memorable songs and lots of cigarette smoke. Ge belts out "L'Amour est un oiseau rebelle" from *Carmen* (twice) as well as "Un bel di, vedremo" dressed as a geisha from *Madame Butterfly*, but she is extraordinary when she joyfully erupts with "Ja-Ja-Jambo" because she is in love for the first time.

Ge Lan made over 30 films and had a musical career. Having vocal training since childhood, she also played piano and studied Chinese opera. She was a popular singer, recorded on the Pathe label, and in the United States sang on the Dinah Shore TV show. Pathe rereleased her recordings in the 1990s.

GEN X. Gen-X (from Generation-X) is the term commonly applied to a group of young actors who burst on the scene in the late 1990s, all of whom have appeared in either **Benny Chan's** *Gen-X Cops/Dak ging san yan lui/Te jing xin ren lei* (1999) or *Gen-Y Cops/Dak ging san yan lui 2/Te jing xin ren lei 2* (2000). For the most part, they are singers as well as actors, considered to be attractive, and popular with younger filmgoers. The actors include Edison Chen Koon-hei, Stephen Fung Tak-lun, Sam Lee Chan-sam, Nicholas Tse Ting-fung, Daniel Wu Yin-cho, and Terence Yin Chi-wai. The actors have crossed paths in numerous films.

Edison Chen (1980–). Born in Vancouver, Chen is a popular singer and actor. Arriving a bit later than the others on the Hong Kong film scene, his film debut was in *Gen-Y Cops*, and he has appeared in 18 movies to date. In *Infernal Affairs 1* and *2/Mou gaan dou 1,2/Wu jian dao 1, 2* (2002–2003), he portrayed the younger version of **Andy Lau**.

Stephen Fung (1974–). Fung was born in Hong Kong and raised partly in the United States; his mother, Julie Sek Yin, was a 1960s **Shaw Brothers** actress. He earned a degree in graphic design from the University of Michigan and returned to Hong Kong in the mid-1990s as a guitar player in the band Dry. His film debut was in **Ann Hui's** ***Summer Snow****/Nui Yan Sei Sap/Nuren sishi* (1995); he costarred opposite Daniel Wu as a gay prostitute in **Yonfan's** gay-themed *Bishonen (Love of a Beautiful Boy)/Mei siu nin ji luen/Mei shao nian zhi lian* (1998), a sensual relationship movie and homage to the beauty of the male body. The multitalented Fung has appeared in more than 30 films and has also directed and cowritten several, including *Enter the Phoenix/Daai liu oio mei lai/Da lao ai mei li* (2004) and *House of Fury/Cheng miu ga ting/Jing wu gu ting* (2005).

Sam Lee (1975–). Lee was born in Hong Kong and, more than any of the others, fits the Generation-X slacker edginess, angst, and questioning of authority; however, he also brings a wry humor and coolness to the screen. Lacking the pretty boy good looks of some of the others, Lee was one of the amateurs cast by **Fruit Chan** for *Made in Hong Kong/Heung Gong jai jo/Xiang Gang zhi zao* (1997), and his explosive film debut earned Lee Best Newcomer at the **Hong Kong Film Awards**. In less than a decade, he has appeared in 50 movies, and whether the genre is comedy, drama, horror, or action, Lee delivers memorable performances.

Nicholas Tse (1980–). Tse was born in Hong Kong and is a popular singer as well as actor. He is the son of actor **Patrick Tse Yin**, popular in Cantonese films of the 1950s–1960s, and actress Debra Moore (Deborah Li, Dik Bo-laai), and grew up in Canada and the United States before returning to Hong Kong, where, after singing at his father's birthday party, he was offered a recording contract. The bilingual (American English and Hong Kong Cantonese) Tse made his film debut in *Young and Dangerous: The Prequel/San goo wak chai ji siu nin gik dau pin/Xin gu huo zai zhi shao nian ji dou pian* (1998) as the younger version of **Ekin Cheng's** character, Chan Ho-nam (Sam Lee played the younger version of **Jordan Chan's** character Chicken). He has appeared in almost 20 films to date, including tender portrayals in several romances, such as *Metade Fumaca/Boon chi yin/Ban zhi yan* (1998, also with Terence Yin as the villain) and *Tiramisu/Luen oi hang sing/Lian ai hang xing* (2002), as well as action and comedy. More than the others, Tse has been fodder for the tabloids because of speeding and auto accidents.

Daniel Wu (1974–). Wu was born in San Francisco, was an amateur *wushu* champion, and earned a degree in architecture before coming to Hong Kong to make movies. His film debut was as Chin Kar-lok's younger version, Big Head, in *Young and Dangerous: The Prequel* (1998), and he has appeared in 33 films to date. He has given notable dramatic performances in Yonfan's *Bishonen,* as a closeted gay cop, and *Peony Pavilion/Yau yuen geng mung/You yuan jing meng* (2001), as the attractive young man who comes between two women, and in **Cheung Yuen-ting's** *Beijing Rocks/Bakging lok yue liu/Beijing le yu lu* (2001) as a wealthy Hong Kong songwriter looking for inspiration and love in Beijing's underground music scene.

Terence Yin (1975–). Yin grew up in Los Angeles and earned a degree in philosophy from the University of California before coming to Hong Kong. His mother, Jenny Hu, was a Shaw Brothers actress and his father director Kang Wei. He has appeared in more than 20 movies, many of them **action**, and he is often, but not always, cast as a heavy; sometimes his characters are ambiguous. In *Bishonen*, he played an aspiring pop singer who tempts Daniel Wu; he cameoed in *Lavender/Fan dut cho/Xun yi cao* (2000); in *New Police Story/San ging chaat goo si/Xin jing cha gu shi* (2004), he played one of the gang of five, a videogame-loving, cop-hating gang of rich kids bent on mayhem, led by Daniel Wu.

GENDER. *See* GAY FILMS; WOMEN AND FILMS.

***GIRLS ARE FLOWERS* (1966).** *Girls Are Flowers/Gu niang shi ba yi duo hua*, directed by Wong Yiu, essentially launched the youth genre movie. It stars **Chan Po-chu** as Ng Hoi-yin, a bubbly and talented teen orphan who defends her honor. From Macau, Hoi-yin is taken in by a Hong Kong foster mother, a servant in a rich man's household. Hoi-yin falls for the rich man's son, and not only replaces the son's rich girlfriend, but surmounts class barriers. Downplaying social issues by enhancing song and dance, the movie includes musical-styled interludes that predate MTV-styled video. It also establishes a can-do attitude and independence for the lead, mirroring Hong Kong youthful aspirations.

GOLDEN BAUHINIA AWARDS. Established in 1996 by the **Hong Kong Film Critics Association (HKFCA),** the Golden Bauhinia Awards are Hong Kong's equivalent to the Golden Globe Awards in the United States. According to the HKFCA, the awards were established "to promote film culture, protect film critics' interests and foster exchange between the local and overseas film industry."

GOLDEN HARVEST FILM COMPANY. Raymond Chow, Leonard Ho, and Leung Fung founded Golden Harvest in 1970, and the company became one of the leading Hong Kong film companies. Chow had worked at Shaw Brothers for 10 years, first as a publicity manager and then as head of production, but left to pursue his own vision. Golden Harvest produced eight features its first year and also set up distribution in Hong Kong and across Asia. The studio site is on the old **Cathay** Organization lot, the former Hammer Hill Production complex, located at King Tung Street, originally the home of **Yonghua** Motion Pictures Studio, established in 1947. Many of Golden Harvest's film subsidiaries, including **Golden Way**, Bo Ho

Films, and Hui's Film, have made movies there. Films of **Bruce Lee**, **Jackie Chan**, and **Michael Hui** have been made through the company, and in 1978 Golden Harvest was the largest Chinese-language film production company worldwide.

By 1997, Golden Harvest productions had topped 300. Many have broken into the international market, including Bruce Lee's films and Jackie Chan's *Rumble in the Bronx/Hung faan kui/Hong fan qu* (1995), directed by **Stanley Tong**. Movies earning over US$1 million include *Cannonball Run* (1981) and *Teenage Mutant Ninja Turtles* (1991). At home, one of the company's most profitable films has been the Jackie Chan vehicle *First Strike/Ging chaat goo si ji gaan daan yam mou/Jing cha gu shi zhi jian chan ren wu* (1996), the fourth *Police Story* installment. Among its other hits are **Yuen Wo-ping's** *The Miracle Fighters/Kei moon dun gaap/Ji men dun jia* (1982); **Wu Ma's** *The Dead and the Deadly/Yan haak yan/Ren he ren* (1982, through subsidiary Bo Ho), starring **Samo Hung**; *Mr. Vampire/Geung shi sin sang/ Jiangshi xiansheng* (1985), which started the **vampire** trend; **Stanley Kwan's** *Rouge/Yin chi kau/Yan zhi kou* (1988, through subsidiary Golden Way); and **Tsui Hark's** *Once upon a Time in China/Wong Fei-hung/Huang Feihong* (1991), which reinvigorated the folk hero on-screen.

Beginning in the late 1970s, the studio occasionally rented its complex out to others, but in 1998 the site was selected for government housing projects. In the years that followed, the company reformed several times. That same year, the company produced **Andrew Lau's** computer-generated imagery (CGI)–enhanced *The Storm Riders/ Fung wan hung ba tin ha/Feng yun xiong ba tian xia*, which set a new Hong Kong opening weekend record. Also in 1998, Golden Harvest Group entered a joint venture with Rupert Murdoch's Village Roadshow (Australia), and in 2000 Chow reduced his shares in the company, called Golden Harvest Entertainment, to 22 percent, in the same year taking on Taiwanese technology partner Acer. As Hong Kong generally suffered in the aftermath of the Asian economic crisis, with recession, internal upheaval, and an industry slump the company suffered losses but at the end of 2000 recorded a 5.8 percent increase in box office receipts.

The 30-year-old studio began to reinvent itself, focusing on an increased presence on the Mainland and producing more than a dozen films over the year, including Jackie Chan's vehicle *The Accidental Spy/Dak mou mai shing/Te wu mi cheng* (2001), a Mainland coproduction and its most expensive (US$20 million) production to date. The company also set its sights on theaters and distribution on the Mainland, establishing three screens in Shanghai, which the company sold in 2004, and joining with importer-distributor China Film to offer cinema management training courses on the Mainland. The same year, the company accepted shareholders Li Kar-shing and EMI, and in 2005, opened its first flagship multiplex in Shenzhen as well as acquiring Warner Village, Taiwan's largest cinema circuit. Although the company is publicly listed, currently the 78-year-old Chow still comes in to the office on a regular basis.

GOLDEN HORSE AWARDS. Taiwan's Golden Horse Awards are presented in tandem with the Taipei Golden Horse Film Festival, which screens international features, documentaries, shorts, and animation, but singles out Chinese-language films (including features, documentaries, shorts, and animation) that recognize outstanding figures in Chinese-language cinema. Originating in 1963, the awards celebrated their 40th anniversary in 2003.

GOLDEN PRINCESS. Golden Princess was a sister company of Kowloon Development. It owned many cinemas, with more than one thousand seats each, prior to the multiplex invasion of Hong Kong. In the early 1980s, the company entered the film production business, financing many companies, such as **Cinema City** (Golden Princess owned 51 percent, with **Karl Maka**, **Dean Shek**, and **Raymond Wong** owning the other 49 percent), Always Good (again Golden Princess owned 51 percent, Frankie Chan and his partner Mr. Lai, 49 percent), and **Danny Lee's** Magnum. They also financed films at **Tsui Hark's Film Workshop** and Milestone Pictures. Directors of Golden Princess included Lawrence Louey, Ng Siu-chen, and Gordon Fung.

By 1972, as the Triads began running rampant in the movie business, and actors, directors, and even cinema managers were being threatened, with several key people killed, Lai decided to get out of the business as numerous cinemas were being sold off one by one. Eventually Golden Princess stopped film production altogether. Several years ago,

Ng sold his share; Gordon Fung is the only one of the original directors remaining on the board.

Most of the Golden Princess film library was sold to Rupert Murdoch's Star TV for 38 Asian countries only, while a handful, including **John Woo's** *Hard-Boiled/Kwong sau san taam/ Lashou shentan* (1992), were sold to the Hong Kong company Mei Ah.

Just as **Motion Pictures and General Investment** played an important role in Hong Kong cinema in the 1950s and early 1960s, **Shaw Brothers** in the late 1960s and early 1970s, and **Golden Harvest** in the 1970s, so Golden Princess similarly influenced the 1980s and early 1990s.

GOLDEN WAY FILMS LTD. In 1980, **martial arts** actor and director **Jackie Chan** founded Golden Way, a subsidiary of **Golden Harvest**. The company's first production was *The Young Master(Little Brother's Turn to Shine)/Shi di chu ma* (1980), in which Chan action directed, acted, and directed. The period action movie was Hong Kong's top grosser that year and earned over HK$10 million at the box office. Other successful Chan vehicles produced include *Drunken Master 2/Zui quan 2* (1994), and **Stanley Tong's** *Rumble in the Bronx (Red Indian Territory)/Hung faan kui/Hong fan qu* (1995), which penetrated the international market, and *First Strike (Police Story 4: A Simple Mission)/Ging chaat goo si ji gaan daan yam mou/Jing cha gu shi zhi jian chan ren wu* (1996), which at the time held Hong Kong's highest-grossing film record. By 1996, the company had produced more than 30 films, each earning on average HK$20 million.

Chan's company has also supported art house films, producing *Rouge (Rouge Hook* ["hook" means a Chinese knot or buckle]*)/Yan zhi* (1988) and *Centre Stage/Ruan Lingyu* (1992), both directed by **Stanley Kwan**.

GONG, LI (1965–). Actress Gong Li was born in Jinan, Shangdong province, China to an economics professor father. In 1985, she enrolled in the Central Academy of Dramatic Art in the acting department. A year before graduating, she was cast as the lead in **Zhang Yimou's** *Red Sorghum/Hung go leung/Hong gao liang* (1987). *Red Sorghum* won the prestigious Golden Bear prize at the Berlin Film

Festival. The next year she was cast in **Li Han-hsiang's** *The Empress Dowager/Sai taai hau/Xi tai hou*, a telling of the famed Cixi of the Qing dynasty. After starring alongside Zhang Yimou in **Ching Siu-tung's** *A Terracotta Warrior (*aka *Fight and Love with a Terracotta Warrior)/Chin yung/Qing yong* (1989) and making a few other films, Gong Li and Zhang made *Ju-Dou* (1990). They reunited to make *Raise the Red Lantern* (1991) together, and in the West both are most famous for their Mainland collaborations.

However, Gong has made films with Hong Kong directors and actors as well. She also starred alongside **Stephen Chiau** in *God of Gamblers 3: Back to Shanghai/Do hap 2 seunghoi taan do sing/Du xia 2 shanghai tan du sheng* (1991), in which she played twins. She starred in **Sylvia Chang's** *Mary from Beijing (*aka *Awakening)/Mung seng shut fan/Meng xing shi fen* (1992) alongside **Kenny Bee**, as well as starring in the Zhang Yimou–helmed *The Story of Qi-Jiu*, for which she won the Best Actress award at the Venice Film Festival, and the Mainland Golden Rooster Award. She reunited with Chiau to make *Flirting Scholar/Tong Pak-fu dim Chou-heung/Tang Bohu dian Qiuxiang* (1993). That same year saw the release of the internationally acclaimed *Farewell, My Concubine/Ba wong bit gei/Ba wang bie ji*, directed by Chen Kaige, with Gong Li, **Leslie Cheung**, and Zhang Fengyi. This same year, she won the Berlinale Camera Award at the Berlin Film Festival.

Gong and Zhang collaborated once again to create the epic tale *To Live* (1994), while she also starred alongside another screen goddess, **Brigitte Lin**, in *Dragon Chronicles: The Maidens of Heavenly Mountain*, which was based on a **Louis Cha** novel, as well as *The Great Conqueror's Concubine Parts One and Two/Sai choh ba wong/ Xi chu ba wang*. Gong starred in *La Peintre/Ung wan/Hua hun* (1995), and *Shanghai Triad (Rock a Rock, Rock to the Grandma Bridge)/Yiu a yiu yiu do ngoi poh kiu/Yao ya yao yao dao wai po qiao* (1995) was her last collaboration with Zhang. Though she married in 1996, she still continued to make films. That year, Li once again worked with Chen Kaige on *Temptress Moon/Fung yuet/Feng yue* (a Hong Kong–China coproduction) costarring Leslie Cheung, and was nominated for a Hong Kong film award. Gong made her only English-language film, Wayne Wang's *Chinese Box* (1997), with **Michael Hui**, **Maggie Cheung**, and Jeremy Irons. She starred in the

Chen Kaige–directed *The Emperor and the Assassin/Ging nyn chi chun wong/Jing ke ci qin wang* (1999) with Zhang Fengyi. This film holds the record for the most expensive Chinese film ever made and is an epic tale of the birth of the Chinese empire. The film was nominated for the Golden Palm at Cannes and won an award there for its production design. Gong also starred that year in *Breaking the Silence/Piu leung lut lut/Piao liang ma ma*, in which she plays the working single mother of a deaf child. Unlike the glamorous personae for which she is known, she wore no makeup in the movie. For this performance, she won another Golden Rooster and also won Best Actress at the Montreal World Film Festival. Gong starred alongside **Tony Leung Ka-fai** in *Zhou Yu's Train/Zhou yu de huoche* (2002) and she worked with director **Wong Kar-wai** in *2046* (2004).

GONG, QIUXIA (Kung Chiu-hsia) (1916–). Actress Gong Qiuxia, a native of Jiangsu province, was a member of a song and dance troupe by age 12 and at 18 had set up a film company and starred in her first film, *Parents and Children* (1936). She joined **Mingxing** in 1937, appearing in many of its Shanghai films. Gong came to Hong Kong in 1946 to join Dazhonghua and appear in its first production, **He Feiguang's** Mandarin drama *Gone Were the Swallows When the Willow Flowers Wilted/Liu dut faan baak yin ji fei/Lu hua fan bai yan zi fei* (1946).

Gong worked for **Great Wall** and **Feng Huang**, making 58 films, among them **Yue Feng's** drama *Flower Street/Dut gaai/Hua jie* (1950), **Tao Qin's** comedy *Aren't the Kids Lovely?/Ngai lui ging/Er nu jing* (1953), **Zhu Shilin's** family drama *Festival Moon/Chung chau yuet/Zhong qiu yue* (1953) and his historical dramas *The Eternal Love/Tung meng tut yeung/Tong ming yuan yang* (1960) and *Thunderstorm/Lui yue/Lei yu* (1961), and **Lee Tit's** Cantonese drama *The Lost (Lovely) Pearl/Chong hoi wai chu/Cang hai wei zhu* (1965). *Flower Street* is set during China's chaotic period from the 1920s to the 1940s, during the time the Chinese were ridding themselves of warlords, establishing a republic, and being invaded by the Japanese; the traumas of a family of entertainers mirror the instability and up and down development of China. In *The Lost Pearl*, Gong played a nurse who loses her daughter in a fire only to discover her daughter survived and was raised in a brothel by the madam's servant. The film was produced by leftist Great Wall with Cantonese director, art director, and cinematographers; it was the last of the Northern–Southern Chinese conflict genre films.

Also a popular singer, Gong made numerous recordings.

GRAND SUBSTITUTION, THE* (1965).** Director **Yan Jun's *huangmei diao *The Grand Substitution/Maan goo lau fong/Wangu liufang* began as a **Cathay** project of the director and his wife, **Li Lihua**, and was conceived for Cantonese stars; when the couple moved to **Shaw Brothers**, they brought the story with them and enlisted Mandarin actresses **Ivy Ling Bo** and Li Ting. Li Lihua played the pregnant princess whose Chiu family prince consort is murdered by an evil official who not only manipulates the emperor but kills the 300 members of the Chiu. A loyal servant (**Yan Jun**) sacrifices his newborn son by switching the infants and protecting and raising the prince and heir apparent. The superior production values, aesthetic camerawork, and expressive acting on the parts of the leads make this a superior *huangmei diao*, shot in brilliant Eastmancolor and Shawscope. Ling Bo, in another characteristic cross-dressing role, did her own singing. The film won Best Picture at the 12th **Asian Film Festival**.

GRANDVIEW (DAGUAN) FILM COMPANY, LTD. Grandview (Daguan) was founded in 1933 by Chinese Americans **Kwan Man-ching** and **Joseph Sunn** (Chiu Shu-sun), and produced one of the earliest talking pictures in Cantonese, *The Romance of the Songsters/Gehu Qingchao* (1934). Grandview established itself in Hong Kong in 1935, becoming one of the leading studios there, producing Sunn's *Yesterday's Song/Zuori zhi ge* (1935) and Kwan Man-ching's *The Bandits of Shandong/Shandong xiangma* (1936) and becoming known for its Cantonese productions, with films such as Kwan Man-ching's *Lifeline (Life)/Shengming xian* (1935). Grandview occupied the largest studio space and hired some of the most highly regarded filmmakers. In 1940, the company took over the premises of Leong Yan-fu Villa on Diamond Hill, and was preparing to relocate the studio there, but unfortunately in 1941 the Japanese occupied Hong Kong and building ceased. During wartime (1942–1947), Grandview opened a subdivision in San Francisco, making 22 films, mostly 16mm color.

Few of its early films have survived, but Grandview gave several next-generation filmmakers their start, including **Ng Cho-fan** and **Lee Tit**, when work resumed after the war, and the studio was inaugurated in 1947. Its first production with the new studio was Lau Fong's Cantonese contemporary comedy *Welcome, the God of Wealth/Jie caishen* (1948), starring **Cheung Ying**. The company produced more than 120 films, including *White Powder and Neon Lights/Jinfen nishang* (1947), Hong Kong's first 16mm color film; Sunn and Cheng Shu-kin's *A Woman's Revenge/Yunu qingchou* (1953), its first 3-D movie; Chan Pei's *Madame Butterfly* (1954), its first 35mm color film; Sunn's *New Yu Tangchun/Xin Yu Tangchun* (1954), its first Cinemascope film; and **Ng Wui's** *The End of the Year Means Money/Nian wan qian* (1950). Occasionally, the studio was leased out to **Shaw Brothers**, **Xinlian**, and others. Reorganized in 1954 by Chiu Shu-ken, the studio became Diamond Hill.

GREAT CHINA FILM COMPANY (Dazhonghua). Founded in 1946 by Jiang Boying, Dazhonghua (Great China) Film Company was Hong Kong's first production company established following the war, and one of the companies responsible for the revival of film there following 44 months of Japanese occupation. The studio was located at Pak Tai Street on space rented from the former Nanyang Film Company (headed by **Runde Shaw**, who agreed to serve as a board member for Great China). The studio produced 43 feature films, in Mandarin and Cantonese. Its inaugural production, the first film produced in Hong Kong following the war, was *Gone Are the Swallows When Willow Flowers Wilt/Liu dut faan baak yin ji fei/Lu hua fan bai yan zi fei* (1946), actor **Hong Bo's** film debut. Thirty-four Mandarin films were produced, such as **He Zhaozhang's** *An All-Consuming Love/Chang xiangsi* (1947) and **He Feiguang's** *Madame X/Mou furen* (1947), and nine Cantonese movies made, such as **Yeung Kung-leong's** *The Judge Goes to Pieces/Shensi guan* (1948).

Great China's films were highly commercial entertainments geared to popular taste, including films depicting postwar Hong Kong life, thrillers, romances, melodramas, and family dramas. Following 1949, the company's production rate slowed, the company closed, and it moved to Shanghai.

GREAT WALL FILM PRODUCTION COMPANY. In 1949, **Zhang Shankun** cofounded Great Wall Motion Picture Company with **Yuen Yang-an** as an overseas Mandarin production company. Great Wall was the only other company at the time besides **Yonghua** producing Mandarin films in Hong Kong. The premises of the studio were on the site of Sai Kwong and Yau Kiu studios. Lu Jiankang was the boss behind the company, Zhang Shankun was manager, and Shen Tianyin was studio manager. With four sound stages, Great Wall's first production was **Yue Feng's** *An Unfaithful Woman/Dang fu xin* (1949, starring **Bai Guang**). After Feng's *Blood Will Tell/Hoi tong hung/Hai tang gong* (1949) and *Flower Street/Hua jie* (1950, starring **Zhou Xuan**), **Li Pingqian's** *A Strange Woman/Yat doi yiu gei/Yi dai yao ji* (1950), and Liu Qiong's *The Insulted and the Injured/Haomen niezhai* (1950), the studio was well established.

Around 1950, Great Wall turned pronouncedly left-wing politically, and Zhang himself left the company. That year, the company reorganized as Great Wall Film Company, with Lu Jiankang in charge and Yuan Yang-an as general manager. Its first production was Li Pingqian's *The Awful Truth/Shuo huang shi jie* (1950). Over the next 30 years, Great Wall produced over 150 films. Those with critical and popular success include Yue Feng's *Modern Red Chamber Dream/Xin honglou meng* (1952), Li Pingqian's *The Peerless Beauty/Juedai jiaren* (1953), *Loves of the Youngsters/Da emu jing* (1955), Yuen Yan-an's ***The True Story of Ah Q****/A Q zhengzhuan* (1958), *The Gentleman Who Steals/Liang shang jun zi* (1963), Li Pingqian's *Three Charming Smiles/San xiao* (1964), and **Fu Che's** *The Jade Bow/Yun hai yu gong yuan* (1966). The company also produced **documentaries**, with its greatest commercial success being *The National Games*. Great Wall merged with **Sil-Metropole** in 1982.

GU, LONG (1937–1985). Gu Long is the penname for Taiwanese author Xiong Yaohua, a prolific writer of ***wuxia*** fiction and a contemporary and great friend of novelists **Louis Cha** and **Ngai Hong**. Originally born in Hong Kong, Gu moved with his family to Taiwan at the age of 13. Gu wrote a total of 69 novels, many of which have been adapted into film or **television** series. Perhaps the most famous of these is *Sentimental Swordsman, Ruthless Sword/Duo Qing Jian Ke*

Wu Qing Jian, also sometimes called *The Romantic Swordsman/Siu Lei fei do/Xiao Li fei dao/lit. Little Li's Flying Knife (Dagger)*. This was adapted as a film by **Chor Yuen** starring **Ti Lung** as Li Xunhuan and titled *The Sentimental Swordsman*. The story was also adapted into one of the most popular TV series, *The Romantic Swordsman*, with **Paul Chu Kong** in the part of Li Xunhuan and a top-hit theme song sung by **Roman Tam**. Other famous adaptations of Gu Long novels include Chor Yuen's *Clans of Intrigue* and *The Magic Blade*. Another popular story of the author is *Chor Lau Heung/Chu Liu Xiang*, which is about a sort of dynastic period Chinese James Bond, who was successfully portrayed on television by **Adam Cheng**.

Gu Long's stories are distinctive for their intricate plots with many twists and turns. Another of their distinctive characteristics is their sexist attitude toward **women**. In *Sentimental Swordsman, Ruthless Sword*, he describes women in the following way: "If a woman is smart, pretty, and can drink, even if she talks too much, a man can tolerate her, but otherwise, a woman should talk as little as possible." In real life, Gu was known as a womanizer. He was married and divorced twice; in these two marriages he had a total of three sons. In public, he was always seen with beautiful women on his arm. He was also a great drinker and a self-confessed alcoholic, much like the character Li Xunhuan. Gu died of a hemorrhage caused by excessive drinking, which led to liver failure. He was buried with 48 open bottles of Hennessy XO in his coffin.

GUANGYI FILM PRODUCTION COMPANY. Guangyi (Kong Ngee), one of the Cantonese production companies, was founded in 1955 by director **Chun Kim** and producer Chan Man, backed by Singapore's Guangyi Organization. Over its 20-year history, the company produced 80 films. Its first production was Chun's *The Pretty Tigress/Yan zhi hu* (1955). Other notable films followed, including **Lee Tit's** *The Sad Wife in a Grand House/Zhu men yuan* (1956, written by Chun), Chan Man's *Brothers/Shouzu qingshen* (1956), and Chun's *Dial 999 for Murder/999 Ming an* (1956), *The Fatherless Son/Wei fu zi* (1956), *Intimate Partners/Nan xiongnan di* (1960), and *How to Get a Wife/Zhui qi ji* (1961). Although the company ceased production in 1968, it did not officially dissolve until 1976, following a final film, *Let's Do It/Nu ren ne yang ye* (1976).

– H –

HA, PING (Xia Ping) (1937–). Cantonese actress Ha Ping (real name Lo Siu-ping), a native of Shandong province, began in the film industry in *The Fascinating Messenger (Soul Stealer)/Ang wan sai che/Gou hun shi zhe* (1956) and gained fame with *Little Women/Siu foo yan/Xiao fu ren* (1957). *Driver No. 7/Dai chat hiu shut gei/Di qi hao si ji* is one of her most memorable films. She appeared in numerous **Tso Kea** pictures, often costarring with actor **Cheung Ying** and actress **Pak Yin**. In Tso's *Salvation/Tsz miu sam/Ci mu xin* (1960), she played a servant girl for whom the scion of a family falls; later discovery proves she is the offspring of his disreputable but respected father and a servant, and that the son is infected with syphilis. The film was an adaptation of Henrik Ibsen's *Ghosts*, Hong Kong style. Disintegration of the family, gloomy atmospheric setting, and depressing mood sets the tone. In Tso's *Many Aspects of Love/Laai ha goo miu/Luo xia gu mu* (1961), Ha Ping also played a servant girl in a love triangle involving herself, the revolutionary played by Cheung Ying, and the orphan portrayed by Pak Yin. Adapted from a **Mandarin Duck and Butterfly** novel by Zhang Henshui, the women share a friendship but make the ultimate sacrifice while the male carries on.

Since the 1980s, Ha Ping has also been acting on **television** as well as in supporting roles in recent Hong Kong films.

HAN, FEI (Hon Fai) (1919–1985). Mandarin actor Han Fei (real name Han Youzhi), a native of Ningbo, graduated from secondary school in Beijing and, in 1932, moved to Shanghai. He stood in for another actor onstage on Lu Xun's *The True Story of Ah Q*, which started his stage career, and he appeared in other plays such as *Thunderstorm* and *Family*. The actor's screen debut was *Somber Night* (1940), costarring with **Zhou Xuan**. He also appeared in *Bright Days* (1948) and *Joy and Sorrow of Middle Age* (1949).

Han came to Hong Kong in 1949, making films at **Great Wall** and **Longma**, such as **Li Pingqian's** screwball comedy *The Awful Truth/Suet fong sai gaai/Shuo huang shi jie* (1950), **Zhu Shilin's** comedies *Spoiling the Wedding Day/Neung gaai gei/ Wu jiaqi* (1951) and *Mr. Chen vs. Mr. Chen* (1952), and dramas *Flower Girl/Fa goo* *leung/Hua Guniang* (1951) and *Festival Moon/Chung chao yuet/Zhong qiu yue* (1953). In *The Awful Truth*, Han played a dupe of his bankrupt company manager (**Wang Yuanlong**) and a con man (**Yan Jun**). In *Spoiling the Wedding Day*, one of Zhu's classics, Han played a trumpeter affianced to **Li Lihua**; he performs for various ceremonies, especially weddings, but the couple appears to be unable to follow through on their own wedding plans.

The actor returned to the Mainland in 1954 to work at studios in Shanghai and Beijing, appearing in films like director Zheng Junli's *The Opium War/A pin ching chang/Ya pian zhan zheng* (1959) and *Nie Er* (1959). Han played everyman characters and was called the "Master of Comedy."

HATTORI, RYOICHI (1907–1993). Musician and composer Hattori Ryoichi was born in Osaka, Japan, the son of a poor clay doll maker, and he joined a church choir at six, where he began learning Western instrumentation. He joined a band at 16, and at 19, joined the Osaka Symphony Orchestra, in which he played oboe, and he studied Western music theory privately with the orchestra conductor, Emmanuel Metter. He worked as a composer for a record company at 24, and joined Columbia for the next five years. In 1938, he began composing for Toho Studio, and those films included *Iron Wrist City* (1938), *China Night* (1940), and *My Nightingale* (1943).

In 1938, when he visited Shanghai, the composer met film composer **Yao Min**, and began a student–mentor relationship with Yao. Following the war, he composed music for a Japanese film starring **Bai Guang**, *Koi no rantan* (1951). His relationship with Yao brought him to Hong Kong, and he began composing music for **Motion Pictures and General Investment (MP&GI)** movies, including **Evan Yang's** drama *Miss Secretary/Yan bei shu yim shut/Ren mi shu yan shi* (1960); **Wang Tianlin's** classic ***The Wild, Wild Rose***/*Yau mooi gwai ji luen/Yemeigui zhi lian* (1960), co-composed with Yao Min, and starring **Ge Lan**; the Mandarin drama *A Night in Hong Kong/Heung gong ji yau/Xiang gang zhi ye* (1961); the Mandarin musical *Because of Her/Gaau ngo yue hoh bat seung sze/Jiao wo ru he bu xiang ta* (1963), codirected by Wang Tianlan and Evan Yang, and starring Ge Lan; and Wang Tianlin's family drama ***Father Takes a Bride***/*Siu ngai lui/Xiao er nu* (1963), starring **Lucilla You Min** and **Wang Yin**.

The composer also wrote music for Japanese director **Inoue Umetsugu's** first four **Shaw Brothers** lavish musicals. These included *Operation Lipstick/Mong giu wa/Wang jiaowa* (1967), *Hong Kong Nocturne/Heung Kong fa yuet yeh/Xiangjiang huayue ye* (1967), *King Drummer/Ching chun goo wong/Qing chun gu wang* (1967), and *Hong Kong Rhapsody/Fa yuet leung siu/Hua yue liang xiao* (1968). When Yao Min passed away, Hattori decided not to continue in the Hong Kong film industry.

HE, MENGHUA (Hoh Mung-wa) (1923–). Director He Menghua, born in Guangdong province, grew up in Shanghai and graduated from the Shanghai Drama Institute. In 1955, he began working in the film industry. For a time, he worked as **Yan Jun's** assistant. His directorial debut at **Shaw Brothers** was the romantic tragedy *An Appointment after Dark/Yan yeuk wong fan hau/Renyue huanghun hou* (1957), starring **Zhao Lei** and **Lucilla You Min**. Zhao played a factory worker living with his girlfriend (You) but tempted by a female cousin; he not only abandons his pregnant girlfriend but attempts her murder; however, he cannot escape justice. He made *Model's Romance/Miu dak ngai ji luen/Mo te er zhi lian* (1959) for Sixi and *The Wild Girl/Yau goo leung/Ye gu niang* (1960) for **Cathay**, but returned to Shaw, remaining there until 1980.

The director made more than 50 films in various genres, from melodrama to swordplay, to thriller and costume epic. His Mandarin melodrama *Susanna/Saan saan/Shanshan* (1967), starring **Kwan Shan** and **Lee Ching**, won best film at the 14th **Asian Film Festival** and a special prize from the Japanese minister of cultural affairs. His swordplay films include *The Jade Raksha/Yuk law chaat/Yu luo cha* (1968), *Lady of Steel/Fong kong lui hap/Huang jiang nu xia* (1970), and *The Lady Hermit/Chung kwai leung ji/Zhong kui niang zi* (1971), all starring **Cheng Pei-pei**; *The Flying Guillotine/Huet dik ji/Xie di zi* (1975); and, *The Dragon Missile/Fei lung cham/Fei long zhan* (1976). In *Lady of Steel*, the Fang family is murdered, but a baby girl survives to grow up and seek revenge. Cheng Pei-pei allies with a beggar king (**Yuen Wah**) and his clan to wreak vengeance on the killers. In *The Flying Guillotine*, set during the Qing dynasty, a corrupt emperor requires the invention of an infamous weapon, the spinning beheading device of the title; **Chen Kuan-tai** is best at using it, but realizes it is being used for evil. Fleeing to start a new life, he finds his past catches up with him and he becomes a revolutionary fighting the immoral regime.

Among He's other films is the cult movie *Mighty Peking Man/Sing sing wong/Xing xing wang* (1977), a Shaw Brothers production riff on Merian Cooper and Ernest Schoedsack's Hollywood classic *King Kong* (1933) and John Guillermin's remake (1976), starring **Danny Lee** and Evelyn Kraft, with action by **Corey Yuen**. Since 1980, He has been directing in Taiwan.

HE, YALU (Ho Ah Loke) (1901–1982). A native of Papua New Guinea, producer and manager He Yalu graduated with a degree in mechanical engineering from the University of Hong Kong and in 1926 became involved in film exhibition and distribution. His theater chains were incorporated in International Theaters Limited in 1948, under **Cathay** of Singapore, which later expanded into Loke's Theaters Limited. He became the head of the group, and was section head of film scheduling and board director of Cathay.

He had his own production company, Keris, which in 1953 joined with **Loke Wan Tho** to form Cathay Keris. Together they produced Malay films, including *Bamboo of Yearning/Buloh perindu* (1953), *The Vampire/Potianak* (1957), and *Curse of the Vampire/Sumpah pontianak* (1957). The first was Singapore and Malaysia's first color film; the second was a box office hit; and the third was their first Cinemascope feature.

He had over 30 years' experience in filmmaking production and exhibition, and after he left Cathay in 1959, he established Independent Film Company and coproduced films in Indonesia. He is credited as the writer and director of the Cantonese comedy *Every Cloud Has a Silver Lining/Yan who dak fook/Yin huo de fu* (1960).

***HER TENDER HEART* (1959).** Director **Tang Huang**, assisted by screenwriter **Qin Yifi** and a talented ensemble cast, creates a human drama characteristic of the best Mandarin melodramatic films of the era. In *Her Tender Heart/Yuk lui shut ching/Yunu siqing*, **Lucilla You Min** stars as an innocent high school girl torn between her parents. She discovers that the wealthy aunt (**Wang Lai**) who visits from Italy is really her mother, and that the single father who has raised her

(**Wang Yin**) is not her natural father. Each character earns the viewer's sympathy, including the mother who abandoned her daughter for love.

***HE'S A WOMAN, SHE'S A MAN* (1994).** Director **Peter Chan's** gender-bending *He's a Woman, She's a Man (Golden Branch, Jade Leaf)/Gam chi yuk yip/Jin qi yu ye* satisfied Hong Kong audiences and crossed over internationally. Screened at the 19th **Hong Kong International Film Festival**, the film was described by Chan as "a traditional love story with a dash of contemporary romance"; the director also stated that "the message we want to get across is that feminine men are not necessarily gay and masculine women are not necessarily lesbians." (Chan, who wears his hair long, has sometimes been mistaken as a woman from behind.)

Leslie Cheung plays homophobic music producer Sam Koo, tired of the singing star (and girlfriend) Rose (**Carina Lau**) he has promoted; both he and she fall for an ordinary person, Wing (**Anita Yuen**), a fan whom Koo remakes into an androgynous new singing star (actually female but whom both believe to be male). The comedy zeroes in on Hong Kong's fascination with celebrity, and while the music industry is focused upon, it applies to the film industry as well.

The film was a big hit in Hong Kong, a pure fairy tale, capped by a kiss between the heterosexual couple (Cheung and Yuen). Reality set in, however, with its sequel, *Who's the Woman, Who's the Man?/Gam chi yuk yip/Jin qi yu ye* (1996), inspired by Stanley Donen's *Two for the Road*, as the producer and new star try to live together, which included a lesbian kiss and sex scene, which local audiences could not accept. Chan's exploration of gender identity in both films is groundbreaking.

HO, FEI-FAN (He Feifan) (1919–1980). Cantonese opera actor and producer Ho Fei-fan (real name He Henian, also called He Kangqi) was born in Guangdong province and began in Chinese opera at an early age, studying under three masters, Li Jiaotian, Chen Xingzhang, and Shi Yanzi. He began a professional opera career at 16, performing under the stage name He Xiaonian for the Fengqiuhuang opera troupe, starting with *lache* (menial) parts and leading to *xiaosheng* (handsome young men, usually scholars or military generals) leading roles, then for the Wenyi Troupe before founding his own company, Feifanxiang. He became an opera star, playing Jia Baoyu in *The Romantic Monk*, an opera adaptation of the classic novel *Dream of the Red Chamber*, which broke box office records and sold out for 367 performances.

The actor's film debut was Wong Toi's *Monk in Love* (1950). He appeared in over 80 films, most of them adaptations of operas, including **Zhou Shilu's** *The Mad Monk by the Sea/Bik hoi kwong chang/Bi hai kuang seng* (1953), **Tong Tik-sang's** *The Impatient Bride/Goo lui chui ga yuk long/Man nu cui jia yu lang* (1954), Cheung Wai-gwong's *Two Immortals at the Pavilion of the Moon* (1958), and Chan Pei's *Poor Lady Ping* (1963). He costarred with **Hung Sin-nui** in the contemporary romantic comedy *The Impatient Bride*, playing the mechanic she loves; to repay her aunt's debts, she must marry a rich heir (**Leung Sing-po**), but Ho impersonates the bride during the wedding ritual to comic effect, disrupting the plans and winning his love. In *Two Immortals at the Pavilion of the Moon/Seung sin baai yuet ting/Shuangxian baiyue ting,* loosely based on Guan Hanqing's *Moon Worship Pavilion* and the Hunan opera *Paying Tribute to the Moon*, Ho costarred with Ng Kwan-lai. She plays the daughter of the prime minister, and he pledges his love to her; separated by war, they each believe the other to be dead. He sits for the imperial exam under a pseudonym and becomes the number one scholar. When the prime minister wants him to marry his daughter, both decline, yet are reunited when they meet at each other's grave.

In 1953, Ho founded Yuzhou Studio, which produced **Chun Kim's** *The Romantic Monk/Ching chang yue diy siu seung goon/Qingseng tou dao Xiaoxiang guan* (1956), and director-writer Ling Yun's *A Murder Case/Hak yau fei tau gei/Hei ye fei tou ji* (1961), in both of which he starred. He retired in 1966. Ho died of throat cancer in Hong Kong and is buried in Macau. *See also* CHINESE OPERA FILMS.

HO, LILY (He Lili) (1952–). Actress Lily Ho was born in Taiwan and came to Hong Kong in 1963, signing, and making all her films, with **Shaw Brothers**. She was one of the "sour beauties" or sex kittens, of 1960s Hong Kong films, making 40 films of various genres, including **melodrama**, **musical**, and **martial arts**, and over her career appearing in several films each for directors **Chun Kim**, **Tao Qin**, **Inoue Umetsugu**, and **Chang Cheh**. The height of her popularity was in the early 1970s.

Her second film, *Song of Orchid Island/Laan jui ji goh/Lan yu zhi ge* (1965), won Best Color Photography at the 12th **Asian Film Festival**, and she played an unmanageable wealthy Chinese heiress; in her third film, Chun Kim's *Till the End of Time/Hoh yat gwan joi loi/He ri jun zai lai* (1966), she played a spoiled and unsympathetic wealthy cousin. In Inoue Umetsugu's musical *Hong Kong Nocturne/Heung Kong fa yuet yeh/ Xiangjiang huayue ye* 1967), she costarred (with **Cheng Pei-pei** and **Qin Ping**) as the vain and impractical eldest daughter of a magician father who squanders his daughters' earnings; each daughter sets out to make her own way, and Ho's character gets the worst of it. Lured by a supposed Japanese movie producer who will make her a star, she finds herself an object of exploitation; to make matters worse, she is ogled by another Japanese pornographer, and when she finally finds a sincere trumpet player, he breaks it off because of the slim chances of them succeeding in a personal relationship if they both want entertainment careers. One seduction scene, risqué for its time and place, features her in a bath towel only (although tame by current standards).

In Tao Qin's melodrama with music, *My Dreamboat/Suen/Chuan* (1967), a story of mismatched lovers, Ho plays a woman promised to a soft-spoken man (Yang Fan) who loves a robust outdoors type (Chin Han); the former falls into a life of dissolution and despair that affects everyone. The youthful optimism of the first half of the story is replaced by the melodramatic tragedy of the second, and through it all, Ho's character maintains her determination. It would be in Chang Cheh's curious martial arts musical, *The Singing Detective/Daai diy goh wong/Da dao ge wang* (1969), that Ho would choose a similarly strong male, signaling a shift in movie images of preferred masculinity. She plays a wealthy playgirl fascinated by a reformed cat burglar/singer framed for some robberies; she plays films of his performances from her bed, even during a lovemaking scene with him.

Ho would also appear in martial arts movies, including Chang Cheh's *The Water Margin (Outlaws of the Marsh, Seven Blows of the Dragon)/Shui hui chuen/Shui hu zhuan* (1972) and **Chor Yuen's** *Intimate Confessions of a Chinese Courtesan (Ai Nu)/Oi No/Ai Nu*

(1972). Ho plays the protagonist of the Mandarin title (Ai Nu), and she breaks the weak female/lady knight stereotype by using sex and seduction to trap male and female tormentors. The campy and voyeuristic film, with decent martial arts action, has the distinction of being Shaw's first **gay** (lesbian) **film**, with the procuress played by Betty Pei Ti (Bei Di) in love with Ai Nu.

Lily Ho retired from film in 1972. She had opened a European-style fashion boutique in Hong Kong in 1971, called Act One, after the clapperboarding that starts the first step in film shooting. With her husband, a Hong Kong shipping magnate, she moved to Canada in 1988, where he maintained a garment business. She ran a cleaning business and in 1995 introduced network marketing and Lifestyles, a food supplement company, that has resulted in a very successful business.

HO, LOOK-YING (He Luying) (1913–2003). Cinematographer Ho Look-ying, a native of Zhejiang province, joined Shanghai's **Mingxing** studio as an apprentice at 12 and later became an assistant cameraman. He came to Hong Kong in 1937, working for Hezhong Film Company, filming *The Pioneer* (1937).

Ho was a journalist during the war; after, he returned to Hong Kong, resuming his career at Dazhonghua. He continued working at various studios, staying the longest at **Motion Pictures and General Investment (MP&GI)**. Ho's outstanding cinematography includes *Young Lovers* (1959) and **Tang Huang's** *Little Lotus/Hoh dut/He hua* (1963), both at MP&GI, which won him awards at the sixth **Asian Film Festival** and third **Golden Horse Awards**, respectively. **Li Han-hsiang's** *Rear Entrance/Hau moon/Hou men* (1960), for **Shaw Brothers**, won Best Picture at the seventh **Asian Film Festival**. The same director's *Enchanting Shadow/Sin lui yau wan/Qian nu you hun* (1960), with camerawork by Ho, screened at the Cannes Film Festival.

HO, PAK-KWONG. Affectionately known as "Uncle Ho," this ubiquitous elderly actor has appeared, since the early 1960s, in more than 230 movies in small roles, from **Chang Cheh's** *Have Sword, Will Travel/Biu biu/bao bao* (1969) and *The Heroic Ones/Sap saam taai biu/Shi san tai bao* (1970) as an action extra to a lightshop owner whose store is visited by **Chow Yun-fat** in James Foley's *The Corruptor* (1999).

HONG, BO (1921–1968). Actor Hong Bo (real name Wang Jiajie), a Beijing native, graduated from China University and became an actor in the Guangxi Arts Center drama group. His film debut was the Mandarin drama *Gone Were the Swallows When the Willow Flowers Wilted/Liu dut faan baak yin ji fei/Lu hua fan bai yan zi fei* (1946). He became famous in the role of the deceitful eunuch Li Lianying in **Zhu Shilin's *Sorrows of the Forbidden City*** (1948). In 1952 alone, Hong appeared in at least 12 films, including **Tu Guangqi's** Mandarin musical *The Moon Blanch'd Land/Yuet ngai waan waan chiu gau chow/Yue er wan wan zhao jiu zhou* and **Bu Wancang's** Mandarin comedy (written by **Evan Yang**) *Portrait of a Lady (Rich Men Hunting)/Buk lui tiu/Shu nu tu*. The latter starred Hong as the father of three daughters, two of whom have disappointed him; Shi Hui played the youngest and most promising daughter of the title, whom he successfully marries off to a banker's son. He becomes the wiser when he learns status and money are not the end-all.

Hong wrote and directed the Mandarin crime *Demon of Lust* (1952) and Mandarin comedy *Heavenly Beauty/Tin tong mei lui/Tian tang mei nu* (1954). In *Demon of Lust*, Hong starred and wrote the lyrics to the theme song. He played Shen Huanwen, who comes to Hong Kong driven from China by war, and brings a fortune with him, which he manages to squander through gold speculation. When unsuccessful at convincing a friend to invest, he murders him, invests his money, and becomes rich. He takes on a coquette, strangles his wife, and kills a sycophantic friend, only to die in a gun battle with police.

During the 1950s, Hong worked in Mandarin productions for **Shaw Brothers** and **Yonghua**, often appearing in **Li Han-hsiang** features, including the director's debut ***Blood in the Snow*** *(Red Bloom in the Snow)/Suet lee hung/Xue lihong* (1956), **Yan Jun's** *Golden Phoenix/Gam fung/Jin feng* (1956, written by Li Han-hsiang), Evan Yang's drama *Over the Rolling Hills/Gwaan saan hang/Guan shan xing* (1956), and Li Han-hsiang's drama *A Mellow Spring/Chun gwong miu haan hiu/Chun guang wuxian hao* (1957) and historical drama ***The Kingdom and the Beauty****/Kong saan mei* *yan/Jiangshan meiren* (1959). The actor also appeared in Cantonese productions such as **Yang Gongliang's martial arts** movie *Heroes of the Five Sacred Mountains/Ng ngok ying hung chuen/Wu yue ying xiong zhuan* (1961). Hong specialized in playing villains with a characteristic sneer, but in the fantasy comedy *Ji Gong, the Living Buddha/Chai gung wood bat/Ji gong huo fo* (1964) he played against type as a positive character. In *Golden Phoenix*, Hong played an exploitative landlord. Li's *Blood in Snow* was adapted from Shi You's *Big Circus/Da Maxituan*, and Hong played the local despot to whom a naïve father, persuaded by a jealous songstress (**Li Lihua**), arranges a marriage for his daughter (**Ge Lan**), despite her love for another (**Lo Wei**), but thankfully, the mother intervenes and the couple wed.

Hong was married to actress **Li Mei**. His career spiraled downward when news broke that he had a drug problem, although director Li Han-hsiang cast him in the epic *Beauty of the Beauties* (1964) and produced him in Song Congshou's *When Dawn Breaks*. Hong worked in nightclubs as a comic singer and later committed suicide.

HONG KONG FILM ARCHIVE. Established in 1993 by the Urban Council (superseded by the Leisure and Cultural Services Department in 2000) and joining the International Federation of Film Archives (FIAF) in 1996, the Hong Kong Film Archive (HKFA) secures and preserves films and film-related materials, publishes relevant books and monographs, and presents film programs and exhibitions. Its cinema, exhibition hall, and resource center is located at 50 Lei King Road, Sai Wan Ho, Hong Kong. The public-accessible organization promotes Hong Kong film culture and facilitates research on its rich cinema history. Its film library includes close to six thousand movies, from an early Thomas Edison documentary on Hong Kong (1898) and films of the 1930s and 1940s, such as **Cai Chusheng's** wartime drama *Orphan Island Paradise/Gudao tiantang* (1939), to popular movies of the 1990s. The archive publishes a quarterly newsletter (also available online) and is compiling a complete film catalogue (also online) as well as publishing a bilingual (Chinese and English) detailed descriptive filmography in numerous volumes, beginning with volume 1 (1913–1941) and currently up to volume 5 (1960–1964). The organization is headed by Angela Tong and employs film scholars Wong Ain-ling, Sam Ho, and Mable Ho. Veteran film scholar and critic **Law Kar** has until recently served as its programmer. The online site is located at www.filmarchive.gov.hk.

HONG KONG FILM AWARDS (HKFA). Established in 1981 by the Hong Kong Film Awards Association (HKFAA), the Hong Kong Film Awards are Hong Kong's equivalent to Hollywood's Oscars. The HKFAA consists of eight film industry associations and a board of directors.

HONG KONG FILM CRITICS SOCIETY. The Hong Kong Film Critics Society was established in 1994, and members include reputable film critics and scholars, both local and international, from **Li Cheuk-to** and **Law Kar** to Esther Yau and Stephen Teo. Financially supported by the Hong Kong Arts Development Council (HKADC), the organization is housed at 1/F, 30 Bowring Street, Jordan, Kowloon.

HONG KONG FILM SERVICES OFFICE. Established under the Television and Entertainment Licensing Authority in 1998 (following the Special Administration Region's chief executive's 1997 policy address), the Film Services Office (FSO) exists to ensure long-term development of the film industry; this office attempts to overcome difficulties encountered in film production. Functions range from facilitating location shooting and governing the use of pyrotechnics to maintaining a resource center on services available, administering a film guarantee fund, and assisting in film festival and exhibition organization.

HONG KONG INTERNATIONAL FILM FESTIVAL (HKIFF). Established in 1977 through Hong Kong's Urban Council, the yearly Hong Kong International Film Festival was founded by Paul Yeung, who was manager of city hall when he sat as a member on the festival's organizing committee. The festival is recognized for the breadth and scope of its programming, and has evolved over its more than quarter century of existence. The first festival offered 27 exhibition programs, with no competition or awards, but aimed to put Hong Kong on the map as a film center. Roger Garcia organized the third festival, which established an Asian Cinema section. Scholars and researchers Lin Nien-tong and Lau Shing-hon, film critics **Li Cheuk-to**, Freddy Wong, and Jerry Liu, and others served as programmers in its early decades. Beginning with the 15th festival (1991), **Law Kar** (Hong Kong retrospectives), Li Cheuk-to (international), and Wong Ain-ling, followed by Jacob Wong (Asian and Hong Kong) served as the programming team; since 2000, Li has served as general manager. The retrospectives of Hong Kong cinema screened at the festival (and written about in its publications) have helped fill the hole in information and available resources on Chinese cinema.

Through its 20th year, the festival published themed retrospectives; since the 21st festival, the retrospectives have been superseded by the panorama, and additional publications have appeared under the auspices of the **Hong Kong Film Archive**. In the mid-1990s, the festival began including **independent film** and video on its slate, and in 1999 added "The Age of Independents: New Asian Film and Video," including the screening of more independent film and digital production. That same year, the festival established the International Film Critics Federation Award (FIPRESCI) for young Asian cinema, another way of recognizing a newer generation of filmmakers. The Hong Kong Arts Development Council (HKADC) took over as festival organizer in 2002, and in 2004, the independent and nonprofit Hong Kong International Film Festival Society took the helm, with Peter Tsi as the executive director and Li as artistic director. At the 28th festival (2004), more than 300 films from 40 countries and regions were screened over the 16-day event.

HONG, SHUYUN (Hung Suk-wan) (1913–). Director and writer Hong Shuyun, a native of Jiangsu province, graduated from the Shanghai Academy of Arts and joined **Lianhua**, working in its arts and publicity departments. When war broke out, he traveled to Hong Kong with his brother Hong Zhonghao (grandfather of **Samo Hung**); together they directed *How Luo Bu Rescued His Mother* (1939). The same year he directed the **martial arts** movie *Shattering the Copper Net Array (Breaking through the Bronze Net)/Daai poh tung mong chan/Da po tong wang zhen* (1939) and with his brother, director Hung Chai (Hung Chung-ho), set up Zhongnan, producing films such as *The Story of Meng Lijun* (1938) and *Marry-*

ing Young Is a Woman's Merit (1938). (Another brother of Hong was playwright Hung Sum.)

In 1939 Hong began directing at Nanyang (the former **Tianyi**, which became **Shaw Brothers**). Popular films included the Cantonese romances *When Will My Love Return?/Hoh yat gwan joi loi/He ri jun zai lai* (1940) and *A Smile of a Thousand Dollars (Smile of a Woman)/Chin gan yat siu/Qian jin yi xiao* (1940). When Hong Kong fell to the Japanese, Hong formed the China Drama Group, which performed in Guangzhou.

After the war, Hong resumed directing, with a total of 18 films, including the Cantonese comedy *Stage Fan Husband/Fai mai goo yau/Xi mi gu ye* (1948) and the Cantonese contemporary melodramas *Wild Flowers Are Sweeter/Yau dut heung/Ye hua xiang* (1950) and *A Girl Named Liang Lengyan 1* and *2/Leung Laang Yim/Liang Lengyan* (1950). *Stage Fan Husband* starred **Ma Sze-tsang** and **Pak Yin** as opera performers in love who are both promised to others in marriages their families are arranging; it was Pak Yin's first opportunity to display her opera talent on-screen in a *huadan* role. In the two-part *A Girl Named Liang Lengyan*, **Fong Yim-fan** (Fong Yim-fung) starred in her third feature and first contemporary role; she survives the death of her grandfather, attempted rape, domestic employment, scheming between a concubine and the attempted rapist, drugging and rape, an unwed pregnancy, and banishment before she is reunited with her lover.

Hong also directed Mandarin films, including the romance tragedy *Don't Tell My Husband/Bit yeung cheung foo chi diy/Bie rang zhang fu zhi dao* (1952), produced by Dianyi and starring Ouyang Shafei and Bai Yun. "Don't tell your husband" is a line delivered to Ouyang in *Don't Tell My Husband*; she stars as a famous singer who marries a painter with whom she leads a happy life until her husband's sister brings home Bai's childhood sweetheart, who will not let her go. His last film was the Mandarin historical drama *The Story of Yang E/Yeung Ngo/Yang E* (1955, codirected with **Evan Yang**). He settled in Canada.

HONG, SIN-NUI (Hong Xiannu) (1924–). Actress Hong Sin-nui (real name Kang Jiankang), a native of Guangdong province, grew up in Macau. She learned opera from her aunt, Ho Fun-lin. Discovered by **Ma Sze-tsang** when she was only 15, she costarred with Ma in numerous stage operas and opera films, the latter including *I'm Crazy about You/Ngo wai hing kwong/Wo wei qing kuang* (1947), *A Spoilt Brat (An Unruly Princess)/Diu goo gung chu/Diao man gong zhu* (1948), and *The Judge Goes to Pieces/Sam sei goon/Shensi guan* (1948). She made her first film, *Unforgettable Love/Ang due shut lin/Ouduan silian* (1947), in Hong Kong, costarring as the blind wife of an opera star (Ma Tze-tsang) who regains and again loses her sight because of traumatic events, including her abduction, rape, and destined separation from her husband and child. (The story was adapted from an opera made famous by the celebrated opera actors Ma and **Tan Lanqing**.)

Hong made approximately 100 films, including **Chun Kim's** Cantonese drama *A Mother's Tears/Tsz miu lui/Ci mu lei* (1953), family drama *Neighbors All (Mutual Tears)/Ga ga woo woo/Jia jia hu hu* (1954), and historical drama *The Rouge Tigress/Yin chi foo/Yan zhi hu* (1955). In the first, Hong plays daughter-in-law to mother-in-law **Wang Man-lei**, and the women are at odds with husband/son **Cheung Ying** in the middle. A series of incidents bring the women together and lead to their mutual understanding, despite differences. In the last, Hong played the title lead character, a young woman who learns of her mother's rape and abandonment by the local elder, which leads to her death. She plots her revenge, seducing both father and son and turning them against each other before escaping with her lover, **Patrick Tse Yin**. The film was **Guangyi's** inaugural production.

Ma Tze-tsang was Hong's husband, and they returned to Guangzhou in 1955, where they ran the Guangdong Opera School and Troupe and performed in numerous operas. During the Cultural Revolution, Hong left the stage, only to return in 1980, in one of her most famous operas, *Princess Zhao Jun*. In 2005, she was awarded an honorary doctorate by Hong Kong Baptist University.

HOWE, JAMES WONG (Wong Tsung-jim, Huang Zhongzhan) (1899–1976). Cinematographer James Wong Howe was born in Guangzhou and came to the United States with immigrant parents at five. He worked as a professional boxer before he joined Cecil B. DeMille as an editing assistant and slate boy; he became an assistant cameraman and then a director of photography in 1922. He went on to work on 162 films, as cinematographer on 125 of them, and his work spans movies from Hollywood's silent era to full-color sound pictures. He won two Oscars, for his camerawork on *The Rose Tattoo* (1955) and *Hud* (1963). He was famous for his artful, low-key, deep focus lighting, innovative but unobtrusive camerawork, and use of the handheld camera, many new practices of his day that have become standard. His cousin was actress **Anna May Wong**.

HSIA, MOON (Xia Ming) (1933–). Actress Hsia Moon (real name Yang Meng), a native of Suzhou, was born in Shanghai and came to Hong Kong in 1947, studying at Maryknoll Convent School where she developed an interest in theater. Her film debut was as lead in **Li Pingqian's** Mandarin comedy *A Nighttime Wife/Gam fan gei/Jin hun ji* (1951).

Hsia made close to 40 films for **Great Wall**, **Feng Huang**, and **Longma** between 1951 and 1967, among them the Mandarin historical dramas *A Torn Lily/Chuet doi gaai yan/Niehai hua* (1953), *Peerless Beauty* (1953, directed by Li Pingqian), *The Wedding Night/San fan dai yat yau/Xinhu diyiye* (1956), *A Widow's Tears/San gwa/Xin gua* (1956), ***The Eternal Love****/Tung meng tut yeung/Tong ming yuan yang* (1960, directed and written by **Zhu Shilin**), and *Garden of Repose/Goo yuen mung/Gu yuan meng* (1964, directed and written by Zhu Shilin), and the Mandarin comedy *Oh! The Spring's Here/Ying chut dut/Ying chun hua* (1968). She played a variety of roles, from loyal wives to imperial concubines. In *Peerless Beauty*, Hsia starred in the title role as a peasant girl who meets a nobleman willing to sacrifice her for a cause; she enters the Wei palace as an imperial concubine to bend the ear of the king to send troops to Zhao to break the siege of the Qin army. For her efforts, she is executed. In *The Eternal Love*, adapted from the traditional opera *After the Reunion*, from Fujian province, Hsia played the new wife who discovers her mother-in-law's secret, unintentionally causing her death; she accepts responsibility by drinking poisoned wine and joining her husband in death. *Garden of Repose*, adapted from Ba Jin's novel of the same title, set during the Sino–Japanese War, concerns decadent and decaying families, and was Zhu Shilin's last film, shot in Eastmancolor.

The actress retired in 1968, went to Canada for two years, returned to Hong Kong, and opened a garment factory. She officially retired in

1978, but formed **Blue Bird Film Company**, producing films of two significant **New Wave** directors, **Ann Hui's** *Boat People/Tau ban liu hoi/Touben nuhai* (1982) and **Yim Ho's** *Homecoming/Chi shui lau nin/Si shui liu nian* 1984).

HSU, FENG (Xu Feng, Hsu Fong) (1950–). The Taiwanese actress Hsu Feng is best known as the star of many of director **King Hu's** classic ***wuxia*** films. Hsu was a 16-year-old newcomer to the Lianbang (Union) studio when Hu cast her with fellow Taiwan native **Polly Shangkuan Ling-fong** in *Dragon Gate Inn/Lung moon haak chan/Longmen kezhan* (1967) and then as the lead in his enormously successful swordplay epic *A Touch of Zen/Hap lui/Xia nu* (1971). When King Hu left Liangbang to form his own production company, Hsu joined him to star in some of the most beautiful and compelling *wuxia pian* ever made. Films like *The Fate of Lee Khan/Ying chun gok ji fung boh/Ying chun ge zhi feng bo* (1973), *The Valiant Ones/Chung lit tiu/Zhong lie tu* (1975), and *Legend of the Mountain/Saan chung chuen kei/Shanzhong chuanqi* (1979) not only broke box office records in Asia, but also attracted considerable attention in the West. Hsu Feng had no formal training in **martial arts**, but she was a gifted actress, and she projected a fierce intensity that made her an ideal martial heroine.

After a brief retirement in the 1980s, Hsu Feng returned to the world of film as a producer. Her notable work in this field includes the **Brigitte Lin**–vehicle **Yim Ho**–directed *Red Dust/Gun gun hong chen* (1990) and the international sensation *Farewell My Concubine/Ba wang bie ji* (1993). She was twice the recipient of the Best Actress prize from Taiwan's **Golden Horse Film Awards**, for her roles in *Assassin/Lui chi haak/Ci ke* (1976) and *The Pioneer/Yuen/Yuan* (1980).

HU, KING CHIN-CHUAN (Hu Jinquan) (1931–1997). King Hu was one of the first Chinese directors to gain international recognition for his filmmaking. His 1971 film *A Touch of Zen*, which won a special technical award at the Cannes Film Festival (1975), was the first Chinese film to win an award there. Hu was born in Beijing; his paternal grandfather was an imperial officer of the Qing dynasty, his father studied in Japan, and his mother was a traditional Chinese painter.

His primary and secondary education was at an American Protestant school, and he studied at the prestigious National Art Institute in Beijing, educated in the classics, Chinese studies, and painting. He had a strong interest in **Peking (Beijing) opera** and loved drawing cartoons. He came to Hong Kong penniless in 1949, worked as a proofreader, and painted postcards and billboards. He joined **Great Wall**, working in the art department, and then switched to **Yonghua**, working as an art director and actor, but learning all the departments. When Yonghua closed, he worked for Voice of America.

Upon **Li Han-hsiang's** recommendation, Hu joined **Shaw Brothers** in 1958, working as an actor, writer, and ultimately, director. He codirected the ***huangmei diao The Love Eterne*** *(Eternal Love)/Leung saan pak yue chuk ying toi/Liang shan bo yu zhu ying tai* (1963) and the costume drama *The Story of Sue San/Yuk tong chun/Yu tang chun* (1964) with Li. His war drama *Sons of the Good Earth/Daai dei ngai lui/Da di er nu* (1964) was censored for its anti-Japanese theme and failed at the box office, but it was with his **martial arts** debut, *Come Drink with Me/Daai chui hap/Da zui xia* (1966), starring **Cheng Pei-pei**, that he broke through and also established a new ***wuxia pian*** (martial chivalry) style. He reestablished the female warrior on-screen, paced his movies like spaghetti Westerns, and created classic mise-en-scène and masterful, rhythmical editing. In *Come Drink with Me*, Cheng Pei-pei plays Golden Swallow, the governor's daughter out to rescue her kidnapped brother. Joining forces with the Drunken Knight (**Yueh Hua**), they defeat the villainous Jade-Faced Tiger and his cohorts. Hu's rhythms came from **Chinese opera**, and he inventively told the story, moved the characters, choreographed the action as dance, and built and released tension through camera shots and editing.

In 1965, Hu moved to Taiwan and joined Union (Lianbang) Film Company; the first film he made there was *Dragon Gate Inn (Breakthrough,* aka *Dragon Inn)/Lung moon haak chan/Longmen Kezhan* (1967), which was a commercial hit, breaking all box office records, thereby sealing his reputation as a powerful martial arts director and as an artist of nuance and atmosphere. *Dragon Gate Inn* likewise uses the inn setting and choreographs the action to the rhythms of opera, and in that film a band of Ming loyalists protect the children of an honest minister from a corrupt eunuch and his forces. Producer **Tsui**

Hark would remake the film as *Dragon Inn* (1992, directed by Raymond Lee). Hu made *A Touch of Zen (The Gallant Lady)/Hap lui/Xia nu* (begun 1968, released 1971) in two parts; the film took three years to complete. The "gallant" or "knight lady" of the title (**Hsu Feng**), hiding out in an abandoned fortress, prepares to fight against the corrupt eunuch forces that have attacked her minister-father. A sensitive scholar (Shi Jun) assists with the strategy. Adapted from **Pu Songling's** *Strange Stories from Liu Jai*, this film won a special award for superior technique at the Cannes Film Festival in 1976. The film features a poetical bamboo forest fight that influenced **Ang Lee's** *Crouching Tiger, Hidden Dragon* (2000). Hu's films lovingly create atmosphere, combined with character development, careful plot construction, and original editing style.

Hu started his own company, King Hu Film Production Company, in 1970, and produced *The Fate of Lee Khan/Ying chun gok ji fung boh/Ying chun ge zhi feng bo* (1973), *The Valiant Ones/Chung lit tiu/Zhong lie tu* (1975), *Raining in the Mountain/Hung saan leng yue/Kongshan lingyu* (1979), and *Legend of the Mountain/Saan chung chuen kei/ Shanzhong chuanqi* (1979). His subsequent martial arts films of the 1970s are highly regarded, although none of his films in the 1980s was successful. In 1989, producer-director Tsui Hark invited Hu to direct *Swordsman (Smiling Proud Warrior)/Siu ngo gong wu/Xiaoao jianghu* (1990), starring **Sam Hui**; although Hu departed early on due to disagreements with Tsui, he remains credited as director. Hu's last film, *Painted Skin (Painted Skin: The Yin Yang Method King)/Wa pei ji yam yeung faat wong/Hua pi zhi yinyang fawang* (1993), starred **Samo Hung** and **Joey Wang**. Hu moved to Los Angeles, hoping to find financial backing for *The Battle of Ono*, a drama about the hardships and contributions of overseas Chinese building the transcontinental railroad. Director **John Woo** and producer partner **Terence Chang** secured the funds for the film; meantime Hu returned to Taiwan to undergo treatment for heart disease. Sadly, he died in Taipei as he was preparing for heart surgery.

Hu was named one of the world's top five directors in 1978 by the British International Film Guide. His art is one of concealment and explosiveness. His martial artists perform supernatural feats courtesy of small trampolines (concealed by trees and branches) and little wirework, leaping and slashing in and out of frame. Hu combined the acrobatic stagecraft and sounds of Peking (Beijing) opera, shooting action like a ballet with percussion. He rapidly cut action scenes, and boasted he was the first Hong Kong director to use only eight frames per second. His artistic sensibility on-screen was reflected offscreen as well. He was a scholar of Chinese literature and an authority on contemporary author Lao She.

HU, XIAOFENG (Woo Siu-fung) (1926–). Director Hu Xiaofeng was born in Shanghai and at 16 joined the Tianfeng Drama Society, where he first worked in a stage production of ***Sorrows of the Forbidden City***, responsible for its stage effects. He later served the same function for Fei Mu's Shanghai Art Drama Society. In 1950, Hu debuted as an actor in the Lianyi Drama Society, appearing in numerous plays.

Meanwhile, in 1946 **Great China** invited Hu to come to Hong Kong as an actor; there, he moved to **Yonghua**, appearing in films such as *Life and Death* and *The Angry Tide*. At **Longma**, he assisted director **Zhu Shilin** on *The Flower Girl/Fa goo leung/Hua guniang* and *Spoiling the Wedding Day (The Little Trumpeter and A Cui)/Neung gaai gei/Wu jiaqi* (both 1951), and he took Zhu as his mentor.

Hu joined **Great Wall** in 1952, acting in *Blossoms in the Heart/Baak dut chaai fong/Bai hua qi fang* (1952) and *The Gold-Plated Man/Huahua shijie* (1953). He codirected and cowrote *Loves of the Youngsters/Daai ngai lui ging/Da emu jing* (1955) and *Sunrise/Yat chut/Richu* (1956) with Su Chengshou (So Shing-sau); thereafter, he turned to writing and directing. He directed more than 30 films for Great Wall, including *Seventeen/Sap chat sui/Shi qi sui* (1960) and *The Gentleman Who Steals/Leung seung gwan ji/Liang shang jun zi* (1963). Hu and **Zhang Xinyan** have been the two leading directors of the company since the 1960s. *The Hut on the Hilltop/Ngu/Wu* (1970), *Hawk of the Yi's/Yee chuk ji/Yi zu zhi* (1973) and *One Pound of Flesh/Yat bong yuk/Yi bang ron* (1976) are among the director's films that mirror the ideology and aesthetics of the later stages of the Cultural Revolution.

HUALIAN FILM COMPANY. Founded by actor/director **Ng Cho-fan** and director/writer **Lee Sung-fung** in 1954, Hualian made only four films over six years, but most are classics. Films include **Yeung**

Kung-leong's *This Wonderful Life/Jinxiu rensheng* (1954), Lee Sung-fung's *Cold Nights/Han ye* (1955) and *The Orphan/Renhai guhong* (1960), and **Lee Tit's** *Father Is Back/Huo ku you lan* (1961).

HUANG, HE (1919–2000). Mandarin actor Huang He (real name Huang Shijie), a native of Guangdong province, dropped out of medical school in Shanghai to join a drama group. He came to Hong Kong in 1939, and Su Yi cast him in the Mandarin drama *The Flowers of the Earth/Daai dei dut/Da di zhi hua* (1939). He returned to Shanghai and appeared in *Spring Warms Up with the Fragrant Quilt* (1941). During wartime, he appeared in 14 films, including *Universal Love* (1942), *The Next Generation* (1942), *The Better Halves* (1943), and *Sex Trap* (1943). Following the war, he returned to films with **Zhu Shilin's** Mandarin drama *Two Persons in Trouble Unsympathetic to Each Other/Tung ban bat seung lin/Tong bing bu xiang lian* (1946).

Huang simultaneously appeared in Cantonese and Mandarin films, such as **Lo Dun's** Cantonese comedy *Intimate but Quarrelsome/Foon choi yuen ga/Huan xi yuan ga* (1947) and **Wang Yin's** Mandarin drama *The Open Road* (1948). He hit his stride in the 1950s, playing the lead in more than 60 films, including **Li Pingquian's** Mandarin romantic drama *A Strange Woman/Yat doi yiu gei/Yi dai yao ji* (1950), Wang Yin's Mandarin musical *Red Rose/Hung mooi gwai/Hong mei gui* (1952), the multi-director Mandarin drama *Sweet Memories* (1952), **Chun Kim's** Mandarin contemporary family drama *Sweet Seventeen/Lui yee sam/Nu er xin* (1954), and the multi-director Mandarin historical drama *Blood-Stained Flowers/Bik huet wong dut/Bixue hua* (1953). Nine directors and five writers were involved in the latter production, a Kuomintang-slanted history lesson about a handful of 1911 revolutionaries who sacrifice to stage an uprising against the Qing dynasty in Guangzhou. In *A Strange Woman*, Huang played a revolutionary protected by a woman (**Bai Guang**). In *Red Rose*, Huang played a teacher in love with the title character (**Li Lihua**), but she is pursued by a warlord, so he is arrested and imprisoned, but never forgets her, reunites with her, and is then executed. In *Sweet Seventeen*, **Lin Cui's** debut in the title role, Huang played another teacher, whose support and understanding, after initial troubles, leads to a new life for the tender youth. During 1952 alone, Huang starred in 15 films. Shot in Taiwan, one of his most critically acclaimed films was *The Cliff* (1959).

Scandal affected his life; feeling betrayed by a woman in the mid-1950s, he attempted suicide unsuccessfully. In 1960, he publicly stated he would make an autobiographical film that never happened. He retired and went into business.

HUANG, YEBAI (1917–1998). Producer and manager Huang Yebai was a Shanghai native who graduated from Xinhua Art Academy and was an editor for Shanghai newspapers as well as founder of his own paper, *Cheng Post*. In 1952, he entered the film industry as a publicity officer at **Yonghua**, then in the same position at International Film Distributing Agency (later restructured as **Motion Pictures and General Investment**, Cathay) as Yonghua was absorbed by the company.

In 1969, Huang left Cathay and worked briefly at **Shaw Brothers**. In 1970, he started New Century Film Company, producing four films, among them *My Love, My Wife* (1970). In 1974, he founded Wanxing Film Company, producing three films. He was chairman of the Hong Kong and Kowloon Cinema & Theatrical Enterprise Free General Association Limited from 1966 to 1973.

Huang's contributions to film earned him awards from the Taiwanese government.

HUANGMEI DIAO. *Huangmei diao* (literally, yellow plum opera) refers to a cultural phenomenon and distinctive film genre popular for roughly 10 years, beginning in the late 1950s. **Motion Pictures and General Investment** (Cathay) and **Shaw Brothers** studios were primarily its producers. Based on traditional Chinese stage opera, the films integrated stage arts, singing styles, and performance methods with current cinematic techniques. On-screen an imaginary China resulted. *Huangmei xi* (opera) originated in Huangmei, Hubei province, and gained recognition in performances in other cities as theatrical troupes traveled around Eastern China. The style is still practiced in Anhui province today. The Communist Party chose the style to develop indigenous culture, and promoted it throughout the country in the early 1950s, standardizing the language as Mandarin.

As in Western opera, the stories were well known by audiences, who also knew the songs and sang along in movie theaters. It borrowed from Beijing opera, and used modern orchestration. *Huangmei diao* (tune) was an older name for the opera style, which was used to describe the new movies. Elaborate costumes, sets, and spectacle; use of screens and curtains; moments of silence relying on facial and hand expression; and emotion and character expressed through music and lyrics sung characterize the film genre. The first film produced was *Heavenly Match* (1954) and the first Hong Kong film produced was *To Borrow a Wife* (1958), using non-opera trained performers and produced by the **Great Wall** studio. Classics include **Li Han-hsiang's** *Diau Darling* (1958), Yuan Qiufeng's *The Dream of the Red Chamber* (1961), Li Han-hsiang's ***The Love Eterne*** (1962), and **Yan Jun's *The Grand Substitution*** (1965). *See also* CHINESE OPERA FILMS.

HUAQIAO FILM COMPANY. Huaqiao was founded in 1957 by actor **Cheung Ying** and backed by Macau tycoon Ho Yin. Its first production was *A Tale of Laughter and Tears/Tai siu yan yuen/Ti xiao yin yuan* (1957). The company specialized in adaptations of **Mandarin Duck and Butterfly** novels by Zhang Henshui, with roles tailor-made for Cheung. Besides its inaugural film, other Zhang adaptations included **Lee Sung-fung's** *The House of Kam Topples/Jin fen shi gu* (1961) and **Tso Kea's** *Many Aspects of Love/Luo xia gu mu* (1961) and *Time Flows Like a Stream/Si shui liu nian* (1962). Other productions were **Ng Wui's** melodramas *Thunderstorm/Lei yu* (1957) and *Little Women/Xiao fu ren* (1957); Cheung Ying's realist *Driver No. 7/Di qi hao si ji* (1958), in which Cheung acted and directed; Ng Wui's fantasy *Ten Brothers/Shi xiong di* (1959); and Tso Kea's family melodrama *Salvation/Ci mu xin* (1960). Huaqiao's last production was *Miss, Mr., Mrs.* (1967).

HUI, ANN ON-WAH (1948–). Born in Manchuria to a Chinese father and a Japanese mother, director Ann Hui earned a master's degree at Hong Kong University before attending the London Film School. When she graduated in the mid-1970s, she returned to Hong Kong and worked as an assistant to **King Hu** and became a **television** director of dramatic series and documentaries at Hong Kong Television Broadcasts Limited (TVB), under production chief Selina Chow, where other burgeoning filmmakers dubbed Hong Kong's **New Wave** were working. Among them was **Patrick Tam**, who had directed the first season of the series *CID*, and was senior to Hui. Lau Fong-kong was the supervisor who established the film unit and Hui's boss at TVB and supervisor. While working at TVB, Hui was offered work on four occasions by the Independent Commission against Police Corruption (ICAC), but refused. When her father died and she was responsible for supporting her family, she agreed, at a salary four times her present one. She made seven episodes for a series called *ICAC*. Two episodes were deemed controversial and banned. Subsequently, Hui received offers from Hong Kong Television Broadcasts Limited (TVB), Rediffusion Television (RTV), and Radio Television Hong Kong (RTHK) and was undecided; she followed the advice of a fortune-teller who told her that since she wanted to make movies, she should choose the company with the smaller workload, so Hui chose RTHK. By 1978, eager producers were pursuing the group that would become Hong Kong's New Wave filmmakers to make movies, and Hui agreed to work with producer Wu Sau-yee (who had produced Hu's *Raining in the Mountain*), and she brought along her scriptwriter partner Joyce Chan.

Hui's directorial debut was *The Secret/Fung gip/Feng jie* (1979), a supernatural psycho-thriller with many layered secrets to peel away, followed by *The Spooky Bunch/Chong do jing/Zhuang dao zheng* (1980), a film suggested by star **Josephine Siao** who liked **Cantonese opera** and imagined a story revolving around an opera troupe haunted by mischievous spirits. While at RTHK, Hui directed the drama *The Boy from Vietnam*, having researched the plight of Vietnamese "boat people" in Hong Kong. With *The Story of Woo Viet (Woo Yuet's Story)/Woo Yuet dik goo si/Hu Yue de Gushi* (1981), starring **Chow Yun-fat**, Hui readdressed the plight of Vietnamese "boat people," reconstructing the refugee problem as a thriller set in hell. Chow played a young ex-soldier arriving along with a boatload of Vietnamese refugees in Hong Kong. In a refugee camp, he gets in trouble with Vietnamese secret agents. He escapes, planning to go to the United States with a fake passport. He ends up in the Philippines, betrayed by the Triad that had smuggled him. He meets and befriends another refugee (**Cherie Chung**), sold into prostitution while working for a vicious Triad boss in Manila's Chinatown.

Boat People/Tau ban liu hoi/Touben nuhai (1982) was set in 1970s Vietnam under an oppressive regime, starring **George Lam** as a visiting Japanese photojournalist expecting to find utopia and **Andy Lau** as a political victim. The latter film was viewed as a thinly veiled allegory for Hong Kong's future after 1997, and censored by Beijing authorities (although they had previously approved the script). It was a box office hit in Hong Kong upon its release and became one of Hong Kong's top-10 grossing films, also garnering numerous film awards, including Best Director for Hui at the **Hong Kong Film Awards** and receiving distribution in the United States. Both films are harrowing experiences. *Love in a Fallen City/King sing zi Luen/Qingcheng zhi lian* (1984), also starring Chow and Cora Miao, won awards at the fourth Hong Kong Film Awards and the 25th **Golden Horse Awards**.

With *Romance of Book and Sword (Book Sword Gratitude Revenge Record)/Sue gim yan sau luk/Shu jian en chou lu* (1987), Hui directed a two-part **martial arts** epic based on **Louis Cha's** first novel; shot on location in China, the film portrayed Hui's imaginary China, where different races and cultures can peacefully coexist. This theme again appeared in Hui's autobiographical film, ***Song of the Exile*** *(Exile and Autumn Sorrow)/Haak to chau han/Ketu qiuhen* (1990), starring **Maggie Cheung** as a stand-in for Hui as the daughter who learns as an adult to understand her Japanese mother and discovers her Japanese mother's family's class superiority to her father's Chinese one. The British-educated daughter returns home to Hong Kong to resume a difficult relationship with her mother. Important issues of identity and exile are raised in the film, and reflected through multiple points of view.

Summer Snow *(Woman, Forty)/Nui Yan Sei Sap/Nuren sishu* (1995) is a heartbreaking Alzheimer's-themed drama starring **Josephine Siao** and **Roy Chiao** that celebrates an ordinary housewife as hero. Siao's daughter-in-law juggles home, family, and work as she cares for her Alzheimer's-ridden father-in-law. Hui also acted in the film, running a day care center for the elderly, and the filmmaker managed to indicate Hong Kong's housing shortage and inadequacies in elder care programs, also pointing an accusatory finger at a younger generation too involved in their lives to remember they come from a culture that traditionally reveres (and cares for) its elderly. The film won numerous awards at the Berlin Film Festival that year. Hui and Siao were two of the last Hong Kong citizens to be awarded titles by Queen Elizabeth. With *Ordinary Heroes/Chin yin maan yue/Qian yan wan yu* (1999), starring **Anthony Wong** playing real-life Italian activist priest Franco Mella, Hui recreated the excitement, frustrations, and hope of social activists in Hong Kong in the 1980s. The movie won Best Film at the 19th Hong Kong Film Awards. More recently, Hui tackled poetry and a midlife crisis in *July Rhapsody/Laam yan sei sap/Nan ren si shi*, starring **Jacky Cheung** as a middle-aged secondary school teacher married to **Anita Mui**, who relates to a nubile student through lyrical verse. Hui's *Goddess of Mercy/Yu Guangyin* (2004) is a Hong Kong–Mainland coproduction that opened the 28th **Hong Kong International Film Festival**. Written by frequent collaborator **Ivy Ho** and characteristic of Hui's forte, the story, shot on location in Yunnan province, concerns individuals caught in uncontrollable historical circumstances, starring Mainlander Zhao Wei and Hong Konger **Nicolas Tse**. She reunited with Chow Yun-fat for *This Aunt's Postmodern Life* (2006).

Hui is a rarity in Hong Kong, both a female director and a humanistic filmmaker who has never given in to the commercialism of Hong Kong movies generally. Careful storytelling, meticulous contextualization of characters into the social fabric and specific locations, stylistic and intimate camerawork, and individual and emotional characterization all contribute to the personal becoming political in her work.

HUI BROTHERS.

Hui, Michael Koon-man (1942–). Born in Guangdong Province, actor, director, and writer Michael Hui graduated from Union College, Chinese University, in Hong Kong and became a schoolteacher. He also managed an advertising agency before joining Hong Kong Television Broadcasts Limited (TVB) as a television host in 1968. He achieved success as a performer with *The Hui Brothers' Show*, mixing sketches and musical numbers, also starring younger brother Sam Hui. The show got **Li Han-hsiang's** attention, and Hui made his film debut in Li's *The Warlord/Daai gwan fat/Da jun fa* (1972), starring in three more films by the director. He began directing at **Golden Harvest**, with *Games Gamblers Play/Gwai ma seung sing/Gui ma shuang xing* (1974), which became Hong Kong's biggest blockbuster at the time. The movie was first in a comedy series that came to be called

Mr. Boo movies in Japan, after the character Hui played. (Others include *The Last Message/Tin choi yue baak chi/Tian cai yu bai chi*, *The Private Eyes/Boon gan baat leung/Ban jin ba liang*, *The Contract [Sold Body Contract]/Maai san kai/Mai shep qi*, and *Security Unlimited [Modern Bodyguards]/Lut dang biu biu/Mo deng bao biao* [1975, 1976, 1978, and 1981, respectively]). Hui won Best Actor at the 1992 **Hong Kong Film Awards** for his characterizations. Hui's brothers also played key roles in many of these films. He executive produced and wrote **Ronny Yu**'s *The Trail (The Trial)/Chui gwai chat hung/Zhui gui qi xiong* (1983), and began producing, through the **Hui's Film Production Company, Ltd.**, movies including **Clifton Ko's** food comedy *Chicken and Duck Talk (Chicken with Duck Talk)/Gai tung aap gong/Ji tong ya jiang* (1988), also written by Hui, starring him with brother Ricky and Sam in a cameo, for which Hui was awarded Best Performance Actor by the American Film Institute; the tabloid-set *Front Page/San boon gan baat a/Xin ban jin ba ya* (1990), for which the **Hong Kong Artists' Guild** named him Actor of the Year; *The Magic Touch/San suen/Shen suan* (1992), which screened at the Art Institute of Chicago and for which Hui, playing a tax-evading psychic, was named Distinguished Film Artist by the Illinois governor, and the Chicago mayor declared March 14, 1992, Michael Hui Day; and the tender family story *Always on My Mind/Cheung chin foo chai/Chuang qian fu qi* (1993), in which he starred opposite **Josephine Siao**, and which was named Best Asian Film at the Tokyo Film Festival and one of the Best Five of the Year at the Hong Kong Film Awards. Hui appeared in the Hollywood movie *Cannonball Run* with **Jackie Chan** and **Wayne Wang's** *Chinese Box*, filmed in Hong Kong with Jeremy Irons, **Maggie Cheung**, and **Gong Li** during the return of Hong Kong to the Mainland.

Michael Hui is responsible for reinventing Hong Kong comedy in the mid-1970s. His family-friendly humor involves situation comedy (with settings such as gambling dens, mental hospitals, restaurants) with a marked sense of place, physical comedy with visual gags, recognizable everyman characterizations, and social satire. Typically Hui would play a self-centered and cunning character too smart for his own good. His plans backfire on him. Brother Ricky would play the subservient sidekick and scapegoat who ultimately served as Michael's conscience. Brother Sam would play the ladies' man.

Hui, Ricky Koon-ying (1946–). Actor Ricky Hui Koon-ying was born in Guangdong Province. He had been working for the French Press Agency (AFP) in Hong Kong when he joined his brothers to make *The Private Eyes* (1976). He has made a career of playing the somewhat out of it supporting character in a number of comedies, not only those involving his brothers, but also **Chor Yuen's** *House of 72 Tenants/Chat sap yee ga fong hak/Qi shi er gu fang ke* (1973) and **John Woo** comedies like *Money Crazy/Faat chin hon/Fa qian han* (1977), *From Riches to Rags/ Chin jok gwaai /Qian zuo guai* (1980), and *Plain Jane to the Rescue/Baat choi Lam A Jan/Ba cai Lin Ya Zhen* (1982, opposite Josephine Siao). He costarred in Ricky Lau's seminal comic *Mr. Vampire/Geung shi sin sang/Jiangshi xiansheng* (1985), as a Taoist apprentice who sets the action in motion by disturbing an eternal flame and releasing a roomful of corpses. The film began the vampire trend, with 24 **vampire movies** released between 1986 and 1990; the film ranked number six at the local box office and earned nominations for Best Picture and Director at the Hong Kong Film Awards. Ricky Hui's malleable face has made him a memorable comic character but also one deserving of pathos in over 50 films.

Hui, Sam Koon-kit (1948–). Actor Sam Hui Koon-kit was born in Canton. He achieved fame as a singer and is called the "Father of **Cantopop**," credited with developing a new musical style that used Cantonese lyrics and themes with Western instruments and music. While he appeared on-screen as early as **Lo Wei's** *Back Alley Princess/Ma liu siu ying hung/Ma lu xiao ying xiong* (1973), he really joined the film industry by singing the theme song and appearing in brother Michael's *Games Gamblers Play* (1974), and when **Karl Maka** cast him as star in the *Aces Go Places* series (1980s) at **Cinema City**, a string of urban-set zany comedy **action** pictures spoofing James Bond movies, with the stunt action involving lots of gadgetry, with fashion trends, adventure, and romance thrown in, and featuring Hui's singing. Hui appeared in five of these films between 1982 and 1989. He also starred in **Tsui Hark's** production of the preternatural *Swordsman (Laughing and Proud Warrior)/Siu ngo gong wu/Xiao ao jianghu* as the affable title character (who prefers drinking wine to fighting) in search of a sacred scroll. The film was freely adapted from **Louis Cha's (Jin Yong)** novel *The Wandering Swordsman*. Hui also composed the musical score for several of his films.

HUI, KARA YING-HUNG (Wai Ying-hing) (1960–). Kara Hui Ying-hung, a Hong Kong native, started her performing career at age 13, when she quit school to study with the Miramar dance troupe. Based in the Miramar nightclub in Hong Kong, the troupe was famous for traditional Chinese dance, and among the instructors teaching young Hui was recent Chinese immigrant and *wushu* expert Bow Sim Mark, mother of future **martial arts** star **Donnie Yen**. Three years later Hui signed on with the **Shaw Brothers** studio, where she soon became a favorite of **kung fu** director **Lau Kar-leung**. She starred in a number of Lau's hit films, including *Mad Monkey Kung Fu/Fung hau/Feng hou* (1979) and *Lady Is the Boss/Cheung moon yan/Zhang men ren* (1983). Although her characters appeared to be fragile and demure, she displayed determination and a dancer's speed and agility in the fight scenes. Her trademark role was in *My Young Auntie/Cheung booi/Zhang bei* (1981), where she played the young widow of an aged martial arts master, and rallied the rest of his family into helping to preserve his legacy. Her nickname, after the film's release, became "Auntie."

Hui branched out into a variety of roles in the early 1980s, even appearing in non-fighting drama and comedy roles. She also cultivated a slightly more risqué image. At the same time, she continued to appear in traditional kung fu and ***wuxia*** films like *Long Road to Gallantry/Yap hap ching/You xia qing* (1984) and *Zen of Sword/Xia nu chuan qi* (1993), and she has contributed solid martial performances to a number of successful **television** series, such as *The Master of Tai Chi/Tai ji zong shi* (1997). She remains a favorite of knowledgeable martial arts fans around the world.

THE HUI'S FILM PRODUCTION COMPANY LTD. In 1975, comedic actor and director **Michael Hui** founded Hui's Film, a subsidiary of **Golden Harvest**, and the company is known for the **Hui Brothers**' comedies as well as other Michael Hui vehicles such as **Jacob Cheung's** *Always on My Mind/Chuang qian fu qi* (1993), starring Hui and **Josephine Siao Fong-fong**. The company's inaugural production was *Games Gamblers Play/Gui ma shuang xing* (1974). Other brother comedies include *The Last Message/Tian cai yu bai chi* (1975), *The Private Eyes (*aka *Mr. Boo)/Ban jin ba liang* (1976), *The Contract (Sold Body Contract)/Mai shep qi* (1978), *Security Unlim-*

ited (Modern Bodyguards)/Mo deng bao biao (1981), and *Chicken and Duck Talk (Chicken with Duck Talk)/Ji tong ya jiang* (1988), the latter a food comedy written and directed by and starring Michael Hui (and brother **Ricky**, and brother **Sam** in a cameo) that earned Hui Best Performance Actor recognition by the American Film Institute.

HUNG, SAMO KAM-BO (1950–). Born in Hong Kong, actor and director Samo Hung was one of four children born to Shanghainese parents. As a child he was sent to train at Yu Zhangyuan's (Yu Jim Yuen) Chinese Drama Academy, a Peking/Beijing **Chinese opera** school in the old style (and mirrored to a lesser degree in **Alex Law's** *Painted Faces*, starring Hung in the part of his former master, and for which he won a **Golden Horse Award** for Best Actor in 1988). Hung was the oldest boy at the school, and hence referred to as "*dai go dai*," or "Big Brother," by the others, including **Jackie Chan**. Hung was the leader of the **Seven Little Fortunes**, Yu's children's performing troupe. Called the "Fat Dragon" because of his rotundity, Hung has nonetheless always been agile on his feet. Like many in the opera schools, Hung began working in the movies as an extra and stuntman in the 1970s, using the skills he acquired through opera training. His first film appearance, at age 11, was in Chung Kai-man's *The Education of Love/Oi dik gaan yuk/Ai de jiao yu* (1961), in which he played a shy, quiet student from a single-parent home. **Golden Harvest** Studios invited him to choreograph the fight scenes in *The Fast Sword/Do meng gam kim/Duo ming jong jian* (1971), the beginning of a fruitful partnership that ended in 1989. Hung appears briefly in the opening fight of **Bruce Lee's** ***Enter the Dragon****/Lung chang foo dau/Loong zheng hu dou* (1973), among many other action movies.

Hung has worked as director on 28 films, actor in 110, producer of 31, and **action** director of 49. He is considered one of the all-time great fight choreographers, staging amazing feats and setting styles to story and character. Not only has he directed the action of numerous action films, but some out of the ordinary ones, including **Jeff Lau's** postmodern parody *Eagle-Shooting Heroes/San diu ying hung chuen ji dung shing sai jau/Shediao yingxiong zhi dongcheng xijui* (1993) and **Wong Kar-wai's** meditative and stylish Eastern–Western ***Ashes of Time*** *(Evil East Malicious West)/Dung chea sai duk/Dong xie xi du*

(1994). Hung's directorial debut was with *The Iron-Fisted Monk (Monk Sam Tak and Chung Mai-luk)/Saam Dak who seung* (1977). He produced, among others, *Long Arm of the Law* (1984), *Mr. Vampire* (1985), and *Yes, Madam* (1985), through his **Bo Ho Films** (1980–1992), a subsidiary of Golden Harvest. Hung also created Samo Hung's Stuntmen's Group, his stunt team, which has worked on more than 30 films.

Hung's collaborations with "little brothers" Jackie Chan and **Yuen Biao** include *Wheels on Meals (Fast Food Car)/Faai chaan che/Kuai can che* (1984) and *Dragons Forever/Fei lung maang cheung/Fei long meng jiang* (1988); with Chan, *Project A/A gai waak/A ji hua* (1983), *Heart of the Dragon (Dragon's Heart)/Lung dik sam/Long de xin* (1985), and *Mr. Nice Guy/Yat goh hiu yan/Yi ge hao ren* (1997); with Biao, *Prodigal Son (Son Ruining the Family,* aka *Pull No Punches)/Bai ga jai/Baijia zi* (1982). Hung has a knack for action comedy as both director and performer, as in the ghost comedy, *Encounters of the Spooky Kind (Ghost Strikes Ghost)/Gwai chuk gwai/Gui da gui* (1980), and *Millionaire's Express/Foo gwai lit che/Fu gui lie che* (1986), a Hong Kong version of *It's a Mad, Mad, Mad, Mad World*. But Hung also proved himself with dramatic action, as in the Vietnam War–set *Eastern Condors/Dung fong tuk ying/Dong fang tu ying* (1987). *Pedicab Driver (A Group of Dragons Playing Phoenix)/Kwan lung hei fung/Qun long xia feng* (1989), considered by many to be his best, mixes drama and humor with traditional exciting and dynamic martial arts filmmaking. Hung plays one of a hardworking family group of pedicab drivers in 1940s Macau who get embroiled with the Triads.

Hung has proved equally strong in dramatic parts, as signaled by the unusual Chan film *Heart of Dragon* (1985), in which Chan plays an atypical selfish brother trying to escape the responsibility of his mildly retarded brother (Hung). In **Cheung Yuen-ting's** *Eight Taels of Gold/Baat a gam/Ba ya jin* (1989), he played a Chinese immigrant who falls deeply in love with his affianced cousin. He also played a no-nonsense action director in **Ann Hui's** *Ah Kam (The Stuntwoman)/Ah Gam dik koo si/A Jin de gu shi* (1996), costarring **Michelle Yeoh**, and revealing the camaraderie and sacrifice of Hong Kong's stunt people; real life mirrored the movies with a stunt gone wrong in which Yeoh was dangerously injured. In 1998, Hung starred as a Chinese cop in Los Angeles in the comedic action U.S. television show, *Martial Law*, executive produced by **Stanley Tong**. After two seasons, he returned to Hong Kong and has acted in several films, including two Mainland features, as well as directing the action in *The Medallion/Fei lung joi sang/Fei long zai sheng*, starring Chan, and **Wilson Yip's** detective martial arts actioner *Sha Po Lang* (2005), opposite **Donnie Yen**. Hung's nickname, "Samo," means "three hairs."

– I –

INDEPENDENT FILM. While Hong Kong cinema has been dominated by mainstream, 35mm features, pre-1997 and second-generation independent filmmakers have carved a niche in Hong Kong filmmaking. Independent shorts have provided an alternative perspective and expression as well as training for young filmmakers eager to enter the mainstream.

Independent film development really began with various cine clubs, starting with the College Cine Club, developed around the monthly college magazine *College Life* (1966), aimed at idealistic and open-minded college students during the years of the Cultural Revolution in China and the burgeoning underground and experimental movements in Europe and the United States, inspiring important figures such as critics **Law Kar**, **Sek Kei**, critic/filmmaker Kam Ping-hing, and filmmaker **John Woo**.

The Phoenix Club, established in 1976 and dissolved in the late 1980s, served as a gathering for filmmakers and cinephiles, showing Western independent films and classics as well as super-8 and 16mm Hong Kong experimentals. Also in the mid-1970s, the Communications Department at Hong Kong Baptist College began offering film and video training, and students included post-grad **Allen Fong**. In 1977, a group of young **television** directors and filmmakers established the Film Culture Centre, which not only offered technical support and training for aspiring filmmakers, but programmed alternative Hong Kong and Chinese cinema, ranging from the experimental, such as Dominique Lui's *Legend of the Dragon* (1981), an interpretation of ancient Chinese poems, to Joyce Lam's straightforward **documentary** *Chiu Chow Opera* (1979). Both new-waver **Terry Tong** and second-waver **Eddie Fong** have been part of this group.

Independent film in Hong Kong has gathered strength since 1993, when the Hong Kong Urban Council (renamed in 2000 as Leisure and Cultural Services Department) revived independent shorts as part of the **Hong Kong International Film Festival** (HKIFF) and the Hong Kong Arts Center organized the first Hong Kong Independent Short Film and Video Awards simultaneously. The attention since has encouraged independent production, although financing remains difficult to secure; digital video production has somewhat eased the problem. In 2001, the **Hong Kong Film Archives** presented "I-Generations, a retrospective of independent, experimental, and alternative creations from the 60s to now," which recovered several decades of film history and contributions. Reasons for the lack of product include the local market being small, as well as the apolitical nature of Hong Kong itself, with an emphasis on conformity and family, as opposed to self-expression, as well as the expensive price of film prior to digital production.

Since the mid-1990s, the Hong Kong International Film Festival has included independent film and video, encouraging the production of such media, and during the late 1990s, the scene began to change. Kwan Park-heun's *Landscape* (1988) was the first independent feature, bookended by **Fruit Chan's** trilogy, starting with *Made in Hong Kong* (1997), almost a decade later. Chan studied filmmaking at the Film Culture Centre and worked as a cinematographer throughout the 1980s before his directorial debut. William Kwok's *And So and So* (2000) provided 10 portraits of contemporary Hong Kong, while **Nelson Yu's** drama *Love Will Tear Us Apart* (1999) depicted lost Mainlanders in Hong Kong and **Evans Chan's** *Map of Sex and Love* (2001) depicted three interrelated stories of the **diaspora**, sexual preference, and identity. Hong Kong independent film continues to push the envelope and expand artistic creation. *See also* NEW WAVE.

IN-GEAR FILM PRODUCTION COMPANY LTD. The 1960s Cantonese actor **Alan Tang**, who had previously founded the Wing-Scope Company, founded In-Gear in 1987. Its first production was Joe Cheung's *Flaming Brothers/Jiang hu long hu men* (1987), starring Tang and **Chow Yun-fat**. In-Gear produced two of director **Wong Kar-wai's** films, *As Tears Go By (Mongkok Carmen, Carmen of the Streets)/Wong kok Ka Moon* (1988) and *Days of Being Wild*

(The True Story of Ah Fei)/Ah Fei ching chuen/A Fei zhengzhuan (1990). In-Gear is representative of independent filmmaking, producing independent films and not being associated with any major companies. **Clarence Ford's** *Black Panther Warriors (Warriors: The Black Panther)/Hei bao tian xia* (1993), also starring Tang in his last screen role, was an In-Gear production.

INOUE, UMETSUGU (1923–). Born in Kyoto, director Inoue Umetsugu (his name means "above the well") earned a degree in economics from Keio Gijuku Daigaku and joined Shin Toho (New Toho) as an assistant director in 1947. His directorial debut was *Koi No Oendancho* (1952). He joined Nikkatsu in 1955 and made *Man Who Causes a Storm/Arashiwo Yobu Otoko* (1957), which made actor Ishihara Yojiro famous. He continued directing action, light comedy, and **musicals**, and, in 1959, traveled to the United States to study new film technologies.

Inoue joined **Shaw Brothers** in 1965, signing an indefinite contract to make 100 movies; when he came to Hong Kong in 1966, he brought with him his own team, including assistant director, art director, lighting specialist, martial arts director, dance instructor, and dancers. His first film for Shaw was *Operation Lipstick/Mong giu wa/Wang jiaowa* (1967), with composer **Hattori Ryoichi** composing the music. He also used Hattori for the musicals *Hong Kong Nocturne/Heung Kong fa yuet yeh/ Xiangjiang huayue ye* (1967), *King Drummer/Ching chun goo wong/Qing chun gu wang* (1967), and *Hong Kong Rhapsody/Fa yuet leung siu/Hua yue liang xiao* (1968). All of these films, with the exception of *Operation Lipstick*, were adapted from his previous Japanese films, *Tokyo Cinderella/ Tokyo Shinderera Musume* (1954), *Man Who Causes a Storm*, and *Tonight We'll Dance* (1963).

With the musical *Hong Kong Nocturne* Inoue made his male characters the moral measure of the story, by which the females learn lessons about life and fantasy. Three sisters (**Lily Ho**, **Cheng Pei-pei**, and Qin Ping) leave their father's magic act after he is blinded by a gold digger and absconds with their money. Each daughter follows a different path that structures the story; all three meet men, the eldest (Lily Ho) wants to marry a movie producer she discovers is out to exploit her, escaping only to be further ogled by a lecherous Japanese pornographer. The youngest (Qin Ping) dreams of being a ballet dancer, but is drawn into a sadomasochistic relationship with her dance master. The middle daughter (Cheng Pei-pei), who remains with the father, becomes the star of his magical striptease act, to her horror. She is rescued by an aspiring composer (**Peter Chen Hou**), and they marry, but he dies in a plane crash. The story concludes with the family reunited in a Hong Kong recording studio.

Inoue was a prolific and versatile director who could make films rapidly, and specialized in **action** and musicals. His films were carefully structured and designed, and emphasized youth and energy. His favorite actors were Peter Chen Ho and Lily Ho (He Lili). Between 1967 and 1971, he directed 17 features for Shaw; he made 160 films altogether, writing 99 of the scripts. Since the mid-1970s he has worked in **television** and theater. He also wrote the book *Yujiro beneath the Window: The Secret of Films, the Secret of Living* (1987).

– J –

JIANG, GUANGCHAO (1924–). Actor Jiang Guangchao (real name Jiang De), a native of Zhejiang province, was born in Beijing, where he was educated. Interested in the performing arts, especially **Peking/Beijing Chinese opera**, he studied the *huqin*, a classical Chinese two-stringed instrument. He worked as a civil servant in Nanjing in the 1940s, before immigrating to Hong Kong in 1950.

At Longma, Jiang appeared in **Zhu Shilin's** *Spoiling the Wedding Day/Neung gaai gei/ Wu jiaqi* (1951) as a wealthy worshipper of foreign things. In 1951, Jiang signed with **Shaw Brothers**, recommended by actor **Wang Yin**. At Shaw, he usually played comic characters or villains. Screen appearances there include **Yue Feng's** Mandarin comedy *The Other Woman* (1959) and many **Tao Qin** movies, including the screwball comedy *Beware of Pickpockets/Dai fong siu sau/Ti fang xiao shou* (1958), the romance *Love without End/Bat liu ching/Bu liao qing* (1961), the Mandarin musical *The Dancing Millionairess/Maan dut ying ching/Wan hua ying chun* (1964), and the drama *The Blue and the Black/Laam yue hak/Lan yu hei* (1966). In *Beware of Pickpockets*, disguised thieves have a millionaire (Liang Xianbo) and his daughter's fiancé (Jiang) believing they are kleptomaniacs. Jiang's outstanding performance has been compared to a combination of early Cary Grant and Harpo Marx, while Liang's has been likened to Oliver Hardy. In 1958, Jiang appeared in and produced *Wild Fantasies/Seung yap fai fai/Xiang ru fei fei*. In the late 1950s, he also appeared in several **Motion Pictures and General Investment** features, including **Wang Tianlin's** sci-fi comedy *Riots in Outer Space/Leung soh daai laau taai hung/Liang sha da nao tai kong* (1959).

Jiang turned to a career in Taiwan, starting in 1969. By 1981, he had appeared in more than 70 films and was also active in **television**, hosting variety shows, and touring in theaters and clubs. In 1981, he set up his own broadcasting company, and produced and hosted his own variety show *East, West, South, North*.

JIANG HU. Literally meaning rivers and lakes, the term *jiang hu* is used both in reference to the world of martial heroes and villains and to the modern-day world of the gangsters and even film production in Hong Kong. In the introduction to the **Tsui Hark**–produced *Swordsman 3: The East Is Red/Dong fang bu bai feng yun zai qi* (1993), the Spanish admiral asks his Ming escorts what they mean when they say "jiang hu." They themselves are unable to precisely explain to the foreigner what they are talking about, yet the audience understands perfectly what they mean.

In terms of **martial arts** heroes, *jiang hu* can be defined as a parallel world in which martial artists exist and interact that is separate from the non-martial world. This subculture has its own specific set of rules and regulations, and can be very competitive. Members who do not abide by these codes of conduct are villains and usually punished for their misdeeds. Thousands of Chinese **swordplay** and martial arts movies are set in the *jiang hu* world, from Wen Yimin's early *Red Heroine/Hong xia* (1929, China) and **Wang Tianlin's** *Strange Hero/Jianghu qixia* (1956, Hong Kong), to **Chang Cheh's** *One-Armed Swordsman/Du bi dao* (1967) and **King Hu's** *A Touch of Zen* (1971), from Tsui Hark's *Zu: Warriors from the Magic Mountain/Suk san sun suk san geen hap/Zuo shan shen zuo shan jian xia* (1983) and ***Swordsman Trilogy****/Xiao ao jianghu* (1990–1993), to **Ang Lee's** *Crouching Tiger, Hidden Dragon/Wo hu cang long* (2000, Hong Kong–Taiwan–United States) and **Zhang Yimou's** *Hero/Ying xiong*

(2000, Hong Kong–China). From supernatural knight-errant characters with swordplay and palm power to the masculine brotherhood of **kung fu**, the code both defines and measures characters. Even **John Woo's** contemporary martial-arts-with-automatic-weapons heroic bloodshed stories, starting with ***A Better Tomorrow*** *(True Colors of a Hero)/Yang hung boon sik/Ying xiong bense* (1986), allude to a modern *jiang hu* world. It all began with the knight-errant figure of Chinese history some two thousand years ago, becoming a part of the popular imagination by the ninth century and recorded in countless myths and legends, later adapted to the screen.

The connection between the *jiang hu* and the real world is that the power struggles that occur in the *jiang hu* often affect who has power in the day-to-day world of ordinary people. Triads (Hong Kong's version of organized crime) have appropriated the term for themselves. Sam Ho, in his introduction to the 2002 Hong Kong Film Festival Archive retrospective focusing on Tsui Hark, notes that many individuals today describe the world of their own profession as a *jiang hu*. The term could just as easily be used to describe the world of corporate CEOs or government officials.

JIANG, MING (1909–). Actor Jiang Ming (real name He Yucun), a native of Liaoning province, was enrolled at the Northeast University in Manchuria when the September 18th incident caused him to flee to Beijing, where he joined the China Travelling Drama Group, touring and performing across China. His performances in Lu Xun's *The Story of Ah Q* and Ba Jin's *Thunderstorm* established him as an acting talent. He appeared in **Cai Chusheng's** *Orphan Island Paradise/Goo do tin tong/Gudao tiantang* (1939) and with **Zhou Xuan** in **Wu Zuguang's** *Waste Not Our Youth/Mok foo ching chun/Mofu qingchun* (1949), the latter based on a mythical story, *A Xiu*, collected in **Pu Songliang's** classic *Strange Tales from a Chinese Studio*.

In Hong Kong, Jiang joined **Longma** as an actor, appearing as one of the bourgeois evacuees in *The Flower Girl/Fa goo leung/Hua guniang* (1951) with **Li Lihua**, an adaptation of Guy de Maupassant's *Boule de Suif*. Transposed to the Sino–Japanese War, the story deals with the class hypocrisy of the bourgeois in their attitude toward the "flower girl" (prostitute), pressuring her to offer herself to the Japanese commander who waylays them.

Jiang appeared in numerous **Zhu Shilin** films, including the drama *Map of 100 Treasures/Baak bo tiu/Bai bao tu* (1953), the historical drama *Thunderstorm/Lui yue/Lei yu* (1961), and the comedies *Spoiling the Wedding Day/Neung gaai gei/ Wu jiaqi* (1951), *The Wedding Night/San fan dai yat yau/Xinhu diyiye* (1956, which Jiang codirected), *Husband Hunters/Cheung san long/Qiang xin lang* (1958), and *Love's Miracle/Ching dau choh hoi/Qing dou chu kai* (1958). He worked for the leftist studios **Great Wall** and **Feng Huang**. His Great Wall films include *Honeymoon* (1952), *The Inspector General* (1955), *Emperor Takes a Holiday* (1965), and *The Gold Diggers* (1965). His Feng Huang films include *Husband Hunters* (1958), *Love's Miracle* (1958), and *The Cricket and the King* (1966). His last film was **Johnnie To's** *Enigmatic Case (Warrant of Assassination)/Bik shui hon saan duet meng gam/Bi shui han shan duo ming jin* (1980), after which he retired.

Jiang also took part in the actor training programs of the leftist film companies, directed dramas for the Yinxing Performing Group, and served as manager for Feng Huang.

***JOYS AND SORROWS OF YOUTH* (1969). Chor Yuen's** *Joys and Sorrows of Youth/Laang nuen ching chun/Lengnuan Qingchun* (1969) is an unusual youth film of the late 1960s, because rather than young people being betrayed by their elders, here, they betray each other. The story concerns a group of university students, rich and poor, in late 1960s Hong Kong, each with a problem. Rich and spoiled Tommy Hu is the extravagant prodigal who causes his father's bankruptcy; his girlfriend Angel (Tina Ti) turns to prostitution and inadvertently causes her mother's suicide (a former prostitute, she is appalled to learn her daughter is in the trade and jumps from a building to her death). Tommy's sister is raped by the vicious King (Fung Tsui-fan). Poverty-stricken Hui-kit (**Kenneth Tsang Kong**) smuggles drugs to earn money for himself and his roommate; his righteous roommate (**Paul Chu Kong**) feels betrayed to learn the truth of his activities. The film borrows from Nicholas Ray's *Rebel without a Cause* (1955), including a knife fight and car race "playing chicken." The movie was produced independently by New Films (Xin Dianying), the company set up by the director and cast members set on reviving the declining Cantonese film industry. (Short-lived, the company produced only one other film, *Wise Wives and Foolish Husbands/Congming Taitai Ben Zhangfu*, 1969). The film would be influential with later problem youth films, ranging from **Wong Kar-wai's** *Days of Being Wild/Ah Fei ching chuen/A Fei zhengzhuan* (1990) to Lawrence Lau Kwok-cheung's *Arrest the Restless/Laam Gong juen ji faan fei jo fung wan/ Lan Jiang zhuan zhi fan fei zu feng yun* (1992).

– K –

KA, PATSY LING (Jia Ling) (1935–). Actress Ka Ling (real name He Peiying) was born in Guangdong province; she moved with her family to Hong Kong in 1949 and was educated at True Light Girls' College. In 1953, she began acting courses at Ling Guang Film Company, adopting the stage name "He Jialing." When Ling Guang began making Mandarin films, she and actor **Patrick Tse Yin** joined Di Hua Film Company, managed by Pan Binquan, and her first role was the detective story *Mystery of Three Wives (Murder of Three Wives, The Strange Case of Three Wives)/San qi qi'an* (1955). When director **Chun Kim** asked Pan to serve as production manager for his newly created Guang Yi, Jia Ling (having dropped her surname) followed, as did Patrick Tse Yin. She was the most popular female star at Guang Yi.

Over her 12-year career, Ka Ling appeared in 50 films and was usually cast as the mature, sympathetic, and sophisticated woman, often opposite Patrick Tse Yin. She performed in numerous Chun Kim films, including the dramas *The Fatherless Son/Wai fook ji/Wei fu zi* (1956), *Autumn Leaf* (1960), and *Blossom in Rainy May 1* and *2/Ng yuet yue chung dut/Wu yue yu zhong hua* (1960), as well as the comedies *How to Get a Wife/Chui chai gei/Zhui qi ji* (1961) and *The Beau/Dut dut gung ji/Hua hua gong zi* (1964). In *Blossom in Rainy May*, she plays an unwed mother whose fiancé has died on her wedding day; left to raise a daughter, she first adjusts to the loss and begins a life, only to be wooed by her boss, Patrick Tse Yin. Part one ends as she rejects his proposal;part two picks up 10 years later, after she has made her own life and happiness, when her boss returns and encounters resentment from her daughter. Ka Ling also costarred with Patrick Tse Yin in *How to Get a Wife*, playing both the movie star object of his dreams and the look-alike secretary who is also mistress to his boss.

Ka Ling played the sympathetic director of a rehabilitation center where Patrick Tse Yin's discharged prisoner finds himself in **Patrick Lung Gong's** *Story of a Discharged Prisoner/Ying hung boon sik/Yingxiong bense* (1967). The latter film served as the basis for **John Woo's** ***A Better Tomorrow*** *(True Colors of a Hero) Ying hung boon sik/Yingxiong bense* (1986), with **Kenneth Tsang's** taxi company replacing the center and Tsang as a reformed ex-con himself.

The actress married a Chinese from Thailand in 1963, and after playing the lead as a psychologically disturbed young woman in **Wong Yiu's** *The Strange Girl/Yan hoi kei dut/Ren hai qi hua* (1967), she retired and moved to Thailand.

KANESHIRO, TAKESHI (Gum Sing-mo) (1973–). Born in Taiwan to a Japanese father and Taiwanese Chinese mother, the multilingual Kaneshiro Takeshi grew up in Taiwan, attending a predominantly English-language international school. He started working in commercials as a teenager, and began producing music and making films, the first being **Johnnie To's** *The Executioners/Yin doi ho hap chuen/ Xian dai hao xia zhuan* (1993). His breakthrough film was **Wong Kar-wai's** *Chungking Express (Chungking Forest)/Chung Hing sam lam/Zong qing sen lin* (1994) in which he wooed the older **Brigitte Lin** in many languages and by cleaning her shoes with a toothbrush. His performance was so strong, Wong chose him for the sensitive deaf mute in *Fallen Angels/Doh lok tin si/Duoluo Tianshi* (1995), in which he delivered a moving performance without words. **Lee Chi-ngai's** *Lost and Found (Edge of the World)/Tin aai hoi gok/Tian ya hai jiao* (1996) found the actor delivering a moody and effective performance (the soundtrack used Canadian Leonard Cohen); the actor also appeared in the U.S. independent *Too Tired to Die* (1998), directed by Wonsuk Chin and costarring the actor with Mira Sorvino and Ben Gazarra. More recently, Kaneshiro has costarred with **Andy Lau** and Zhang Ziyi in Mainland director **Zhang Yimou's** continued tribute to Hong Kong style in *House of Flying Daggers/Sap min maai fook/ Shimian maifu* (2004) and in **Peter Chan's** musical *Perhaps Love/Yu guo aoi/Ruoguo ai* (2005).

KEUNG, CHUNG-PING (Jiang Zhongping) (1922–1999). Actor Keung Chung-ping (real name Jiang Baolin), a native of Guangdong province, was born in Hong Kong. When Hong Kong fell to the Japanese, Keung's secondary education ended and he joined the resistance, became a member of the Cultural Workers' Group, and staged patriotic dramas. Following the war years, he set up Zhongying Drama Group with Zheng Junmian, and directed famous plays like *Thunderstorm*. In 1964, he led the Hong Kong Drama Group and staged *The House of the 72 Tenants*.

Keung's film career began with an appearance in *Tomorrow Is Another Day* (1947). In 1955, he signed with Guangyi and remained there for eight years, making **Lee Tit's** *The Sad Wife in a Grand House/Jue moon yuen/Zhu men yuan* (1956), Kong Ngee's *Dragnet/Jiu jiu jiu ming'an* (1956), and Chen Wen's *Murder on the Beach/Gau gau gau hoi taan taan meng ngon/Jiu jiu jiu haitan ming'an* (1957), the latter two detective thrillers featuring Jiang's first roles as a villain. In *Murder on the Beach*, he played a murderer who makes a husband's death appear to be a case of drunk driving, and blackmails the wife (**Patsy Ka Ling**) by kidnapping the son. **Patrick Tse Yin** plays the cousin of the victim who is hot on Jiang's trail. (The same cast had played in *Dragnet*.)

A versatile character actor, Keung played in over 400 films between 1947 and his retirement in 1985. He became typecast as villains. Well-known movies include **Tso Kea's** *Love Trilogy/Oi ching saam biu kuk/ Aiqing sanbuqu* (1955), Wong Hang's Cantonese family comedy *The Wall/Cheung/Qiang* (1956), and Tso Kea's Cantonese family comedy *The Chair/Jinshan dashao* (1959), among others. In *The Chair*, a son (**Cheung Ying**) leads a life of debauchery; his mother hides a diamond bracelet in a chair, and when she falls ill, tells her son to find it. The chair has been sold by the son's mistress, and he tries to retrieve it from Keung, the current owner.

Keung appeared alongside **Chow Yun-fat** in **Ann Hui's** nostalgic *Love in a Fallen City/King sing zi Luen/Qingcheng zhi lian* (1984) and in the **Wong Jing** comedy *Romancing Star/Cheung chong chui lui chai/Jing zhuang zhui nu zai* (1987); he came out of retirement to appear in **Roy Chiao's** *Sometimes, Miracles Do Happen/Tin sai ji shing/Tian shi zhi cheng* (1999), Chiao's last film, made for the Christian Church, in Hong Kong.

Besides acting, Keung was active in other parts of the entertainment industry. He set up Baohua Recording Company in the 1950s, in collaboration with Toho, dubbing Japanese and Hong Kong movies into English and Japanese, respectively. When Hong Kong Television Broadcasts Limited (TVB) was founded in 1968, the company recruited him for dubbing. In 1972, Keung created Tianping Film Company to distribute Hong Kong and Taiwanese movies, and to produce them as well, producing *Vanquishing the Tiger and the Dragon* (1972) and *The Desperado/Lung lee gai/Long li ji s* (1980). He also worked as the Hong Kong sales representative of Xinsheng Theater Circuit in New York.

***THE KID* (1950).** Actor-director **Fung Fung's** Cantonese contemporary realist melodrama *The Kid/Sai lui Cheung/Xilu Xiang* starred the 10-year-old **Bruce Lee** as Kid Cheung, an orphan who survives selling comic books in the slums in order to care for his siblings. Their guardian, Uncle Ho (Yee Chau-shui), a former teacher, brings a factory boss (**Lee Hoi-chuen**, Bruce Lee's father) to the slum; when the wealthy boss is robbed by a member of Flash Knife's (Fung Fung) gang, Kid Cheung abets the gangster, who becomes his mentor. Uncle Ho, meantime, is employed by the factory boss, whose eldest son (Yuen Po-wan) is stealing from the company. The story pits the kid between his two father figures, Uncle Ho and Flash Knife. As events progress, Cheung becomes a delinquent under Flash Knife's influence, but a factory worker (Chan Wai-yu) persuades him to reform and convincingly pleads his case to Flash Knife to release him. The family moves to the countryside to start a new life. The film was adapted from Yuen Po-wan's comic strip.

KILLER CLANS* (1976).** Directed by **Chor Yuen** and based on a **Gu Long *wuxia novel, *Killer Clans/Lau sing woo dip kim/Liu xing hu die jian* details the intrigues in the clan of a famous **martial arts** master played by **Ku Feng**. In this **Shaw Brothers** production, **Zhong Hua** plays an assassin sent to kill the master on orders from an unknown party. Instead of showing us the story from the assassin's point of view, the film reveals the events from the perspective of an observer. There are numerous betrayals on the parts of the characters and several surprises for the audience along the way. What sets *Killer*

Clans apart from many of its contemporaries are its elaborate settings and costumes and the many subplots in the film. In addition, this film can be seen as a transition to the **New Wave** martial arts films due to the corruption found in the *wuxia* code in the film.

KIN SING FILM ORGANIZATION. Formerly **Dacheng**, Kin Sing was founded in 1968 by brothers Kwan Chi-kin and Kwan Chi-sing. The studio property, formerly **Grandview's**, was reorganized twice, as Diamond Hill and Hong Kong Film Studio. Beginning in 1970, the studio property was rented to other companies for productions; in the 1980s, **D&B Studios** leased its space. Operations ceased in 1988.

THE KINGDOM AND THE BEAUTY* (1959).** Director **Li Han-hsiang's** first ***huangmei diao *The Kingdom and the Beauty/Jiangshan meiren*, made for **Shaw Brothers**, won 12 awards at the sixth **Asian Film Festival** in 1959. Adapted from the folktale "Meilong Township," the drama is essentially a love story set against a historical background. It concerns a runaway emperor (**Zhao Lei**), tired of the luxury and beauty of the cloistered palace, the atmosphere expressed in an incredible opening scene of dawn, with historical props and architecture, candles, and bell ringing and visualized through a variety of shots. He visits Jiangnan after hearing of its beauty in a song, a traditional *huangmei diao* number featuring a chorus of elaborately costumed beauties who sing and dance; there he falls for local girl Li Feng (**Linda Lin Dai**) through her song, and he promises to marry her. Three years pass and he has forgotten his vow while she is raising an illegitimate son, to the disapproval of the locals. Her relative (Jin Quan) travels to the capital on her behalf; the emperor repents and sends for her, but too late, as she dies on the way, unleashing an emotional response from the audience. Li's epical reach and unified aesthetics make the film a classic, not only part of a genre but a unified vision with a place in film history.

KO, CLIFTON CHI-SUM (1958–). Director and screenwriter Clifton Ko was born in Zhongshan, Guangdong province. After graduating from Hong Kong's Maryknoll College, he began working in **television** in 1977 as a scriptwriter and production assistant. He started working in the film industry in 1979, associated with director Clifford Choi. Early writer credits include Choi's *No U-Turn* (1981) and *Teenage Dreamers (Lemon Cola)/Ling mung hoh lok/Ning meng ke le* (1982), as well as **John Woo's** comedy caper *Once a Thief (Criss Cross Over Four Seas)/Jung waang sei hoi/Zhong heng si hai*, starring **Chow Yun-fat**, **Leslie Cheung**, and **Cherie Chung**. In 1982, he joined **Cinema City**, working on scripts for *Till Death Do We Scare* (1982) and *Esprit d'Amour* (1983). His directorial debut was with *The Happy Ghost* (1985). He has since worked steadily in comedy, making numerous **Lunar New Year's** films. Those include the **Hui Brothers**' food comedy *Chicken and Duck Talk (Chicken with Duck Talk)/Gai tung aap gong/Ji tong ya jiang* (1988), written by **Michael Hui**; the ensemble family comedies *All's Well, Ends Well (Family Has Happy Affairs)/Ga Yau hei si/Jia you xi shi* and *All's Well Ends Well, Too (Happy Event in the Flower Fields)/Fa tin hei si/Hua tian xi shi* (1993) and *It's a Wonderful Life (Big Rich Family)/Daai foo ji ga/Da fu zhi jia* (1994). The latter starred **Leung Ka-fai**, Leslie Cheung, **Teresa Mo**, **Raymond Wong**, **Lau Ching-wan**, **Tso Tat-wah**, **Fung Bo-bo**, **Anita Yuen**, and **Carol Cheng**, and featured **Kwan Tak-hing** as the patriarch of a lost family brought together by Leslie Cheung's good-natured outsider. The feel-good quality of Ko's films is characteristic of his work.

In 1989, Ko founded his own **Ko Chi sum (Clifton Ko) Productions Company**. He has produced and directed more than 30 films and written 20.

KO CHI SUM PRODUCTIONS COMPANY LTD. Ko Chi Sum was founded in 1989 by director **Clifton Ko**. *The Wild Ones/Wo wei cheng nian* (1989) was its inaugural production. During the next eight years, the company produced more than 60 films. Among them are Ko's touching dramas *I Have a Date with Spring/Wo han chun tian you ge yue hui* (1994), *One of the Lucky Ones/Ban wo tong hang* (1994), and *Umbrella Story/Ren jian you qing* (1995). The company also produced **Shu Kei's** *Hu-Du-Men/Hudumen* (1996), starring **Josephine Siao Fong-fong** in a tour de force tribute to life on and off stage, with its many entrances and exits.

KOO, JOSEPH KAR-FAI (1933–). Composer Joseph Koo got his big break in the music industry after he trained at the Berklee School of

Music in Boston in the early 1960s. Koo's older sister Gu Mei is a well-known Chinese singer. Koo's training was paid for by Sir **Run Run Shaw**, and when Koo completed his work, he returned to Hong Kong to work for Shaw at his **television** station, Hong Kong Television Broadcasts Limited (TVB). Koo became the musical director at TVB, in addition to working for **Golden Harvest**. Koo wrote the first **Cantopop** hit, "The Binding Force of a Wedding That Cries and Laughs" in 1971. Koo would collaborate with **James Wong** to write many of the greatest Cantopop hits, including "Shanghai Beach," "Family Struggle," and "Forget the Love in My Heart."

Koo's film work includes such notable films as *Fist of Fury/Jing mou moon/Jing wu men* (1972), *Games Gamblers Play/Gwai ma seung sing/gui ma shuang xing* (1974), **John Woo**'s directorial debut *The Dragon Tamers/Lui Ji Toi Kuen Kwan Ying Kooi/Nu Zi Tai Quan Qun Ying Hui* (1975), and ***A Better Tomorrow****/Ying hung boon sik/Yingxiong bense* (1986). Koo retired from the industry in the early 1990s and emigrated to Canada.

KU, FENG (Gu Feng) (1930–). The actor Ku Feng, born Chan Szeman, joined the **Shaw Brothers** studio in the mid-1960s and rapidly established himself as one of the most valued members of the Shaw repertory company. Whether cast in a minor character part or given costar status, he could be counted on to deliver a solid, pitch-perfect performance. He worked with all the great directors at Shaw: **King Hu** (*Come Drink with Me/Daai chui hap/Da zui xia* [1966]); **Chang Cheh** (*New One-Armed Swordsman/San duk bei diy/Xin du bidao* [1971], *The Brave Archer/Sau diu ying hung chuen/She diao ying xiong zhuan* [1977]); **Chor Yuen** (*The House of 72 Tenants/Chat sap yee ga fong hak/Qi shi er gu fang ke* [1973], ***Killer Clans****/Lau sing woo dip kim/Liu xing hu die jian* [1976]); **Li Han-Hsiang** (*Tiger Killer/Wu Sung* [1982]); and, especially, **Sun Zhong** (*Avenging Eagle/Laang huet sap saam ying/Leng xie shi san ying* [1978], *Deadly Breaking Sword/Fung lau duen kim siu siu diy/Feng liu duan jian xiao xiao dao* [1979], *Kid with a Tattoo/Tong tian xiao zi hong qiang ke* [1980]). He made an early impression as the villain of *The New One-Armed Swordsman*, using a trick weapon to maim his opponents. He was also memorable as the evil mastermind in *Avenging Eagle*, who raised his adopted sons to pillage and kill for him, until one, played by **Ti Lung**, rebels. Ku wasn't limited to playing the heavy. As the ***jiang hu*** patriarch in *Killer Clans*, he overcomes the plotting of **Yueh Hua** to triumph at the end. He took on comic roles, too, from the dotty leader of the Beggar Clan in *Brave Archer* to the befuddled merchant in *Kid with a Tattoo*, whose overimaginative son (Wong Yue) mistakes him for a notorious outlaw. Ku Feng was also a favorite of Shaw choreographers **Lau Kar-leung** and **Tang Chia**; Lau cast him as Wong Kei-ying, father of the famous kung fu master **Wong Fei-hung**, in *Martial Club/Wu guan* (1981).

In 1982, Ku won a **Golden Horse Award** for Best Supporting Actor for his role in *Tiger Killer*, an adaptation of the story of Wu Sung, one of the heroes of the epic novel *The Water Margin*. Ti Lung stars as Wu Sung and Ku plays his older brother, who is murdered by his vain, cold-hearted wife and her lover. Tradition holds that the elder Wu brother was a dwarf, and the story is a popular Chinese opera subject. Ku Feng consulted with Shaw stunt experts **Yuen Wah** and Yuen Bun, former members of the **Seven Little Fortunes** opera troupe, and trained to walk on his knees in a specially constructed costume to play the part.

From the mid-1980s, when the Shaw studio shut down their film production unit, until the present, Ku has continued to work steadily as a character actor in productions by many top Hong Kong filmmakers. He has notable roles in **Tsui Hark's** *Peking Opera Blues/Do ma daan/Dao ma dan* (1986), **Michael Hui's** *Chicken and Duck Talk/Gai tung aap gong/Ji tong ya jiang* (1988), **Clara Law's** *The Reincarnation of Golden Lotus/Poon Gam-lien ji chin sai gam sang/Pan Jinlian zhi qian shi jin sheng* (1989), and **Jacob Cheung's** *Cageman/Lung man/Long min* (1992). He has appeared in more than 200 films.

KUNG FU. *See* MARTIAL ARTS FILM.

KWAN, MAN-CHING (Moon Kwan, Guan Wenqing) (1896–). Director Kwan Man-ching was born in Guangdong province and followed his brother to the United States when very young. He graduated from the University of California and worked in Hollywood as an extra, actor, and cook, becoming the resident authority on Chinese customs and culture and advising D. W. Griffith on *Broken Blossoms*

(1919), starring Lillian Gish. In Hollywood, Kwan learned filmmaking, in 1921 returning to China and unsuccessfully attempting to start a production company. In 1923, he joined **Li Minwei's Minxin** (China Sun) as an acting coach and assisted on *Lipstick (Rouge)* (1925). In 1926, Kwan began directing in Guangzhou, and became known as a patriotic filmmaker in the 1930s, making anti-Japanese war movies.

The director's career spanned 43 years and more than 50 films, and he was a key figure at **Grandview**, having cofounded the company with **Joseph Sunn** in 1933 and setting up in Hong Kong in 1935. The company became one of Hong Kong's leading studios, known for its Cantonese productions, and Kwan influenced many filmmakers who worked there, including **Ng Cho-fan** and **Lee Tit**.

Kwan's better-known films include *Lifeline (Life)/Sang meng geng/Shengming xian* (1935), *New Life/San sang meng sin/Xin sheng ming xian* (1948), *Sorrows of a Neglected Wife/Laang laai duen cheung dut/Leng la duan chang hua* (1950), *Wealth Gone Like a Dream/Sap joi faan wa yat mung siu/Shi zai fan hua yi meng xiao* (1952), *The Crushed Flower/Chaan dut lui/Can hua lei* (1953), *Is Parents' Love Ever Rewarded?/Sim chin dik shui/Yanqian dishui* (1955), *Filial Piety/Haau diy/Xiaodao* (1956), *Poor Mother/Hoh lin dik lut lut/Ke lian de ma ma* (1961), and *To Catch a Cat/Cha lei chuk cho maau/Cha li zhuo cu mao* (1969). *Lifeline* was one of Kwan's Chinese national defense films, initially banned in Hong Kong because of British law (Britain had not yet taken sides), but the ban was lifted after Kwan brought court action explaining the film did not specifically mention which country had invaded China. The film also won an award from the Guangzhou Drama and Film Censorship Committee. The story concerns a young engineer (Ng Cho-fan) who is developing China's railway system for its defense and progress; he undergoes numerous hardships, including being put out of work because of economic depression, but overcomes difficulties to continue his work for the cause.

The Cantonese family melodrama *Is Parents' Love Ever Rewarded?* stars **Pak Suet-sin** and **Cheung Ying** as a married couple, she as a former singsong girl and he as a rich heir. They have a daughter but argue over his son from a previous marriage. She leaves home and lives miserably until the family is reunited after she saves the daughter from being raped.

KWAN, ROSAMUND CHI-LAM (1963–). Rosamund Kwan was born the daughter of noted leading man **Kwan Shan** and actress Cheung Bing-sai, who worked for **Great Wall**; Kwan made her screen debut alongside **Chow Yun-fat** in *The Head Hunter (Killer in Love, Long Goodbye)/Lip tau/Lie tou* (1982). During the early 1980s, Kwan was married to a businessman for a short time and entered the fashion world. Neither her marriage nor her fashion career lasted very long, however. After the breakup of her marriage, the self-proclaimed introvert went back to acting. She starred as one of the female leads in the **Samo Hung**–helmed *Twinkle Twinkle Lucky Stars* (1985) and in two **Jackie Chan** films, *Armor of God (Dragon Elder Brother, Tiger Younger Brother)/Lung hing foo dai/Long xiong hu di* and *Project A 2/A gai waak chuk/A ji hua xu ji* (both 1987). Starting in 1988, Kwan began to star in more and more films. Some of these were *Three against the World* (1988) with **Andy Lau**, Tony Au's *Profiles of Pleasure* (1988), *Casino Raiders/Chi juen miu seung/Zhi zun wu shang* (1989) also with Andy Lau, *Brief Encounter in Shinjuku/Choi joi san sau/Cu zai xin su* (1990), and *Inspector Pink Dragon/San taam ma yue long/Shen tan ma ru long* (1991).

It was not until 1991, however, in her role as Aunt Yee in **Tsui Hark's *Once upon a Time in China*** *(Wong Fei-hung)/Wong Fei-hung/Huang Feihong* (1991), that Kwan gained international notoriety when she acted alongside *wushu* great **Jet Li** along with an A-list cast of actors and martial artists in a film that led to a renaissance of the **kung fu** genre. Kwan would reprise this same role in *Once upon a Time in China 2 (Wong Fei-hung 2: A Man Should Be Self-Sufficient)/Wong Fei-hung ji yi naam yi dong ji keung/Huang Feihong zhi er nan er dang zi qiang* (1992), *Once upon a Time in China 3 (Wong Fei-hung 3: The Lion King Struggles for Supremacy)/Wong Fei-hung ji saam si wong jaang ba/Huang Feihong zhi san shi wang zheng ba* (1993), *Once upon a Time in China 5 (Wong Fei-hung 5: Dragon City's Murderous Tyrant)/Wong Fei-hung chi neung lung shing chim and/Huang Feihong zhi wu long cheng jian ba* (1994), and *Once upon a Time in China and America (Wong Fei-hung: West Territory Mighty Lion)/Wong Fei-hung chi sai wik hung shut/Huang Feihong zhi xi yu xiong shi* (1997).

During this same period Kwan starred in a plethora of other films including the **Stephen Chiau** zany comedy *Tricky Brains (Tricky Expert)/Jing goo juen ga/Zheng gu zhuan jia* (1991), **Tony Ching**

Siu-tung's *Swordsman 2* (1991), Samo Hung's *Blade of Fury/Yat do king shing/Yi dao qing cheng* (1993), *All's Well End's Well Too (Happy Event in the Flower Fields)/Fa tin hei si/Hua tian xi shi* (1993), *The Great Conqueror's Concubine/Sai choh ba wong/Xi chu ba wang* (1994) alongside **Gong Li**, and *The Scripture with No Words* (1996) with Jet Li. After the final installment of the *Once upon a Time in China* series, Kwan took a hiatus, only to return in 2001 in Feng Xiaogong's international *Big Shot's Funeral* alongside Donald Sutherland and Mainland actor Yao Ge. In 2002, Kwan returned to Hong Kong to make *The Wesley's Mysterious Story* and *Mighty Baby/Chuet sai hiu b/Jue shi hao b*.

KWAN, SHAN (Guan Shan) (1933–). Actor Kwan Shan came to Hong Kong following the outbreak of civil war and was hired by **Great Wall**; his title role as a naïve villager in the satirical melodrama ***The True Story of Ah Q***/*A Q Jing chuen/ A Q Zhengzhuan* (1958) won him the Best Actor award at the 12th Locarno Film Festival. Kwan became a dramatic leading man, especially playing vulnerable male romantic leads, from the late 1950s through the 1960s, and he made many films for **Shaw Brothers**, such as **Tao Qin's** *The Blue and the Black 2/L Laam yue hak/Lan yu hei, xia ji* (1966), a romantic epic of star-crossed lovers in two parts. Kwan Shan played the sensitive lover opposite **Linda Lin Dai**. Kwan and Lin played orphans brought up by foster families who oppose their union.

Kwan has appeared in more than 70 movies, moving into more mature parts as he grew older. He was cast as **Brigitte Lin's** father in **Tony Au's** *Dream Lovers/Mung chung yan/Meng zhong ren* (1986) and played the double-crossing partner of **Dean Shek** in **John Woo's** *A Better Tomorrow 2 (True Colors of a Hero 2)/Ying hung boon sik 2/Yingxiong bense 2* (1987). He is the father of actress **Rosamund Kwan**.

KWAN, STANLEY KAM-PANG (1957–). Born in Hong Kong, Stanley Kwan studied communications at Baptist College and worked at Hong Kong Television Broadcasts Limited (TVB), first as an actor and then in production. He started in film in 1979, working as assistant director to many significant directors, including **Ann Hui** (*The Spooky Bunch/Chong do jing/Chuang dao zheng* [1980], *The Story of*

Woo Viet/Woo Yuet dik goo si/Hu Yue de gu shi [1981], *Boat People/ Tau ban liu hoi/ Touben nuhai* [1982]), **Peter Yung**, **Ronny Yu** (*The Postman Strikes Back/Chun shing ma/Xun cheng ma* [1982]), **Patrick Tam** (*Nomad/Lit feng ching chun/Lie huo qing chun*, [1982]), **Leong Po-chih**, **Tony Au** (*The Last Affair/Dut shing/Hua cheng* [1983], *Dream Lovers/Mung chung yan/Meng zhong ren* [1986]), and **Yim Ho**. He also worked as assistant director to **Eric Tsang** on **Jackie Chan's** *Armor of God/Lung fong foo dai/Long xiong hu di* (1987), an Indiana Jones–type adventure shot in Yugoslavia. His directorial debut came with *Women/Lui yan sam/Nu ren xin* (1985), and in this, as in many other films, the director has addressed difficulties **women** experience while negotiating romantic love, personal freedom, and societal constraint. He has drawn comparison with Douglas Sirk's 1950 melodrama weepies. According to Kwan, he expresses the gay spirit in the form of heterosexual love, not necessarily eager to embrace gay issues. His collaboration with art director/editor **William Chang** (who also collaborates with **Wong Kar-wai**) on several films contributes to their distinctive aesthetics.

Rouge (Rouge Hook ["hook" means a Chinese knot or buckle]*)/Yin chi kau/Yan zhi* (1988), a doomed love story and ghost story starring **Anita Mui** and **Leslie Cheung**, puts Kwan's talent on display. Relying on few special effects, Kwan created an ethereal atmosphere through mood and atmosphere and direction of his actors and their strong performances, especially Mui as the ghost Fleur. Not only was the arty film commercially successful, it won Best Picture and Best Director at the **Hong Kong Film Awards** that year. *Centre Stage* (aka *Actress)/Yuen Ling-yuk/Ruan Lingyu* (1992) was critically acclaimed but not a commercial success (Jackie Chan produced). Based on the life of Chinese silent screen goddess **Ruan Lingyu**, the movie includes footage of her extant films, loving recreations of the same, outtakes and documentary footage, and on-screen interviews with Ruan's surviving contemporaries as well as the actors in the film, including **Maggie Cheung** and **Tony Leung Ka-fai**. The film not only pays homage to the woman generally regarded as China's greatest actress, but to the Hong Kong film industry and Hong Kong itself even as it examines the power of image making in film and media.

Kwan is also gay, and he is one of the few public figures in Hong Kong to acknowledge and embrace his sexual orientation; he discusses his sexual orientation with his mother in part of the **documentary** *Yang and Yin: Gender in Chinese Cinema* (1996), which dissects portrayals of male and female in 100 years of Chinese cinema, and explored a gay love story in *Lan Yu/Laam Yue/Lan Yu* (2001), the latter not well-received at the box office but receiving international critical recognition. *Lan Yu*, with a budget of only US$900,000, was nominated for 10 Taiwanese **Golden Horse Awards** and won three, including Best Director for Kwan and Actor for Liu Ye. Based on a mid-1990s anonymous Internet novel posted from the Mainland, the film tackled Chinese taboos, including gay relationships and the Tiananmen Square massacre. Kwan's latest film, *Everlasting Regret* (2005), starring Sammi Cheng, Leung Ka-fai, Hu Jun, and Daniel Wu, revisits old Shanghai and is based on a popular and much loved novel, *Chang Hen Ge/Love Hate Song*, about a 1930s–1940s Shanghai woman.

Besides feature films, he has produced independent and experimental films, including **Nelson Yu's** independent feature *Love Will Tear Us Apart* (1999), **Julian Lee's** *The Accident/Sam yuen yi ma/Xin yuan yi ma* (1999) and *Night Corridor/Yiu yau wooi long/Yao ye hui lang* (2003), and **Carol Lai's** *The Floating Landscape/Luen ji fung ging/Lian zhi feng jing* (2003). Kwan has also directed stage plays. *See also* GAY FILMS.

KWAN, TAK-HING (1906–1996). Born in Guangzhou, Kwan Tak-hing was a lifelong **martial arts** practitioner. He began his career as a **Cantonese opera** actor, well known for his portrayal of the red-faced General Kwan, his namesake. During the Sino–Japanese War, his troupe toured throughout Guangdong, Guansi, and Hunan provinces, entertaining Chinese soldiers with patriotic shows. In fact, the Japanese put a price on his head. Kwan even traveled to the United States to raise funds for the war effort in China. At war's end, Kwan moved to Hong Kong. His first acting role, however, was in a U.S. film, *Romance of the Songsters* (1934), and his Hong Kong film debut was in *Yesterday's Song*. He acted in over 130 films, but became synonymous with the real-life character **Wong Fei-hung**, whom he portrayed in 85 films between 1949 and 1979. The majority of the films were produced in the 1950s, with 25 of them being made in 1956 alone. He also appeared in a 13-episode Wong Fei-hung **television** series in Hong Kong. Kwan Tak-hing was also well known for his fine calligraphy, and an exhibition of his work was held in Hong Kong in the early 1960s.

Kwan portrayed Wong Fei-hung as an archetypal righteous and stern Confucian master and a Chinese nationalist. He emphasized the ethics of the martial arts in tandem with the physical prowess and health benefits, thus presenting the knightly values of Chinese ***wuxia*** highlighted in literature and legend, reifying values of the past in a Hong Kong dramatically changed since the 1950s. Kwan Tak-hing's Wong fights only when absolutely necessary; he protects the weak and oppressed; he reforms (rather than defeats) villains. He also participates in numerous local customs of the region, from lion dancing to calligraphy.

Similarities between the lives of Wong Fei-hung and Kwan Tak-hing led audiences to blur reality and illusion. Like Wong Fei-hung, Kwan Tak-hing was born in Guangdong province and was a martial arts practitioner. Wong specialized in the tiger crane style of *hung gar* and a fighting technique known as the "nine special fists"; Kwan originated the "omni-directional gangrou fist" and specialized in the white crane style. While Wong Fei-hung's school was on the Mainland, his last wife opened a martial arts school in Hong Kong, as did Wong Fei-hung's favorite student Lam Sai-wing. Kwan opened a martial arts school in Hong Kong and also practiced traditional Chinese medicine (as did Wong Fei-hung). In his later years, Kwan opened a chain of stores selling traditional Chinese health food, marketed under the name Po Chi Lam, taken from Wong Fei-hung's school and clinic. Both Wong Fei-hung and Kwan Tak-hing were expert lion dancers (and Kwan performed many lion dances in the Wong Fei-hung movies).

KWAN, TEDDY ROBIN (1948–). The diminutive actor, director, producer, and composer was born in Hong Kong and began performing at an early age. At 17 he formed a popular 1960s pop band called Teddy Robin and the Playboys (he called himself "Teddy" after teddy boy) for which he was lead singer and also performed on **television**. His film debut was **Shaw Brothers**' romance *The Price of Love/Oi ching dik doi ga/Ai qing de dai jia* (1970). He tried experimental filmmaking before leaving for Europe and Canada; he returned to Hong Kong in 1979, producing or executive producing films such as **Ann Hui's** *The Story of Woo Viet/Woo yuet dik goo si/Hu yue de gu* *shi* (1981) and **Clara Law's** *The Other Half and the Other Half/Ngoh oi taai hung yan/Wo ai tai kong ren* (1988), *The Reincarnation of Golden Lotus/Poon gam lin ji chin sai gam sang/Pan jinlian zhi qian shi jin sheng* (1989), and *Farewell, China/Oi joi bit heung dik gwai chit/Ai zai bie xiang de ji jie* (1990). He has also composed scores for more than 20 films, including *Aces Go Places 1* and *2/Chui gai pak dong/Zui jia pai dang* (1982), **Ringo Lam's** *City on Fire/Lung foo fung wan/Long hu feng yun* (1987), **Wong Kar-wai's** *As Tears Go By/Wong kok Ka Moon/Wang jiao Ka Men* (1988), and **Wai Ka-fai's** *Fantasia/Gwai ma kwong seung kuk/Gui ma kuang xiang qu* (2004). His edgy and jazzy score with saxophone for *City on Fire* is characteristic of his work, in synch with the tone and mood of the film.

Kwan has appeared in 20 movies, and is usually cast as a warm-hearted schemer, as in John Woo's *Run Tiger Run/Leung chek liu foo/Liang zhi lao hu* (1984, for which he also wrote and performed the theme song). He delivered an impressive performance in **Jacob Cheung's** *Cageman/Lung man/Long min* (1992). He has directed four movies, including *The Legend of Wisely/Wai shut lee chuen kei/Wei si li chuan ji* (1987), starring **Sam Hui**.

KWOK, AARON FU-SING (1965–). Born in Hong Kong, pop star singer and actor Aaron Kwok studied dancing and acting at Hong Kong Television Broadcasts Limited (TVB) and became a TVB contract player, starting as a backup dancer on TVB shows and acting in **melodramas** and **swordplay** series. He came to public attention for a Taiwanese motorcycle commercial that paid tribute to **Chow Yun-fat's** chocolate-loving character in *God of Gamblers/Do san/Du shen* (1989). He nurtured a singing career, becoming one of the "Four Sky Kings of **Cantopop**" (along with **Jacky Cheung**, **Andy Lau**, and **Leon Lai**).

Kwok's film debut was in *The Big Heat/Shing dak ging/Cheng te jing* (1988), but his breakthrough movie was **Johnnie To's** *The Barefoot(ed) Kid/Chek geuk siu ji/Chi jiao xiao zi* (1993), alongside veteran **Ti Lung**. Other notable performances include the brooding, vengeful Striding Cloud in **Andrew Lau's** *Storm Riders/Fung wan hung ba tin ha/Feng yun xiong ba tian xia* (1998), the novice cop in **Stanley Tong's** *China Strike Force/Lui ting chin ging/Lei ting zhan jing* (2000), the beleaguered computer expert in **Gordon Chan's** *2000 A.D./Gung yuen 2000 A.D./Gong yuan 2000 A.D.* (2000), and a selfish DJ in the romantic comedy *And I Hate You So/Siu chan chan/Xiao qin qin* (2000).

KWOK, AMY OI-MING (1967–). Actress Amy Kwok earned a degree in engineering at California State University; in 1991, she was chosen Miss Hong Kong. She appeared in more than 10 **television** series. Her film debut was in **Leung Po-chi's** *The Island/Sang sei sin/Sheng si xian* (1985), and she has appeared in a half dozen films. She stood out in **Ringo Lam's** *The Victim/Muk lau hung gwong/Mu lo xiong guang* (1999) as a distraught wife, opposite **Sean Lau Ching-wan**, whom she later married.

KWOK, PHILIP CHUN-FUNG (1951–). Ethnic Taiwanese actor and **martial arts action** director Philip Kwok studied at a **Peking (Beijing) opera** school and has acted in more than 50 movies and has also action directed more than 50. His film debut was **Chang Cheh's** *Marco Polo/Ma goh boh law/Ma ge bo luo* (1975), and he acted in many martial arts films, including Chang's *Five (Deadly) Venoms/Ng Duk/Wu du* (1978), in which he played "The Lizard," and he is a phenomenal martial artist on-screen. He is well known for his role as Mad Dog, a villain with a sense of justice, in **John Woo's** *Hard-Boiled/kwong sau san taam/Lashou shentan* (1992, for which he was also action director, orchestrating operatic violence on-screen). Other notable action direction includes Woo's *Once a Thief/Jung wang sei hoi/Zong heng si hai* (1991), **Ronny Yu's** *Bride with White Hair/Baak faat moh nui /Bai fa mo nu chuan* (1993), and **Jeff Lau's** *Treasure Hunt/Dut kei siu lam/Hua qi shaolin* (1994). Kwok also choreographed **Michelle Yeoh**'s action scenes in the James Bond film *Tomorrow Never Dies* (1997, in which he also played General Chang), and in the Yeoh vehicle *The Touch/Tin mak cheun kei/Tian mai chuan ji* (2002) as well as the French-Canadian production *Brotherhood of the Wolf (Pacte des loups*, 2001).

– L –

LAI, CAROL MIU-SUET (1966–). A native of Hong Kong, Carol Lai is one of a new generation of young filmmakers fluent in the language of world cinema. Her early background was in marketing, although at one point she also taught at a school for "problem" children, giving her firsthand experience with the disaffected youth of modern Hong Kong. In 1989, she began to work in the local film industry in a variety of roles, including assistant director and screenwriter. From 1993 to 2000, she handled on-air promotion as a producer at Star TV, one of the largest cable and satellite **television** companies in the world. During this period, Lai began to branch out into independent filmmaking, producing *After the Crescent/Yuet mei liu/Yue wei lao* (1997) for Bryan Chang Wai-hung and directing a short film, *Father's Toys*, which was well received.

Her first feature film, *Glass Tears/Boh lee siu lui/Boli shaonu* (2001), which she wrote and directed, is also notable for the last onscreen appearance of veteran Hong Kong actor **Lo Lieh**. Lo, who was lured out of retirement to play the aging cop searching for a runaway granddaughter, anchors the film with a rueful melancholy. *Glass Tears*, which was nominated for a Camera d'Or award at the Cannes Film Festival in 2001, was edited by fellow hotshot filmmaker **Danny Pang**, but the film remains a highly personal and heartfelt exploration of adolescent angst. Lai's second feature, *Floating Landscape/Luen ji fung ging/Lian ai feng jing* (2003), was produced by **Stanley Kwan** and filmed in Qingdao, China, with a cast consisting of both Hong Kong (**Ekin Cheng**, **Karena Lam**) and Chinese (Liu Ye) actors. The film earned a Best New Director nomination at the 2004 **Hong Kong Film Awards**, marking Carol Lai as a rising star of the new generation.

LAI, GIGI CHI (1971–). Born in Hong Kong, actress Gigi Lai is the granddaughter of film pioneer Lai Man-wai, who founded the first Hong Kong film studio, Chinese American Film, in 1913; wrote *Zhuangzi Tests His Wife/Chong Ji shut chai/Zhuangzi shiqi*; and appeared in the female role. In the mid-1980s, she appeared in small roles and **television** series and began a singing career in 1992. She has acted in 40 films, and her most recognizable role is as the character Smartie, the love interest of gang leader Nam (**Ekin Cheng**), in the Triad-boyz *Young and Dangerous/Goo wak jai ji yan joi gong woo/Gu huo zai zhi ren zai jianghu* series (1996–2000). She also had a dramatic role in the bittersweet comedy/drama *Okinawa(n) Rendezvous/Luen chin chung sing/Lian zhan chong sheng* (2000).

LAI, KELLY CHEN (Lei Zhan) (1933–). A native of Pudong province, actor Lai Chen was born in Shanghai and brought up by his maternal grandmother when his parents died. He joined **Motion Pictures and General Investment** in 1955, and his film debut was in **Yue Feng's** drama *Green Hills and Jade Valleys/Ching saan chui guk/Qingshan cuigu* (1956). With Yue Feng's historical drama *Golden Lotus/Gam lin dut/ Jin lianhua* (1957, opposite **Lin Dai**) and **Tao Qin's** romance *Little Darling/Siu ching yan/ Xiao qingren* (1958) he became a Cathay star, associated with gentle, vulnerable, and sensitive characterizations, whether in dramas, comedies, or musicals.

In **Evan Yang's** comedy *Our Dream Car/Heung che mei yan/ Xiang che mei ren* (1959), Lai costarred with **Ge Lan** as a newlywed couple who reach beyond their means to buy a car from the wife's former boyfriend. In **Chung Kai-man's** tender drama *The Education of Love/Oi dik gaau yuk/Ai de jiao yu* (1961), he played the tireless doctor and fiancé of **Lin Cui**, who is torn between remaining in Hong Kong and teaching, and leaving for the West for her future husband's educational job opportunities. And in **Wang Tianlin's** drama ***Father Takes a Bride***/*Siu ngai lui/Xiao er nu* (1963), he played the patient boyfriend of a grown daughter (**You Min**) whose widowed father (**Wang Yin**) decides to remarry.

Lai's sister was actress **Le Di** (Betty Loh Ti), and with her and director Yuan Qiufeng, they founded the Golden Eagle Film Company, which produced ***wuxia*** films, among them *The Vagabond Swordsman* (1968). He retired from the screen in 1971 and managed his own film laboratory for more than 20 years. He made an appearance as **Maggie Cheung's** boss in **Wong Kar-wai's** award-winning Hong Kong 1960s Shanghainese community love letter *In the Mood for Love/Fa yeung nin wa/Hua yang nian hua* (2000).

LAI, LEON MING (1961–). Born in Beijing, actor-singer Leon Lai is one of the Four Heavenly Kings of **Cantopop**. He came to Hong Kong in 1983, and like others before him, entered a new talent contest (he was second runner-up). He joined the Hong Kong Television Broadcasts Limited (TVB) actors' program and began working in **television** as he developed his music career. Memorable performances include his roles in **Tsui Hark's** *Wicked City/(Monster City)/Yiu sau do si/Yao shou du shi* (1992) as a half human-half mutant raptor, as a troubled son in **Jeff Lau's** *Love and the City/Diy shut ching* *yuen/Dou shi qing yuan* (1994), as a lonely hit man in **Wong Kar-wai's** *Fallen Angels/Doh lok tin si/Duoluo tianshi* (1995), and as a fish out of water Mainlander newly arrived in Hong Kong in **Peter Chan's** *Comrades, Almost a Love Story (Honeysweet)/Tim mat mat/Tian mi mi* (1996). His characterizations have ranged from cool and aloof to sensitive and needy. Lai's boy next door good looks and stature (six feet) have won him rabid fans and a fan club to which he pays attention; just as **Leslie Cheung's** fans developed a rivalry with those of **Alan Tam**, so Lai's challenge **Andy Lau's**.

LAM, CHING-YING (1952–1997). Actor and **martial arts** director Lam Ching-ying was born in Hong Kong and entered acting classes, specifically studying **Chinese opera**, at an early age at Madame Fan Fok-fa's opera school; one of his classmates was actor John Lone (lead in Bernardo Bertolucci's *The Last Emperor*). At 17, he was a stuntman and stunt double (with a lithe frame, he doubled for many female stars at **Shaw Brothers**) and, at 19, a martial arts director in movies when he moved to **Golden Harvest**, the latter debut being as co-martial arts director with Han Yingie in **Bruce Lee's** *The Big Boss* (1971). Lam worked on all of Lee's films with the exception of *The Way of the Dragon*. During the 1970s, Lam worked on numerous martial arts action movies.

Lam became a member of **Samo Hung's** martial arts team and was his chief collaborator behind the camera during the 1980s; in *Prodigal Son/Bai ga jai/Baijia zi* (1981), he also established the characterization of the considerate, calm master. He was also famous as an actor for a series of **vampire movies**, in which he played a wise and capable Taoist priest, and which reinvigorated the genre, with movies like *Mr. Vampire/Geung shi sin sang/ Jiangshi xiansheng* (1985). Among his dramatic roles are a sympathetic anachronistic Chinese opera performer in **Alex Law's** *Painted Faces/Chat siu fuk/Qi xiao fu* (1988) and a deaf mute hit man in **Jacob Cheung's** *Lover's Tears/Sai bat mong ching/Shi bu wang ching* (1992). He directed *Vampire vs. Vampire/Yat mei diy yan/Yi mei dao ren* (1989) and directed and produced *The Green Hornet/Ching fung hap/Qing feng xia* (1994), acting in both. In the mid-1990s, he reprised his Taoist priest role in a **television** series. Lam acted in over 100 films and was action director in over 30. He died prematurely of liver cancer.

LAM, GEORGE CHI-CHEUNG (1947–). Born in Hong Kong, George Lam was a popular singer and actor in the 1980s–1990s. He began as cohost of a children's **television** show with **Alan Tam** and **Carol Cheng**. He is married to singer/actress **Sally Yeh**. He has appeared in more than 30 films and sang a popular version of the **Wong Fei-hung** movie theme song. Outstanding performances include the Japanese reporter living in Vietnam during the war in **Ann Hui's** *Boat People (Escaping Anger through the Sea)/Tau ban no hoi/Touben nuhai* (1982) and the conflicted closeted 40-year-old gay in **Shu Kei's** *A Queer Story/Gei liu 40/Ji lao 40 (Gay Man at 40)* (1996).

LAM, KA-SING (Lin Jiasheng) (1933–). Cantonese opera actor Lam Ka-sing (real name Lin Manchun) was born in Guangdong province, graduated from primary school, and attended the Lanfang Cantonese Opera Training School and the Meigui Music Institute. His teachers included Dengxiao Lanfang, Huang Zhiyun, Li Hairong, and Wang Yuesheng, with the latter two giving him a sound basis in opera music. He also trained in martial arts with Yaun Xiaotian (who became a **kung fu** actor) and Guo Hongbin. In 1945, Lam began performing professionally and four years later was accepted by Cantonese opera actor **Sit Kok-sin** as his last student. In 1956, Lam founded the Yuesheng Opera Troupe, honoring his master, named after him and performing his most famous plays. Over the next 20 years, the actor performed opera widely, in Hong Kong and overseas, and founded three opera companies, one of which was Songxinsheng, one of the most famous and long lasting. He also had a large fan following.

The actor's film debut was director/writer Hung Chung-ho's Cantonese opera *An Orphan Raised on Love (Prostituting to Raise the Orphan)/Maai yuk yeung goo ngai/Mai rou yang gu er* (1947). His first lead role was in Cheung Wai-gwong's *Why Not Return?/Woo bat gwai/Hu bugai* (1958). The original script, by Feng Zhifen, is considered by many to be the most complete of Cantonese operas, and was often adapted to film. Here, Lam played the son torn between his mother (a cross-dressed **Poon Yat On**) and his wife (**Fong Yim-fan**). When he goes off to war, the situation escalates between mother-in-law and daughter-in-law, leading to suffering before resolution. Lam often collaborated with director **Wong Hok-sing**. Lam's famous opera works adapted for film include Wong's historical dramas *Battling*

Sounds/Lui ming gam goo chin fung sing/Lei ming jin gu zhan jia sheng (1963) and *The Pitiless Sword/Miu ching bo kim yau ching tin/Wu qing bao jian you qing tian* (1964), and his Cantonese opera *Uproar in Jade Hall/Ching hap laau suen gung/Qing xia nao xuan gong* (1967).

Lam also appeared in contemporary films, such as **Chun Kim's** ***Parents' Hearts****/Foo miu sam/ Fumu Xin* (1955) and **Lee Tit's** *Everlasting Love (**Eternal Love**)/Tin cheung dei gau/Tianchang dijiu* (1955). In the former, he played the elder son of an opera performer (**Ma Sze-tsang**) who falls on hard times and becomes a street performer; the son works to support himself through school while his younger brother is forced into an opera troupe as an apprentice. His last film was Wong's opera *Li Shishi/Lee Bye Bye/Li Shishi* (1967).

In 1981, Great Britain's queen honored Lam for his contributions to Cantonese opera and film. He is married to opera performer Hong Douzi. *See also* CHINESE OPERA FILMS.

LAM, PATRICIA FUNG (Lin Feng) (1940–1976). Actress Lam Fung (real names Feng Shuyan and Feng Jiting), a native of Guangdong province, was educated at the Precious Blood Girls' School. In 1956, she began training at **Shaw Brothers**, and made her debut in **Zhou Shilu's** musical myth *The Fairy's Sleeves/Sin chow kei yuen/Xian xiu qi yuan* (1957), followed by the director's teenage drama *A Pretty Girl's Love Affair/Yuk lui chun ching/Yu nu chun qing* (1958) and realist *A Virtuous Girl from a Poor Family (from a Humble House)/ Fung moon suk lui/Peng men shu nu* (1958). In all three films, she was the damsel in distress; in the first as a famed courtesan coveted by a prime minister's son; in the second as a teen who foolishly involves herself with a teddy boy and is almost traded as a taxi dancer; and in the third as a cotton mill worker who gives in to vanity and is raped and abandoned by the manager of the factory, who attempts to pimp her to a wealthy client.

Lam made more than 30 films at Shaw, including Zhou's Cantonese thriller *A Sweet Girl in Terror/Yuk lui geng wan/Yu nu jing hun* (1958) and Mandarin comedy *When the Poles Meet/Naam bak yan yuen/Nan bei yin yuan* (costarring **Chen Ho**), and Ng Dan's debut Cantonese musical romance *A Fragrance of Durians (When Durians Bloom)/Lau lin piu heung/Liulian piaoxiang* (1959). In the latter, set in Singapore, Lam played a Malay worker who marries the son overseeing a rubber plant business for his father; his envious uncle conspires against them, with the son being sent home and the wife and daughter suffering until the couple reunite eight years later. The film was shot in Singapore and Malaysia. The theme song used the film's title and became a popular tune.

The actress's 10-year career included over 100 films, and she was immensely popular; her 1960s fan club had 30,000 members, and for nine years running she was on the chart of the 10 most popular stars, sponsored by the *Wah Kiu Daily* paper. Other films include Mok Hong-si's *A Wealthy Family/Daai foo ji ga/Da fu zhi jia* (1963), in which she played twins, of very different temperaments, whose identities are mistaken; **Ng Cho-fan** and Cheung Ying played their potential suitors, the former an unfaithful husband and the latter a playboy. In Lo Yu-kei's comedy *Queen of the Marketplace (Market Queen)/Gaai shut wong hau/Jie shi huang hou* (1964), which was based on a radio play, she starred as the title character, a vegetable hawker and community activist whose caring has earned her the title name. She is pursued by both a *shaoye* (rich young master) and his father, in a social realist comedy that brings together the poor and the rich for a common cause.

Lam retired after completing the Cantonese drama *The Full Moon/Yuet heung kwong fong yuen/Yue xiang na fang yuan* (1967) and marrying; she committed suicide nine years later.

LAM, RINGO LING-TUNG (1955–). Born in Hong Kong, director Ringo Lam joined Hong Kong Television Broadcasts Limited's (TVB) training program in 1973. He began in the industry as an actor, but decided acting was not his forte and he would rather be behind the camera. He worked as an assistant producer and producer of serials for five years at Commercial Television (CTV). He immigrated to Canada in 1978 and attended York University in Toronto to study film, returned to Hong Kong in 1981, and directed the ghost comedy *Esprit D'Amour (Dark and Light Are Wrong for Each Other)/Yam yeung cho/Yin yang cuo* (1983, starring **Alan Tam**) for **Karl Maka** at **Cinema City**. After several comedies, Maka gave him the chance to make whatever kind of film he wanted, and Lam's breakthrough film was *City on Fire* (1987), starring **Chow Yun-fat**

and **Danny Lee**, the first of a *Fire* trilogy (including *Prison on Fire* and *School on Fire*). These films are character-driven stories of gritty realism, based on 1980s and 1990s social issues involving street violence and police abuse, dismal prison conditions, and authoritative and outdated school systems. Unlike most Hong Kong directors, Lam has made a habit of selecting the English titles for his films.

City on Fire (Dragon Tiger Turbulence)/Lung foo fung wan/Long hu feng yun starred Chow Yun-fat as an undercover cop and Danny Lee as a career criminal, a reversal of the roles they usually played (Chow had already made *A Better Tomorrow*, and Lee was known for playing cops in many films). Based on newspaper stories Lam had read about a jewelry store robbery and extensive interviews he carried on with cops and criminals, the movie has the ring of authenticity. Jazzy, driving saxophone riffs and the raspy voice of **Maria Cordero** belting out the theme song contributed to Lam showing the hard life endured not only by the so-called criminals but by the cop used by the system. (Director Quentin Tarantino took the plot from *City on Fire* for his breakthrough *Reservoir Dogs*.) With *Prison on Fire (Prison Turbulence)/Gaam yuk fung wan/Jian yu feng yun* (also starring Chow), Lam conveyed real-life prison experience (**Nam Yin** wrote scripts for *Prison 1* and *2* films). **Leung Ka-fai** costarred as the innocent Chow takes under his wing, and **Roy Cheung** played the abusive prison guard (Cheung also appeared in *City on Fire* as a tyrannical police officer and a sadistic Triad in *School on Fire*, and Leung would reappear in Lam's *The Victim*). With *School on Fire (School Turbulence)/Hok gaau fung wan/Xiao jiao feng yun*, Lam asks why youth behave as they do, and the answers aren't easy; he found himself the victim of **censorship** because of the disturbing psychological needs of the students he unearthed, the neglect of the society, and the resulting violence and destruction. *School on Fire* was banned across Asia; after 40 cuts, the movie played in Taiwan with a half hour running time.

Lam has made a practice of collaborating with actors on several films, including **Simon Yam** in *Full Contact (Chivalrous Thief Ko Fei)/Haap dou Ko Fei/Xia dao Gao Fei* (1992) and *Full Alert (High Level Prevention)/Go do gaai bei/Gao du jie bei* (1997), and more recently with **Lau Ching-wan** in *Full Alert* and *The Victim/Muk lau* *hung gwong/Mu lo xiong guang* (1999). Only Lam could imagine casting Chow Yun-fat as a biker with a buzz cut in *Full Contact* (1992). Lam also codirected *Twin Dragons (Twin Dragons Meet)/ Seung lung wooi/Shuang long hui* (1992, with **Tsui Hark**), appearing briefly, along with many other directors, to benefit the **Hong Kong Directors' Guild**. The movie starred **Jackie Chan** in the role of twins.

Lam, like **John Woo** and Tsui Hark, agreed to direct a Jean-Claude Van Damme vehicle. *Maximum Risk* (1996) was the first of several, including *The Replicant*, *The Savage*, and *After Death*, to date.

LAM, SUET. Character and supporting actor Lam Suet has appeared in close to 100 films since 1991; actor/action director **Lam Ching-ying** introduced him into the film industry. He has worked most often with director **Johnnie To** and **Milkyway Image** productions, such as *The Odd One Dies (Only One between the Two Can Live)/Leung goh ji nang woot yat goh/Liang ge zhi neng huo yi ge* (1997), *Lifeline (Extremely Urgent, Ten Thousand Fire Urgent)/Sap maan feng gap/Shi wan huo ji* (1997), *The Longest Nite/Aau dut/An hua* (1998), *The Mission (Gunfire)/Cheong feng/Qiang ho* (1999), *Running out of Time 2 (Hidden War 2)/Aau chin 2/Anzhan 2* (2001), and *PTU* (2003), among others, and is chameleonlike in his characterizations. He recently appeared in **Stephen Chiau's** *Kung Fu Hustle/Gung foo/Gong fu* (2004) as an axe gang leader.

LAST HURRAH FOR CHIVALRY. Literally "Chivalrous Knight," **John Woo's** ***wuxia pian*** *Last Hurrah for Chivalry/Ho hap/Hao xia* (1979), produced by **Raymond Chow**, is much like **Chang Cheh's** *Blood Brothers/Chi ma/Ci ma* (1973), telling the tale of a group of three male compatriots, one of whom betrays the other two for power, and in that sense is a precursor to Woo's later works ***A Better Tomorrow*** and *A Bullet in the Head.*

The complexity of the plot is characteristic of the genre. Kao Pun (Lau Kong), after having his wedding crashed by his family's sworn enemy, Pak Chun-tong (Lee Hoi-san), and nearly being killed, recuperates at his **martial arts** teacher's cabin and seeks revenge. His teacher refuses to give him his sword, wary of Kao's ambition. To get Chang (Wei Pai), a great fighter, on his side, Kao buys medicine for

Chang's mother, making him feel indebted to Kao. Kao hires assassin Green (**Damian Lau**) to assist Chang. Chang and Green become fast friends. Kao also hires Pray (**Fung Hak-on**), a swordsman looking to build his reputation, to kill his master and give him his master's sword. Pray does not succeed and is later killed when he challenges Chang. Kao does take advantage of his master's wounds to kill him himself and take the sword.

After Green and Chang kill Pak, Green reveals that Kao has paid him to kill Chang as well. Green cannot do it, and he and Chang unite to face Kao, who now has superpowers thanks to his master's sword. Green sacrifices himself to save Chang and take out Kao. Woo has remarked that the character of Green is the same character, Mark Gor, that **Chow Yun-fat** played to much acclaim in *A Better Tomorrow*. Many of the shots that Woo uses in this film also foreshadow what would develop into the director's signature style.

LAU, ANDREW WAI-KEUNG (1960–). Born in Hong Kong, Andrew Lau started in the film industry in 1980, working first as a camera grip and as a cinematographer beginning in 1985, including on *As Tears Go By (Mongkok Carmen, Carmen of the Streets)/Wong kok Ka Moon Wang jiao Ka Men*, *City on Fire/Lung foo fung wan/Long hu feng yun*, *Gunmen/Tin law dei mong/Tian luo di wang*, *He Ain't Heavy, He's My Father!/San naam hing naan dai/Xin nan xiong nan di*, and *Chungking Express (Chungking Forest)/Chung Hing sam lam/Zong qing sen lin* (along with **Chris Doyle** for the latter), and learning from directors **Wong Kar-wai**, **Ringo Lam**, **Kirk Wong**, and **Peter Chan**, among others. Lau has had a nose for the way the wind blows. He began directing in 1990, forming the **BOB & Partners** production company to make *Young and Dangerous (Young Rascals)/Goo wak jai ji yan joi gong woo/Gu huo zi zhi ren zai jiang hu* series (1996–2000) and *The Storm Riders (Wind Cloud: Heroic Tyrant Heaven Earth)/Fung wan hung ba tin ha/Feng yun xiong ba tian xia* (1998). Both set new directions for Hong Kong filmmakers. The former recycled old stories with an obsession for the new, based on a Hong Kong comic book and featuring speedy, handheld camerawork and stylish young gang members ("rascals") doing business. **Ekin Cheng** and **Jordan Chan** stood out, and Cheng sang the theme songs. The latter, a **martial arts** fantasy that pushed Hong Kong postproduction work to new heights with computer-generated special effects (courtesy of **Centro Digital Pictures**), set a new all-time local opening day for box office receipts.

In 2000, Lau became head of production for the Teamwork production company, and started his own studio, Base Productions, in 2002. He has paired with Alan Mak to codirect the three-part *Infernal Affairs/Mou gaan dou/Wu jian dao*, the romantic comedy *Cat and Mouse/Low sue oi seung mau/Lou shue ai shang mau*, and the street-racing picture *Initial D/Tau man chi D/Tou wen zi D*. *Infernal Affairs* beat both *Harry Potter and the Chamber of Secrets* and Zhang Yimou's martial arts themed *Hero* at the Hong Kong box office (prior to 1997, Hong Kongers preferred local fare over Hollywood product). Featuring a talented ensemble cast (**Anthony Wong**, **Eric Tsang**, **Andy Lau**, **Tony Leung Ka-fai**, **Edison Chen**, and **Shawn Yue**) and strong story of the intertwined lives of cop and Triad moles, the trilogy hones character with action. The film won six awards at Taiwan's 40th **Golden Horse Awards** and seven awards at the 22nd **Hong Kong Film Awards** (Best Film, Director, Actor, Supporting Actor, Editing, and Song). Miramax has secured distribution rights in North America and Warner Brothers has purchased remake rights.

LAU, ANDY TAK-WAH (1961–). Born in the poor village of Taipo in Hong Kong's New Territories in 1961, actor and singer Andy Lau was one of six children determined to succeed. His father was a fireman and wanted him to be a doctor, but Lau, banking on his good looks (he is known for an aquiline nose), enrolled in Hong Kong Television Broadcasts Limited's (TVB) artists' training program at 18, learning acting, singing, writing, and fighting. Following, he signed a contract with TVB, appearing on its **television** shows in mostly minor roles for several years, but after a contract dispute, he was kept under contract for a year without working for the studio and ended up singing in a piano bar.

Lau's breakthrough film was **Ann Hui's** *Boat People* (1982); he has made 115 films to date, and because of his output he is recognized as the hardest working actor in Hong Kong. In 1991 alone, Lau averaged a movie a month, at one time shooting four films at different locations and sleeping in his car. Lau is also known as one of the Four Heavenly Kings of **Cantopop**. Although he recorded his first album in 1985, it was with his fifth release, *Would It Be Possible?* (1990), that he first became popular as a singer. The recording went multiplatinum, and Lau has released more than 60 platinum recordings to date and holds countless music awards. In the early 1990s, Lau formed his own production company, Teamwork, and his own recording company. Lau was the first Asian singer to sign a contract with Pepsi, and also the first Hong Kong star to open a private museum, Andy Lau's Showcase, in 1995, with all proceeds going to charity.

Lau has worked with some of Hong Kong's outstanding directors, including **Eddie Fong**, **Ringo Lam**, **Tsui Hark**, **Derek Yee**, and **Ronny Yu**. He has repeatedly worked with some of them, including **Benny Chan**, **Gordon Chan**, Samson Chiu, Ann Hui, **Samo Hung**, David Lai, **Andrew Lau**, **Lau Kar-leung**, **Johnnie To**, **Eric Tsang**, Taylor Wong, **Herman Yau**, and **Corey Yuen**. He has appeared in 25 **Wong Jing** productions, Hong Kong's most commercial director and producer.

In *Boat People (Escaping Anger through the Sea)/Tauben nuhai/Tou ben nu hai* Lau costarred as a sympathetic political victim, and his performance got attention. Wong Kar-wai cast him as the costar (with **Jacky Cheung**) in his Hong Kong version of Martin Scorsese's *Mean Streets*, *As Tears Go By (Mongkok Carmen, Carmen of the Streets)/Wong kok Ka Moon/Wang jiao Ka Men* (1988), and Lau played a small time Triad torn between responsibility for his trouble-making "little brother" and wanting to get out of the gangster life for the sake of his love for a cousin (**Maggie Cheung**). Wong chose him again, as the moody cop Tide in *Days of Being Wild (The True Story of Ah Fei)/ Ah Fei ching chuen/A Fei zhengzhuan* (1990). He costarred with **Chow Yun-fat** in Wong Jing's *God of Gamblers/Do san/Du shen* (1989), the movie that began a new **gambling** craze in the early 1990s. Benny Chan's *A Moment of Romance (If Heaven Has Love)/Tin yeuk yau ching/Tian ruo you qing* (1990) was a defining moment for Lau, and in this movie he established his character as the scarred loner gangster with romantic flair. In Johnnie To's *Running Out of Time (Hidden War)/Aau chin/Anzhan* (1999), Lau starred as a dying jewel thief set against a determined cop, and the mind games that play out between the two created a new action subgenre. Lau won the Best Actor Award at the 2000 **Hong Kong Film Awards** for his performance. For To's romantic comedy *Love on a Diet/Sau geun laam lui/Shou juan nan nu* (2001), Lau donned a fat suit.

With Andrew Lau's *Infernal Affairs/Mou gaan dou/Wu jian dao* (2002) and *Infernal Affairs 3/Mou gaan dou chung gik miu gaan/Wu jian dao zhong ji wu jian* (2003), Lau costarred in two of the three films in the trilogy as a Triad mole in the Internal Affairs Department of the Hong Kong Police. He plays a conflicted character who wants to be the good guy. The character-driven trilogy received much attention in Hong Kong, seen as reviving a suffering industry and pointing in a new direction for Hong Kong movies. Johnnie To punned on his previous English title *Running Out of Time* with *Running on Karma/Daai chek liu/Da zhi lao* (2003), starring Lau as a former monk and current bodybuilder/male stripper. Lau donned an Arnold Schwarzenegger-like body suit for the part and won Best Actor from the 10th **Hong Kong Film Critics' Association** Awards and Best Actor at the 23rd Hong Kong Film Awards for his portrayal.

A versatile actor who has played in every genre, from horseback riding in Samo Hung's *Moon Warriors Warriors (Legend of the War Gods)/Chin san chuen suet/Zhan shen chuan shui* (1992, costarring **Anita Mui**) and motorcycle racing in Derek Yee's *Full Throttle (Flaming Chariot)/Lit foh jin che/Lieho zhanche* (1995), to costume swordplay in Andrew Lau's *The Duel/Kuet chin chi gan ji din/Jue zhan zi jin zhi dian* (2000) and **Zhang Yimou's** *House of Flying Daggers/Shimian maifu* (2004), to Herman Yau's luxury liner–island set romance *Fascination Amour/Oi ching mung waan ho /Ai qing meng huan hao* (1999), Lau has done it all, from various grueling action genres to love stories and comedies. He has also participated in a number of groundbreaking movies that have established new trends in Hong Kong cinema. A recent survey conducted by Beijing's *China Labor Daily* newspaper reported that elementary school children in China know more about Andy Lau than about Mao Zedong.

LAU, CARINA KA-LING (1965–). Actress Carina Lau came to Hong Kong as a teenager and graduated from Kiangsu College. She joined Hong Kong Television Broadcasts Limited (TVB) in 1983 and appeared in numerous **television** dramas, often alongside boyfriend **Tony Leung Chiu-wai** (with whom she has appeared in some films as well). In *The Duke of Mount Deer*, she played one of many wives to Leung's scholar Wai Siu-bo. Her film debut was *Naughty Boys/ Lau gai chap paai gwan/Niu ji za pai jun* (1986), but her breakthrough performance was in **Wong Kar-wai's** *Days of Being Wild (The True Story of Ah Fei)/Ah Fei ching chuen/A Fei zhengzhuan* (1990), in which she played a lovesick and wounded club girl. She also appeared in several **Jackie Chan action** movies, namely *Armor of God/Lung hing foo dai /Long xiong hu di* and *Project A 2/A gai waak chuk/A ji haa xu ji* (both 1987).

Lau has been nominated numerous times as Best Actress at the **Hong Kong Film Awards** for her performances, especially in dramatic roles, in which she communicates a womanliness and sexuality that heats up the screen, but she is equally strong in establishing believable relationships with **women**. In **Stanley Kwan's** *Centre Stage (Actress)/Yuen Ling-yuk/Ruan Lingyu* (1992), for example, her portrayal of Li Lili opposite **Maggie Cheung's Ruan Lingyu** was totally convincing; in **Jacob Cheung's** *Intimates (Self-Combed)/ Ji soh/Zi shu* (1997), she played a mistress and future wife of a factory owner who falls in love with a "self-combed" woman, Chinese working women who pledge to remain virgins and live together in solidarity. The lesbian love story is unusual for Hong Kong film, and Lau's sensitive performance opposite Charlie Yeung was strong.

Lau fares equally well in comedy, especially comedy in which there is some depth, such as Peter Chan's 1993 *He Ain't Heavy, He's My Father (New Two of a Kind)/San naam hing naan dai/Xin nan xiong nan di* (1993), ***He's a Woman, She's a Man*** *(Golden Branch, Jade Leaf)/Gam chi yuk yip/Jin qi yu ye* (1994), and *Who's the Woman, Who's the Man? (Golden Branch, Jade Leaf 2)/Gam chi yuk sip 2/Jin qi yu ye 2* (1996). Recently, she has returned to television in the 64-episode *Showbiz Tycoon*, a look inside the Hong Kong film industry from the 1960s to the millennium.

LAU, HARK-SUEN (Liu Kexuan) (1910–1983). Actor and director Lau Hark-suen, a native of Guangxi province, graduated from Guangxi Provincial Middle School and was among the first group trained by the Opera Actors Training Class of the Chinese Artists' Association of Guangzhou. He performed with several opera troupes, including director **Ma Sze-tsang's** Taiping **Cantonese Opera** Troupe, and he was particularly skilled in singing *Maqiang*, the singing style named after Ma. Lau also served as instructor of the Lidu Cantonese Opera Institute in Hong Kong.

Lau's screen debut was in *Sorrow of the Chinese Redbud (Mourning of the Chaste Tree Flower)/Yap ging dut/Qi jing hua* (1935). His first starring role was in *Hearts and Ways* (1936). Liu's career spanned close to 50 years and he acted in more than 500 films, in many of which he was stereotyped as a malicious and crafty villain. Features include *Madame Li (Wanton Woman)/Lai foo yan/Li fu ren* (1936), **Hong Shuyun's** *A Girl Named Liang Lengyan/Leung laang yim/Liang leng yan* (1950), Zhou Shilu's *Mother Who Walks the Streets* (1950), and *Mother's Heart Is Broken (Mother's Broken Heart)/Ngai sam sui miu sam/Er xin sui mu xin* (1958). In the two-part Cantonese contemporary melodrama *A Girl Named Liang Lengyan*, he played the villain who attempts rape, schemes against, drugs, rapes, and impregnates the heroine of the title, only to shoot the concubine who helps him in his villainy before falling to his death.

In the 1950s, Lau directed half a dozen features, among them the fantasy Cantonese opera *The Immortal He Xiangu's Six Crossings (Crosses the River Six Times)/Luk diy hoh sin goo/Liu du he xian gu* (1950) and the period piece tragedy *The Sad Tale of the Golden-Leaf Chrysanthemum/Chai leung gam yip guk/Qi liang jin ye ju* (1955). The latter, based on a folktale, tells the story of a man murdered because he has taken two sworn sisters as wives, one of whom had rejected the queen's brother. Years later, the sons of the murdered man become the number one literary and warrior scholars and avenge their father's death.

Lau took a hiatus from acting from 1970 to 1977, following the decline of Cantonese cinema in the late 1960s; he returned to the screen with the drama *Money on the Way/Faat choi maai bin/Fa cai mai bian* (1978), produced by his son, Lui Zhirong. He took on character actor and comedic roles in **Ann Hui's** *The Spooky Bunch/Chong do jing/Zhuang dao zheng* (1980), **John Woo's** comedy *Plain Jane to the Rescue/Baat choi Lam A Jan/Ba cai Lin Ya Zhen* (1982, with **Josephine Siao** and **Ricky Hui**), **Samo Hung's** *Winners and Sinners/Kei mau miu gai ng fook sing/Qi mou miao ji wu fu xing* (1983), and **Jackie Chan**'s *Project A/A gai waak/A ji hua* (1983), the latter his last screen appearance before his death. He also appeared on the **television** soap operas *Don't Look Now* (1980) and *Love Forever* (1981)

LAU, JEFF CHUN-WAI. Director Jeff Lau grew up in a Catholic family in Cheung Chau. At 16, he studied design in England and returned to Hong Kong where he worked for a brief time at an advertising agency. He then was employed at a trading company managing Philippine business interests before turning to film as a producer, director, and screenwriter. He worked for the **Century Film Company** in an administrative capacity. His debut feature was *The Haunted Cop Shop/Maang gwai cha goon/Menggui* (1987).

In 1987, Lau joined in Gear, beginning a relationship with **Wong Kar-wai**; Lau directed and wrote *The Eagle Shooting Heroes/Seh diu ying hung chuen ji dung shing sai jau/Shediao yingxiong zhi dongcheng xijiu* (1993), which Wong produced. Loosely based on **Louis Cha's** ***wuxia*** novel *The Brave Archer*, the movie is a frantic, freewheeling phantasmagoria of poisonous drum-dancing centipedes, toad **kung fu**, flying boots, and fairy love, with an ensemble cast (including **Brigitte Lin**, **Leslie Cheung**, **Maggie Cheung**, **Tony Leung Chiu-wai**, **Carina Lau**, **Tony Leung Ka-fai**, and **Veronica Yip**) first planned as a sequel to Wong's ***Ashes of Time****/Dung chea sai duk/Dong xie xi du* (also based on *The Brave Archer*). Together Wong and Lau formed Jet Tone in 1993. Actually, their themes of lost love and fate are similar, but their treatments different.

Lau also shares a productive partnership with **Corey Yuen Kwai**, begun with *Mortuary Blues/Shut ga chung dei/Shi jia zhong di* (1990). Their collaboration *Savior of the Soul/Gau yat san diu hap lui/Jiu yi shen diao xia lu* (1991) originated from a Wong Kar-wai script Lau revised, loosely based on Louis Cha's *The Eagle Lovers*, and starred **Andy Lau**. Lau also wrote the screenplays for Yuen's *Today's Hero/Chi joi chut wai/Zhi zai chu wei* (1999) and *So Close/Chik yeung tin sai/ Xiyang tianshi* (2002).

Unlike many other two-part Hong Kong films, Lau's *A Chinese Odyssey (Journey to the West) Parts 1* and *2/Sai yau gei 101 wooi yuet gwong bo hap tin: Chaai sing dung/Xi you ji 101 hui yue guang bao he: Qi tian da sheng dong you* (1995) form an integral whole. Peripherally drawing on the popular tale *The Journey to the West*, the movie presents a fantastical and ingenious time-traveling plot underscored by disillusionment with mortal love and bad timing. The Joker (**Stephen Chiau**) travels back in time to escort the monk Xuanzang on his journey to retrieve holy sutras. In *Part One: Pandora's Box*

(Moonlight Treasure Box), the Joker (Chiau) loves a woman, who cannot forget their past life together. Toward the end, the Joker opens Pandora's Box to time travel and prevent her from suicide. In *Part Two: Cinderella (Fairy Slipper Magic Encounter)*, he meets and falls for another, Cinderella, even though his former love remains in his heart. The Joker only understands his heart after his death when he reappears before Cinderella as Sun Wukong, the Monkey King, now immortal and immune to human passion.

Lau's **Chinese New Year** tragicomedy, *Chinese Odyssey 2002/Tin ha mo seung/Tian xia wushuang* (2002) starred Leung Chiu-wai, **Faye Wong**, and Athena Chu, and Lau reinterpreted the legend of the Butterfly Lovers Liang Shanbo and Zhu Yingtai in a Ming dynasty–set story that redefines genres and reworks the themes of identity, love, and fate constant in his other movies. As in the retro *92 Legendary La Rose Noire/92 Hei mei gui dui hei mei gui* (1992), *Rose, Rose I Love You/Mooi gwai mooi gwai ngo oi lei/Mei gui mei gu wo ai ni* (producer, 1993), and *The Black Rose 2/Hak mui gwai yee git gam laan/Hei mei gui yi jie jin lan* (1997), Lau both pays homage to genre and creates a postmodern pastiche that takes its measure.

LAU, KAR-LEUNG (Liu, Jialiang) (1937–). Director, **martial arts** director, and actor Lau Kar-leung brings genuine martial arts techniques, especially applied to swordplay, to the movies. His father, Liu Zhan, was a student of Lam Sai-wing, **Wong Fei-hung's** favorite pupil. The martial arts lineage is an interesting one to trace, not only to Wong Fei-hung, but all the way back to the Shaolin Monastery in Northern China that was burned through treachery and betrayal. Wong Fei-hung learned martial arts from his father, Wong Kei-ying, one of the Ten Tigers of Guangdong, and from Lu Ah Tsui, who taught the younger Wong drunken boxing; Lu was also teacher of Wong Kei-ying. Lu Ah Tsui specialized in Flower Fist, and his teacher was Zhi Shan, who reestablished and refined Shaolin martial arts and may have invented wooden dummies and the 36 chambers testing. His teacher, Zhi Kong, was a fugitive monk from the North, who founded the Southern Jiulianshan Shaolin Monastery in Fujian.

Lau began studying martial arts at age nine, and when his family moved to Hong Kong in 1948, he entered the film industry, playing hundreds of minor roles and stunt parts. He became a martial arts director in 1963, working alongside martial arts director and director Tong Kai. He worked with him on *The Jade Bow/Wan hoi yuk gung yuen/Yun hai yu gong yuan* (1966) and *The One-Armed Swordsman/Duk bei diy/Du bi dao* (1967). Lau worked as martial arts director of numerous **Shaw Brothers** productions, including those of **Chang Cheh**. His directorial debut was *The Spiritual Boxer/San ckui/Shen da* (1975), which explicated the true meaning of Shaolin, involving both spiritual and physical aspects. His ***36th Chamber of Shaolin*** *(Shaolin 36th Chamber)/Siu lam sa luk fong/Shaolin sa liu fang* (1978) portrays its protagonists as mere mortals undergoing secretive initiation rites through strenuous training and tests. It won the Best Martial Arts Award at the 24th **Asian Film Festival**. Lau's step-brother **Gordon Liu** (Liu Jiahui, Lau Kar-fai) starred as the real-life Han commoner hiding out from Manchu oppressors, and he learns to exercise his "mind muscle." Lau would cast Liu in many of his films.

Lau directed the **Jet Li** vehicle *Martial Arts of Shaolin (North and South Shaolin)/Nan bei Shaolin* (1986), but temporarily halted work due to health problems. He returned to filmmaking in the 1990s, when **Jackie Chan** invited him to direct *Drunken Master 2 (Drunken Fist 2)/Jui kuen 2/Zui quan 2* (1994), following the success of the first film. Lau's classic old-style **kung fu** enhanced the martial arts movements, but without rapid cuts, wirework, and film speed manipulation; Lau appeared in the film and his fight with Chan underneath a moving train is inventive. Although Lau is credited, Chan directed on the film as well, at least 30 percent of it. At the time, the movie broke box office records across Asia. Lau also directed *Drunken Monkey/Chui ma lau/Zui ma li* (2002) in Mainland China. Most recently, he has played an important role as an actor and action director for **Tsui Hark's** *Seven Swords/Chat kim/Qi jian* (2005).

LAU, LAWRENCE KWOK-CHEONG (Lawrence Ah Mon) (1949–). Born in Pretoria, South Africa, director Lawrence Ah Mon received his secondary education in Hong Kong and his Master of Arts in Film from the University of Southern California. Following this, he returned to Hong Kong, and worked as assistant director to **Tsui Hark** on *The Butterfly Murders (Butterfly Transformation)/Dai bin/Die bian* (1979). He joined Radio Television Hong Kong (RTHK) directing drama episodes for *Under (Below) the Lion Rock*, *Faces and Places*, *Crossroads*, *Profile*, and *Miracle of the Orient*. He left RTHK in 1986. His directorial feature debut was *Gangs (Child Gang)/Tung dong/Tong dang* (1988), and he is a director with class-consciousness. *Arrest the Restless/ Laam Gong juen ji faan fei jo fung wan/Lan Jiang zhuan zhi fan fei zu feng yun* (1992) was a youth problem movie starring **Leslie Cheung** as an innocent 1960s teddy boy caught up in small time gangster life, with Charles Heung as the good cop who tries to help him. *Spacked Out (No One at the Wheel)/Miu yan ga sai/Wu ren jia shi* (2002), set in the housing blocks of the New Territories' Tuen Mun, follows four angst-ridden working-class schoolgirls, two of them lesbians. An update on *Arrest the Restless*, the movie shows the intoxication and misery of wasted lives.

LAU, SEAN CHING-WAN (1964–). Born in Guangdong province, Lau Ching-wan joined the actors Hong Kong Television Broadcasts Limited (TVB) studios at 17, encouraged by his father. He played many working-class characters and swordsmen before moving into his film debut *Silent Love/Teng bat diy dik suet wa/Ting bu dao de shui hua* (1986). He continued working in **television** and film, with TV success in *The Great Man* and *Police Cadet*. He gained audience attention in **Derek Yee's** romantic melodrama *C'est la Vie, Mon Cherie (New Not End Love, New Endless Love)/San bat liu ching/Xin bu liao qing* (1993), in which he costarred with **Anita Yuen** and was nominated for Hong Kong's Best Actor film award. With significant screen presence and large physical stature, Lau appeared in a wide variety of films, from **melodrama**s like *Sea Root/Hoi gan/Hai gen* (1995) to **action** like *Big Bullet (EU Strike Force)/Chung fung dui liu gaai tau (EU chung fung dui)/Chong feng dui nu huo jie tou (EU chong feng dui)* (1996) to comedies like *It's a Wonderful Life (Big Rich Family)/ Daai foo ji ga/Da fu zhi jia* (1994). Dark complected, he was early on the butt of numerous racist jokes in films, called "darkie" or "Charcoal Lau," and not considered a matinee idol.

However, the intensity of his performances, as well as his maturity, have led to him being held in high regard for his depth of characterization, and for his characters never playing the same. He has worked with some of Hong Kong's best directors, including **Ringo Lam** on *Full Alert/Go diy gaai bei/Gao du jie bei* (1997) and *Victim/Muk lau* *hung gwong/Mu lo xiong guang* (1999); **Patrick Leung** on *Beyond Hypothermia (32 Degrees Celsius)/Sip si 32 doe/She shi 32 du* (1996), *La Brassiere/Chuet sai hui bra/Jue shi hao bra* (2001), *Mighty Baby/Chuet sai hiu b/Jue shi hao b* (2002), and *Good Times, Bed Times/Luen seung lei dik cheng/Lian shang ni de chuang* (2003); **Derek Yee** on *Viva Erotica/Sik ching laam nui/Se qing nan nu* (1996) and *Lost in Time/Mong bat liu/Wang bu le* (2003); **Patrick Yau** on *The Longest Nite/Aau dut/An hua* (1998) and *Expect the Unexpected/Fai seung dat yin/Fei chang tu ran* (1998); and **Wai Ka-fai** on *Too Many Ways to Be No. 1/Yat kuo chi tau dik daan sang/Yi ge zi tou de dan sheng* (1997) and *Fantasia/Gwai ma kwong seung kuk/Gui ma kuang xiang qu* (2004).

Foreshadowing Lau's trademark signature is his performance in Leung's *Beyond Hypothermia* (1996), in which he combined action with character, playing a former Triad and noodle stall proprietor who cooks for and falls in love with an icy and alienated hit woman (Wu Sien-lin). Lau's most productive work has been in partnership with director **Johnnie To** and his **Milkyway Image Productions**. To has directed him in moody action pictures, including *Lifeline (Extremely Urgent, Ten Thousand Fire Urgent)/Sap maan feng gap/Shi wan huo ji* (1997, a Hong Kong appropriation of Ron Howard's *Backdraft*), *A Hero Never Dies/Chan sam ying hung/Zhen xin ying xiong* (1998), *Running Out of Time 1* and *2 (Hidden War)/Aau chin/Anzhan* and *(Hidden War 2)/Aau chin 2/Anzhan 2* (1999, 2001), and *Where a Good Man Goes/Joi gin a long/Zai jian a lang* (1999), all of which are character-driven stories. Yau and Wai also worked with Lau under To's shingle.

Variety named Lau one of its 10 actors to watch in 1999. Lau is married to actress **Amy Kwok**.

LAW, ALEX. Born in Hong Kong, screenwriter, director, and producer Alex Law earned a BA in Chinese and English Literature from the University of Hong Kong and worked as a producer and director at Radio Television (RTV) from 1978 to 1981, directing over 20 dramas, including *Goodbye, Suzie Wong*, *Gethsemane*, *Castle of Sand*, *Suffer the Little Children*, and *Farewell, My Concubine*. He traveled to the United States and earned an MFA in Film Production from New York University and was awarded their Best Cinematographer

Award for his student film *Blue Christmas* (1984). There he met (and married) director **Cheung Yuen-ting**, and the two have been productive partners since. For her he wrote the *Immigrant Trilogy*, including *The Illegal Immigrant/Fai faat yee man/Feifa yimin* (1985), *An Autumn's Tale (An Autumn's Fairy Tale)/Chau tin dik tung wa/Qiu tian de tong huo* (1987), and *Eight Taels of Gold/Baat a gam/Ba ya jin* (1989), all award-winning films. Law won Best Screenplay for *An Autumn's Tale* at the 1987 **Hong Kong Film Awards** and the same from the 1987 Hong Kong Film Directors' Choice Awards. They have also collaborated on *Painted Faces (Seven Little Fortunes)/Chat siu fuk/Qi xiao fu* (1988), *Love . . . Now You See It, Now You Don't (Now You See Love, Now You Don't; I Love Nau Man-chai; Rogue Meets Warrior)/Ngoh oi Nau Man-chai (lau man yue do bing)/Wo ai Niu Wenchai (liu mang yu dao bing)* (1991), *The Soong Sisters* (1997), *City of Glass/Boh lee je shing/Bo li zhi cheng* (1998), and *Beijing Rocks/Bakging lok yu lo/Beijing le yu le* (2001). Both *The Soong Sisters (The Sung Family Dynasty)/Sung ga wong chiu/Song guhuang chao* and *City of Glass* were nominated for Best Screenplays at the Hong Kong Film Awards. The **Hong Kong International Film Festival** has described them as "intelligent, kind, gentle people [who] can make films with those qualities that entertain and engage the emotions in real ways" (1992 program, p. 220).

Law's directorial feature debut was the drama *Painted Faces* (1988), starring **Samo Hung**, and based on the real-life experience of Hung, **Jackie Chan**, **Yuen Biao**, **Corey Yuen**, and others as children at the Chinese Drama Academy, a traditional Chinese Opera School, of Master Yu Jim Yuen. Hung plays the role of the master, and the film carefully delineates the arduous training practices of future opera stars as well as the decline of opera in popularity, as its participants turned to the film industry for their livelihood. Law and Cheung cowrote the screenplay, and although Hung and others say the training was more extreme than depicted, the story registers a real sense of loss for an art and way of life. The film won seven **Golden Horse Awards** in Taiwan, including Best Picture, Director, and Screenplay, as well as the Silver Hugo Award for Best First Feature at the 1989 Chicago International Film Festival.

Law followed that film with a **Lunar New Year's comedy** *Love . . . Now You See It, Now You Don't* (1991), costarring **Chow Yun-fat**,

Carol Do Do Cheng, **Anthony Wong**, and **Teresa Mo**, and recorded in the Hakka dialect (what Law calls "native Hong Kongese [and] probably the only film that uses it"). Set in an indigenous fishing village on a New Territories island, the story evolved from Chow Yun-fat's own experience as a country boy who goes to the city to find love and happiness, and according to producer Terence Chang, became "a statement about love." Law reteamed with Samo Hung to produce and write his first **martial arts** film, *The Moon Warriors/Chin san chuen suet/Zhan shen chuan shui* (1992). He produced and wrote the epic *Soong Sisters*, and intimate *City of Glass*, both exploring individual stories set against the rush of history and Hong Kong–Mainland relations. Unsurprisingly, with *Beijing Rocks* (2001), Law developed a contemporary cross-cultural story set in the underground rock music culture in Beijing and examines what it means to be Chinese (supported by interesting casting of Chinese American Daniel Wu, Taiwanese Hong Konger **Shu Qi**, and Mainlander Geng Le in the leads).

LAW, CLARA CHEUK-YIU (1957–). Born in Macau, expatriate director Clara Law studied English literature at the University of Hong Kong, graduated from the National Film and Television School in the United Kingdom in 1985, and worked for Radio Television Hong Kong (RTHK) before directing her own feature films as part of Hong Kong's second wave. She became one of the few female directors in Hong Kong. She and husband **Eddie Fong** are internationally known for their collaborations (generally, but not always, he writes and she directs). They immigrated to Australia in the early 1990s in anticipation of the return of Hong Kong to the Mainland.

While Law's early work was in the comic vein (for example, the farcical divorce-themed *The Other Half and the Other Half [I Love Astronaut]/Ngoh oi taai hung yan/Wo ai tai kong ren* [1988]), her preoccupation with sexual politics, temptation, eroticism, and passion, and the Chinese **diaspora** and identity have defined her work. The hard-hitting *Farewell China (Demon Love Painting)/Moh wah ching/Mo hua qing* (1990), starring **Leung Ka-fai** and **Maggie Cheung**, dramatizes the coming apart of a relationship and the adversities faced by Mainlander emigrants in New York that destroy them. *Temptation of a Monk (Seduction of a Monk)/Yau jang/You seng* (1993), set in the seventh-century early Tang dynasty (starring Wu Hsin-kuo and **Joan Chen**) repeats questions of Hong Kong identity and relationship to the Mainland introduced in the adaptation of *Reincarnation of Golden Lotus (Poon Kam-lien's Past World, This Life)/Poon Gam-lien ji chin sai gam sang/Pan Jinlian zhi qian shi jin sheng* (1988), loosely drawing from an episode of *The Water Margin*. *Temptation of a Monk* inventively visually draws upon Zen painting and empty space, and the titular temptation of former warrior now monk General Shi, rejecting a great passion with Princess Scarlet, is seduced by a vindictive assassin nun, in a memorable lovemaking scene between two bald-headed acolytes.

Similarly, Law's Australian features *Floating Life* (involving a separated and adaptive Chinese family) and *The Goddess of 1967* (linking an abused Aussie female and a Japanese fish out of water enamored of the titular French Citröen) , and the **documentary** *Letters to Ali* (2004, concerning an Afghan boy seeking Australian asylum, whose situation is similar to Chinese emigrants) all explore the diasporic experience in Australia and associate the emptiness of the landscape with the lack of wholeness in characters' lives. Interestingly, Law herself has always been a Hong Kong outsider, first working as a **woman** in a male-dominated industry, and now, as an expatriate. She continues to push the envelope regarding women's sexuality.

LAW, KAR. Affectionately referred to as "Uncle Kar," veteran film critic and scholar Law Kar worked in **television** at Hong Kong Television Broadcasts Limited (TVB) and fostered cinema through the Film Culture Centre of Hong Kong, of which he was one of the founders. There, he organized several Chinese cinema retrospectives. In 1983, **Li Cheuk-to** invited him to write for the **Hong Kong International Film Festival** program; following that, he acted as panel advisor and then as programmer for the Hong Kong retrospective programs of the Hong Kong International Film Festival for many years. He has also been a powerhouse at the **Hong Kong Film Archives** as its advisor since 1993 and programmer from 2001 to 2005. He coauthored the informative and insightful diverse study of Hong Kong film, *Hong Kong Cinema: A Cross-Cultural View* (2005) with Frank Bren.

LAW, KAR-YING (1947–). Born in Guangzhou, son of **Cantonese opera** star Law Ka-kuen, Law Kar-ying was a popular Cantonese opera performer in the 1970s, having studied with his uncle Law Ka-shu, who taught Cantonese opera at the Cantonese Opera Academy in Guangzhou. (Law even transformed *Macbeth* into a Cantonese opera.) By 1966, Law had become a *man mo sheng* (male lead), working in Hong Kong and touring Southeast Asia with small opera companies. With opera's decline in popularity, Law joined Radio Television Hong Kong (RTHK) in 1981 as a radio editor and host of Cantonese opera programs for several years.

The actor began making movies in the 1990s, and he has become a popular character actor and appeared in more than 50 films; he is equally good in drama as comedy. Comedic roles that stand out include his mad inventor opposite **Stephen Chiau's** "Ling Ling Chat" (007) in the James Bond spoof *From Beijing (China) with Love/Gwok chaan Ling Ling-chat/Guo chan Ling Lingqi* (1994), and his failed restaurateur and exasperated father of **Anita Yuen** in *The Chinese Feast (Gold Jade Full Hall)/Gam yuk moon tong/Jin yu man tang* (1995). Impressive dramatic roles include **Josephine Siao's** inadequate husband in **Ann Hui's** ***Summer Snow*** *(Woman, Forty)/**Nui Yan Sei Sap**/Nuren sishu* (1995), in which he is also the son of an Alzheimer's-ridden father (**Roy Chiao**), a film that dramatizes the lives of ordinary Hong Kong people; and the transvestite father of **Jordan Chan** wishing to undergo a sex change operation in **Yim Ho's** *Kitchen (I Love Kitchen)/Ngoh oi chuifong/Wo ai chu fang* (1997), based on the Banana Yoshimoto novel, a role in which he really took risks (he won the Best Supporting Actor award at the **Hong Kong Film Awards** for *Summer Snow* and was nominated for *Kitchen*). He is the longtime boyfriend of television star and opera singer **Lisa Wang** (Wong Ming-chuen). They met in 1988 when Law learned Wang was interested in pursuing Cantonese opera.

In 2005, the University of Hong Kong's museum celebrated Law's opera performances, spanning 50 years, in an exhibition.

LAW, KWUN-HUNG (Lo Kwan-hung, Luo Junxiong) (1919–). Cinematographer Law Kwun-hung, a native of Guangdong province, started in the film industry as a continuity assistant at Daguan (**Grandview**) in Hong Kong, and became an assistant cameraman and head of the stills department. Law's first film as director of photography, *Eternal Flame* (begun 1941), was never completed due to the war. During wartime, the cameraman worked across southwest China shooting newsreels. The first completed feature he filmed was *Remorse in a Grand House* (1948).

Law worked for Nanguo, **Great Wall**, and **Feng Huang** film companies. He filmed **Wang Weiyi's** ***Tears of the Pearl River*** *(Dawn Must Come)/Chu kong lui/Zhujiang lei* (1950), and several **Zhu Shilin** movies, including the situation comedy *Mr. Chen vs. Mr. Chen* (1952), the realist comedy *House Removal Greeting/Kiu chin ji choi/Qiao qian zhi xi* (1954), and the satirical comedy *Husband Hunters/Cheung san long (laai long pooi)/Qiang xin lang (La lang pei)* (1958), the latter adapted from the Sichuan opera *A Forced Match*. In the leftist tradition of Shanghai filmmaking, *Tears of the Pearl River* has a social conscience and high production values for its time. One of Law's famous shots is of the exploitative landlord (**Cheung Ying**), bruised and prone on the ground, overtaken by the moving shadows of oppressed peasant passersby.

Law's directorial debut was *Fantasy of Youth/Ching chun waan seung kuk/Qing chun huan xiang qu* (1959) in which a fresh graduate (Chu Hung) dreams of stardom, and blinded by her dreams, is nearly raped, makes a porn movie, is injured in a car accident, and awakens in the hospital resolving to start fresh. He also codirected several films, including Mandarin comedies codirected by **Chen Jingbo** *Troubles with the Bachelors/Nan da dang hun* (1957) and *A Girl in Disguise/Chan ga chin gam/Zhen jia qian jin e* (1959).

LAW, YIM-HING (Luo Yanqing) (1930–). Actress Law Yim-hing (real name Luo Dahong), who specialized in Cantonese **martial arts** and opera films, was born in Guangdong province and had learned to perform Cantonese opera by age 10. She began guest appearances onstage in 1942, performing in numerous opera troupes, including her own Yantanghuang. She also studied northern and southern martial arts style during her Cantonese opera training. Opera performers Luo Pinchao and **Sit Kok-sin** were her teachers. She was one of the "Eight Peonies," including renowned opera actress **Tang Pak-wan**.

Law's film debut was Wong Gam-yan's martial arts movie *Five Rascals in the Eastern Capital/Ng sue laau dung ging/Wushu nao dong jing* (1948), followed by Koo Man-chung's martial arts period piece *Thirteen Heroes with Seven Swords/Chat kim sap saam hap/Qijian shisan xia* (1949), which sold out 152 straight shows upon release. Law played the Red-Garbed Lady Knight who joins the 13 swordsmen who declare their loyalty to the Ming emperor and fight against rebels. She was one of the first martial arts heroines, starring in numerous martial arts films, including *Heroine in Red/Hung dut lui hap/Hongyi nuxia* (1951), *White Lotus, the Heroine/Nuxia Bailianhua* (1952), *The Heroine Yu Jifeng/Yu Kam-Fung/Nuxia Jinfeng* (1956), *Sword of Blood and Valor (Romance of Blood and Valor)/Bik huet kim/Bi xie jian* (1958), and *The Seven Swordsmen from Tianshan* (1959). In the former, she starred in the title role as the daughter of a rich man, instructed by a chivalrous knight named "Red Blood" in martial arts for many years, clothed in red and nicknamed "Red Heroine"; a series of misadventures follows. Others include *A Beggar Named Su/So hat ngai fook chau gei/Su qi er fu chou ji* and *The Killing Spear/Saam sap luk dim soh hau cheong/San shi liu dian suo hou qiang* (both 1953).

Between 1948 and 1969, Law appeared in close to 300 features, including operas and modern-dress films. The actress starred in numerous opera films, among them *The Playboy Emperor/Fung lau tin ji/Feng liu tian zi* (1953) and *The Festive Lantern/Dut dang gei/Hua deng ji* (1960), opposite **Yam Kim-fai**; *Spanking the Princess/Chui ckui gam chi/Zui da jin qi* (1955); and *Rescue at the West River/Sai hiu kooi chai/Xi he hui qi* (1960) and *Poor Lady Ping/Fung yue yap ping gei/Feng yu qi ping ji* (1963), costarring her second husband **Ho Fei-fan**. Contemporary features include *Comet of Laughter Lands on Earth/Siu sing gong dei kau/Xiao xing jiang di qiu* (1952), ***The Romance of Jade Hall**, 1 and 2 (My Kingdom for a Husband)/Suen gung yim shut/ Xuangong yanshi* (1957–1958), *Typhoon Signal No. 10/Sap hiu fung boh/Shi hao feng bo* (1959), *The Prodigal's Wife/Long ji giu chai/Lang zi jiao qi* (1959), *Coffee Girl/Fung fau lui long/Ka fei nu lang* (1963), and *Our Big Sister/Daai ga che/Da gu jie* (1964). In Leung Fung's contemporary comedy *A Comet of Laughter Lands on Earth*, Law played the female part of a couple whose jealous cousin attempts to separate them; they are mirrored by a working-class couple with another sower of discord, intent, with the cousin, on stealing money from the family.

The actress's final film was *The Sword That Vanquished the Monster/Fook moh gon kwan kim/Fu mo gan kun jian* (1969). Due to rheumatic disease, the actress retired in 1966, and moved to the United States. Her second marriage, to Cantonese opera actor Ho Feifan, ended in divorce. *See also* CHINESE OPERA FILMS.

LE, DI (Lo, Betty Tieh) (1937–1968). Born in Shanghai and a native of Pudong province, actress Le Di (real name Xi Zhongyi) was brought up by her maternal grandmother, after the death of her parents. She developed an interest in acting at a young age because her grandfather, Gu Zhuxuan, owned a Shanghai opera house. She came to Hong Kong in 1949 and joined **Great Wall** in 1953, where her film debut was in the historical costume epic *The Peerless Beauty/Chuet doi gaai yan/Juedai jiaren* (1953). She joined **Shaw Brothers** in 1958, starring in *The Deformed/Gei yan yim foo/Jiren yanfu* (1960) and *The Enchanting Shadow/Sin lui yau wan/Qian nu you hun* (1960). In *The Deformed*, she played a poor Macao nurse bribed by a doctor to marry his humpbacked, buck-toothed son (**King Hu**, who was a character actor in the 1950s and 1960s, before turning to masterful ***wuxia*** directing). Complications ensue when a handsome cousin appears, and the woman must choose between the men. Director **Yue Feng's** melodrama was based on *Beauty and the Beast*.

Le Di (her nickname was "Classical Beauty") was one of Shaw's top female stars before she moved to **Motion Pictures and General Investment** (MP&GI, Cathay) in 1964, appearing in many of the studio's films, including *The Beggar's Daughter/Gam yuk liu/Jin yunu* (1965), *The Longest Night* (1965), *The Lucky Purse/Siu gam long/Suolin nang* (1966), and *The Magic Fan/Sin chung yan/Shanzhong ren* (1967), among others. She costarred with **Ling Bo** as the female lead disguised as a male scholar in **Li Han-hsiang's *huangmei diao The Love Eterne*** *(Liang Shanbo and Zhu Yingtau)/Leung Saan Ang yue Chuk Ying Toi/Liang Shanbo yu Zhu Yingtai* (1963), based on the story of the Butterfly Lovers.

In 1967, she formed Gold Eagle Film Company with her brother, actor **Kelly Lai Chen** (Lei Zhen), and director Yuan Qiufeng, which made a series of *wuxia* films, such as *Duel at the Supreme Gate* (1968), distributed by MP&GI, but unsuccessful at the box office.

She married actor **Peter Chen Ho** in 1962, but they divorced five years later. She died at 31 from an overdose of sleeping pills.

LEE, ANG (1954–). Born in Pingtung, Taiwan, internationally recognized Taiwanese director Ang Lee graduated from the National Taiwan College of Arts in 1975, studied theater at the University of Illinois in 1978, and earned his MFA from New York University's Film School. He began writing screenplays and teamed with current producer James Schamus for his first feature, *Pushing Hands* (1991), which examined an interracial marriage and a generational Chinese family adjusting to life in the United States, while the cross-cultural comedy follow-up *The Wedding Banquet* (1993) explored similar territory but added a gay couple to the mix. Both of these films, and Lee's next endeavor, *Eat Drink Man Woman* (1994), were popular in Taiwan and internationally. Lee has consistently won kudos, winning numerous nominations and awards and support from critics and audiences for his films, whether staging the piquant sexual politics of Jane Austen's England (*Sense and Sensibility*, 1995) or the 1970s upper middle-class suburbs of Connecticut (*The Ice Storm,* 1997). Lee's only miss, according to critics and audiences, was *The Hulk* (2003), an ambitious attempt to adapt the Marvel comic into an allegory for U.S. foreign policy by questioning technological progress and power politics. Lee also examined psychological trauma, anger, and how to control our "inner hulks."

While Lee is a filmmaker who defies pigeonholing based on the look and focus of his films, he nonetheless develops character-driven stories with an acute sense of detailed customs and proprieties that are telling regarding a society and time. Lee's greatest coup to date is *Crouching Tiger, Hidden Dragon* (2000, starring **Chow Yun-fat**, **Michelle Yeoh**, **Cheng Pei-pei**, Zhang Ziyi, and Chang Chen). An epic homage to the Chinese **swordplay** movies Lee remembers fondly from his youth, the film not only employed Hong Kong stars but used **martial arts** director **Yuen Wo-ping** as action choreographer to capture the Hong Kong action style. Lee even added an homage to **King Hu's** bamboo forest scene from *A Touch of Zen* (1971), one-upping the master by setting the scene in the bamboo treetops, more than 30 feet above ground, courtesy of wirework. In the United States, the film won, among others, three Golden Globe Awards (Best

Director, Foreign-Language Film, and Original Score) and four Oscars (Best Foreign-Language Film, Art Direction, Original Score, and Cinematography). The film also won numerous **Golden Horse** and **Hong Kong Film Awards**.

LEE, BRUCE SIU-LUNG (1940–1973). Bruce Lee was born in San Francisco during the Chinese year of the Dragon. He was named Lee Jun-fan, meaning "gaining fame overseas." His father, Cantonese comic actor **Lee Hoi-chuen**, and his mother were part of a touring troupe that returned to Hong Kong several months later. He spent his formative years in Hong Kong as a child actor, appearing in over a dozen dramas and comedies. While filming the comedy *The Kid (My Son A-chang)/Sai liu cheung/Xilu Xiang* (1950), based on a popular Chinese comic book, Lee was given the nickr
Dragon") by the cartoonist Yuan Buyun. Lee's
child star was in *The Orphan/Yan hoi goo hu*
leased 1960, but filmed prior to 1958). Directe
the leftist-leaning Hualian production company
duction values and striking location work. A
starred as a juvenile delinquent pickpocket be
fan, a reform school headmaster who lost his w
Lee discovers he is the headmaster's lost son w
a criminal gang leader (who posed as his father)
ful ending, as Lee's character Ah Sam is redee
mism but also trouble brewing on the horizon
economic factors reflected in the film. *The Orp*
first Hong Kong leftist films to address juveni
also deals with the effects of rapid economic gr
of age of the late and postwar generation.

Growing up in Hong Kong, Lee studied the
martial arts with Yip Man, who also taught hir
of **kung fu**; he won the Crown Colony Cha-
1958. At age 18, he returned to the United Stat
where he completed his high school diploma
School and attended the University of Washingt
phy. There he met Linda Emery; they married a
Brandon and Shannon Lee (both of whom would
was developing his approach to the martial arts

Do ("The Way of the Intercepting Fist"), as a master of all and none. He opened a martial arts school in Seattle, a second in Oakland, California, and a third in Los Angeles.

Producer William Dozier watched footage of Lee's performance at the 1964 Long Beach International Karate Championship. Producer of the TV series *Batman*, starring Adam West, Dozier capitalized on its success by creating another action hero series, *The Green Hornet* (1966–1967), based on a 1930s radio serial. Lee played Kato, the Hornet's "manservant" and sidekick, and he fought for less stereotypical characterization and more prominence on the show. Fans watched, not for Van Williams's newspaper editor-publisher by day/crime fighter Hornet by night, but Lee's cool and focused Kato, in black suit, mask, and chauffeur's cap, with his sudden and deadly strikes. Although the show lasted only six months, Lee gained in popularity and attention, all the while continuing with kung fu demonstrations at public events and tournaments.

Meantime Lee appeared as a guest on numerous **television** shows and worked on several films, even developing a story based on a Shaolin priest and kung fu master roaming America and finding himself drawn into various situations on his travels. Warner Brothers Studio decided to create a martial arts TV series and contacted Lee for involvement; Lee contributed many ideas to the series *Kung Fu* but was never officially offered the part, which went to actor David Carradine. The studio informed Lee that he had never been considered for the part, claiming he wasn't a big enough name and too inexperienced, too small, and too Chinese. Hollywood actors who worked with him on-screen and off, including James Coburn and John Saxon, disagreed, as did those who received Lee's private martial arts instruction, including Steve McQueen and Kareem Abdul-Jabbar. But Lee's inability to break the color barrier in Hollywood resulted in his return to Hong Kong. The popularity of *The Green Hornet* series there (known as *The Kato Show*) got the studios' attention. **Shaw Brothers** and **Golden Harvest** vied for Lee; Lee felt the deal offered by Shaw was insulting (the studio offered its basic starting salary) and signed with **Raymond Chow**.

Prolific filmmaker **Lo Wei** directed Lee in his first Golden Harvest release, *The Big Boss* (known in the United States as *Fists of Fury)/Tong saan daai hing/Tang shan da xiong* (1971); Lee had little control over the production (Han Ying-chieh, of **King Hu's** *Dragon Gate Inn* [1967] and *A Touch of Zen* [begun 1968 released 1971] was action director), but he was able to invest the film with some Jeet Kune Do and crafted the brutal ice house fight. The movie became Hong Kong's first international commercial success. Although Han Ying-chieh was credited as action choreographer on Lo Wei's and Lee's second collaboration, *Fist of Fury* (known in the United States as *Chinese Connection)/Jing mou moon/Jing wu men* (1972), Lee took control over his fight scenes. *Fist of Fury* broke box office records throughout Asia. In *The Big Boss*, Lee had played a trusting provincial character who discovers that the ice factory where he works is a front for drug smuggling and explodes into action when pushed too far. In *Fist of Fury* he played Chen Jun, a martial arts hero in Japanese-occupied Shanghai who seeks justice for his master's murder by a rival Japanese dojo and stands up to the foreign invaders. As such he became an icon for Chinese nationalism. Besides the outstanding fights and a tightly structured plot, two famous scenes include him breaking a signboard the Japanese present identifying the Chinese as "the sick men of Asia" and the final freeze frame where he hurls himself at the Japanese bearing guns aimed at him.

Way of the Dragon (aka *The Return of the Dragon)/Maang lung guo kong/Meng long guo jiang* (1972) served as Lee's directorial debut and expanded Hong Kong filmmaking to an international reach. Lee filmed on location in Rome and played another provincial and gullible character whose eyes are opened. He fought both American action star Chuck Norris and Korean martial arts master Whang In Shik, with a climactic fight in the Roman Coliseum. Working on his next film, *Game of Death/Sei miu yau fai/Si wang you goo* (released posthumously, 1978), Lee halted for the Hong Kong–U.S. coproduction ***Enter the Dragon****/Lung chang foo dau/Loong zheng hu do* (1973), directed by Robert Clouse. The film achieved great success in the United States; prolific Chinese actor **Shek Kin** played the villain and Lee choreographed the famous mirror scene fight. A month before *Dragon's* U.S. premiere, while working on *Game of Death*, Lee unexpectedly died. His premature death was listed as cerebral edema caused by allergic reaction to Equagesic, a painkiller he had taken for a headache. However, there was some mystery surrounding his death and conspiracy theories still abound. Years later Brandon

Lee's accidental death in 1993 while filming *The Crow* added to the specter of a Lee family curse. Bruce Lee is buried at Lake View Cemetery in Seattle.

As an adult, Bruce Lee completed only four signature films but became a legend. All four films emphasize straightforward plots and characters, and Lee's physical talents, maintained through training, not special effects. With a distinctive howl, Bruce Lee burst onscreen not as an emasculated Chinese master but as a streetwise and exciting presence. Strong and virile, sexual and shirtless, charismatic and effective, he came to represent Chinese nationalism and pride, not only to native Chinese but those spread worldwide in the **diaspora**. Showing face rather than losing it, he combined realistic acting with his martial arts philosophy on-screen, changing the style of Hong Kong martial arts filmmaking and influencing contemporary **action** stars like **Donnie Yen** and **Jet Li**, and affecting the lives of many who study the martial arts. A Bruce Lee library is available through Tuttle Books and ranges from published letters and interviews to biography and instructions. A portion of the proceeds goes to the Bruce Lee and Brandon Lee Medical Scholarship Endowment at the University of Arkansas and the Brandon Lee Drama Scholarship at Whitman College in Walla Walla, Washington.

LEE, CHI-NGAI. Lee was one of the founding members (along with **Peter Chan**, **Eric Tsang**, Claudie Chung, and **Jacob Cheung**) of **United Filmmakers Organization** (known as UFO) in 1990. The partners created the company in order to function in a collaborative spirit, encouraging first-time directors, sharing credits for writing and directing, and producing movies other than the **action** genre. Mostly known for twenty- and thirty-something contemporary urbanite stories, running the gamut from tender and gentle dramas to dramedies and lightweight comedies, the production company merged with studio **Golden Harvest** in 1996. Known for his talent as a writer, Lee's directorial debut was with the rape revenge *Vengeance Is Mine* (1988) starring **Rosamund Kwan**. He has also worked as art director on several films, including **Eddie Fong's** *Cherry Blossoms (When Tat Fu Was Young, Legend of Yu Ta Fu)/Wat data foo chuen kei/Yu da fu chuan qi* (1988). His collaborations with director Peter Chan, as writer and codirector, on films such as *Alan and Eric: Between Hello* *and Goodbye/Seung shing goo si/Shuang cheng gu shi* (1991), *Tom, Dick and Hairy (Three World-Weary Heroes)/Fung chan saam hap/ Feng chen san xia* (1993), and *He Ain't Heavy, He's My Father (New Two of a Kind)/San naam hing naan dai/Xin nan xiong nan di* (1993), led to a productive and rewarding period of filmmaking.

Lee's magical, contemplative, and bittersweet *Lost and Found (Edge of the World)/Tin aai hoi gok/Tian ya hai jiao* (1996) reflects his previous work as well as bringing to the foreground a predominant theme in his work, that of loss and love relationships. The film opens with a black-and-white sequence courtesy of director of photography **Bill Wong** set to Leonard Cohen's "Dance Me to the End of Love," establishing its wistful mood. Because of the polished script and talented ensemble cast (**Kaneshiro Takeshi**, **Michael Wong**, Cheung Tat-ming, **Jordan Chan**), the simple plot of a woman dying of leukemia (**Kelly Chan**) choosing whom and how to love richly develops an emotional resonance and nostalgia (especially for Hong Kong on the verge of its return to the Mainland in 1997).

Lee also directed and wrote (adapted from a novel by Seishu Hase) *Sleepless Town/Bu ye cheng* (1998), a Japanese-financed, Hong Kong–Japan coproduction that garnered Best Cinematography and Best Art Design awards at the 1998 **Hong Kong Film Awards**. Both magical romance and neo-noir urban thriller, the film was shot in the nighttime neon of Tokyo's Shinjuku district. Voice-over narration, a femme fatale, and other noir clichés are wedded to a story of outsiders, competing gangsters from Taiwan, Shanghai, and Beijing fighting in Japanese territory. Starring Kaneshiro Takeshi (himself part Japanese and part Chinese) as a romantic Taiwanese gangster, the film incorporates Lee's preoccupations of love and loss with stylish images (sumptuous camerawork provided by **Arthur Wong**). His latest endeavor, the **Lunar New Year's** offering *Magic Kitchen/Moh waan chuifong/Mo huan chu fang* (2004), is a romantic comedy starring **Andy Lau**, Sammi Cheng, and Jerry Yan.

LEE, CHING (Li Qing) (1914–). Actor Lee Ching (real name Li Hanqing), a native of Guangdong province, was born in Kuala Lumpur and attended secondary school in Shanghai. There, he enrolled in the actors' training course at **Mingxing**, first appeared on-screen in *Jade Horse* (1935), and became well known after making *Life and Death*

Together (1936). He joined **Lianhua** in 1937, starring in "The Moonlit Scene," an episode in *The Lianhua Symphony* (1937).

Lee came to Hong Kong in 1938 and starred in seven movies over four years, including the Cantonese features *Bloodshed in Baoshan City (The Blood-Stained Baoshan Fortress)/Huet chin bo saan shing/Xie jian bao shan cheng* (1938, directed by **Situ Huimin**) and *Behind the Shanghai Frontline* (1938), and the Mandarin films *Orphan Island Paradise/Go do tin tong/ Gudao tiantang* (1939) and *Ten Thousand Li Ahead (Big Future, Boundless Future)/Chin ching maan lee/Qian cheng wan li* (1941), both directed by **Cai Chusheng**. In the latter, Lee starred as a Mainland refugee in 1940 Hong Kong, working at menial labor to survive. He refuses to work as a coolie after discovering the merchandise he is loading is destined for the Japanese. At the film's conclusion, the Mainlanders turn their backs on Hong Kong to return to the Mainland and fight the Japanese. During wartime, the actor performed with the Hong Kong Drama Group in plays like *Sunrise* and *Thunderstorm*.

Following the war, Lee returned to film acting and appeared in more than 100 movies before retiring in 1976. He usually played the hero, a man of impeccable integrity, earning him the name "The Sturdy Guy." Occasionally he played villains. The actor's films include both Cantonese and Mandarin classics such as **Wang Weiyi's** ***Tears of the Pearl River*** *(Dawn Must Come)/Chu kong lui/Zhujiang lei* (1950), **Chun Kim's** *Following the Gentle Light (The Guiding Light)/Foo hoi ming dang/Ku hai ming deng* (1953), **Zhu Shilin's** Mandarin contemporary social realist movie *Between Fire and Water/Shui feng ji gaan/Shui huo zhi jian* (1955), and Chun Kim's romantic melodrama *Rouge Tigress (Pretty Tigress)/Yin chi foo/Yan zhi hu* (1956). In *Tears of the Pearl River*, Li played a corrupt master, Japanese collaborator, seducer, and rapist. In *Between Fire and Water*, Lee was part of the ensemble cast of eight families cramped in a small apartment that learn to cooperate after a fire breaks out. In *Rouge Tigress*, he played the son of a local tyrant (**Lo Dun**) who causes the death of a mother. Her daughter, the "rouge tigress" of the title (**Hong Sin-nui**), seeks revenge, turning father against son, leading to the son shooting his father.

Lee was one of the founding members of the cooperative **Zhonglian** Film Company. He retired after making the drama *The Best Friends/Chi oi chan pang/Zhi ai qin peng* (1976).

LEE, DANNY SAU-YIN (1953–). Born in Shanghai, director/producer/actor Danny Lee came to Hong Kong at six months of age. In 1970, he enrolled in actors' training programs through **Shaw Brothers** and Hong Kong Television Broadcasts Limited (TVB). **Chang Cheh** cast him in *The Water Margin* (1972), based on the classic *All Men Are Brothers,* and his first lead role was in Zhang Zhenzher's *River of Fury/Kong woo hang/Jiang hu hang* (1973), which also starred **Lilly Ho**. He worked with Shaw Brothers appearing in **martial arts** flicks for seven years before developing his own production company, Magnum Films. The name reflects characterizations he became known for, a Hong Kong Dirty Harry, which reflects his participation in the Hong Kong film industry, similar to Clint Eastwood, as actor, producer, and director. He gained notoriety for his direction of *Doctor Lamb (Lamb Doctor)/Go yeung yi sang/Gao yang yi sheng* (1992), starring **Simon Yam** as a serial killer, in which he played the tough-minded cop; indeed, he has become known for his strong cop persona as a dogged but unflinching cop, willing to bend the rules to achieve justice. However, he has also been recognized for his strong and nuanced performances in numerous films directed by others, namely **Ringo Lam's** *City on Fire (Dragon Tiger Turbulence)/Lung foo fung wan/Long hu feng yun* (1987) and **John Woo's** *The Killer (A Pair of Blood-Splattering Heroes)/Dip huet seung hung/Die xie shuang xiong* (1989), in both of which he held his own against **Chow Yun-fat**, and **Kirk Wong's** *Organized Crime and Triad Bureau (True Record of Important Case: Department O)/Chung ngon sat luk O gei/Chong an shi lu o ji*, in which he played his trademark cop set against **Anthony Wong's** desperate criminal. More recently, he appeared in **Herman Yau's** *Shark Busters/Baan san chuk dak hin dui/Fan shou shu te qian dui* (2002) as a cop burdened by debts to loan sharks.

LEE, HOI-CHUEN (Li Haiquan) (1898–1965). Cantonese opera actor Lee Hoi-chuen was born in Guangdong province and worked on staff in a teahouse. He joined the Xinzhonghua Opera Group, playing *xiaosheng* (handsome young men, either scholars or military generals) roles. He turned to *chou* (clown, Shakespearean-style fools) roles, and was one of the "four great *chous*" alongside Liao Xiahuai, **Poon Yat On**, and Ye Furuo. Lee retired from the stage in 1958.

Lee's film debut was as the lead in *Hundreds of Birds Adoring a Phoenix/Baak diu chiu wong/Bai niao chao huang* (1947). He appeared in close to 100 films, including **Zhou Shilu's** melodrama *Two Drug (Opium) Addicts Sweep the Long Dike/Leung goh yin cheng siu cheung/Liangge yanjing sao changdi* (1948), **Fung Fung's** realist melodrama ***The Kid****/Sai luiCheung/ Xilu Xiang* (1950), and Cheung Wai-gwong's *A Buddhist Recluse for 14 Years/Feng mong faan gong sap sei nin/ Huowang fangong shisi nian* (1958). *Two Drug Addicts Sweep the Long Dike* was first performed as a stage play by the Lung Fung Opera Troupe, featuring Lee and others; in the movie, he starred as the only son of a landlord who cannot overcome his addiction, and is imprisoned three times with his servant and fellow addict, and punished in other ways as well. In *The Kid*, Lee played the factory boss to his real-life son **Bruce Lee's** orphan turned delinquent of the title.

Lee's last film was *The Orphan's Adventure/Goo ngai gau jo/Gu er jiu zu* (1961). A devout Catholic as well as dedicated to training the young in opera arts, he trained opera actress **Fong Yim-fan** and comedian Xin Haiquan. He died in Hong Kong.

LEE, HONG-KUM (Li Xiangqin) (1932–). Actress Lee Hong-kum (real name Li Ruiqin), a native of Guangdong province, was raised and educated in Macau. She trained in Cantonese opera and was performing onstage at 16, becoming a supporting actress for numerous opera troupes and earning herself the title *"Erbang Huang"* (Queen of Supporting Ladies). At one point she served as deputy chairman of the Cantonese Artists Association of Hong Kong and was enthusiastic about setting up a Cantonese opera institute to train young actors.

Lee made her screen debut in **Wong Fei-hung** serials. Thereafter she appeared in hundreds of movies, often playing villains, especially treacherous concubines in opera films. Her features include *The Dream Meeting between Emperor Wu of Han and Lady Wei/Han Wudi menghui Wei Furen* (1959) and the Cantonese drama *Market Queen/Gaai shut wong hao/Jie shi huang hou* (1964). In the former, a Cantonese opera, she played the jealous Empress Chan, who puts a favored courtesan (**Yam Kim-fai**) under house arrest and plots to kill her. For her scheming, she ended up imprisoned for life. Lee's first starring role was in the comedy *The Country Bumpkin/Daai heung* *lee/Da xiang li* (1974), produced by Huanle, a company founded by Lee and Tan Bingwen. In 1976, the actress also founded Lishi Film Production Company and produced *You Are Wonderful/Lei hai dak gei/Ni xi de ji* (1976).

In 1972, Lee joined Hong Kong Television Broadcasts Limited (TVB) and hosted the variety show *Enjoy Yourself Tonight*. She also appeared in the **television** soap operas *The Good, the Bad and the Ugly* (1980) and *Brothers* (1980), playing kindhearted and gentle mother figures.

LEE, KA-SING. Although not an entertainment personality per se, self-made multimillionaire Lee Ka-sing, who made his fortune in real estate, is often referenced in Hong Kong films as an icon of the self-made man. He is generally regarded as the richest man in Hong Kong. An example is Waise Lee's characterization of him in **Peter Chan's** *He Ain't Heavy, He's My Father!/San naam hing naan dai/Xin nan xiong nan di* (1993), the Hong Kong version of Hollywood's *Back to the Future*, in which Tony Leung Chiu-wai's character gives him real estate tips by which he makes his fortune.

LEE, SIU-WAN (Li Shaoyun) (1916–2002). Cantonese opera librettist, writer, and producer Lee Siu-wan (real name Li Bingda) was born in Guangdong province to a family of scholars. He began as a jazz club performer before he became a librettist. Opera actor **Sit Kok-sin** was drawn to his first opera, *Return of the Swallows*, and invited him to work for his Juexiansheng troupe, and Lee was popular before the war, with operas such as *The Tough and the Unreasonable* and *The Cuckoo's Soul in March*.

Lee produced more than 100 operas, not including those he cowrote with others. His most famous works include *Poor Lady Ping* (starring **Ho Fei-fan**), *Emperor Guang Xu's Nocturnal Sacrifice to Zhen Fei* (starring **Ma Sze-tsang**), *Red and White Peonies* (starring Ma and **Hong Sin-nui**), *The Crab Beauty* (starring **Yu Lai-jan**), and *Wan Pan'an and His Impersonator* (starring **Yam Kim-fai**). He wrote to please a mainstream audience.

The librettist also founded and managed opera troupes, for which he wrote popular pieces, including the popular Da Feng Huang, where most famous Cantonese opera performers worked; Lishi, cofounded with Yu Lai-jan; and Songxinsheng (cofounded with **Lam Ka-sing**).

Lee debuted as a screenwriter with a remake of *Camille/San cha dut lui/Xin cha hua nu* (1950), and he wrote over 100 scripts during the next 20 years, mostly adaptations of his own operas. Lee founded the Lishi Production Company, and its inaugural production was **Wong Hok-sing's** *The Fourth Son of the Yang Family Visits His Mother (Fourth Brother Yeung of the Yang Family Visits His Mother)/Sei long taam miu/Silang tanmu* (1959). This historical Cantonese opera included the ensemble cast of Ma Sze-tsang, Yu Lai-jan, Lam Ka-sing, **Fung Wong-nui**, and **Poon Yat On**. The Yang family father and son are ambushed and the fourth brother is captured by the Liao princess who pressures him to marry her; when the Yang matriarch falls ill, her daughter-in-law peddles songs as she travels to the Liao kingdom to find her husband; they convince the princess to allow him to visit his mother. A sequel, *Eighth Sister Yeung (Miss Yang) Seizes the Gold Blade/Yeung baat mooi chui gam diy/Yang bamei qu jindao* (1959) followed, with the same cast.

Over nine years the company produced close to 100 features, most of them traditional Cantonese opera movies, among them Wong Hok-sing's *Seven Phoenixes/Gam fung cham gaau lung/Jin feng zhang jiao long* (1961), *Uproar at the Palace/Gam gaan liu sui aau on din/Jin jian nu sui yin an dian* (1962), and *Who Should Be the Commander-in-Chief?/Lung fung chang gwa sui/Long feng zheng gua shuai* (1967). Many of them starred *huadan* (young women or maidens, vivacious or shrewish, with emphasis on recitation and acting) performer Yu Lai-jan (also Lee's wife). Lee also produced contemporary films, such as Wong Toi's *A Girl Named Leng Qiuwei, 1* and *2/Laang Chau Mei/Leng Qiuwei* (1963), **Fung Chi-kong's** *My Four Children, 1* and *2/Sei ngai lui/Si er nu* (1964), and Wong Hok-sing's *All Packed into a Small House/Muk nguk qui din yue/Mu wu sha dian yu* (1965) and *Selling, Pawning and Borrowing/Maai dong che/Mai dang jie* (1967).

In the 1970s, Lee immigrated to Canada and later died there.

LEE, SUN-FUNG (Li Chenfeng) (1909–1985). A native of Guangdong province born in Guangzhou, director and writer Lee Sun-fung was orphaned at an early age when his parents died and was raised by his grandmother and aunt. In 1927, he entered the Drama School of Lingnan University and graduated from the Guangdong Drama Institute (founded by Quyang Yuqian). His early work on stage was experimental, and he organized the Drama Group of Modern Actors.

Lee moved to Hong Kong in 1933, first working as a teacher, and he started in the film industry there between 1935 and 1936, writing scripts and codirecting. He began directing after the war, with *Wait Till the Moon Shines through the Clouds* (1948) and *Perseverance Rewarded (It Will Pay Off)/Sau dak wan hoi gin yuet ming/Shou de yun kai jian yue ming* (1949). Always literary minded, he generally wrote his own scripts, often adapting them from fiction, which allowed him more control than others. The author Ba Jin was a favorite source for Lee, including the films *Spring/Chun/Chun* (1953), *Cold Nights/Hon yau/Han ye* (1955), and *A Sketch of Humanity/Yan lu/Ren lun* (1959). He also adapted the novel *Wanderings of a Poor Child* for *Everyone's Darling/Diy chue yau yau lin/Dao chu re ren lian* (1952), Cao Yu's play for *Sunrise/Yat chut/Richu* (1953), a novel by Xu Zhenya of the **Mandarin Duck and Butterfly** School for *Jade Pear Spirit (Soul of the Jade Pear)/Yuk lee wan/Yu li hun* (1953), Leo Tolstoy's *Anna Karenina* for *Broken Spring Dreams/Chun chaan mung duen/Chun can meng duan* (1955), and a Zhang Hen-shui novel for *A Tale of Laughter and Tears/Tai siu yan yuen/Ti xiao yin yuan* (1957), among others.

Lee's heyday was the 1950s and early 1960s, in Cantonese melodrama, and themes explored include anti-feudalism, whether it be the decadence of feudal families, an examination of the consequences of arranged marriages, ineffectual intellectuals, preparing the young for the future, or the contrast between city and village life, common to many progressive filmmakers of the time, especially those working for **Zhonglian**. Influenced by **Cai Chusheng**, Lee joined the Motion Pictures Cooperative program in the 1950s, and he was influenced by the north to south migration of filmmakers. He also made seven or eight Mandarin features as well as 10 in the Swatow dialect. Family as a sacred institution and depicting its members' emotions is also prominent in his work. **Ng Cho-fan** was a frequent actor and **Pak Yin** an actress in the director's films. He made the first color Cantonese film, *The Orphan/Yan hoi goo hung/Renhai guhong* (1960), starring Ng and the teenaged **Bruce Lee**. Lee wrote screenplays for director **Ng Wui**, including the ghost story *The Haunted House/Gwai nguk/Gui wu* (1950), the drama *Plum Blossom in the Snow/Suet ying hong mooi/Xue ying han mei* (1951), and *A Dream of Red Mansions (The Dream of the Red Chamber)/Hung lau san mung/Hong lou xin meng* (1951), adapted from Cao Xueqin's classic *The Story of a Stone*. He also made the occasional comedy, **martial arts**, and filmed opera movie, among them the comedy satire *A Man of Prosperity (Nouveau Riche)/Faat data ji yan/Fada zhi ren* (1956), the opera *The Wooden Hairpin (The Humble Wife)/Ging chaai gei/Jing cha ji* (1958), and the martial arts movies *Sword of Blood and Valor 1* and *2/Bik huet kim/Bi xie jian* (1958 and 1959). *A Man of Prosperity* begins in the 1930s, with a big family celebrating New Year's; the second brother leaves to work in the United States, returning in the late 1940s. The first and third brothers believe him to be wealthy, but he is poor and finds himself playing out their fantasy for the sake of appearances. Rooted in the tradition of moral folktales, the film offers an object lesson and is a humorous satire on the social pretensions of the nouveau riche.

Cold Nights (1955) is generally regarded as Lee's masterpiece. Set in Chongqing during the Japanese occupation, and adapted from a Ba Jin novel, it concerns a tubercular intellectual (Ng Cho-fan) who submits to his domineering feudalistic mother, to the disgust of his modern wife (Pak Yin). The wife leaves, only to return at war's end, to discover her physically and emotionally wasted husband. Unlike Ba's novel, in this version mother and daughter-in-law unite over the man's gravesite. Entirely shot on set, lighting and camerawork strengthen the strong emotions of the story, from anger and bitterness to regret and sadness. It takes a hard look at the cost of war and its pyrrhic victory, at the loss of idealism and cost of family.

Lee's career spanned more than 30 years and nearly 100 films, all told. *Spring* (1953), an adaptation of Ba Jin's semiautobiographical novel, won honorable mention by China's Ministry of Culture in 1957. Li retired in 1978.

LEE, TIT (1913–1996). Director Lee Tit developed an early interest in drama and at 18 appeared in **Lianhua** Studios Hong Kong branch's silent *Midnight Shot* (1932), directed by **Kwan Man-ching**. He joined the studio's acting class in Hong Kong and learned filmmaking. In 1933, he turned to intensive study of directing, writing, cinematography, editing, film scoring, and film developing. He began directing in the 1940s, making more than 70 films spanning a more than 30-year career. He was known for social realist Cantonese melodramas of the 1950s and opera films, such as *The Tragic Story of Liang Shanbo and Zhu Yingtai/Leung Chuk Han Shut/Liang Zhu Henshi* (1958), ***The Purple Hairpin****/Chi chaai gei/ Zichai ji* (1959), *Snow Storm in June/Luk yuet suet/Liu yue xue* (1959), and *Butterfly and Red Pear/Dip ying hung lee gei/ Dieying hongli ji* (1959).

Lee's social consciousness can be seen in his *Space Is Gold* (aka *Land Is Precious*)/*Cunjin chitu* episode for the omnibus film *Kaleidoscope/Yan hoi maan dut tung/Ren hui wan hua tong* (1950), produced by the South China Film Worker's Union; it presents adverse living conditions and city people as greedy and selfish; its solution suggests people return to the countryside. The director is perhaps most famous for *In the Face of Demolition/Aau lau chun hiu/Weilou chunxiao* (1953), produced by the Chung-luen (Union) film company. The story revolves around difficulties facing working-class people inhabiting one apartment (the ensemble cast featured distinguished Cantonese actors including **Cheung Ying**, **Ng Cho-fan**, Tzi Lo-lin, **Mui Yee**, and the young **Bruce Lee**). The film fits in the genre of classic tenement movies going back to 1930s Shanghai films and forward to *The House of 72 Tenants* (1963, 1973) and **Jacob Cheung's** *Cageman* (1992). Lee would return to class consciousness in some of his 1960s films, including *The Lost Pearl/Chong hoi wai chu/Cang hai wei zhu* (1965), produced by **Great Wall**, in which a seemingly orphaned, amnesiac girl grows up poor and is dismissed by the wealthy family of her boyfriend. The story later reveals her as the long-lost child of the wealthy mother. **Pak Yin** starred (her last screen performance) as the servant who rescued and raised the child. With a change in gender, the film is similar to **Lee Sun-fung's** *The Orphan* (1960, with Bruce Lee), and also fits the pattern of many 1960s melodramas focusing upon familial conflicts between Northern and Southern Chinese, with sharply delineated class distinctions. *Lost Pearl* is the last film in this genre.

Among Lee's opera films is ***Eternal Love**/Chat choi woo bat gwai/Qicai hu bugui* (1966), which starred **Josephine Siao** and **Chan Po-chu**, and was based on the **Cantonese opera** *Hu Bugui (Why Not Return?).* Both Chan and Siao were trained in Cantonese opera, and the movie remains one of the best opera films of the decade.

Lee also directed *The Little Warrior/Siu miu si/Xiao lou shi* (1969) as part of a martial arts series starring **Fung Bo-bo** as the Little White Dragon. (This film was preceded by *The White Dragon*, 1968.) In this story, Little White Dragon helps a loyal general (**Kenneth Tsang Kong**) protect the prince from assassins (led by **Shek Kin**). Like George Lucas's *Star Wars* (1977), the film not only drew its plot from Kurosawa Akira's *Hidden Fortress* (1958), but Fung Bo-bo's sword-fighting style (choreographed by **Lau Kar-leung**) was also influenced by popular Japanese samurai movies. **Samo Hung** would remake *The Little Warrior* as *Moon Warriors* (1992), starring **Anita Mui**, **Andy Lau**, and **Maggie Cheung**.

All told, Lee directed more than 100 features, including close to 100 Cantonese, 10 Mandarin, a handful of Swatow dialect, and one Amoy dialect. He remains, with **Chun Kim** and **Lee Sung-fung**, one of the three most important 1950s Cantonese directors. Deep focus was his forte signature, and his films criticize the established social hierarchy and indicate the rise of a middle class.

LEE, WAISE (Lei Chi-hung) (1959–). Born in Hong Kong, actor Waise Lee started his career in the entertainment industry as a model. Appearing in a **television** commercial, he gained the attention of producer **Tsui Hark**. His first film role was as the villain Shing in **John Woo's** *A Better Tomorrow/Ying hung boon sik/Yingxiong bense* (1986). In the next few years, Lee would appear in several big **Cinema City** productions, including *Gunmen/Tin law dei mong/Tian luo di wang* (1988) and *A Chinese Ghost Story 2/Sin nui yau wan 2 aan gaan diy/ Qiannu youhun 2 ren jian dao* (1990). Lee's most critically acclaimed role was as Paul in John Woo's *Bullet in the Head/Dip huet gaai tau/Die xue jie tou* (1990). In the early 1990s, Lee appeared in *Centre Stage/Yuen ling yuk/Ruan ling yu* (1992) and ***Swordsman** 2/Siu ngo gong wu2: Dung fong bat bai/Xiao ao jianghu2: Dongfang Bubai* (1992). After appearing in 10 films in 1993, Lee began acting in fewer and fewer films, though he did recently appear in *Inner Senses/Yee diy hung gaan/Yidu kongjian* (2002) and *Crazy n' the City/San ging hap lui/Shen jing xia lu* (2005). He also frequently appears on Hong Kong television.

LEE, YUEN-MAN (Li Yuanwen) (1912–1997). Cantonese opera librettist, composer, writer, and producer Lee Yuen-man was born in Guangdong province into a family of scholars, so he early on developed an interest in literature while simultaneously being gifted in music and writing. By age 13, he was playing a variety of Cantonese opera instruments; by age 16, he was writing Cantonese opera songs; and by age 18, he became coordinator of the Guangzhou Sports Association music group and lectured at the Chinese music study section at the Guangdong National Education Institute. Also a singer, Lee sang on the provincial radio station and appeared onstage. Following the war, he opened a nightclub featuring music and magic shows.

The musician entered the film industry at Guangzhou's Asia Studio as a musician for its first sound movie, *The Animal Intelligence* (1933). He began working for Hong Kong's Yongye Film Production Company in 1949 as a producer, with the films *End of the Day* (1949), *Dark Paradise* (1950), and *Red Rose, the Songstress* (1952).

Lee's most productive period was in the 1950s, when he composed music and soundtracks for numerous films. Among them are *Soul of the Jade Pear* (1953), ***Romance of Jade Hall**, 1* and *2* (1957–1958), *Swallows Come Home (The Swallow's Message)/Yat nin yat diy yin gwai loi/Yi nian yi du yan gui lai* (1958), and *Twelve Beauties/Sap yee laan gon sap yee chaai/Shi er lan gan shi er chai* (1964). Over an extensive career, Lee worked for the major studios, including **Shaw Brothers**, Dianmao, **Zhonglian**, **Guangyi**, and **Dacheng**.

Lee's first screenplay was **Ng Wui's** fantasy **Cantonese opera film** *The Precious Lotus Lamp/Bo lin dang/Bao lian deng* (1956), which was part of a new trend. The plot follows the son of a forbidden match, the Holy Mother of Mount Hua and a mortal, who enlists a fairy to retrieve a magical Lotus lamp. The film has an authentic stage atmosphere with the orchestra's drums and gongs recorded live on set. Two sequels followed. Other scripts and librettos include *The Romantic Monk/Ching chang yue diy siu seung goon/Qingseng tou dao Xiaoxiang guan* (1956), *Return on a Snowy Night/Yilou Fengxue ye guiren* (1957), *Xi Shi, the Eternal Beauty/Sai Si/Xi Shi* (1960), *Romance (Rescue) at the West River/Sai hiu kooi chai/Xi he hui qi* (1960), and *Romance of the Phoenix Chamber/Fung gok yan chau ching mei liu/Feng ge en chou qing wei le* (1962).

In 1966, Lee retired from the film industry but turned to recording; he established Fung Hang Records and produced traditional music, opera, and pop. He retired in 1973 and later died in Hong Kong.

LENG, CHI-PAK (Jing Cibo) (1905–1992). Cantonese opera actor Leng Chi-pak (real name Li Guoxiang) was born in Guangdong province and early on developed an abiding interest in **Chinese opera**. His third eldest brother, opera actor Xintaizi Xiang, performed with the Huanqiule Troupe, along with opera luminaries **Sit Kok-sin**, Zhu Cibo, and Xin Shaohao; Leng joined and out of respect adopted master Zhu Cibo's name for his stage name. Leng performed as third *wusheng* (male stage fighting roles) in the Zhuhuanian Troupe, and as lead *wusheng* in another, in 1924. With his brother, Liang Shaojia, he formed the Shengshounian Troupe. The fourth son in his family, Leng was called "Fourth Uncle" in the opera world.

Over the intervening years, Leng performed with various opera troupes and appeared in some of the most popular operas, including *The Impeachment of Yim Sung (Yan Song)*, *Judge Bao's Night Trial of the Wicked Guo Huai*, *The Butterfly Lovers*, *Romance of Mount Fuji*, and *Red Maid, the Matchmaker*. With the creation of the Xianfengming Troupe in 1956, Leng joined with **Yan Kim-fai**, **Leung Sing-po**, and **Pak Suet-sin**, laying the foundations of Cantonese opera cinema.

The actor's film debut was *A King Speaks His Heart (in the Cuckoo's Song)/Dai yuen chun sam dut do guen/Diyuan chunxin hua dujuan* (1951), and his first lead role was in *Judge Bao's Night Trial of the Wicked Guo Hai/Sang Baau gung yau sam gaan gwok waai/Bao Gong yeshen guo huai* (1952). The latter, a Song dynasty palace chamber piece directed by Bi Hu, is based on a folktale in which the wicked eunuch Guo Huai conspires with one of the emperor's concubines for power, stealing the emperor's newborn son by another concubine and replacing him with a leopard cat. The truth comes out and Judge Bao, disguised as the King of Hell, metes out justice. Leng appeared in over 100 features, most of them opera films, and his definitive screen performance is perhaps **Kwan Man-ching's** period Cantonese opera *The Immortal Han Xiangzi Refuses Love on a Snowy Night (An Immortal Refuses Love)/Han Xiangzi xueye guo qingguan* (1958). Leng played the uncle of a devout Buddhist follower (**Ho Fei-fan**) who arranges a marriage for him; the Buddhist refuses and becomes an immortal. When the uncle is demoted and his family suffers, the immortal descends from heaven to help.

Leng remained active in opera until the 1980s, working with the Chufengming Troupe and developing new stage talent, including actress Mei Xueshi. He died of illness in Hong Kong.

LEONG, PO-CHIH (1939–). Director Leong Po-chih, a native of Guangdong province, was born in London and educated in the United Kingdom at Leighton Park School, the University of Exeter (where he earned a degree in philosophy), and the London Film School. He worked for the BBC for two years as a film editor and came to Hong Kong in 1967 to set up a film crew for Hong Kong Television Broadcasts Limited (TVB). The next year, he was promoted to executive producer and produced a variety of programs per week, including pop, quiz, and talk shows. In 1969, he formed his own advertising production company, Adpower Ltd., with cinematographer Tony Hope, producing some U.S–award-winning commercials.

Leong began directing with **Josephine Siao** on *Jumping Ash/Tiu fooi/Tiao hui* (1976). A precursor of **New Wave** cinema, the film, a Hong Kong–style *French Connection* (1971), emphasized suspense over action and used fast pacing, freewheeling editing, and realistic documentary style to vividly capture the underworld of drugs, cops, and informants. Leong directed **Chow Yun-fat** in *Hong Kong 1941 (Waiting for Dawn)/Dang doi lai ming/Deng dai li ming* (1984), a gripping and tragic story of the Japanese occupation and resistance in Hong Kong, costarring **Cecilia Yip** and Alex Man, which won Chow Best Actor at the **Golden Horse Awards** and the **Asian Pacific Festival**. He also directed **Leslie Cheung** and **Cherie Chung** in *Fatal Love/Saai ji luen/Sha zhi lian* (1988), and John Lone in *Shanghai*

1920/Seunghoi 1920/Shanghai 1920 (1991). Leong and his daughter, Leong Sze-wing, codirected a fascinating four-part video, *Riding the Tiger* (1997), documenting the last several years of British rule in Hong Kong and examining the hopes, fears, and uncertainties of people from various walks of life.

The next year, the director made a curious **vampire film**, *Wisdom of Crocodiles* (1998), starring Jude Law and Elena Lowensohn, and has since directed several U.S. thriller **television** series, including *Cabin by the Lake* (2000) and *Wolf Lake* (2001), the latter starring Lou Diamond Phillips and American Indian actor Graham Greene.

LEUNG, GIGI WING-KEI (1976–). Born in Hong Kong with the name Leung Pei Chi and a graduate of Hong Kong Polytechnic University, actress Leung made her film debut in the romantic comedy *Dr. Mack* with **Tony Leung Chiu-wai** after she appeared in a Hong Kong commercial. She followed that up by appearing alongside **Stephen Chiau** in *The Sixty Million Dollar Man/Baak bin sing gwan/Bai bian xing jun* (1995). Her first big break, however, came with **Derek Yee's** *Full Throttle (Flaming Chariot)/Lieho zhanche* (1995) alongside superstar **Andy Lau**. Leung is known for her girl-next-door average-type beauty. She also starred in **Joe Ma's** *Feel 100%/Baak fan baak gam gaau/Bai fen bai gan jiao* (1996), one of the most popular romantic films of the 1990s, and *Feel 100% Once More/Baak fan baak aau feel/Bai fen bai yan feel* (1998), both of which had all-star casts including **Ekin Cheng** and Sammi Cheng. Leung has continued to appear in prominent films, including *Hit Man/Saai sau ji wong/Sha shou zhi wang* (1998) with **Jet Li**, and the unusual **Sylvia Chang**–directed and **Jackie Chan**–produced *Tempting Heart/Xing dong* (1999). More recently Leung has appeared in a string of comedies including *La Brassiere/Chuet sai hui bra/Jue shi hao bra* (2001) and *Mighty Baby/Chuet sai hiu b/Jue shi hao b* (2002), where she played opposite **Louis Koo**, and *Driving Miss Wealthy/Chuet sai hui ban/Jue shi hao bin* (2004), costarring **Sean Lau**. Leung also has a successful singing career and has released over 15 albums to date.

LEUNG, PATRICK PAK-KIN (1959–). Born in Hong Kong, director Patrick Leung graduated from Hong Kong Baptist College in

1982. He began in the film industry working for **John Woo** on script continuity and later as assistant director, scriptwriter, second unit director, and associate producer. Woo produced his directorial debut, *Somebody Up There Likes Me/Long maan fung biu/Lang man feng bao* (1996), and that same year he directed the gender-bending hit woman drama *Beyond Hypothermia (32 degrees Celsius)/Sip si 32 doe/She shi 32 du*. Recently he has turned his hand to comedy, directing *La Brassiere/Chuet sai hui bra/Jue shi hao bra* (2001), *Mighty Baby/Chuet sai hiu b/Jue shi hao b* (2002), and *Good Times, Bed Times/Luen seung lei dik cheng/Lian shang ni de chuang* (2003). He often collaborates with actor **Sean Lau Ching-wan**.

LEUNG, SAAN-YAN (Liang Shanren) (1920–1991). Cantonese opera librettist and writer Leung Saan-yan (real name Liang Jintong) was born in Guangdong province and completed secondary school in Nanhai. Leung joined Ren Huhua's Cultural Opera Troupe in 1942 as a performer and appeared in new-style operas like *Hong Kong's Fading Beauty*. Later on, he started writing scripts for the troupe, such as *The History of the Eastern Jin Dynasty*. During the war, the opera troupe was based in Guangzhou; after the war, in 1949, Leung moved to Hong Kong and became assistant librettist to **Tong Tik-sang** and **Lee Siu-wan**. In the 1950s, he worked independently, writing dozens of operas, many performed by **Ma Sze-tsang**, **Tang Pak-wan**, **Mak Bing-wing**, Ng Guan-lai, and others.

The librettist began writing for film in 1950. He wrote more than 100 scripts, including librettos, during the next 16 years. His popular opera films include Chan Cheung-sang's *Two Heroes/Yat chue king tin seung foo cheung/Yi zhu qing tian shuang hu jiang* (1961) and **Wong Hok-sing's** *Princess Ping Yang/Ping Yeung gung chu tai ji sau cham ying/Ping Yang gong zhu ti zi shou zhan xing* (1962). Screenplays for contemporary films include Cheung's comedy *Larceny/Ging chaat chuk siu tau/Jing cha zhuo xiao tou* (1961) and Wong's comedy *Two Mouthy Ladies from the North and South/Naam bak tit joh gai/Nan bei tie ju ji* (1965). He also wrote music and songs for films, among them the comedy *A Bachelor's Love Affair* (1953), and Wong's comedies *Half a Bed/Boon cheung luk fung chong/Ban zhang lu jia chuang* (1964) and *Teddy Boy in the Gutter/Fei goh dip laai hang kui/Fei ge die la keng qu* (1967). In the former, **Leung Sing-po** and **Fung Wong-nui** become partners after he poses as a wealthy man, although unemployed, and she is also a swindler.

In 1967, Leung retired but continued helping others write operas, like Ye Shaode, and Cantonese operas *Zhu Bian's Return to the Government* and *Farewell to Winter*. In the 1980s, he wrote a column on Cantonese opera for the *Macau Daily* newspaper. Leung died in Hong Kong following an illness.

LEUNG, SING-PO (Liang Xingbo) (1908–1981). Actor and producer Leung Sing-po (real name Liang Guangcai, known as Liang Ruhai) was a native of Guangdong province born in Singapore, where he received private tuition and was raised in an actor's family (his father and sister performed in **Cantonese operas**). He became interested in acting during childhood and appeared onstage for the first time at nine. He became one of the iconic Cantonese opera stage and screen stars.

By his early twenties, Leung was a distinguished Cantonese opera actor in both Singapore and Malaysia, earning the title of one of "The Four Kings of Cantonese Opera." He performed a singing style called "Maqiang," made famous by renowned actor **Ma Sze-tsang**. Leung joined Ma's troupe and came to Hong Kong in 1939; during wartime he performed Cantonese opera throughout Mainland China. Later he started an opera troupe with actress **Tan Lanqing** (Tam Lan-hing).

Director Ren Yuhua brought him into the film industry. His first starring role was *The Elderly Gentleman Searches for Romance/Lam liu yap dut/Lin lao ru hua cong* (1950). His career spanned more than 30 years and 400 films, including innumerable adaptations of Cantonese operas, such as Cheung Wai-gwong's *The Story of a Sing Song Girl/Dut laai kong naam nim sei kiu/Hua luo jiang nan er shi si qiao* (1960), **Tso Kea's *The Romance of Jade Hall*** *1* and *2 (My Kingdom for a Husband)/Suen gung yim shut/Xuangong yanshi* (1957 and 1958), **Lee Tit's *The Purple Hairpin*/***Chi chaai gei/Zichai ji* and *Butterfly and Red Pear/Dip ying hung lee gei/Dieying hongli ji* (both 1959), **Mok Hong-si's** *The Fairy of Ninth Heaven/Gau tin yuen lui/Jiu tian xuannu* (1959), and **John Woo's** *Princess Chang Ping/Dai Nui Fa/ Dinu Hua* (1976). In the classic *The Purple Hairpin*, he played the poor Cui Yunming, indebted to **Pak Suet-sin's** courtesan, and the reincarnation of the Man in the Yellow Robe, the disguised fourth imperial prince, empathetic to her suffering. In librettist **Tong Tik-sang's** adaptation of the Fujian opera *Lychee for Red Peaches*, *The Fairy of Ninth Heaven*, Leung played the master to a scholar (cross-dressed **Yam Kim-fai**) in love with a famous beauty (Pak Suet-sin); the master teacher serves as their go between and makes the mistake that words alone can save.

Leung's versatility as an opera actor was equally matched by the feeling he emoted in performance. He turned to comedy as he began gaining weight; no longer playing *wenwu sheng* (young roles) in opera, he played *chou sheng* (comic roles) and *xu sheng* (middle-aged roles); he earned the moniker "King of Comedians." His comedies often taught lessons. He played calculating hypocrites who get their comeuppance as well as kindhearted and generous men.

Leung also made Mandarin comedies like **Tao Qin's** *Beware of Pickpockets/Dai fong siu sau/Ti fang xiao shou* (1958) and *The More the Merrier/Saam sing boon ming/San xing ban yue* (1959), and **Wang Tianlin's** *The Greatest Civil War on Earth/Naam bak who/Nan bei he* (1961), *The Greatest Wedding on Earth/Nam bak yut ga chan/Nan bei yijia qin* (1962), and *The Greatest Love Affair on Earth/Naam bak hei seung fung/Nan bei xi xiang feng* (1964), the latter three written by **Eileen Chang**. He also made Cantonese comedies such as *Money for Marriage* (1964) and **Chor Yuen's** *The Lady and a Thief (Maiden Thief)/Yuk lui san tau/Yu nu shen tou* (with **Josephine Siao**, 1967), and dramas like *Four Darling Daughters/Sei fung kau wong/Si feng qiu huang* (1969).

The Romance of Jade Hall was a romantic musical comedy with Western elements. Leung and Tan Lanqing played a pair of overweight servants paralleling a royal couple. Tan's exaggerated gestures and mugging were set against Leung's more subtle humor and slow responses. The **North–South trilogy** of comedies Leung made with Wang Tianlin (*The Greatest . . .*) pair him with another portly actor, **Liu Enjia**, pitting Leung's Cantonese character against Liu's Northerner to great comic effect.

In 1953, Leung helped organize the Chinese Artist Association of Hong Kong, an organization of Cantonese opera performers; he was four times elected its president. He also established two film companies, Liying and Dafeng, producing films such as the Cantonese drama *Precious Daughter* (1956) and Cantonese opera *The Dunce Attends a*

Birthday Party (1956). He turned to **television** and hosted the popular Hong Kong Television Broadcasts (TVB) variety show *Enjoy Yourself Tonight* in 1967. In 1976, he was among the first actors in Hong Kong to be knighted as a Member of the Order of the British Empire (OBE) because of his contributions to the performing arts. He was affectionately referred to as "Uncle Bo." He died of colon cancer, but his legacy survives in three daughters who are actresses, Liang Baozhen in television dramas, Wen Lan in films, and Liang Baochu in Cantonese opera.

LEUNG, TONY CHIU-WAI (1962–). Born in Hong Kong, actor Tony Leung Chiu-wai (not to be confused with actor **Tony Leung Ka-fai**) started in the Hong Kong Television Broadcasts Limited (TVB) training program and began in **television**, costarring in the series *Police Cadet* (with **Lau Ching-wan**, **Carina Lau**, and **Maggie Cheung**), and he became famous for his role as Wai Siu-bo in the popular show *The Duke of Mount Deer* (also starring **Andy Lau**). He segued into films in the early 1980s, appearing alongside **Chow Yun-fat** in both *The Lunatics (Lunatics: True Story)/Din lo jing juen/Dian lao zheng zhuan* (1986) and **Stanley Kwan's** *Love unto Waste (Underground Love)/Dei ha ching/Di xia qing* (1986). He has been much lauded and has managed to run the gamut from serious films to action, legends, soaps, and crazy comedies. Leung costarred in two **John Woo** films, the autobiographical *Bullet in the Head (Bloodshed on the Streets)/Dip huet gaai tau/Die xue jie tou* (1990), in which he played Woo's alter ego, and *Hard-Boiled (Hot-Handed God of Cops)/Lat sau san taam/ Lashou shentan* (1992), in which he portrayed an undercover cop opposite Chow Yun-fat's detective. He has also acted in six **Wong Kar-wai** films, those being *Days of Being Wild (The True Story of Ah Fei)/ Ah Fei ching chuen/A Fei zhengzhuan* (1990), *Chungking Express (Chungking Forest)/Chung Hing sam lam/Zong qing sen lin* (1994), ***Ashes of Time*** *(Evil East, Malicious West)/Dung chea sai duk/Dong xie xi du* (1994), *Happy Together (A Sudden Leak of Spring Light)/Chun gwong ja sit/Chun guang zha xie* (1997), *In the Mood for Love/Fa yeung nin wa/Hua yang nian hua* (2000), and *2046* (2004). In his first Wong film, his screen presence amounted to a cameo, but in *Chungking Express*, his character's indecisiveness and moon-eyed, soulful longing contributed to the importance of proximity and chance in the relationships defined by the story. He played the blind swordsman in *Ashes of Time* and one of the partners (along with **Leslie Cheung**) in a gay love story in the controversial *Happy Together*, for which he was awarded Best Actor at the Cannes Film Festival. His most expressive nonverbal character to date has been the lead in Wong's *In the Mood for Love*, set in the Shanghainese community in Hong Kong in the early 1960s and costarring Maggie Cheung. He costarred in several **Peter Chan** films, including *He Ain't Heavy, He's My Father! (New Two of a Kind)/San naam hing naan dai/Xin nan xiong nan di* (1993) and *Tom, Dick, and Hairy (Three World-Weary Heroes)/Fung chan saam hap/Feng chen san xia* (1993), in both of which he played urban yuppie characters searching for themselves and trying to make sense of their relationships. He served as the moral center of Mainland director **Zhang Yimou's** *Hero/Ying xiong* (2002), the director's first **martial arts action** movie.

Unlike many others, Leung never took part in the Hong Kong method of filming that allowed a hot star to work on several films at once (using photo doubles in every possible shot), and complete up to 20 or more films a year. He has opted instead to mix one or two long-term projects with a couple of "quickies." His film output has therefore remained fairly stable, even with the Hong Kong industry's decline. He has won Best Actor awards for *Chungking Express*, *Happy Together*, *In the Mood for Love*, and *Infernal Affairs/Mou gaan dou/Wu jian dao* (2002) at the **Hong Kong Film Awards**.

Leung also launched a successful singing career with the help of his best friend, singer **Jacky Cheung**. He wore a men's skirt to accept a music award on a 1995 show, ridiculed the hostesses' ball gowns when they commented on his attire, and thanked his music label, his friend Cheung, and himself in his acceptance speech. Leung speaks Cantonese, Mandarin, and more than passable English. He grew up in desperate circumstances in Hong Kong, as his father deserted the family when he was six years old. He considers himself to be "horribly shy," and pursued acting from his youth as a way to get an emotional release while hiding himself. He does not actively promote himself or his career. He is reported to be as intense in his personal life as he is on-screen. He has sustained a long relationship with actress Carina Lau since the 1980s. *Time* magazine listed him as number nine of its 10 Most Interesting People of 2000.

LEUNG, TONY KA-FAI (1958–). Prolific actor Tony Leung's mother worked in the box office at a theater showing Hollywood movies, and Leung grew up watching them. Born in Hong Kong in 1958, he studied design and graduated from the Hong Kong Institute of Technology and entered the Hong Kong Television Broadcasts Limited (TVB) training program, but dropped out to earn a living, forming a short-lived entertainment magazine with friends. He met director **Li Han-hsiang** (Li Hanxiang, Lee Hong-cheun), who cast him as a lead in *The Burning of the Imperial Palace/Huoshao yuanming yuan* (1983). (He would later turn down the role of last emperor in Bertolucci's film of the same title out of respect for Li, who would become like a father to him.) Li's film, like Bertolucci's, covered the same time period and subject and was shot on the Mainland. Leung won Best Actor at the **Hong Kong Film Awards** in 1983. (Unfortunately, Taiwan, Hong Kong's largest export market at the time, would blacklist him for two years for appearing in a film shot on the Mainland.)

The actor began working off-camera at **Cinema City**, connecting with **Tsui Hark** (he starred in Tsui productions *King of Chess [Chess King]/Kei wong/Qi wang* [1992], *A Better Tomorrow 3: Love and Death in Saigon [True Colors of a Hero 3]/Ying hung boon sik 3/Yingxiong bense 3* [1989], and *Dragon Inn [New Dragon Gate Inn]/San lung moon haak chan/Xin longmen kezhan* [1992]). In the first, he played a sensitive and talented peasant chess player in the **Yim Ho**–directed sequences; in the second, he costarred with **Chow Yun-fat** and **Anita Mui** in Tsui's Vietnam-set apocalypse with allusions to Tiananmen Square and Hong Kong–China relations; and in the third, a remake of **King Hu's *wuxia*** classic, he costarred with **Brigitte Lin**, **Maggie Cheung**, and **Donnie Yen** as a legendary swordsman of the ***jiang hu***. He starred in Peter Wang's comedic *Laser Man* (1986), shot in New York with an international cast, produced by Tsui, and he costarred again with Chow in **Ringo Lam's** *Prison on Fire (Prison Turbulence)/Gaam yuk fung wan/Jian yu feng yun* (1987) as an innocent and naive inmate taken under the wing of Chow, running through a range of emotions including fear, compassion, comradery, righteous anger, hopelessness, horror, and aggression.

In 1990, Leung won Best Actor at the Taiwanese **Golden Horse Awards** for his harrowing portrayal of a Chinese immigrant lost in New York in **Clara Law's** drama *Farewell China (Demon Love Painting)/Moh wah ching/Mo hua qing* (also starring Maggie Cheung, 1990). The two have appeared together in many films. In 1991, he gained international reach as the lead in French director Jean-Jacques Arnaud's *The Lover*, based on the autobiographical novel by Marguerite Duras, an eroticized and sexually explicit art house film. Leung was cast as director **Cai Chusheng** in **Stanley Kwan's** postmodern portrayal of the great silent screen star **Ruan Lingyu**, *Centre Stage (*aka *Actress)/Yuen Ling-yuk/Ruan Lingyu* (1992), an homage to Chinese filmmaking and period 1930s Shanghai; Leung reunited with the director for another Shanghai-set ambience in *Everlasting Regret/Chui chung aan chin yan/Zhui zong yan qian ren* (2005). Leung continued making movies in Hong Kong, a dozen in 1993 alone, many of those comedies that have exploited his physical and voice talents. Among them was **Tony Au's** *A Roof with a View (The Moonlight from Heaven's Windowsill, aka Love on the Roof)/Tin toi dik yuet gwong/Tian tai de yue guang* (1993), in which Leung demonstrated great and natural rapport with a child actor as well as chemistry with **Veronica Yip**. In Wong Jing's off-the-wall comedy *Boys Are Easy (Chasing Boys) /Chui lam chai/Zhui nan zi* (1993), he was paired with Brigitte Lin and delivered a hilarious bowling alley song set to the tune of the theme from John Huston's *Moulin Rouge* (1952). He also broke out into the well-known **Ge Lan** song "Ja-Ja-Jambo" from Wang Tianlin's ***Wild, Wild Rose*** (1960) in **Peter Chan's** *Tom, Dick and Hairy (Three World-Weary Heroes)/Fung chan saam hap/Feng chen san xia* (1993), as a shameless womanizer who realizes the value of love too late. That same year, he again won Best Actor at the Hong Kong Film Awards for a dead-on imitation of **Lui Kei** in **Jeff Lau's** spoof of 1960s *Black Rose* spy vehicles,*'92 Legendary La Rose Noire ('92 Black Rose vs. Black Rose)/Hak mui gwai dui hak mui gwai/92 Hei mei gui dui hei mei gui*.

Like many Hong Kong actors, Leung has worked in all genres, as adept at comedy as drama, as capable in period piece as contemporary action; he has consistently generated sexual heat on-screen. His portrayal of renowned swordsman Huang Yaoshi (Evil East) in **Wong Kar-wai's** Eastern-Western ***Ashes of Time*** *(Evil East, Malicious*

West)/Dung chea sai duk/Dong xie xi du (1994), based on chapters from **Louis Cha's** (Jin Yong) *wuxia* novel *The Eagle Shooting Hero*, involved a philosophical and emotionally wounded swordsman who drinks to forget, and Leung costarred with a wonderful ensemble cast including **Leslie Cheung**, Brigitte Lin, Maggie Cheung, **Tony Leung Chiu-wai**, **Jacky Cheung**, and **Carina Lau**. The next year, he played a Japanese writer in Tony Au's sensual art house *Christ of Nanjing/Laam ging dik gei duk/Nan jing de ji du* (1995). An actor who enjoys taking risks and trying new things, he starred in (and produced) **Nelson Yu Lik-wai's** experimental *Love Will Tear Us Apart (Ah Ying)/Tian shang ren jian* (1999), an official Cannes Film Festival selection from Hong Kong in 1999, and Cheng Hui-lung's *The Gua Sha Treatment (Ghu Sha: The Treatment)/Gwaat Sa/Gua Sha* (2002), produced by the Beijing Television Art Center, filmed in St. Louis, and based on a true story of cultural misunderstanding. Leung costarred with David Morse in *Double Vision/Seung Tung/Shuang Tong* (2002), a Hong Kong–Taiwan–United States coproduction psychological horror film, and with **Gong Li** in Sun Zhou's *Zhou Yu's Train/Zhou yu de huoche* (2002), a China–Hong Kong coproduction. He appeared opposite **Sylvia Chang** in her romantic comedy *20:30:40* (2004), a story of three women at various stages in their lives.

Leung won Best Supporting Actor for his role in **Edmond Pang's** *Men Suddenly in Black/Daai cheung foo/Da zhang fu* (2003) at the 23rd Hong Kong Film Awards. Recently he starred with Charlene Choi in **Herman Yau's** comedy *Papa Loves You/Jei goh ah ba chan baau ja /Zhe ge ba ba zhen bao zha* (2004), and with both **"Twins"** (Choi and Gillian Chung) in **Patrick Leung's** *Huadu Chronicles: The Blade of the Rose (Twins Effect 2)/Chin gei bin 2: Dut diy daai chin/Qian ji bian 2: Hua dou da zhan* (also 2004, with action directed by **Corey Yuen**), the action fantasy sequel to popular *Twins' Effect*, in which Leung plays adoptive father to the future emperor and ally to the Twins. Donnie Yen plays the villainous swordsman general who wants to rule the world but must first overcome the Lord of Armor (**Jackie Chan**). Leung also appears in Chan's *The Myth/San wa/Shen hua* (2005). Leung has appeared in over 75 movies to date. In 1996, he released a recording in Mandarin on Rock Records in Taiwan.

LI, CHEUK-TO. Film critic Li Cheuk-to joined the editorial board of *Film Bi-weekly* in 1980 and was its editor in chief (1983–1986). He has been a programmer for the **Hong Kong International Film Festival** for 17 years, in charge of its Hong Kong cinema retrospectives (1983–1990) and international cinema (1990–2000), and beginning in 2001, was its general manager; in 2004 he became its artistic director. A founding member of the **Hong Kong Film Critics Society**, he served as its president (1995–1999).

LI, HAN-HSIANG (LI HANGXIANG) (1926–1996). Director Li Han-hsiang was born in Jinzhou, Lianing Province, and he studied Western painting at the prestigious National Art Institute in Beijing. He came to Hong Kong in 1948, and he began working in the film industry, first as an extra and actor at **Great China**, and then as a set designer at **Grandview**, next working as a scriptwriter and an assistant director at **Yonghua**, and eventually director. His directorial debut was with ***Blood in the Snow*** *(Red Bloom in the Snow/Suet lee hung/Xue lihong* (1956). He began working for **Shaw Brothers** in 1954 and became one of their finest directors, specializing in films with Northern Chinese settings and subjects, making over 25 films in seven years. He left Shaw in 1963, and went to Taiwan where he created his own film company, Guolian, making 20 films; he returned to Hong Kong in 1970, rejoining Shaw in 1972 and worked there for another 10 years, introducing the theme of duplicity in movies such as *Legend of Cheating* (1971) and *Cheating in Panorama* (1972).

Blood in the Snow (1956) is a behind-the-scenes story of a small-time folk opera troupe and other performers in Northern China in the 1930s; the movie is a melodrama with songs integrated into the story as the characters stage their performances. Starring **Li Lihua**, **Ge Lan**, **Lo Wei**, and **Wang Yuanlong**, the movie is well crafted, with all major characters introduced in a chain of intersecting actions. A background of authentic street life, markets, and courtyards, along with lively renditions of Beijing folk songs, captures the shades of Northern Chinese folk culture, further enhanced by a strong ensemble supporting cast of Mandarin actors of Northern origin, including the young **King Hu**.

With ***The Kingdom and the Beauty****/Kong saan mei yan/Jiangshan meiren* (1959) and ***The Love Eterne*** *(Eternal Love)/Leung saan ang* *yue chuk ying toi/Liang shanbo yu zhu yingtai* (1962), Li set the standard for ***huangmei diao*** genre pictures in Hong Kong and Taiwan in the 1960s. *Huangmei diao* is a traditional aesthetic form of Chinese stage opera that exploited cinematic technique and individual actors' singing and performance styles, creating a rich cinematic Chinese past. The latter is based on one of China's most famous love stories, that of Liang Shanbo and Zhu Yingtai, a scholar and a female beauty who dons a male disguise to attend school. The doomed lovers are subjected to parental and class prejudices.

The Kingdom and the Beauty (1959) won the sixth **Asian Film Festival** Best Picture. *The Warlord/Daai gwan fat/Da jun fa* (1972), starring **Michael Hui**, won Best Comedy and Best Character Development at the 19th Asian Film Festival. *The Empress Dowager/King gwok king shing/ Qing Guo Qing Cheng* (1975), a historical costume epic with an all-star cast (including **Ti Lung**), authentic costumes and props, and extensive sets, won Honorable Mention for Drama at the 12th **Golden Horse Awards**, Best Actress for **Lisa Lu**, and Best Color Art Design for Chen Ching-shen. *Burning of the Imperial Palace/Huoshao yuanming yuan* (1983) was released during the Sino-British negotiations regarding Hong Kong's future. This historical epic features scenes of the British plundering and destroying the Summer Palace in 1860, but Empress Dowager Cixi is the undisputed power behind the throne as the Qing dynasty crumbles under the burden of foreign imperialism. At the time, Beijing declared the film "patriotic." For *The Empress Dowager*, *Burning of the Imperial Palace*, and *Reign behind the Curtain/Shui lim teng ching/Chui lian ting zheng* (also 1983 and starring **Tony Leung Ka-fai** in the latter two), Li was invited by Beijing to shoot the historic epics on authentic locations. Li also directed another version of *The Empress Dowager/Sai taai hau/Xi tai hou* (1989, with **Gong Li**) and a version of *The Last Emperor/Feng lung/Huo long* (1986), also starring Leung, focusing on the latter years of former emperor Pu Yi, not to be confused with Bernardo Bertolucci's film of the same title.

Meticulous in his research, Li will be remembered for his ability to handle historic themes with microscopic attention to the details of life and manners in ancient China, presented as spectacles set in the past with his highly polished lavish productions, as well as for the simplicity and plainness of films like *A Mellow Spring/Chun gwong miu haan hiu/Chun guang wuxian hao* (1957) and *The Winter/Dung nuen/Dong nuan* (1969). He was an important figure of the first generation of postwar directors and influenced those who followed in Hong Kong and Taiwan.

LI, HELEN MEI (1929–1994). Born in Jilin province, actress Li Mei (real name Li Jingfang) had a civil servant father and a well-educated mother. She spent her childhood in Hebei, later moving to Shanghai and Nanjing. At the war's end she moved to Beijing and attended the University of North China. She came to Hong Kong in 1949, starting with **Great Wall** (although she never made a film there) and joining Minsheng in 1950 as a screenwriter. Her first screenplay was *The Golden World/Wong gam sai gaai/Huang jin shi jie* (1953). When she took part in the Miss Hong Kong pageant in 1952 she changed her name to Li Mei. She became known as one of the "sour beauties," a strong female character with sex appeal, a "sex kitten." Her film debut was *Strayed Beauty* (1953) and she caught the public eye with other films the same year, including *The Secret Life of Lady So Lee (Notorious Woman)/Ming lui yan bit chuen/ Ming Nuren Biezhuan*, *Returning the Pearl (Return of the Pearl)/Suen chu gei/Huan zhu ji*, and *A Woman of Throbbing Passions/Dong foo ching chi/Dang fu qing chi*. She joined International Films, forerunner of **Motion Pictures and General Investment (MP&GI)**, in 1955, appearing in *Calendar Girl/Lung cheung fung mo/Longxiang fengwu* (1959) and *It's Always Spring/Tiu lee chang chun/Tao li zheng chun* (1962), dancing and singing in both. In *Calendar Girl*, she played the eldest daughter of estranged parents, and when she and her sister are both entered in the calendar girl pageant, she lets her sister win; later both sisters perform in the father's musical show.

In 1956 Li founded the Beidou Film Company, appearing in and producing *Wild Fire (Prairie Fire)/Ye huo* (1958), **Chang Cheh's** tragic melodrama, and *Romance in Bangkok* (1958). In *Wild Fire*, she played an abandoned daughter who suffers for love. She falls in love with her rescuer, who changes his affections to another. After being raped and tried on a false charge, she is about to reunite with her lover when more tragedy ensues. Her last film for MP&GI was *The Imperial Lady/Sai taai hau yue jan fei/Xi tai hou yu zhen fei* (1964). She appeared onstage in Japan in the play *Hong Kong*

(1961), modeled swimsuits for the United States sportswear company Jantzen, and married an American who was a former CIA agent in 1967, after which she retired from acting and lived in the United States until her death from cancer.

LI, HENG (1913–). Screenwriter, actor, and director Li Heng, a native of Guangdong province, was born in Macau. He began working on stage in 1937 and joined the China Travelling Drama Group, acting in many plays. During the war, he formed the Yilian Acting troupe, touring the Mainland. After the war, he wrote and directed plays for the Hong Kong Drama Troupe.

Li appeared in a Cantonese classic, *Tears of the Pearl River (**Dawn Must Come**)/Chu kong lui/Zhujiang lei* (1950). Directed by **Wang Weiyi** and produced by **Cai Chusheng**, the movie narrates the lives of uneducated Guangdong peasants exploited by a greedy landlord who forces them to work in Guangzhou.

Li began writing screenplays with *The Prodigal Son/Baijia zai*(1952). **Lo Dun** played a father who goes to work in the United States to make a better living; his wife, believing her husband is doing well, spoils her son, who grows up to be profligate. When the father returns, he runs a laundry and ends up hiring his son's abandoned wife. When the son is rejected by the sycophants around him, he repents and returns to his wife and father. Li's stories were moralistic, family tales.

In Li's screen roles, he became known for kindhearted, gentle characters with good breeding. In 1973, Li turned to television. Among his greatest contribution, however, has been the training of actors, through the actors' training course offered by **Great Wall** and **Xinlian**, as well as at Rediffusion Television's (RTV) seventh and Asia Television Limited's (ATV) third, actors' training programs.

LI, JACK PINGQIAN (1902–1984). Born in Hangzhou, Li Pingqian began his filmmaking career in Shanghai in the 1920s after graduating from university. His father encouraged an interest in photography, leading Li to drama and film. In 1920, Li signed with Shanghai's **Mingxing** and enrolled in the company's film training course. His first film, which he directed and wrote, was *A Perfect Romance*

(1924). He made more than 100 silent films and as many in Mandarin.

First as an apprentice and gradually a screenwriter and translator, he established himself as a director by the 1930s, coming to Hong Kong in 1947, and bringing with him the tradition of leftist filmmakers to make comedies, melodramas, and thrillers of social introspection and criticism. At the **Great Wall** Studio, he served on the scriptwriter–director committee established after the company's 1950 reorganization, and became one of the creative minds behind the company, directing more than 25 films there. A leftist filmmaker, Li addressed social corruption and human foibles, but he was also the most commercial filmmaker at the studio, making light-hearted films that gently poked fun at human weaknesses.

A Strange Woman/Yat doi yiu gei/Yi dai yao ji (1950), for example, set in Beijing in the 1910s and 1920s, criticizes the decadence and corruption of rapacious warlords. The story was based on *Tosca*, and the heroine, a songstress (**Bai Guang**), sacrifices herself to a cruel warlord to save her revolutionary lover. *Awful Truth/Suet fong sai gaai/Shuohuang Shijie* (1950), written by **Tao Qin**, is a screwball comedy and exposé of human foibles, set in Shanghai during the last days of the Kuomintang, when inflation has skyrocketed. Speculators and con men lie, cheat, and beguile others to squeeze out the last profit as the regime nears collapse. In the plot of *Tales of the City/Diy kooi gaau heung kuk/Duhui jiaoxinag qu* (1954), an unemployed young man wins the lottery and is suddenly everyone's best friend. *Laugh, Clown, Laugh/Siu siu siu/Xiao xiao xiao* (1960), set in Tianjin during the Japanese occupation, features an accountant (**Bao Fang**) who loses his job but hides it from his family; he takes up with a partner to perform *xiangsheng* (Chinese stand-up comedy dependent on Mandarin banter), a few steps down from his previous employment because of the low status assigned to entertainers. The film is a tragicomedy as the family suffers embarrassment and humiliation when they discover the truth. With *Forever Waiting/Mong foo saan gwong/Wangfu shanxia* (1957) and *Rendezvous/Gaai yan yau yeuk/Jiaren youyue* (1960), Li tried his hand at suspense thrillers in the Hitchcock style. Li was a versatile director who masterfully handled comedies, satires, melodramas, operas, and historical costumers, yet satirical comedy remained his signature.

LI, JET LIAN-JE (1963–). Born in Beijing, Jet Li was two when his father died. Li started training in *wushu* at the age of eight in a government-run summer sports camp. Li was part of an elite group that was asked to come back for further training every day after school for two hours. After three months, out of the 20 students remaining, all but four were eliminated from the program. At the age of nine, Li won the award for excellence in the first **martial arts** exhibition held since the Cultural Revolution. Afterward, Li no longer attended regular school and moved into the dormitory of the sports school; during the day, he usually trained for eight hours. At the age of 11, Li was part of a group of Chinese martial artists that traveled to the United States and met then president Richard Nixon who asked Li if he would be his bodyguard when he grew up. Li precociously replied, "No, I don't want to protect any individual. When I grow up, I want to defend my one billion Chinese countrymen!" That same year, Li won his first national championship title.

At the age of 17, Li retired from *wushu* competition and later began his film career in the **Zhang Xinyan**–directed ***Shaolin Temple*** *(Siu lam chi/ Shaolin si)* (1982). The film made Li famous on-screen and two sequels were made. From 1987 to 1990, Li was married to Huang Qiuyan, with whom he had two daughters. Li's next big career move came when he teamed up with director/producer **Tsui Hark** to make *Once upon a Time in China (Wong Fei-hung/Huang Feihong)* (1991), which breathed new life both into the martial arts genre and into the august **Wong Fei-hung** character. Li also reprised the role in three out of the five sequels in the ***Once upon a Time in China* series**, whose popularity will indelibly identify him with the character in audiences' minds. Li also starred in the *wuxia* revival ***Swordsman*** *2/Siu ngo gong woo ji Dung Fong Bat Baai/Xiao ao jianhu zhi Dongfang Bubai* (1992), directed by **Ching Siu-tung** and produced by Tsui Hark.

Li has also worked with **Gordon Chan**, director of *Fist of Legend/Cheung miu ying hung/Jing wu ying xiong* (1994), a remake of *Fist of Fury*, in which Li reprised **Bruce Lee's** role as Chen Zhen, with the action directed by **Yuen Wo-ping**, earlier with Yuen Woping on *Tai Chi Master/Taai gik cheung saam fung/Tai ji zhang san feng* (1993, costarring **Michelle Yeoh**), and on *Hit Man/Saai sau ji wong/Sha shou zhi wang* (1998, produced by Gordon Chan); he also worked with Tsui collaborator Daniel Lee on Lee's *Black Mask/Hak hap/Hei xia* (1996, costarring **Karen Mok**). Obviously, Li's characterizations have always been part of action-driven stories, to allow him to demonstrate his physical talents, and his characters have always been "the good guys," more specifically, the heroes.

Most productive have been Li's collaborations with director **Corey Yuen Kwai**, with whom he has made numerous films, including *Fong Sai-yuk 1* and *2/Fong Sai-yuk/Fang Shiyu*, *Bodyguard from Beijing/Chung naam hoi biu biu/Zhong nan hai bao biao*, and *My Father Is a Hero (A Letter to Father)/Kap ba ba dik sun/Gei ba ba de xin* (1993, 1994, and 1995, respectively), as well as Yuen's action direction for **Wong Jing's** *High Risk (Mouse Courage, Dragon Might)/ Sue daam lung wei/Shu dan long wei* (1995, costarring **Jacky Cheung**). Ironically, Li's first Hollywood introduction to audiences would cast him as a villain (*Lethal Weapon 4*, 1998). In recent years, Li has starred in a number of Hollywood films, often teaming him with African American hiphop artists. Corey Yuen Kwai would serve as action director on Li's Hollywood films. Li returned to Hong Kong to star in **Zhang Yimou's** *Hero/Ying hung/ Ying xiong* (2002), again as the "hero" of the title. Li resides with his second wife, actress Nina Li Chi, with whom he has one child, in the United States.

LI, LIHUA. Actress Li Lihua was discovered in Shanghai by director **Yue Feng**, who cast her at 16 in her film debut *Three Smiles/San xiao* (1940). She was a teenage star in Shanghai, starring during wartime in *Qiu Haitang, Part One* and *Two/Qiu Haitang, Shangxia ji* (1943), an adaptation of a novel and play that has the notoriety of being used as propaganda by the Japanese, and costarring in the comic postwar satire *Phony Phoenixes/Jiafeng xuhuang* (1947). She came to Hong Kong in 1947 and worked with the best directors there, including Yue Feng, **Zhu Shilin**, **Li Pingqian**, and **Li Han-hsiang**. Li remained one of Yue Feng's favorite actresses (along with **Lin Dai**), costarring in his *Three Women/Saam lui shing/San nuxing* (1947), in which she played an independent career woman bringing up the daughter of a prostitute, and *Modern Red Chamber Dream/San hung lau mung/Xin honglou meng* (1952), a modern adaptation of the classic novel *Dream of the Red Chamber*, in which she starred as a sympathetic orphan adopted into a powerful feudal family. She falls in love with the family's son (played by her future husband, actor and director **Yan Jun**), only to be abandoned when the family's class politics and self-interest outweigh their humanity.

Similar in theme but quite different in tone, Li Pingqian's screwball comedy *Awful Truth/Suet fong sai gaai/Shuohuang shijie* (1950) was another film set in the last days of Shanghai before the fall of the Nationalists, and a money-crazed, materialistic cast of characters, led by Li and Yan Jun, is hilarious. She also starred alongside Han Fei in Zhu Shilin's *Spoiling the Wedding Day/Neung gaai gei/ Wu jiaqi* (1951) as half of a working-class couple attempting to overcome obstacles in the way of them arranging their wedding. In producer **Zhang Shankun** and director **Evan Yang's** *What Price Beauty?/ Xiao bai cai* (1954), she portrayed a wife accused of conspiring with her lover and murdering her husband. Based on the famous 19th-century case of Yang Naiwu and Xiao Bai Cai, the story had been the subject of several operas and films before; this time the perspective presented is the woman's, and even though pardoned by the Empress Dowager herself, the innocent woman enters a monastery.

Described as a "sour beauty," Li Lihua portrayed exceptionally strong women, attractive to men, who preserved their femininity. She shone in Zhu Shilin's *Flower Girl/Fa goo leung/Hua guniang* (1951), adapted from Guy de Maupassant's *Boule de Suif*, and set on the Mainland during the Sino–Japanese War. She played a prostitute ("flower girl") who sacrifices to aid in the patriotic cause against the Japanese; the film takes the measure of a hypocritical bourgeoisie that thinks little of her. One of her most memorable roles is as Xiao Fengxian ("Little Phoenix") in **Tu Guanqi's** film of that title, *The Little Phoenix/Siu fung sin/Xiao fengxian* (1953). She played a singsong girl opposite Yan Jun's revolutionary general Cai Songbo. Based on a true story, the plot revolves around their plotting to overthrow the first president of the Chinese Republic who planned to proclaim himself emperor. Equally memorable performances were in Li Han-hsiang films, including the melodrama ***Blood in the Snow** (Red Bloom in the Snow)/Suet lee hung/Xue lihong* (1956), his directorial debut, and the historical *gongwei* (palace chamber) drama *Empress Wu Tse-tien/Mo Jak Tin/Wu Zetian* (1963). In the latter film, she played the title role with feminist flair.

Li Lihua was courted by Hollywood's Cecil B. DeMille, who cast her as a war bride (opposite Victor Mature) in Frank Borzage's *China Doll* (1958), but she returned to Hong Kong and she and her husband signed with **Shaw Brothers** shortly thereafter, where she continued filming. She costarred in Yan Jun's ***huangmei diao***, ***The Grand Substitution***/*Maan goo lau fong/Wangu liufang* (1965), and when they both retired, they relocated to New York in 1972. After his death and her remarriage, she settled in Singapore. Her film career spanned over 40 years.

LI, MINWEI (Lai Man-wai) (1893–1953). Born in Yokohama, Japan, Li Minwei was one of the pioneers in developing Hong Kong and Chinese cinema. He advocated "national salvation through cinema" and believed in the power of movies, artistically and educationally, to bring about reform and education. He was educated at St. Paul's College in Hong Kong, and followed his father into business. He took part in the 1911 Revolution that ended the dynasties in China.

Li was interested in photography and theater, and he helped form the Qingpingle Drama Group and was one of its principal actors and directors, involved in numerous plays. In 1913, he met the American Benjamin Polaski, and they joined the Huamei Film Company, to produce the silent film *Zhuangzi Tests His Wife (Chuang Tzu Tests His Wife)/Chong Ji shut chai/Zhangzi shiqi* (1913), adapted from a **Cantonese opera**, which Li made and starred in, playing the female role. While there was a ban at the time on women appearing on the theatrical stage, there was not one in film; however, due to disapproval of family and society, Li's wife, Yan Shanshan, appeared only in a supporting role. The film was the earliest Chinese movie shown in the United States, and had been financed by and technically assisted by Americans. In 1922, along with his brother Li Beihai and cousin Li Haishan, he established Hong Kong's first local film company, **Minxin** (China Sun Film Company Limited), and he also became an instructor in its actors' training class. He coordinated and photographed Hong Kong's first **documentary**, *Chinese Competitors at the Sixth Far East Sports Games in Japan* (1923) and the company produced (and Li directed and acted in) *Lipstick (Rouge)/Yin chi/Yanzhi* (1925), financed, acted, and made by locals. Li Minwei and Li Haishan also opened Hong Kong's first movie theater, the New World Cinema, in 1924.

In 1925, Li moved the company to Shanghai, helping to develop the burgeoning film industry there. Other silent films included *Romance of the Red Chamber* (1927), *Cai Gongshi* (1928), and *Mulan Joins the Army* (1929). *Romance of the Red Chamber*, adapted from one of China's earliest operatic plays, has survived and prints are archived in Beijing and Taipei. The company was later incorporated into **Lianhua** Film Company in 1930. It became the biggest studio in China and produced many classics of early Chinese cinema, including **Cai Chusheng's** award-winning *Song of the Fishermen* (1934), Wu Yonggang's *The Goddess* (1934), and **Cai Chusheng's** *New Woman* (1937), the latter two films starring **Ruan Lingyu**.

Li was an enthusiastic documentarian and photographer and is perhaps best known for his documentary footage of Dr. Sun Yat-sen, leader of the 1911 Chinese Revolution that ended the dynasties and eventually led to the establishment of the Chinese Republic. Li followed Sun from 1926 to 1927 on the Northern Expedition to destroy the warlords and unify the country, a goal Sun did not live to achieve (but which was left to his successor, Chiang Kai-shek). Li's footage of Sun and other Republicans remains as historical record and also concretizes Li's belief in film as a medium that can subscribe to a political cause.

Li reestablished Minxin in 1936 and produced *Mother's Love* (1936) and *New Humanity* (1937). He returned to Hong Kong in 1937 to work for Qiming Film Company and specialized in film processing. Following the war, he managed a cinema until his death. He left behind a further legacy for the film industry; his wives, Yan Shanhan and Lin Cuocuo, his daughter, Li Xuan, and his granddaughter, Li Zi, were all actresses.

LI, NINA CHI (1961–). A native of Shanghai, actress Nina Li is the daughter of a respected stage actor who taught theater in Shanghai and Guangzhou. When she was 19, her father moved to Hong Kong (after her parents had separated) and she followed him there and for a brief stint in the United States. She returned to Hong Kong in 1986, entered and won the Miss Asia contest, and began working in the film industry, completing 30 films. She acted with **Chow Yun-fat** in five

Cover: Peter Chan's Perhaps Love *(2005). Permission of Peter Chan and Andre Morgan, Ruddy Morgan Organization.*

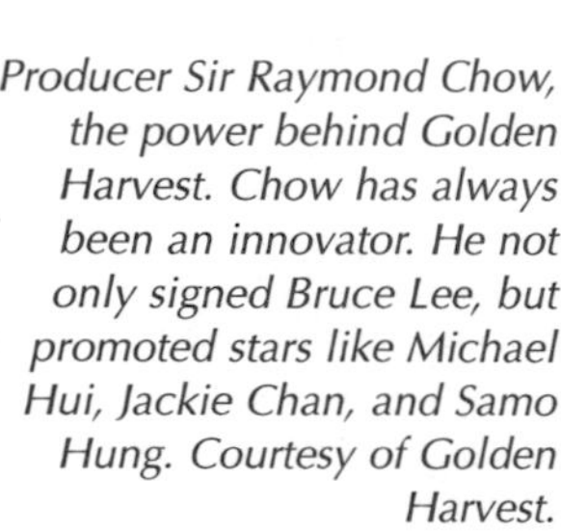

Producer Sir Raymond Chow, the power behind Golden Harvest. Chow has always been an innovator. He not only signed Bruce Lee, but promoted stars like Michael Hui, Jackie Chan, and Samo Hung. Courtesy of Golden Harvest.

Actor Tony Leung Ka-fai. The prolific and talented Leung has appeared in more than 75 films to date, the pictures ranging across all genres. He has appeared not only in Hong Kong but international features and is equally good in comedy and drama. Courtesy of Leung Ka-fai.

Director Stanley Kwan Kam-pang (foreground). Kwan is part of Hong Kong's New Wave, and is recognized for his art house cinema. Many of his films are described as "women's pictures." Courtesy of Stanley Kwan.

Actress Karen Mok. The multitalented Mok is involved in the music as well as the film industry. She has gained attention at home and internationally with Wong Kar-wai's Fallen Angels *(1995) and Corey Yuen's* So Close *(2002). Courtesy of Karen Mok.*

Producer Andre Morgan. Morgan worked for Sir Raymond Chow at Golden Harvest and was part of the group responsible for bringing Bruce Lee to stardom and reshaping Chinese masculinity onscreen. He formed Ruddy Morgan Organization in 1984 and is producer of Peter Chan's musical Perhaps Love *(2005). Courtesy of Andre Morgan, Ruddy Morgan Organization.*

Director Tsui Hark. The multitasking Hark (primarily a director, but also a producer and actor) is cofounder (with his wife and partner Nansun Shi) of Film Workshop. Tsui is one of the New Wave filmmakers, and his trademark appears on films he directs and produces; he is known for reinventing the martial arts epic with the Once upon a Time in China *series. Courtesy of Tsui Hark.*

Actor Anthony Wong Chau-Sang. The classically trained Wong has appeared in more than 100 film and television series, and he has created memorable and extreme characters in the films he has made with frequent collaborative directors Herman Yau, Kirk Wong, and Johnnie To. He also performs regularly onstage. Courtesy of the Hong Kong Repertory Theatre. Photograph by Benny Luey.

Director John Woo. Woo is among a handful of directors responsible for the artistic and commercial prominence of the Hong Kong film industry in the 1980s. He remains one of the few directors successfully transitioning to Hollywood. His A Better Tomorrow (1986) and The Killer (1989) reinvented the gangster genre and led to the introduction of the label "heroic bloodshed." Courtesy of John Woo.

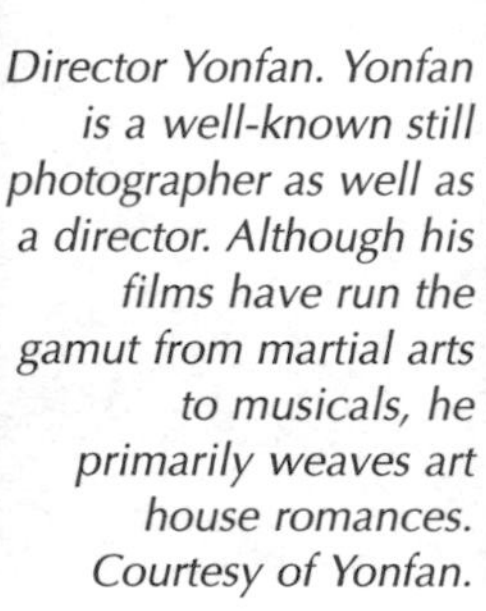

Director Yonfan. Yonfan is a well-known still photographer as well as a director. Although his films have run the gamut from martial arts to musicals, he primarily weaves art house romances. Courtesy of Yonfan.

Director Ronny Yu Yan-tai. Yu has worked locally and internationally in varied films that create an atmospheric sense of place where location is almost a character. His Phantom Lover *(1995) was the first Hong Kong film to incorporate the Digital Theater System (DTS). Courtesy of Ronny Yu.*

Golden Harvest Multiplex Theater in Shenzhen, China. Opened in 2005, this state-of-the-art flagship multiplex represents Golden Harvest's interest in theaters and distribution on the Mainland. Courtesy of Golden Harvest.

From left to right, actor Chow Yun-fat, director John Woo, and the late actor Leslie Cheung, shooting Once a Thief *(1991), a film influenced by Alfred Hitchcock's* To Catch a Thief *and Cary Grant's debonair style. Woo added orphans and a love triangle to the story. Woo's collaboration with Chow on this and other films led to Westerners describing their partnership as reminiscent of the one shared by Martin Scorsese and Robert De Niro. Woo worked with Chow and Cheung together on* A Better Tomorrow 1 *and* 2 *prior to this internationally set action comedy caper. Courtesy of John Woo.*

Kaneshiro Takeshi in Peter Chan's Perhaps Love *(2005). In this Shanghai-set romantic musical, Chan reinvents the Chinese musical via Hollywood, combining large-scale and splashy musical numbers with a tragic love triangle. In the story, a film director discovers that his lead (Kaneshiro) is the old flame of his female star (and the director's great love). Permission of Peter Chan and Andre Morgan, Ruddy Morgan Organization.*

Wang Tianlin's The Wild, Wild Rose *(1960), with costars Ge Lan standing and Chang Yang at the piano. While a Mandarin musical in the doomed songstress genre, Wang added a film noir element that makes the film unique, and Ge Lan's electrifying musical numbers popularized several songs. Pictured here, the mise-en-scène foreshadows the love story that will develop between Ge's singer (the "wild, wild rose" of the title) and the conflicted pianist. Permission of Cathay, Singapore.*

Actor/director Donnie Yen's martial arts actioner Legend of the Wolf *(1997). Yen directed and starred in this moody period piece that laments the passing of a time when the values of kung fu reigned supreme. Yen used experimental camerawork and rhythmic editing. Pictured here, Yen's character, a stranger, approaches a poor and victimized village. Permission of Donnie Yen.*

films, from *Seventh Curse/Yuen jan hap yue wai shut lee/Yuan zhen xia yu wei si li* (1986) to **Johnnie To's Lunar New Year's comedy** *The Fun, the Luck, and the Tycoon/ Gat sing gung jiu/Ji xing gong zhao* (1990). She went through her paces in **Stanley Tong's** *Stone Age Warriors/Moh wik fei lung/Mo yu fei long* (1991), shot on a shoestring budget in Papua New Guinea with dangerous komodo dragons. She also starred in a heart-wrenching performance as a deaf mute in **Jacob Cheung's** *Lover's Tears/Sai bat mong ching/Shi bu wang qing* (1992).

Li retired from films in 1999 when she married action star **Jet Li**.

LIANHUA. Lianhua (United China) was a Shanghai film company established in 1930 and run by Hong Kong–born and Beijing-educated Luo Mingyou. The studio grew by merging **Minxin** and Da Zhonghua Ba He. Lianhua is associated with Shanghai's golden age of filmmaking prior to the Sino–Japanese War, starting in 1937.

LIN, BRIGITTE CHING-HSIA (1954–). Born in Taiwan, Brigitte Lin would become one of the most sought after film actresses in Asia. Her film debut was in the Taiwanese film *Outside the Window* (1973), and even though the film went unreleased due to legal issues, Lin drew enough attention to continue her career. Throughout the 1970s, Lin's star continued to rise in Taiwan and she was frequently cast alongside **Chin Han** or Charlie Chin in melodramas. After leaving Taiwan for personal reasons, Lin went to the United States to make **Patrick Tam's** *Love Massacre/Ai Sha* (1981), a film with a Hong Kong cast and crew including **Ann Hui**. After this misstep, Lin returned to Taiwan and starred in a number of rather unremarkable action films.

Lin's first Hong Kong film was *Zu: Warriors from the Magic Mountain (Zu Mountain: New Legend of the Zu Mountain Swordsmen)/ Suk san sun suk san geen hap/Zuo shan shen zuo shan jian xia* (1983). Dividing her time between Hong Kong and Taiwan, Lin was also cast as one of the female leads in **Jackie Chan's** *Police Story/Ging chaat goo si/Jing cha gu shi* (1985). Both *Zu* and *Police Story* earned Lin Best Actress nominations at the **Hong Kong Film Awards**, yet Lin's major breakthrough as an actress in Hong Kong came with **Tsui Hark's** *Peking (Beijing) Opera Blues (Knife, Horse, Dawn [name of*

Beijing Opera character])/Do ma dan/Dao ma dan (1986). Lin's career slowed in the late 1980s; she starred in **Yim Ho's** *Red Dust (Swirling Red Dust)/Gwan gwan hung chan/Gun gun hong chen* (1990), which won her a **Golden Horse Award** (Taiwan). Lin did not make another film until the Tsui Hark–produced ***Swordsman*** *2 (Smiling Proud Warrior: Invincible Asia/Siu ngo gong woo ji Dung Fong Bat Baai/Xiao ao jianhu zhi Dongfang Bubai* (1992), adapted from a **Louis Cha** novel, in which she played "Asia the Invincible," a villainous kung fu master who changes from a man to a woman during the course of the film. This is the role for which Lin has gained the most recognition from Western audiences.

After this, Lin would be cast in many roles where she was either a woman disguised as a man, as in *Handsome Siblings/Chuet doi seung giu/Jue dai shuang jiao* (1992), or in one case, *The Three Swordsmen (Knife Sword Smile)/Diy kim siu/Dao jian xiao* (1994), an actual man. Lin was nominated for best actress at the Hong Kong Film Awards for both *Swordsman 2* and *Handsome Siblings*. Lin's trademark became a close-up glaring stare, which filmmakers would continue to exploit throughout the rest of her career. Lin also starred in the Taiwanese film *Peach Blossom Land/Aau luen tiu dut yuen/An lian tao hua yuan* (1992), a filmed version of a Taiwanese play written in 1981 and now recognized as a classic piece of Taiwanese theater. She reprised the role of "Asia the Invincible" for **Ching Siu-tung's** *The East Is Red (Invisible Asia: Turbulence Rises Again)/Dung Fong bat Baai: Fung wan joi hei/Dong Fang Bu Bai: Feng yun zai* (1993), and was also cast as the titular character in *The Bride with White Hair (The Evil White-Haired Lady)/Baak faat moh nui/Bai fa mo nu* (1993), starring alongside **Cantopop** legend **Leslie Cheung** in the **Ronny Yu**–directed international favorite.

Lin starred in two of the most cinematically important Hong Kong films, both of them directed by **Wong Kar-wai**. The first, ***Ashes of Time*** *(Evil East, Malicious West)/Dung chea sai duk/Dong xie xi du* (1994), is Wong's Eastern–Western philosophical take on the Louis Cha novel *The Eagle Shooting Heroes/Seh diu ying hung chuen ji dung shing sai jau/Shediao yingxiong zhi dongcheng xijiu*. The second, *Chungking Express (Chungking Forest) /Chung Hing sam lam/ Zong qing sen lin* (1994), is a modern-day tale set in Hong Kong's Chungking Mansions. *Chungking Express* is Lin's last film, in which, interestingly enough, we never see her trademark stare as she wears sunglasses and a wig partially covering her face whenever she is onscreen. Lin retired, married in the summer of 1994, and now has two children. She has returned only to do a voiceover in **Yonfan's** *Bishonen (Love of a Beautiful Boy)/Mei siu nin ji luen/Mei shao nian zhi lian* as a favor to a friend.

LIN, JEANETTE CUI (Lin Tsui) (1936–1995). A native of Guangdong province, actress Lin Cui (real name Zheng Yizhen) came to Hong Kong in 1949 and studied at St. Stephen's College. She joined Liberty Film in 1953 and her feature debut was *Sweet Seventeen/Lui yee sam/Nu er xin* (1954); she also made *Life and Love of a Horse-Cart Driver/Ma che foo ji luen/Ma che fu zhi lian* (1956) and *Season of Budding Roses/Cheung mei chue chue hoi/Qiang wei chu chu kai* (1956) for the studio. On loan to Yihua, she made *Girl in Disguise* (1956). She joined **Motion Pictures and General Investment** (MP&GI Cathay) in 1957 even as she was making *He Has Taken Him for Another/Yee dut chip muk/Yihua jie mu* (1957) for **Shaw Brothers**. Lin soon worked exclusively for Cathay, making ***Our Sister Hedy*** *(Four Daughters)/Se chin gam /Si qianjin* (1957), *Spring Song/ Ching chung ngai lui/Qingchun ernu* (1959), *Education of Love/Oi dik gaan yuk/Ai de jiao yu* (1961), *An Affair to Remember/Ching tin cheung han/Qingtian changhen* (1964), and *Wife of a Romantic Scholar/So siu mooi/Su xiao mei* (1967). Her last film was *No Time for Love/Yau lung fai fung/Youlong xifeng* (1968). A popular actress of young people, she was known as the "students' darling."

In **Tao Qin's** Mandarin musical *Our Sister Hedy* (1957), Lin starred as the title character and third sister in a family of four daughters; she is introduced to an engineer (**Peter Chen Ho**) as a suitor, but he is taken by her elder sister. A rich heir pursues her but she shows no interest until he finally wins her at the film's conclusion. Lin Cui also starred in **Chung Kai-man's** *The Education of Love* (1961) as the daughter who replaces her bedridden father as an elementary school teacher. At first reluctant because she detests children, as she learns more about their situations and realizes the influence her father has played in their lives, she decides to follow in her father's footsteps as a teacher.

Lin Cui was the sister of actor **Tsang Kong**. She married director Chun Kim in 1959, divorced him in 1967, and married Shaw Brothers

martial arts actor **Jimmy Wang Yu**, but divorced him in 1975. That year she started Jeanette Film Company, producing *Sup Sap Bup Dup/Sap saam bat daap/ Shisan bu da* (1975) and *Divorce Hong Kong Style/Heung gong sik lee fan/Xiang gang shi li hun* (1976). The former, directed by **Tang Shuxuan**, is a comedy about mahjong, and the title refers to a match in mahjong (with that hand of 13 tiles all disconnected one gets a sure win). So the title alludes to isolation and the disorderly yet energetic lifestyle of Hong Kong. In 1977, she immigrated to San Francisco and opened a restaurant. She came out of retirement for the Chinese–American coproduction *Iron and Silk* (1990), based on the autobiographical novel by Mark Salzman, and acted in Taiwanese soap operas. She died in 1995 in Taiwan.

LIN, LINDA DAI (1934–1964). Born in Guangxi province, Lin Dai (real name Cheng Yueru) spent her childhood in Guilin, Chongqing, and Nanjing. Her father, Cheng Siyuan, was a political figure. She came to Hong Kong in 1948 and joined **Great Wall** in 1950, but did not appear in films at Great Wall because of her father's politics. She joined **Yonghua** in 1952, and her film debut was *Singing under the Moon/Chui chui/Cui cui* (1953), an overwhelming success with *chaqu* episodes (song numbers) that made her a star. She played in romantic comedies but became known for playing victimized women caught in star-crossed romances. She starred in *Golden Phoenix/Gam fung/Jin feng* (1956), with **Yan Jun** credited as director and **Li Han-hsiang** listed as assistant director and screenwriter (although Li was responsible for the film). In this musical melodrama, Lin Dai played a country shepherd girl (Golden Phoenix) wooed by two suitors, a country boy (Yan Jun) and an evil landlord (**King Hu** played a dumb village boy). In the climax, she defeats the villain single-handedly. *Golden Lotus/Gam lin dut/Jin lianhua* (1957) won her the first of her Best Actress Awards at the **Asian Film Festival**, which she also won for three **Shaw Brothers** productions, *Diau Darling/Diu sim/Diao chan* (1958), *Les Belles/Chin giu baak mei/Qian jiao bai mei* (1961), and *Love without End/Bat liu ching/Bu liao qing* (1961).

In the mid-1950s, Lin Dai competed with **Li Lihua** for popularity both on and offscreen. While actor/director Yan Jun contributed to her screen success, he married Li Lihua in 1957. Lin Dai enrolled in

Columbia University in 1959, and met and married business tycoon Long Shengxun when she was 26. She continued making movies, including Li Han-hsiang's ***The Kingdom and the Beauty/Kong saan mei yan/Jiangshan meiren*** (1959). Lin Dai starred as a tavern girl who has a love affair with the emperor and brings up an illegitimate son; traveling to the capital to reunite with a repentant emperor, she is too weak to survive the journey.

Love without End (1961) remains the peak of Lin's collaboration with director/writer **Tao Qin**. Lin Dai plays a songstress caught up in a romance and suffering from leukemia; she gives her body to a corrupt businessman to save her lover (**Kwan Shan**). She won her fourth and last Best Actress Award at the Asian Film Festival for her portrayal, and it remains her most memorable role. Their final film, in two parts, *The Blue and the Black/Laam yue hak/Lan yu hei* (1966), won the 13th Asian Film Festival best picture, and the fifth **Golden Horse Awards'** honorable mention for dramatic feature.

In the romantic epic *The Blue and the Black*, Lin Dai is again paired with Kwan Shan, and in part two plays the misunderstood and self-sacrificing songstress who plays up to the Japanese while her lover is away at war. The actress committed suicide at 30 before the second film was finished, and some scenes were shot with a stand-in. Eerily, some of the incidents in *Love without End* paralleled her life. Over an 11-year career, she made 50 films for Yonghua, Guotai, Shaw Brothers, and **Motion Pictures and General Investment** (MP&GI Cathay) studios.

LING, IVY BO (Ching Miao) (1939–). Born Jun Hai-tang, an Amoy child adopted during the Chinese civil war by parents who immigrated to Hong Kong, actress Ivy Ling Bo began as a child star and appeared in numerous mid- to late 1950s movies under the name of Xiao Juan. She joined **Shaw Brothers** in 1962 and provided the vocals for Ren Jie in the role of Jia Bao Yu in *Dream of the Red Chamber* (1962). She will forever be identified with her cross-dressing role as the male scholar (*shusheng*) Liang Shanbo in ***Love Eterne/****Leung saan ang yue chuk ying toi/Liang shanbo yu zhu yingtai* (1963), the **Li Han-hsiang**–directed ***huangmei diao*** that served as her breakthrough role. As a singer of *huangmei diao*, she always recorded her own songs. She won Outstanding Artist at the second **Golden Horse**

Awards for *Love Eterne*. Starring opposite **Le Di** (Betty Lo Tieh) as the female who disguises herself to be educated and sit for the Imperial exams, Ling's male character spends half the movie attracted to his schoolmate before discovering her true identity. More than 30 songs throughout highlight the singing abilities of the leads, thematically tied to every occasion—friendship, medicinal herbs, heartbreak, etc. When obstacles intervene to prevent the lovers marrying, they commit suicide (to music) and are transformed into butterflies, hence referred to as "the Butterfly Lovers."

Ling Bo became known for her cross-dressing roles. She starred as the historical figure Hua Mulan, long before Disney sanitized the story, in director **Yue Feng's** *Lady General Hua Mulan/Dut muk laan/Hua Mulan* (1964) as the title character from the historical fifth century figure, who stood in as a warrior for her father. She also appeared in the ***wuxia pian*** *Temple of the Red Lotus/Kang woo kei hap/Jiang hu qi xia* (1965), produced by **Chang Cheh** and directed by Hsu Cheng-hung, as the Red Sword Lady, who rescues **Jimmy Wang Yu's** Wu, a naïve husband who has married into a family of ruthless bandits posing as Buddhist monks. The film brought into play the shift from fantastical effects to more realistic and violent combat. In **Yan Jun's** *huangmei diao* *The* ***Grand Substitution****/Maan goo lau fong/Wangu liufang* (1965), which won Best Picture at the 12th Asian Film Festival, she played Chiu Wu, the prince saved by a loyal servant to the prince consort, who, according to Confucian values, sacrifices his own child to protect the prince from an evil official. Ling Bo was incredibly expressive in her singing and acting when the prince discovers his true identity and is reunited with his mother. She also starred in Yue Feng's *huangmei* comedy *The Three Smiles/Saam siu/San xiao* (1969) as a famous scholar (the *shu sheng* part) who disguises himself as a page in the household of the Grand Tutor in order to be near the beautiful maid Autumn Fragrance (Li Ching).

After 12 years at Shaw Brothers, Ling Bo left the studio and participated in various genres, not only *huangmei diao*, but *wuxia*, historical, and contemporary drama. In 1975, she began **television** work in Taiwan, and produced movies with her husband, Chin Han, including the historical drama *Dream of the Red Chamber/San hung lau mung/Xin hong lou meng* (1978) and the romance *Imperious*

Princess/Gam chi yuk yip/Jin zhi yu ye (1980). She retired in the mid-1980s and moved to Canada with her husband. Among her three sons, her second son, Kenneth Bi, is an independent director in Hong Kong, and her third son a singer and songwriter in Taiwan. Among her awards are Movie Queen in 1964 at the 11th **Asian Film Festival** for *Lady General Hua Mulan*, Most Versatile in 1965 at the 12th Asian Film Festival for *The Grand Substitution*, Movie Queen in 1968 at the sixth Golden Horse Awards for *Too Late for Love/Fung feng maan lee ching/Feng huo wan Lee Ching* (1967), and Best Supporting Actress in 1975 at the 22nd Asian Film Festival for *Empress Dowager/King gwok king shing/ Qing Guo Qing Cheng*, an historical costume epic directed by Li Han-hsiang, with an all-star cast, authentic props and costumes, and spectacular sets.

LIU, ENJIA (1916–1968). Comic Mandarin actor Liu Enjia, one of the foremost comedians of the Mandarin cinema, was a native of Hebei province who spent his childhood in Jilin. He was recruited by the Manchuria Movie Association in 1937, when he started his career as an actor. He came to Hong Kong in 1949, invited by director Zhang Junxiang to appear in the **Yonghua** drama *Hearts Aflame (Peasant's Tragedy)/Saan hiu lui/Shan he lei* (1949) and appeared in films for Lihua, Qinghua, and **Asia** studios. In 1956, he joined **Motion Pictures and General Investment** (MP&GI Cathay), appearing in numerous films by studio directors **Yue Feng**, **Evan Yang**, **Wang Tianlin**, and **Tang Huang**, in movies such as Yue's historical drama *Golden Lotus/Gam lin dut/ Jin lianhua* (1957) and comedy *The Battle of Love/Ching cheung yue chin cheung/Qingchang Ru Zhangchang* (1957, written by **Eileen Chang**, in which Liu almost stole the movie as a lecherous professor), Yi's Mandarin musical ***Mambo Girl****/Maan boh lui long/Manbo nulang* (1957) and comedy *Our Dream Car/Heung che mei yan/Xiang che mei ren* (1959), Wang's science fiction comedy *Riots in Outer Space/Leung soh daai laau taai hung/Liang sha da nao tai kong* (1959) and ***The Wild, Wild Rose****/Yau mooi gwai ji luen/Yemeigui zhi lian* (1960), and Tang's dramatic comedy with song *June Bride/Luk yuet san leung/Liuyue xinniang* (1960) and comedy *Sister Long Legs/Cheung tui che che/Changtui jiejie* (1960). Whether as lead or supporting actor, in comedies and dramas, Liu added an all-too-human dimension to the story. In *Our Dream Car*, for example, he plays landlord to the overextended couple, with the constant refrain that his lodging holds good feng shui; in Evan Yang's *Bachelors Beware/Wan yau hing/Wen rou qing* (1960), he is the house servant to the playboy fiancé who seems to have outgrown his Mainland cousin, and Liu is sympathetic toward the girl (**Lin Dai**). In the war-set ***Sun, Moon, and Star*** *2/Sing sing yuet leung taai yeung/Xingxing, Yueliang, Taiyang* (1961), he appears in clown face to rally the troops Shanghai-style.

One of Liu's most popular performances was in Wang Tianlin's **North–South trilogy**, two written by Eileen Chang. He costarred with **Leung Sing-po** in all three. In each case, Liu played Northerners (Mainlanders) with an aversion to Cantonese people, to great comic effect. In the first film, *The Greatest Civil War on Earth* (1961), he plays a tailor sharing an apartment with a Cantonese family whose father (Leung) is also a tailor; in the second, *The Greatest Wedding on Earth/Nam bak yut ga chan/Nan bei yijia qin* (1962), he is the Northern restaurateur whose competition across the street is a Cantonese restaurant owner (and his future in-law, played by Leung); in the final film, *The Greatest Love Affair on Earth/Naam bak hei seung fung/Nan bei xi xiang feng* (1964), Liu plays Northern guardian to cousins wanting to marry prospects of whom he disapproves. In each case, Liu's growing frustrations erupt in riotous comedy, although all stories result in growing toleration and cooperation.

Appearing in more than 100 films, the portly actor, with his appearance a feature that contributed to his characterizations, died prematurely at 52 of a heart attack, but left behind a legacy of laughter in remarkable performances for their time.

LIU, GORDON CHIA-HUI (Lau Kar-fai) (1955–). Born in Guangdong, starting from his early teens, **martial arts** actor Gordon Liu began practicing martial arts under the tutelage of Lau Charn, father of **Lau Kar-leung**, and grand student of **Wong Fei-hung**. He became Charn's adopted son. Liu's true love has always been martial arts, and he was cast in the **Shaw Brothers** films directed by stepbrother Lau Kar-leung. Though appearing in some of Lau's earlier films such as *Executioners from Shaolin/Hung Hei-kwun/Hong Xiguan* (1977), Liu's most notable role was as the determined monk San Te, who progresses through the 35 tests in Lau Kar-leung's ***The 36th Chamber***

of Shaolin*/Siu lum qui luk fung/Shaolin sa liu fang* (1978). The film was a huge success and is one of the best-known Shaw Brothers films from the late 1970s.

Liu would go on to star in some of the best martial arts films of the period, including *Dirty Ho/Laan tau hoh/Lan tau he* (1979), *My Young Auntie/Cheung booi/Chang bei* (1981), *Legendary Weapons of China/Sap baat boon saam ngai/Shi ba ban san yi* (1982), and *Cat vs. Rat/Nga maau saam fai gam mo sue/Yu mao san hu jin mao shu* (1982). He also starred in Lau's masterpiece *Eight Diagram Pole Fighter/Ng long baat gwa gwan/Wu lang ba gua gun* (1983). Liu directed *Shaolin and Wu Tang/Siu lam yue miu dong/Shaolin yu wu dang* (1981, in which he also acted).

With audiences' changing tastes in the 1980s, traditional period martial arts films fell out of favor, and though Liu continued to make martial arts films, he was forced to expand his range. He played a villain alongside **Chow Yun-fat** in *Tiger on Beat/Liu fu chut gang/Lao hu chu geng* (1989). Liu continued making also-ran modern-day action films until the early 1990s when he rode the martial arts revival wave generated by **Tsui Hark**. Liu appeared alongside Chow Yun-fat again in *Treasure Hunt/Dut kei siu lam/Hua qi shaolin* (1994). Liu continues to work in the industry sporadically, recently in Quentin Tarantino's two *Kill Bill* movies (2003–2004), in the first as the masked bodyguard, Johnny Mo, and the second as the white-haired, powerful master, Pai Mei, who takes Uma Thurman's character as his student.

LIU, QI (Lau Kei) (1930–). Actress Liu Qi, a native of Hebei province, was born in Beijing. Her father, an army officer, traveled widely where his orders sent him; consequently, Liu grew up in various provinces. She went to school primarily in Shanghai and Chongqing. At 16, she was part of actor Jin Shan's China Art Troupe, and during the Sino–Japanese War, she performed for the Long Live China drama troupe. Liu's film debut was in *Heavenly Dream* (1947). She became well known with *To Betray Oneself* (1948).

The actress came to Hong Kong in 1948, starring in **Cheng Bugao's** Mandarin drama *A Fisherman's Honor/Hoi sai/Hai shi* (1949) for **Yonghua**. She worked for Yonghua, **Shaw Brothers**, Yihua, and **Asia** studios, and by the end of the 1950s, she had appeared in more than 50 films, playing good and bad women of various ages. Her films include **Hong Bo's** Mandarin crime movie *Red Rose* (1952), **Tu Guangqi's** Mandarin drama *The Moon Blanch'd Land/ Yuet ngai waan waan chiu gau chow/Yue er wan wan zhao jiu zhou* (1952), the Mandarin comedy *Long Live the Bride (Wedding Affairs)/ San leung maan sui/Xin niang wan sui* (1952, written by **Evan Yang**), **Yang Gongliang's** Mandarin drama *Good Faith/Cheung mei chue chue hoi/Qiang wei chu chu kai* (1952), and the Mandarin historical drama *Blood-Stained Flowers/Bik huet wong dut/ Bixue hua* (1953). In *Red Rose/Hung mooi gwai/Hong mei gui*, **Li Lihua** played the title character, a popular song girl performing in Daguanyuan fairground, and Liu played her maid; Red Rose loves a teacher, and to save him, she must submit to a warlord. Tragedy ensues. In the first postwar film of Yihua, *Long Live the Bride*, Liu played a coquette and the object of a rich man's (**Wang Yuanlong**) attentions. He inadvertently causes his son's (Hong Bo) death, although the couple (Zhou Manhua and **Huang He**) of the title, despite obstacles, including the abduction of the bride by the son's thugs, wed.

While at Asia Film Company, Liu was called the "Pearl of Asia," appearing in **Tang Huang's** Mandarin dramas *Tradition/Chuen tung/Chuantong* (1955) and *Half Way Down/Boon gwong lau sau kooi/Ban xia liu she hui* (1957). The latter was the right's answer to leftist films of the day, dramatizing the lives of the "lower depths," that is, middle-class people living as working-class people in Hong Kong, blaming the Communists, and wanting to reclaim the Mainland. Joining together, the expatriates survive as a social group in Hong Kong.

Liu retired in 1960.

LO, DUN (1911–2000). Renaissance man Lo Dun, actor, director, screenwriter, and producer, was born in Guangzhou, and he enrolled at the Guangdong Drama Research Center after abandoning medical studies. There he studied under distinguished **Peking (Beijing) opera** actor, playwright, and director Ouyang Yuqian (1889–1962). When the school closed, Lo helped form the Contemporary Drama Group with **Lee Sun-fung**, **Ng Wui**, and others, starting the modern Cantonese drama movement. He started in the film industry in Guangzhou in 1931 in silent films and first appeared on-screen in

Verdict in the Palace (1933) and Hezong Film Company's *Bombing the Five-Fingered Mountain*, followed by others at Zimei. In 1935, he moved to Shanghai to learn film production, working in publicity and screenwriting at *Xinhua* and *Mingxing* (Star). He was also active as an actor there.

Lo Dun came to Hong Kong in 1936; with Lee Sun-fung and Ng Wui he organized the Shidai drama group, active in schools. He also starred in the films *Modern Diao Chan (Modern Seductress)/Lut dang diu sim/Mo deng diao chan* (1936) and *Beauty in Distress* (1936). During the Japanese occupation, he was in Guilin, but returned to Hong Kong following the war and joined South China Film Corporation. In 1949, he cofounded the South China Film Industry Workers Union. In 1952, he also cofounded the **Xinlian** film company with others. In 1963, Lo established the Feilong Film Company that produced **Mok Hong-si's** comedy *The Girl in the Bus/Ang si aau haau poh ho moon gai/Ba shi yin qiao po hao men ji* (1965) and Choi Cheong's *The Jugglers/Gon daam chiu kong woo/Gan dan zhao jiang hu* (1970).

Over a 40-year career, he appeared in more than 100 films, including Cantonese and Mandarin features. Cantonese films include *Behind the Shanghai Front/Seung hoi feng sin hau/Shanghai huo xian hou* (1938), *The Perfect Match (Heavenly Union)/Tin chok ji gap/Tian zuo zhi he* (1941), and *The Morning Bell Rings (Tolling Bell)/Daai dei san chung/Da di chen zhong* (1940). Mandarin films include *Under the Roofs of Shanghai/Shanghai wuyan xia* (1941), *Everlasting Sorrow (Everlasting Regret)/Chi han pin min mouchute gei/Cihen mianmian wu jueqi* (1948), *Prodigal Son/Baijia zai* (1952), *Family/Ga/Jia* (1953), *In the Face of Demolition/Aau lau chun hiu/Weilou chunxiao* (1953), and *The Grand Party (Feast of a Rich Family)/Ho moon yao yin/Hao men ye yan* (1959). He retired from the screen following *The Jugglers* (1970), but he made a comeback with *Long and Winding Road/Gam sau chin ching/Jin xiu qian cheng* and *1941 Hong Kong on Fire/Heung gong lun haam/Xiang gang lun xian* (both 1994). He also reappeared onstage and in several **television** dramas.

As a screenwriter, Lo began by writing for director Lee Sun-fung. He wrote or cowrote *Everlasting Sorrow* (1948), *In the Face of Demolition* (1953), *Driver No. 7* (1958), and *The Grand Party* (1959), among others. His directorial debut was *Heaven on Earth* (1941), and 27 other features followed, including *Everlasting Sorrow* (1948), *Tragedy in Canton (*1951), and *Typhoon Signal No. 10* (1959). *Typhoon Signal No. 10/Shi hao fengbo* was based on a novel by Liu Yat-yuen and starred **Ng Cho-fan** as father of a family living in a rooftop squatter hut constantly threatened by typhoons and a loan shark. His neighbor (**Law Yim-hing**) works as a taxi dancer to pay off debts. As in **Lee Tit's** *In the Face of Demolition*, in which Lo had appeared, the motto of "one for all, all for one" is close to the Cantonese neighborhood's hearts, as they work hard and stick together to solve a crisis. Characteristic of leftist cinema of the time, Lo Dun's art was put at the service of politics.

LO, LIEH (Law Lit) (1939–2002). Although virtually unknown in the West, the astoundingly prolific character actor Lo Lieh made his mark in hundreds of **kung fu** epics, classy dramas, exploitation films, and the occasional oddball **independent film**. Lo was born in Indonesia, but his parents sent him back to China at a young age to be educated in their homeland. He later mourned the early loss of a "warm" family life. The close teamwork of filmmaking must have provided a satisfying surrogate experience. Lo seems to have been genuinely liked by his coworkers, the actors and directors of the golden age of Hong Kong films.

Compared to fluid modern actors like **Jackie Chan** and **Jet Li**, Lo's fighting style was harder, probably derived from popular Southern Chinese schools of fighting arts. A high point of his career occurred in 1972, when he was cast as the star of the **martial arts** classic *King Boxer* (aka *Five Fingers of Death*)/*Tin gwong dai yat kuen/Tian xia di yi quan*. *King Boxer* rapidly became an early cult favorite, profiting from the growing fan base in the United States for the films of **Bruce Lee** and the *Kung Fu* TV show. It might be supposed that Lo Lieh had a shot at being the next big crossover kung fu star; instead, he seems to have disappeared from American radar screens after his one international hit.

Nevertheless, Lo went on to carve out one of the longest running and well-respected careers in Hong Kong. Directors **Lau Kar-leung** and **Chang Cheh** at the **Shaw Brothers** studio cast Lo in many of their iconic kung fu films. He worked with swordswoman **Cheng**

Pei-pei (Jade Fox in *Crouching Tiger, Hidden Dragon*, 2000) early in her career. He shared the screen with top stars **Chow Yun Fat**, **Angela Mao**, and **Gordon Liu**. He created some of the most memorable villains of the era, including the prototype of the cruel Pai Mei of *Kill Bill: Volume 2* (2004). And he produced a handful of straight dramatic roles that reveal a mastery of the actor's craft (see *The Story of Woo Viet [God of Killers]/Woo yuet dik goo si/Hu yue de gu shi* [1981], or *Hong Kong, Hong Kong/Naam yue nui/Nan yu nu* [1983]).

Lo has done trash, too (see *Black Magic 1 & 2/Gong tau/Xiang tou* [1975], *Human Lanterns/Yan pei dang lung/Ren pi deng long* [1972], or *Sex and Zen/ Yuk po tuen chi tau ching biu gaam/Yu pui tsuan zhi tou qing bao jian* ([991]). One consideration about Lo Lieh is that he did not embarrass easily. He also liked to work, another quality common to Hong Kong film people. He used to brag that he only needed four hours of sleep at night, and calculated that it allowed him "sixteen hours to make money" every day. He did not mind working overtime, in multiple productions simultaneously. In fact, he once claimed that he never wanted to direct another film after his debut, *Fists of the White Lotus (Clans of the White Lotus)/Hung man deng saam poh baak lin gaau/Hung wen tin san po pai lien chiao* (1980), because the director's pay was about the same as acting, and the responsibilities interfered with his ability to work on other projects.

It is ironic that the international stardom that had eluded Lo Lieh for so long once more beckoned just before his death in November 2002. His subtly humorous performance in **Carol Lai's** *Glass Tears/Boh lee siu lui/Boli shaonu* (2001) earned him a ticket to the Cannes Film Festival the previous year, and he was Quentin Tarantino's original choice for the recreated Pai Mei role. Much of Lo's best work is now finding a new audience with the release of the Shaw Brothers film library on DVD.

LO, WEI (1918–1996). Director, producer, and character actor Lo Wei (Luo Wei) was born in Jiangsu province and became an actor in Shanghai and Sichuan province during the Sino–Japanese War. Following the war, he came to Hong Kong in 1948 and joined **Yonghua** Motion Picture Industries Limited. His Hong Kong film debut was as Yuan Shikai in **Zhu Shilin's** ***Sorrows of the Forbidden City****/Ching gung bei shut/Qinggong mishi* (1948). Following Yonghua studio's closure, he starred in numerous films, including *The Husband's Diary (Diary of a Husband)/Cheung foo yat gei/Zhangfu Riji* (1953), *The Secret Life of Lady So Lee (Notorious Woman)/Ming lui yan bit chuen/Ming Nuren Biezhuan* (1953), and *Rose, Rose I Love You/Mooi gwai Mooi gwai ngo oi lei/Meigui Meigui Wo ai ni* (1954).

Lo Wei made his directorial debut with *Love River (River of Romance)/Doh ching hiu/Duoqing he* (1957) after forming Siwei Film Company. Next he directed the box office hit *Romance on Lake Emerald (Jade Green Lake)/Fei chui woo/Feicui hu* (1958), a sensual and bold love story. He joined **Motion Pictures and General Investment (MP&GI)** in 1961 and directed the drama *Song without Words/Miu yue man chong tin/Wu yu wen cangtian* (1961), one of his most representative works of the period, while continuing to act in other films. In 1965, Lo joined **Shaw Brothers** and remained there for five years, making 17 movies, first directing spy films like *The Golden Buddha/Gam piu saat/Jin pu sa* (1966), but later directing ***wuxia*** pictures such as *Dragon Swamp/Duk lung taam/Dulong tan* (1969), *The Shadow Whip/Ying ji san bin/Yingzi shen bian* (1971), and *Vengeance of a Snow Girl/Bing tin hap lui/Bing tian xianu* (1971), most of them starring female **martial arts** actress **Cheng Pei-pei**.

In 1970, Lo Wei joined **Golden Harvest Studios** and directed one of its first releases, *The Invincible Eight/Tin lung baat cheung/Tian long ba jiang* (1971), starring **Angela Mao Ying**. His next film was *The Big Boss* (known in the United States as *Fists of Fury)/Tong saan daai hing/Tang shan da xiong* (1971), the movie that made **Bruce Lee** a star and began a new style of **kung fu** movie making. Lo and Lee made only one more film together for Golden Harvest, *Fist of Fury* (known in the United States as *Chinese Connection)/Jing mou moon/Jing wu men* (1972). Lo continued making kung fu movies, many starring **Jimmy Wang Yu**, such as *A Man Called Tiger/Laang min foo/Leng mian hu* (1973) and *Seaman No. 7/Hoi wan chat hiu/Haiyuan qi hao* (1973).

In 1975, Lo created his own company, Lo Wei Motion Picture Company Limited, yet none of its films were commercially successful, including those Lo directed himself with **Jackie Chan**, among them *New Fist of Fury/San jing mou moon/Xinjing wumen* (1976), *The Killer Meteors/Feng yu shuang liu xing* (1976, also starring Jimmy Wang Yu and Chan as the villain), *To Kill with Intrigue (Sword Flower Mist*

Beach South)/Gim fa yin yue gong naam/Jian hua yan yu jiang nan (1977), *Spiritual Kung Fu (Fist Spirit)/Kuen jing/Quan jing* (1978), and *Dragon Fist/Lung kuen/Long quan* (1979). Although Lo Wei could claim he discovered Jackie Chan, he was unable to channel his talent. With these films, Lo Wei, like others, was trying to create the new Bruce Lee after the actor's untimely demise. A prolific filmmaker, Lo retired from directing in the 1980s. In 1997, Taiwan's **Golden Horse Awards** posthumously presented him a lifetime achievement award. He appeared in over 90 films and directed more than 50.

LOKE, WAN THO (Lu Yuntao) (1915–1964). A Malaysian Cantonese born in Kuala Lumpur, Malaysia, Loke was educated in Malaysia and Switzerland and received a BA in Literature and an MA in History from Cambridge University. His father was the tycoon Loke Yew. The son's early career was focused on photography and ornithology, two of his great loves. His career changed when he inherited his father's business, taking over the management of 60 theaters in Malaysia and Singapore, and distributing movies made by Hong Kong's **Yonghua** studio, which he took over in 1955 and reorganized as International Films and later **Motion Pictures and General Investment (MP&GI)**, creating a modern movie empire, Hong Kong–old Hollywood style, with integrated production, distribution, and exhibition. MP&GI productions were renowned in the Southeast Asian and Hong Kong markets throughout the late 1950s and early 1960s, and the company was a major force in Hong Kong cinema.

Loke traveled between his base in Singapore and Hong Kong, and was known for allowing his contract actors and directors creative freedom. Loke was famous for his philanthropy, and his contributions to the arts and education in both Singapore and Malaysia earned him knighthoods from Malaysia, Great Britain, and Japan. Unfortunately, Loke, his wife, and other MP&GI executives were killed in a freak plane crash after attending the 11th **Asian Film Festival** in Taiwan in 1964. His legacy continues. Loke's brother-in-law, Choo Kok-leung, took over and renamed and reorganized the company as Cathay Organization Hong Kong. **Raymond Chow** and Leonard Ho's **Golden Harvest** was initially supported by Cathay, which gave them Yonghua's studio and equipment in exchange for distribution. Choo's daughter, Meileen, took the company public in 2000.

LONGMA FILM COMPANY (1950–1955). Longma, meaning "dragon-horse," was a leftist film studio cofounded by businessman Wu Xingzai and run by director Fei Mu and his brother Fei Lu-yi. Wu had an appreciation for art and **Chinese opera**, and became involved in the film industry in 1924 by establishing the Lily Film Company in Shanghai and supporting Fei Mu's opera films *Murder in the Oratory* (1937) and *Remorse at Death* (1948), and the **Wenhua** Film Company in 1947, producing Fei's *Spring in a Small Town* (1948). Wu came to Hong Kong in 1948 and set up Longma in 1950; the company was so named because Wu was born in the year of the dragon and Fei in the year of the horse. Its first production was **Zhu Shilin's** *The Flower Girl/Fa goo leung/Hua guniang* (1951). Fei died in 1951, and Wu left the next year, with director Zhu Shilin taking over.

Over five years, the company made nine films, all directed by Zhu (sometimes overseeing the work of his students) except one. Zhu's films include *Spoiling the Wedding Day/Wu jiaqi* (1951), *Sons of the Earth* (1952), *The Dividing Wall/Yi ban zhi ge* (1952), *House Removal Greeting/Qiao qian zhi xi* (1954), and *Between Fire and Water/Shui huo zhi jian* (1955). One of the company's exceptional films was *Woman Shut behind the Door* (1953), directed by Fei Lui-yi. Longma was one of the studios that early organized an artistic committee (Yonghua had done so in 1948), helmed by Zhu.

THE LOVE ETERNE* (1963).** *The Love Eterne (Leung Saan-ang yue Chuk Ying-toi/Liang Shanbo yu Zhu Yingtau)* is a classic ***huangmei diao that integrates music, choreography, cinematic techniques, and storytelling. Directed and written by **Li Han-hsiang** in collaboration with **King Hu**, the **Shaw Brothers** production starred **Ivy Ling Bo** and **Le Di** (Betty Lo Tieh). The film won four major awards at the 10th **Asian Film Festival** and Best Drama at the second **Golden Horse Awards**. It played for 62 days running in Taiwan upon its release. Ling Bo plays *shusheng* (male scholar) character Liang Shanbo, who falls in love with fellow scholar Zhu Yingtai (Le Di), a young woman disguised as a male so that she can receive an education and sit for the Imperial exams. When she reveals her true gender, Liang Shangbo swears to marry her, although her father opposes their union and has arranged her marriage to another. The lovers commit suicide and are transformed into butterflies, hence referred to as "the Butterfly Lovers." Based on a well-known Chinese folktale, the story has been cinematically portrayed numerous times, among them by **Runje Shaw** in *The Disheartening Story of Liang Shanbo and Zhu Yingtai (Liang Zhu tong shi*, 1928), Bi Hu (But Fu) in *Liang Shanbo and Zhu Yingtai* (1952), **Yan Jun** in another *huangmei diao Liang Shanbo and Zhu Yingtai* (1964), and **Tsui Hark** in *The Lovers (Liang Zhu*, 1994).

LU, LISA (Lu Yan, Lo Yin) (1927–). Actress Lisa Lu (Lu Yanqing), a native of Guangdong province, was born in Beijing but raised in Shanghai. She graduated from Shanghai University and the University of Hawaii. Her parents immigrated to the United States in 1948, and in 1956, she finished at the Pasadena Playhouse and began a career as an actress, appearing onstage in *Flower Drum Song* and *The World of Suzie Wong*. She attempted to popularize Chinese opera in the United States by touring universities and performing in English. Although she costarred (with James Stewart) in Daniel Mann's war movie *The Mountain Road* (1960), she did not successfully break into mainstream Hollywood movies and instead taught Mandarin in an army language school and worked as a magazine reporter and Chinese program radio broadcaster.

In the 1970s, the actress began appearing in Chinese films in Hong Kong and Taiwan, including **Tang Shuxuan's** drama *The Arch/Dung foo yan/Dong fu ren* (1970), **Cheng Gang's** *The Fourteen Amazons/ Sap sei lui ying ho/Shi si nu ying hao* (1972), and **Li Hanhsiang's** historical dramas *The Empress Dowager/King gwok king shing/Qing Guo Qing Cheng* (1975) and its sequel *The Last Tempest/Ying toi yap huet/Ying tai qi xie* (1978). In *The Arch*, Lu starred as the widow who chooses to observe social conventions rather than give in to love and to whom the arch of the title is built as a sign of honor; Lu brought a sense of humanity, both reluctant and accepting, to the character in a film that serves as a precursor to **New Wave** style with its experimental visuals that suggest psychological states. The historical epic *The Empress Dowager*, drawing from **Zhu Shilin's *Sorrows of the Forbidden City*** (1948), features a strong ensemble cast, indulgent atmosphere, and fatalistic, loaded melodrama; Lu played Empress Cixi (Tzu Hsi) and the story covers the latter part of the 19th century, with political intrigue and the empress outmaneuvering the reformist emperor Guangxu (Kuang Hsu).

Lu also worked in Hollywood again, appearing in Donald Cammell's sci-fi horror film *Demon Seed* (1977) with Julie Christie, Peter Bogdanovich's *Saint Jack* (1979) with Ben Gazarra, Daryl Duke's adaptation of James Clavell's *Tai Pan* (1986), and **Wayne Wang's** *The Joy Luck Club* (1993), adapted from Amy Tan's novel. She also was featured in Italian director Bernardo Bertolucci's *The Last Emperor* (1987), the first Western production to film in the Forbidden City. In *The Joy Luck Club*, Lu played one of four mothers to Chinese American daughters, and the film examined the relationships and misunderstandings between them; the mothers experienced the last of feudal China, and Lu's An-mei, a second wife to a wealthy man, who sacrificed her well-being for her daughter, relates an emotionally devastating experience and wonderment at her survival.

The actress played onstage in Hong Kong at the Hong Kong Repertory Theater in Lillian Hellman's *The Little Foxes* (1985). She has also produced **documentaries** and supervised production and written commentary for the **television** series *Tibet* (1987).

LU, YUQI (Lo Yu-chi, Lo Yue-kei) (1917–1981). Writer, director, and actor Lu Yuqi was educated at Wah Yan College in Hong Kong, and, after graduation, worked in a family business while he nurtured a deep interest in art, literature, and music. He began as a screenwriter in 1951, encouraged by Zheng De of Yongmao film company. He wrote *When a Lady Bestows Her Favors (When a Lovely Girl Bestows Her Favors)/Mei yan yan/Mei ren en* (1954), which was directed by **Ng Wui**, and between the early 1950s and 1969, wrote close to 100 screenplays. His scripts include *Motherly Love* (1954), *Wong Fei-hung and the Lantern Festival Disturbance/Wong Fei-hung daai laau dut dang/Huang Feihong da nao hua deng* (1956), and *The Bitter Lotus (Bitter-Hearted Lotus)/Foo sam lin/Ku xin lian* (1960). *Let's Sing and Dance to Celebrate a Good Year/Gap foon goh miu hing wa nin/He huan ge wu qing hua nian* (1969) was his last script.

Lu began directing with **Mok Hong-si** in *Homeless Girl/Piu ling lui/Piao ling nu* (1954). His solo directorial debut was *Beauty in Tears/Lui ping ting/Lei ping ting* (1960). His popular films include *Market Queen/Gaai shut wong hau/Jie shi huang hou* (1964) and *Un-*

der the Same Roof (Upstairs and Downstairs)/Tung nguk gung chu/Tong wu gong zhu (1964). In *The Maid Who Sells Dumplings/Hiu che maai fan goh/Hao jie mai fen guo* (1965), which Lu wrote and directed, **Tang Pak-wan** stars as a strong and determined woman who finds the wherewithal to fire her master and establish her own grocery. Lu's last film was *Iron Fist of the Devil (Blood Stains the Iron Fist)/Huet yim tit moh cheung/Xie ran tie mo zhang* (1967).

In 1974, Lu turned to **television**, scripting serials and dramas. In the 1980s, he began acting on TV, appearing in the dramas *Fatherland* (1980) and *Fame* (1981). Lu died of lung cancer.

LUI, KEITH KEI (Lu Qi). Cantonese actor Lui Kei (real name Tong kok-man, Tang Juemin) is a native of Taishan, Guangdong province. His first leading role was in **Chan Wan's** *Lost Girl/Sat chung dik siu liu/Shi zong de shao nu* (1961). He became a star with Chan Wan's *Romantic Love/Gung ji doh ching/Gong zi duo qing* (1965) and by the mid-1960s was one of the most popular actors in romances and dramas. He starred in several **Chor Yuen** films, including the Cantonese experiment *I Love Violet (Violet Girl)/Ngo oi chi law laan/Wo ai zi luo lan* (1966), in which he played a hotel telephone operator caught up in an amnesiac woman's mysterious past, an unusual film blending romance, thriller, and comedy, and *The Lady and a Thief (Maiden Thief)/Yuk lui san tau/Yu nu shen tou* (1967), in which he played a professional cat burglar. He costarred with **Chan Po-chu** in numerous films, including **Wong Yiu's** musical *Girls Are Flowers/Goo leung sap baat yat deu dut/Gu niang shi ba yi duo hua* (1966), the first youth movie of the 1960s, and the drama *Movie-Fan Princess/Ying mai gung chu/Ying mi gong zhu* (1966). He also began writing, scripting films like the dramas *Forget Not Tonight/Mok mong gam siu/Mo wang jin xiao* (1966) and *The Strange Girl/Yan hoi kei dut/Ren hai ji hua* (1967). In the 1970s, he began directing adult films and retired after *The Seductress/Meng daai tiu dut/Ming dai tao hua* (1987) and immigrated to Taiwan.

Among Lui's parts alongside Chan Po-chu is Ng Dan's *Waste Not Our Youth/Mok foo ching chun/Mofu qingchun* (1967), a problem youth movie that ignored class prejudices and represented the adults as tolerant of youthful transgressions. Lui stood out as the responsible youth, playing the butler's son that upper-middle-class spoiled rich girl Ruby (Chan) falls for, abandoning her wealthy boyfriend. When the former boyfriend abducts her, she survives the trauma but develops mental problems. In Chor Yuen's screwball comedy *Young, Pregnant and Unmarried/Yuk lui tim ding/Yunu tianding*(1968), Lui played next-door neighbor to Chan Po-chu, whose status-conscious father is unaware of his elder daughter's out of wedlock pregnancy. As the younger and favorite daughter, Chan feigns pregnancy to help her sister and names Lui Kei as the father. The parents of both youngsters are delighted with the match, while Lui attempts to identify the real father, at one point hilariously disguised as an official of the Abortion Society questioning Chan. The story serves as a humorous Cantonese antiestablishment statement as well.

Producer **Jeff Lau's** genre blending *Rose, Rose I Love You* (1993) includes **Tony Leung Ka-fai's** spot-on imitation of Lui Kei.

LUI, RAY LEUNG-WAI (1955–). Actor Ray Lui was born in Vietnam and came to Hong Kong as an adolescent, joining the Hong Kong Television Broadcasts Limited (TVB) actors' training class and becoming a TVB star in the 1980s; he costarred with **Chow Yun-fat** in *The Bund/Seunghoi tan/Shanghai tan* (1983, aka *Shanghai Beach*, which was later remade as a film starring **Leslie Cheung** and **Andy Lau**). His film debut was *The Informer/Gam sau chi/Jin shou zhi* (1980), and the movie which put him on the map was Poon Man-kit's true crime story, *To Be Number One/Bai ho/Bo hao* (1991), which clocked at 2 hours and 30 minutes, one of the longest Hong Kong releases ever, in which he played the limping lead character based on real-life gangster Limpy Ho. He played the irresponsible but charming Triad husband in **Tony Au's** *A Roof with a View/Tin toi dik yuet gwong/Tian tai de yue guang* (1993) and starred in Poon's two-part *Lord of the East China Sea/Sui yuet fung wan ji Seunghoi wong dai/Sui yue feng yun zhi Shanghai huang di* (1993) in the titular role as the real-life former illiterate fruit seller turned gambler who became one of the most powerful men in early 20th-century Shanghai. Lui has appeared in more than 60 movies.

LUK, JAMIE KIM-MING (1956–). Born in Hong Kong, director, screenwriter, and actor Jamie Luk entered the film industry at 17 while still in high school (he later graduated), working for director **Chang Cheh**'s Chang's Film Company in numerous martial arts films, such as *Heroes Two/Fang Shiyu Yu Hong Xiguan* and *Men from the Monastery/Shaolin Zidi* (both 1974); when Chang returned to **Shaw Brothers**, Luk followed, making films with director **Chor Yuen**, such as *Jade Tiger/Bai Yu Laohu* (1977) and more films with Chang, like *The Brave Archer/She Diao Yingxiong Zhauan* and *The Chinatown Kid/Tangrenjie Xiaozi* (both 1977). Luk has acted in more than 125 films, not exclusive to martial arts and action, but including comedy and drama, usually in supportive or smaller parts. Like **John Woo**, Luk claims Chang Cheh as his mentor. As a young man at Shaws, he was able to observe all areas of filmmaking; by 1980, Luk co-wrote (with **Derek Yee**) the screenplay for *The Legend of the Owl/Maau tau jing/Mao tou ying* (1981), for which he was also assistant director. Thereafter, he worked as production manager, stunt coordinator, and actor for many years.

Luk made his directorial debut in 1984 with *In Love with a Perfect Stranger/Choh dim yuen yeung/Cuo dian yuan yang*, which he also wrote, starring Yee and newcomer Pauline Wong Hsiao-feng. Wong won Best Actress and Luk won Best Screenplay for that film at the 5th **Hong Kong Film Awards**. In 1986, he directed **Chow Yun-fat** and **Carol Cheng**, equally matched in the battle-of-the-sexes comedy *My Will, I Will/Lei ching ngo yuen/Ni qing wo yuan.* In 1995, he directed *The Case of the Cold Fish/Yuet hak fung go/Yue hei feng gao*, set in a small fishing village, Tai O, on Lantau Island. The film was recognized by the **Hong Kong Film Critics Society** as one of the eight Hong Kong films of merit that year, and it played numerous international film festivals. In cult circles, Luk is remembered for the Category III flick *Robotrix/Nui gei haai yan/Nu ji xie ren* (1991), co-starring Hong Kong, Taiwanese, and Japanese actresses (respectively) Amy Yip, Hui Hsiao-dan, and Chikako Aoyama. Personally, Luk prefers comedy. He is currently, like many Hong Kong filmmakers, working on coproductions in film and television on the Mainland; his most recent project is as coproducer (along with producers John Woo and **Terence Chang**) on director Alexi Tan's *Blood Brothers/Tin tong hau/Tian tang kou*, a remake of Woo's *A Bullet in the Head*, shifted to 1930s Shanghai, and starring Daniel Wu, Chang Chen, and Shu Qi.

LUNAR NEW YEAR'S COMEDIES. Lunar New Year (rather than the Western New Year of January 1) is celebrated in Hong Kong, China, and throughout Southeast Asia on the first full moon of the first month of the lunar calendar (which can fall anytime between January 21 and February 21). Families prepare prior to Lunar New Year's Eve by housecleaning, honoring ancestors, sending greeting cards, and making holiday food. Families feast together on Lunar New Year's Eve, close up the house tightly, and the head of household opens the doors at dawn to let in good fortune. On Lunar New Year's Day, families visit each other and exchange gifts and give the children red envelopes of lucky money. The film industry celebrates Lunar New Year's with the release of comedies during a two-week period, equivalent to Hollywood's Christmas and summer blockbusters. People anticipate the releases and going to the movies. In all of them, the movie concludes with obstacles overcome and a happy ending; often cast (and sometimes crew) wish each other (and the audience) "*gung hei fat choy*," wishes for good health, wealth, happiness, and fortune. Lunar New Year's releases have included such films as **Peter Chan's** ***He's a Woman, She's a Man***, **Tsui Hark's** *The Chinese Feast*, **Jackie Chan's** *Drunken Master 2*, and **Raymond Wong's** numerous comedic productions.

LUNG, PATRICK GONG (Long Gang) (1934–). Actor and director Patrick Lung Gong (real name Long Qianyao) is a native of Anhui province, born into a family of actors. He joined **Shaw** and Sons and made his screen debut in **Zhou Shilu's** *A Hotel Murder Case (Crime of Passion in the Hotel)/Chow dim ching saai ngon/Jiu dian qing sha an* (1958) and played male leads in close to 50 films, chiefly Cantonese, for various studios through the 1960s, including the anti-Triad story *Murder on Black Dragon Street/Huet chow hak lung gaai/Xie sa hei long jie* (1961). He is one of the most successful actors turned directors of that era, serving as assistant director on **Chun Kim's** *The Big Circus/Daai ma fai tuen/ Da Maxituan* (1964) and making his directorial (and writing) debut with the drama *Broadcast Prince/Boh yam wong ji/Bo yin wang zi* (1966). The latter story is built around a popular broadcaster (**Patrick Tse Yin**) and the schoolgirl (Chen Qisong) he loves. Her wealthy father (played by Lok Gong) values his social standing more than his daughter's happiness, and intervenes to break up the couple. The film set the pattern for Lung projects to follow, with innovative camerawork, props, and music, as well as themes of love, power, and hypocrisy (this last especially among the rich) with social critique.

Story of a Discharged Prisoner (Upright Repenter)/Ying hung boon sik/Ying xiong ben se (1967), which Lung directed and wrote, also starred Patrick Tse Yin as the title character, a reformed ex-con hounded by a detective (the director) who wants him to play informant and is drawn back into the life by the One Eye Dragon (**Shek Kin**), who needs his expertise as a safecracker. Lung Kong's eye for detail focused on the social aspects of 1960s underworld life. Location shooting, fast rhythm, and inventive camera angles and editing characterize the director's strengths and make this one of his best films. It served as the model for **John Woo's *A Better Tomorrow*** (1986), that spawned the heroic bloodshed genre.

Juvenile delinquency was the social problem the director tackled in the Cantonese melodrama *Teddy Girls/Fei liu jing chuen/Feinu zhengzhuan* (1969). After a rumble with boys in a disco, the rebellious Josephine Tsui (**Josephine Siao**) chooses a girls' reform school (where **Kenneth Tsang Kong** is the rector) over becoming the ward of her mother's shady lover (the director). As the title suggests, focus is on characterization of the disaffected youth or ***ah fei*** characters, and Siao's righteous-angered angel face dominates the screen; despite her violent bent, she has a strong code of morality in tune with a generation that felt betrayed by its elders (an uncommon theme for the time). Siao gave one of her best performances of the 1960s.

Beginning in 1970, Lung turned to Mandarin cinema. *Yesterday, Today and Tomorrow/Chok tin gam tin ming tin/Zuotian jintian mingtian* (1970), a response to the explosive 1967 riots, was withheld for two years and then severely cut before its release. Loosely based on Albert Camus's *The Plague*, it portrayed an apocalyptic Hong Kong, infested with plague, with the message that only love can save the world. *Hiroshima 28/Gong do nim baat/Guang dao ershiba* (1974) was criticized at the time for its sympathy toward the Japanese, but the film, shot on location in Hiroshima, follows the horror carried by the next generation of the nuclear holocaust survivors, 28 years later, with a strong antinuclear theme. *Call Girls/Ying chiu lui long/Yingzhao nulang* (1973, in Cantonese) followed the lives of five prostitutes, probing the causes for their situations and actions. Lung never abandoned social criticism, and even his other melodramas, like *Pei Shih/Pooi si/Pei shi* (1972) and *Nina/Sze/Ta* (1976), convey themes of loneliness and dissatisfaction among the hypocrites of the upper classes. By 1978, Lung had directed a dozen features, four in Cantonese and eight in Mandarin.

Realism remained his credo throughout his directorial career, with large themes. Educated in Catholic schools, Lung used religious motifs as dramatic and visual cues throughout his films. Lung stopped making films in the late 1970s, but produced **Patrick Tam's** *Love Massacre* (1981) and returned for on-screen appearances in films including **Tsui Hark's** *Shanghai Blues/Seung hoi ji yau/Shanghai zhiye* (1984), *Black Mask/Hak hap/Hei xia* (1996), and **Samo Hung's** *Once upon a Time in China and America/Wong Fei-hung ji sai wik hung shut/Huang Feihong zhi xi yu xiong shi* (1997).

LUNG, TO (Long To) (1910–1986). Director, writer, and librettist of **Cantonese opera** movies, Lung To (real name Pan Weilin) was born in Guangdong province in an operatic family. From an early age, Lung was trained in Cantonese opera and was interested in writing and arranging music. Among his most acclaimed librettos are *Hong Niang*, *The Matchmaker*, and *The Faithful Wife from the Great Wall*.

In 1938, Lung entered the film industry as an assistant director on *One Night Couple*. His first film script was for Kwun Siu's *The Peacock's Plumage (The Peacock Shows Its Tail)/Kongque kaiping* (1939), a patriotic story with music. His directorial debut was *Blossoming Flower* (1941). During the Sino–Japanese War, Lung worked in Guangxi; he returned to Hong Kong and directed *No More Retreat/Bihu tiaoqiang* (1949). The latter was a contemporary wartime melodrama with social significance. A family is beset by more powerful and corrupt forces; **Tso Tat-wah** stars as an honorable son, husband, and prisoner who extracts revenge, but suffers the consequences.

Between 1941 and 1946, the director made over 110 films, one-third of which he wrote as well. Most of his films were Cantonese opera adaptations, among them *The Happy Wedding/Kwa fung shing lung/Kua feng cheng long* (1959) and *The Dream Comes True* (1960).

Non-opera films include *The True Story of Xiao Yuebai, 1* and *2/Siu Yuet Baak jing cheung/Xiao Yuebai zheng chuan* (1955) and *The World Is a Big Family/Sei hoi yat ga chan/Si hai yi gu qin* (1963). In the former, a contemporary tragedy, **Cheung Ying** stars, defrauded by his elder brother and betrayed by his fiancée. Lung's specialty was the use of special effects and experimentation with freeze-frame, revolving, and split screens. The director also made films in Mandarin and the Chaozhou dialect. The director's experimentation can be seen in films like *The Magic Cup, 1* and *2/Yau gwong booi/Ye guang bei* (1961) and *The Powerful Gunman and the Super Kid/San cheong siu ba wong/Shen qiang xiao ba wang* (1965).

After retirement, Lung dedicated himself to Christian church work. He died in Hong Kong.

LUO, JIANLANG (Law Kim-long). Cantonese opera actor and producer Luo Jianlang (real name Luo Fuwen) was born in Guangdong province. He studied under Huang Hesheng, performed in Liang Xiao feng's opera troupe, and developed a career in Singapore in *Sweet Girl*, consolidating his career as *xiaosheng* (male lead, as a young man, scholar, or general) in *Cool Emperor Husband*, standing in for star Gui Mingyang.

The actor's film debut was Yam Woo-dut's Cantonese comedy *Nothing Counts but Love/Yau ching yam shui baau/You qing yin shui bao* (1952). During the next 10 years, he played leading roles in more than 180 features. In 1960, he appeared in 39 Cantonese films. Most of his films were adaptations of Cantonese operas, among them, **Zhou Shilu's martial arts** film *Nocturnal Mourning for White Lotus/Yau diu baak foo yung/Ye diao bai fu rong* (1956), with **Law Yim-hing**, and his Cantonese opera *How an Honest Official Passed the Death Sentence on a Chaste Widow/Ching goon cham chit foo/Qing guan zhan jie fu* (1958); **Lung To's** *Red Maid, the Matchmaker* (1958); **Wong Hok-sing's** *Sweet Girl/Lui ngai heung/Nu er xiang* (1959); **Tso Kea's** *The Story of Wong Baochuan/Wong Bo Chuen/Wan Bao Chuan* (1959), all opposite **Fong Yim-fan**; *The Beauty's Grave/Heung law chung/Xiang luo zhong* (1957), with **Yam Kim-fai**; and Tso Kea's *The Swallow's Message/Yin ji sau loi yin ji chin/Yan zi xie lai yan zi jian* (1959), with **Tang Pak-wan**.

Luo's contemporary films included *Pretty Girl from Kuala Lumpur/Ban shing yim/Bin cheng yan* (1954), *Bitter Lotus, 1* and

2/Foo sam lin/Ku xin lian (1960), and *The Affairs of Miss Ping, 1* and *2/Piu Ping han/Piao Ping hen* (1960–1961). The producer founded Guozhen Studio and made *Lovers at the Mercy of the Sword* (1957). The studio also produced *Prince Kang Crosses the River on a Clay Horse* (1958) and *The World Is a Big Family/Sei hoi yat ga chan/Si hai yi gu qin* (1963).

Luo retired in 1964 and in 1965 immigrated to the United States and participated in the catering business. He died of asthma in San Francisco.

LUO, ZHEN (Lo Chun) (1923–2003). Writer and director Luo Zhen (real name Li Mengfei) was born in Shanghai and studied journalism at Shanghai's Hujiang University. Early on he was reputed to be one of the three leading poets in Shanghai; Luo was also interested in drama and joined the China Art Troupe.

Luo came to Hong Kong in 1948, working as a translator and newspaper supplement editor. In 1949, he joined **Great China Film Company** and became an assistant director; he also began writing scripts. His first, for **Great Wall**, was the tragic melodrama *The Haunted House/Qionglou hen* (1949, directed by **Ma-Xu Weibang**), in which a nurse who resembles her patient's deceased daughter learns the secrets hidden in the country mansion, solves a murder, and reveals the culprits.

The screenwriter worked for various companies making Mandarin films, including Haiyan, Pacific Film, and Guotai, between 1949 and 1957, writing the screenplays for Wang Hao's Mandarin family drama *Love Song* (1953), Ma-Xu Weibang's drama *Resurrected Rose/Fook wood dik mooi gwai/Fu huo de mei gui* (1954), and **Yan Jun's** action movie *The Valley of the Soul* (1957). Luo won best screenplay for **Bu Wancang's** family drama *The Long Lane/Cheung hong/Chang xiang* (1956) at the third **Asian Film Festival**. *The Long Lane* tells the story of a mother (**Chen Yanyan**) who abandons her newborn daughter and adopts a male infant so that her husband (**Wang Yin**) will have an heir. The baby girl grows up with a good-hearted prostitute while the son grows up shiftless. Seventeen years later, the wife reveals her action to her husband on her deathbed, and he seeks out their daughter, but seeing the love between mother and adopted daughter, leaves without revealing the truth.

Luo's directorial debut was the tragic drama *The Fresh Peony/Sin maau daan/Xian mu dan* (1957), from his own screenplay. He also directed the period **martial arts** movie *The Story of Lu Siniang/Lui sei leung/Lu Siniang* (1958) and the contemporary comedy *Welcome, God of Wealth* (1959). In *The Story of Lu Siniang*, **Li Lihua** starred as the granddaughter of a Ming scholar whose family has been wiped out by the Qing court; she trains in the martial arts to seek revenge and assassinates the emperor.

In 1960, Luo joined **Shaw Brothers** as a director and head of the script department. Over the next 15 years, he directed 28 films, many of them based on his own scripts, including *Flames of Passion* (1960), the Mandarin opera *The Shepherd Girl/Saan goh luen/Shan ge lian* (1964), the drama *Vermillion Door/Hung ling lui/Hong ling lei* (1965), and the drama *Swan Song/Shui sei tin ngo/Chui si tian e* (1967). Other films Luo directed include the martial arts movie *Mad Killer/Fung kwong saai sau/Feng kuang sha shou* (1971), *A Warm Family* (1973), the fantasy *The Snake Prince/Sau wong ji/She wang zi* (1976), and *A Beast in Human Shape* (1982).

– M –

MA, JOE WAI-HO (1964–). Director, producer, and screenwriter Joe Ma began as a writer during high school, winning Best Director, Best Actor/Actress, and Best Cast in a drama contest for the stage play *Scholar Chu*, which he wrote and directed in Secondary Six. The play would later be adapted for the film *Happy Ghost/Hoi sam gwai/Kai xin gui* (1984). After graduating in 1987 from the University of Hong Kong with a major in Contemporary Chinese History, Ma became a full-time writer. His directorial debut was *Rich Man/Hoh yat gam joi loi/He ri jin zai lai* (1992), and he also wrote and directed *Over the Rainbow, Under the Skirt/Gei dak heung chiu shing suk shut 2 choh luen ching yan/Ji de xiang jiao cheng shou shi 2 chu lian qing ren* (1994); the latter, consisting of the bittersweet memories of a youth growing up and falling in love, was produced by **Peter Chan**. *Feel 100%/Baak fan baak gam gaau/Bai fen bai gan jiao* (1996), starring **Ekin Cheng**, Sammi Cheng, and **Gigi Lai**, established him as a box office success and gained him an audience (two other *Feel* films followed). Other box office hits include *The Lion Roars/Ngo ga yau yat chek hiu dung shut/Wo gu you yi zhi he dong shi* (2002) and *Love Undercover/San chat bye mooi/Xin za shi mei* (2002).

Ma's territory is romantic comedy and youth romance. He works efficiently and produces fast-paced films. He believes in youthful innocence and captures its warmheartedness and purity on-screen; he himself is warmhearted and sympathetic to the stories he portrays, and Ma serves as the Hong Kong equivalent to Hollywood director Cameron Crowe. Dramatizing youthful aspirations, Ma always pays careful attention to the troubled teenage soul, and is one of the few who speaks its language and follows its heartbeat, albeit with a light touch, always finding the brighter side of life. Carson Lau describes the director best as capable of portraying death "with a smell of perfume" in his *Funeral March/Seung joi ngo sam/Chang zai wo xin* (2001) (personal correspondence, November 21, 2005). The film was a change of tone for the director, but he was still able to portray a life-affirming story. Eason Chan played a funeral director and Charlene Choi Cheuk-yin of the popular **Twins** singing duo played a dying young woman making her funeral arrangements. Ma has showcased several of the newer female pop idols like Sammi Cheung, Gigi Leung, Miriam Yeung, and the Twins in his trendsetting films.

As a screenwriter, Ma has written all of the 23 films he has directed, including *Love Undercover*, which won the Audience Award at the 2002 Far East Film Festival in Undine, Italy. In this screwball comedy told from a **woman's** point of view (unusual in male-dominated Hong Kong cinema), Miriam Cheung and Daniel Wu starred, and Cheung's character, Fong Lai-kuen, became a household name. Ma has also written for other directors, in films such as Daniel Lee/**Tsui Hark's** *Black Mask/Hak hap/Hei xia* (1996), **Benny Chan's** *The Big Bullet/Chung fung dui liu feng gaai tau/Chong feng dui nu huo jie tou* (1996), and **Ringo Lam's** *The Victim/Muk lau hung gwong/Mu lo xiong guang* (1999).

In 1997, Ma founded the film company Brilliant Idea Group Limited. Its first feature, Ringo Lam's *Full Alert (High Level Prevention)/Go do gaai bei/Gao du jie bei* (1997), received five nominations at the 17th **Hong Kong Film Awards**. As a producer, Ma has guided several directors toward recognition early in their careers, producing

Wilson Yip, for *Bullets over Summer/Baau lit ying ging/Bao lie xing jing* (1999); Alan Mak, for *A War Named Desire/Oi yue shing/Ai yu cheng* (2001); and Cheang Pou-soi, for *Love Battlefield/Oi chok chin/Ai zuo zhan* (2004). He produced Wilson Yip's *Juliet in Love (Juliet and San-pok, Butterfly Lovers)/Jue lai yip yue leung saan ang/Zhu li ye yu liang shan ba* (2000), starring **Francis Ng** and **Sandra Ng**, which received several nominations at the 20th Hong Kong Film Awards, and **Carol Lai's** *Glass Tears/Boh lee siu lui/Boli shaonu* (2001), which was invited to screen at the Director's Fortnight at the 2001 Cannes Film Festival, the Hong Kong International Film Festival, and the Filmfest Munchen.

To date, Ma has worked on 40 feature films. His latest film as director, *Embrace Your Shadow/Jeung oi/Zhi ai* (2005), is a heartbreaking fable of a girl, a pirate, and a cripple that uses natural sound and minimalism to approach pure cinema. His collaboration with **Wong Kar-wai** (producer) on the boundary-crossing fairy-tale Christmas story *Sound of Colors/Dei gwong tit/Di xia tie* (2003), as well as others mentioned above, demonstrates his ability to work within and outside the romantic comedy genre.

MA, SZE-TSANG (Ma Shizheng) (1900–1964). Legendary **Cantonese opera** actor Ma Sze-tsang (real name Ma Bolu) was born in Shunde, Guangdong province, into a scholar family. At an early age, he ran away from home to learn Cantonese opera in Guangzhou, and, at 18, he joined an opera troupe that performed in Singapore. Ma began as a *madan* (a very minor supporting character) and was listed as "Madan Chang" in a role that he disliked, and he soon quit. He stepped up from third supporting to first supporting character in four years' time. He began playing *xiaosheng* parts (male leads, either handsome young men, scholars, or generals), and he changed his name to "Fenghua Zi." Ma studied opera under the famous actor Liang Yuanheng, and he became his stage partner. By 1923, he came to Hong Kong and joined the Renshounian Opera Group as its main comedian, becoming well-known for his performance in the opera *A Perfect Match*. In 1925, the actor created the Daluotian Opera Troupe with Chen Feinong, and in 1933, he established the Taiping Opera Troupe with **Tan Lanqing**; during wartime, he also started the Kangzhan Opera Troupe, which performed for frontline soldiers. In

1955, he returned to the Mainland and joined the Guangdong Cantonese Opera Group, along with his wife, **Hong Sin-nui**.

Ma was a versatile opera performer known for his distinctive singing style, "Maqiang" (the Ma pitch), which gradually became an established mode of Cantonese opera. He was also a reformer, and his opera troupe was the first to have both sexes performing together onstage. Along with **Sit Kok-sin** (Xue Juexian), he remains the most significant Cantonese opera figure.

The actor's film career began with *Wild Flowers Are Sweeter (Scent of Wild Flowers)/Yau dut heung/Ye hua xiang* (1935). Prewar movies are mostly adaptations of his stage performances, such as *Flying General of Dragon Town (The General of Dragon City)/Lung shing fei cheung/Long cheng fei jiang* (1938) and *Prince of Thieves (The Vagabond Prince)/Chaak wong ji/Ze wang zi* (1939). Postwar opera films followed, such as *I'm Crazy about You/Ngo wai hing kwong/Wo wei qing kuang* (1947) and *A Spoilt Brat (An Unruly Princess)/Diu goo gung chu/Diao man gong zhu* (1948). Ma was also one of the founders of **Zhonglian** Film Company, and he starred in some of its classics, such as ***Parents' Hearts****/Foo sam/Fumu Xin* (1955).

MA-XU, WEIBANG (Ma Shui Wei Pan) (1905–1961). Director Ma-Xu Weibang, a native of Zhejiang province, studied in Shanghai and entered the film industry there in 1922. He began directing in 1926, and made more than 30 films in Shanghai and Hong Kong between 1926 and 1959. His forte was the horror film. He is best remembered for *Song of Midnight* (1937). He died in a car accident in 1961.

Regarded as a masterpiece of suspense in its day, *Song of Midnight (Midnight Charm)* concerns a 1930s male singer with an avant-garde style that offended the local elders. But his problems only begin there. When he falls in love with a powerful warlord's daughter, the warlord burns down his theater. The Chinese are under Japanese occupation, so the singer dons a mask and becomes a freedom fighter. **Ronny Yu** drew from his memories of this movie when making *Phantom Lover* (1995), shifting the emphasis to class differences and prejudices and away from anti-Japanese sentiment, and fashioning a romantic story of unconditional love. Ma-Xu also reworked his film as *Qiu Haitang* (1943), featuring a **Peking (Beijing) opera** actor who specializes in female roles and is disfigured by a powerful warlord. The film was based on a novel by Qin Shouou, also adapted into a play in 1942. The Japanese used it as propaganda to promote humiliating Chinese tendencies. The film was produced by Huaying, a company set up in Shanghai by the Japanese during the Sino–Japanese War to control Chinese filmmakers. Still, Ma-Xu incorporated elements of his other films, including an anguished hero, a villain unable to appreciate aesthetics, the urge to right wrongs, and a call for reform in China. Since **Leslie Cheung** starred in *Phantom Lover*, and also starred in Chen Kaige's *Farewell, My Concubine* (1993) as the opera actor of female roles, the coincidences between the three films are striking.

Ma-Xu's *Leper Girl/Mafeng nu* (1939) reinforced elements of his work, a combination of expressionist and noir cinema. A beautiful woman saves a scholar and falls in love with him, only to lose her looks to leprosy. Facial disfigurement was a constant in his films, even a fetish, and provides an interesting subtext for understanding human nature. *The Haunted House (A Maid's Bitter Story)/King lau han/Qiong louhen* (1949) likewise repeated the grand guignol but interwove his signature motifs, facial disfigurement, spiritual weakness, and an urge toward improving the nation. While the satire *Booze, Boobs, and Bucks (Wine, Women and Money)/Chow sik choi lei/Jiuse caiqi* (1957) seems unrelated to his other films, the contrast between surface and depth or appearance and reality relates the Mandarin musical to the horror genre. **Ge Lan** stars as a woman on the make, in a story of lovers, mistresses, and scamming, where greed and lust rule and altruism is a bore. Real life can be ugly.

MAK, BING-WING (Mai Bingrong) (1915–1984). Cantonese opera actor and producer Mak Bing-wing (real name Mai Hanming) was born in Guangdong province and attended Wah Yan College in Hong Kong. At 13, he ran away from home to study Cantonese opera, finding teacher Ziyou Zhong (literally "Freedom Bell," real name Liang Zhong). He became a supporting player with the Renshounian (Good Health) Opera Troupe; in 1934, he joined Xinshenghuo (New Life) Opera Troupe, playing *xiaosheng* (handsome young men or military generals) roles. During wartime, he performed in the United States, returning in 1947 to Hong Kong where he performed Cantonese opera until 1966, when he retired.

The actor paired with *huadan* (young women or maiden roles, often vivacious or shrewish) **Fung Wong-nui**, lead actress of Dalongfeng (Great Dragon Phoenix), the opera troupe he was a part of, and most representative of his performances. Mak was talented as a melodramatist and martial artist. He possessed a distinctive voice and skillfully interpreted the body movements of opera.

Mak's film debut was in *Xu Minggao's Secret Visits to General Ning's Mansion (Triple Visits to the Conspirator's Residence)/Ming Bei saam taam Ling wong foo/Tu Mingbei san Tan Ning wang fu* (1940). He appeared in more than 100 films, mostly in lead roles; the majority of his operas were adapted to films, including **Wong Hok-sing's** *Return from Battle (for His Love)/Baak chin wing gwai ying choi fung/Bai zhan rong gui ying cai feng*, Wong Fung's *Meeting on the Weedy River/Liu dut hiu kooi miu/Lu hua he hui mu*, Wong's *Three Battles to Secure Peace for the Nation/Saam chin deng kong saan/San zhan ding jiang shan*, *Woman General Hua Mulan/Dut Muk Laan/Hua Mulan* (all 1961), and *Banners of Victory/Feng hoi sing chi kei/Huo hai sheng zi qi* (1962). The actor also guest starred in the classic opera films Law Chi-hung's *The Nymph of the River Lo/Lok san/Luo shen* (1957) and Cheung Wai-gwong's *A Buddhist Recluse for Fourteen Years/Feng mong faan gong sap sei nin/Huo wang fan gong shi si nian* (1958). In the latter, a Cantonese period opera, he played the ruthless elder brother of the cross-dressed **Yam Kim-fai**, paired with actress **Fong Yim-fan**. After ascending the throne, he challenges his brother to compose a poem within seven steps of his suffering and dying lover, who must drink poisonous wine and is transformed into the nymph of the Lo River. Librettist **Tong Tik-sang** was inspired by the famous poem "Cooking Peas" for the characterization of the ambitious and ruthless villain.

In 1963, with martial arts actress Yu Suqiu (who became his second wife), Mak founded Rongfend Film Company. He died in the United States of a heart attack.

MAK, JOHNNY TONG-HONG (1949–). Born in Hong Kong, producer Johnny Mak joined **television** station RTV (now ATV) as a director, after graduating from high school; he directed episodes in the series *Ten Sensational Cases* (1975), *Ten Assassinators* (1976), and *Operation Manhunt* (1977), before becoming controller of the station from 1978 to 1981, when he formed his own production company, producing films such as *Rich and Famous/Kong woo ching/Jianghu qing* (1978), *Tragic Hero/Ying hung hiu hon/Ying xiong hao han* (1987), and *The Greatest Lover* (1988), all starring **Chow Yun-fat**, and *To Be Number One/Bai ho/Bo hao* (1991, which he also cowrote), among others. He directed one film, *Long Arm of the Law/Saang gong kei bing/Sheng gang qi bing* (1984), which mimicked the style of *Ten Sensational Cases* and started the "big timer" gangster trend of biopics.

MAKA, KARL (Karl Mak) (1944–). Producer, director, and actor Karl Maka was born in Taishan, Guangdong province, and came to Hong Kong in 1958, in 1963 attending the Tsung Tsin English College before emigrating to New York and entering the RCA Institute of Technology, where he majored in electronics. In 1973, he returned to Hong Kong and began working in the film industry, first as an assistant director and debuting as director with *The Good, the Bad and the Ugly/Yat chi gwong gwan chow tin aai/Yi qi guang gun zou tian ya* (1976). Maka made a series of successful **kung fu** parodies with minimal plot but lots of action, such as *Dirty Tiger, Crazy Frog/Liu foo tin gai/Lao hu tian ji* (1978), becoming a comedic filmmaker and comic actor working through the early 1990s, directing a dozen movies and acting in more than 30.

He formed **Cinema City** with friends **Dean Shek** and **Raymond Wong** in 1980, and the production company became known for Maka's madcap style of comedy, which included the use of contemporary settings, fast plotting, large stunts, wacky pratfalls, visual and linguistic puns, and inane, irreverent, and vulgar humor, still family-oriented. He is most famous for his comedic roles as a bald-headed and bearded character by turns good-natured, annoying, cowardly, cunning, and for his development of the *Aces Go Places/Chui gai pak dong/Zui jia pai dang* series (1982–1989), starring **Sam Hui**. Cinema City also had an interest in the production of numerous **Tsui Hark Film Workshop** movies and produced **Ringo Lam's** *On Fire* trilogy.

***MAMBO GIRL* (1957).** Director **Evan Yang's** *Mambo Girl/Maan boh lui long/Manbo nulang* is the epitome of the mature modern Mandarin

Hong Kong musical. Opening in stark black-and-white, with a lively mambo dance sequence that features a close-up of **Ge Lan's** legs dancing the mambo steps, a dramatic crane pullback follows, revealing the ensemble group of young people in a joyful wild dance. The story thrives on melodramatic elements, but little time is spent on plot development. Ge Lan stars as the free-spirited title character, tailor-made for her; in this movie she sang and danced her way to stardom, becoming the face of the Mandarin musical genre. Her character discovers that her happy family is not her own, that she was abandoned by a fallen woman to an orphanage but it is from her that she got her dancing talent. Dance became an element of character in the story, as the mambo and cha cha were regarded as wild and representative of her disreputable origins.

MANDARIN DUCK AND BUTTERFLY. Mandarin Duck and Butterfly (*yuanyang hudie*) refers to a style of romantic literature that was hugely popular across China and Hong Kong in the 1910s and 1920s. Serialized stories first appeared in Beijing and Shanghai newspapers and were later published in book form, and they appealed to the masses, not to intellectuals. The stories became a major source for Chinese film melodrama, primarily in the 1930s and 1940s in Shanghai, and in postwar Hong Kong.

The stories centered on tragic love stories and family conflicts between males and females. Typical scenarios involve kindhearted and beautiful songstresses who meet their doom and gentle students finding their first loves only to be thwarted by powerful, evil warlords or the prejudiced wealthy.

Zhang Henshui (1895–1967) was one of the style's famous writers. Film adaptations of his novels were favored by **Tso Kea**, who directed several, including *Many Aspects of Love* (1961), *Sunset on the River* (1962), *Somber Night* (1962), *Time Flows Like a Stream* (1962), and *The Songstresses* (1963). **Wang Tianlin** also directed an adaptation, ***The Story of Three Loves*** (1964).

On May 4, 1919, more than 3,000 university students in Beijing assembled at the Gate of Heavenly Peace to protest the Versailles Peace Conference following World War I and the decision to award Japan parts of Shandong province previously held by Germany, setting off protests across the country in the students' support. In subsequent years, the May Fourth Movement came to represent the students' desire for a modern and strong China, a break with the past, especially the feudal structure. There was a call for a new literature, in the vernacular, that would speak to the Chinese people. In the years following the May Fourth Movement, Mandarin Duck and Butterfly novels were frowned upon as cheap fictions with little, if any, artistic merit or literary importance. They were rejected for conforming to the decadent traditions of the old society and labeled nonprogressive. However, the current perception is that the genre served an important part of the literary heritage of the early republic at the turn of the 20th century. Some have become classics.

MANDARIN FILM COMPANY (1993–). Mandarin was founded by actor/producer **Raymond Wong**. Its first production was **Clifton Ko's Lunar New Year's comedy** *All's Well Ends Well, Too/Hua tian xi shi* (1993), which Wong cowrote and in which he costarred. The company also produced **Ronny Yu's** lyrical classic *The Bride with White Hair (The Evil White-Haired Lady)/Bai fa mo nu* (1993), starring **Leslie Cheung** and **Brigitte Lin**. Other productions have included **Tsui Hark's** *The Chinese Feast (Gold Jade Full Hall)/Gam yuk moon tong/Jin yu man tang* (1995), also starring Cheung, and another Lunar New Year's comedy, *All's Well Ends Well '97* (1997), with **Roy Chiao**, **Stephen Chiau**, **Francis Ng**, and Wong. Currently, **Philip Chan** helms Mandarin, although this is subject to change.

MAO, ANGELA YING (1952–). In her prime as a **kung fu** star, Angela Mao was the female counterpart to **Bruce Lee**: tough, fierce, and deadly serious about **martial arts**. The Taiwan native enrolled in a Chinese opera school as a child, and was a star performer in her teens. In 1969, director Wong Fung, who joined producer **Raymond Chow** in founding the **Golden Harvest** studio, soon to become one of the most powerful production companies in Hong Kong, recruited her. Angela Mao was one of the major players at Golden Harvest, starring in their very first production, *The Angry River/Gwai liu chuen/Gui nu chuan* (1970), which was loosely based on a famous opera.

In films like *Lady Whirlwind/Tit cheung suen fung tui/Tie zhang xuan feng tui* (1972) and *Hapkido/Gap hei diy/He qi dao* (1972), Mao played a typical kung fu hero, motivated by honor or the desire for revenge in her confrontations with bad guys. Her colleagues at Golden Harvest included the future stars **Jackie Chan** and **Samo Hung**, and she frequently worked with Hung, who served as action director and supporting actor in many of her productions, while Chan was stunt coordinator on two of her films, *Hapkido* and the later *Dance of Death/Miu kuen/Wu chuan* (1980). Her opera training had given her a dancer's flexibility, and she earned a black belt in the *hapkido* style, adding a fighter's power to her high kicks. As the star of *Dance of Death*, she played a beggar boy to learn different kungfu styles—a role similar to the kind of kung fu comic parts Jackie Chan had made famous, and she carried off Chan's choreography with style and verve.

Mao also worked with another female kung fu star, **Polly Shangkuan Lingfeng**, in *Back Alley Princess/Ma liu siu ying hung/Ma lu xiao ying xiong* (1973) and **King Hu's** *The Fate of Lee Khan/Ying chun gok ji fung boh/Ying chun ge zhi feng bo* (1973). Her portrayal of a young pickpocket who signs on as an undercover revolutionary in the latter film is a highlight of the intricately crafted tale of politics and betrayal. Also in 1973, she had a cameo in Bruce Lee's international hit ***Enter the Dragon****/Lung chang foo dau/Loong zheng hu dou*, playing Lee's sister. Before her retirement in the early 1980s, she costarred with well-regarded kung fu actors like Dorian Tan and **Lo Lieh** in a handful of excellent Taiwanese productions, including *Scorching Sun, Fierce Wind, Wild Fire/Lit yat kwong fung yau feng/Lie ri kuang feng ye huo* (1978) and *Bandits, Prostitutes and Silver/Bo ming* (1978).

MARTIAL ARTS FILM. The martial arts film is derived from a centuries-old Chinese tradition of the ***wuxia***, stories of chivalrous knights-errant who roamed the country righting wrongs. These expert martial artists occupied a hidden realm known as the ***jianghu***, an underworld interwoven with mainstream Chinese society and characterized by power struggles between secret societies. *Wuxia* storytelling is unique in its utter indifference to conventional social roles. **Women** and men meet as equals, and a beggar may outrank a high government official in the martial clans. The complex network of the *jianghu*, with its hereditary feuds and alliances, mirrors the arcane history of traditional martial arts in China. Combat techniques have been associated with regions (Northern kicks vs. Southern stances), religious centers (Shaolin staff vs. Wu Tang sword), and prominent historical figures (Chen Wang Ting, Yim Wing Chun). Opera schools trained young performers in authentic **kung fu** and swordplay methods, and helped to popularize the stories of noble bandits and fearless swordswomen (***nuxia***/*xianu*) through staged dramatizations. Martial arts movies include kung fu (the skill resulting from hard work), which is Cantonese slang for *wushu* (literally, war arts); *quan shu* (empty hand); and the use of weaponry. Many pairings result, from empty hand/weapons, to internal/external styles, to long/short weapons. **Swordplay films** are usually drawn from *wuxia* literature and myth and therefore tend toward semilegendary abilities on the part of the heroes, with lightness, running, flying, and fighting simultaneously. Overlapping in genres is frequent, although swordplay retains more of a fantasy element while kung fu includes more physical combat. More than 200 kung fu movies were made in Hong Kong over the 35 years since the end of World War II.

The first martial arts films were produced in the early Chinese film industry in Shanghai. The most significant films from this period were a series of 18 films entitled *The Burning of the Red Lotus Temple* (1928) made by Zhang Shichuan. These early films contained the building blocks that would go on to form the major characteristics of the genre: characters with a clear and simple sense of morality, who are often legendary heroes; dramatic events, such as the murder of a master; and a resolution to the film that involves martial arts.

The first Cantonese martial arts films in Hong Kong were a series of films about Cantonese folk hero Wong Fei-hung, starring **Kwan Tak-hing** as Wong. Unlike the earlier Shanghainese films and their offshoots, these films used realistic martial arts instead of mythical abilities. Wong himself was a traditional Confucian patriarch, continuing the tradition of simple good-and-evil morality. Starting in the 1960s, Mandarin films came into vogue again, and with them the works of **King Hu**, who would later move to Taiwan. Hu's swordplay films, such as *A Touch of Zen* (1971), were like Chinese scroll paintings with beautiful scenery and stylish martial arts. At the same time, in contrast to the aristocratic style of Hu's films, **Shaw Brothers** was releasing the violent works of **Chang Cheh**, whose breakthrough came with *The One-Armed Swordsman* (1967). Chang went on to produce increasingly more violent films with the duo of **Ti Lung** and **David Chiang**. Chang's films also included the liberal use of fake blood, taking the violence to a new level. Chang's films appealed to the common and working people of Hong Kong, with heroes that mostly came from the lower social orders.

In the early 1970s, **Bruce Lee** changed the character of the martial arts film by using real martial arts and showing real street fights onscreen. After his death, this style would continue to influence filmmakers until the late 1970s when **Jackie Chan** united kung fu with comedy in *Snake in the Eagle's Shadow* (1978). During the 1980s, Chan relegated the traditional form of martial arts film to the past by making comedic films with an average protagonist instead of a morally superior superman.

In the 1990s, **New Wave** director **Tsui Hark** revitalized the traditional martial arts film with **wirework** and stunning fight sequences when he released ***Swordsman***/*Siu ngo gong wu/Xiao ao jianghu*(1990) and a film redefining **Wong Fei-hung**, ***Once upon a Time in China***/*Wong Fei-Hung/Hwang Fei Hong* (1991). From then until the mid-1990s, martial arts films remained popular. Recently, the martial arts film has been revived yet again, this time by comedian **Stephen Chiau** with *Kung Fu Hustle (Gung foo/Gong fu)* (2004), which incorporated computer-generated imagery (CGI) with traditional wirework and broke Hong Kong box office records (and is the highest grossing domestic product to date) and by **action** director **Ching Siu-tung's** ravishing art film collaborations with Mainland director **Zhang Yimou**.

Hong Kong's unique cinematic specialty is martial arts action, for several reasons. First, movie budgets were limited and filmmakers found practical and inexpensive ways to express the action, for example, using baby powder to register the hardness of a punch; these techniques have been passed on. Second, the film industry has always drawn on the acrobatics and staging expertise of the **Peking (Beijing) opera**, and benefited greatly from the exodus of Mainland opera professionals after the 1949 revolution. Third, Hong Kong filmmakers and actors, unlike other film producers, know how to direct the action to the camera and the camera to the action. And fourth, unlike others, Hong Kong continues to prefer hands-on involvement, with actors, wirework, and stunt choreography, rather than mechanical control and inordinate special effects. *See also* SWORDPLAY FILMS.

MEDIA ASIA FILM COMPANY. Media Asia was founded in 1994 by Ma Fung-kwok and others, and is a self-described "integrated, distribution-driven group of companies in the media and entertainment industries," that is, film, video, and **television**. The company distributes and finances Hong Kong movies and film production, often seeking overseas investment. The company also created Media Asia Film Partners, a film fund investing in Chinese-language film production. Through its subsidiary Media Asia Distribution, Media Asia runs a distribution chain that distributes post-1970 Chinese and foreign movies, primarily Hong Kong films. Its subsidiary Mega Star Video, active since 1997, has released more than 500 films on VCD and DVD, most recently the trilogy-conceived *Infernal Affairs/Mou gaan dou/Wu jian diao* (2002–2003), codirected by **Andrew Lau** and Alan Mak, a contemporary riff on the cop–Triad genre, with less action, more tension, depth, and character development.

Some of the company's productions include **Clifton Ko's** drama *I Have a Date with Spring/Wo han chun tian you ge yue hui* (1994, coproduced with **Ko Chi-sum**), which earned HK$22 million; Mainland director Xie Fei's *A Mongolian Tale/Hei jun ma* (1995), a simple and moving story of hard life in Mongolia and its effects on relationships that won Best Director at the 1995 Montreal World Film Festival; and, **Gordon Chan's** bullet ballet *First Option (Flying Tiger)/Fei hu* (1996). Gordon Chan's *Beast Cops/Ye shou xing jing* (1998) scooped five awards at the 1999 **Hong Kong Film Awards**. Besides testosterone-laden fare, Media Asia has also produced romances like **Sylvia Chang's** *Tempting Heart/Xing dong* (1999) and **Ann Hui's** horror twist *Visible Secret/ Youling renjian* (2001).

In 2000, **action** actress **Michelle Yeoh** set up her own production company, Mythical Films, and signed a five-year first-look deal with Media Asia. To date, two films, **Peter Pau's** *The Touch/Tian mai chuan ji* (2002) and Jingle Ma's *Silverhawk/Fei ying nu xia* (2004), have been released. Both action films star Yeoh.

MELODRAMA. Chinese melodramas, ***wenyi*** *pian*, can be traced back to late 1920s Shanghai movies, when few film genres existed, and the term *wenyi*, combining *wenxue* (literature) and *yishu* (art), was applied to denote movies emphasizing drama, plot, and character. The term was generally used to distinguish these films from another prevalent type, ***wuxia pian***, or martial chivalry movies, emphasizing action through **martial arts** and swordplay. As more genres developed, including horror, detective thrillers, and comedies, critics and intellectuals regarded *wenyi pian* as superior, with their deeper meanings and significance, while the other genres were thought of as simple entertainment.

Elements of Chinese melodrama include an emphasis on plot, coincidences and fortuitous events, and emotional extremes developed with depth of characterization secondary, although characters stand out and usually have exaggerated backstories to explain their behavior. Melodramas established a film convention, but the best of them transcend the limitations of convention and provide memorable characters, in part due to the talent of the actors and actresses.

In the 1950s, the Mandarin melodramas were viewed as more sophisticated than those of the Cantonese flavor, based on the historical traditions on the Mainland. Ironically, in films based on both literature and the arts, some were considered to characterize weak men in soft occupations, hence the presence of weak men in the movies. *Wenyi pian*, however, were not limited to literary or stage adaptations, since original stories were developed as well. Whatever the origins, *wenyi pian* were intended to evoke an emotional response from the audience and centered on the family and romantic, often tragic, relationships.

Exemplary of melodramatic standouts is *Everlasting Love **(Eternal Love**)/Tin cheung dei gau/ Tianchang dijiu* (1955), an innovative **Zhonglian** production, the first to come to terms with a changing Hong Kong and its individualistic-oriented growing and affluent middle class. The movie sets up the dialectic between new Western and traditional Chinese values, and the protagonist's nostalgia for the past in a changing world. It draws on **Cai Chusheng**/Zheng Junli's Shanghai classic *Spring River Flows East* (194?) in both theme and frame composition. A humiliated hotel manager (**Ng Cho-fan**) steals from work to get the money to elope to Macau with a peasant girl (**Hong Sin-nui**) on staff; after encountering numerous obstacles, including a miscarriage, she abandons him to pursue a career as an opera singer. Following her success, she recognizes him in the audience, now homeless and suffering from tuberculosis.

In the 1960s, Cantonese melodrama superseded its Mandarin counterparts, emphasizing family films and **women's** issues. Its contradictory themes of filial piety and transgression by youth dominated melodrama. A notable example would be **Chor Yuen's** *Remorse/Yuen loi ngo foo hing/Yuanlai wo fu qing* (1965), in which a widow supports her younger brother-in-law, leading to romantic complications. More typical of the genre is Chor's *Parents' Love (The Great Devotion)/Hoh lin tin gwong foo miu sam/Kelian tianxia fumu xin* (1960), in which a teacher (**Zhang Huoyou**) loses his job and falls ill when his wife becomes pregnant again, after having birthed four other children; his students come to his rescue. The movie combines melodrama with social realism, transcending the genre in another way. Another, **Lee Tit's** *Eternal Love (Qicai hu bugui)* (1966), starring **Josephine Siao** and **Chan Po-chu**, was adapted from the **Cantonese opera** *Hu Bugui (Why Not Return?)*. Chan plays the male role opposite Siao's female. With two female leads, the film transferred the theme of filial piety from filial sons to dutiful daughters, and is exemplary of 1960s Cantonese movies seriously treating women as equal to men. Other titles of the time that emphasize the melodramatic bent include **Ng Wui's** *The Story of a Family/Tin lun/Tianlun* (1961) and **Wang Tianlin's** ***The Story of Three Loves****/Ti xiao yin yuan* (1964).

The melodrama declined in the 1970s, as kung fu action superseded it locally and globally. However, in the early 1990s, **Derek Yee's** *C'est la Vie, Mon Cheri (New Endless Love)/San bat liu ching/Xin bu liao qing* (1993) revived the genre. The movie played for two months in Hong Kong and earned HK$30 million, praised by audiences and critics alike.

MIAO, JINFENG (1941–). Actress Miao Jinfeng (real name Lin Husihan) was a native of Guangdong province. She graduated from Chonglan Girls' College in Hong Kong and was immediately recruited by **Ganglian** Film Company. In her screen debut, *Revenge of the Twin Phoenixes/Seung fung chau/Shuang feng chou* (1962), she played twin sisters of very different natures, which won her kudos and stardom. Even though Cantonese film production declined during the

1960s, Miao's films drew audiences and she was nicknamed "Box Office Panacea" and "Treasure of Ganglian."

Miao starred in 17 features, among them **Tso Kea's** *Tears of Pearl/Jan chu lui/Zhen zhu lei* (1965) and ***The Story between Hong Kong and Macau****/Yat sui gaak tin aai/Yi shui ge tian ya* (1966). In the former, she played Pearl, a dance hall girl whose love of **Cantonese opera** and vanity are manipulated by a corrupt Kuomintang official (**Ng Cho-fan**), leading to her degradation; she is rescued by a playwright who recognizes her talents. In the latter, Miao sang the theme song and costarred with **Cheung Ying.** She played a single mother with a checkered past who overcomes numerous ordeals (seduction and abandonment, the death of her son, the loss of her lover to her sister, an amputated leg) to find a new life.

Miao's last film was **Lee Sun-fung's** *Four Girls from Hong Kong/Kwan fong biu/Qun fang pu* (1972), after which she turned to television, appearing in soap operas and dramas such as *Lok Sun* (1975) and *Seven Women* (1976). Miao was an active member of the Hong Kong Drama Group. She immigrated to Australia in 1985 but periodically returned to Hong Kong to appear in TV movies like *Once in a Lifetime* (1995).

MILKYWAY IMAGE PRODUCTIONS. Directors **Johnnie To** and **Wai Ka-fai** founded Milkyway Image in 1996. To produced Wai Ka-fai's *Too Many Ways to be No. 1* (1997) and movies for directors **Patrick Leung** (*Beyond Hypothermia*) and **Patrick Yau** (*The Longest Nite, The Odd One Dies*, *Expect the Unexpected*) and began collaborations with writer Yau Nai-hoi (*Lifeline*, *A Hero Never Dies*, *Running Out of Time 1* and *2*, *The Mission*, *Running on Karma*). Wai Ka-fai and To have codirected films since 2000. To's first three films produced by the company, *A Hero Never Dies* (1998), *Running Out of Time* (1999), and *The Mission* (1999), offered distinctive stylishness. The first plays out like a Sergio Leone Western as two rival hit men (Lau Ching-wan and **Leon Lai**) face off before joining forces. With the second, an elaborate game of cat and mouse ensues between a desperate, dying jewel thief (**Andy Lau**) and a determined cop (**Lau Ching-wan**). The third film is a lean ensemble, thinking person's action movie with little action and lots of waiting, dependent upon strong performances and played-with conventions.

MINGXING. Mingxing (Star Motion Picture Company) was founded in 1922 by Zhang Shichuan, Zheng Zhengqiu, and Zhang Juchuan. The company produced China's first talkie, *Songstress Red Peony* (1941) starring **Butterfly Wu**. It turned out numerous **martial arts** fantasies in the 1920s, and became China's largest film company by the 1930s.

MINXIN. Minxin, or the China Sun Film Company Limited, was the first film company founded in Hong Kong in 1923 by **Li Minwei** and others, beginning a rudimentary film industry there. The studio produced *Lipstick/Yanzhi* (1925) and relocated to Shanghai in 1926 because of a general strike in Hong Kong and Guangzhou. By 1930, the company was absorbed into **Lianhua**.

MO-LEI-TAU. Literally, *mo* (none), *lei* (come), *tau* (head or source), *mo-lei-tau* means something that comes out of nowhere and makes no sense, a non sequitur. But a common explanation among locals is "nine follows eight, but nine has nothing to do with eight." The term (also *mo-lay-tau*) refers to obscure puns and nonsense language associated with the comedian **Stephen Chiau**. Early in his career, Chiau served as a representative for disaffected Hong Kong youth because of his cinematic irreverence. He capitalized on the Cantonese language as spoken in Hong Kong and the quickly changing slang of Hong Kong youth. Those who are not Hong Kong belongers and of a certain age have difficulty understanding his puns and humor. For example, Chiau's various characters will often tell others to "have some tea and dumplings." What he means is "relax." *Cha* means tea and *bau* means dumplings, but the slang means "take it easy, sit and think about it."

MO, TERESA SHUN-KWAN (1953–). Actress Teresa Mo worked in television for more than 10 years before she entered the film industry, appearing in 30 films, mostly in comedic roles, with a sardonic wit but an all-around likeable persona. She was extremely popular in the early 1990s, in movies like *92 Legendary La Rose Noire ('92 Black Rose vs. Black Rose)/Hak mui gwai dui hak mooi gwai/92 Hei mei gui dui hei mei gui* (1992, for which she was nominated for Best Supporting Actress at the **Hong Kong Film Awards**), **Alex Law's**

Now You See Love . . . Now You Don't (I Love Nau Man-chai [Rogue Meets Warrior])/Ngoh oi Nau Man-chai (lau man yue do bing)/Wo ai Niu Wenchai (liu mang yu dao bing) (1992), and the **Lunar New Year's** family comedies *All's Well, End's Well (Family Has Happy Affairs)/Ga yau bei si/Jia you xi shi* (1992), *All's Well, End's Well, Too (Happy Event in the Flower Fields)/Fa tin hei si/Hua tian xi shi* (1993), and *It's a Wonderful Life (Big Rich Family) Daai foo ji ga/Da fu zhi jia* (1994). Mo was often paired with actor **Leslie Cheung**, and an on- and offscreen chemistry and friendship existed between them.

She is famous for being matched with **Chow Yun-fat** in *Hard-Boiled (Hot-Handed God of Cops)/Lat sau san taam/ Lashou shentan* (1992), as a savvy female cop; recently she played the harridan of henpecked husband **Tony Leung Ka-fai** in *Men Suddenly in Black/ Daai cheung foo/Da zhang fu* (2003), which hilariously borrows the gangster genre format to create a battle of the sexes comedy.

Mo is married to director **Tony Au Ting-ping**.

MOK, HONG-SI (Mo Kangshi) (1908–1969). A native of Guangxi province, director and writer Mok Hong-si was a law graduate from Shanghai's Hujiang University. He joined the city's Sucheng Film Company to study screenwriting, and he wrote *Shadow* (1932), with Feng Zhigang. **Feng Huang Film** hired him to direct its silent feature *Sunset* (1935) in Hong Kong, but the company declared bankruptcy before the film's release. He left for Nanjing and from 1936 to 1938 he managed the Nanjing Theater, translating for American film companies in the meantime.

Mok returned to Hong Kong in 1939 and began a full-fledged writing career, many films receiving critical acclaim, such as *A Beauty in the Limelight* (1940), *The Gold Worshipper* (1952), and *A Young Girl's Desires* (1954). His directorial debut was *When Spring Comes (Spring Returns to the Good Earth)/Daai dei wooi taai/Da di hui chun* (1940). He directed *Flames of Lust/Ching jim/Qing yun* (1946), the first production of Dahua Film and the debut of Li Lan, a former Miss Hong Kong, that began the film revival following the war. The **melodrama** *A Wealthy Family/Daai foo ji ga/Da fu zhi jia* (1963) was a popular film. He excelled in Cantonese comedies and among his best known are the *Broker La (Lai)* series of the 1950s. Based on a popular newspaper serial novel by Ko Hung (Sam So) called *The Di-*

ary of Broker Lai, the movies focused on the rising entrepreneurial class in a budding capitalist society (they include *Broker Lai [La]* [original title *Gold and Beauty*]/*Ging gei Laai/Jing ji La [Huangjin yu meiren]*, *The Adventures of Broker Lai [La] and the Smart Fei-tin Nam/Ging gei Laai yue fei tin naam/Jing ji La yu Feitian Nan*, and *Misarranged Love Trap/Baai cho mai wan chan/Bai cu mihun zhen* [all 1950]). Cheaters, schemers, and middlemen abound, greed is good, or at least funny, but misadventures create a heady euphoria for a city on the move. **Cheung Ying** starred as Broker Lai, the real estate broker enmeshed in numerous conflicts and disputes over business and profits. *Crossroads/Sap chi gaai tau/Shi zi jie tou* (1955) is another comedy, basically a remake of an earlier late-1930s Mandarin classic of the same title directed and written by Shen Xiling, featuring two lovers who pretend to be well-off, but actually are not, this time around adding another hard-working and honest couple as foils. During a 30-year career, Mo directed over 130 films.

MOK, KAREN (1970–). Born in Hong Kong, actress/singer Karen Mok (Karen Joy Morris) was born to a half-Welsh, half-Chinese father and a Persian, German, and Chinese mother. She was educated at Hong Kong's elite Diocesan Girls' School, United World College in Italy, and London University. Gifted in languages, Mok speaks fluent Cantonese, Mandarin, Italian, French, and English. She began singing while in London, collaborating with Hong Kong fellow student Mark Lui (now a top producer in Hong Kong who pens **Cantopop** songs for many Hong Kong singers).

Mok began in the music industry with a 1993 release, with more than 20 albums following and numerous solo concerts in Hong Kong, Taiwan, and Singapore. One concert series included Mok, legs painted gold, leaping into a foamy bathtub to be sponged down by dancers; she has always played with her image. As a pop diva, Mok holds the distinction of being the first-ever Hong Kong singer to win the Best Female Vocal Performance Award at the Taiwan 2003 Golden Melody Awards, recognized and acknowledged as Asia's Grammy Awards. She has performed theme songs for several films and was recently handpicked for the female lead role in the "*Rent* 10th Anniversary World Tour," again making history as the first Asian to star in a Broadway show.

Mok entered the film industry in 1993, appearing in *Tigers—The Legend of Canton/Gong dung ng foo ji tit kuen miu dik suen chung saan/Guang dong wu hu zhi tie quan wu di sun zhong shan* (1993), and she began the first of her seven collaborations with actor-director **Stephen Chiau** in 1995's *A Chinese Odyssey, 1* and 2 *(Journey to the West)/Sai yau gei/Xi You Ji, Part One: Pandora's Box/Dai yat baak ling yat wooi ji yuet gwong bo hap/Di yi bai ling yi hui zhi yue guang bao he (Moonlight Treasure Box)* and *Part Two: Cinderella/Daai git guk ji sin lei kei yuen/Da jie ju zhi xian lu qi yuan (Fairy Slipper Magic Encounter*) (1995), based on the Chinese classic *A Journey to the West*. Unlike many other two-part Hong Kong films, these formed an integral whole, and Mok played the love of the Joker/Monkey King (Chiau) who time travels to prevent her suicide.

Mok gained international attention with her risk-taking performance as a shocking red-haired, half-crazed, jilted girlfriend in **Wong Kar-wai's** *Fallen Angels/Doh lok tin si/Duoluo tianshi*, for which she won Best Supporting Actress at both the 1995 **Hong Kong Film Awards** and the Hong Kong **Golden Bauhinia Awards**. She continued to take on quirky and daring roles, from gangsters to schizophrenics to no-nonsense cops, always suggesting intelligence, spontaneity, and sexuality in her characterizations. She is not afraid of disguising her beauty, or of taking on characters out of the ordinary. In Chiau's *God of Cookery (The Eating God)/Jeung san/Shi shen* (1996), Mok was disfigured with buckteeth and a scarred face to play the noodle seller Sister Turkey, earning her Best Actress nominations at both the Hong Kong Film Awards and the Golden Bauhinia. In the comedy *Irresistible Piggies (Irresistible Women)/Chu ong daai luen mang/Zhu ba da lian meng* (2002), she costarred as a masculine security guard with uncontrollable body hair growth. In *Tempting Heart/Sam dung/Xin dong* (1999), she was a bisexual interested in both the male and female costars. Mok played girlfriend to **Leslie Cheung** in *Viva Erotica (Sex Man Woman)/Sik ching nam nui/ Se qing nan nu* (1996), which opened with a fairly steamy sexual fantasy (played for comedy), and won her Best Original Song at the 1996 Hong Kong Film Awards for her singing. In Mainland director Shi Runjiu's *All the Way/Zou dao di* (2001), she starred as the single female among the guys in a Mainland road movie.

Of special note is her starring role opposite one of China's top male leads in *Crash Landing/Jinji pojiang* (2001), a most important film especially selected and dedicated to the 16th Congress of the People's Republic of China. For *So Close/Chik yeung tin sai/ Xiyang tianshi* (2002), **Corey Yuen's** female action riff on *Charlie's Angels*, she trained in **martial arts** for a month and a half and shared an on-screen lesbian kiss. (Mok was approached by British director Peter Greenaway for *8½ Women*, but turned down the part because she was reluctant to perform the full-frontal nudity and graphic sexual scenes required.) Her playful on-screen sexuality is more in the promise than the delivery, and never disguises the talent that has allowed her to act in more than 35 films covering a wide range of acting styles to date. The actress's first foray into Hollywood is in **Jackie Chan's** *Around the World in 80 Days*.

MORGAN, ANDRE. Born in French Morocco to a United States navy man and English mother, producer Andre Morgan traveled widely and was educated mostly in England and the United States. He attended the University of Kansas, majoring in Chinese in what was then the Department of Oriental Languages; there, the Chinese department chair connected him with a close friend, **Raymond Chow**, who had just established **Golden Harvest** in Hong Kong. In 1972, producer Andre Morgan joined the studio responsible for bringing **Bruce Lee** to an international audience, prior to the actor's untimely demise in 1973, and Morgan was part of the team that recognized Lee's talent as a **martial artist** and an actor that was instrumental in reshaping masculinity in Hong Kong cinema. At the studio, Morgan produced numerous films, including Lee's *The Way of the Dragon* (aka *The Return of the Dragon*)/*Maang lung guo kong/Meng long guo jiang* (1972), ***Enter the Dragon***/*Lung chang foo dau/Loong zheng hu dou* (1973), and *Game of Death/Sei miu yau fai/Si wang you ju* (1978), as well as more than 20 other Chinese films. In 1974, when Golden Harvest acquired Panasia Films, Morgan became managing director of the local distribution company. In 1976, the conglomerate formed Golden Communications (which included Panasia, Golden Communications Overseas Ltd., and Golden-Towa), with Morgan as president and CEO; the company distributed big pictures across Asia, such as Dino DeLaurentis's *King Kong* (1976). The company was the largest English distribution company in Asia. Beginning in 1976, Golden Communications also produced international movies like *Cannonball Run 1* and *2* (1981, 1984), with an ensemble cast, including **Jackie Chan**; *Death Hunt* (1981), starring Charles Bronson and Lee Marvin; and *Lassiter*, starring Tom Selleck.

Morgan's business acumen and global perspective have led to a rewarding career. In 1984, he sold his interest in Golden Communications and returned to Los Angeles, where he formed Ruddy Morgan Productions with Al Ruddy, who previously produced *The Godfather* (1972). The independent production company has produced over 35 Hollywood feature films, including *Farewell to the King* (1989), *Bad Girls* (1994), *Mr. Magoo* (1997), and *Million Dollar Baby* (2004), as well as 200 hours of television, including several successful television series, such as *Walker, Texas Ranger* (1993–2001, starring Chuck Norris) and *Martial Law* (1998–2000, starring **Samo Hung**) and movies of the week, such as *Miracle in the Wilderness* (1992) and *Running Mates* (2000). Additionally, the company produced the first three seasons of *World Series of Poker* and other cable series. It also has a management company, handling Hong Kong directors such as the **Pang Brothers**, **Peter Chan**, and **Stanley Tong**. In 2000, Ruddy Morgan set up shop in China, producing Tong's *China Strike Force/Lui ting chin ging/Lei ting zhan jing* (2000) and others. Recent productions include *The Longest Yard* (2005), a remake of Ruddy's original, *Out of the Blue* (2005), and the James Ivory drama *The White Countess* (2005). Morgan is also producer of Peter Chan's latest film, a musical, *Perhaps Love/Yu guo aoi/Ruoguo ai* (2005), that was the closing film at the Venice Film Festival.

Fluent in Cantonese and Mandarin, and having lived in Asia for more than 30 years, 12 in Hong Kong, and Hollywood in between, Morgan has recently been instrumental in establishing Shanghai's Hweilai Studios in Shanghai, a state-of-the-art production and postproduction facility providing permanent production and postproduction resources, where U.S. and international production of English-language television and movies is ongoing. He is also a member of the Academy of Motion Pictures Arts and Sciences and the Writers Guild of America.

MOTION PICTURES AND GENERAL INVESTMENT LTD. (MP&GI, Dianmou). Motion Pictures and General Investment (MP&GI), one of the two most powerful studios in Hong Kong for its time, producing predominantly Mandarin-language films, began because of the need to integrate film production, distribution, and exhibition. A Guangdong native, Loke Yew (Lu You), **Loke Wan Tho's** father, made the family fortune in Malaya through operating mines and plantations, and through banking in Kuala Lumpur during World War I. After his death in 1917, his fourth wife (and mother of Wan Tho) ran the family business. In Singapore, Loke's mother had established the Pavilion Theater in 1936 and the Cathay Building in 1939. Eventually the Loke family, through the Cathay Organization, owned one of the three largest movie theater chains across Southeast Asia.

Following World War II, Loke Wan Tho, rooted in Singapore, signed to distribute the films of the British firm J. Arthur Rank. He established International Theater Ltd. in 1948 and the next year began building more state-of-the-art theaters with widescreen, advanced projection, air-conditioning, and stereo sound. In 1951, he formed International Film Distribution Agency (Guoji), and established a branch in Hong Kong, International Films Distributing Agency, headed by Albert Odell, to ensure a steady supply of films for his theaters. The Hong Kong company supported other independents, all with *guo* (country) in their Chinese titles, in exchange for distribution rights. These companies included Guotai, headed by **Yan Jun**, which produced several films, including *Golden Phoenix/Jin feng* (1956) with **Lin Dai**; Guofeng, headed by Zhu Xuhua, which produced **Bu Wancang's** *Nobody's Child/Kuer liulang ji* (1960) with **Wang Yin**, **Josephine Siao Fong-fong**, and **Butterfly Wu**; Guoguang, headed by **Bai Guang**, which produced *Red (Fresh) Peony/Xian mu dan* (1956); and, Guoyi, headed by **Chun Kim**, which produced *The Big Circus/Da Maxituan* (1964).

Odell also aggressively developed Mandarin films and worked with other production companies like **Yonghua** in order to do so. The first Hong Kong production was *My Wife, My Wife* (1955), made by the Cantonese film unit. Cathay took over Yonghua in 1955 after the company fell into financial difficulty. Loke restructured, named himself as chairman (operating from Singapore), **Robert Chung Kai-man (Zhong Qiwen)** as general manager, Lam Wing-tai as distribution manager, and **Stephen Soong** (Song Qi) as production manager, and renamed the company MP&GI in 1957. Its first production was **Yue Feng's** *Golden Lotus/Jin lianhua* (1957).

Even before MP&GI formed, Cathay had created an actors' training course; **Kitty Ting Hao** and **Dolly Soo Fung** started there. Some of its contract directors included **Lo Wei**, **Tao Qin**, **Wang Tianlin**, Wang Yin, Yan Jun, **Evan Yang,** and Yue Feng. Famous contract actresses included **Chen Man-ling**, **Ge Lan**, **Li Mei**, Lin Dai, **Lo Di**, **Ting Hao**, **Wang Lai**, **Ye Feng**, **You Min**, Zhang Zhongwen, and **Zhong Qing**. Among the notable contract actors were **Chang Yang**, **Liu Enjia**, and **Wang Yin**.

The company operated under the old Hollywood studio system. Loke had received a Western education, and the studio's films were aimed at middle-class tastes, popular but not unsavory, sophisticated but not too deep. Its chief competitor was **Shaw Brothers**, and rivalries flared in the 1950s and 1960s, with each rushing to sign stars, raid talent, and beat the other to the screen with the latest popular trend. The competition stimulated industry growth and production quality. MP&GI's most productive period was from the late 1950s to the mid-1960s (between 1956 and 1965), when over 100 films were released, primarily high-quality Mandarin-language films, specializing in comedy, musicals, and melodrama, including box office record-breakers and award winners.

The studio's output included more than 140 films. MP&GI was the first Hong Kong studio to win a major prize at the fourth **Asian Film Festival** (Best Actress for Lin Dai in *Golden Lotus*, 1957), and in 1958 won Best Picture for Tao Qin's ***Our Sister Hedy*** *(Four Daughters)/Si qianjin* (1957). Also well-received were the new-look Mandarin musical directed by Evan Yang, ***Mambo Girl****/Manbo nulang* (1957), Yue Feng's *The Battle of Love/Qingchang Ru Zhangchang* (1957), Tao Qin's *Calendar Girl/Lung cheung fung mo/Longxiang fengwu* (1959), **Tang Huang's** ***Her Tender Heart****/Yunu siqing* (1959), Tang Huang's romantic comedy *Sister Long Legs/Chang tui jie jie* (1960), Evan Yang's historical epic ***Sun, Moon and Star, 1*** and ***2****/ Xing xing yue liang tai yang* (1961), and Wang Tianlin's North–South comedy written by **Eileen Chang**, *The Greatest Civil War on Earth-Naam bak who/Nan bei he* (1961).

When Loke, his wife, and a group of MP&GI executives were killed in a plane crash in Taichung in 1964, after attending the 11th Asian Film Festival, a crisis resulted. Loke's brother-in-law **Zhu Guoliang** (Choo Kok-leung) took over and in 1965 reorganized the company as Cathay Organization Hong Kong, delegating production to **Paul Yui** (Yu Piqing), and later himself. Its first production was Wang Tianlin's *The Lucky Purse/Xiao jin nang* (1966). The company produced close to 90 films, among them **Tang Huang's** *The Haunted/Liao zhai zhi yi xu ji* (1967), Evan Yang's *The Boat Girl/Shui shang ren gu* (1968), **Wang Xinglei's** *Escorts over Tiger Hills/Foo saan hang/Hushan hang* (1969), Zhang Zengze's *From the Highway/Luke yu daoke*, and Tang Huang's *The Monkey in Hong Kong/Sun wu kong da nao xiang gang* (1969); its last film was *Please Sir, We're Sorry!* (1972).

Yui died in 1969 and operations were downsized, with the company closing in 1971. By that time, **Raymond Chow** and Leonard Ho had left Shaw Brothers and with Cathay support, established **Golden Harvest**; Zhu turned over the Yonghua studio (costumes, props, etc.) and equipment to them, in exchange for distribution rights across Southeast Asia. Cathay became a public company in 2000.

MP&GI. *See* MOTION PICTURES AND GENERAL INVESTMENT LTD.

MUI, ANITA YIM-FONG (1963–2003). Born in Hong Kong, actress and singer Anita Mui dropped out of school to help support her family after her father's premature death. She started singing opera and pop songs in theaters and clubs in 1968 at age five. Her break came in 1982 when she was 19 and won Hong Kong Television Broadcasts Limited's (TVB) New Talent Singing contest, leading to recordings. Her 1985 album *Bad Girl* went platinum eight times, selling 400,000 copies, for which she remains the all-time best-selling Hong Kong recording artist. She recorded over 30 albums, won more than 80 music awards, set musical trends, and was dubbed the "Asian Madonna" for her musical style and outrageous costumes and raunchy performances. She starred in over 40 films over 20 years, entering the film industry with *Behind the Yellow Line/Yuen ban/Yuan fen* (1985, costarring **Leslie Cheung**), for which she won Best Supporting Actress at the **Hong Kong Film Awards**. She follows the line of "sour beauties" from the 1960s like **Li Lihua**.

Like many Hong Kong actors, she appeared in movies of all genres, from comedy to drama and everything in between, including martial arts fantasy, period pieces, and heroic bloodshed. Notable performances include the comic book action heroine Wonder Woman in **Johnnie To's** *Heroic Trio (The Three Asian Heroines)/Dung fong saam hap/Dong fang san xia* and *The Executioners (Legend of the Modern Day Wonder Heroes)/Yin doi ho hap juen/Xian dai hao xia zhuan* (both 1993), a pop idol not unlike herself in Peter Chan's *Who's the Woman, Who's the Man (Golden Branch Jade Leaf 2)/Gam chi yuk yip 2/Jin qi yu ye 2* (1996), and the woman who teaches **Chow Yun-fat's** gangster everything he knows in the prequel *A Better Tomorrow 3: Love and Death in Saigon (True Colors of a Hero 3)/Ying hung boon sik 3/Yingxiong bense 3* (1989). She costarred with Leslie Cheung in **Stanley Kwan's** *Rouge (Rouge Hook* ["hook" means Chinese knot or buckle]*)/Yin chi kau/Yan zhi kou* in two roles, as the broken-hearted betrayed lover and the ethereal and tortured ghost Fleur, for which she won Best Actress both at the 23rd **Golden Horse Awards** and the eighth Hong Kong Film Awards. She was close friends with **Jackie Chan** and appeared in several of his movies, including *Mr. Canton and Lady Rose (*aka *Miracles)/Gei jik/Qi ji* (a Hong Kong version of Frank Capra's *Lady for a Day* and *Pocketful of Miracles*, 1989), *Rumble in the Bronx/Hung faan kui/Hong fan qu* (1995), and *Drunken Master 2 (Legend of the Drunken Master)/Chui kuen 2/Zui quan 2* (in which she plays mother to Chan's Wong Fei-hung, 1994). She sang on-screen as the doomed songstress/soulful chanteuse in **Tony Au's** *Au Revoir, Mon Amour (Will Mr. Sun Come Back?, Till We Meet Again)/Hoh yat gwan joi loi/He ri jun zai lai* (costarring **Leung Ka-fai**, 1991), a tragic love story set during the Japanese occupation of Shanghai. She also won Best Supporting Actress at the 1998 Hong Kong Film Awards for her performance in **Ann Hui's** *Eighteen Springs/Boon sang yuen/Ban seng yuan* (1997) opposite **Leon Lai**. Her last role was in Hui's *July Rhapsody/Laam yan sei sap/Nan ren si shi* (2002).

Mui was not only married to her career; she was also involved in public life. In 1989, she publicly called for democracy on the Mainland after the events of Tiananmen Square. In 1993, she helped found the Hong Kong Performing Artists Guild. After the SARS outbreak, she organized the 1:99 concert as a fundraiser. Mui was diagnosed with cervical cancer shortly after her sister had died of cancer. She died on New Year's Eve 2003, and 20,000 fans subsequently paid tribute. She was posthumously awarded a lifetime achievement award at the 23rd Hong Kong Film Awards.

MUI, YEE (Mei Qi) (1923–1966). Actress and producer Mui Yee (real name Jiang Duanyi) was born in Beijing; her family came from Guangdong province where her father was a high-ranking official. Although she was trained to be a teacher, as early as age six she appeared in a **Great Wall** film under the name of Jiang Lili. In 1937, she joined Nan Yang Film Company and debuted in *Survival after a Hundred Wars (War and Survival)/Baak chin yue sang/Bai zhan yu sheng* (1937). During the war, Mui, a talented **Cantonese opera** singer, performed onstage with renowned opera actor **Ma Sze-tsang** and the Tai Ping Opera Troupe in plays like *The Precious Lotus Lamp*.

Mui was a versatile actress and was cast in a wide range of roles in more than 70 films, including Wong Toi's contemporary romance *Madame Butterfly/Woo dip foo yan/Hu die fu ren* (1948), Hong Kong's first 35mm color film, and contemporary romantic comedy *My Beloved Is Like the Spring Wind (My Love Is Like the Wind of Spring)/Long shut chun yat fung/Lang shi chun ri feng* (1949); Lau Fong's *Who Are Happy, Who Are Sad (Laughter and Tears)/Gei ga foon siu gei ga/ Jijia huanxiao jijia chou* (1950); **Lee Sung-fung's** drama *Sunrise/Yat chut/Richu* (1953); and **Ng Wui's** drama *Sworn Sisters/Gam laan che mooi/Jin lan jie mei* (1954). She played an old superstitious maidservant who loses her niece's life in the latter. In **Lo Dun's** *Everlasting Regret (Everlasting Sorrow)/Chi han pin min mou chute gei/Cihen mianmian wu jueqi* (1948), the actress starred as a virtuous young woman forced into prostitution to help her family when the youngest falls ill and money is needed for medical care; the director himself played her father, a poor but honest accountant who refuses to involve himself in shady money-making schemes but ultimately does so when he discovers his daughter's actions; the daughter joins her jailed father when she murders her father's boss when he takes advantage of her. The family tragedy reflected life's struggles as well as the insidious spread of corruption.

The actress also appeared in **Tso Kea's** comedy *The Chair/Jinshan dashao*, as a greedy mistress fixated on money. She sells a set of antique chairs owned by the mother (Wong Man-lei) of her lover (**Cheung Ying**), an unfaithful husband and squanderer of his inheritance. The mother has hidden a valuable diamond bracelet in one of the chairs, and as the search for the chair ensues, absurd coincidences and physical comedy play out, until the son learns a valuable lesson.

Mui starred in and produced the contemporary **melodrama** *Sunrise*. In 1956, she published an autobiography, *A Life of Drama*. A devout Christian, she took up missionary work in Southeast Asia after retiring from the film industry in the early 1960s. She died of cancer.

MUSICALS. In the post–World War II years, exiled Shanghai film industry veterans developed a sophisticated and effective production mode with excellent technical standards and professionalism with the Mandarin musicals that dominated in Hong Kong from the 1940s to 1960s, and in many others, operating under the rationale of "a song in every film." Early musicals were influenced by Shanghai nightlife entertainment, set in the nightclub (singing and dancing halls), with a singer, invariably female, behind the microphone. Early on, many of the musical scenes had little to do with the rest of the film, and the songs were there simply to satisfy audience demand or due to the cross-pollination between the film and music industries. For instance, Zhou Xuan's solo "The Spring Morning" in 1948's *Orioles Banished from the Flowers/Huawei Liuying*, is sung on a picnic to friends; other than it being spring and that the characters are out of doors, the song has no relevance to the story.

The suffering songstress became the dominant figure in early musicals, and the setting was definitely Shanghai. By the mid-1950s, music became integrated into the story; many films were romances or rooted in the music of country life, especially those set in Northern China. For example, in 1956's *Song of the Peach Blossom River/Taohua Jiang*, Wild Kitten's (**Zhong Qing**) courtship is carried out through a series of musical numbers; music is rooted in country life and thereby associated with innocence, reinforcing the Chinese association of nature with goodness, spontaneity, and creativity. The music was also represented as having redemptive powers. When war breaks out, Wild Kitten escapes to an idyllic Hong Kong where she succeeds as a singing star. *Song of the Peach Blossom River* introduced the farmer's daughter figure, which replaced the doomed songstress as a primary element. It also, for the last third of the film, featured Hong Kong, and began the transition to Hong Kong settings.

As music was more integrated, another shift occurred. By the late 1950s, the urban and authentic middle-class Hong Kong girl appeared, in movies like ***Mambo Girl/****Manbo nulang* (1957) and *Air Hostess/Kongzhong xiaojie* (1959). In *Mambo Girl*, dance became an element of the drama and character, and established an attitude of youthfulness and fun. Hong Kong replaced the Mainland as a setting, and the movie world reaped the benefits of unparalleled stability, prosperity, and optimism around since the mid-1950s in the then colony. Rather than decadent nightclubs or rich rice fields, domestic settings in the city prevail, emphasizing family life and places where business is conducted. The Mambo Girl's family home, for example, is also a toy store. Family values, modernity, and thriving commerce exist side by side. In the golden age of the Mandarin musicals, from the late 1950s through the 1960s, like Hollywood, the films presented fantasies of the good life, opulence, glamour, and modernity. Typical is **Inoue Umetsugu's** *Hong Kong Nocturne/Heung Kong fa yuet yeh/ Xiangjiang huayue ye* (1967), starring **Cheng Pei-pei**, **Lily Ho**, Chin Ping, Ling Yun, **Peter Chen Ho**, **Yueh Hua**, and Tina Chin Fei. Three sisters leave their father's magic act to follow different career paths; all three meet their dream men, yet only one (Cheng Pei-pei) marries, only to have her husband (Peter Chen Ho) die in a plane crash. Women are the stars of these musicals, while all the men exist simply as moral centers.

The popularity of the musical waned over the next several decades; however, Hong Kongers did not forget the stricture of "a song in every film," and from **John Woo's** heroic bloodshed opera ***A Better Tomorrow*** *(True Colors of a Hero)/Ying hung boon sik/Yingxiong bense* (1986) to **Peter Chan's** comedy ***He's a Woman, She's a Man*** *(Golden Branch, Jade Leaf)/Gam chi yuk yip/Jin qi yu she* (1994), songs are prevalent, tied to character, theme, and mood as an integral part of the story. Part of this may also be due to the fact that so many actors in Hong Kong are also singers (**Leslie Cheung** sings in both of the aforementioned films).

Currently, director Peter Chan is reviving the musical with *Perhaps Love/Yu guo aoi/Ruoguo ai* (2005), a musical/romantic drama starring **Kaneshiro Takeshi**, Mainland star Zhou Xun, **Jacky Cheung**, and Korean star Ji Jin-hee, with **Peter Pau** as cinematographer.

– N –

NAM, HUNG. Actress and producer Nam Hung (Nan Hong, real name Su Manmei) was educated at Mingde Middle School and studied accounting courses in Guangzhou. When she came to Hong Kong, she studied English at St. Rose of Lima. Her mother Chen Jianna was a stage actress before the war and her older sister Su Ziaomei was a **Cantonese opera** singer. Nam's mother introduced her to actress **Hong Sin-nui**, who became fond of her, taught her singing and acting, and gave Nam her theatrical name, which means "fame of the south." She began performing in 1950 with the Bao Feng Operatic Troupe, but soon turned to film.

She appeared in the three film adaptations of Ba Jin's *Torrent Trilogy*, **Ng Wui's** *Family/Ga/Jia* (1953), **Lee Sun-fung**'s *Spring/Chun/Chun* (1953), and **Chun Kim's** *Autumn/Chau/Qiu* (1954). In 1956, she joined Guang Yi Film Company, and her first lead role was in *Seven Heavens* (1956). She became famous with Chun Kim's *Tears of a Flower/Sin dut chaan lui/Xian hua can lei* (1958, costarring **Patrick Tse Yin**) and also starred in the Guang Yi studio comedy *Intimate Partners (My Intimate Partner)/Laan fong laan dai/Nan xiongnan di* (1960, directed by Chun), costarring Patrick Tse Yin and Wu Feng. Nam plays the woman (with a fiancé abroad) that two men working as real estate agents (Tse and Wu) fall for; when the fiancé dies, his sister is matched with Tse and Nam with Wu, but only after urban situation comedy ensues based on the contrasts in personalities. In a restaurant scene where both men expect to court Nam, the laughs come from a skillful combination of props, space, and supporting cast (a surly waiter).

Nam set up Rose Film Company in 1962, named after her favorite flower, together with director **Chor Yuen** (whom she later married). She starred in many of his films as well as those of director **Chan Wan**, and she was often cast opposite actor Patrick Tse Yin and with actress **Patsy Ka Ling**. Although she was mostly cast in melodramas as the woman holding traditional values, both tolerant and compliant, she also starred in Chor's *Black Rose/Hak muigwai/Hei mei gui* (1965) in the title role, which blended Chinese swordplay and the Western detective genre, and led to the sequel *Who Is That Rose?* (1966), taking its cue from James Bond flicks and lavish sets. She also was part of the ensemble cast in Chor's *The House of 72 Tenants/Chat sap yee ga fong hak/Qi shi er gu fang ke* (1973).

Nam began working at Hong Kong Television Broadcasts Limited (TVB) in 1976, appearing in soap operas like *A House Is Not a Home* and *No One Is Innocent*.

NAN KUEN FILM COMPANY (Nanqun). Nan Kuen was a small independent company, founded in 1948, with Xia Yan, Ouyang Yuqian, Zhang Min (Cheung Man), and Ge Qin working on its productions. Its goal was to find a way to use the art of film to educate and mobilize its audience. The company produced two films, Ouyang Yuqian's *The Way to Love/Lian'ai zhi dao* and Zhang Min's *Wind and Rain in Jiangnan (Quietly Flows the Jialing River, Gia Liang Kiang be My Destiny)/Jingjing de Jialingjiang* (both 1949). The company contributed to late 1940s Hong Kong film development.

NEW WAVE. Borrowing the term from the French New Wave, Hong Kong New Wave filmmakers include those young filmmakers, mostly in their twenties and thirties in the late 1970s and 1980s, who redefined Hong Kong cinema. What these innovators had in common was that most were Hong Kong belongers (they grew up in Hong Kong and defined home as Hong Kong rather than the Mainland) who trained in **television** locally or were educated at international film schools. While their styles differed, these filmmakers operated outside mainstream expectations; were technically proficient; tackled difficult and disturbing subject matter; exhibited social conscience and multicultural aesthetics; experimented with visuals, story, and character; and contributed a new voice on the Hong Kong scene, ushering in the creative explosion of 1980s Hong Kong cinema. They also explored Hong Kong identity as a theme, either directly or as subtext, and were also attentive to **gender** issues. Among those associated with the New Wave are (alphabetically) Alex Cheung, Clifford

Choi, Selina Chow, **Allen Fong**, **Ann Hui**, Kam Kwok-leong, Lau Shing-hon, **Johnny Mak**, Stephen Shin, **Patrick Tam**, **Terry Tong**, **Tsui Hark**, **Kirk Wong**, **Yim Ho**, Dennis Yu, and Peter Yung. They have influenced a generation of filmmakers who followed. *See also* INDEPENDENT FILM.

NG, CARRIE KA-LAI (1963–). Born in Kowloon, actress Carrie Ng has appeared in close to 90 movies. She began at Hong Kong Television Broadcasts Limited (TVB) and made her film debut in **Ringo Lam's** *City on Fire/Lung foo fung wan/Long hu feng yun* (1987) as **Chow Yun-fat's** impatient girlfriend. She had impressive roles in **Kirk Wong's** *Gunmen (Dragnet)/Tin law dei mong/Tian lun di wang* (1988) and **Tony Au's** *Au Revoir, Mon Amour (Will Mr. Sun Come Back?, Till We Meet Again)/Hoh yat gwan joi loi/He ri jun zai lai*, both starring **Tony Leung Ka-fai**. While she won a **Golden Horse Award** for Best Actress in the Category 3 *Remains of a Woman/Long sam yue tit/Lang xin ru tie* (1993) and Best Supporting Actress at the **Hong Kong Film Awards** for *The Kid/Lau sing yue/Liu zing yu* (1999), she is famous for her portrayal of a lesbian assassin in Clarence Ford's Category 3 *Naked Killer/Chik loh go yeung/Chi luo gao yang* (1992). She delivered another sympathetic performance as a mother, similar to *The Kid*, in **Carol Lai's** independent *Glass Tears/Boh lee siu lui/Bo li shao nu* (2001).

NG, CHO-FAN (Wu Chufan) (1911–1993). Actor, director, and producer Ng Cho-fan was born in Tianjin, studied at St. Paul's College in Hong Kong, and at 15 began working as a salesman and textile factory worker. In 1932, he performed in a fund-raising play for victims of a flood in Northern China, getting the attention of a **Lianhua** manager who immediately signed him. He acted in silent films as well as Guan Wenqing's first talkie, *Lifeline* (1935), with strong anti-Japanese sentiment, in which he sang the theme song. His performance in *Melody of Life (Song of Life, A Lost Woman)/Yan sang kuk/Ren sheng qu* (1937) earned him the title "Movie King of South China."

During wartime, he left for Macau, organizing the Ming Xing Theater Group that toured Guangdong province. He returned to Hong Kong following the war, helping initiate the "clean-up campaign" to raise the quality of films produced; he set up Hua Nan (South China)

Filmmakers' Collective in 1948 and he founded **Zhonglian** Studio (with **Pak Yin**, **Lee Tit**, and others) in 1952.

In 1955, Ng organized **Hualian** Film Company and produced **Lee Sun-fung's** *Cold Nights/Hon yau/Han ye* (in which he starred), and in the early 1960s he cowrote, produced, and starred in the director's *The Orphan/Yan hoi goo hung/ Renhai guhong* (1960) and founded Xin Chao, that produced Li's *A Wealthy Family* (1963), the first Cantonese color cinemascope movie. *The Orphan* costarred a teenaged **Bruce Lee** as a juvenile delinquent and Ng as the sympathetic reform school headmaster who changes his life, despite economic and social difficulties. Ng often collaborated with directors Lee Sun-fung and Lee Tit. He starred in Li's *Humanity/Yan diy/Ren dao* (1955) as a Shanxi farmer and scion who enters the university at the sacrifice of his family, only to be seduced by the distractions of city life; in a moving symbolic scene, he strips off his Western suit and dons peasant clothes. In Lee Tit's *In the Face of Demolition/Aau lau chun hiu/Weilou chunxiao* (1953), he was part of a distinguished ensemble cast of Cantonese actors playing working-class residents losing their homes. Ng frequently was paired with actress **Pak Yin**, as in *Spring/Chun/Chun* (1953), *Cold Nights* (1955), *The Grand Party (Feast of a Rich Family)/Ho moon yau yin/Hao men ye yan* (1959), *The Orphan* (1960), and *A Woman in Hong Kong* (1964). Referenced in director **Nelson Yu Lik-wai**'s *Love Will Tear Us Apart/Tin seung yan gaan/Tian shang ren jian* (1999, starring **Tony Leung Ka-fai**), the couple and their films appear symbolically in contrast to the disenfranchised Mainlanders bewildered by Hong Kong.

Ng won the Gold Award in China for his role in Lee Sun-fung's *Spring* (1953), and in 1956 he was selected as one of the best actors. In *Spring*, based on Ba Jin's second semiautobiographical novel in a trilogy, he starred as Juemin, one of two third-generation brothers in a family who fights for reform. He began directing as early as 1934 with the silent film *Coming Home*, and later in *A Woman in Hong Kong* (1964). He appeared in close to 400 films.

NG, FRANCIS CHUN-YU (1961–). Actor Francis Ng began in Hong Kong Television Broadcasts Limited's (TVB) training program (failing three times before graduating in 1985). He appeared in minor roles in film and worked in **television** early in his career, but his portrayal of the reprehensible Ugly Kwan in **Andrew Lau's** breakthrough "Triad-boyz" *Young and Dangerous (Young Rascals: Man of the World)/Goo wak jai ji yan joi gong woo/Gu huo zi zhi ren zai jiang hu* (1996) got attention, cemented by a performance as an apprehensive gang member in the irreverent spin-off *Once upon a Time in a Triad Society (Mongkok's Man in Charge)/Wong kok cha FIT yan/Wang jiao zha FIT ren* the same year. The **Hong Kong Film Critics' Society** has awarded him Best Actor three times, for **Wong Ka-fai's** *Once upon a Time in a Triad Society* (1996), *Bullets over Summer/Baau lit ying ging/Bao lie xing jing* (1999), and *2000 A.D./Gung yuen 2000 A.D./Gong yuan 2000 A.D.* (2000), the latter a small but impressive role as a character much older than he. He also won the Best Supporting Actor Award from the **Hong Kong Film Awards** for that portrayal. He won the Taiwanese **Golden Horse Award** for **Johnnie To's** ensemble piece, *The Mission (Gunfire)/Cheong feng/Qiang ho* (1999). His performances have ranged from quirky and maniacal to comedic or contemplative. He can play sensitive and subtle, as in **Wilson Yip's** *Juliet in Love (Juliet and San-pok, Butterfly Lovers)/Jue lai yip yue leung saan ang/Zhu liye yu liang shanbo* (2000).

To date Ng has directed (and appeared as an actor in) two of his films, *9413* (1998) and *What Is a Good Teacher?/Chi chung sze lo liu/Zi cong ta lai le* (2000). He also performs onstage in the theater, including *Naughty Couple* (1994–1995), and in stand-up comedy with Dayo Wong and Cheung Tat-ming in *Free Man Show* and *Free Man Show 2* (1998 and 2000). He has recently appeared in the TVB series *Triumph in the Skies* as an airline pilot.

NG, MAN-TAT (1952–). Actor Ng Man-tat has appeared in several hundred films over more than 20 years. Although he is known in more recent years for his partnerships with comedian **Stephen Chiau** and very broad comedy, he began at the Hong Kong Television Broadcasts Limited (TVB) actors' training program and appeared in **television** variety shows and dramas. His early roles were in crime dramas, one of them being as a crooked cop in **Yuen Wo-ping's** *Tiger Cage* (1988). He won Best Supporting Actor at the 1990 **Hong Kong Film Awards** for his performance in *A Moment of Romance (If Heaven Has Love)/Tin yeuk yau ching/Tian ruo you qing* (1990) and shone alongside **Chow Yun-fat** in **Ringo Lam's** *Prison on Fire 2*

(Escaped Criminals: Prison Turbulence Sequel)/To faan gaam yuk fung wan juknjaap/Tao fan jian yu feng yun xu ji (1991).

Ng was first paired with Chiau in *All for the Winner/Diy sing/Du sheng* (1990) and began developing the characterization for which he would become known. He chews up scenery and his gestures are large. Exaggerated expressions, eyes enlarged, and mouth agape, his body language resembles that of **Liu Enjia**, except Ng's characters are more scheming, out for themselves and figuring the angles; however, his schemes rarely come to a good end, and he sweats out the results. Although a sycophant, he also plays the everyman with a soft underbelly so audiences in Hong Kong find him difficult to dislike. The shtick between Chiau and Ng ranges from two antagonists sizing each other up and mutually using each other until the scales tip one way or the other; ultimately there is genuine affection underneath. The two actors have collaborated on more than 20 films to date. In 1992 alone, the prolific Ng made 17 films.

NG, RICHARD YIU-HON (1939–). Actor Richard Ng left Hong Kong in 1955 to go to school in London, graduating from the Central School of Speech and Drama, and appearing on the BBC in the late 1960s, as well as in two British films, *The Gamblers* and *Tomorrow*. He returned to Hong Kong in 1970 and began working with the **Hui Brothers** on their television show, which gave him an entry into their films. Though his first film in Hong Kong was the Robert Klause–directed actioner *Golden Needles/San kei duet meng gai/Shen ji duo ming ji* (1975), in which he acted alongside Jim Kelly and Burgess Meredith, Ng was also cast in Michael Hui's *The Private Eyes/Boon gan baat leung/Ban jin ba liang* (1976). Ng's first starring role was in *The Yellow Panther/Dim chi chuk chaak gam gaan daan/Dian zhi zhuo ze gan jian chan* (1977). He is most famous for his somewhat zany comedic roles, particularly those in the series of *Lucky Stars* films produced by **Samo Hung**. However, he has taken more dramatic roles as well, as in **Ann Hui's** *Starry Is the Night/Gam yau sing gwong chaan laan/Jin ye xing guang can lan* (1988) and **Yim Ho's** *Red Dust/Gwan gwan hung chan/Gun gun hongchen* (1990). Though he has slowed down considerably, he still makes the occasional film, most recently *Legend of the Dragon/Lung wai foo ji/Long wei fu zi* (2005) with Hung. Ng is also the father of actor Carl Ng.

NG, SANDRA KWUN-YU (1965–). Born in Hong Kong, actress Sandra Ng is a second-generation actor, her father being a television contract player at Asia Television Limited (ATV). Ng started at Hong Kong Television Broadcasts Limited (TVB) and had small parts in films during the mid-1980s, but found her comedic side by the late 1980s, appearing in films like *The Greatest Lover/Gung ji dok ching/Gong zi duo qing* (1988), alongside **Chow Yun-fat** and **Anita Mui**. Her characterizations were usually obnoxious, unattractive pushy women who were also very funny, making her one of the leading comediennes. She made numerous ensemble comedies with **Wong Jing** in the later 1980s into the 1990s, including *All's Well End's Well (Family Has Happy Affairs)/Ga yau bei si/Jia you xi shi* (1992) and its sequel *All's Well, End's Well, Too (Happy Event in the Flower Fields)/Fa tin hei si/Hua tian xi shi* (1993) as well as *Boys Are Easy (Chasing Boys)/Chui lam chai/Zhui nan zai* (1993).

In the mid-1990s, she turned to drama, delivering a convincing bravura performance by playing four characters in four stories in the arty **independent** *Four Faces of Eve/4 Min ha wa/4 Mian jia wa* (1996), working with four directors, namely Kam Kwok-leung, Eric Kot Man-fai, Eric Kwok, and Jan Lam Hoi-fung. While the film failed at the box office, it did not disappoint critics. In another drama, *Juliet in Love (Butterfly Lovers)/Jue lai yip yue leung saan ang/Zhu li she yu liang shan ba* (2000), Ng delivered a touchingly deep performance, playing a lonely woman who finds love with **Francis Ng**.

Ng also appeared in four films of the *Young and Dangerous/Goo wak jai ji/Gu huo zi zhu* series (1996–2000) as the tough Sister 13, and although the character was not a lead, Ng was memorable and the character was given a spin-off, a gender-bending gang movie, *Portland Street Blues/Goo waak chai ching yee pin ji hung hing sap saam mooi/Gu huo zai qing yi pian zhi hong xing shi san mei* (1998), for which Ng won the Best Actress **Hong Kong Film Award**.

More recently, Ng has returned to comedy in two films, *Golden Chicken 1* and *2/Gam gai/Jin ji* (2002, 2003), the title a reference to her character's profession as a prostitute. She also played the housewife whose henpecked husband (**Leung Ka-fai**) is under house arrest in the smart and humorous *Men Suddenly in Black/Daai cheung foo/Da zhang fu* (2003), shot as a gangster crime movie with the

Triad war here between men and women, and appears in Peter Chan's musical *Perhaps Love/Yu guo aoi/Ruoguo ai* (2005).

NG, SEE-YUEN (1944–). Director, producer, and writer Ng See-yuen was born in Shanghai and educated in Hong Kong. He was a teacher before entering the film industry in 1967 at **Shaw Brothers,** working as a script continuity person and then assistant director. He left Shaws in 1971 and directed such films as *The Bloody Fists* and *The Good and the Bad* (both 1972). He established **Seasonal Films** in 1975, and wrote and directed the crime thriller *Anti-Corruption/Lianzheng fengbao* (1975), as well as producing **Jackie Chan** films like *Drunken Master (Drunken Monkey in the Tiger's Eye)/Chui kuen/Zui quan* and *Snake in the Eagle's Shadow (Snake Form Trick Hand)/Sau ying diu san/She xing diao shou* (both 1978). He also produced **Tsui Hark**'s *Butterfly Murders (Butterfly Transformation)/Dai bin/Die bian* (1979) and **Cheung Yuen-ting**'s *The Soong Sisters(The Sung Family Dynasty)/Sung ga wong chiu/Song gu huang chao* (1997). Prolific as a writer, director, and producer, he has served as president of the Hong Kong Film Directors Guild.

NG, WUI (Wu Hui) (1913–1996). Director and actor Ng Wui, a native of Guangdong province, was born in Guangzhou and in 1940 began as an actor with Daguan (**Grandview**). His directorial debut was *Reunion at Full Moon* (1941). He temporarily retired during the war when he refused to make films for the Japanese; together with **Lo Dun**, Li Chen, **Wong Cho-san**, and Li Yueqing, he formed a theater group and toured Southeast Asian countries to aid in the war effort.

Among his best-known films are *Family/Ga/Jia* (1953), based on Ba Jin's first novel in a semiautobiographical trilogy, and *Wilderness/Yuan yau/Yuan ye* (1956), adapted from a Cao Yu original. He made numerous dramas and historical dramas, but also comedies like *End of the Year Means Money/Nin man chin/Nian wan qian* (1950) and *A Chao Is Getting Married/Chan chiu git fan/Chen chao jie hun* (1958), starring **Patrick Tse Yin**, and a fantasy **Chinese opera** like *Precious Lotus Lamp/Bo lin dang/Bao lian deng* (1956). Ng often worked with the actress **Pak Yin** and actors **Ng Cho-fan** and **Cheung Ying**. In *Father and Son/Foo yue ji/Fu yu zi* (1954), an underpaid clerk (**Zhang Houyou**) invests his savings and hope in his son, sending him to a private school, where he is looked down upon; the film, produced by **Zhonglian**, anticipates the social dramas to follow, like **Allen Fong's** 1980s film of the same title. *The Story of a Family/Tin Lun/Tianlun* (1961), made in two parts, is a savage indictment of male weakness and middle-class values. Pak Yin plays wife to Ng Cho-fan; the wife is expecting a second child and the husband gets promoted, only to take a mistress, gamble, and embezzle to cover his debt. Numerous catastrophes ensue as a result of the man's infirmities, and they must be lived through before some semblance of normality reappears.

Ng directed over 250 films, his last in 1979. He joined Rediffusion Television (RTV) in 1970 as an actor, but later turned to program planning and production. He acted in 40 films, specializing in greedy and cowardly characters; he appeared in the **Stephen Chiau** vehicle *Hail the Judge/Gau ban chi lut goon baak min baan ching tin/Jiu pin zhi ma guan bai mian bao qing tian* (1994) before his death in Hong Kong two years later.

NG, YAT-SIU (Wu Yixiao) (1906–1964). Cantonese opera librettist and writer Ng Yat-siu was born in Guangdong province and began his Chinese opera career at a young age. In Guangzhou, he was a member of the Feisheng Drama Group, playing servile *lache* (literally, "to drag or pull," parts that require the actor to fill in between acts by playing to the house) roles. With Liu Zhenqiu he began writing scripts and composing librettos; he also wrote many opera songs for performers such as Xiao Mingxing, Xu Liuxian, Xiao Yanfei, and **Yam Kim-fai**.

Ng began composing for films with *Official Mei* (1938). Libretti he adapted for the screen include *Third Master Sha and Lady Yin/Sha Sanshao yu Yinjie* (1947), *Prostituting to Raise the Orphan/Maai yuk yeung goo ngai/Mai rou yang gu er* (1947), *The Love Chain* (1952), *Emperor Guang Xu's Nocturnal Lament/Goh Cheung Gwong Sui wong taan ng gang/Ge Chang Guang Xu wang tan wu geng* (1952), and *The Humiliated Rickshaw Puller* (1953). *Third Master Sha and Lady Yin* was based on a Guangdong incident in which the son of an official uses his power to exploit those weaker, killing the husband of a servant to whom he is attracted; ultimately, his own father puts him on trial. In *Prostituting to Raise the Orphan*, Cheung Yuet-yee starred as a popular songstress who has an affair with a scoundrel who leaves her to raise a son alone; in order to do so, she prostitutes herself to raise the boy to adulthood. *The Humiliated Rickshaw Puller (Driver)/Laai che bei yuk/Xin mazai lache bei ru* featured nine songs, and starred **Sun Ma Tze-tsang** in the title role.

Ng also worked in the radio and recording industries, but his outstanding achievement is the reforms he instituted in Cantonese opera by using Cantonese folk melodies, popular songs, and foreign film soundtracks in his operas. Also a prolific songwriter, Ng had songs that appeared in movies like *Prostituting to Raise the Orphan/Mairou yang guer* (1947) and *Homeward the Swallow Flies/Duoqing yanzi gui* (1956). For **Wu Pang's** contemporary **melodrama** *Parting under Sky's End/Bieli ren dui naihetian* (1951), Ng composed the songs "Amorous Butterflies" and "Pain of Farewell," sung by Siu Yin-fei, playing a Guangzhou singer thwarted in her love for Cheung Ying; she makes her way to Hong Kong and only too late does he discover she carried his child.

The composer was also a screenwriter. He wrote the first episode of the popular **Wong Fei-hung** series. Others include *How Ten Heroes of Guangdong Slew the Dragon/Gong Dung sap foo tiu lung gei/ Guangdong shi hu tu long ji* (1950) and *Punish the Unfaithful/Paang ckui bok ching long/Bang da bo qing lang* (1955).

Ng died in Hong Kong.

NORTH–SOUTH TRILOGY. The huge box office success North–South trilogy of the early 1960s includes three comedic films, the first written by **Stephen Soong** and the latter two written by **Eileen Chang**, directed by **Wang Tianlin**, starring popular actors from Cantonese and Mandarin cinema (including actors **Leung Sing-po** and **Liu Enjia**), and featuring contrasts between Cantonese and Northern (Mandarin) language and customs, to humorous effect. In the first film, *The Greatest Civil War on Earth/Naam bak who/Nan bei hei* (1961), Leung and Liu play rival tailors living in the same apartment. The Cantonese Leung and the Mandarin Liu find their daughters falling in love with a Shanghainese and Cantonese, respectively; the fathers face off by singing their regional operas.

In the second film, *The Greatest Wedding on Earth/Nam bak yut ga chan/Nan bei yijia qin* (1962), the two actors play competing restaurateurs serving Cantonese and Northern cuisines. Leung's son and

Liu's daughter hide their romance, the son (a health inspector) pretending to be from Shandong and the daughter pretending to be skilled in making a specialty Cantonese cake. When the fathers discover their children's pretense, they face off in a hilarious **Wong Feihung** school–Tianjin tai chi fight in a restaurant (that would be reprised in numerous Hong Kong comedies of the 1980s and 1990s); the younger siblings serve as mediators and another cross-cultural romance develops.

In the third film, *The Greatest Love Affair on Earth/Naam bak hei seung fung/Nan bei xi xiang feng* (1964), the laughter stems more from the plot's comedy of situation. Two Cantonese- and Mandarin-speaking female cousins fall in love with two poor teachers; their Northern guardian (Liu Enjia) disapproves, especially of one of them who speaks only Cantonese, until he discovers the teacher has a wealthy aunt willing to invest big money. When the aunt fails to appear, Leung Sing-po, disguised in drag to avoid creditors, poses as the aunt.

In all three films, the cultural and language differences and disagreements ultimately give way to cooperation, tolerance, and love, especially through the romance of the younger generation and gradual acceptance by the elders. Still, the humor is infectious, unforgettable, and influential, both for the physical comedy of the mismatched men as well as the language confusions. In the second film, for instance, Leung plays the Cantonese "Shen Jingbing," whose name, pronounced in Mandarin means "insanity." Likewise, Liu plays the Northerner Li Shipu, whose name, pronounced in Cantonese means "nonsense." When the two meet through a mutual friend and mediator to resolve matters, things get off to a bad start, as Shen announces himself by name, which the other infers to mean his adversary thinks their meeting is insanity, and then, the other deduces Li believes it to be nonsense. In this film, as the others, details of cultural differences are introduced, as the Cantonese father is preoccupied by the bride's dowry, not the groom's gift, and the Northerner the reverse.

NUXIA* (*xianu*)**. *Xia* is a Chinese term usually translated as "knight" or "swordsman," and *nu* means "female"; therefore, *nuxia/xianu* refers to a swordswoman or female knight. The astonishing images of female warriors seen in Chinese **martial arts** films may seem to be inspired by modern feminism, but these images of gender equality can be traced back at least to the late 19th century. In the waning years of the Qing dynasty, books describing the adventures of male and female martial artists living in the realm of the ***jiang hu, the "martial underworld," created the genre of ***wuxia*** in 20th-century Chinese pop culture. Tracing the stories back further leads to the classic literature of Imperial China, and the *dao ma dan* ("broadsword horse actress" or woman warrior) roles of **Peking (Beijing) opera**.

The martial underworld is a shadow society. It exists intermingled with the everyday world but with its own power structure, including arcane rules and ancient feuds. One tenet of the *wuxia* world is that it is impossible to know who is friend or foe. Anyone can be a hidden "dragon" or a secret master, regardless of gender or social status. While the *jiang hu* stories dramatized in Hong Kong films are exaggerated to an extreme of fantasy, tales of woman masters of swordplay and kung fu appear to have some basis in fact. The female generals Hua Mulan and Mu Guiying are the subjects of popular operas. The actual martial arts lineages, real world equivalents to the *wuxia* clans, pass down accounts of the exploits of their originators that are not dissimilar to tales of the *jiang hu*. Women masters are credited in the lineages with creating and popularizing fighting systems, such as *wing chun*. How true are the stories? Certainly there are no taboos against women learning martial arts in China, and there are a number of documented modern female masters, including **Samo Hung's** grandmother Chin Tsi-ang, and **Donnie Yen's** mother, Bow Sim Mark.

Chinese martial arts (*wushu*) have been heavily influenced by Taoist philosophy, in which duality (yin/yang) has very fluid boundaries. Many of the writers and directors working in the *wuxia* genre have used this fluidity of gender roles to create strong, vibrant, and sublimely confident heroines. Some of the earliest surviving films of China are *wuxia pian* with sword-fighting heroines. These young women forswear romance for a life of martial training and protecting the innocent. Xu Qin Fang was the star of a typical early *nuxia* film, *Swordswoman of Huangjiang/Huangjiang nuxia* (1930). Western audiences were first introduced to *nuxia* through the luminous films of director **King Hu**. Working with actresses like **Hsu Feng** and **Cheng**

Pei-pei, he created a new cinematic language for the magic of *wuxia* and the perils of life in the *jiang hu*.

Film technology has gradually advanced to the point where the lyrical visions of directors like Hu, **Tsui Hark**, **Ching Siu-tung**, and **Zhang Yimou** can be reproduced on-screen. All have incorporated images of *nuxia* into their films. A *nuxia* actress might be an elegantly beautiful sword fighter in one film, and the tough-as-nails sidekick in another. As icons of female power, the great *nuxia* actresses, including Cheng Pei-pei, Hsu Feng, **Hui Ying-hung**, **Angela Mao**, Shih Szu, **Polly Shangkuan Lingfeng**, **Connie Chan Po-chu**, **Michelle Yeoh**, **Brigitte Lin**, and Zhang Ziyi, bring to life a world in which women stand tall and fight on their own behalf.

– O –

O-MEI FILM COMPANY. Founded in 1958 by Wan Wu and managed by Lin Yan, O-mei specialized in **martial arts** movies and was the first company to adapt novels of **Louis Cha** (Jin Yong) and Liang Yu-sheng. Its first production was Wu Pang's *Story of the Vulture Conqueror/Shediao yingxiong zhuan* (1958). Other films include *Story of the White-Haired Demon Girl/Bai fa mo nu chuan* (1959) and *The Blind Swordsman/Man xia chuan xin jian* (1965). Over seven years, the company produced 34 films.

ODELL, ALBERT (1924–2004). Born and raised in Hong Kong of British, Russian, and Jewish origin, Albert Odell worked briefly at the British Embassy in Chongqing during the Japanese occupation, and joined Republic Pictures in Singapore after the war. In 1951, he joined Singapore's **Cathay** Organization, heading its International Film Distribution Agency. In 1954, at the direction of **Loke Wan Tho**, he went to Hong Kong as general manager, establishing the Hong Kong branch, International Films Distributing Agency, producing a number of well-regarded Cantonese films. While managing operations, he oversaw the takeover of **Yonghua Studios** and the building of a new studio at Hammer Hill Road. He resigned in 1957 to set up his own company, but shortly thereafter joined **Shaw Brothers**. He owned video stores in Singapore before his death.

***ONCE UPON A TIME IN CHINA* SERIES.** With the first *Once upon a Time in China (Wong Fei-hung)/Wong Fei-hung/Huang Feihong* (1991), director **Tsui Hark** became responsible for reviving the Chinese **martial arts** films in the early 1990s and creating a new trend after the **gambling** and gunplay films of the 1980s. All six films tell tales of legendary Chinese folk hero, martial arts master, and herbal doctor **Wong Fei-hung**. The series has a strong pro-Chinese, anti-imperialist sentiment as well as themes of inexorable progress and celebration of Chinese cultural identity and humanistic ideals. Tsui mixed historical figures with fictional characters, related the past to the present, delivered political messages in relation to identity and gender, and used arty camerawork, including multiperspective angles.

The first film in the series has Wong (**Jet Li**) along with his new pupil Leung Foon (**Yuen Biao**) and his disciples at Po Chi Lam confronting the Sha He gang and a corrupt American slave trader tricking Chinese people into going to America through promises of gold. On top of this, he also must battle an impoverished martial arts master (**Yam Sai-koon**) all the while tiptoeing around his romantic interest, Wong's 13th aunt Yee (**Rosamund Kwan**), who is actually younger than Wong. Typical of Tsui's signature approach, the first film served as an allegory of the Tiananmen Square tragedy.

Li would continue to play Wong in the next two films. The second film, *Once upon a Time in China 2* (*Wong Fei-hung 2: A Man Should Be Self-Sufficient)/Wong Fei-hung ji yi naam yi dong ji keung/Huang Feihong zhi er nan er dang zi qiang* (1992, director Tsui Hark) has Wong confront both the corrupt Chinese government as personified by **Donnie Yen** and the insane nationalist White Lotus Society, whose members believe that their magic protects them from modern weaponry. Max Mok replaced Yuen Biao as Leung Foon for the rest of the series. The third film, *Once upon a Time in China 3 (Wong Fei-hung 3: The Lion King Struggles for Supremacy)/Wong Fei-hung ji saam si wong jaang ba/Huang Feihong zhi san shi wang zheng ba* (1993), is a marked departure in tone from the first two, taken over by series producer Tsui Hark's tendency toward too much spectacle. In this entry, Wong is forced to enter the Empress Dowager's lion dance competition to stop a Russian, who is also a romantic rival for Aunt Yee's affections, from assassinating Prime Minister Li Hung-chang. Along the way he must also defeat a local gang harassing his father, Wong Kei-ying (Lau Shun). This film also introduces Wong's disciple Club Foot (Hung Yan-yan).

For the fourth and fifth films, Chinese *wushu* champion Zhao Wenzhou replaced Jet Li as Wong. The series waned at this point through relatively undeveloped plots as compared to the previous films. In the fourth film, *Once upon a Time in China 4 (Wong Fei-hung 4: Royal Demeanor)/Wong Fei-hung ji 4 wong je ji fung/Huang Feihong zhi 4 wang zhe zhi feng* (1993, Yuen Bun), the foreign powers trying to carve up China have their own lion dance competition with specially designed lions, and the Chinese government asks Wong to attend since he won the last competition. Wong misses the first competition and the Chinese officers are killed. In retaliation, Wong challenges the foreign powers, which accept his invitation. Despite winning the battle, Wong loses the war as the foreign troops seize Peking. In the fifth film, *Once upon a Time in China 5 (Wong Fei-hung 5: Dragon City's Murderous Tyrant)/Wong Fei-hung chi neung lung shing chim and/Huang Feihong zhi wu long cheng jian ba* (1994), Wong defends a town from pirates who are stealing the food.

After five films, the series went on hiatus only to return with **Samo Hung** directing and action-directing the final installment and Jet Li back in the role of Wong Fei-hung for a **Lunar New Year** release. This time, in *Once upon a Time in China and America (Wong Fei-hung: West Territory Mighty Lion)/Wong Fei-hung chi sai wik hung shut/Wong Feihong zhi xi yu xiong shi* (1997), Wong travels to America to set up a branch of his herbal clinic and loses his memory when he nearly drowns after a battle. While Aunt Yee searches for Wong and helps set up Po Chi Lam with Club Foot, she must also contend with the local sheriff and his anti-Chinese attitude. She receives help in the form of Billy the Kid. When Wong returns with the Indians and regains his memory, he and his disciples are arrested for robbing the bank (for which the corrupt sheriff and a gang of bandits are actually responsible). Billy saves Wong and his friends from the stockades and Wong battles the leader of the bandits. As Wong prepares to return to China, Billy is made sheriff and the film ends with a lion dance. The sixth film was shot on location in Texas.

***ORIOLES BANISHED FROM THE FLOWERS* (1948).** *Orioles Banished from the Flowers/Dut ngoi lau aau/Huawai liuying* was directed by **Fang Peilin** and stars **Zhou Xuan**. This Mandarin musical situation comedy tells the story of two feuding neighbors who eventually fall in love. (It was remade four years later as a Cantonese comedy, *Night of the Romance*, which introduced characters hiding in small spaces, a sight gag that would reappear in lots of 1980s comedies.) Signature stylized devices of Fang Peilin are evident, from quick pans and lots of camera movement to cross-cutting, point-of-view shots, and poetical inserts.

ORPHAN ISLAND PERIOD. The Orphan Island period dates from November 1937 to December 1941, and refers to the Japanese occupation of Shanghai during the Sino–Japanese War. When the Kuomintang army retreated, the Japanese overran Shanghai, with the exception of the foreign concessions. Foreign powers remained neutral at this time. The term originally meant Shanghai as surrounded by foreign powers, literally, an island. But the term came to be used to refer to the filmmakers who moved into the concessions and continued to make movies. Perhaps 20 film companies operated during this period and 200 films a year were made. The period ended when the Japanese moved into the concessions and neutrality was no longer an option. Many Shanghai filmmakers then fled to Hong Kong.

***OUR SISTER HEDY* (1957).** Director and writer **Tao Qin's** musical melodrama *Our Sister Hedy/Se chin gam/Si qianjin* (the Chinese title is *Four Daughters*) was produced at **Motion Pictures and General Investment** and features a bevy of female beauties. Taiwanese actress Mu Hung plays the eldest sister who has been shouldered with family responsibilities since her mother's early death; **Julie Ye Feng** (her screen debut) is the second daughter and selfish flirt; **Jeanette Lin Cui** appears as the English title character, an energetic, tomboyish character on the cusp of womanhood who concerns herself with others' well-being; and, **Dolly Soo Fung** plays the youngest and meekest daughter. Wang Yuanlong is cast as the hapless widowed father, and the movie is a story of sibling rivalries as each daughter finds romance and love. Above all the squabbling, catfights, and stolen boyfriends is a positive message about sisterly love and the importance of family through thick and thin.

Composer **Qi Xiangtan** (Kei Shang-tong) was responsible for the music, and the songs are interwoven into the dramatic action. Ye Feng does a sultry and seductive version of "You Come with Me" and Lin Cui conducts a singing-dancing-and-fencing gym class with her charges. The film won numerous awards, among them best film at the fifth **Asian Film Festival** and 11 Golden Harvest Awards, including Best Screenplay, Director, Leading Actor and Actress (**Peter Chen Ho** and Lin Cui), Supporting Actor and Actress (Wang Yuanlong and Mu Hong), Photography, Music, Recording, Sets, and Editing.

A sequel, *Wedding Bells for Hedy/Langui fenyun* (1959), written by Tao Qin and directed by Shen Zhong, with the same cast, followed.

– P –

PAK, CHRISTINE LU-MING (Bai Luming) (1937–). Actress Pak Lu-ming (real name Xu Liqiong), a native of Guangdong province, attended the Tack Ching Girls' Middle School in Hong Kong. Interested in acting from an early age, she trained under famous opera actor **Sit Kok-sin** (Xue Juexian) and his wife Tong Suet-hing (Tang Xueqing) and performed opera onstage. Encouraged by her godmother, celebrated opera actress **Yam Kim-fai** (Ren Jianhui), she joined Tai Seng (Dacheng) Film Company in 1953. Her first starring role was *Now That I've Got a Daughter, Everything's Okay (Everything's Okay When You Have a Daughter)/Yau lui maan si chuk/You nu wan shi ju* (1955), director-writer Chiang Wai-kwong's Cantonese comedy that takes its cue from a well-known saying that favors males over females in families. Yam Kim-fai played a young woman who also disguises herself as her lost twin brother, and Pak played the brother's fiancée, with a lover on the side; Yam's husband also becomes infatuated with the fiancée, and the humor comes from the bizarre relationships. Other films included *The Wise Guys Who Fool Around/Chat lut laap fook/Zha ma na fu* (1956) and *Mother's Broken Heart/Ngai sam sui miu sam/Er xin sui mu xin* (1958).

Pak joined **Motion Pictures and General Investments (MP&GI)** in 1957 and starred in *Memories of Love (A Lovely Girl's Lovely Dreams)/Mei yan chun mung/Mei ren chun meng* (1958); she made

14 Cantonese films at MP&GI. In **Tso Kea's** *Memories of Love*, she starred opposite **Ng Cho-fan** as a smitten songstress who falls for him, despite their age differences. Since he is married, her mother defies the match, and she takes ill. A rich heir (**Cheung Ying**) proposes to no avail, so he shoots the lover. The movie was an adaptation of a Hollywood movie, Richard Fleischer's *The Girl in the Red Velvet Swing* (1955), starring Ray Milland and Joan Collins. *Bitter Lotus/Foo sam lin/Ku xin lian* (1960) broke box office records from the previous ten years. Pak appeared in Mandarin features as well, including *Four Brave Ones/Dip hoi sei chong si/Die hai zhuang shi* (1963), which won at the third **Golden Horse Awards**; the comedy *The Greatest Civil War on Earth/Naam bak woh/Nan bei he* (1961), part of the **North–South trilogy**; the melodrama *Father and Son/Yan ji choh/Ren zhi chu* (1963); and the costume drama *The Magic Lamp* (1964).

Pak's last film was *Mistaken Love/Chi chok doh ching/Zi zuo duo qing* (1966). She retired in 1965 to marry a lawyer.

PAK, SUET-SIN (Bai Xuexian) (1926–). Actress Pak Suet-sin (real name Chen Shuliang) was born in Guangzhou and completed her secondary education in Hong Kong. Under the influence of her father, famous opera performer Bai Jurong/Pak Kui-wing, she came under the spell of Chinese opera, trained under **Sit Kok-sin** (Xue Juexian), performed with the Juexiansheng Opera Troupe, and began using the stage name Pak Suet-sin (Bai Xuexian) at 12. During wartime, she performed with various opera troupes, among them the New East Asia Opera Troupe. She specialized in *huadan* roles (vivacious young women) for the Jintianhua Opera Troupe at 16. She joined the Xinsheng Troupe with actress **Yam Kim-fai** (Ren Jianhui), who specialized in male roles, beginning a beautiful partnership throughout their movie careers, in close to 60 Cantonese opera films alone in the 1950s. Their mutual contribution to Cantonese opera and films is great, and the duo were much beloved. The duo Pak–Yam, partners in their private lives, formed the Xianfengming Opera Troupe in 1956, which continued until their retirements for health reasons in 1966.

Pak's film debut was *Wife in the Morning, Sister-in-Law at Night/San chai miu siu/Chenqi musao* (1947). The contemporary family **melodrama** was set during the Sino–Japanese War, and Pak played a cousin loved by two brothers. One of them impregnates her, but is believed dead at the front, so the other brother intends on marrying her; when the brother reappears, crippled, the couple, after overcoming obstacles, is eventually reunited. The film was adapted from the stage opera and the playwright, Auyeung Kim, also played the male lead. In Yeung Kung-leong's family melodrama *Red and White Peonies/ Hung baak maau daan dut/Hongbai mudan hua* (1952), she played the young and inexperienced daughter who foolishly reveals her older sister (**Hong Sin-nui**) is adopted on the sister's birthday, and that the real father (**Ma Sze-tsang**) is a gangster.

Pak appeared in 200 films from 1947 to 1968, and was the lead in more than 100 of them. Opera films include, among numerous others, **Mok Hong-si's** *Romance of Mount Fuji (Fuji Mountain)/Foo si saan ji luen/Fushishan zhi lian* (1954), **Lee Tit's** ***The Purple Hairpin****/Chi chaai gei/Zichai ji* and *Butterfly and Red Pear/Dip ying hung lee gei/Dieying hongli ji* (both 1959), Jiang Weiguang's *Gold-Braided Fan/Chuen gan bo sin/Chuan jin bao shan* (1959), Yu Liang's *Triennial Mourning on the Bridge/Aaam nin yat huk yee long kiu/Sannin yiku erlang qiao* (1959), and **Lung To's** (actually, uncredited **Tso Kea**) *Princess Cheung Ping [Tragedy of the Emperor's Daughter]/Dai lui dut/ Dinu hua* (1959). In both *The Purple Hairpin* and *Butterfly and Red Pear*, Pak played courtesans to Yam's cross-dressed male scholars. In the latter, they are a pair of would-be lovers, who keep trying to meet but are thwarted; when they finally meet, Pak cannot reveal her identity. Librettist **Tong Tik-sang** frequently collaborated with these actresses, and in both of these films he achieves a lingering air of sadness. Tong also adapted *Triennial Mourning on the Bridge* from the stage opera both actresses had starred in; **Leung Sing-po** became the third corner of a love triangle, with Pak playing the woman caught between two brothers (with Yam playing the other brother), and Leung's character making the ultimate sacrifice for the couple's love.

The actress produced *Tragedy of a Poet King/Lee hau chu/Li hou zhu* (1968) for her own company. After retirement, she and Yam remained active supporting and training new talent through the Chufengming (Young Phoenix) Opera Troupe. *See also* CHINESE OPERA FILMS.

PAK, YIN (Bai Yan) (1920–). Actress and producer Pak Yin (real name Chen Yuping) was born in Guangzhou and educated at Jiao Zhong Girls' School. In 1936, she started at Guo Ji Film Company, and was starring in *Twin Lotus*, but the company manager absconded with funds and the film was uncompleted. The film's director, Chen Tian, came to Hong Kong in 1937, and Pak followed him, appearing in his *Glorious Country (Magnificent Country)/Gam sau hiu saan/Jin xiu he shan* (1937) alongside **Ng Cho-fan** and Lin Liping.

Pak was nicknamed the "evergreen tree" of Hong Kong Cantonese movies. She appeared in more than 250 movies, and was typically cast as an oppressed woman, victimized by China's feudalism, who endures her fate. She often acted as a virtuous mother. Sometimes, however, she played a strong and determined **woman**, as in director **Tso Kea**'s adaptation of novels by Zhang Henshui, *Somber Night* and *Sunset on the River/Moon kong hung/Man jiang hong* (both 1962). She worked regularly with directors Wong Toi, **Ng Wui**, and **Lee Sun-fung** and was often paired with the actor Ng Cho-fan, as in *The Lover's Belated Return (Never Too Late to Come Home)/Long gwai man/Lang gui wan* (1947), *The Shackles of Sin (The Waves of Sin) 1* and *2/Chui nyn soh lin/Zui e suo lian* (1950), *Blood-Stained Azaleas/Huet yim do guen hung/Xie ran du juan hong* (1951), *A Dream of Red Mansions (The Dream of the Red Chamber)/Hung lau san mung/Hong lou xin meng* (1951), *Following the Gentle Light (The Guiding Light)/Foo hoi ming dang/Ku hai ming deng* (1953), *Spring/Chun/Chun* (1953), *Cold Nights/Hon yau/Han ye* (1955), *The Road/Liu/Lu* (1959), *The Orphan/ Yan hoi goo hung/ Renhai guhong* (1960), and *A Hong Kong Woman/ Heung gong yat foo yan/Xiang gang yi fu ren* (1964). Pak shined in her last film before retirement, **Lee Tit's** *The Lost Pearl/Chong hoi wai chu/Cang hai wei zhu* (1965). She plays a brothel madam's servant who becomes foster mother to a lost child, willing to do anything for the girl's happiness. Using family conflict to contrast Northern and Southern Chinese language and customs, and reflect class differences, the film is one of the last of the genre made. Its story is similar to Lee Sun-fung's *The Orphan* (1960, in which Pak also costarred), featuring a female rather than male young person.

In 1952, Pak established **Zhonglian** (Union) Film Company with actor Ng Cho-fan and others, initially serving as its deputy director and in 1961 as chief director. In 1954, she also founded **Shanlian** Film Company with director **Ng Wui** and actor **Cheung Wood-yau**, which produced *Parents' Love (Great Devotion)/Hoh lin ting gwong-foo miu sam/Ke lian tian xia fu mu xin* (1960) among others. Pak's autobiography, *Glorious Youth*, was published in 1966. In **Nelson Yu Lik-wai's** *Love Will Tear Us Apart/Tin seung yan gaan/Tian shang ren jian* (1999, starring **Tony Leung Ka-fai**), Leung's character describes her as having "the perfect face."

PAN, PETER LEI (Poon Lui) (1927–). Director and writer Pan Lei (real name Pan Rongsheng), a native of Guangdong province, was born in Haiphong, Vietnam. During World War II, he was an army lieutenant on the Cambodian front, afterwards he attended the Jiangsu National Medical Institute in Shanghai, and in 1949 he moved to Taiwan. There, he began writing poetry and worked as a writer and literary magazine editor. He wrote more than 20 novels, among them *Red Valley* and *Devil Tree*, and won the China Literary Award for 1957, 1958, and 1959.

Pan first became involved in the film industry in Taiwan as a script editor at the Central Motion Picture Company; he also helped found Hua Guo studio. He wrote *Dawn Has Broken* (1955) for the former company, which starred Zhang Zhongwen and Tang Qing; he also wrote *The Leper Girl Mafeng Nu* (1956). His directorial debut was *On Mount Hehuan (The Mountain of Mutual Happiness)/Hehuan-shan shang* (1958), followed by several others. *Typhoon/Tai feng* (1962), shot in Scope and in black-and-white, focused on a love triangle and sexual attention. The film played at the seventh **Asian Film Festival**, and Pan's experimental subject matter gained the attention of **Run Run Shaw**, who invited him to Hong Kong.

In 1963, the director came to Hong Kong and joined **Shaw Brothers**, where he directed 10 films, mostly romantic **melodramas**, including *The Rock (Lover's Rock)/Ching yan sek/Qing ren shi* (1964) and *Song of Orchid Island/Laan jui ji goh/Lan yu zhi ge* (1965), both starring actress **Cheng Pei-pei**. He adapted *Purple Shell/Chi bou hok/Zi bei ke* (1967) from a Qiong Yao novel; he also adapted his own novels, including *End of Spring*, which became the drama *Fallen Petals/Lai dut shut chit/Luo hua shi jie* (1967), and *Third Kind of Love*, which became the drama *Tomorrow Is Another Day/Ming yat* *yau tin aai/Ming ri you tian ya* (1969). Other films included the **action** drama *Downhill They Ride/Saan chaak/Shan ze* (1966), written by **King Hu**, and the **martial arts** movie *The Fastest Sword/Tin gwong dai yat kim/Tian xia di yi jian* (1968).

The writer-director founded Pan Lei Film Company in Taiwan in 1971, directing and producing *The Sword/Kim/Jian* (1971), in which Wang Yu starred as a ruthless aristocrat intent on possessing the finest blade in the world, who rejects Confucian values and ignores moral codes; the results are disastrous. Pan's swordplay movies of the 1960s–early 1970s are underpinned by philosophical contemplation. In 1975, he returned to Shaw Brothers, writing and directing the ghost fantasy *The Evil Seducers* (1975) and the musical *Cuties Parade/Miu miu lui long/Miaomiao nulang* (1975). He also wrote for others, including for He Fan's *The Long Haired Girl (The Girl with Long Hair)/Cheung faat goo leung/Chang fa gu niang* (1975) and **Lo Wei's** *New Fist of Fury/San jing mou moon/ Xinjing wumen* (1976).

The director is also known for spotting and nurturing talent, and several famous actresses began their careers in his movies, including Cheng Pei-pei, **Lily Ho**, and **Betty Ting Pei**. Since 1979, Pan worked in Taiwan, directing for his company, including, among others, *Strange Story (Mysterious Case) of the Crematorium/Feng chong cheung kei ngon/Huo zang chang ji an* (1980). Now retired, he studies antique jades and is writing an autobiography.

PAN, REBECCA DI-HUA. Although she has appeared in only a half-dozen movies, singer and actress Rebecca Pan, a Shanghai native, better known for her singing career, has chosen roles in important art house films, including **Ann Hui's** *Starry Is the Night/Gam yau sing gwong chaan laan/Jin ye xing guang can lan* (1988), **Wong Kar-wai's** *Days of Being Wild/ Ah Fei ching chuen/A Fei zhengzhuan* (1990) and *In the Mood for Love/Fa yeung nin wa/Hua yang nian hua* (2000), as well as Taiwanese director Hou Hsiao-hsien's *Flowers of Shanghai/Hai shanghua* (1998). She began a singing career in the late 1950s, sang with a band, and became a solo performer, singing in Chinese, English, Japanese, French, and Spanish, extremely popular in the 1960s–early 1970s. She not only toured worldwide but staged Hong Kong's first Mandarin pop musical, *Madam White Snake* (1972), which influenced the **Cantopop** scene to come.

PANG BROTHERS (Oxide and Danny) (1965–). Born in Hong Kong, the twin Pang Brothers established themselves in Hong Kong, Oxide as a Telecine color grader and director of television commercials and Danny as an editor of commercials and features, with Danny editing 17 features. Oxide's directorial debut was *Who's Running?/Ta fa likit?* (1997) and Danny's editorial debut was **Andrew Lau's** *The Stormriders/Fung wan hung ba tin ha/Feng yun xiong ba tian xia* (1998), which earned him a Best Editor award at the **Hong Kong Film Awards**. They are currently located in Thailand and collaborated on *Bangkok Dangerous* (1999) and the horror films *The Eye 1* and *2/Gin gwai/Jian gui* (2002, 2004). Danny directed *Leave Me Alone/Ah ma yau nan* (2004, also coproducer with Oxide) and Oxide *Ab-normal Beauty/Sei mong se jun* (2004, writer, and coproducer with Danny).

PANG, EDMOND HO-CHUNG. Pang quit high school and entered the film business after taking a scriptwriting course and becoming a screenwriter and writer. He directed his first short, *Summer Exercise*, in 1999. His directorial feature debut was an alternative hit man story, *You Shoot, I Shoot/Maai hung paak yan/Mai xiong pai ren* (2001), a satirical film that draws parallels between the hit man's situation and the film industry, making numerous allusions to Hong Kong's current social and economic climate. He is also a writer and **Johnnie To** adapted one of his novels, *Fulltime Killer*, to the screen in two parts.

Pang's offbeat battle-of-the-sexes comedy *Men Suddenly in Black/Daai cheung foo/Da zhang fu* (2003) was a critical success and crowd pleaser, gathering an all-star ensemble cast including **Tony Leung Ka-fai**, **Eric Tsang**, **Jordan Chan**, Chapman To, **Teresa Mo**, Candy Lo, Tiffany Lee, Marsha Yuan, Spirit Blue, **Maria Cordero**, Jenny Raven, **Sandra Ng**, Nat Chan, **Lam Suet**, **Samo Hung**, and Ellen Chan. Pang also acted in the film and picked up the Best New Director Award at the 2003 **Hong Kong Film Awards**. The film is shot as a gangster crime movie, with the "Triad" war here between men and women. Leung plays Ninth Uncle, a supposedly incarcerated criminal (he is actually henpecked by his wife, played by Ng) revered by his cronies. Pang's latest film is *AV* (2005), in which a handful of Hong Kong slackers use government money to hire a Japanese porn star and make a movie.

***PARENTS' HEARTS* (1955).** *Parents' Hearts/Foo miu sam/Fumu Xin* is an enduring classic of Cantonese **melodrama** and one of **Zhonglian** production company's undeniable masterpieces, directed and written by **Chun Kim**. The plot involves a **Cantonese opera** singer (**Ma Sze-tsang**) who stretches beyond his limits to put his oldest son through college. When the opera troupe disbands, he works as a clown. Shamed, the son refuses his father's support and secretly works to finance his education. Ill and saddened over his wife's death, the father turns to his second son. Superior and moving performances by Ma, **Wong Man-lei** as the wife, and Lin Jiasheng and Yuan Zhaofei as the sons are more than matched by the acute observation of human behavior and the environment. A cultural history lesson as well, the story parallels the decline of Cantonese opera's popularity with the economic and social misfortunes of the family.

PAU, PETER TAK-HEI (1952–). Cinematographer Peter Pau was born in Hong Kong. He is the son of actor **Bao Fang**. Although he directed and photographed *Temptation of Dance/Cheuk si ga diy/Jue shi jia dao* (1985), he would not direct another film until *Misty/Miu diy ching chau/Wu dou qing chou* (1992), followed by *The Touch/Tin mak chuen kei/Tian mai chuan ji* (2002), which he also shot, and which stars **Michelle Yeoh**.

Instead, Pau established himself as a cinematographer, and he has shot more than 30 films, many of them poetic and sumptuous in their camerawork. Some are **John Woo's** *The Killer (A Pair of Blood-Splattering Heroes)/Dip huet seung hung/Die xie shuang xiong* (1989, for which Pau was co-cinematographer); **Tony Au's** *Au Revoir, Mon Amour/Hoh yat gwan joi loi/He ri jun zai lai* (1991); **Ronny Yu's** *Bride with White Hair/Baak faat moh nui /Bai fa mo nu* (1993) and *Phantom Lover/Ye boon goh sing/Ye ban ge sheng* (1995); **Ang Lee's** *Crouching Tiger, Hidden Dragon/Ngo foo chong lung/Wo hu cang long* (2000); **Cheung Yuen-ting's** *Beijing Rocks/Bakging lok yue liu/Beijing le yu lu* (2002), and co-cinematographer for **Peter Chan's** musical *Perhaps Love/Yu guo aoi/Ruoguo ai* (2005). Pau is also one of the founders of the Society of Cinematographers.

PEARL CITY FILM LTD. Mrs. Vicky Lee Leung founded Pearl City in 1979, a company, like **Century Film Company**, dedicated to producing the films of alternative, either arty or edgy, **New Wave** filmmakers. Pearl City produced 13 films during its seven years of existence until 1988. Features included **Alex Cheung's** *Cops and Robbers/Dian zhi bing bing* (1979), **Ann Hui**'s *The Story of Woo-Viet/Woo Yuet dik goo si/Huyue de gu shi* (1981), **David Lai's** *Lonely Fifteen/Jing mei zai* (1982), **Tony Au's** *The Last Affair/Hua cheng* (1983) and *Dream Lovers/Meng zhong ren* (1986, co-produced with **D&B**), and **Stanley Kwan's** *Women/Nu ren xin* (1985). Actor **Chow Yun-fat** starred in all of the films above (except *Cops and Robbers* and *Lonely Fifteen*).

PEKING (BEIJING) OPERA FILMS. *See* CHINESE OPERA FILMS.

PING, FAN (Ping Faan) (1919–). Actor Ping Fan (real name Ping Yongshou) was born in Beijing and raised in a family of acrobats; he started performing magic and bicycle routines at an early age. He joined several drama groups, including the Yasheng Theater Group, the Yinren Stage Group, and the Plum Blossom Musical Group. He appeared in several patriotic plays in 1938, including *The Eight Hundred Heroes*. During the Japanese occupation, he moved to Vietnam and ran a restaurant there.

At war's end, Ping came to Hong Kong and joined the film industry. His film debut was the Mandarin fantasy *The New 1001 Nights (New Arabian Nights)/San tin fong yau taam/Xin tian fang ye tan* (1946), produced by Da Zhonghua film company. Other films followed, such as the romance *A Beauty from the Sea (Beauty Adrift in the Sea)/Hoi hun aan/Bi hai gong yan* (1948) and the action movie *Four Heroes from the Wang's (Young Heroes)/Ngai lui ying hung/Er nu ying xiong* (1948). Over a screen career of more than 30 years, Ping appeared in 70 features, all from leftist studios.

A versatile actor, Ping has appeared in diverse genres, including the historical drama *A Torn Lily/Yuen yeung on (Yuan yang an)/Niehai hua* (1953); the Mandarin **martial arts** movies *Between Vengeance and Love/Suet dei ching chau/Xue di qing chou* (1963, directed by **Li Pingqian**) and **Albert Young's** *The Jade Bow/Wan hoi yuk gung yuen/Yun hai yu gong yuan* (1966); the Mandarin dramas *Father Marries Again/Yat ga chun/Yi jia chun* (1952, directed by **Tao**

Qin) and *Garden of Repose/Goo yuen mung/Gu yuan meng* (1964, directed by **Zhu Shilin**); and the Mandarin comedies *Awful Truth/Suet fong sai gaai/Shuo huang shi jie* (1950, directed by Li Pingqian) and *The Gentleman Who Steals/Leung seung gwan ji/Liang shang jun zi* (1963). In the family **melodrama** *Father Marries Again*, Ping stars as a widower who decides to remarry and chooses a colleague (Xia Meng); the story revolves around the difficulties encountered by the stepmother in being accepted by her sister-in-law and her husband's daughters. In *Gentleman Who Steals*, a comic social satire produced by **Great Wall**, Ping plays a self-serving lawyer (with a disproportionate nose) who prevents a thief (**Fu Che**) from going straight. Not only satirizing the rich who prosper at the expense of the poor, but implying that representatives of legal and security systems are corrupt, the story has Ping's lawyer scheming with a cop (**Shi Lei**) who needs an easy target to arrest.

Ping left the big screen for the small one, working at Asia Television Limited (ATV) and appearing in numerous soap operas.

PONG CHAU-WA (Pang Qiuhua) (1926–1991). Cantonese opera librettist, writer, composer, and assistant director Pong Chau-wa was born in Guandong province and attended Ba Gui Middle School there. Influenced by an operatic family, Pong pursued an opera-related career and by 1950, he was a writer and librettist for opera troupes. His first, cowritten with Chen Tianzong, was *An Immortal Refuses Love*. Later works were made famous by their performers, **Ma Sze-tsang** in *Pan Bizheng's Temple Love Affair*, and Liang Wuxiang in *The Qin Palace's Legacy of Hatred*.

Pong's screenwriting debut was *The Story of Lun Wenxu and Li Chunhua/Lun Man Chui yue Lee Chun Dut/Lun Wenxu yu Li Chunhua* (1955). He often cowrote with librettist **Lee Yuen-man**, and from 1955 to 1968, they wrote more than 30 scripts or librettos for opera films. The duo also wrote song lyrics for films like *The Little Prince Minister (The Valiant Prince)/Yau lung ching hap/You long qing xia* (1961), *The New Magic Cup/San yau gwong booi/Xin ye guang bei* (1962), *Loyalty/Ching cheung yee gang cheung/Qing chang yi geng chang* (1965), and *Lau Kam Ding the Female General* (1967). Pong wrote the lyrics for Xu Zilang's dramatic *A Ten Year Dream* (1961) and comedic *Romance of the Phoenix Chamber* (1962).

Pong's solo efforts include *The Precious Fan (Romance of the Precious Fan)/Bo sin yuen/Baoshan yuan* (1957) and *Flag of Pearls/Fooi ching saam chui jan chu kei/Hui qing san qu zhen zhu qi* (1968), his final film. Adapted from the folktale "The Precious Jade Fan," the former starred **Ho Fei-fan** and **Tsi Lo-lin** as a couple whose marriage has been arranged since childhood and sealed by a precious royal fan as a keepsake. Tsi's father, financially strained, attempts to break the pact, and she contemplates suicide; after many plot twists, her lover returns as a high official and the couple is reunited.

Pong also served as assistant director for **Lee Sun-fung** on *The Humble Wife/Ging chaai gei/Jing gai ji* (1958) and **Lee Tit** on ***The Purple Hairpin***/*Chi chaai gei/Zichai ji* (1959) and *Butterfly and Red Pear/Dip ying hung lee gei/Dieying hongli ji* (1959). During the 1960s, Pong wrote songs for EMI Record Company and was a production officer at Fung Hang Record Company. He also worked for seven years at Rediffusion **television**. After retiring, he continued writing music for television and record companies until his demise.

POON, CHEUK (Pan Zhuo) (1921–). Cantonese opera librettist and writer Poon Cheuk was born in Guangdong province, graduated from Shunde Agricultural High School, and in 1948 began writing opera songs.

Poon's screen debut was the libretto for *The Romantic Story of the West Chamber/Sai seung gei/Xi xiang ji* (1956), for which he teamed with librettist **Lee Yuen-man**. Other collaborations between the pair included *The Precious Lotus Lamp/Bo lin dang/Bao lian deng* (1956) and *Liu Yi Sends His Letters/Lau ngai chuen shi/Liu yi chuan shu* (1958). The former, a Cantonese fantasy opera, featured the taboo marriage of an immortal and mortal; when their son (**Lam Ka-sing**) matures, he enlists the aid of a fairy (**Mui Yee**) to gain the magic Lotus lamp, and he frees his trapped mother from the foot of Mount Hua with a powerful ax. Poon's script *Awaiting the Return of the Prodigal at the Pavilion, 1* and *2/Mong ngai ting/Wang er ting* (1960) was produced; he wrote screenplays and composed libretti for over 30 opera films by 1965, among them director **Wong Hok-sing's** *The Pitiless Sword/Miu ching bo kim yau ching tin/Wu qing bao jian you qing tian* (1964), starring **Lam Ka-sing** as a prince who betrays his clan for love of a woman and suffers the consequences. In this production, character and situation are emphasized and cinematic techniques, instrumentals, and libretto well integrated.

Since 1965, Poon has written operas for stage troupes including Xinma, Dalongfeng, and Qingxinsheng, among others. Some of his popular operas are *Two Heroes in Chu City*; *Horse, Sword, and Love*; and *Fearless Lin Chong*. He also wrote for music companies, composing songs recorded and made popular by opera singers. Poon retired in 1976.

POON YAT ON (Banri An) (1904–1964). Cantonese opera actor Poon Yat On (real name Li Hong'an) was born in Guangdong province. He studied under opera performer **Ma Sze-tsang** (Ma Zhizeng) for half a year and began performing onstage, initially playing *dahuamian* roles (literally, big colorful face) and then *chou* (literally, clown) roles. The actor worked in various famous opera troupes, including Ma Sze-tsang's Baluotian and Tai Ping, as well as **Sit Kok-sin's** Juexiansheng Troupe.

Poon Yat acted in more than 650 operas, and was best known for his mother-in-law impersonations, as in **Ng Wui's** *Why Not Return?* (1952) in which he costarred with his wife Shanghai Mei and actor Sit Kok-sin (Xue Juexian), or in **Lee Tit's** *Snow Storm in June/Luk yuet suet/Liu yue xue* (1959), in which he played the sympathetic mother-in-law of victimized daughter-in-law **Fong Yim-fan**. The actor was one of the four great *chous* (including **Lee Hoi-chuen**, Ye Furuo, and Liao Xiahuai). His stage name literally means "stealing half a day of leisure."

The actor joined the film industry with the Cantonese opera *Cao Fooled by Zuo Ci* (1941), the first of more than 140 films he made. Title roles included Chan Pei's *A Good Girl Covers for Both Sides/Hiu lui leung tau moon/Haonu liangtou man* (1948) and **Chu Kei's** *Twin Heads Selling Martial Arts/Seung yan tau maai miu/Shuang ren tou mai wu* (1948). The former, originally titled *Buying Beauty's Heart with Gold*, was a contemporary **melodrama** while the latter featured a group of justice fighters (including Poon Yat) set on eliminating corrupt officials and bullies in the brothels; the film featured over 100 **martial arts** masters performing both Northern and Southern styles.

Opera films include, among others, Law Chi-hung's *The Nymph of the River Lo/Lok san/Luo shen* (1957), Chan Pei's *Why Not Return/ Woo bat gwai/Hu bugui* (1958), Cheung Wai-gwong's *The Gold-Braided Fan/Chuen gan bo sin/Chuan jin bao shan* (1959), **Chu Kei's** *The Dream Meeting between Emperor Wu of Han and Lady Wei/Hon miu dai mung kooi wai foo yan/Han Wudi menghui Wei Furen* (1959), **Wong Hok-sing's** *Battling Sound/Lui ming gam goo chin fung sing/Lei ming jin gu zhan jia sheng* (1963), and **Sun Ma Sze-tsang's** *Lust Is the Worst Vice/Maan nyn yam wai sau/Wan e yin wei shou* (1963). In *Why Not Return?*, Poon Yat cross-dressed as the mother-in-law who, pressured by her relatives with ulterior motives, expels her daughter-in-law (Fong Yim-fun) supposedly suffering from tuberculosis, while her son (Lam Kar-sing) is away serving in the army. In *The Gold-Braided Fan*, he played the father of a daughter (**Pak Suet-sin**) who disavows her marriage to a scholar (cross-dressed **Yam Kim-fai**); the gold-braided fan is a testimonial to the elder-arranged marriage.

Shortly after completing his last film, *Rich and Prosperous/Foo gwai moon wa tang/Fu gui man hua tang* (1964), Poon Yat died. He had continued performing during a terminal illness and died onstage.

PU, SONGLING (1640–1715). Qing dynasty famous author Pu Songling failed as a scholar in his youth and gave up his dream of becoming an official. He opened a teahouse and listened to customers tell stories, which he compiled, in approximately 1679. Drawing on the oral tradition, *Strange Tales from a Chinese Studio (Strange Stories from Liu Jai)/Liaozhai zhiyi* consists of more than 400 atmospheric stories that blur the lines between reality and the supernatural. Scholars, court officials, ghosts, vixens, unusual animals, and spirits lead the cast of characters. Often the humans are weak, uncertain, and easily manipulated while the spirits serve as moral and trustworthy, but not always, wherein lies the rub.

The collection has been appropriated by numerous filmmakers, including, among others, Lai Pak-hoi in *Rouge/Yin chi/Yan zhi* (1925); **Li Han-hsiang** in *The Enchanting Shadow/Sin nui yau wan/Qian nu you hun* (1960), the precursor of **Ching Siu-tung's** similarly influenced *A Chinese Ghost Story, 1, 2,* and *3/Sin nui yau wan/Qiannu youhun* (1987, 1990, 1991); **Wong Hok-sing** in *Magic Sword/Xian* *jian shen mo* (1963); numerous directors with the portmanteau *The Four Moods/Xi nu ai lei* (1970); and **King Hu** with the **martial arts** atmospheric piece *A Touch of Zen/Xia nu* (1971).

***THE PURPLE HAIRPIN* (1959).** A classic of Cantonese opera film, *The Purple Hairpin (The Legend of the Purple Hairpin)/Chi chaai gei/Zichai ji*, directed by **Lee Tit**, was based on a staple and much revived opera by Ming dynasty librettist Tang Xianzu (actually drawing on an earlier Tang dynasty story) and aided by the screen adaptation by librettist and screenwriter **Tong Tik-sang**. The romantic story follows the love between Huo Xiaoyou, a famous courtesan (**Pak Suet-sin**), and Li Yi, a famous scholar (**Yam Kim-fai**, cross-dressed in the male part). During a full moon evening, she drops and he retrieves a purple jade hairpin, which symbolizes their pledge of love and union. When he becomes the number-one scholar, the Taiwei, a powerful court minister (**Leng Chi-pak**), connives to separate the couple and secure the scholar for his daughter. Huo suffers financial loss and illness, even selling the hairpin that means so much. Three years later, Li returns from exile, and led to believe that Huo has remarried, is engaged to the official's daughter. Fate intervenes with the Man in the Yellow Robe (**Leung Sing-po**), actually the disguised fourth imperial prince, interceding to redress Huo's injustice. The couple is eventually reunited and the Taiwei punished. The five acts of this romantic opera include "Picking Up a Jade Hairpin in a Lantern-Lit Street," "Rendezvous in the Garden," "Go Not Beyond the Yang Pass," "Meeting a Knight Before the Blossoms," and "Reunion." *See also* CHINESE OPERA FILMS.

– Q –

QI, XIANGTANG (Kei Shang-tong) (1911–). Musician and composer Qi Xiangtang, a native of Hunan province, born in Guangdong, graduated from the National Music Academy and performed with the Chinese Symphony Orchestra. During World War II, he served with the Hong Kong Youth Association and its drama troupe. In 1950, he began his musical career in Hong Kong, producing the hit songs "You Are So Pretty" and "Unreasonable Girl" for **Yan Jun's** *Singing* *under the Moon/Chui chui/Cui cui* (1953), starring **Linda Lin Dai**. Other songs followed, including "Sweet Dance" for **Tao Qin's** ***Our Sister Hedy***/*Se chin gam/Si qian jinSi qianjin* (1957), "Forget Your Sorrows" and "My Heaven" for **Ge Lan's** star vehicle ***Mambo Girl***/*Maan boh lui long/ Manbo nulang* (1957), and the theme songs for **Evan Yang's** comedies *Our Dream Car/Heung che mei yan/Xiang che mei ren* (1959) and *Bachelors Beware/Wan yau hing/Wen rou qing* (1960).

The composer began writing film scores with Yan Jun's historical drama *Golden Phoenix/Gam fung/Jin feng* (1956), starring Lin Dai and Yan Jun, and continued writing them for **Motion Pictures and General Investment** productions, including *Our Sister Hedy*, its sequel *Wedding Bells for Hedy/Laan gwai fung wan/ Langui fengyun* (1959), *Tragedy of Love/Ching tin huet lui/Qing tian xie lei* (1959), and *Song without Words/Miu yue man chong tin/Wu yu wen cang tian* (1961). He also wrote scores for **Li Han-hsiang's** drama *Rear Entrance/Hau moon/Hou men* (1960) for **Shaw Brothers** and *The Winter/Dung nuen/Dong nuan* (1969) for Guolian. Between composers **Yao Min** and Qi, the style of the music and songs in most of the Mandarin movies (operating under the belief that every movie must have a song) and musicals of the 1950s–1960s was established.

In 1973, Qi immigrated to Canada.

– R –

RATINGS SYSTEM. While an official system was first implemented in 1953, when a censor's office was established in Hong Kong, in 1977, film and television were examined and rated by a government office called the Television and Licensing Authority (TELA), under a regulatory code named the Film **Censorship** Regulations provided by the Places of Public Entertainment Ordinance. Basic criteria were laid down in a guidebook called *Film Censorship Standards: A Note of Guidance*, establishing three categories for movies. They are namely: Category I: For exhibition to persons of any age subject to the condition that any advertising material that relates to the film shall display the appropriate classification symbol; Category II is subdivided into Category IIA and Category IIB: For exhibition to persons of any age subject to the condition that any advertising material that relates to the film shall display the appropriate classification symbol and contain the following notice, or notice to the like effect, that next to or adjacent to the symbol in block letters and Chinese characters prominently and legibly displayed—for IIA "NOT SUITABLE FOR CHILDREN" and for IIB, "NOT SUITABLE FOR YOUNG PERSONS AND CHILDREN"; and Category III: For exhibition only to persons who have attained the age of 18 years subject to the condition that any advertising material that relates to the film shall display the appropriate classification symbol and contain the following notice, or a notice to the like effect, next to or adjacent to the symbol, in block letters and Chinese characters prominently and legibly displayed "APPROVED FOR EXHIBITION ONLY TO PERSONS WHO HAVE ATTAINED THE AGE OF 18 YEARS." Examples of the preceding include the Category I **Lunar New Year's comedy** *It's a Wonderful Life/Daai foo ji ga/Da fu zhi jia* (1994); the Category II heroic bloodshed *The Killer/Dip huet seung hung/Die xie shuang xiong* (1989); and the Category III soft-core *Sex and Zen (The Prayer Mat of Flesh: The Treasured Almanac of Secretive Affairs)/Yuk po tuen chi tau ching biu gaam/Yu pui tsuan zhi tou qing bao jian* (1991). Category III emerged on the scene in the late 1980s. Regarding the ratings, sex and politics count more than violence for exclusion.

REIS, MICHELLE (Lei Kar-yan) (1968–). Michelle Reis (also known as Michelle Lee, Lei Kar-yan) was born in Macau to a Portuguese father and a Chinese mother. Reis started out as a teenage model and won the Miss Hong Kong pageant in 1988. Her film debut came with **Ching Siu-tung's** *A Chinese Ghost Story 2 (Sien, the Female Ghost Human Realm Tao)/ Sin nui yau wan/Qiannu youhun* (1990). While appearing in more run-of-the-mill Hong Kong fare during the early 1990s, Reis garnered the attention of many as the beautiful Windy in the **Tsui Hark**–produced sci-fi cult classic *The Wicked City (Monster City)/Yiu sau do si/Yao shou du shi* and as **Jet Li's** sidekick Kiddo in ***Swordsman*** *2 (Smiling Proud Warrior: Invincible Asia)/ Siu ngo gong woo ji Dung Fong Bat Baai/Xiao ao jianhu zhi Dongfang Bubai*, another Ching Siu-tung film. After this Reis worked with Jet Li again in *Fong Sai-Yuk/Fong Sai Yuk/Fang Shiyu* and *Fong Sai-Yuk 2/Fong Sai Yuk chuk chap/Fang Shiyu xu ji*. Until 1995, Reis's roles had been relatively undemanding and she was often used only for window dressing. However, Reis proved her mettle in **Wong Kar-wai's** *Fallen Angels/Doh lok tin si/Duoluo tianshi* as the cleaner who falls for the hit man for whom she works. After this, Reis went on to star in *Armageddon/Tin dei hung sam/Tian di xiong xin* (1997), a film loaded with references to the imminent reunification with China, alongside superstars **Andy Lau** and **Anthony Wong**. Reis starred in the critically acclaimed Taiwanese art house film *The Flowers of Shanghai* (1998), directed by Hou Hsou-Hsien. Since then, Reis has continued to make a few films every year, in addition to her modeling career.

REN, PENGNIAN (Yam Paang-nin) (1892–1968). Director Ren Pengnian was born in Shanghai and began as a bookbinder for the Commercial Press before becoming an assistant in the newly established film department of the company in 1918. His first short, *The Gambler* (1919), was one of 19 films he made there, including *Yan Ruisheng* (1921) and *Lovers' Tragedy* (1925). Many believe the murder thriller *Yan Ruisheng* to be the first feature film made in China.

Ren founded Dong Fang Diyi Film Company (renamed Yue Ming) in 1926, and by 1936, 40 films were made there, including *The Worker's Wife* (1926) and *Frenzy* (1935). When war broke out, Ren immigrated to Hong Kong, where he directed *The Strange Hero Yi Zhimei* (1941) and *The Woman Security Guard/Lui biu bye/Nu biao shi* (1941). He was one of the first to resume making **martial arts** movies in Hong Kong following the war. Indeed, his work serves to provide continuity in the martial arts genre from its prewar to postwar stages of development. Beginning in 1948, over the next decade he directed nine films, including *Female Robin Hood/Lui law ban hon/Nu luo bin han* (1947), *The Female Warrior (The Amazon)/Lui yung si/Nu yong shi* (1949), and *The Lady Escort (Protector) and the Knight with the Whip/Lui biu bye saam fai san bin hap/Nu biaoshi sanxi shenbian xia* (1949). In *The Lady Escort and the Knight with the Whip*, **Wu Lizhu** costarred in the title roles with **Kwan Tak-hing**. She played a master of the flying dart and expert in hand and leg combat in search of missing jewels; he is a whip master who helps her overcome the villains. *The Three Swordswomen from Guangdong (Three Gallant*

Ladies of Guangdong)/Gwaan dung saam lui hap/Guangdong san nuxia (1961) is a period drama swordplay that reunites three sisters (Yu Suqiu, Wu Lizhu, and Mei Lan) estranged since childhood. Together they search for their father's murderer to take revenge.

Ren reestablished Yue Ming in Hong Kong in 1960, his last film being *The Irascible Lady at Imperial City (The Tigress' Adventures in the Capital)/Chi foo laau ging wa/Ci hu nao jing hua* (1961), after which he retired. He was married to actress Wu Lizhu, "the queen of ***wuxia pian***" in its early days, who starred in many of his films. He died in Hong Kong.

REN, YIZHI (Yam Yi-ji) (1925–1978). Shanghainese director and actress Ren Yizhi had famous parents; her father, **Ren Pengnian**, was a director of ***wuxia*** films, and her mother, **Wu Lizhu**, was an actress. Ren attended school in Hong Kong and was active in drama; during wartime, she performed across China with several stage troupes. Her film debut was the Mandarin thriller *Female Spy No. 76/Hiu lui gaan dip/Hao nu jian die* (1947), and the following year she appeared in a Cantonese thriller, *The Girl Warrior (The Amazon)/Lui yung si/Nu yong shi* (1948).

Director **Zhu Shilin** was impressed by Ren, who performed as one of the guerilla nurses in his *The Flower Girl/Fa goo leung/Hua guniang* (1951), produced by Longma; they developed a mentor–student relationship, and he taught her screenwriting and directing. Ren was among the group of film workers, led by Zhu Shilin, who joined **Feng Huang** in 1953, and she codirected (with Zhu Shilin) the drama *Festival Moon/Chung chau yuet/Zhong qiu yue* (1953), the company's first feature. She and Wen Yimin codirected the drama *The Lone Woman/Suet chung lin/Xue zhong lian* (1957), and with Zhu and **Chen Jingbo** she codirected the comedies *Love's Miracle/Ching dau choh hoi/Qing dou chu kai* (1958) and *Precious Little Moon/Siu yuet leung/Xiao yue liang* (1959), both of which she wrote. In *Love's Miracle*, produced by Feng Huang and one of its best comedies, two neighboring middle-aged couples feud over minor things; when their children (Fu Che and Zhu Hong) fall in love the couple try everything to reconcile their families.

Ren began directing on her own in 1960, making seven films, including *A Perfect Match/Ching tau yi gap/Qing tou yi he* (1960), *That*

Certain Age/Ham baau doi fong/Han bao dai fang e (1966), *The Fair Ladies/Baak leng lai yan/Bai ling li ren* (1967), and *Three Seventeens/Saam goh sap chat sui/San ge shi qi sui* (1972). In the comedy *A Perfect Match*, a prospective husband (Fu Qi) convinces his prospective wife (Shi Hui) that he has no bad habits; after marriage, the wife discovers her husband's vices—smoking, drinking, and gambling. A war breaks out between husband and wife, and each plays strategist—the husband to hide his indulgences, the wife to expose them.

Ren died in Hong Kong.

***THE ROMANCE OF JADE HALL* (1957).** Director **Tso Kea's** *The Romance of Jade Hall (My Kingdom for a Husband)/Suen gung yim shut/Xuangong yanshi* is a romantic musical comedy with Western elements that premiered **Cheung Ying** singing **Cantonese opera** songs. The plot revolves around a wandering musician whose carefree life ends when he marries the queen of the Snow Kingdom. Paralleling the royal couple is an overweight pair of servants played by **Leung Sing-po** (Liang Xiangbo) and **Tan Lanqing**, lending visual and situation comedy. The lead couple experiences difficulties but is reunited through the servants' wedding, with a happy ending for all. A second film came out the following year.

ROTHROCK, CYNTHIA (1957–). An American **martial artist** from Scranton, Pennsylvania, actress Rothrock is one of the few non-Chinese performers to win top billing in Hong Kong action films. She began her training at age 13, taking black belts in a variety of Chinese and Korean combat styles. Rothrock soon became one of the top U.S. champions, dominating the tournament circuit in the early 1980s. Her sassy personality and agile fighting style caught the eye of producers at the **Golden Harvest** studio in Hong Kong, and she made her film debut opposite **Michelle Yeoh** in *Yes, Madam (Royal Hong Kong Police Woman)/Wong ga si je/Huang jia shi jie* (1985), a high-spirited female cop comedy/drama. Rothrock continued to work with Golden Harvest for several years, often costarring with **kung fu** aces **Samo Hung** and **Yuen Biao**. Her knockabout fight with Hung is a highlight of the action-packed *Millionaires' Express (Shanghai Express)/Foo gwai lit che/Fu gui lie che* (1986). Other notable films include *Above the Law (Righting Wrongs)/Chap faat sin fung/ Zhi fa xian feng* (1986) and *Blonde Fury/Bye che daai sai/Shi jie da shai* (1989). She continues to make martial arts films in the United States, including the *China O'Brian* series (1990–1991), and has made a number of **television** appearances.

RUAN, LINGYU (1910–1935). Silent film actress Ruan Lingyu (real name Ruan Fenggen) was born in Shanghai to working-class Cantonese parents; after her father's early death, she and her mother lived with another Cantonese family as servants, and at 16, Ruan became the common-law wife of the fourth son, Zhang Damin. In 1927, she made a screen test at **Mingxing** (Star) studios and began making films there and at **Lianhua**, completing close to 35 films. She formally separated from Zhang in 1935, at the height of her popularity, moving in with a married businessman, Tang Jishan. The resultant scandal, particularly Ruan's hounding by the press, led to her suicide. One of her three suicide letters read, "*renyan kewei*" ("the words of others [gossip] is a fearful thing").

Ruan's incredible acting abilities, including subtle expressiveness, from joy and tenderness to sorrow and anger, in a flash, led her to be nicknamed "the Chinese Garbo," and she has been compared not only to Garbo, but Marlene Dietrich, Lillian Gish, and Mary Pickford combined. She was the biggest film star China has had. She was known for her tragic roles, in life and on-screen. She collaborated with leading Shanghai directors, including Sun Yu on *Spring Dream in the Old Capital/Guru chunmeng* (1930) and *Wild Flower (Wild Grass)/Yecao Xianhua* (1931); **Bu Wancang** on *The Peach Girl (Peach Blossom Weeps Tears of Blood)* (1931) and *Love and Duty/Lianai yu yiwu* (1931); Wu Yonggang on *The Goddess/Shennu* (1934), in which she played a sympathetic and suffering prostitute; and **Cai Chusheng** on *The New Women/Xin nuxing* (1934), in which she played an independent and educated woman who is persecuted by society. Most of her early films have not survived, but a print of *Love and Duty* was found in the early 1990s in Uruguay among the effects of a late Kuomintang general. Like other Shanghai talent, she came to Hong Kong during the Battle of Shanghai, but returned after a brief sojourn.

In 1959, director **Zhu Shilin** planned to film Ruan's story, but the project was never realized. **Stanley Kwan's** art house and experimental docu-drama *Centre Stage* (1992) recreates the Shanghai era and incorporates found footage from Ruan's movies as well as recreating famous scenes. **Maggie Cheung** stars in an amazing performance as Ruan Lingyu, **Tony Leung Ka-fai** plays sympathetic director Cai Chusheng, and **Chin Han** appears as her lover. Besides celebrating Chinese film history, Kwan also draws parallels between contemporary Hong Kong cinema figures and media mania to the past situation. A gorgeous meditation on the past, the film pays homage to a legend.

– S –

SAI, GUA-PAU (Xigua Bao). Actor Sai Gua-pau (real name Lin Shugen and also known as Lin Gen) was born in Guangzhou, where he grew up and was educated. He came to Hong Kong in 1937 and worked as a custodian at Fanglian Middle School. Actor **Wong Cho-san** helped him secure a position as property keeper at Nanyang Film Company; he later transferred to the makeup and costume departments. In 1945, he returned to Guangzhou and appeared as an extra in films, becoming a professional extra, and later a supporting character actor.

Sai returned to Hong Kong after the war. He appeared in *Mother Who Walks the Streets* (1950), the film on which he first used his stage name. "Sai Gua-pau" (*Xigua Bao*, literally, "melon scraper") became a popular Cantonese nickname for anyone with prominent front teeth. Sai played the part of Shuaya Su (Bucktooth So) in 80 sequences of the **Wong Fei-hung** series, such as *How Wong Fei-hong Vanquished the 12 Tigers/Wong Fei-hong liu tan sap yee shut/Huang Feihung nu tun shi er shi* (1956), creating an indelible screen image as a comic stuttering character.

The actor has appeared in hundreds of movies in supporting roles, usually playing naïve, helpless, or just plain dumb characters, usually taken advantage of by others; however, despite a distinguishing simplemindedness, Sai's characters were kind and righteous, endearing them (and him) to audiences. The actor turned to **television** in the mid-1960s, appearing in Rediffusion Television (RTV) and Hong Kong Television Broadcasts Limited (TVB) dramas, action, and comedy.

SEASONAL FILM CORPORATION. Seasonal is an independent company that has had commercial success, and was founded in 1975 by director **Ng See-yuen**. Its first production was *Anti-Corruption/Lian zheng feng bao* (1975), written and directed by Ng and coproduced with the Eternal Film Company. *Drunken Master/Zui quan* (1978) followed, a film that gained director **Yuen Wo-ping** and **martial arts** actor **Jackie Chan** recognition. The company's *All for the Winner/Du sheng* (1990), a **Corey Yuen–Jeff Lau** comedy, set a new box office record, earning over HK$40 million. Other important productions include the Chan vehicles *Snake in the Eagle's Shadow/She xing diao shou* (1978) and *Fearless Hyena/Xiao quan guai zhao* (1979) and **Tsui Hark's** *The Butterfly Murders* (1979) and *Dragon Inn (New Dragon Gate Inn)/Xin longmen kezhan*(1992).

SEK, YIN-JI (Shi Yanzi) (1920–1986). Cantonese opera actor Sek Jin-ji (real name Mai Zhisheng) was born in Guangdong province and since childhood was interested in Chinese opera, studying with famous opera performer Xi Qi and performing onstage at age 11, known as the "Superkid." Many famous actors took him under their wings, including Luo Jiaquan, **Leng Chi-pak**, and Chen Feinong. He stood out in *wusheng* (**martial arts** and military roles), as a practitioner of Northern-style martial arts.

Prior to the outbreak of the Sino–Japanese War, Sek performed in the United States and Southeast Asia. He founded the Yanxinsheng opera troupe in Hong Kong following the war, performing onstage until 1984 in a charity show with Chen Feinong.

The actor made his screen debut as the lead in *Fang Shiyu and Miao Cuihua/Fong Sai Yuk yue Miu Chui Dut/Fang Shiyu yu Miao Cuihua* (1948). He appeared in more than 100 features, although he is best known for his portrayal of the Shaolin rebel Fang Shiyu in an 18-episode series.

Other well-known movies include **Lee Tit's** period martial arts movie *The Bloody Fight between Big Knife Wong Wu (Fifth) and the Invincible Kid/Daai diy Wang Ng huet Chin siu ba wong/Da dao Wang Wu xie zhan xiao ba wang* (1950) and *Her Majesty's Imperial Warrant/Gam paai gai/Jin pai ji* (1962). Sek's final role was in **John Woo's** *A Better Tomorrow/Ying hung boon sik/Yingxiong bense* (1986), in which he played a sympathetic out-of-date Triad boss; the actor died shortly after shooting completed, ironically, on his birthday.

The actor was also well known as an artist, especially for his paintings of Buddhist imagery. His widow, **Yam Bing-yi**, was an opera performer and sister of **Yam Kim-fai**.

SEVEN LITTLE FORTUNES. Seven Little Fortunes is the name of the performance troupe of children from Master Yu Zhangyuan's (Yu Jim Yuen) Chinese Drama Academy, a traditional **Beijing Opera** School in Hong Kong. The children sang, danced, acted, learned weapons, and performed acrobatic feats, all required for Beijing Opera performance. There were actually many more than seven children as members, with children leaving the school and newcomers replacing them. However, seven have become famous in the film industry. All were required to take the name of their master, or *sifu*; some, such as **Yuen Biao** and **Yuen Wah**, retain the name today. When the traditional theater died out, opera performers turned to the movie industry, beginning as extras, stuntmen, and stunt doubles, becoming actors, **action** choreographers, and directors.

The seven famous little fortunes included **Jackie Chan** (Yuen Lan), probably the most recognizable Chinese actor in the world, because of his **action** comedies, and **Samo Hung** (Yuen Chu), Chan's elder at the school and the most accomplished director of the group, these two being the most prominent. Yuen Biao became an action actor and appeared in *The Prodigal Son* and *Eastern Condors* (both directed by Hung). Yuen Kwai **(Corey Yuen**) became a **martial arts** performer in movies like *Dance of the Drunken Mantis* (1979), turned to action choreography, and became an action director, guiding **Jet Li** in *Fong Sai-yuk* (1993) and *My Father Is a Hero* (1995). Yuen Wah became **Bruce Lee's** action double and went on to play villains in *Eastern Condors* (1987), *Dragons Forever* (1988), and *Iceman Cometh* (1989). Yuen Mo is a stuntman, supporting actor, and action director, and appeared as the Monkey Boxer in **Yuen Woping's** *Magnificent Butcher* (1979) with Samo Hung. Ng Ming Choi (Yuen Choi) has worked as an actor (he played in **King Hu's** *The Valiant Ones*, 1975, and Lam Sai-wing in *Butcher Wing*, 1979) but is now a producer. (Even Yuen Wo-ping was a day student at the school, along with Samo Hung, before Jackie Chan and the others came.) Yuen Tak worked as a **Shaw Brothers** actor and as an action choreographer.

Fortune has smiled on all these talents, and they have worked together on many occasions. Yuen Tak and Yuen Kwai collaborated on *Fong Sai-yuk*, and Yuen Tak was action director (with Yuen Wah and Yuen Biao's Stuntmen's Association) on *Iceman Cometh* (1989), with Yuen Biao, Yuen Wah, and Yuen Kwai acting in the movie. Jackie Chan, Samo Hung, Yuen Biao, and Yuen Wah last appeared together on-screen in *Dragons Forever* (1988). Yuen Biao, Yuen Wah, and Yuen Tak appeared in Yuen Kwai's *Hero* (1997).

SHANGKUAN, POLLY LINFENG (Shang Kuan Ling-fong) (1949–). Polly Shangkuan Lingfeng is a **martial artist** from Taiwan, with black belt rankings in tae kwan do, judo, and karate. In 1966, she signed on with the Union (Lianbang) Film Company, which was soon to become the home of popular ***wuxia*** director **King Hu**. One of her earliest films was made with Hu, *Dragon Gate Inn/Lung moon haak chan/Longmen kezhan* (1967). Also in 1973, she made *Back Alley Princess/Ma liu siu ying hung/Ma lu xiao ying xiong*, with **Sam Hui** and **Angela Mao**, for **Golden Harvest**, and won a Best Actress prize at the Taiwanese **Golden Horse Awards** for her portrayal of a young street kid. She went on to make dozens of **kung fu** films in Hong Kong and Taiwan through the 1970s, frequently playing male roles or cross-dressing for stretches of the film. Her most famous movies include *Eighteen Bronzemen/Siu lam chi sap baat tung yan/Shaolin si shi ba tong ren* (1975) and *Kids of Shaolin/Siu lam siu ji/Shaolin xiao zi* (1977). Tiny in stature but tough and powerful in her fight scenes, Shangkuan was one of a handful of female kung fu stars who created memorable screen personae in the golden age of Hong Kong film. She retired and moved to the United States in the early 1980s.

SHANLIAN FILM COMPANY. Founded by **Cantonese opera** actress **Pak Yin** and actor **Cheung Wood-yau** in 1954, Shanlian produced only six films over 10 years, but most are classics, including **Chu Kei's** *Madame Yun/Yun Niang* (1954), **Ng Wui's** *The Pagoda of Long Life* (1955), and **Chor Yuen's** *The Great Devotion (Parents'*

Love) Hoh lin tin gwong foo miu sam /Ke lian tian xia fu mu xin (1960), *Eternal Regret/Nie hai wei hen* (1962), and *A Mad Woman/ Feng fu* (1964).

***SHAOLIN TEMPLE* (1982).** *Shaolin Temple/Siu lam ji/Shaolin si*, **Jet Li's** debut film, was in many ways a milestone in the history of **martial arts** filmmaking. Not only was it the first martial arts collaboration between the Hong Kong film industry and the People's Republic of China (PRC), as well as being the first production made on the grounds of the actual Shaolin Temple, revered as the birthplace of Chinese **kung fu**, but it also introduced the world to an acrobatic form of standardized *wushu*, or martial arts, that had become the most popular sport in the PRC. In 1979, a consortium of Hong Kong companies that included the Great Wall Movie Enterprises Ltd., the Chung Yuen Film Co., and the **Feng Huang Film Company** of Hong Kong made arrangements to shoot at the temple, under the direction of **Zhang Xinyan** (Chang Hsin-yen, Cheung Yam-yim). Filming was already underway when a number of Japanese investors in the project discovered that the original cast had little training in real Shaolin kung fu. The resulting uproar caused the producers to reconsider, and the decision was made to recast *Shaolin Temple* with young martial artists and coaches from the professional *wushu* teams.

In 1980, the reigning national *wushu* champion was Li Lian-jie (Jet Li), who had taken gold medals for five years straight as the star of the Beijing Wushu Team. Li was cast as Zhang Xiaohu (Little Tiger Zhang), one of the Thirteen Chivalrous Monks of Shaolin, from an old story of the early days of the temple that served as the basis of the plot. In the film, the monks save the life of future Tang dynasty emperor Li Shih-min from the murderous general Wang Ren-ze. General Wang was played by Shandong *wushu* coach Yu Cheng-wei. Coaches Pan Qing-fu and Ji Chun-hua played his villainous henchmen. The young *wushu* champions Hu Jian-qiang, Du Chuan-yang, and Sun Jian-kui portrayed Li's fellow monks, and Yu Hai, another coach from Shandong, was cast as the stern but benevolent master monk. The sole female role was filled by actress Ding Lan, who underwent *wushu* training for the part. Action choreography was handled by Pan and Yu, with assistance from coaches Ma Xian-da and Wang Chang-kai. Shooting began in Henan province in July 1980, wrapping in

September of the following year, and included a six-week sojourn in Hong Kong for interior scenes filmed at the **Clearwater Bay Studio** in Kowloon. *Shaolin Temple* premiered in Hong Kong in early 1982 to universal acclaim. The film was an international success, spawning two sequels, *Kids from Shaolin/Siu lam siu ji/Shao lin xiao zi* (1984) and *Martial Arts of Shaolin/Naam bak siu lam/Nan bei Shaolin* (1986), and propelling its star, soon renamed Jet Li, to the top rank of action heroes.

SHAW BROTHERS (Shaoshi). Sir Run Run (1907–) and Runme (1901–1985) Shaw first came to Southeast Asia in 1926; based in Singapore, they bought land and built a theatrical chain to support their film distribution business. At the peak of their success, they owned over 160 theaters in Malaysia and Singapore. In 1957, Sir Run Run relocated to Hong Kong to develop movie production in order to support his brother's theater chains. Runme remained in Singapore, where he built a studio concentrating on Malay-language films (which disappeared after 1965 when Singapore became independent of Malaysia and the Malaysian government promoted a homegrown film policy).

The origins of Shaw Brothers go back to Shanghai, where brother Runje (1896–1975) had rented a theater in the French Concession to show *wenming xi* (civilized plays) and films; in 1925 he and his younger brothers formed Shanghai's **Tianyi** (Unique Film Company), which moved from Shanghai to Hong Kong during the Sino–Japanese War. Its manager was Runde Shaw (1898–1973). The company changed its name to Nanyang, and it specialized in Cantonese commercial films. Its studio was located in Kowloon on Pak Tai Street, and when **Great China** was founded, it used the Nanyang studio until moving to Shanghai.

In 1950, Nanyang reclaimed its studio and changed its name to Shaw Brothers Studio; simultaneously, the production branch renamed itself Shaw and Sons Company Ltd. (Shaoshifuzi) and began producing Mandarin films for the Shaw Brothers chain in Hong Kong and across Southeast Asia. Directors working for the company included **Li han-hsiang**, **Tao Qin**, **Tu Guangqi**, **Yan Jun**, and **Wang Yin**.

Shaw and Sons decided to challenge the market leader in Southeast Asian Chinese cinema, **Motion Pictures and General Investment**

(MP&GI), and to do so reorganized and expanded. In 1957, Sir Run Run Shaw came to Hong Kong from Singapore and headed the new company, Shaw Brothers (Hong Kong) Ltd. (Shaoshi). Shaw and Sons Company continued, but turned to theater management and distribution. In 1961, Shaw Movietown, a new and larger studio, was built in Clearwater Bay, occupying 65,000 square feet, and producing an average of 30 films a year (between 1961 and 1985, 750 films were produced). Incorporating 13 sound stages, various outdoor sets and scenery (with streets, full-scale palaces, pavilions, pagodas, temples, and bridges), extensive costume wardrobes and props, color labs, and dubbing facilities, the studio was a self-contained entity and earned the status of the largest in Asia. Dormitories and facilities were provided for contract players; thus the "town" in Shaw Movietown was fact. In Hong Kong, Shaw Movie Studio officially went into operation in 1961.

By the mid-1960s, Shaw was running 35 companies across Asia and owned 130 theaters, nine amusement parks, and three production studios (in Hong Kong, Singapore, and Kuala Lumpur). Shaw Brothers made over 300 films, including **Asian Film Festival** award winners Li Han-hsiang's ***huangmei diao The Kingdom and the Beauty***/*Jiangshan meiren* (1959), the company's inaugural production, *Back Door/Houmen* (1960), ***The Grand Substitution***/*Wan gu liu fangWanggu liufang* (1965), the romance *The Blue and the Black/Laam yue hak/Lan yu hei* (1966), and *The Three Smiles/San xiao* (1969). Taiwanese **Golden Horse Award** winners included Li Han-hsiang's lavish period pieces *Yang Kwei Fei/Yang Guifei* (1962), ***The Love Eterne***/*Liang Shanbo yu Zhu Yingtai* (1963), and *The Empress Wu Tien/Wu Zetian* (1963). Other outstanding films are *The Enchanting Shadow/Qian nu you hun* (1960) and *Love without End/Bu liao qing* (1961), as well as the **martial arts** films that signaled a new direction for martial arts **action** filmmaking, namely **Chang Cheh's** maverick *The One-Armed Swordsman/Du bi dao* (1967) and **Jimmy Wang Yu's** *The Chinese Boxer/Long hu men* (1970).

In 1965, when MP&GI reorganized as Cathay and the company entered a period of decline, many of its directors and actors joined Shaw Brothers. Shaw also ran an actors' training school, directed by veteran Gu Wenzong, as well as a **television** and film artists' training center, headed by **Zhu Xuhua**.

Between 1970 and 1985, Shaw Brothers (Hong Kong) produced over 500 films. Among its **Asian Film Festival** award winners are **Lau Kar-leung's** ***The 36th Chamber of Shaolin****/Shaolin sa liu fang* (1978) and *Heroes of the East/Zhong hua zhang fu* (1978); **Chor Yuen's** *Intimate Confessions of a Chinese Courtesan/Oi No/Ai Nu* (1972), chosen as one of the world's 10 best; *King Boxer (Five Fingers of Death)/Tian xia di yi quan* (1972), Hong Kong's first international release; and, Chor's realist comedy *The House of 72 Tenants/ Chat sap yee ga fong hak/Qi shi er gu fang ke* (1973), a Cantonese remake that contributed to reviving Cantonese cinema. Other important films include Li Han-hsiang's *The Warlord/Da jun fa* (1972), starring **Michael Hui**, and *The Empress Dowager/Qing Guo Qing Cheng* (1975), starring **Lisa Lu**; Chor Yuen's ***Killer Clans****/Liu xing hu die jian* (1976); and **Alfred Cheung's** *Let's Make Laugh/Biao cu qi ri qing* (1983). Shaw also coproduced films with foreign companies, such as *Legend of the Seven Golden Vampires/Oi jin shi* (1974) with Britain's Hammer Films, *Blood Money/Xie han jin qian* (1983) with American and Spanish companies, and *Mighty Peking Man/Xing xing wang* (1977) with a German company.

A handful of people played key roles at Shaw Brothers. Managing director Sir Run Run Shaw and a series of general managers, Zhou Duwen, Lin Sicong, and Albert Chan (Chen Liduan), oversaw the company. **Raymond Chow**, vice general manager, was first in charge of production, followed by production manager Yuan Qiufeng. Since the 1970s, Mona Fong has run the studio, overseeing administration and production.

Famous Shaw Brothers contract directors included **Bu Wancang**, Chang Cheh, Chor Yuen, **He Menghua**, **King Hu**, Li Han-hsiang, **Lo Wei**, **Sun Zhong**, Tao Qin, **Yuen Chau-fong** (Yuan Qiufeng), **Yue Feng**, and **Zhou Shilu**. Famous contract actresses were **Cheng Pei-pei**, **Lily Ho**, **Betty Le Di**, **Li Lihua**, **Lin Cui**, **Linda Lin Dai**, **Ling Bo**, and Zhang Zhongwen. Famous contract actors included **Chen Hou**, **David Chiang**, **Chin Han**, Li Ching, **Lo Lieh**, **Ti Lung**, **Wang Yin**, Wang Yue, **Yueh Hua**, and **Zhao Lei**.

Sir Run Run Shaw launched Television Broadcasts Limited (TVB) in Hong Kong in 1973; TVB operated two channels and became a leading producer of Chinese-language programs. Starting in 1985, the studio was used for making television, particularly TVB miniseries. In

1990, TVB1 began operating as a franchised video chain in Vancouver, and in 1994, in the United Kingdom. In 1988, Shaw began making movies again and formed a subsidiary, Metropolitan, also investing in other companies, and producing films that included *Painted Faces* (1988, coproduced with **Golden Harvest**), and actor **Stephen Chiau's** *Out of the Dark/Wooi wan yau/Hui hun ye* (1995), actor **Lau Ching-wan's** *Loving You/Mo mei san taam/Wuwei shentan* (1995), and actor **Kaneshiro Takeshi's** *Hero/Ma wing ching/Ma yong zhen* (1997).

In 2000, Shaw sold its entire film library, spanning more than 800 films, to the Malaysian conglomerate Celestial Pictures for HK$600 million (approximately US$84 million), which continues restoring and releasing Shaw classics on DVD.

Since 1973, the Hong Kong Shaw Foundation has given over US$125 million around the world, to hospitals, educational institutions, college scholarships, and teacher training programs, including the Institute for Chinese Studies at Oxford University.

SHAW, SIR RUN RUN (Shao Yifu) (1907–). Born in Zhejiang province, producer Sir Run Run Shaw, the most famous of the **Shaw brothers**, made immense contributions to the Hong Kong film industry. He came to Southeast Asia with brother Runme in 1926, where they based themselves in Singapore, building a chain of theaters and shoring up distribution, eventually owning more than 160 theaters throughout Malaysia and Singapore. In 1957, he relocated to Hong Kong, focusing on movie production; he bought an 800,000 square foot property on Clearwater Bay from brother Runde and built the Shaw Movie Studio, and in 1958 Shaw Brothers Ltd (HK) was created as a production company. The facilities, the largest in Asia, were completed in 1964, and more than 1,000 films were made. Shaw modeled his studio after the old Hollywood system, signing contract players and directors, building impressive permanent sets on the property, accumulating expansive wardrobe for period piece movies. Shaw became chairman of Television Broadcasts Limited (TVB) in 1980, gradually diverting his interests from movies to **television**, and in 1987, sharply curtailing movie production. In 1984, Shaw established the Blood Transfusion Center under the Hong Kong Red Cross. In 2000, he sold Shaw's extensive film library (some 800 movies) to the Malaysian conglomerate Celestial Pictures, currently restoring and releasing classic Shaw movies on DVD. That same year, Shaw successfully obtained a pay-TV operating license in Hong Kong for his Galaxy Satellite Broadcast Ltd. He also joined a consortium to purchase a 90,000 square meter property in Tseung Kwan O to build new television studios.

SHEK, DEAN TIN (1950–). Born in Beijing, actor and producer Dean Shek was educated at Raimondi College in Hong Kong and joined the actors' training course at **Shaw Brothers**, and his film debut was *Dark Semester/Tiu lee chun fung/Tao li chun feng* (1969). He appeared in numerous Shaw films through 1974, usually playing the villain. He continued in **martial arts** films elsewhere, with a definite turn to comedy, in movies like **Michael Hui's** *Games Gamblers Play/Gwai ma seung sing/Gui ma shuang xing* (1974) and **Yuen Wo-ping's Jackie Chan** vehicle *Drunken Master/Chui kuen/Zui quan* (1979). He also made a dramatic turn as a retired Triad boss who cannot escape his past in **John Woo's** *A Better Tomorrow 2/(True Colors of a Hero 2)/Ying hung boon sik 2/Yingxiong bense 2* (1987) opposite **Chow Yun-fat**. He starred in a remake of the 1958 comedy, *Beware of Pickpockets/Foon lok san sin wing/Huan le shen xian who* (1981), directed by **Wu Ma**. He has appeared in over 90 films and directed a handful.

Shek formed Cinema City with **Karl Maka** and **Raymond Wong** in the early 1980s.

SHEK, KIN (Shih Kien) (1913–). The most prolific and recognizable villain in Hong Kong cinema of the 1950s and 1960s, "Bad Man Kin" appeared in hundreds of **martial arts** movies with stars like **Kwan Tak-hing** and **Chan Po-chu**. A trim, elegant man with an expressive face, he perfected the sneers, leers, cringes, and snarls necessary to play the stylized roles of bully and thug in films like *A Goddess' Sword/Lui din tin sin kim/Lei dian tian xian jian* (1963) and *Jade in the Red Dust 1* and *2/Bik laai hung chan/Bi la gong chen* (1966). Later in life, when he was cast in mostly benevolent parts, in films like *Young Master/Si dai chut ma/Shi di chu ma* (1980) and *A Friend from Inner Space/Gaan yan gwai/Jian ren gui* (1984), a hint of devilry remained in the expertly cocked eyebrow or sinister smile.

Shek Kin studied martial arts and traditional **Chinese opera** from childhood. His debut as a film actor was in *Flower in a Sea of Blood/Huet hoi dut/Xie hai hua* (1940). His on-screen chemistry with the martial arts actor Kwan Tak-hing in the long running **Wong Fei-hung** film series of the 1950s, where Shek took on a number of villainous roles opposite Kwan's heroic portrayal of Wong Fei-hung, helped to propel the films into cult status. Many of the top-ranked stuntmen and action directors of the era worked on the Wong Fei-hung series, like Lau Cham (father of **Lau Kar-leung**) and **Yuen Siu-tin** (father of **Yuen Wo-ping**). Shek Kin's ability to execute complex choreography and handle a variety of weapons meant that the films were able to showcase real martial technique, and Shek frequently choreographed his own scenes.

International audiences recognize Shek Kin from his iconic role as Mr. Han, the villain of **Bruce Lee's *Enter the Dragon*** (1973). Despite the nearly 30-year difference in their ages, Shek acquits himself well in the fight scenes with Lee. He also was seen in a number of **television** dramas from the mid-1970s until his retirement in the mid-1990s. Shek was awarded the Lifetime Achievement Award from the **Hong Kong Film Critics' Society** in 1996, and in 2002 the **Hong Kong Film Awards** gave him their Professional Achievement Award, in recognition of his contributions to the development of Hong Kong cinema.

SHI DAI QU* (Mandarin Pop).** Popular songs sung in Mandarin, they dominated the 1940s–1960s in movie musicals, generally melodramas or comedies disguised with song and dance sequences, leading to the expression "a song in every film," with songs usually sung simply for the sake of singing, not to drive the narrative. Songs were generally simple, to satisfy audience demand. Composers included He Luding, Chen Gexin, and **Yao Min**. Duets were not uncommon, but female solos outnumber them. Leading singers included **Zhou Xuan**, **Bai Guang**, **Ge Lan**, Yao Li, and Xi Jingting. There is some dispute as to whether the term originated in Shanghai or Hong Kong, but undoubtedly the migration of Mandarin films and music from prewar Shanghai to Hong Kong during the period had a tremendous impact on the Hong Kong industry. Cathay Organization (**Motion Pictures and General Investment**) and **Shaw Brothers** were the biggest studios producing Mandarin films, but their musical output was not as great as some independent studios like **Xinhua**. One trend was toward ethnic character in the songs, reflected by Shaw Brothers' introduction of ***huangmei diao opera films (that would also include several Mandarin pop tunes or regional folk songs). By the mid-1960s, songs were increasingly Westernized with Western songs being written with Chinese lyrics or old Chinese songs rewritten with English lyrics. By the 1970s, **Cantopop**, Cantonese popular song, began usurping Mandarin pop as the dominant form.

SHI, LEI (Sek Lui). Actor Shi Lei (real name Li Mengzhi), a native of Hebei province, was a university graduate and music lover, adept in Chinese calligraphy. His film debut was **Ma-Xu Weibang's** *A Maid's Bitter Story/King lau han/Qiong lou hen* (1949) for **Great Wall**. He was invited to join the newly formed **Feng Huang** in 1952 and appear in its first feature, *Festival Moon/Chung chau yuet/Zhong qiu yue* (1953), directed by **Zhu Shilin**. Shi made 40 films over a 30-year career, mostly for leftist studios.

Shi's best known films include *Year In, Year Out/Yat nin ji gai/Yi nian zhi ji* (1955) and *The Cricket and the King/Sik sut wong dai/Xi shuai huangdi* (1964). In the former, a contemporary Mandarin family melodrama, the families of two brothers (Shi Lei, **Bao Fang**) live together with their mother. The disparity between the brothers' financial circumstances causes bickering among the couples and puts the mother in an awkward situation. But when the older brother suffers losses from speculation, the younger brother helps. The film was the winner of the Excellence Award presented by the Ministry of Culture of the People's Republic of China.

Although Shi usually played villains, he also had comic talent and performed in *Love's Miracle/Ching dau choh hoi/Qing dou chu kai* (1958, codirected by Zhu Shilin, **Ren Yizhi**, and **Chen Jingbo**) and the social satire *Gentleman Who Steals/Leung seung gwan ji/Liang sang jun zi* (1963). In the former, Shi played one of the middle-aged partners of two neighboring couples who argue over small things; when their children fall in love, attempting to reconcile their families, the disputes escalate and situational comedy ensues. In the latter film, Shi played a cop in 1935 Shanghai who schemes with a lawyer (**Ping Fan**) to keep a thief (**Fu Che**) from reforming; both will prosper as long as the thief robs (the lawyer defending the criminal and the cop by arresting him and being promoted).

Shi also appeared in some Cantonese features, including **Allen Fong's** *Father and Son/Foo ji ching/Fu zi qing* (1981). Shi immigrated to Canada in 1983.

SHIN, STEPHEN GEI-YIN (1950–). Born in Hong Kong, director Stephen Shin graduated from Chinese University. He began in **television** as an assistant director and scriptwriter in 1975 and made his directorial film debut with the three-episode *Affairs/Yuen ga/Yuan gu* (1979), followed by the romance *Innocence/Ching gip/Qing jie* (1980) and the drama *Eclipse/Bok hoh fung fau/Bo he ka fei* (1982). Others include the **action** movie *Brotherhood/Fong dai/Xiong di* (1986), costarring **Danny Lee** and Alex Man, and the historical drama *The Great Conqueror's Concubine/Sai choh ba wong/Xi chu ba wang* (1994), starring **Ray Lui** and **Gong Li**.

Shin has also produced a number of films, including **Eddie Fong's** *An Amorous Woman of the Tang Dynasty/Tong chiu ho fong lui/Tang chao hao fang nu* (1984) and *Cherry Blossoms/Wat data foo chuen kei/Yu da fu chuan qi* (1988) and **Yuen Wo-ping's** *Tiger Cage/Dak ging tiu lung/Te jing tu long* (1988).

SHING, FUI-ON (1955–). Supporting actor Shing Fui-on was working on a film crew when someone spotted him and based on his appearance (large build and powerful, some say scary, face), began casting him as villains on-screen. He has appeared in more than 200 movies, usually cast as a villain or Triad. One of his most memorable roles is as the nasty double-crosser Johnny Weng in **John Woo's** *The Killer/Dip huet seung hung/Die xie shuang xiong* (1989), but he has also played against type in movies like **Clarence Ford's** battle of the sexes comedy *The Greatest Lover/Gung ji doh ching/Gong zi duo qing* (1988), as **Chow Yun-fat's** buddy.

SHU, KEI (1956–). Born in Hong Kong, writer-director Shu Kei graduated from the University of Hong Kong and began writing screenplays for **television** dramas. He has written scripts for many of Hong Kong's illustrious directors, including **John Woo**, **Ann Hui**, **Yim Ho**, **Patrick Tam**, and **Allen Fong**. He made his directorial debut with

Sealed with a Kiss (1981). In the mid-1980s, he worked as a programmer for the **Hong Kong International Film Festival**. He is also a published novelist, film distributor, and film scholar. His *Hu-Du-Men (Entrance from the Platform Side)/Fu do moon/Hu du men* (1996) was adapted by Raymond To from his own play. When **Cantonese opera** actors make their first entrance onstage, they are said to have crossed the "*hu-du-men*." In the film, **Josephine Siao** plays a successful opera actress who has had 20 years' experience and has a successful husband and daughter. When difficulties arise, she uses what she has learned onstage in life.

Shu Kei also directed and wrote *A Queer Story (Gay Man at 40)/Gei liu 40/Ji lao 40* (1997), a gay love story between an older and younger man, starring **George Lam** and **Jordan Chan**; the film stands out for its realistic and sympathetic portrayals in a film culture that remains mostly homophobic. *See also* GAY FILMS.

SHU, QI (1976–). Taiwanese actress Shu Qi (Hsu Chi) was discovered by producer Manfred Wong, who brought her to Hong Kong; her film debut was in a Category 3 film, *Sex and Zen 2/Yuk po tuen 2 yuk lui sam ging/Yu pui tsuan 2 yu nu xin* (1996); that same year, among other movies she appeared in **Derek Yee's** insider comedic look at the film industry, *Viva Erotica/Sik ching laam nui/Se qing nan nu* (1996), in a role that related to her own life (her nude photographs at age 18 are widespread, and an attractive body served as her entry into the movie industry); she won Best Supporting Actress at the **Hong Kong Film Awards** for her portrayal. Shu crossed over into the mainstream, difficult to do for Hong Kong actresses after doing nudity, and she has since appeared in **action** and drama such as the Triad-boyz *Young and Dangerous* spin-off *Portland Street Blues/Goo wak chai ching yee pin ji hung hing sap saam mooi/Gu huo zai qing yi pian zhi hong xing shi san mei* (1998); **Andrew Lau's** mythic *Storm Riders (Wind Cloud: Heroic Tyrant Heaven Earth)/Fung wan hung ba tin ha/Feng yun xiong ba tian xia* (1998); **Yonfan's** drama *Bishonen (Love of a Beautiful Boy)/Mei siu nin ji luen/Mei shao nian zhi lian* (1998); **Cheung Yuen-ting's** indie-feeling *Beijing Rocks/Bakging lok yue liu/Beijing le yu lu* (2001), set in Beijing's underground music scene; **Ann Hui's** horror movie *Visible Secret/Yau leng yan gaan/Youling renjian* (2001); and **Corey Yuen's** grrrl power actioner *So Close/Chik yeung* *tin sai/ Xiyang tianshi* (2002), among others. In her best roles, Shu is caught in complex relationships, usually between three characters, and she uses an open face to communicate a variety of emotions, although in some movies she is either simply sweet or bubbly. Shu has made more than 50 movies in less than a decade, including the Hollywood actioner *The Transporter* (2002), opposite Jason Stratham.

SHU, SHI (Shu Sik) (1916–). Actor and director Shu Shi (real name Shu Changge), a native of Zhejiang province, grew up in Shanghai and studied at Shanghai's Fudan University. He participated in a variety of dramas during his schooling and studied under the tutelage of **Beijing opera** actor Mei Lanfang, a family friend. In 1933, he joined the Qingdao Troupe, acting in many plays.

Shu Shi's debut as a film actor was the lead in *Sensational News* (1938) opposite actress Lu Luming. Starting in 1940, for the next five years he appeared in a dozen Shanghai films for studios including Jinxing, **Zhonglian**, and Huaying, among them *The Family of Qin Huai* (1940) and *Tears of the Flower/Sin dut chaan lui/Xian hua can lei* (1941), although he also returned to theater after the outbreak of war. He briefly worked in Taiwan as a section chief of a transportation company.

In the late 1940s, the actor came to Hong Kong to work for **Yonghua** and **Great China**, appearing in Zhang Shichuan's Mandarin drama *An All-Consuming Love/Cheung seung si/Chang xiangsi* (1947), **Zhu Shilin's** Mandarin romance *A Dream of Spring/Chun zhi meng* (1947) and his classic historical drama ***Sorrows of the Forbidden City****/Ching gung bei shut/ Qinggong mishi* (1948), and Wu Zuguang's drama *Kinship Marriage/Chun fung chau yue/Chunfeng qiu yu* (1949). In *An All-Consuming Love*, set in Shanghai's foreign concession during the Japanese occupation, Shu costarred as a teacher and the good friend of a married couple (**Zhou Xuan** and Liang Fu) who falls for Zhou but respects his friend and their relationship. In *Sorrows of the Forbidden City*, process shots, particularly those of the Summer Palace, are outstanding, and the total budget for the film is estimated at HK$1 million.

At the end of the 1940s, Shu returned to Shanghai, appeared in several films, and codirected *Witch Devil, Gambler (Witch, Devil, Man)/San, gwai, yan/Shen, gui, ren* and directed the contemporary

Mandarin melodrama *Unknown Father/Bat chi diy dik foo chan/Bu zhi dao de fu qin* (both 1952), starring **Chen Juanjuan**, **Han Fei**, and **Yan Jun**. Adapted from a Russian play, *Unknown Father* focuses on a student playing an unmarried pregnant girl in a play; a neighbor overhears her rehearsing and believes she is pregnant. The misunderstanding leads to complications, but also better understanding.

Shu was deported by the Hong Kong government in 1953, along with more than 20 other filmmakers, for supposedly instigating a workers' strike. He settled in Shanghai and worked for Shanghai Film Studio, starring in *Letter with Feathers* (1954), *Li Shizhen* (1956), and *Red Day* (1961). He directed Wu Yonggang's *Lin Chong* (1958), and shared writing, directing, and acting with Lin Bin, and *The Pearl and the Phoenix* (1963). He also wrote Zhu Shilin's *Map of 100 Treasures/Baak bo tiu/Bai bao tu* (1953). During the Cultural Revolution, he spent time in a labor camp. In the mid-1970s, he was sent to Beijing, worked as a manual laborer at film schools and in a textile factory, and was eventually sent back to Shanghai Film Studio.

Shu's first wife, Murong Wan'er, died of breast cancer during the Cultural Revolution, but he found actress Feng Huang ("phoenix"), not through film, but through his daughter. She had played his son in *Li Sanniang* (1939), and he comforted the child after (s)he fell from a horse; years later, through proximity and Shu's daughter's suggestion, after Feng had also lost her husband and was left with three sons, they married.

SHUM, JOHN KIN-FUN (John Sham) (1952–). Actor and producer John Shum was educated in Hong Kong, Great Britain, and the United States. He began working in **television** while he was editor of Hong Kong's *City* magazine. He joined forces with entrepreneur Dickson Poon, and at Poon's direction began **D&B Films** with **Samo Hung**. The company produced numerous films, including **Leung Po-Chi's** *Hong Kong 1941/Dang doi lai ming/Deng dai li ming* (1984); **Ronny Yu's** *Legacy of Rage/Lung joi kong woo/Long zai jiang hu* (1986), starring Brandon Lee; **Stanley Kwan's** *Love unto Waste/ Dei ha ching/Di xia qing* (both 1986); and **Patrick Tam's** *Final Victory/Chui hau sing lei/Zui hou sheng li* (1987). Shum began another company, Maverick Films, with writer-producer John Chan in 1986. Their productions included **Derek Yee's** *People's Hero/Yan man ying hung/Ren* *min ying xiong* (1987), a Hong Kong version of Sidney Lumet's *Dog Day Afternoon*; **David Chung-Tsui Hark's** *I Love Maria/Tit gaap miu dik lut lei a/Tie jia we di ma li ya* (1988); and **Cheung Yuen-ting's** *Eight Taels of Gold/Baat a gam/Ba ya jin* (1989).

As an actor, Shum has appeared in close to 40 films, including comedies but also dramas, such as Derek Yee's *The Lunatics (Lunatics: True Story)/Din lo jing juen/Dian lao zheng zhuan* (1986) and the **Yim Ho–Tsui Hark** codirected *King of Chess (Chess King)/Kei wong/Qi wang* (1992). In the latter, Shum played a major character in the contemporary Taiwan story who as an adult flashes back to his childhood on the Mainland during the Cultural Revolution.

In the 1990s, Shum became a visible and vocal political activist as a part of Hong Kong's prodemocracy movement, although he continues in film, most recently in the **Jackie Chan** vehicle directed by **Benny Chan**, *New Police Story/San ging chaat goo si/Xin jing cha gu shi* (2004).

SHUM, LYDIA (1947–). Actress Lydia Shum was born in Shanghai and came to Hong Kong as a young child. She began as a child actor with **Shaw Brothers** at 12, debuting in *When the Peach Blossom Blooms/Yat shu tiu dut chin deu hung/Yi shu tao hua qian duo gong* (1960). As a child-teen actress, she appeared in numerous films alongside **Josephine Siao** and **Connie Chan Po-chu**, including youth problem films like *Waste Not Our Youth/Mok foo ching chun/Mofu qingchun* (1967), *Teenage Love/Yuk lui sam/Yu nu xin* (1968), and *Teddy Girls/Fei lui jing chuen/ Feinu zhengzhuan* (1969).

Since childhood, the robust Shum has played the overweight friend or comic relief. She was part of the ensemble cast in **Chor Yuen's** *The House of 72 Tenants/Chat sap yee ga fong hak/Qi shi er gu fang ke* (1973), a color remake of **Wang Weiyi**'s 1963 film, and in the 1980s she appeared in the zany *It's a Mad, Mad World/Foo gwai bik yan/Fu gui bi ren* series (1987–1992) opposite Bill Tung; she was well-used in **Yuen Wo-ping's** *Drunken Tai Chi/Siu taai gik/Xiao tai jii* (1984) in which she was more than a match for **Donnie Yen**.

Shum has appeared in over 100 films, but became a popular host of the **television** show *Enjoy Yourself Tonight* where she was a regular for more than 20 years. She remains a popular entertainment personality.

SIAO, JOSEPHINE FONG-FONG (1947–). Born in Shanghai, actress Josephine Siao (real name Xiao Liang) has had a film career spanning 43 years and over 200 films, with the lead in close to 150 of them; there are three separate phases to her career, as a child star, a teenage princess, and a mature actress. She began in the Mandarin cinema as a child actress, debuting in *A Child's Tears (Tears of a Young Concubine)/Siu sing lui/Xiao xing lei* (1954); she costarred with **Yan Jun** and **Lin Dai** in *The Orphan Girl/Mooi goo/Mei gu* (1956), for which she won the Best Child Actress at the second Southeast Asian Film Festival. She starred opposite **Butterfly Wu** and **Wang Yin** in **Bu Wancang's** *A Tender Story* (1960), in which she played the orphan girl adopted by a street vendor; the story follows their experiences as they travel the country with a monkey and three dogs.

In 1960, Siao began making **martial arts** movies, starting with **Tu Guangqi's** *Nineteen Swordsmen of Ching City (Daring Gang of Nineteen from Verdun City)* (1960), in which she played the heroine seeking to avenge her parents' murder, and including many others like *Burning of the Red Lotus Monastery, Parts 1* and *2/Feng shui hung lin chi/Huo shao gong lian si* (1963). She also began making Cantonese films, including **melodramas** and **musicals**, starting with **Chu Kei's** *Madame Yun (Filial Piety)/Haau diy/Yun niang* (1960), also starring Butterfly Wu. They appeared together again in Chu's *Mother Love/Miu oi/Mu ai* (1961), another Cantonese melodrama in which the teenaged Josephine Siao plays youngest daughter to the widow Butterfly Wu. Abandoned by her older children, the mother suffers, facing degradation after degradation, all painfully experienced by the young daughter so attached to her. At film's end, the absentee eldest son miraculously reappears to save his mother and affirm values of filial piety, loyalty, and love.

Siao also costarred as the female lead opposite **Chan Po-chu** as the male lead in **Lee Tit's Cantonese opera** *Eternal Love/Chat choi woo bat gwai/Qicai hu bu gui* (1966). Siao studied Cantonese opera with masters Fen Juhua and Qi Caifen, and her singing performance is outstanding. At the peak of her career, 1966–1969, Siao was one of the two most popular female stars. She and Chan Po-chu (with whom she often costarred) virtually launched the contemporary youth genre movie. **Chan Wan's** *Romance of a Teenage Girl/Siu lui sam/Shaonu* *xin* (1967) was Siao's first youth musical, in which she played a reporter. Assigned to interview a young student (Wu Fung) in difficult circumstances, she concocts a scheme to help him financially. She takes on two other personae, a spoiled rich girl and a Vietnamese nightclub dancer. In one scene, all three characters appear, and the movie combines comedy and drama with video-style musical sequences (including Vietnamese folk dance, modern dance, and Cantonese opera). That same year she starred in **Mok Hong-si's** (Mok Kangshi) *Tender Love/Yu lui chan ching/Yunu qinqing* as an innocent reform school escapee (she was framed as a drug dealer by her cousin) who masquerades as the lost granddaughter of a tycoon (**Shek Kin**). Charmed by the girl, the old man and everyone else end up playing along with the ruse as the good-bad girl joins the rich household.

Siao starred in **Patrick Lung Gong's** *Window/Cheong ngoi ching/Chuang wai qing* (1968) and *Teddy Girls/Fei liu jing chuen/Feinu zhengzhuan* (1969). In *Teddy Girls*, she played the rebellious Josephine Tsui, who, after a rumble with boys, chooses a girls' reform school (where **Kenneth Tsang Kong** is the rector) over becoming the ward of her mother's shady lover (Lung Gong, also the film's director). As the title suggests, focus is on characterization of the disaffected youth or ***ah fei*** characters, and Siao's righteous-angered angel face dominated the screen; despite her violent bent, she has a strong code of morality in tune with a generation that felt betrayed by its elders (an uncommon theme for the time). Siao gave one of her best performances here.

Siao left Hong Kong to pursue an education and graduated from Seton Hall University in New Jersey with a degree in Communications in 1973. While in the United States, she also worked as an assistant producer at NBC Television in New York. She returned to Hong Kong in 1974, and starred in Lung Gong's *Hiroshima 28/Gong do nim baat/Guang dao ershiba* (1974), controversial in its day, in which Siao played a Japanese victim of post-Hiroshima syndrome, and Li Xing's *Rhythm of the Sea* (1974); she also codirected and starred in **Leong Po-chih's** action-drama *Jumping Ash/Tiu fooi/Tiao hui* (1976), a **New Wave** precursor. She founded Hi-Pitch Film Company in 1977, and produced *Lam Ah Chun/Lam A Jan/Lin Ya Zhen* (1978), in which she starred as the title character (one she had created in an earlier 1977 **television** series) and that she would reprise in **John Woo's** *Plain Jane to the Rescue/Baat choi Lam A Jan/Ba cai Lin Ya Zhen* (1982) with **Ricky Hui**. The company also produced **Ann Hui's** horror-comedy *The Spooky Bunch/Chong do jing/Zhuang dao zheng* (1980), in which Siao starred with **Kenny Bee**. She won a Best Actress Award at the seventh **Hong Kong Film Awards** for her performance as a single woman opposite **Richard Ng's** seaman fighting for custody of his young daughter in **David Chiang's** *The Wrong Couples/Bat shut yuen ga bat chui tau/Bu shi yuan gu bu ju tou* (1987).

Siao suffered from a hearing disability since early childhood, which worsened with age. She married Hong Kong media executive Clarence Chang Ching-po in the early 1980s; they have two daughters. She continued to make films, among them **Corey Yuen's** *Fong Sai-yuk 1* and *2/Fong Sai-yuk/Fang Shiyu* (1993), in which she played **Jet Li's** titular character's mother; **Jacob Cheung's** *Always on My Mind/Cheung chin foo chai/Chuang qian fu qi* (1993), a family drama in which she played opposite **Michael Hui**; and **Shu Kei's** *Hu-Du-Men (Entrance from the Platform Side)/Fu do moon/Hu du men* (1996), a story built upon the metaphors of the stage and life, adapted by Raymond To from his own play. When Cantonese opera actors make their first entrance onstage, they are said to have crossed the "*hu-du-men*," and Siao's opera actress uses what she has learned onstage in life. Her last film was *Mahjong Dragon (Mahjong Flying Dragon)/Lut cheuk fei lung/Ma que fei long* (1997), in which she starred opposite Zhao Wen-zhou as a cop with a gambling problem out to fix her jinx. She won Best Actress at the 1995 Berlin Film Festival and **Golden Horse Awards** for Ann Hui's ***Summer Snow*** *(Woman, Forty)/Nui Yan Sei Sap /Nuren sishi* (1995), an Alzheimer's-themed drama starring Siao and **Roy Chiao** that celebrates an ordinary housewife as hero. Siao's daughter-in-law juggles home, family, and work as she cares for her Alzheimer's-ridden father-in-law (Chiao). The reality and humor of everyday life cuts both ways in a heartbreaking and life-affirming story.

Siao was awarded an MA in Child Psychology from Regis University in Denver, Colorado, and currently practices in Hong Kong. She also founded the End Child Sexual Abuse Foundation there in 1999.

SIL-METROPOLE ORGANIZATION LTD. Formed in 1982, from the merger of **Great Wall**, **Feng Huang**, **Xinlian**, and Sun Luen studios, Sil-Metropole Organization is headed by Liu Yat-yuen. In the early 1980s, the company made a series of documentaries on Chinese folk traditions and scenic attractions. The studio also made **Jet Li** a star, with Cheung Yam-yim's ***The Shaolin Temple***/*Shaolin si* (1982), which was released internationally, and *Kids from Shaolin/Shaolin xiao zi* (1984).

In its first 15 years of operation, the company produced more than 60 films. Notable productions include **Allen Fong's** *Father and Son/Foo ji ching/ qing* (1981, shared with Feng Huang) and *Ah Ying/ Ban bian ren* (1983), both of which won Best Film at the **Hong Kong Film Awards**; **Stanley Kwan's** *Full Moon in New York/Yan joi nau yeuk/Ren zai niu yue* (1989), which won Best Film at Taiwan's **Golden Horse Awards**; and **Jacob Cheung's** realist *Cageman/Long min* (1992), which won Best Film at the Hong Kong Film Awards. The company also coproduced (with Mainland China) *The Story of Qiu Ju/Qiu ju da guan si* (1992), which won Best Director (**Zhang Yimou**) and Best Actress (**Gong Li**) at the Venice Film Festival.

SIQIN, GAOWA. Of Chinese, Mongolian, and Swiss decent, Mainland dramatic actress Siqin Gaowa has appeared in moving performances in films by several Hong Kong directors, including **Yim Ho's** *Homecoming/Chi shui lau nin/Si shui liu nian* (1984) and *The Day the Sun Turned Cold/Tin gwok ngaak ji/Tian guo ni zi* (1995) and **Stanley Kwan's** *Full Moon in New York/Yan joi nau yeuk/Ren zai niu yue* (1989). Among her famous Mainland roles is as the daughter of an Alzheimer's patient mother in *Gone Is the One Who Held Me Dearest in the World* (2001). She costars with **Chow Yun-fat** in **Ann Hui's** *The Postmodern Aunt's Life* (2006).

SIT, KOK-SIN (Xue Juexian) (1904–1956). Cantonese opera actor Sit Kok-sin (real name Xue Zuomei), a native of Guangdong province, was born in Hong Kong and educated there. At 18, he started training under Xin Shaohua and played *lache* (literally, "to drag or pull," parts that require the actor to fill in between acts by playing to the house) roles in the Huanqiule (Universal Joy) Opera Troupe. Also inspired by his idol Cantonese opera performer Zhu

Cibo, Sit turned to *chou* (clown) roles for the Renshounian (Good Health) Opera Troupe. He became an opera star with *The Three Noblemen*, and strengthened his standing with parts in other plays, including *The Rainbow Gate*, *The Pear's Spirit*, *White Gold Dragon*, *Romance of Jade Hall*, and *Queen of the Stage*.

In *Why Not Return?* the actor played both lead roles, including the *huadan* (maiden) as a female impersonator. Sit's versatility resulted in him being described as *wanneng laoguan* ("all-purpose hired hand"). Sit founded a singing style known as Xue qiang ("Xue style"), and was known as a reformer of Cantonese opera, introducing Northern-style opera elements and Western musical accompaniment. He inspired a younger generation, including his students **Lam Ka-sing** and **Pak Suet-sin**.

Sit's film debut, under the name Zhang Fei, was as the lead in *The Loverboy* (1926), produced by the Feifei Film Company, which he founded the same year. Sit played two brothers, one rich, one poor; both brothers appeared in dialogue scenes together and fought each other. The actor also starred as a rich playboy in the first Cantonese language film made, *White Gold Dragon/Chuk baak gam lung/Yu bai jin long* (1933), produced by Shanghai's **Tianyi**; its success, in Guangzhou, Hong Kong, and overseas communities, helped lead to the rise of Cantonese-dialect film production. A sequel appeared four years later. Sit's film career spanned 27 years and 35 films, including adaptations of stage works such as *Sisters-in-Law in Danger* (1939), *Why Don't You Return (Why Not Return)?/Woo bat gwai/Hu bugui* (1940), and *Queen of the Stage (The Spotlight)/Aau dang chiu yuk yan/Yindeng zhao yuren* (1940). In **Fung Chi-kong's** *Why Don't You Return?*, Sit starred as the son who loves his wife and mother, but whose mother tries to, and almost succeeds in, separating the couple. In the contemporary romance *Love Affairs of the Opera Master/Ling wong yim shut/Lingwang yanshi* (1953), Sit starred in the title role as an opera master in love with Pak Suet-sin; she falls for **Yam Kim-fai**, disguised as a man but really a woman; Yam admires the opera master, so she stirs discontent between the couple, until she repents. Sit and Pak performed excerpts from the opera *White Gold Dragon's Altercation in the Garden*, while Yam and Pak performed from *Rendezvous with Camille*. Sit sang "Worshipping the Queen of Flying Phoenix."

During wartime, Sit suffered a mental breakdown. Although he continued performing, his career following the war suffered until he joined the Guangzhou Cantonese Opera Troupe in 1954. He died two years later from a cerebral hemorrhage.

SIT, NANCY KAR-YIN (Xue Jiayan) (1950–). Actress Sit Kar-yin, a native of Fujian province, was one of the "Seven Princesses," a group of teenage females including **Petrina Fung Bo-bo** and **Josephine Siao**, namely in *Seven Princesses 1* and *2/Chat gung chu/Qigong zhu* (1967), among others. She appeared in close to 70 movies, becoming a star in the title role in *Bunny Girl/Tiu lui long/Tu nu lang* (1967); her most famous films include the teen **musical** ***Girls Are Flowers****/Goo leung sap baat yat deu dut/Gu niang shi ba yi duo hua* (1966) and teen problem movie *Teddy Girls/Fei lui jing chuen/Feinu zhengzhuan* (1969). In the 1970s, she worked in **television** and codirected and cowrote *Dog Bites Dog Bone/Gau aau gau gwat/Gou yao gou gu* (1978), in which she also starred, after which she turned to business interests. In the 1990s, she made a successful comeback and has become a popular TV star.

SITU, HUIMIN (Szeto Wai-man) (1910–1987). Director Situ Huimin was born in Guangdong and educated in China, Canada, and Japan, and in the United States at Columbia University in New York. In 1931, he returned to China and became a member of the Communist Party. In 1933, he became head of the Diantong film studio. When Shanghai fell to the Japanese, Situ moved to Hong Kong in 1937, where he made anti-Japanese films and cowrote several scripts with **Cai Chusheng**, such as *Blood Splashes on Baoshan Fortress (The Blood-Stained Baoshan Fortress)/Huet chin bo saan shing/Xie jian bao shan cheng* (1938, awarded a prize of excellence by the Guangzhou Film Jury Committee) and *March of the Guerillas (Song of Righteousness, Song of Retribution)/Youji jingxing qu (Zhenqi ge)* (1938, released 1941).

Situ's *March of the Guerillas* was intended to rally the Chinese on the Mainland in the war effort against the Japanese. It was banned in Hong Kong because the British at the time wished to remain neutral. When the ban was lifted in 1941, the Cantonese-speaking cast was seen on-screen, many actors for the first time. Set in a village overrun by Japanese soldiers (there are some who question their government's intervention), a young man tries to organize a local resistance movement but is injured. When he recovers, he joins mountain guerillas to resist, but learns his girlfriend has been captured. As the rebels attack the Japanese camp, the couple briefly reunites before she dies.

Later Situ became deputy director of the film bureau under Mao Zedong's government.

***SONG OF A SONGSTRESS* (1948).** *Song of a Songstress/Goh lui ji goh/Genu zhi ge* is a Mandarin **musical** directed by **Fang Peilin** and starring **Zhou Xuan**, a semibiographical depiction of the singing actress. As a young girl, the protagonist Zhu Lan is brought up by foster parents and pressured into a performing life. Lan (Zhou) becomes a nightclub singer, torn between two men, a struggling painter she loves and a heartless playboy (**Wang Hao**) revealed to be the son of the man who attempted to rape and then killed her mother. The tragic character of the songstress is a staple of early Mandarin musicals; she is helpless and hapless but eventually reveals her strength to go on. This popular characterization spoke to audiences of the 1930s and 1940s, who had lived through a long war, economic hardship, and political turmoil. The filmmakers (with or without Zhou Xuan's consent) exploited events from her own life in this particular story, which the audience read as hers—an unhappy childhood, introduction into the profession by her foster parents, involvements with men who used her. Her final song is both heart wrenching and hopeful.

***SONG OF THE EXILE* (1990). New Wave** director **Ann Hui's** *Song of the Exile (Exile and Autumn Sorrow)/Haak to chau han/Ketu qiuhen* (1990), is an autobiographical film that addresses Chinese–Japanese relations as well as important issues of the Hong Konger's identity and exile, reflected through multiple points of view. The film stars **Maggie Cheung** as Hui's stand-in, as the British-educated daughter who returns home to Hong Kong to resume a difficult relationship with her mother (Lu Shao-fen). Taught from childhood by her grandparents living in Macau to look down upon her mother's Japanese origins and to elevate her Chinese heritage, the daughter finds the tables are turned when she visits Japan with her mother, is viewed as an outsider, and learns of her mother's class superiority. As an adult, she begins to understand her mother and the complexity of their relationship as well as to reevaluate the past and her beliefs. The intimate film was shot in Hong Kong and on location in London, Japan, Guangzhou, and Macau and also addresses the Chinese diaspora as well as the conflict between tradition and modernity.

***SONGS OF THE PEACH BLOSSOM RIVER* (1956).** *Songs of the Peach Blossom River/Tou Fa Kong/Taohua jiang*, codirected by **Zhang Shankun** and **Wang Tianlin**, is a Mandarin **musical** in which music is not only fully integrated into the story, but also plays a significant and positive role in the characters' lives. In the pastoral setting of the Peach Blossom River, farmer's daughter Wild Kitten (Little Wild Cat) (**Zhong Qing**) is courted by two suitors, actors **Lo Wei** (who sings and is collecting folk tunes along the river) and **Chen Hou** (who does not sing), cast as a tone-deaf country boy. One of the musical courtship numbers is the hit "Moonlight Duet." War interrupts the peacefulness of the village and Wild Kitten escapes to an idyllic Hong Kong where she finds a mother, singing success, and love. Surely the movie hit home with Mainland Chinese refugees content to settle in stable Hong Kong but nostalgic for the home left behind. A big hit upon its release, the movie also made Zhong a major box office star (she was called "Wild Kitten") and established the farmer's daughter phase of Mandarin musicals. A dozen songs were included, among them the title song, "Peach Blossom River."

SOO, DOLLY FUNG (Su Feng) (1939–). Actress Dolly Soo Fung (real name Li Shaojuan), a native of Guangdong province, was born in Shanghai where her father ran a pharmaceutical company, and she received her secondary education and took part in a school drama group. In 1942, she moved with her family to Hong Kong, and 11 years later joined **Motion Pictures and General Investment (MP&GI)**.

The actress's film debut was in **Evan Yang's** romance *Green Hills and Jade Valleys/Ching saan chui guk/Qingshan cuigu* (1956), also the debut of **Kelly Lai Chen**, **Kitty Ting Hao**, and **Tian Qing**. Soo played Lai's cousin, whose parents arrange their marriage; but Lai and Soo love others and evade the elders' plans. She also appeared in Yang's

musical *Air Hostess/Hung chung siu che/Kongzhong xiaojie* (1959), **melodrama** *My Darling Sister/Che mooi dut/Jie mei hua* (1959), comedy *Bachelors Beware/Wan yau hing/Wen rou qing* (1960), and epic drama ***Sun, Moon and Star***, *Part 1* and *2/Sing sing yuet leung taai yeung/Xing xing yue liang tai yang* (1961).

A supporting actress with simple presence but an unobtrusive demeanor, Soo supported star **Ge Lan** in movies like *Air Hostess*, Yang's *My Darling Sister*, **Tang Huang's** *June Bride* (1960), and **Wang Tianlin's** musical ***The Wild, Wild Rose*** (1960), and star **Linda Lin Dai** in Tang Huang's *Cinderella and Her Little Angels/Wan seung yim hau/ Yunchang yanhou* (1959), and Yang's *Bachelors Beware* (1960). In **Tao Qin's** musical melodrama ***Our Sister Hedy*** *(Four Daughters)/Se chin gam/Si qianjin* (1957), she played the youngest in a family of four daughters; her widowed father wishes she attend university, but she elopes with a pilot, and the couple proceed to move in with the family. In *The Wild, Wild Rose/Yau mooi gwai ji luen/ Yemeigui zhi lian*, Soo played the loyal girlfriend whose boyfriend turned lounge lizard piano player is seduced and loved by Ge Lan. In *Cinderella and Her Little Angels* (1959), Soo was the glasses-ridden student at the orphanage where Lin Dai teaches. Soo made 12 films during her years at MP&GI and retired after her marriage in 1962.

SOONG, STEPHEN (Song Qi, Sung Kei) (1919–1996). A native of Zhenjiang, Stephen Soong studied Western Literature at the University of Yanjing and was a teacher there. In the 1930s and 1940s, he began writing for and became involved with the stage, leading the renowned Jindu Drama Troupe. He came to Hong Kong in 1948, working at the United States Information Service (USIS) as a publication and translation officer. He often published under the pseudonym Lin Yiliang.

In 1955, **Loke Wan Tho** hired him for the newly formed International Films Distributing Agency (later **Motion Pictures and General Investment, MP&GI**), and he was one of four core script committee members. Soong was responsible for bringing famous writer **Eileen Chang** into MP&GI as a screenwriter. In 1957, Soong became production supervisor at the company, instrumental in shaping the stories (**melodramas**, comedies, and **musicals**), for which the studio would become known. Soong not only initiated the ***North–South***

Trilogy by writing the first episode, but he will always be credited with movies like **Evan Yang's** *Air Hostess* (1959), starring **Ge Lan** in the title role, as a modern woman looking for meaning in a career, and **Wang Tianlin's** musical noir ***The Wild, Wild Rose*** (1960), also starring Ge Lan as both femme fatale and doomed songstress. After Loke's death and company reorganization, Soong moved to **Shaw Brothers** as head of the script department. Beginning in 1968, he served as special assistant to the vice-chancellor and head of the Department of Translation Studies at the University of Hong Kong. He died in Hong Kong.

***SORROWS OF THE FORBIDDEN CITY* (1948).** Director **Zhu Shilin's** masterpiece *Sorrows of the Forbidden City/Ching gung bei shut/Qinggong mishi* is perhaps his most well-known work. It was **Yonghua's** second production. Adapted from Yao Ke's play and based on his script, the story is set during the final decade of the 19th century, toward the end of the Qing dynasty; it dramatizes a family story that reverberates as a national dilemma. Three figures, the Empress Dowager Cixi (Tang Ruoqing), the reformist emperor Guangxi (**Shu Shi**), and his concubine wife Zhenfei (**Zhou Xuan**) are the central characters in the family story, which boils down to a conflict between mother-in-law and daughter-in-law. The Empress Dowager "reigns behind the curtain" by manipulating the emperor and plotting against his favorite, all of this set against the building of the Summer Palace, an internal reform movement, naval defeat in the 1894 Sino–Japanese War, the Boxer Rebellion, and foreign invasion. She wins, and the film ends with a dead concubine, grieving husband, and collapsing country. In this film, as in others by the director, the ethics underlying the family foundation and the nation are questioned.

The struggle between conservative and reformist forces and the transition between old and new was perceived at the time as a distortion of history by many, but none could deny the aesthetics of the film's direction, casting, camerawork, narrative structure, and art design. Scenes of the imperial palaces of the Forbidden City and the Summer Palace were created through expensive process shots. Mao Zedong denounced the film during the Cultural Revolution but it was rehabilitated in 1976.

SOUTH CHINA FILM INDUSTRY WORKERS UNION. Formed in 1949, the South China Film Industry Workers Union was the first professional organization of Hong Kong's filmmaking industry, including all positions, from minor supporting actors to big stars, from technical crews to directors and producers, and the first to demand national dignity and social welfare for its members. Early activist members of the group included **Ng Cho-fan**, **Cheung Ying**, **Lo Dun**, **Lee Tit**, **Kwan Man-ching**, **Ng Wui**, Ng Kei-man, and Chan Pei. It remains active presently.

SOUTHERN FILM COMPANY (Nam Kwok, Nanguo). The Southern Film Company (Nam Kwok) was founded in 1948 to make Cantonese-language films, to satisfy the early postwar population that, through large-scale migrations, had settled in Hong Kong. The filmmakers wanted to appeal directly to their audience and to more intimately transfer Hong Kong life on-screen; they promoted energetic and serious filmmaking. Three films were made: **Wang Wei-yi's** *Tragedy on the Pearl River/Zhu jiang lei* (1950), Zhang Min's *Spring Follows Winter (Spring Comes and Winter Goes)/Don qu chun lai* (1950), and **Lo Dun's** *Tragedy of Canton/Yang cheng hen shi* (1951). The company contributed to late 1940s Hong Kong film development until 1951.

***THE STORY BETWEEN HONG KONG AND MACAU* (1966).** Director **Tso Kea's** *The Story between Hong Kong and Macau (Beyond the Horizon)/Yat sui gaak tin aai/Yi shui ge tian ya* is an intricately plotted **melodrama** set apart from many others. **Miao Jinfeng** plays a woman leading a life with a checkered past, a single mother who falls in love with her son's headmaster (**Cheung Ying**). He discovers her secret, that she is an unwed mother who was seduced and abandoned by her boss and earns a living as a nightclub singer (considered disreputable). When her son is hospitalized and the woman must also support an ailing father in Macau, the headmaster helps pay, and, in return, she offers herself to him but he refuses her. Their friendship leads to love, but the man's aunt in Macau objects, having selected one of her students (Li Min) for her nephew. The singer discovers the student's love for the man, so she pretends their affair has just been a fling, and sacrifices for his happiness. The man becomes gravely ill and is taken back to Macau, and as a result, the child, who has become very attached to him, dies. The singer not only learns that the other woman is her sister, but she also loses a leg in an accident and is cared for by a supportive doctor. In a climactic scene, all the parties come together and realize the sacrifices made and the suffering woman's strength. Despite the coincidences the plot depends upon, Tso Kea's symbolic mise-en-scène through sets and props and exacting camerawork, as well as the strong cast, make this a memorable tragic love story.

***THE STORY OF THREE LOVES* (1964). Wang Tianlin's melodrama** *The Story of Three Loves/Tai siu yan yuen/Ti xuao yin yuan*, adapted from **Mandarin Duck and Butterfly** author Zhang Henshui's famous romantic novel, was released in two parts with an all-star cast, featuring **Lin Cui**, **Ge Lan**, **Zhao Lei**, **Roy Chiao**, **Wang Yin**, and **Wang Lai**. Zhao plays a wealthy Huangzhou student temporarily living with his cousin (Wang Lai) who develops feelings for two street performers, one, a **kung fu** practitioner (Lin Cui), the other, a singer (Ge Lan). He helps in the recovery of the former's father (Wang Yin), but plans on marrying the latter. When he is called away by an ill mother, his absence ensures that the latter will fall victim to a villainous warlord general (Roy Chiao). She is forced into marriage by him, and driven mad by his cruelty. The opera song "Lady Pan Jinlian" is symbolically used to represent her situation. Eventually, the kung fu performer and student unite to defeat the warlord, and Zhou's character realizes her love for him. Ge Lan not only sings opera songs, but plays a dual role as a modern socialite attracted to the wealthy student. Although the novel had previously been adapted in two 1950s Cantonese versions, this Mandarin production has far superior production values.

SUEN, LUN (Sun Lun) (1919–2001). Cinematographer Suen Lun, a native of Guangdong, was brought up and educated in Guangzhou; he came to Hong Kong in 1932, and began in the film industry in 1935, first briefly working at **Feng Huang** as a laborer, then in the lighting department at Jinqiu, employed on the production of *The New Generation* (1936). He continued working for various studios, in charge of lighting and special effects, including **Cai Chusheng's** *Orphan Island Paradise/Goo do tin tong/ Gudao tiantang* (1939).

Suen's debut as cinematographer was *Blood Stains the Rainbow Robe* (1948). He worked as director of photography for many studios, including **Zhonglian**, Huaqiao, Lingguang, Hualian, Shanlian, and **Xinlian**. Suen was one of the foremost cinematographers of Cantonese cinema, working with leading directors, among them **Chun Kim**, **Lee Tit**, **Lee Sun-fung**, **Ng Wui**, and **Tso Kea**. Between 1948 and 1983, Suen was responsible for shooting more than 300 movies, including classics like Ng Wui's *The Prodigal Son/Baijia zai*(1952), Lee Tit's *In the Face of Demolition/Aau lau chun hiu/Weilou chunxiao* (1953), Chun Kim's *A Mother's Tears/Tsz miu lui/Ci mu lei* (1953), Lee Sun-fung's *Cold Nights/Hon yau/Han ye* (1955), Chun Kim's ***Parents' Hearts****/Foo miu sam/ Fumu Xin* (1955), Wong Hang's Cantonese comedy *The Wall/Cheung/Qiang* (1956), Lee Tit's ***The Purple Hairpin****/Chi chaai gei/ Zichai ji* (1959), Tso Kea's *The Chair/Jinshan dashao* (1959), and *The Grand Party/Hao men ye yan* (1959). The latter, a comedy collectively written and codirected by Lee Sun-fung, Lee Tit, Ng Wui, and Luo Zhixiong, celebrated the 10th anniversary of the **South China Film Industry Workers Union** and was peopled by stars of Cantonese and Mandarin cinema. Suen's first color feature was Lee Sun-fung's *The Orphan/Yan hoi goo hung/ Renhai guhong* (1960), with **Ng Cho-fan**, **Bak Yin**, and **Bruce Lee**.

***SUMMER SNOW* (1995).** Ann Hui directed, produced, and acted in *Summer Snow (Woman, Forty)/ Nui Yan Sei Sap /Nuren sishu*, which won numerous awards at the Berlin Film Festival; swept the **Hong Kong Film Awards**, winning awards for Best Picture, Director, Actor (**Roy Chiao**), Actress (**Josephine Siao**), Supporting Actor (**Law Kar-ying**), and Screenplay (Chan Man-keung); and won best picture and actress at the second Annual **Hong Kong Film Critics Society** Awards. A comedy-drama about the effects of Alzheimer's disease on a family, *Summer Snow* celebrates an ordinary housewife (Siao) as hero. Siao's daughter-in-law juggles home, family, and work as she cares for her Alzheimer's-ridden father-in-law (Chiao). Law Karying plays the ineffectual but caring husband and son. Hui acted in the film, running a day care center for the elderly, that includes her aged husband, and she succumbs to stomach cancer, heartbreakingly leaving him behind. Hui makes the political personal and indicates Hong Kong's housing shortage and inadequacies in elder care programs, also pointing an accusatory finger at a younger generation too involved in their lives to remember they come from a culture that traditionally reveres (and cares for) its elderly.

Hui's strength is in depicting the day-to-dayness of middle-aged people's lives and their feelings and responsibilities as well as those of the elderly, alive but missing. She captures a spectrum of human nature in people's responses to problems, including a self-centered but insecure daughter and a greedy and selfish son, as well as the sheer joy of living, despite everything. As Chiao's character remarks, "Do you know what life is all about? . . . Life is all about fun."

SUN, JINSAN (1914–1962). Writer Sun Jinsan was a graduate of Qinghua University and the first Gengzi Compensation scholar to study drama at Harvard University. He taught drama and comparative literature at Nanjing Central University. Sun was invited by International Films (later **Motion Pictures and General Investment**) to join its scriptwriting committee, working with **Yao Ke** and **Stephen Soong**. Sun's single script was the Mandarin drama *Till the End of Time/Hung pan ching dang mei liu ching/Gong pin qing deng wei le qing* (1961), directed by **Evan Yang**. It starred **Jeanette Lin Cui**, **Cheung Yeung**, and **Helen Li Mei**. Sun also published *Time and Tide*, a fine literature and arts magazine.

SUN, MOON, AND STAR **(1961).** Director **Evan Yang's** *Sun, Moon, and Star/Sing sing yuet leung taai yeung/Xingxing Yueliang Taiyang* is a romantic and historical epic with song in two parts, set just prior to, during, and following the Sino–Japanese War, and based on a popular novel. **Chang Yang** stars as Xu Jianbai, a weak and favored son who falls in love with three women, each represented by the title. **You Min** plays Zhu Lan (Star), the innocent country girl who is his abandoned first love because of class differences; **Ge Lan** plays Ma Qiuming (Moon), his city cousin and the traditional Chinese woman approved by both families for marriage; and **Julie Ye Feng** plays Su Yanan (Sun), the modern woman who has survived through sheer determination. In the first film, the scion travels from the village to the city and North to further his education (or escape making a decision between two women); the first film ends as he has awakened to politics, patriotism, and commitment through Sun's influence and war breaks out. The second film takes place mostly during wartime, with star-crossed lovers against the backdrop of chaos. The film features **Liu Enjia** in clown face attempting to rally the troops. At war's end and story's end, Star is dead, Sun has lost a leg, and Moon has taken orders, so the protagonist is left to contemplate his life choices and remember the women. The strength of the story relies on the sharp characterizations of the women, their bonding, and their love for and understanding of the man.

SUN, ZHONG (Sun Chung) (1941–). Director Sun Zhong, born in Shandong province, graduated from the directing and screenwriting department of the National Arts Institute in Taiwan. He spent a year as a production intern at Taiwan Central Motion Picture Company, and worked as a continuity assistant then assistant director, then assistant to directors Li Xing and Bai Jingrui.

Sun's directorial debut was the Taiwanese comedy *Tops in Every Trade* (1969). He joined **Shaw Brothers** at the suggestion of its production manager **Yuan Qiufeng** and directed the martial arts movie *The Devil's Mirror/Fung lui moh geng/Feng lei mo jing* (1970). Over the span of 11 years, he directed close to 30 films, four of them under the name Dong Mingshan.

Early on, Sun directed satirical comedies such as *Sugar Daddies/Tiu sik ging gei/Tao se jing ji* (1973, which he also wrote). He moved on to **action** movies, such as *Big Bad Sis/Qui ming ying/Sha ming ying* (1976), starring Chen Ping. He became most well-known for his **martial arts** movies, beginning with *The Avenging Eagle (Cold Blooded Eagles)/Laang huet sap saam ying/Leng xie shi san ying* (1978), starring **Ti Lung** as a reluctant Ming-era gang member befriended by a stranger (**Alexander Fu Sheng**) he meets in the desert upon his escape. Together they fight the gang and learn a curious history that unites them in strange ways. The fights, executed with weapons, feature Ti Lung specializing with a trisectional staff and Fu Sheng with blades attached to his wrists. Ti Lung also starred in the director's *The Deadly Breaking Sword/Fung lau duen kim siu siu diy/Feng liu duan jian xiao xiao dao* (1979) and *Kung Fu Master/Gaau tau/Jiao tou* (1979).

In the 1980s, Sun made a variety of thrillers, including the horror-martial arts *Human (Skin) Lanterns/Yan pei dang lung/Ren pi deng long* (1982), starring **Lo Lieh** as an insane renowned lantern maker using the skins of female victims to make beautiful objects; the thriller *Lady in Black/Duet meng gaai yan/Duo ming jia ren* (1987), starring **Brigitte Lin** as an abused wife and **Tony Leung Ka-fai** as a nasty, sadistic and greedy husband: and the heroic bloodshed *City War/Ye daam hung sun/Yi dan hong chun* (1988), costarring Ti Lung and **Chow Yun-fat** as renegade cop partners who must go outside the law to preserve justice.

SUN MA, SZE-TSANG (Sun Ma Shizeng) (1916–1999). Actor Sun (new) Ma Sze-tsang (real name Deng Yongxiang) was born in Guangdong province, and at the age of nine was studying **Cantonese opera** and was performing professionally in his teens. His imitation of renowned Cantonese opera singer **Ma Sze-tsang** (Ma Shizeng) was so dead-on that the boy's teacher suggested he take the stage name Sun Ma Shizeng, literally meaning "the new Ma Shizeng." Sun Ma is also adept at performing Peking (Beijing) opera. Appearing since the 1930s with well-known opera groups like Juexiansheng and Dingqiankun, he also organized his own troupe, the Xinma Cantonese Opera Group. The actor is famous for his singing style, known as Xinmaqiang, "the Xinma voice." His performances, many for charity, have earned him the name "Opera King of Charity."

Sun Ma's first film was a Cantonese comedy *A Happy Marriage (The Perfect Match)/Mei moon yan yuen/Mei man yin yuan* (1936). Early on, his roles were obviously in period opera dramas utilizing his singing talents with the songs serving as the main event; later, he appeared in comedy farces. He starred in nearly 300 films. Cantonese opera film adaptations include *Xiang, the Dragon Boatman/Lung chow cheung/Long zhou Xiang* (1952) and *Paying Nocturnal Sacrifice to Qiuxi/Yau diu Chau Choi/Ye diao Quixi* (1954). Comedies include **Yang Gongliang's** "Two Fools" series, including *Two Fools in Hell/Leung soh yau dei yuk/Liang sha you di yu*, *Two Fools in Paradise/Leung soh yau tin tong/Liang sha you tian tang* (1958), *Two Fools Capture the Criminal/Leung soh kam hung gei/Liang sha qin xiong ji*, and *Two Fools Capture a Ghost/Leung soh chuk gwai gei/Liang sha zhuo gui ji* (1959), and **Wong Hok-sing's** "Mr. Wang" series, including *Mr. Wang Is in His Wife's Shoes by Mistake/Wong sin sang chue cho liu poh huai/Wang xian sheng zhao cuo lao po xie*, *Mr. Wang's Adventures with the Unruly Girl/Wong sin sang gei jing yin chi ma/Wang xian sheng ji zheng yan zhi ma*, *Mr. Wang Advertises for a Wife/Wong sin sang chiu chan/Wang xian sheng zhao qin*, and *A Stroke of Romance for Mr. Wang/Wong sin sang hang jing tiu dut wan/Wang xian sheng xing zheng tao hua yun* (1959). As one of the "two fools" (the other being **Deng Jichen**), Sun Ma delivered the vigilance and quick-wittedness to his partner's clumsiness and slowness. His usual screen persona was unemployed, exploited, and lewd. He hunts for a job in the "Two Fool" series, and in the "Mr. Wang" movies, he preys on the opposite sex. One of the actor's last film appearances was *Mr. Kwong Tung and the Robber/Gong dung sin sang yue saan dung heung ma/Guang dong xian sheng yu shan dong xiang ma* (1980).

The performer directed one film, *Lust Is the Worst Vice/Maan nyn yan wai sau/Wan e yin wei shou* (1963), for his own company, Yongxiang. He created another company to produce recordings of his Cantonese and Beijing opera songs, and he has served more than once as president of the Chinese Artists' Association of Hong Kong, an organization of Cantonese opera performers. Sun Ma was awarded an honorary degree from Oxford University in 1977 and a knighthood in 1978.

SUNN, JOSEPH (Chiu Shu-sun, Zhao Shusang) (1904–). Director Joseph Sunn was born in Guangdong province, spent his youth and was educated in the United States, and worked in Hollywood in production design and photography. In 1933, he cofounded **Grandview** with **Kwan Man-ching** in San Francisco to make the Cantonese talkie *Singing Lovers/Romance of the Songsters*, which instantly became very popular in Hong Kong, Canton, and Southeast Asia. In 1934, Sunn moved to Hong Kong, where he later established the Grandview studio there and where he directed more than 50 films spanning a 23-year career. Sunn is responsible for the San Francisco production of the first Cantonese 16mm color film, *White Powder and Neon Lights/Gam fan aau seung/Jinfen nishang* (released in Hong Kong in 1947, directed by **Wong Hok-sing**); its first 3-D movie, *A Woman's Revenge/Yunu qingchou* (1953, which Sunn codirected); and its first

Cinemascope film, *New Yu Tangchun/Xin Yu Tangchun* (1954, which Sunn directed).

Sunn's better-known films include *The Entangling Ones/Kwong fung long dip/ Kuangfeng langdie* (1946), *Great Lover/Ching hoi ying hung/Qing hai ying xiong* (1947), *Two Women after One Man/ Seung fung kau wong/Shuang feng qiu huang* (1949), *A Small Gift from Afar/Chin lee sung ngo mo/Qian li song e mao* (1950), and *A Woman's Revenge/Yunu qingchou* (1953). *A Woman's Revenge* is a detective story involving a love triangle. Two men are in love with the same woman, and when she chooses one over the other, the other murders the couple. Twenty years later, the murderer and his son both desire the daughter of the couple.

Sunn retired and moved to the United States in the late 1950s and lived in San Francisco.

SWORDPLAY FILMS. Post–World War II Hong Kong has made more than 800 Cantonese and Mandarin swordplay movies; immediately following the war, Cantonese-language films dominated for two decades, only to be superseded by Mandarin-language films in the 1960s; by the 1980s, Mandarin cinema declined.

All of these movies have relied on modern Chinese chivalric literature, drawing on the texts but refashioning them for cinema, and it is a cinematic mythology that continues to this day. Although the stories, conveyed orally and through song, can be traced back to 400 B.C.E., they entered popular culture in the late ninth century during the Tang dynasty, when heroes provided courage and justice in times of chaos. In modern times, beginning with the 1919 May Fourth Movement, writers began transferring its anti-Confucian slogans to literature, with characters opting for personal freedom over traditional, feudalistic beliefs. Novels of Wang Dulu and Huanzhu Louzhu in the 1930s and Hong Kong-based Liang Yusheng, **Louis Cha** (Jin Yong), and **Gu Long** from the 1950s on were influential. While the ***wuxia*** films of the 1950s reflected Confucian values, especially in the master–disciple relationship, by the 1960s, those values were questioned and became a source of conflict.

Swordplay movies tend toward semilegendary abilities on the part of the heroes, with lightness, running, flying, and fighting simultaneously, as swordplay retains more of a fantasy element, while **kung fu** includes more physical combat. Martial talent and noble character are the chief characteristics of the heroes and heroines of the genre. Confucian, Buddhist, and Taoist values are blended to stress altruism, loyalty, courage, generosity, and justice. Men's training is more emphasized than women's. Early representative films include Wen Yimin's *Red Heroine/Hong Xia* (1929), a 13-part silent serial from Shanghai featuring a woman warrior (***nuxia***), a maiden of the clouds who flies across the sky to rescue the innocent, and *Swordswoman of Huangjiang/Huangjiang nuxia* (1930), another 13-episode series featuring the swordswoman Fang Yuqin and her martial brother Yue Jianqiu, who roam the countryside helping those in need. *Revenge of the Great Swordsman/Daai hap fook chau gei/Daxia fuchou ji* (1949) would be remade by **Chang Cheh** as *The Blood Brothers/Chi ma/Ci ma* (1973). In the 1950s, **Wang Tianlin's** *Strange Hero/Kong woo kei hap/Jianghu qixia* (in two parts, 1956) pitted a husband and wife against evil monks of the Red Lotus Monastery.

Notable 1960s films include **Ren Pengnian's** *Three Swordswomen from Guangdong/Guangdong san nuxia* 1961), starring the director's actress-wife, **Wu Lizhu,** known in the 1920s as "the Queen of *wuxia pian*"; **King Hu's** *Come Drink with Me/Daai chui hap/Dai zui xia* (1966), starring **Cheng Pei-pei**; and Chang Cheh's *One-Armed Swordsman/Duk bei diy/Du bi dao*(1967), starring **Jimmy Wang Yu**, the former movie featuring a *nuxia* and the latter a *xia*. In the 1970s, Hu's classic *A Touch of Zen/Hap lui/Xia nu* (1971) elevated the genre to new artistic heights, while Cheh's disciple, **John Woo**, followed Cheh's *Blood Brothers* and other masculine-themed stories with ***Last Hurrah for Chivalry****/Ho hap/Hao xia* (1979). Tsui Hark reinvigorated the genre with *Zu: Warriors from the Magic Mountain/Suk san sun suk san geen hap/Zuo shan shen zuo shan jian xia* (1983), followed by the cult classic *Swordsman/Siu ngo gong wu/Xiao ao jianghu* (1990) and current *Seven Swords/Chat kim/Qi jian* (2005). *See also* MARTIAL ARTS FILMS; *SWORDSMAN* SERIES.

SWORDSMAN **SERIES (1990–1993). Tsui Hark** produced a series of three films in the early 1990s that reinvigorated the ***wuxia*** genre with fantasy, gender politics, slice-and-dice action, and surrealism. The tamest of the three was the first, with an affable swordsman who prefers drinking wine to the competitive world of the ***jiang hu***, the martial world. The success of the first, creatively and financially, led to the making of a second, which continued where the first left off, but brought in new actors to play the major roles. The third film served as an excuse to go wild with a character introduced in the second. Lots of wire work, incredible feats of palm power, and razor-slicing editing characterize the series, but the final installment goes where film has rarely ventured, and as such, remains a unique specimen of cinema, combining many motifs from **martial arts** movies of the past and the sophisticated playfulness of Tsui Hark's creative vision.

Swordsman/Siu ngo gong wu/Xiao ao jianghu (1990) is based on the **Louis Cha** (Jin Yong) novel of the same name and helped to revive the traditional *wuxia* movie. Directed by **King Hu**, Tsui Hark, **Ching Siu-tung**, Raymond Lee, Andrew Kam, and **Ann Hui**, the film chronicles the adventures of Ling Wu-chung (**Sam Hui**) and his traveling companion Kiddo (**Cecilia Yip**) as he gets involved in the quest for the Sacred Volume, a scroll stolen from the Ming Imperial Archives that promises to give whoever masters its teachings supernatural powers. Also searching for the scroll are a power-mad eunuch (Lau Shun) and his two assistants Yeung and Zhor (**Jacky Cheung** and **Yuen Wah**). As Ling searches for the scroll and runs from the villains he also learns that his own teacher, who is also Kiddo's father, master Ngok of the Wah Mountain School (Lau Siu-ming), is also out for the scroll to increase his own personal power. Assisting Ling are Ying (Cheung Man) and Blue Phoenix (Fennie Yuen) from the Sun Moon Sect. In the end, Ling and company overcome the eunuch, and Ling defeats his master and decides to retreat from the *jiang hu* with his friends.

The second installment in the series, *Swordsman 2 (Smiling Proud Warrior: Invincible Asia)/Siu ngo gong woo ji Dung Fong Bat Baai/Xiao ao jianhu zhi Dongfang Bubai* (1992) came out with an all-new cast with the exception of Fennie Yuen and Lau Shun (in a different part). One year later, Ling (**Jet Li**) and Kiddo (**Michelle Reis**) are traveling to meet up with their Wah Mountain brethren and Ying (**Rosamund Kwan**). Meanwhile, the Sun Moon sect has been taken over by Ying's power-hungry uncle Asia the Invincible (**Brigitte Lin**) who has the Sacred Scroll and has allied himself with renegade Japanese ninjas (**Waise Lee** and Chin Kar-lok) and imprisoned Master Wu (**Yam Sai-koon**), the sect's former leader and Ying's father. Ling meets Asia and finds him beautiful, not realizing that Asia is a man. (Asia is in the process of a sex change due to the secret of the scroll, and undergoes transformation from male to female.) Meanwhile, Ling, with the assistance of the loyal Zen (Lau Shun), rescues Master Wu from prison. Wu drags Ling and his brothers into the power struggle between Asia and himself while Asia's former concubine Snow (Candice Yu) is made to sleep with Ling, who thinks that she is Asia, as Asia fights with Wu and mistakenly kills Ling's brothers along with Blue Phoenix. The film ends with a climactic showdown in which Asia falls down a cliff, supposedly dead, and Ling and Kiddo retreat from the *jiang hu*. The film broke box office records across Asia and revitalized Brigitte Lin's career.

The final installment in the series is a complete diversion from the Louis Cha novel. *Swordsman 3: The East Is Red/Dong fong bu bai feng yun zai qi* (1993), directed by Ching Siu-tung, is a character study of Asia the Invincible (Brigitte Lin) taking place 23 years later. The film starts off with Koo (**Yu Rongguang**), a Ming dynasty official, and his assistant (Eddie Ko) leading a Spanish general to help recover the Dutch warship that was stolen by Asia. The general is actually only after the Sacred Scroll and turns on the officials, who are saved by the aged warden of the Sun Moon sect (Lau Shun) whom Koo rightly suspects to be Asia in disguise. Koo makes a deal with Asia, who is enraged about the fake Asia the Invincibles that have arisen since her faked death. Asia then goes on a killing spree, taking out the fake Asias until she comes across Snow (**Joey Wang**), masquerading as Asia, and feels both pity and anger. In the end, Asia battles Koo for Snow with a Japanese submarine against the Spanish ship. However, Snow dies and the film ends with only Asia surviving the carnage. Anything and everything goes, from the awesome stare and destructive power of Asia to a dwarf full sprung from a suit of samurai armor or Asia riding a giant sailfish. Unlike the first two installments, this film shifts tone frequently, plays with gender bending, and is full of comic book action. It is regarded by many today as a cult classic. *See also* SWORDPLAY FILMS.

– T –

TAI KWONG MING FILM COMPANY (Daguangming). Tai Kwong Ming was founded in 1948 by Zhang Junguang, Gu Eryi, and Gao Zhanfei; Ouyang Yuqian, Qu Baiyin, Ye Yiqun, and Shu Xiuwen came on board. All of these filmmakers had initially come to Hong Kong at the invitation of **Great China**, but formed their own independent company. They pledged to educate and mobilize people through art by reflecting people's needs and pointing them on the way to a better life, according to Gao Zhanfei. The company's first production was Ouyang Yuqian's *Wild Fire and Spring Wind/Ye huo chun feng* (1948). Its second was Gu Eryi's *Floating Family/Shuishang renja* (1949). After its fourth production, the company relocated to Shanghai, responding to a rapidly changing China. **Tao Qin** directed its fifth film, *The Peace Dove* (1951). Following its sixth production, the company became part publicly owned. Founded in Hong Kong, the company was dissolved in China in 1954, but contributed to the development of late 1940s Hong Kong film.

TAISHAN FILM COMPANY. Director **Bu Wancang** founded Taishan in 1951 as an independent company, after having worked for **Yonghua** since he arrived in Hong Kong in 1947. Taishan had financial backing from Southeast Asian entrepreneur Wang Daoming. The company was based in the Daxing studios in Diamond Hill. Besides production, Taishan created an actors' training course, and actresses like **Ge Lan** and **Zhong Qing** started there.

The company's first film was the director's *The Affairs of Diana/Nuren yu Laohu* (1951). Over four years, the company produced eight films, among them *Portrait of a Lady* (1952), Shi Hui's debut; *The Song of Spring/Chun qu* (1953); *Beauty in Disguise/Hua juan yan ying* (1953); and *Seven Sisters/Qi zimei* (1953), the debut film of Ge Lan, Zhong Qing, Li Qiang, and Liu Lianghua (the latter became director **Lo Wei's** wife). *It Blossoms Again/Zai chun hua* (1954) was Taishan's last production. Independent companies prospered in the early 1950s, but when audiences dropped in 1954, the first companies to go under were the independents.

TAM, ALAN WING-LUN (1952–). Growing up in Hong Kong, actor and singer Alan Tam became a singer in a band during secondary school and, in 1970, he won best singer at the Hong Kong Beach Festival. He began in the entertainment industry in 1974 when he formed a rock group with singer/actor **Kenny Bee** and producer/actor Anthony Chan Yau and others. They entered the All Hong Kong Singing Contest as "The Losers," won first place, and changed their name to "The Wynners." Their lyrics mixed Cantonese and English and they became extremely popular, making several teen movies, debuting with *Let's Rock/Daai ga lok/Da gu le* (1975). The band broke up in the early 1980s, with Tam and Bee pursuing solo careers as singers and actors. Tam became one of the biggest music stars during the 1980s and was famous for his **Cantopop** romantic ballads.

Tam has appeared in over 50 movies, most of them made in the 1980s–1990s, as romantic lead and often balladeer, including **Ringo Lam's** ghost story romance *Esprit D'Amour/Yam yeung cho/Yin yang cuo* (1983) and romantic comedy *The Other Side of Gentlemen/Gwan ji hiu kau/Jun zi hao qiu* (1984), costarring **Brigitte Lin**; **Jackie Chan's** Indiana Jones vehicle *Armor of God/Lung foo dai/Long xiong hu di* (1987); and **Peter Chan's** directorial debut drama *Alan and Eric: Between Hello and Goodbye/Seung shing goo si/Shuang cheng gu shi* (1991). Tam also starred in **Wong Jing's** *Casino Raiders/Chi juen miu seung/Zhi zun wu shang* (1989), which revived the gambling genre. He won a **Golden Horse Award** for his performance in the Taiwanese drama *If I Were Real/Ga yue ngo shut chan dik/Jia ru wo shi zhen de* (1981). Presently he oversees several international companies and charities.

TAM, PATRICK KA-MING (1948–). Director Patrick Tam was born in Hong Kong and is associated with the group of Hong Kong belongers (the first generation to regard Hong Kong, rather than the Mainland, as home) who became the **New Wave**. While attending Wah Yan College, Tam began writing film reviews. In 1967, he joined Hong Kong Television Broadcasts Limited (TVB) as a production assistant, became a producer in 1975, and trained further in San Francisco. His **television** work includes episodes on series such as *CID* (1976) and *Social Worker* (1977) and his own series *Seven Women* and *13* (both 1977). He left TVB in 1977.

Tam's directorial debut on-screen was *The Sword/Ming kim/Ming jian* (1980), starring **Adam Cheng**, a moody **swordplay** saga in which he modernized the feel of the ***jiang hu***, just as he would the teenage angst story *Nomad (Flaming Youth)/Lit foh ching chun/Lie huo qing chun* (1982), starring **Leslie Cheung**. Tam also explored **gender** issues in his television and film work, making him a thematic innovator as well as a stylistic one; his use of color symbolism, disjunctive editing, rich mise-en-scène, and pop songs would influence **Wong Kar-wai**, who wrote Tam's *Final Victory/Chui hau sing lei/Zui hou sheng li* (1987) on which Tam doubled as art director. Tam also worked as supervising editor on Wong's *Days of Being Wild/Ah Fei ching chuen/A Fei zhengzhuan* (1990) and coeditor on his *Ashes of Time/Dung chea sai duk/Dong xie xi du* (1994). Since 1996, Tam has worked as scriptwriter at HVD Company (Malaysia). Tam came back to teach at the Creative Media Centre, the City University of Hong Kong, and he edited **Johnnie To's** *Election* (2005). He returned to Malaysia to direct *Father and Son* (2005), after an interruption of 15 years.

TAM, ROMAN (LAW MAN) (1949–2002). Born Tam Bak-sin in Guangxi province, singer Roman Tam immigrated to Hong Kong with his family in 1962. In 1967, he formed his first band, Roman and the Four Steps, performing as a lounge singer solely in English. Tam brought a new aesthetic to musical performance with his flamboyant style, an aesthetic that continues to influence contemporary artists to this day, and paved the way for **Leslie Cheung**. After having a hit, Tam left the band to sing with **Lydia Shum**, and then broke up the alliance as she began singing in Cantonese while he still sang only in English. Facing a changing music scene, Tam traveled to Japan in 1974, where he recorded a hit **television** theme. Returning to Hong Kong in 1976, Tam signed a contract with Hong Kong Television Broadcasts Limited (TVB) to sing the themes for its series. Tam pioneered the TV theme song as pop song in Hong Kong with such memorable songs as "Under (Below) the Lion Rock" ("Si Ji Saan Ha"), which was quoted in a speech by Hong Kong Financial Secretary Anthony Leung. As Tam continued to record songs for TVB, often singing duets with **Jenny Tseng**, he also recorded songs for films, including **John Woo's** ***Last Hurrah for Chivalry*** and the Hong Kong version of **Bruce Lee's** last film, *Game of Death*. Tam was also godson to the wife of director **Chang Cheh**. In 1979, Tam became the first Asian to perform at the Royal Albert Hall.

In 1983, Tam was named one of Hong Kong's 10 Outstanding Youths; that same year he also became the first male singer to pose nude in a magazine. As Tam continued to successfully sing both theme songs for television and movies as well as release his own albums, he did some film work, including appearances in Woo's *Plain Jane to the Rescue/Baat choi Lam A Jan/Ba cai Lin Ya Zhen* (1982), **Eric Tsang's** *Trouble Couples/Hoi sam mat yue/Kai xin wu yu* (1987), and *Twilight of the Forbidden City/Chung gwok chui hau yat goh taai gaam dai yee cheung giu bit chi gam shing/Zhong guo zui hou yi ge tai jian di er zhang gao bie zi jing cheng* (1992), playing the villain in the latter.

Unlike other **Cantopop** artists, Tam branched out into other genres of music and recorded jazz-style albums, Mandarin albums, and even worked with a Russian orchestra. Tam was known for his perfect singing skills, with clear pronunciation and voice. Always a strong contributor to charity, after retiring in 1996, Tam dedicated himself to helping charitable causes by performing around the world before coming back and releasing a newly arranged collection of classics in 1998. Tam mentored actors **Ekin Cheng** and **Jordan Chan**, and pop star Joey Yung. When Tam was diagnosed with liver cancer, he continued to work for charity and help his protégée Joey Yung, despite knowing the disease was terminal. Always a gentleman, Tam faced paparazzi with grace, never using a harsh word despite his condition. Tam's impact on Chinese popular culture was so large that it is difficult to underrate him. Perhaps nothing speaks of this more eloquently than the calligraphy epitaph written for Tam by legendary author **Louis Cha** that simply read "Song In Our Hearts."

TAN, LANQING (Tam Lan-hing). Comedienne Tan Lanqing used her plumpness and exaggerated her facial expressions to make herself one of the outstanding comediennes of Cantonese movies. She was trained in **Cantonese opera**, and appeared in numerous Chinese opera movies, including *Why Not Return?/Woo bat gwai/Hu bugui* (1952) and as the plotting mother-in-law with a change of heart in

Lee Tit's ***Eternal Love****/Chat choi woo bat gwai/Qicai hu bu gui* (1966). Although in comedies she was typecast as unsympathetic mothers-in-law, calculating owners, and tough cops, she really was more of a speak-your-mind character than an evil one. In many scenarios, she was a victim of misinformation or circumstance and when she learned of her mistakes, she repented.

Tan is remembered for her performances as the servant matched with **Leung Sing-po** in ***The Romance of Jade Hall*** *(My Kingdom for a Husband)/Suen gung yim shut/Xuangong yanshi* (1957) and the overweight wife of a skinny, elderly miser in a series of "Mr. Wang" movies opposite **Sun Ma Sze-tsang**, directed by **Wong Hok-sing**, starting with *A Stroke of Romance for Mr. Wang/Wong sin sang hang jing tiu dut wan/Wang xian sheng xing zheng tao hua yun* (1959), as well as a policewoman in Wang Feng's *The Strange Hero Yi Zhimei/Guai xia Yi Zhimei* (1967). The latter blended crime, thriller, martial arts, slapstick, soft-core sex, and opera songs in a fast-paced comedy. The plot focuses on a wimpish heir who will not gain his inheritance until he avenges his father's death; he recruits two cops (one of them, the chief, played by Gao Luquan, and the other, a sergeant played by Tan) to help. In one sequence, Tan fights a bikini-clad vixen.

TANG, CHIA (Tong Kai) (1937–). The influential **martial arts** choreographer Tang Chia was born in Hong Kong, into quite a large family—his father had two wives, and each wife had 10 children. Feeling lost in a crowd of siblings, Tang set off on his own at an early age. He became a student of **Yuen Wo-Ping's** father **Simon Yuen Siu-tin**, and even moved in with the Yuen family at age 19, training daily with Wo-ping and his brothers over the next couple of years. At that time, Yuen Siu-tin was working as a stuntman and choreographer on the popular **Wong Fei-hung** film series starring **Kwan Tak-hing**. It was on the Wong Fei-hung sets that Tang Chia got his first taste of **kung fu** choreography.

In 1963, Tang Chia partnered with **Lau Kar-leung**, himself a veteran of the long-running series, on the ***wuxia*** film *South Dragon, North Phoenix*. The pair went on to co-choreograph a series of martial arts films during the 1960s. Lau specialized in empty hand techniques and kicks, and Tang was responsible for the weapon routines. Eventually both were recruited by **Shaw Brothers**.

More than anyone else, even more than auteurs like Lau and **Chang Cheh**, Tang was responsible for creating the kung fu sequences that defined the Shaw "look." Back when the Shaw Brothers movie studio was churning out dozens of titles each year through the 1970s into the early 1980s, he was the "go-to" guy for combat choreography. Tang Chia was a virtuoso of bladed weapons, often designing his own swords—he was especially fond of using a "halberd," a kind of long-handled sword. Tang's choreography was steeped in the intrigue and mystery of the world of the ***jiang hu***. In his best movies, like *The Magic Blade/Tin aai ming yuet diy/Tien ya ming yue dao Tian ya ming yue dao* (1976), *The Avenging Eagle/Laang huet sap saam ying/Leng xie shi san ying* (1978), and especially *The Deadly Breaking Sword/Fung lau duen kim siu siu diy/Feng liu duan jian xiao xiao dao* (1979), the weapons change in unexpected ways, morphing into other shapes or revealing hidden capabilities.

Tang was also adept at tailoring a weapon to the actor's skill. In *The Deadly Breaking Sword*, **Alexander Fu Sheng** uses a short knife, which he twirls and juggles in a playful manner. In the earlier film *The Avenging Eagle*, Tang had choreographed Fu Sheng with a similar weapon but completely different techniques. In *The Avenging Eagle*, his weapon consists of two short chopper-shaped blades that lock into wrist guards, in effect becoming extensions of his hands. This fact, that the blades are fixed rather than held, plays a crucial role in the final outcome of the film.

Despite his success, Tang was modest and unambitious. He had to be prodded to direct his first film. *Shaolin Prince/Siu lam chuen yan/Shaolin chuan ren* (1982) starred **Ti Lung** and **Derek Yee**, and featured a cameo by Tang himself. The film was successful, and Tang went on to direct two more films for the Shaws, but the era of dominance of the Shaw Brothers studio was coming to a close. Tang Chia was never to regain his eminence in the Hong Kong film world.

TANG, HUANG (Tong Wong, Tang Wang) (1916–1976). Director Tang Huang, a native of Shanghai, graduated from the National University of Politics in Nanjing. He joined Zhongyang Film Studio in 1939, working on newsreels and writing and producing them for a period of eight years. His directorial debut feature was *The Story of Dream-Chasing* (1947). His Hong Kong debut was *Diary* *of a Husband* (1953), for Asia Pictures. He made *Springtime in Paradise/Fung loi chun nuen/Peng lai chun nuan* (1957) for **Shaw Brothers**. In 1958, he joined **Motion Pictures and General Investment** (MP&GI Cathay), and is best remembered for ***Her Tender Heart****/Yunu siqing* (1959), the first film he made there. Adapted from Du Ning's novel, the melodrama starred **You Min**, **Wang Yin**, and **Wang Lai**. Strong direction, writing (Qin Yufu), and performances prevented the film from falling into predictability and raised it to a human and heart-breaking story, very much a film of its time.

Between 1958 and 1971, Tang directed more than 30 films, among them the Mandarin **musical** *Cinderella and Her Little Angels/Wan seung yim hau/Yun chang yan hou* (1959). Starring **Lin Dai** as an orphan and **Chen Ho** as a fashion designer, the musical uses a fashion show to benefit orphans as its raison d'etre for lots of songs and gorgeous costumes and integrated music. Chen chooses Lin for a model, the orphanage is destroyed by a storm, but the show must go on and it does as the orphanage undergoes reconstruction and the couple wed. Others films at Cathay include the comedy *Sister Long Legs* (1960), the dramatic comedy with song *June Bride/Luk yuet san leung/Liuyue xinniang* (1960, written by **Eileen Chang** and starring **Ge Lan**), and *A Resort Called Hell/Shewang yu yanwang* (1972), his last film at Cathay before it ceased operations. In 1972, he moved to Rediffusion TV (RTV), working as a **television** director and scriptwriter.

TANG, PAK-WAN (Deng Biyun, Dang Bik-wan) (1926–1991). Actress and producer Tang Pak-wan (real name Deng Shaofu), a native of Guangdong province, was born in Guangzhou and attended Pooi To Middle School in Hong Kong. She began studying **Cantonese opera** as a child, became the lead actress of Jintianhua Cantonese opera troupe by age 15, and set up her own opera group Biyuntian in 1965, performing both male and female roles and earning the name "Cantonese Opera Queen." In her early film roles, mostly operas, she played male roles. This carried over into comedies in which she sometimes impersonated males and resumed her female identity at film's end; it is also reflected in the strong, energetic, and decisive females she played, with a sharp wit and shrewdness.

Tang entered the film industry in 1950 and by 1967 had appeared in over 250 movies, including, among many others, the Cantonese comedies *A Nagging Wife Meets Her Fierce Mother-in-Law/Niuwen Xinbao e Jiagu* (1956), *An Anxious Bride/Cheung chap san leung/ Chuang zha xin niang* (1964), *Funny Girl Joins the Army/Soh daai che dong bing/Sha da jie dang bing* (1965), *Selling, Pawning and Borrowing/Maai dong che/Mai dang jie* (1967), and the Cantonese opera *The Immortal Han Xiangzi Refuses Love on a Snowy Night (An Immortal Refuses Love)/Hong Seung ji suet yau goh ching gwaan/ Han Xiangzi xueye guo qingguan* (1958). In *A Nagging Wife Meets Her Fierce Mother-in-Law*, she played the determined and strong-willed daughter-in-law who stands up to a shrewish mother-in-law.

Tang made numerous comedies with director **Wong Hok-sing**, among them *Mr. Wang's Adventures with the Unruly Girl/Wong sin sang gei jing yin chi ma/Wang xian sheng qi zheng yan zhi ma* (1959). Over the course of a year, four films featuring Mr. Wang, a Shanghai cartoon character from 20 years earlier, were resurrected. In this version, the lecherous and miserly Mr. Wang (**Sun Ma Sze-tsang**) pursues the young and fashionable "unruly girl" of the title (Tang). Tang's chic character manipulates and pokes fun at Mr. Wang, and **Tan Lanqing** as Mrs. Wang adds to the comedy, which includes songs and improvised jokes. In **Lu Yuqi's** *The Maid Who Sells Dumplings/Hiu che maai fan goh/Hao jie mai fen guo* (1965), she fired her master and opened her own grocery.

Tang was perhaps the most popular and certainly the most ubiquitous Cantonese comedy actress; she was extremely popular with **women** because of the strong women she played in humorous situations. She often played authority figures, including cops and detectives. After 1967, Tang did not appear on-screen until **Ringo Lam**'s *Esprit D'Amour/Yam yeung cho/Yin yang cuo* (1983).

Tang formed three film companies, Baobao, Baohua, and Jinbi, which produced 39 films. She turned to **television** in 1968, starting with Hong Kong Television Broadcasts Limited's (TVB) soap opera *Love the Children*, and others for **Rediffusion Television** (RTV), Commercial Television (CTV), Asia Television Limited (ATV), and Radio Television Hong Kong (RTHK), as well as a variety show for Rediffusion Television (RTV) in 1970, and in the 1980s she became a household idol with her performance of "Mother" in the long-running soap series *Seasons*.

TANG, SHUXUAN (Cecille Tong Shu-shuen) (1941–). Director Tang Shuxuan, a native of Yunnan, grew up in Hong Kong. She graduated from the University of California, remaining in the United States for a while directing commercials. Her first feature, *The Arch/Dung foo yan/Dong fu ren* (1970), was based on a folktale, played the San Francisco and Cannes film festivals, and won awards for Best Actress, Best Photography, and Best Art Direction at the ninth **Golden Horse Awards**.

The Arch, set in the Ming dynasty in southwest China, stars **Lisa Lu** as a widow from a scholarly background who works as a teacher and doctor to local villagers and supports her daughter and mother-in-law. She falls in love with a soldier (**Roy Chiao**) billeted in the village, but due to traditional custom, she cannot remarry, much less reveal her love, so she marries her daughter off to the soldier. Meantime the villagers are erecting an arch in the village in her honor. The widow chooses to support tradition, despite her independence and intellect, rather than defy it, which leads to an ambiguous read of the film. In the essay "The Significance of the Arch," in *A Comparative Study of Post-War Mandarin and Cantonese Cinema: The Films of Zhu Shilin, Chun Kim and Other Directors*, Law Kar described it as "starting a revolution, in spirit if not in practice . . . posing an uncompromising challenge to commercial cinema" because of the director's revelation of psychological states through subtle visual metaphors and juxtapositions throughout.

The director filmed *China Behind (Goodbye China)/Joi gin chung gwok/Zaijian zhongguo* (1974) in Hong Kong and Taiwan; the story follows five intellectuals escaping the Cultural Revolution in China for Hong Kong; there, the complex disillusionment they face suggests Hong Kong provides no viable alternative for them. The film was banned in Hong Kong for almost 15 years, but originally screened in France. Tang's next film, *Sup Sap Bup Dup/Sap saam bat daap/Shisan buda* (1975), is a surrealistic series of comedic sketches indicting materialism and capitalism; the title is a double entendre, referring to the sound of shuffling mahjong tiles as well as to a match in mahjong (with that hand of 13 tiles all disconnected one gets a sure win). So the title refers to the isolation and disorderly yet energetic lifestyle of Hong Kong people. Tang opened a restaurant in Los Angeles, and she remains in the United States, but she made a Chinese–American coproduction **television** drama in Beijing in 1981.

TANIGAKI, KENJI (Guk Woon Kin-chi) (1970–). Born in Nara Prefecture, Japan, stuntman and assistant action director Kenji Tanigaki joined a Japanese stunt team in the late 1980s and worked on several films before moving to Hong Kong in 1991. He is known for working closely in various capacities (stuntman, stunt double, assistant action director) with action director and actor **Donnie Yen** on several films, such as *Legend of the Wolf (War Wolf Legend)/Jin long chuen suet/Zhan lang chuan shuo* (1997), *Ballistic Kiss (Kill a Little, Dance a Little)/Saat saat yan tiu tiu mo/Sha sha ren tiao tiao wu* (1998), and *Moonlight Express/Sing yuet tung wa/Xing yue tong hua* (1998). He also appeared in **Benny Chan's** *Gen-X Cops/Dak ging san yan lui/Te jing xin ren lei* (1999) as a terrorist and was action director on **Carol Lai's** *Glass Tears/Boh lee siu lui/Bo li shao nu* (2001).

TAO, QIN (Doe Chin) (1915–1969). A native of Cixi in Zhenjiang province, director Tao Qin (real name Qin Fuji) studied Chinese literature at St. John's University in Shanghai and became a playwright, writing *Tears on the Scented Flower*. He translated film dialogue and synopses for Nanjing and Meiqi cinemas, thereby learning film structure. During wartime, he translated into Chinese the American author Helen Snow's biography *The Soong Sisters*, which was serialized in **Chen Dieyi's** monthly magazine *Wanxiang*. He was discovered by producer **Zhang Shankun**, who saw his play, and Tao joined China Film as a screenwriter, with *Sail of Kindness through the Sea of Human*.

Tao moved to Hong Kong in 1950, working first as a screenwriter and later as a director, often directing the scripts he had written. He collaborated as screenwriter on several films with director **Yue Feng**, including *An Unfaithful Woman/Dong foo sam/Dangfu xin* (1949), adapted from Leo Tolstoy's novel *Resurrection*, and *Flower Street/Dut gaai/Hua jie* (1950). His codirectorial debuts were *Aren't the Kids Lovely?* and *Night and Every Night* (both 1953). He wrote *Flower Street*, *Awful Truth* (1950), and *A Night-time Wife* (1951). His directorial debut was *Father Marries Again/Yi jia chun* (1952) for

Great Wall. In 1952, Tao moved to **Shaw Brothers** where he directed *Love with a Ghost* (1952), and then to **Motion Pictures and General Investment (MP&GI)** to direct **musicals**. Many of his films were both commercially successful and award winning, including the musical ***Our Sister Hedy****/Se chin gam/Si qianjin* (1957), the comedy *Beware of Pickpockets/Dai fong siu sau/Ti fang xiao shou* (1958), and the musical *Calendar Girl/Lung cheung fung mo/ Longxiang fengwu* (1959).

A masterful director, with 50 films, Tao remains a neglected auteur and brilliant scenarist. He worked in many genres, including **melodrama**, musicals, screwball comedies, and romantic epics. He is best remembered for his work at MP&GI (Cathay) and Shaw Brothers Studios. *Our Sister Hedy* (Cathay) is a musical melodrama of four very different sisters (*Four Sisters* is the Chinese title), the eldest being responsible for the family, the second a free-spirited, selfish fun lover, the third an inexperienced but energetic tomboy concerned for others, and the youngest a timid but naïve young woman. The movie is a story of sibling rivalries, as the daughters of a widowed father find romance and love, when they are not fighting. The film promotes sisterhood and the importance of family, no matter what. It won the Best Film Award at the fifth **Asian Film Festival** and close to a dozen **Golden Horse Awards**. *Beware of Pickpockets* brings to mind the best of screwball comedies as an amorous pair of thieves (**Chen Hou** and **Lin Cui**) turn the tables on a wealthy family. *Calendar Girl* (starring **Li Mei** and Zhang Zhongwen as two talented sisters in their father's performing musical troupe) was his first color film, assigning red, pink, white, and yellow to the characterizations. Influenced by Busby Berkley musicals and ballet, the film also includes a rendition of the popular song "Rose, Rose, I Love You" set against a white background with hundreds of red roses. It won the Best Music Award at the sixth **Asian Film Festival**.

Tao worked with **Linda Lin Dai** on several films, including *Love without End/Bat liu ching/Bu liao qing* (1961) at the peak of their collaboration and *The Blue and the Black/Laam yue hak/Lan yu hei* (1966), a romantic epic in two parts. In *Love without End*, Lin Dai's songstress not only sacrifices her body to save her lover, but dies of leukemia, denied romantic happiness. *The Blue and the Black* also starred **Kwan Shan** and Angela Yu Chien. It won the 13th **Asian**

Film Festival Best Picture, fifth Golden Horse Awards Honorable Mention for Dramatic Feature, and Best Supporting Actress for Angela Yu Chien. With *Les Belles* (1961), Tao won the Best Director at the first Taiwanese Golden Horse Awards.

Tao is one of the most important directors of the first postwar generation of Hong Kong directors. He produced highly literary works with strong characterizations. He died of stomach cancer.

TAO, SANGU (To Sam-ku, Tiu Saam-goo) (1895–1983). Actress Tao Sangu (real name Tao Ying), a native of Guangdong province, started as a **Cantonese opera** actress under the name of Yin Laoshu. She made her film debut in a family **melodrama**, *A Woman in Guangdong* (1935).

From the mid-1930s to the 1960s, Tao appeared in hundreds of movies, including **Cai Chusheng's *Ten Thousand Li Ahead*/*Chin ching maan lee/Qian cheng wan li*** (1941), **Wang Weiyi's** *Tears of the Pearl River (Dawn Must Come)Chu kong lui/Zhujiang lei* (1950), the portmanteau *Kaleidoscope/Yan hoi maan dut tung/Ren hai wan hua tong* (1950), **Chun Kim's** *Nanhai Fisherman's Song/Nam hoi yue goh/Nan hai yu ge* (1950), **Lee Tit's** *In the Face of Demolition/Aau lau chun hiu/ Weilou chunxiao* (1953), Chow Sze-luk's *Life/Yue chi yan sang/Ru ci rensheng* (1954), and **Yang Gonglian's** *The Apartment of Fourteen Families/Yat lau sap sei feng/Yi lou shi si huo* (1964). Tao was known for playing shrews and landladies, usually mean, loud, and greedy and the object of tenants' mockery; she also played matchmakers, gossips, and nouveau riche snobs. Sometimes she was the kindly landlady, like the superstitious one she played in *The Apartment of Fourteen Families*.

Tao retired from film in the early 1970s. She died in Hong Kong.

TEARS OF THE PEARL RIVER **(1950).** Director **Wang Weiyi's** *Tears of the Pearl River (Dawn Must Come)/Chu kong lui/Zhujiang lei* was heavily influenced by Shanghai's left-wing filmmaking tradition (**Cai Chusheng** was producer). With high production values, the film is a classic of Cantonese cinema at the time with a strong cast, including **Cheung Ying**, **Lee Ching**, **Wong San**, and To Sam-ku. The film portrays uneducated Guangdong villager peasants who are oppressed by a greedy landlord and made to work in the city,

Guangzhou, where they face further difficulties. A penultimate shot shows the landlord prone and bruised as the peasants' shadows fall upon him.

TELEVISION. Television came to Hong Kong in 1957, courtesy of Rediffusion cable, which showed English-language news, documentaries, and movies, mostly from British programming. By 1959, the station split into English- and Chinese-language channels. In 1963, **Motion Pictures and General Investment** (MP&GI Cathay) production manager **Robert Chung Kai-man** (Zhong Qiwen) became program director at the Chinese channel (primarily Cantonese, but also Mandarin, Hakka, and Chaozhou dialects), adding new programming, including educational programs as well as drama and film. Film director **Bu Wancang** trained new talent, including **Lisa Wang**, among many others, and Rediffusion eventually moved away from foreign imports to local programming.

By 1967, a second television station emerged, **Shaw Brother's** Hong Kong Television Broadcasts Limited (TVB), creating competition with Rediffusion. At first, TVB imported foreign black-and-white and color programs, and produced its own only live program, *Enjoy Yourself Tonight*, but by 1971 was producing more local programs, including *The Hui Brothers Show*. Beginning in March 1973, Rediffusion transformed from cable to wireless structure, changing its name to RTV, and by year's end producing all-color programming. *Enjoy Yourself Tonight* ran through the 1990s, but for close to the next three decades, TVB reigned in the ratings. TVB imported programs such as *I Love Lucy*, *Doctor Kildare*, and *I Spy*, with only three local programs, but in 1968, its dramatic series *Romance in Heaven/Mengduan Qingtian*, a contemporary drama set against the May 4th Movement won viewers over.

In 1973, Selina Leong Suk-yi became head of programming at TVB, producing popular situation comedies. In 1975, a third television station was added, Commercial Television (CTV), which fell back on Taiwan's Guang Qi station and served primarily educational purposes. A **martial arts** series, *Legend of the Condors* (released 1976), found an audience, recording some of the highest ratings of the time, moving CTV into second place behind TVB in the ratings. TVB's martial arts epic based on **Louis Cha's** *Romance of Book and*

Sword (including **Adam Cheng** in the lead) and the 100-episode soap opera *Hotel* (starring **Chow Yun-fat**), dramatizing the 1960s and 1970s Hong Kong lifestyle, were successful, followed by *A House Is Not a Home* (1977), a family drama focusing on a strong female, starring Wang and featuring Chow, which broke **ratings** records. Meantime RTV competed with **Johnny Mak's** realistic series *Ten Sensational Cases* (1975–1976), and the battle between the stations raged until CTV shut down in late 1978. RTV suffered financial problems and TVB dominated for the next 20 years.

As Hong Kong's economy flourished, Cantonese-dialect television crossed over into the film market and Hong Kong film production, rather than the separate Cantonese and Mandarin markets of the 1950s and 1960s, became singularly Cantonese (for Asian markets, later dubbed into Mandarin). Furthermore, many film actors turned to work in television. And, in the early heyday of television, film production declined due to the growing affluence of Hong Kong and the availability of television in most homes. Television also influenced the kinds of films made, such as Michael Hui's *The Hui Brothers Show* (1971), often compared to the U.S. satirical skit show *Laugh-In*, leading to the Hui feature-film satirical comedies like *Games Gamblers Play/Gwai ma seung sing/Gui ma shuang xing* (1974).

Lau Fong-kong began working in television in 1972, creating the influential docudrama *Crossroads*. (By 1975, TVB was making the similarly toned series *Wonderfun* and *Superstars*.) **Patrick Tam** directed the *CID* series, as well as others, before entering the film industry. In 1976, TVB established the HK-TVB film unit, and there, the **New Wave** directors, including Tam, **Ann Hui**, **Kirk Wong**, and others, who had trained mostly in overseas film schools, would hone their craft on series such as *CID*, *Social Workers*, and *Seventeen*, as TVB turned to video as its production mode. RTV also used the film medium, and Johnny Mak's *Ten Sensational Cases* would lead to Mak's violent gangster films such as *Long Arm of the Law/Saang gong kei bing/Sheng gang qi bing* (1984). Meantime, the government-supported Radio Television Hong Kong (RTHK) attracted multiple talent because of its supportive working conditions and produced the phenomenal docudrama series *Under (Below) the Lion Rock*, employing future film directors such as **Allen Fong**, Ann Hui, **Lawrence Lau Ah Mon**, and Wong Sum.

While television played an important part in training directors and actors since the 1970s (including those directors labeled New Wave and actors such as Chow Yun-fat), and this group filled the need for a newly emerging and more independent film industry outside the older studio system, it had the opposite effect regarding **Chinese opera** performers. Because of the impact of television, people quit attending live opera performances, opting for television programs at home. Opera's death knoll was sounded, and those trained in the opera moved into the film industry, first as extras, doubles, and stuntpeople, then becoming actors and stars. **Jackie Chan**, **Samo Hung**, **Yuen Biao**, and **Yuen Wah** are all good examples.

RTV would eventually become ATV and remain TVB's competitor. By the 1990s, Star TV, one of the largest cable and satellite TV companies in the world, appeared on the scene.

***TEN THOUSAND LI AHEAD* (1941).** *Ten Thousand Li Ahead (Boundless Future, Bright Future)/Chin ching maan lee/Qian cheng wan li*, written and directed by **Cai Chusheng** (of working-class Cantonese Shanghai origins) is set in 1940 Hong Kong and depicts Mainlanders living under hardship in exile in Hong Kong, portraying the city as coarse and unforgiving. Hong Kongers appear materialistic and indifferent to their plight as well as to the Sino–Japanese War effort on the Mainland. The protagonists (**Lee Ching**, **Yung Siu-yi**) work as dockworkers only to discover the merchandise they are loading is bound for the Japanese. The intention of the film was to instill Chinese patriotism in Hong Kongers, but its critique of Hong Kongers' materialism is as strong. The working-class heroes are characterized as willing to become "men," according to a similar line in the film, when they find themselves "at the crossroads of man and ghost." The film ends with the Mainlanders leaving Hong Kong and marching into China to fight. It also includes spellbinding documentary footage of Hong Kong shortly before the Japanese invaded. The film is an example of work made during the **"Orphan Island" period** when 1930s Shanghai filmmakers fled to Hong Kong while Shanghai was occupied (other than the international concessions) by the Japanese.

***THE 36TH CHAMBER OF SHAOLIN (Master Killer)* (1978).** One of the best pure **martial arts** movies ever made, *The 36th Chamber of*

Shaolin/Siu lum saam sap luk fong/Shaolin sa liu fan is **kung fu** director **Lau Kar-leung's** salute to the fabled origins of the *Hung Gar* fighting style. Lau traces his own martial lineage to *hung gar* founder Hung Hsi-kwan, and many of his films are based on stories from this tradition. *36th Chamber* tells the first of these stories, about the martial training and political activism of Hung Hsi-kwan's teacher, a monk named San Te (Three Virtues). The Shaolin Temple, despite its Buddhist orientation, is considered one of the birthplaces of Chinese martial arts. The monks are said to have developed a demanding physical exercise regimen in order to strengthen their bodies for long sessions of meditation. They also learned self-defense methods to defend the temple against bandits. Over the centuries, Shaolin kung fu became famous.

In the film, Lau constructs a metaphor for the disciplined practice of fighting arts by breaking down the skills required into 35 types of training, each with its own "chamber," or dedicated practice space. Novice monks work through each chamber until they have mastered the required skill. San Te, after many trials, persuades the Temple to open a 36th chamber, where he teaches lay disciples and fellow rebels, including Hung Hsi-kwan. The film starred Lau's adopted brother **Gordon Liu**, who made this his signature role. As the young monk fighting the oppressive Manchu overlords, Liu radiates moral courage and tackles each challenge with unstoppable fervor. When the film was made, it was considered commercially risky because it dispensed with the usual love story. But *The 36th Chamber of Shaolin* was a huge success for the **Shaw Brothers** studio, and it remains an international favorite to this day. Lau made a humorous semi-sequel called *Return to the 36th Chamber/Siu lum dap pang dai si/Shaolin da peng da shi* (1980), in which Liu plays a con man who manages to pick up some moves from San Te, just in time to save his village.

TI, LUNG (1946–). Actor Ti Lung (the actor's stage name, roughly translated as "ennobled dragon") was born in Guangdong and educated at Eton School in Hong Kong. He briefly worked as a tailor. He became a student of Chu Wan, a well-known Wing Chun–style **martial arts** master. His film debut was in *The Delinquent* (1968), in which he imitated **Jimmy Wang Yu** from *Chinese Boxer*. Ti auditioned for the leading role in **Chang Cheh's** *Dead End* (1969) based on his acting strengths (but did not get the part). Instead, *Return of the One-Armed Swordsman/Duk bei diy /Du bei dao* (1969) was their first collaboration and Ti's breakthrough. He became identified with the heroic male image through his collaborations with Chang Cheh, in *mo haup* (swordsman hero) movies at **Shaw Brothers** in the 1970s, many costarring **David Chiang**. Other classic examples include *The Heroic Ones (Shaolin Masters, 13 Fighters)/Sap saam taai biu/Shi san tai bao* (1970), *The Water Margin (Outlaws of the Marsh)/Shui hui chuen/ Shui hu zhuan* (1972), *Blood Brothers/Chi ma/Ci ma* (1973), and *Shaolin Temple (*aka *Death Chambers)/Siu lam chi/Shaolin si* (1976).

In *The Heroic Ones*, set during the Tang dynasty, Ti plays one of 13 Tartar warriors in a story of filial duty, loyalty, trust, and betrayal. In a bare-chested fight, Ti's warrior, Shih Chingszu, whose stomach has been sliced open, wraps his open belly with his *gi* and fights on; he dies a hero's death, standing, true to his ideals and attempting to protect his father/Lord against an army raised by his betrayer brothers; his fall, in slow motion, is noble and a heightened emotional moment in the story. In *Blood Brothers*, set during the late Qing dynasty, Ti plays a brooding and tormented mercenary warrior befriended by two bandit brothers who first attempt to rob him. Ti's character added psychological complexity to a story of loyalty, betrayal, and love; to Ti's "yin," actress Li Ching contributed the "yang" as the conflicted woman in a love triangle. Ti won a special performance award for his portrayal at the 11th **Golden Horse Awards**.

Ti appeared in more than 70 Shaw Brothers martial arts movie period pieces. His majestic presence and powerful emotionalism set him apart from others. He starred in numerous **Chor Yuen** movies at Shaw, including *The Magic Blade/Tin aai ming yuet diy/Tianya mingyue dao* (1976), *Clans of Intrigue/Choh lau heung/Chu liu xiang* (1977), *Swordsman and Enchantress/Siu sap yat long/Xiao shi yi lang* (1978), and *Ten Tigers of Kwangtung (Canton Ten Tigers, Kwongdung Pleasure War Five Rain)/Gong dung sap foo hing yik ng sui/Guang dong shi hu xing yi wu xu* (1979). *The Magic Blade* was one of many stories director Chor Yuen adapted from the novels of **Gu Long**, featuring a heroic male image in the new style of martial arts filmmaking. In *Ten Tigers of Kwangtung*, set during the Qing dynasty, Ti plays one of the "ten tigers" and a pawnshop owner who helps a Ming rebel hide from Manchu forces. A story of loyalty and revenge, the film features all styles of fighting, with and without weapons.

After Shaw Brothers closed, Ti remade himself as a character actor, starring in **John Woo's** watershed martial arts-with-automatic-weapons heroic bloodshed film ***A Better Tomorrow*** *(True Colors of a Hero)/Ying hung boon sik/Yingxiong bense* (1986). Cast as the Triad brother trying to go straight, Ti won the **Hong Kong Film Award** for Best Actor that year; the part was tailor-made for him, allowing him to bring the full resonance of his former **swordplay** persona into a contemporary story. He also starred as Judge Pao in a long running **television** series.

Playing with his previous film incarnations, Ti was cast as Wong Kei-ying, stern father of **Wong Fei-hung**, to **Jackie Chan's** Fei-hung in *Drunken Master 2/Chui kuen 2/Zui quan 2* (1994) to both comic and reverential effect, and in **Lau Kar-leung's** *Bare-footed Kid (Bare-foot Kid)/Chik geuk siu ji/Chi jiao xiao zi* (1993), a remake of Chang Cheh's *The Invincible One* (1975), Ti plays a martial arts master hiding out as a weaving mill manager. He teaches the "bare-foot kid" (**Aaron Kwok**) the kid's father's whip chain form and shows him the meaning of love, loyalty, and honor. Ti won Best Supporting Actor at the Hong Kong Film Awards for his role as a sympathetic cop in **Jacob Cheung's** *The Kid/Lau sing yue/Liu xing yu* (1999), starring **Leslie Cheung** in a remake of the 1950 **Bruce Lee** film of the same title. He served as the narrator for **Cheung Yuen-ting's** documentary *Traces of a Dragon: Jackie Chan and His Lost Family/Longde shenchu: Shiluode pin tu* (2003). Ti remains emblematic of the lone hero who follows the masculine code of honor, even to death.

TIAN, QING (1935–1993). Actor Tian Qing (real name Tian Chunsheng), a native of Henan province, was born in Shanghai and in 1949 came to Hong Kong, where he completed his secondary education. He joined International Films (predecessor of **Motion Pictures and General Investment, MP&GI**) and his film debut was **Evan Yang's** romance *Green Hills and Jade Valleys/Ching saan chui guk/Qingshan cuigu* (1956), in which Tian played **Dolly Soo Fung's** love interest.

Tian usually played supporting roles in Mandarin features and was a multifaceted character actor. Films include ***Our Sister Hedy****/Se chin gam/Si qian jin* (1957), *All in the Family/Ga yau choi si/ Jia you xishi* (1959), *Cinderella and Her Little Angels/Wan seung yim hau/ Yunchang yanhou* (1959), ***The Wild, Wild Rose****/Yau mooi gwai ji luen/Yemeigui zhi lian* (1960), and ***Sun, Moon, and Star****/Sing sing yuet leung taai yeung/Xingxing, Yueliang, Taiyang* (1961). In **Tang Huang's** *Cinderella and Her Little Angels*, for example, he supported male lead **Peter Chen Hou** as one of the employees in the tailor shop where Chen works. However, Tian played the lead in *Torrents of Spring/Chun chiu/Chun chao* (1960).

In 1964, the actor transferred to MP&GI's Cantonese division, becoming its primary actor. Some of his starring vehicles were *What Now My Love?/Gau oi san foon/Jiu ai xin huan* (1964) and *Mistaken Love/Chi chok doh ching/Zi zuo duo qing* (1966). In **Wang Tianlin's** North–South comedy *The Greatest Love Affair on Earth/Naam bak hei seung fung/Nan bei xi xiang feng* (1964), written by **Eileen Chang**, he played a Cantonese-speaking poor teacher rejected by the prejudiced guardian (**Liu Enjia**) of his lover, but the guardian softens when he learns Tian's character has a wealthy aunt. Following **Loke Wan Tho's** untimely demise and the closing of the Cantonese unit, Tian returned to making Mandarin films. In **Yuen Chau-fong's** (Yuan Qiufeng) *A Debt of Blood/Luen sai ngai lui/Luan shi er nu* (1966), starring **Roy Chiao**, set during the Japanese occupation, Tian played an underground resistance fighter pitted against a brother collaborator.

In the 1970s, the actor joined **Shaw Brothers**. He played in many **martial arts** genre movies, including Chang Cheh's *Boxer from Shantung/Ma wing ching/Ma yong zheng* (1972), *The Water Margin/ Shui hui chuen/Shui hu zhuan* (1972), and *All Men Are Brothers/ Dong kau jeung/Dang kou zhi* (197 5), and **Chor Yuen's** ***Killer Clans****/Lau sing woo dip kim/Liu xing hu die jian* (1976) and *Clans of Intrigue/Choh lau heung/Chu liu xiang* (1977). In *Killer Clans*, he played the teahouse owner who abets the hero by revealing the villain's presence. In the 1980s, he left Shaw but was active in Hong Kong and Taiwan cinema, appearing in **Yim Ho's** *The Extras/Ke lei fe/Jia li fei* (1978), **Tsui Hark's** *Shanghai Blues/Seung hoi ji yau/Shanghai zhiye* (1984) and *Peking (Beijing) Opera Blues/Diy ma* *dan/Dao ma dan* (1986), **Johnnie To's Lunar New Year's comedy** *Eighth Happiness/Bat sing bo hei/Ba xing bao xi* (1988) and martial arts *The Bare-Foot Kid/Chek geuk siu ji/Chi jiao xiao zi* (1993), and **Jackie Chan's** *Mr. Canton and Lady Rose (Miracles, Hong Kong Godfather, Canton Godfather)/Gei jik/Qi ji* (1989). In *Peking (Beijing) Opera Blues*, he played one of the revolutionary operatives; in *Eighth Happiness*, he played **Cherie Chung's** father; and, in *Mr. Canton and Lady Rose*, he was the flower seller's friend.

Tian acted in more than 150 films. He passed away in Hong Kong.

TIANYI STUDIO. Originally based in Shanghai, where it produced fantasy **martial arts** pictures, Tianyi Studio was built by Shao Zuiweng. Its *White Gold Dragon* (1933, starring **Sit Kok-sin**), the first Cantonese talkie, had been successful in Cantonese-speaking Southern China, so when the government moved to ban a genre it considered morally decadent, Tianyi studio was established in Hong Kong in 1933–1934. Tianyi led the way in local sound production early on, and exported its Shanghai-produced Mandarin films and Hong Kong-produced Cantonese films throughout Southeast Asia. In 1936, a fire destroyed Tianyi, but phoenix-like from its ashes arose Nanyang, run by **Runde Shaw**, who would later reorganize as Shaw and Sons, while Runme Shaw, with his brother **Run Run Shaw**, would start **Shaw Brothers** (Hong Kong) in 1956.

TING, KITTY HAO (Ding Hao) (1939–1967). Actress Kitty Ting Hao (real name Ding Baoyi) was a native of Guangdong province born in Macau. Her father was a senior officer in the army, and the family traveled with his assignments. Following World War II, she lived in Shanghai and came to Hong Kong in 1950, where she enrolled as a teenager in the actor training class at International Films (predecessor of **Motion Pictures and General Investment, MP&GI**) and was discovered by director **Yue Feng** and producer **Robert Chung**.

Ting's debut film was **Evan Yang's** romance *Green Hills and Jade Valleys/Ching saan chui guk/Qingshan cuigu* (1956). *Little Darling/Siu ching yan/Xiao qingren* (1958) made her a star. In the former, she played a street performer who catches the eye of a wealthy young man (**Kelly Lai Chen**); the movie portrays a younger generation making their own decisions rather than following their elders'. In the latter film, set against the lives of puppeteers and featuring puppet show scenes, including one from *Journey to the West/Xi You Ji*, the actress portrayed an orphan taken in by a puppet master (Kelly Lai Chen); a romance blossoms but the lovers have to overcome misunderstandings.

Over the next eight years, the actress made 20 Mandarin films for MP&GI, including *Between Tears and Laughter/Yuk lau saam fung/ Yulou san feng* (1960), *You Were Meant for Me/Yau fai yan gaan/You hu ren jian* (1961), and *Little Lotus/Hoh dut/He hua* (1963). She was often paired with Kelly Lai Chen as her love interest, and she was known for her performances in comedic cultural conflicts as in the North–South films *The Greatest Civil War on Earth/Naam bak who/ Nan bei he* (1961) and *The Greatest Wedding on Earth/Nam bak yut ga chan/Nan bei yijia qin* (1962), in which she played the Mandarin daughter in love with the son (Lai) of a Cantonese family, or as the country girl ostracized by city girls in *Beauty Parade/Tai yuk wong hau/ Tiyu huanghou* (1961).

In 1963, Ting married and began working in the Cantonese cinema, making 10 films, beginning with *The Murderer Is a Ghost/Gwai hung sau/Gui xiong shou* (1964). Her final film was *Four Sisters/Sei che mooi/Si jie mei* (1966). In 1966, Ting went to Los Angeles where she committed suicide at the age of 27. *See also* NORTH–SOUTH TRILOGY.

TO, JOHNNIE KEI-FUNG (1955–). Director Johnnie To began working in **television** for Hong Kong Television Broadcasts Limited (TVB) in 1973, starting as an office assistant, later promoted to production assistant and finally producer and executive producer. He began directing his first film, a **martial arts** action movie, *Enigmatic Case/Bik shui hon saan duet meng gam/Bi shui han shan duo ming jin*, in 1980; seven years later, he began another, a ghost comedy, *Happy Ghost 3/Hoi sam gwai chong gwai/Kai xin gui zhuang gui* (1986). He remained at TVB for nearly 20 years, leaving in 1990. Early on, To worked with **Chow Yun-fat** on the **Lunar New Year's comedies** *Eighth Happiness (Eight Stars Greetings)/Bat sing bo hei/Ba xing bao xi* (1988) and *The Fun, the Luck, and the Tycoon (Lucky Star Join Hands and Shine)/Gat sing gung jiu/Ji xing gong* *zhao* (1990), but also the tearjerker drama *All About Ah-Long (Ah Long's Story)/Ah Long dik goo si/A Lang de gu shi* (1989), a Chinese *Kramer vs. Kramer* (1979) combined with *The Champ* (1979). In the early 1990s, he made two female superhero fantasy movies starring three of Hong Kong's lead actresses—**Maggie Cheung**, **Anita Mui**, and **Michelle Yeoh**—*The Heroic Trio (The Three Asian Heroines)/ Dung fong saam hap/Dong fang san xia* and *The Executioners (Legend of the Modern Day Wonder Heroes)/Yin doi ho hap juen/Xian dai hao xia zhuan* (both 1993). He cast **Lau Ching-wan** in the mainstream drama *Loving You (The Tasteless Detective)/Mo mei san taam/ Wuwei shentan* (1995) as a ruthless cop and bad husband. When Lau's cop is injured in a shootout, he depends on his estranged wife, Carmen Lee, to nurse him. Director To made the movie rich in its psychologically complex characterization and details of daily life, and these features remain in his best films.

To has worked frequently with Lau Ching-wan since *Lifeline (Extremely Urgent, Ten Thousand Fire Urgent)/Sap maan feng gap/Shi wan huo ji* (1997), in films including *Expect the Unexpected (Unusually Sudden)/Fai seung dat yin/Fei chang tu ran* (1998), *A Hero Never Dies (True Heart Hero)/Chan sam ying hung/Zhen xin ying xiong* (1998), *Where a Good Man Goes/Joi gin a long/Zai jian a lang* (1999), *Running Out of Time 1* and *2 (Hidden War)/Aau chin/Anzhan* (1999, 2001), *Fat Choi Spirit/Lik goo lik goo san nin choi/Li gu li gu xin nian cai* (2002), and *My Left Eye Sees Ghosts/Ngo joh aan gin diy dao gui/Wo zuo yan jian dao gui* (2002). He values hard-working actors and also frequently casts actors **Andy Lau**, **Lam Suet**, and **Simon Yam** and actress **Ruby Wong**. Andy Lau donned a fat suit for him in *Love on a Diet/Sau geun laam liu/Shou shen nan nu* (2001) and a bodybuilder physique for *Running on Karma/Daai chek liu/Da zhi lao* (2003).

In 1996, To began **Milkyway Image Productions** with **Wai Ka-fai**. He produced Wai Ka-fai's *Too Many Ways to Be No. 1/Yat kuo chi tau dik daan sang/Yi ge zi tou de dan sheng* (1997) and movies for other directors, including **Patrick Leung's** *Beyond Hypothermia/Lip jeung 32 diy/She shi 32 du* (1996) and Patrick Yau's *The Odd One Dies/ Leung goh ji nang woot yat goh/Liang ge zhi neng huo yi ge* (1996), *The Longest Nite/Aau dut/An hua* (1998), and *Expect the Unexpected*. He also began collaborations with writer Yau Nai-hoi (*Lifeline*, *A Hero*

Never Dies, *Running Out of Time 1* and *2*, *The Mission*, *Running on Karma*). Wai Ka-fai and To have codirected films since 2000. To's first three films produced by the company, *A Hero Never Dies* (1998), *Running Out of Time* (1999), and *The Mission (Gunfire)/Cheong feng/Qiang ho* (1999), offered distinctive stylishness. The first plays out like a Sergio Leone Western as two rival hit men (Lau Ching-wan and **Leon Lai**) face off before joining forces. With the second, an elaborate game of cat and mouse ensues between a desperate dying jewel thief (Andy Lau) and a determined cop (Lau Ching-wan). The third film is a lean ensemble, thinking person's action movie with little action and lots of waiting, dependent upon strong performances and playing with conventions.

In 1999, To became chief operating officer of the local production house for China Star Entertainment, transforming the company into a formidable force in local filmmaking. Two years later he resigned, leaving on good terms but citing the distraction of administrative duties and dissatisfaction with the commercially successful comedies he had to make while there. Since he has returned to the signature of his earlier Milkyway Image movies with *Fulltime Killer/Chuen chik saai sau/Quanzhi shashou* (2001) and *PTU (Police Tactical Unit)* (2003). The former is an imaginative psychological action fantasy pitting two hit men against each other, all seen through an unreliable cop narrator; the latter's cross-cut action occurs during a single night on Hong Kong's back streets. Both demonstrate To's talent as one of the guiding lights in making stylish mainstream movies since the industry's downturn following the 1998 Asian economic crisis. *Running on Karma* was awarded Best Film at the 23rd **Hong Kong Film Awards** while To won Best Director for *PTU*.

TONG, STANLEY GWAI-LAI (1960–). Born in Hong Kong, Stanley Tong moved to Canada where he graduated from high school. Upon returning to Hong Kong, he entered the film industry (in part encouraged by his brother-in-law actor/director Lo Lieh) as a stuntman, a fact he hid from his disapproving parents. As a martial artist and stuntman, he has more than two thousand filmed stunts under his belt. When injuries made his profession apparent to his parents, Tong reconsidered and began working behind the camera. Still, he has become known for always performing the stunts in his action movies for his actors first, including those for **Jackie Chan**. Tong's credited directorial debut, the action adventure *Stone Age Warriors (Magic Territory Flying Dragon)/Moh wik fei lung/Mo yu fei long* (1991), is distinctive and memorable for its action. Shot on four locations, including New Guinea, the film involved using thousands of tribesmen from seven separate tribes (some actually feuding and fighting each other), human-eating komodo dragons, poisonous scorpions, and a precarious trip over a waterfall (Tong, in drag, actually served as a stunt double going over the falls).

With the ambition of the low-budget *Stone Age Warriors*, Tong gained the attention of Leonard Ho at **Golden Harvest**; Ho convinced Tong to direct Jackie Chan in *Police Story 3: Supercop* (known as *Supercop* in the United States)/*Ging chat goo si 3 chiu kap ging chat/Jing cha gu shi 3 chao ji jing cha* (1992). At first reluctant because of Jackie Chan's stature and well-known control over his films, Tong was promised (by Chan as well) that he would be the director and in charge. The film was Jackie Chan's first Hong Kong direct sound movie. In this film and two others, *Rumble in the Bronx (Red Indian Territory)/Hung faan kui/Hong fan qu* (1995) and *First Strike (Police Story 4: A Simple Mission)/Ging chaat goo si ji gaan daan yam mou/Jing cha gu shi zhi jian chan ren wu* (1996), Tong remade Chan by maintaining the screen persona but adding stronger female characters. He also emphasized international themes. The trio of films not only became big box office successes in Hong Kong, but also in the United States, and would serve as Jackie Chan's calling card for a U.S. film career. (*Supercop* was number one in the U.S. box office its opening weekend and finished out the year in Hong Kong as its highest grossing movie.) In *Police Story 3: Supercop*, the story shifts from Hong Kong and Mainland China to Kuala Lumpur. *Rumble in the Bronx* is set in New York City (with Vancouver standing in). *First Strike* is set in Russia and Australia.

Working with **Michelle Yeoh** on Chan's *Supercop* (Chan jumps from the city's tallest building onto a rope ladder hanging off a hovering helicopter in Kuala Lumpur matched by Yeoh's jump from a racing motorcycle onto a rapidly moving train), Tong promised Yeoh he would make an action film with her where she could play the Jackie Chan part. The resultant movie, *Project S (Supercop 2, Once a Cop)/Chiu kap gai waah/Chao ji ji hua* (1993), combines an action movie with a love story, allowing Yeoh to deliver more than a few sharp, swift kicks to the head and featuring Chan in a drag cameo; costarring **Yu Rongguang** as the love interest, the movie culminates in a torrent of water set loose in an underground bank tunnel with a drowned lover.

With *Rumble in the Bronx*, Tong paired Chan with **Anita Mui**, combining action with humor. Set in a Chinese-operated grocery store in New York's Bronx, immigrants work hard to survive against gangs and criminals. A building collapses with Mui caught in the bathroom; Chan survives a bottle attack by a gang, then takes them on in their hangout, fighting with every object at hand, only to lecture them against violence; a breathtaking climactic action scene involves Chan helming a hovercraft, chasing villains through the streets. *First Strike* features Chan (donning a child's polar bear cap), snowboarding through the mountains after villains, leaping from a mountain to a helicopter and dropping from it into a frozen lake, and swimming with a shark.

Tong came to the United States to learn Hollywood style and to contribute Hong Kong style to Hollywood. *Mr. Magoo* (1997) starred Leslie Nielsen (of the *Naked Gun* series). Tong reprised Chan's snowboard feat with Mr. Magoo on an ironing board and borrowed from **Michael Hui's** *Their Private Eyes* (1976) with a comic kitchen chicken preparation scene. Unfortunately, the Disney studio release had no merchandise tie-ins and was competing with another Disney film, *Mouse Hunt* (1997). Meanwhile, Tong pitched a **television** series detective action show to CBS, *Martial Law*, starring a Hong Kong actor (**Samo Hung**) and highlighting Hong Kong–style action and references. The series lasted two seasons.

Tong returned to Hong Kong, continuing his international themes, with *China Strike Force/Lui ting chin ging/Lei ting zhan jing* (2000), starring an international cast (**Aaron Kwok**, Norika Fujirawa, Leehom Wang, Ken Lo, Mark Dascascos, and Coolio), with English-language dialogue and impressive action. That film was followed by *The Myth/San wa/Shen hua* (2005), another Jackie Chan vehicle.

TONG, TERRY KEI-MING (1950–). Born in Hong Kong, director Terry Tong graduated from Chinese University and began working in **television** at Hong Kong Television Broadcasts Limited (TVB) and now defunct Commercial Television (CTV); in 1979 he began working at Rediffusion Television (RTV) (now Asia Television Limited [ATV], directing numerous **martial arts** miniseries. His directorial debut film was *Coolie Killer/Saai chut sai ying poon/Sha chu xi ying pan Shachu xiying pan* (1982), starring Charlie Chin in the titular role as a professional hit man who himself is marked for death when he turns down a job. The film is often cited as the precursor of the "heroic bloodshed" genre credited to **John Woo**, and there are some echoes in Woo's *The Killer/Dip huet seung hun/Die xie shuang xiong* (1989), but unlike the romanticism of *The Killer* and the charm of its hit man, Tong's film is bleak and its hit man paranoiac. Woo's story is entrenched in morality while Tong's is ambiguous regarding the nature of existence and the killer's psychology.

Tong's sophomore film *Yellow Peril/Wong who/Huang ho* (1984) explored racism against Asians and racial hatred between Chinese and Vietnamese, wrapped around an **action** film. In both *Coolie Killer* and *Yellow Peril*, Tong pushed the envelope, experimenting with subject matter and technique; he is considered to be one of Hong Kong's **New Wave**. He made a half dozen movies in the 1980s–1990s.

TONG, TIK-SANG (Tang Disheng) (1917–1959). Cantonese opera librettist, dramatist, playwright, and director Tong Tik-sang was born in Guangdong province, and graduated from Cuihengcun Memorial School in Zhongshan before entering the Shanghai Academy of Arts. After the outbreak of the Sino–Japanese War, he transferred to Hong Kong as a member of the "Juexiansheng" (literally, "Juexian voice"), so named after opera star Xue Juexian (**Sit Kok-sin**), where he arranged music and wrote plays. He studied under renowned librettist Nanhai Shisanlang, "Thirteenth Son of the South Sea." He gained public recognition with *Bird on the Sunset*, written for Baiju Rong. During the 1940s, famous libretti followed, including *The Cuckoo's Soul in March*, *Zhang Xun Slays His Concubine*, and *Gone Like a Dream*. Tong's acme was *White Poplar Red Tears*, *Lonely Moon on a Lonely Bed* (one of **Fong Yim-fan's** definitive parts), *A Buddhist Recluse for 14 Years/Huowang fangong shisi nian*, *Swallows Come Home/Yat nin yat diy yin gwai loi/Yi nian yi du yan gui lai*, *Emperor Wu and Lady Wei*, and *I Cannot Love You*.

In 1954, Tong began a collaboration with the Pak–Yam duo (**Pak Suet-sin** and **Yam Kim-fai**), the two greatest opera stars of their time, and their works are considered classics, among them *Romance of Mount Fuji (Fuji Mountain)/Foo si saan ji luen/Fushi shan zhi lian* (1954), *The Fairy in the Picture/Ung lee tin sin/Hua li tian xian* (1957), ***The Purple Hairpin***/*Chi chaai gei/Zichai ji* (1959), *The Fairy of Ninth Heaven/Gau tin yuen lui/Jiu tian xuannu* (1959), *Triennial Mourning on the Bridge/Sannin yiku erlang qiao* (1959), and *The Happy Wedding/Kwa fung shing lung/Kua feng cheng long* (1959), among many others. In Chiang Wai-kwong's mythological romance opera *The Fairy in the Picture*, Pak Suet-sin is trapped in a painting by a crazy Taoist; Yam played the scholar who releases her, and they fall in love. When the Taoist captures her again, the God of Mountains aids the scholar. Tong's libretto for *The Fairy of Ninth Heaven*, directed by **Mok Hong-si**, was adapted from a Fujianese Min opera called *A Lychee in Exchange for a Crimson Peach*, in which Yam played a painter to Pak's famous beauty.

Besides his musical career, having most of his libretti adapted for film, Tong also worked as a screenwriter and director. His screenwriting debut was *Bell of the Earth* (1939). Others include the contemporary family tragedy *Between Her Own and the Concubine's Children/Dik sue ji gaan laan wai miu/Dishu zhi jian nan wei mu* (1952) and *Mrs. Cheng* (1954). The former was adapted from one of Tong's operas, and complications include a husband who takes a mistress and has children with her, his ailing and dying wife leaving a son behind under the mistress' care, and war. Among the seven films he directed are *The Phoenix's Escape* (1948), *The Story of Dong Xiao-wan/Dung siu yuen/Dong Xiaowan* (1950), *Mysterious Murder* (1951), *A Dream of Love/Dut diy yee mung/Hua dou qi meng* (1955), and *How the Sedan Carrier Raised the Bride/Toi giu liu yeung san leung/Tai jiao lao yang xin niang* (1955). The contemporary family tragedy *Mysterious Murder*, also adapted from a Tong opera, starred Fong Yim-fan as a gardener's daughter who enters into an unconsummated marriage with the dying son of a retreating warlord. She is pregnant by her lover but marries for his sake and that of her father. Fong sang the film's theme song, "Blooming Beauty by the Silver Pond," with lyrics written by Tong. Tong also acted in Chen Pi's *Moving House* (1955).

Tong died at the peak of his career, of a heart attack during the performance of his last opera, *The Reincarnation of Plum Blossom*. He was the most important librettist and screenwriter of the Cantonese opera film, upholding high artistic traditions, influenced by Guangdong opera style, eloquent in his music and lyrics, reflecting a maturity and gravity with rigorous plotting and structure. He possessed the knack of knowing when and where characters should sing or speak their lines. Some of his libretti have been translated and published in French.

***THE TRUE STORY OF AH Q* (1958).** Directed by **Great Wall** founder **Yuen Yang-an**, *The True Story of Ah Q/A Q jing chuen/ A Q Zhengzhuan*, a satirical **melodrama**, won newcomer **Kwan Shan** the Best Actor award at the 12th Locarno Film Festival, for his sympathetic portrayal of the villager in the title role, the first international award won by a Hong Kong actor. The movie was based on Lu Xun's novel of the same title (and made to mark the 20th anniversary since his death), and adapted by **Yao Ke**, who knew the author. Zhang Shizhao, a former teacher of Mao Zedong, advised and was the film titles' calligrapher. The story follows the Wei township native with a "can-do" attitude, from the township, where he attempts to woo a widowed maid but almost drives her to suicide, to the city where he fails as well. Returning home, he is accused of being a revolutionary and executed.

Although Great Wall began the production in 1957, when the film was released, Yuen had left Great Wall and formed Sun Sun, so the film was listed as a coproduction. Sun Sun distributed.

TSANG, ERIC CHI-WAI (1953–). Born in Hong Kong, actor/director/producer Eric Tsang is the son of a famous father, professional soccer player Tsang Fai-wing. As a youth, the athletic son played soccer for Hong Kong's team at the Asian Youth Games in 1970. He began his film career as a stuntman at the suggestion of **Jackie Chan**, and became a **kung fu** actor in the 1970s. His directorial debut was with *The Challenger/Tek goon/Ti guan* (1979) and he cofounded the production company **Cinema City** with **Karl Maka** in 1981, directing and producing the first film in its landmark series, *Aces Go Places/Chui gai pak dong/Zui jia pai dang* (1982), a zany **martial**

arts spy spoof that at the time was the highest grossing Hong Kong film ever. He was uncredited director for half of the *Armor of God/ Lung hing foo dai /Long xiong hu di* (1987) shoot, during which time Jackie Chan suffered a near-fatal injury in Yugoslavia, falling from a tree onto his head and requiring brain surgery.

Throughout the 1980s, Tsang continued directing, producing, and acting for Cinema City, **Golden Harvest**, **D&B Films**, and Impact Films. In 1987, he cofounded Alan and Eric Films with **Alan Tam**, Friend Cheers in 1988, and **United Filmmakers Organization (UFO)** in 1992, each with the goal of developing **independent** and collaborative film production. His most recent venture is Star East Holdings. Tsang has been spending time on the Mainland since Hong Kong's return, interested in nurturing joint productions between the two. He has begun a performing arts school in Beijing.

Tsang has been involved in the Hong Kong film industry for close to 30 years. Short in stature with a malleable face, he has made a career foremost as a comic and as a dramatic character actor. He was awarded Best Actor at the **Hong Kong Film Awards** for his portrayal in *Alan and Eric: Between Hello and Goodbye/Seung shing goo si/Shuang cheng gu shi* (1991) and Best Supporting Actor for his sympathetic Triad figure in **Peter Chan's** *Comrades, Almost a Love Story (Honeysweet)/Tim mat mat/Tian mi mi* (1996). Tsang has produced and directed 20 films and acted in close to 170. His son, Derek, is also an actor.

TSANG, KENNETH KONG (Zeng Jiang) (1938–). Born in Guangdong province, actor Tsang Kong, brother of actress **Lin Cui**, received a degree in architecture from the University of California before he debuted in *The Feud/Tung lam diu/Tong lin niao* (1955) and became a star after *The Big Circus/Daai ma fai tuen/ Da Maxituan* (1964). His ex-wife, Lan Di, and his present wife, Jiao Jiao, are also actresses.

Tsang has appeared in over 150 films, from **Patrick Lung Gong's** youth problem *Teddy Girls/Fei lui jing chuen/Feinu zhengzhuan* (1969) to **John Woo's** ***A Better Tomorrow*** *1* and *2/Ying hung boon sik/Yingxiong bense* (1986, 1987) and **Tsui Hark's** *Peking (Beijing) Opera Blues/Diy ma dan/Dao ma dan* (1986). In recent years, he has played Hollywood villains in *The Replacement Killers* (1998) and

Anna and the King (1999). He continues to work in Hong Kong in **television** serials.

TSE, PATRICK YIN (1936–). Actor Patrick Tse Yin, known in his heyday as the "Movie Prince," was a native of Guangdong province and became one of the most popular leading men of Hong Kong Cantonese film in the 1950s–1960s, making 112 movies. His film debut was a supporting role in *Taps Off, Downstairs!/Lau hu saan shui hau/Lou xia shuan shui hou* (1954), and he became a star with *Dial 999 for Murder/999 Meng ngon/999 Ming an* (1956) alongside costar **Patsy Ka Ling**. Famous roles include the love interest for **Connie Chan Po-chi** in **Chor Yuen's** *The Black Rose/Hak muigwai/Hei mei gui* (1965). Tse would later reappear in **Jeff Lau/Corey Yuen's** *Black Rose 2 (Black Rose Befriends Golden Tulip)/Hak muigwai yi git gam laan/Hei mei gui yi jie jin lan*, a pastiche that pays homage to the earlier film, as well as the titular role in **Patrick Lung Gong's** *Story of a Discharged Prisoner/Ying hung boon sik/Ying xiong ben se* (1967), remade by **John Woo** as ***A Better Tomorrow****/Ying hung boon sik/Yingxiong bense* (1986).

Tse formed his own company, Tse Brothers, in the mid-1960s, and produced Cantonese- and Mandarin-language films, for which he directed *Madness of Love/Chak tai/Ze ti* (1972). He has also appeared in numerous popular **television** dramas. Today he is best known among younger people as the father of Nicholas Tse Ting-fung, one of the newer **Gen-X** actors, considered to be a heartthrob. Like father, like son.

TSENG, JENNY (Yan Lei) (1953–). Singer and actress Jenny Tseng made her acting debut on **television** in 1970. The next year, she released her first album. In 1972, Tseng sang the theme songs for five different films. Her first film role came in 1973 in the Taiwanese film *Life in Danger*. The next year she was cast as **Brigitte Lin**'s college friend in *Moon River/Wan Hiu/Yun He* (1974). That year she also hosted *Jenny Tseng's Hour* and a New Year special on television. In Hong Kong, she appeared in the **Shaw Brothers** film *New Shaolin Boxers/Choi Lee Bat Siu Ji/Cai Li Fo Xiao Zi* (1976) with **Alexander Fu Sheng** and in another film *Forever, My Love/Fung Yip Ching/Feng She Qing* (1976). That same year, she married Alexander Fu Sheng.

Tseng continued appearing in Shaw Brothers films like *The Chinatown Kid/Tong yan gaai siu ji/Tang ren jie xiao zi* (1977), but she is most remembered for singing theme songs for Hong Kong Television Broadcasts Limited (TVB), mostly written by **James Wong** and **Joseph Koo**, including a series of duets with **Roman Tam** for the **Louis Cha** series *Legend of the Condor Heroes*. In 1982, she was awarded "the best singer for the previous 10 years" by the Hong Kong press. In 1983, Fu Sheng was killed in a car crash, and since then Tseng has made a few films including *Flaming Brothers* (1987) with **Chow Yun-fat** and Alan Tang.

Tseng continues with her singing career to this day. She immigrated to San Francisco in the 1980s and had a daughter, Melody, in 1986. Tseng was part of the 1997 Hong Kong handover ceremony and was the female headliner for the reopening of the Hong Kong Coliseum. In 2000, she performed a sold-out concert series at the Coliseum and came back in 2004 for her "Jenny Can't Stop" tour.

TSI, LO-LIN (Zi Luolian) (1924–). Actress Tsi Lo-lin (real name Zou Jielian), a native of Guangdong province, was influenced by opera actress Zou Jieyun, also her sister. Tsi trained in Cantonese opera at 13, and played minor roles in **Ma Sze-tsang's** Tai Ping **Cantonese Opera** Troupe. Her screen debut was *The Eighth Heaven* (1940). Her first starring role was *Jealousy over the Blue Bridge* (1940). She also appeared in four opera films before the Sino–Japanese War. Tsi was forced to appear in *The Capture of Hong Kong* (1948) during the Japanese occupation. She was later kidnapped to Japan for another feature, but escaped to the Mainland where she remained until war's end.

Tsi was most often cast as a soft, quiet woman, and she shone as the tender and loving wife and mother. Between 1947 and 1964, Tsi starred and appeared in more than 110 films. They include Cantonese dramas like **Lee Tit's** *In the Face of Demolition/Aau lau chun hiu/Wei lou chun xiao* (1953) and **Chun Kim's** *The More the Merrier (We Owe It to Our Children)/Ngai lui chai/Er nu zhai* (1955), Wong Hang's drama *The Wall/Cheung/Qiang* (1956), and **Ng Wui's** Cantonese opera fantasy *The Precious Lotus Lamp/Bo lin dang/Bao lian deng* (1956). In *The More the Merrier*, Tsi played a wife who miscarries after an auto accident, but whose husband adopts a baby girl, unaware the child is the daughter of an office staff underling who cannot afford to keep her. The natural mother, however, rests easy because the child is in the arms of a loving couple.

In 1954, Tsi founded Ziluolian Film Company, which produced *Love in Malaya/Ma loi a ji luen/Ma lai ya zhi lian* (1954), in which she also starred. She was also cofounder of **Zhonglian**. After retiring in 1964, Tsi, a devout Christian, committed her time to church work.

TSO, KEA (Cho Kei, Zuo Ji) (1916–1997). From Guangdong province, director and writer Tso Kea (real name Wang Zuoji, Wong Cho-kei) graduated from the University of Guangdong with a degree in sociology. While studying he became involved in drama, which led to him forming a theater group and directing plays. He joined the film industry in 1937 and wrote his first screenplay, *The Flower Girl* (1938). He worked briefly at Qi Ming Film Company as script person, editor, and laboratory technician. In 1940, he began codirecting *Beware of the Husband* with well-known novelist Wang Yun, but production was halted when war broke out. He organized a theater group with actors Feng Feng and Ling Meng, touring Guangdong and environs during the war. After the war, he returned to Hong Kong and completed *Beware of the Husband* (1947).

Tso's directorial debut was *The Dragon Is Teased by the Beautiful Phoenix/Youfeng Xilong* (1948). He directed many hits for **Motion Pictures and General Investment** (MP&GI Cathay), including ***The Romance of Jade Hall*** *(My Kingdom for a Husband)/Suen gung yim shut/Xuangong yanshi* (1957), a romantic musical comedy with Western elements based on Ernst Lubitsch's *Love Parade* (1929), via a late 1930s stage adaptation.

During 26 years in the industry, Tso directed over 70 Cantonese features, including romance, **melodrama**, fantasy, **Chinese opera**, and comedy, regularly handling props, sets, composition, and transitions symbolically. His opera films preserve opera conventions while recognizing the potential of film, using close-ups and tracking shots, in adaptations such as *The Story of Wang Baochuan/Wong Bo Chuen/Wang Baochun* (1959). A loving mother–dissolute son theme ran through many of his films, an exception being *House of Prosperity/Gam yuk moon tong/Jin yu man tang* (1963). In *Salvation/Tsz miu sam/Ci mu xin* (1960), adapted from Henrik Ibsen's play *The Ghosts*, a wealthy father's moral decay leads his daughter to reject him in favor of her poor love and his mother. Most appreciated were his adaptations from popular fiction, including Ba Jin's *Love Trilogy (Three Stages of Love)/Oi ching saam biu kuk/Aiqing sanbuqu* (1955) and *Fire* (1956); the romantic fiction of **Mandarin Duck and Butterfly** novelist Zhang Henshui's *Many Aspects of Love/Laai ha goo miu/ Luo xia gu mue* (1961), *Somber Night/Yau sam sam/Ye shen chen* (1962), *Time Flows Like a Stream/Chiu shui lan nin/Si shui liu nian* (1962), and *The Songstresses/Chun waai sai ga/Qin huai shi gu* (1963); and Cao Yu's *House of Prosperity*. Perhaps his best-known film is the classic melodrama ***The Story between Hong Kong and Macau*** *(Beyond the Horizon)/Yat sui gaak tin aai/Yi shui ge tian ya* (1966), an intricately plotted tragic romance of coincidences in which **Miao Jinfeng** plays a woman leading a life with a checkered past who makes sacrifices and discovers strength through adversity.

Tso was also a prolific screenwriter writing under the pseudonym Ho Yu (He Yu). His interpretation of the Cantonese opera *Princess Cheung Ping (Tragedy of the Emperor's Daughter)/Dai lui dut/Dinu hua* (1959) was credited to Lung To, as Tso had been branded as leftist and his films were prohibited in Taiwan and Southeast Asia at the time. He joined Rediffusion TV in 1968 and produced *Detective Warren's Files* and other **television** series as well as heading its script unit and its actors training program, becoming the creative manager in 1981. He immigrated to Canada in the early 1980s, and there established the Film and TV Association.

TSO, WALTER TAT-WAH (Cao Dahua) (1916–). Actor Walter Tso Tat-wah, born in Guangdong province, grew up in Hong Kong and was educated at St. Peter's College. He joined the film industry in Shanghai in 1931 as an extra at Ming Yue Studio and appeared in the silent film *The Hero of Guangdong* (1931, in 13 parts). **Ren Pengnian's** *Frenzy* (1935) was his first sound film, an anti-Japanese propaganda piece.

In 1935, the actor returned to Hong Kong and joined Da Guan, appearing in **Kwan Man-ching's** comedy *Modern Bride/Lut dang san leung/Mo deng xin niang* (1935) and Zhao Shushen's war-themed *Shanghai under Fire/Seung hoi feng sin hau/Shanghai huo xian hou* (1938), among others. His first lead role was in *Journey of the Heroine* (1939). Tso's first Mandarin film was He Feiguang's contemporary romance *Gone Were the Swallows When the Willow Flowers Wilted/Lu hua fan bai yan zi fei* (1946), produced by **Great China**. With Kwan Man-ching's drama *Tears of the Returned One/Fook wan lui/Fuyuan lei* (1947), Tso returned to Cantonese cinema.

The actor founded two film companies, You Qiao (Yau Kin) and Wen Hwa, in 1947–1948; the former produced the eight-part **martial arts** series *Seven Swords and Thirteen Heroes (Thirteen Heroes with Seven Swords)/Chat kim sap saam hap/Qijian shisan xia* (1949–1967), and the latter produced *World of Fists/Quantou shijie* (1947), among others. The same year, he also began managing the You Qiao (Yau Kin) Studio (which burned in 1951), and in 1953, he began running the Palace Theater (until 1965).

Over a seven-decade career, Tso has appeared in more than 700 films, primarily **martial arts** and detective thrillers, playing the lead in almost half of them, and the sheer volume of his work earns him a place in Hong Kong **action** film history. Close to 70 of his martial arts films were **Wong Fei-hung** stories; Tso played Wong's first disciple, Leung Foon (Liang Kuan). He costarred with **Kwan Tak-hing** in Wu Pang's contemporary martial arts movie *The Brave Archer/Baak chin san gung/Baizhan shengong* (1951) and starred in Hu Peng's *Legend of the Brave Archer, 1* and *2/She diao ying xiong zhuan* (1958) in the title role. The movie was based on a **Louis Cha** (Jin Yong) novel and follows the conflict between Song patriots and Tartars. Tso also collaborated with actress **Yu So-chau** in more than 70 films, including **Yang Gongliang's** *Heroes of the Five Sacred Mountains/Ng ngok ying hung chuen/Wu yue ying xiong zhuan* (1961) and Ling Wan's *The Burning of the Red Lotus Monastery, 1* and *2/Feng shiu hung lin chi/Huo shao gong lian si* (1963). Since Kwan Man-ching's *The Mystery of the Human Head/Yan tau kei ngon/Ren tou qi an* (1955), the actor has appeared in more than 50 detective thrillers, usually as the detective, and **Lung To's** *The Kidnappers/Chan chan geng wan/Zhen zhen jing hun* (1960) is one of his strongest films in this genre.

Throughout most of the 1960s, Tso played in fantasy martial arts movies such as *Buddha's Palm/Yue loi san cheung/Ru lai shen zhang* (1964) and *The Supreme Sword/Kong woo dai yat kim/Jiang hu di yi jian* (1969). He also appeared in several **Shaw Brothers** productions, among them **Chang Cheh's** *Shaolin Rescuers/Gaai shut ying* *hung/Jie shi ying xiong* (1979) and **Lau Kar-leung's** *My Young Auntie/Cheung booi/Zhang bei* (1981), among others.

Tso turned to television in the mid-1970s, appearing in drama series such as *Male and Female King Kong*, and martial arts series such as *Legend of the Condor Heroes*, *Boxers from Canton*, *Dragon Strike*, *Dynasty*, and *Tai Chi Master*. On-screen, throughout the 1980s, he capitalized on his image, playing the police chief throughout the *Aces Go Places/Chui gai pak dong/Zui jia pai dang* (1982–1989) and *My Lucky Stars/Fook sing go chiu/Fu xing gao zhao* (1985–1996) series, as well as chief inspector in **Samo Hung's** *Millionaire's Express/Foo gwai lit che/Fu gui lie che* (1986). He also played the father in **Clifton Ko's Lunar New Year's comedy** *It's a Wonderful Life (Big Rich Family)/Daai foo ji ga/Da fu zhi jia* (1994), playing son to **Kwan Tak-hing** and father to **Raymond Wong**, **Tony Leung Ka-fai**, and **Teresa Mo**.

Tso's sister, Tso Yi-man, was a leading actress in the late 1930s, and his young daughter, Tso Man-yee, was a child actress.

TSUI, HARK (Tsui Man-kwong, Xu Wen-guang, Xu Ke) (1950–). Born in Vietnam, director-producer Tsui Hark came to Hong Kong in 1966. In 1969, he began college at Southern Methodist University in Dallas, Texas, and transferred to the University of Texas at Austin, where his father believed him to be studying medicine, although Tsui was actually studying film. He graduated in 1975. He completed an internship at New York Newsreel and shot his first documentary in New York. He returned to Hong Kong in 1977 and became a **television** director and producer for Hong Kong Television Limited (TVB), and later turned to CTV, directing a **swordplay** television series (based on novelist **Gu Long's** *Golden Dagger Romance*) that caught the attention of **Ng See-yuen**, who hired him to direct his first feature, *Butterfly Murders (Butterfly Transformation)/Dai bin/Die bian* (1979).

Even though the three films of his early efforts were not commercially successful, as Tsui had yet to understand the market, he was invited to join **Cinema City** and **Golden Harvest**, but chose to work first with the former because of its "creation by committee" working method, where they worked as a team and shared differences of opinion. He directed comedies at Cinema City and also directed *Zu: War-*

riors from the Magic Mountain (Zu Mountain: New Legend of the Zu Mountain Swordsmen)/Suk san sun suk san geen hap/Zuo shan shen zuo shan jian xia (1983), a free adaptation of Huanzhu Louzhu's classic novel, for Golden Harvest. In 1984, he formed his own company, **Film Workshop**, with partner and wife Nansun Shi.

Tsui is an important member of Hong Kong's **New Wave**. He is often referred to in the West as the "Steven Spielberg of Hong Kong," based on his commercial and artistic success. "I am looking for ways to make my audience feel. If your audience doesn't have a strong feeling about your story, you fail," he observes (personal interview, October 24, 1998). He has acted in a few films, and directed, written, and produced over 60, with his signature writ large on them. His style is constantly changing; although ravishing mise-en-scène, stately pans, and disorienting and abrupt shots usually compete, there's a mastery of editing and emphasis on strong female roles and gender issues.

Tsui has made a career of reinterpreting traditional stories with a contemporary perspective, that is, his films make political statements, from *Shanghai Blues (Shanghai Nights)/Seunghoi chi yau/Shanghai ye* (among the filmmaker's favorites, a musical romance that evokes and parodies classic Shanghai films, 1984) and *Peking (Beijing) Opera Blues (Knife, Horse, Dawn* [name of Beijing Opera character]*)/ Do ma dan/Dao ma dan* (1986), a pastiche musical-comedy-adventure and **woman's** film, to ***Swordsman*** *2*, a transgendered free reworking of **Louis Cha's** (Jin Yong) *The Condor Lovers*, and *The Lovers/Leung chuk/Liang zhu* (1994), based on the ancient tale of the Butterfly Lovers. "I went to film school because I like to express my feelings on certain issues in film," he explains. He has made numerous period pieces, contemporary urban stories, sci-fi films, and comedies. He has always been fascinated with exploiting state-of-the-art technology, as he did in importing George Lucas's Skywalker Ranch team for *Zu: Warriors from the Magic Mountain*, for its special effects, and revisited 19 years later with the spectacle *Legend of Zu/Suk san sun suk san geen hap/Zuo shan shen zuo shan jian xia* (2001), to recreate the world of the sword gods and swordsmen via computer-generated images (CGI), as well as an animated version of *A Chinese Ghost Story: The Tsui Hark Animation* (1997) and the first reunified Chinese film to use live action and a computer-generated lead in *Master Q 2001/Low foo ji 2001/Lao fu zi 2001* (producer, 2001).

Tsui is well known for the ***Once upon a Time in China* series**, four of which he directed and all of which he produced, based on Chinese hero and folk legend **Wong Fei-hung**. The series possesses the trademarks of much of his work, with an exploration of an East–West dialectic, an anti-imperialist message, and a critique of narrow nationalism and a provincial Chinese attitude toward not accepting things foreign. The series presents a changing China coming into the modern world, as relevant to contemporary Hong Kong coping with change as to the Mainland. Tsui has also made forays into Hollywood, directing Jean-Claude Van Damme in *Double Team* and *Knock Off*. His latest endeavor, *Seven Swords/Chat kim/Qi jian* (2005), reinvents martial arts movies once again, with a realist take on action and more characterization. Set in the 17th century with the Manchus in power, the story, based on writings by Liang Yusheng, promotes unity and character sacrifice. This ***wuxia pian*** debuted at the 62nd Venice International Film Festival, and Tsui hopes this is the first in a new series.

TU, GUANGQI (1914–1980). A native of Zhejiang province, director Tu Guangqi graduated from Wenjiang University in Haungzhou. He began acting in 1939 and directing in 1941.

Tu immigrated to Hong Kong in 1951. He directed numerous films, including *The Moon Blanch'd Land/Yuet ngai waan waan chiu gau chow/Yue er wan wan zhao jiu zhou* (1952), *The First Sword* (1967), and *Crush* (1972). He directed more than 50 films and wrote more than 25 scripts. *A Songstress Called Hong Lingyan/Goh lu hung ling yim/Ge nu gong ling yan* (1953) starred **Bao Fang** and **Bai Guang** as did *New West Chamber/San sai seung gei/Xin xi xiang ji* (1953). *Little Phoenix (General Chai and Lady Balsam)/Siu fung sin/Xiao fengxian* (1953) as well as *Qiu Jiu, the Revolutionary Heroine/Chau Gan/Qiu Jin* (1953), both starring **Li Lihua**, were based on real-life figures and celebrated revolutionary acts. In *Little Phoenix*, set during the Republican revolution era, Li Lihua set fashion trends with her "little phoenix" dress and starred as courtesan Lady Balsam, who helps a general and former governor (**Yan Jun**) thwart evil forces.

Tu retired from the film industry in 1973 and began writing **martial arts** novels. He died in Los Angeles.

TWINS, THE (Choi, Charlene Cheuk-yin [1982–] and Chung, Gillian Yan-tung [1981–]). With the release of their first EP album in August 2001, Emperor Entertainment Group's (EEG) pop packaging sensation known as the Twins has taken the Hong Kong entertainment industry by storm. The Twins relied on the cuteness factor, along with colorful packaging and a sweet nonthreatening pop sound, to succeed in the youth market. Called Ah Sa (Choi) and Ah Gil (Chung) by their fans, the duo stage elaborate stage shows with myriad costumes and perform in an infectious style. Inevitably, the Twins have branched out and now are all over the Asian map, whether starring in films or modeling for advertisements.

As actresses, the duo have worked together in some EEG-backed projects such as the *Twins Effect/Chin gei bin/Qian ji bian* (2003) and its sequel, as well as *Protégé de La Rose Noir/Gin chap hak mooi gwai/Jian xi hei mei gui* (2004) and also ventured out on their own, although these films also usually have EEG ties. Choi is the more prolific of the two, and often acts in comedic parts. She made her debut as a student in the **Francis Ng**–directed comedy *What Is a Good Teacher?/Chi chung sze loi liu/Zi cong ta lai le* (2000), and went on to play a role in the independent *Heroes in Love/Luen oi hei yee/Lian ai qi yi* (2001), a unique film made up of three shorts on love, one of which was directed by **Nicholas Tse** and **Steven Fung**. She played opposite the older **Ekin Cheng** in *My Wife Is Eighteen/Ngo liu poh lut gau ching/Wo lao po wu gou cheng* (2002), and was paired with the much older **Sean Lau** in *Good Times, Bed Times/Luen seung lei dik cheng/Lian shang ni de chuang* (2003). Choi also played an aspiring **Cantopop** queen in *Diva—Ah Hey* (2003), a film that mildly skewers the Hong Kong entertainment industry, alongside **Jordan Chan**. In 2004, Choi appeared in 10 films, including the retro-themed *Fantasia/Gwai ma kwong seung kuk/Gui ma kuang xiang qu* (2004).

Chung made her cinematic debut in *U-Man/Gwaai sau hok yuen/Guai shou xiao yuan* (2002) alongside **Anthony Wong**. Since then, she has worked with Choi in such films as Riley Yip's *Just One Look/Yat luk che/Yi lu zhe* (2002). Chung has also starred alone in such films as *Happy Go Lucky/Dai yat dim dik tin hung/Di yi dian de tian kong* (2003) with **Kent Cheng**, **Wong Jing's** *The Spy Dad/Chuet chung tit gam gong/Jue zhong tie jin gang* (2003) alongside

Tony Leung Kar-fai, and *House of Fury/Cheng miu ga ting/Jing wu gu ting* (2005), again with Anthony Wong. The Twins have legions of fans and have captured the Hong Kong youth market. With each passing year, both Choi and Chung have worked in more and more films in addition to their burgeoning singing careers; with the powerful backing of EEG it does not appear that they will be going away anytime soon.

– U –

UNITED FILMMAKERS ORGANIZATION (UFO) LTD. In 1990, directors **Eric Tsang**, **Peter Chan**, **Jacob Cheung**, and **Lee Chi-ngai** (Chi Lee), and Claudie Cheung cofounded United Filmmakers Organization; writer/director James Yuen later came on board. They had a dual purpose of making movies outside the **action** genre and filling in the gap between very commercial and extremely noncommercial films, producing high quality but commercial films. The company's first production was Blacky Ko Sau-leung's comedy *Days of Being Dumb/Ya Fei yu Ya Ji* (1992), a send-up of **Wong Kar-wai's** *Days of Being Wild (The True Story of Ah Fei)/ Ah Fei ching chuen/A Fei zhengzhuan* (1990), starring **Leung Chiu-wai** and **Jacky Cheung**, two of the latter's cast. Its critical and commercial successes include Lee and Chan's *Tom, Dick and Hairy (Three World-Weary Heroes)/Feng chen san xia*, Chan's ***He's a Woman, She's a Man*** *(Golden Branch, Jade Leaf)/Jin qi yu ye* (1994), Cheung's *Whatever Will Be, Will Be/Xian he piao piao* (1995), and Chan's *Comrades, Almost a Love Story (Honeysweet)/Tian mi mi* (1996).

In 1996, UFO, in need of a major studio, merged with **Golden Harvest**. The group has always functioned in a collaborative spirit, encouraging creative freedom, nurturing first-time directors, and sharing credits for writing and directing.

URBANITY IN FILM. In the 1950s, director **Zhu Shilin** began making films set specifically in Hong Kong and addressing everyday problems that audiences recognized, such as in the comedy *Spoiling the Wedding Day* (1951). Zhu and **Lee Tit's** melodrama *Everlasting Love (**Eternal Love**)* (1955) was one of the first films to come to terms with a changing Hong Kong and its growing, affluent, and self-absorbed middle class. The story set up a dialectic between new Western and traditional Chinese values, and the protagonist's nostalgia for a changing world.

Hong Kong, as colony and now as the Special Administrative Region (SAR) since its return to the Mainland, has always been a place of shifting sands, and a local vernacular of Qing dynasty influences and British colonial–style architecture exist side by side as well as being continually displaced by postmodern commercial buildings, office towers, and 20- to 34-story apartment high rises. During the spring of 1997, more than 10 reclamation projects (using landfill material to expand the islands) were underway. Ackbar Abbas, in his *Hong Kong: Culture and the Politics of Disappearance* (1997), has described the phenomenon as "déjà disparu" (already seen, already gone) and notes "the cultural self-invention of the Hong Kong subject in a cultural space of disappearance." **Lee Chi-ngai's** appropriately titled *Lost and Found/Tin aai hoi gok/Tian ya hai jiao* (1996), for example, open and closes with black-and-white vignettes of ordinary people on Hong Kong streets, set to the seductive lament of Leonard Cohen.

Contemporary filmmakers continue to be inspired by this crowded, bustling, open-24-hours-a-day city, where rich and poor rub shoulders; they have responded to place in a variety of ways, some nostalgic for the past and communities and relationships lost, as in **John Woo's** *A Better Tomorrow* (1986) and *The Killer* (1989), **Jacob Cheung's** *Cageman* (1992), and **Ann Hui's** ***Summer Snow*** (1995), some expressing the dialectic through characterization, as in **Peter Chan's** *Comrades, Almost a Love Story* (1996) and **Cheung Yuen-ting** and **Alex Law's** *Now You See Love . . . Now You Don't/Ngoh oi Nau Man-chai (lau man yue do bing)/Wo ai Niu Wenchai (liu mang yu dao bing)* (1992). The latter's aptly titled *City of Glass* (1998) combines all the approaches, with the love stories of two generations. Often locales are specifically identified, to capture them on-screen before they disappear, as in **Wong Kar-wai's** *Chungking Express*. In numerous gangster films, as chases are underway, streets are named and a territory mapped on celluloid, from **Ringo Lam's** *Expect the Unexpected* (1998), to the Triad-boyz series *Young and Dangerous* (1996–2000). **Fruit Chan's** *Made in Hong Kong* (1997) explored the underbelly of

Hong Kong's neon skyline by following disenfranchised and alienated youth.

– V –

VAMPIRE MOVIES. The earliest vampire movie made in Hong Kong was Yeung Kung-leung's *Midnight Vampire* (1936), and half a dozen films followed sporadically through the 1970s. But the vampire became a popular Hong Kong movie staple from the mid-1980s to the early 1990s, with 24 films made between 1986 and 1990. **Samo Hung's** *Encounters of the Spooky Kind (Ghost Strikes Ghost)/Gwai chuk gwai/Gui da gui* (1980) and *The Dead and the Deadly/Yan haak yan/Ren he ren* (1982) previewed the resurgence. The seminal contribution is Ricky Lau's (Liu Guanwei) *Mr. Vampire (Mr. Stiff Corpse)/Geung shi sin sang/ Jiangshi xiansheng* (1985, produced by Hung's **Bo Ho Films** and stereotyping **Lam Ching-ying** as the Taoist priest fighting vampires). Premised on the custom of corpse driving, whereby a Taoist priest transports the deceased to safe burial grounds, the story draws from Qing dynasty literature about cadavers turning into vampires when they take in the breath or *qi* of a living being. The comic film spawned four sequels and multiple copycats.

Chinese vampires derive from ghost stories based on the traditional Chinese view that the human soul is divided into two parts; upon death, one part (*shen*) enters heaven, joining spiritual beings, while the other part descends to earth. If troubled, this part appears as an erratic, often pernicious ghost (*kuei*). Vampires (literally *gyonsi/ jiangshi*, a "hardened body") result from disrespect in a culture with strong traditions of honoring the dead. Under such circumstances, the soul (*po*) remains inside the body, reanimating it as it sets out for nourishment to survive. Chinese vampires move by hopping on two legs with their arms stretched out in front of them, like mummified kangaroos. Blind, they only detect humans by their breathing. Rather than blood sucking, they suck the life spirit out of their victims and use long sharp nails to rip flesh apart. Taoist talismans mixed with **kung fu** are used to stop them.

Related films include **Tsui Hark's** early *We're Going to Eat You/Dei yuk miu moon/Di yu wu men* (1980) and Samo Hung's aforementioned comedy. A recent vampire revival has occurred with films incorporating hyperkinetic fights and editing, like *The Era of Vampires* (aka *Tsui Hark's Vampire Hunters*, 2002), produced by Tsui Hark, and *The Twins Effect/Chin gei bin/Qian ji bian* (2003), with action direction by **Donnie Yen**.

– W –

WADER FILM STUDIO. Founded in 1953 by Hu Jinkang, Wader was taken over by Singapore's Kwong Ngai Organization upon Hu's demise, and Xu Lizhai became manager. Wader occupied three sound stages on 80,000 square feet at Tsuen Wan. The studio's first production was **Tso Kea's** *Far Away/Shanchang shuiyuan* (1954). Over 20 years the studio produced 1,200 movies, in Cantonese, Mandarin, and Chaozhou dialects, one-fifth of Hong Kong's total production for the period. In the 1970s, as more movies were shooting on location, the studio declined, closing in 1973. A factory currently occupies its site.

WAI, KA-FAI (1962–). Born in Hong Kong, writer-director-producer Wai Ka-fai joined Hong Kong Television Broadcasts Limited's (TVB) scriptwriting course in 1981 and wrote numerous **television** dramas. He began producing them in 1988. His directorial debut was with *Peace Hotel/ Wing ping fan dim/Han ping fan dian* (1995), starring **Chow Yun-fat**, produced by **John Woo**. Set in the 1920s in an isolated way station established by a reformed killer, the film is visually rich and stylish, with arty camerawork **Wong Kar-wai**–style, a combination spaghetti Western and allegory. The killer (Chow) promises sanctuary to all seeking refuge from violence, and his principles are tested when a woman (**Cecilia Yip**) arrives, running from a big gang whose boss she has killed. She lies and is disliked by the residents, and the killer must choose whether to sacrifice her for the good of the group, or remain loyal to his principles. Here, as in future stories by the screenwriter, loyalty and redemption provide major themes.

With director **Johnnie To**, Wai created **Milkyway Image Production Company** in 1996. The company produced Wai's *Too Many Ways to Be No. 1 (The Birth of a Letterhead)/Yat kuo chi tau dik daan* *sang/Yi ge zi tou de dan sheng* (1997) and movies for other directors, including **Patrick Leung's** *Beyond Hypothermia (32 Degrees Celsius)/Sip si 32 doe/She shi 32 du* (1996) and **Patrick Yau's** *The Odd One Dies/Leung goh ji nang woot yat goh/Liang ge zhi neng huo yi ge* (also written by Wai, 1996), *The Longest Night/Aau dut/An hua* (1998), and *Expect the Unexpected (Unusually Sudden)/Fai seung dat yin/Fei chang tu ran* (1998). They were all dark and distinctive films that challenged the mainstream by being more experimental and edgy. A black comedy, Wai's gangster film parody *Too Many Ways to Be No. 1* has two members of an incompetent gang (**Lau Ching-wan** and **Francis Ng**) somehow muddle through, despite the gang boss being killed in the opening minutes of the story (the fleeing gang runs over him with a stolen car, at least in one version). One fight is shot upside down, another in total darkness. The aggressive and inventive camerawork throughout stands in as a perpetrator of crimes, following the gang members relentlessly, creatively, and destructively. With 1997 on the horizon, the early Milkyway productions reflected the uncertain atmosphere of the times and the films were not as commercially successful as some others, but earned the company recognition for its stylish and original productions.

Wai Ka-fai and To have codirected films since 2000, from the commercially successful drama *Needing You/Goo lam gwai lui/Gu nan gua nu* (2000) to mainstream comedies like *Love on a Diet/Sau geun laam liu/Shou shen nan nu* (2001) and *Fat Choi Spirit/Lik goo lik goo san nin choi/Li gu li gu xin nian cai* (2002), romance with *Turn Left, Turn Right/Heung joh chow, heung yau chow/Xiang zuo zou, xiang you zou* (2003), and drama with *Running on Karma/Daai chek liu/Da zhi lao* (2003). Their collaboration *Fulltime Killer/Chuen chik saai sau/Quanzhi shashou* (2001) stars **Andy Lau** as a competitive hit man who yearns to overthrow the reigning number one (Takashi Soramachi); the plotline, however, is deceptive. Viewers discover the story is being told from the point of view of an unreliable cop (**Simon Yam**), and there are numerous flashbacks and various tellings of the story, allowing the filmmakers to play with conventions and genre and nuance mood, atmosphere, and character. Lau's popularity contributed to the movie's commercial success, although it is similar in tone to the early Milkyway productions.

For *Fantasia/Gwai ma kwong seung kuk/Gui ma kuang xiang qu* (2004), Wai directed, produced, and wrote. Homage to and generous parody of the broad-based Cantonese comedies of the 1970s and 1980s (such as those produced by the **Hui Brothers**) and a pastiche of popular culture, from **Bruce Lee** to Harry Potter, the film stars **Cecilia Cheung**, Lau Ching-wan, Louis Koo, Francis Ng, and the **Twins**, each sending up their on-screen personae.

WAN BROTHERS (WAN CHAOCHEN [1906–1992], WAN DIHUAN [1907–], WAN GUCHAN [1899–1995], WAN LAIMING [1899-1997]). All the Wan brothers worked as set designers for live action films, and were painters and followers of Chinese shadow puppet theater. Art directors and animators Wan Guchan and Wan Laiming were twin brothers and natives of Nanjing who studied Western painting and graduated from Shanghai Art College. Both began as set designers but were especially interested in animation. All the brothers began developing **animation** after seeing some American cartoons in a Shanghai theater in 1923; they joined **Great Wall** (Shanghai) in 1926. The twins' first silent animation, a cartoon, *Disturbing the Studio* (1926), was the first made in China and it used live action actors and animation to show a figure in a canvas come to life, disturbing a painter's studio. During the early 1930s, Wan Dihuan left the group to become a photographer, and the remaining brothers worked for **Mingxing** (Star) and **Lianhua** studios during the 1930s, making anti-Japanese animated shorts, such as *The Price of Blood* (1932), inspired by a Japanese attack on Shanghai. For Yuan Muzhi's *Scenes of City Life* (1935), they contributed the musical sequence animation. During the war, they created animations for the songs in *Popular Chinese War Songs*.

The twins' first animated feature, *Princess Iron Fan/Tit sin gung chu/Tieshan Gongzhu* (1941), was the first Chinese and Asian animated film. Younger brother Wan Chaochen worked on the human models but was not credited. Both clay and human models were used to trace action and movement, resulting in a unique style, and the quality of the animation was recognized as the best worldwide at the time. The brothers took their story, of the Monkey King defeating the Ox King, from the classic and popular *Journey to the West*, but were also inspired by animators Walt Disney and Max Fleischer. The controversial aspect of the film, made in Shanghai, was that United China Motion Picture Corporation, sponsored by the Japanese, produced it, although the film's hidden allegory contains an anti-Japanese statement.

Wan Chaochen immigrated to the United States in 1946 to study animation techniques and returned to Shanghai in the mid-1950s. The Wan twins came to Hong Kong following the war and worked as art directors for Great Wall; they returned to Shanghai in 1955 to join the animation group built by caricaturist Te Wei (1915–) and painter Jin Shi (1919–1997); the group shortly became the Shanghai Animation Studio, employing 200 workers. Wan Gushan and his artists spent a year developing a paper-cut animation technique based on the traditional folk art of paper-cutting; he made several animations using the technique, including *Zhu Baijie (Piggy) Eats the Watermelon* (1958), *The Fisherboy* (1959), and *The Spirit of Ginseng* (1960). The latter told the tale of a small boy who defeats a landlord with the spirit of the ginseng plant. *Havoc in Heaven, Parts 1* and *2* (1961, 1964) is the epitome of Shanghai's golden age of animation. Also based on *Journey to the West* (chapters 3, 4, and 5), the cel animation visualized the popular story of the Monkey King battling a series of heavenly hosts. The well-loved animation served as an allegory of Mao Zedong as heroic rebel for the Chinese and also won international acclaim at the Locarno (Italy) Film Festival in 1965.

WANG, HAO (Wong Ho) (1917–1991). Mandarin dramatic actor Wang Hao (real name Wang Zhongkang), a native of Tianjin, made his film debut at 18 in *The Wedding Night* (1936). He alternated between stage and screen, in theater in Chongqing in 1943, and onscreen for China Film Studio in *Tremendous Momentum* (1944).

Following the war, the actor came to Hong Kong, appearing in a dozen films for **Great China Film**, including **Yue Feng's** Mandarin drama *Three Women/Saam lui sing/San nuxing* (1947) and **Fang Peilin's** Mandarin **musical** *Song of a Songstress/Goh lui ji goh/Ge nu zhi ge* (1948), and for other studios in *Blood for Justice* (1948) and **Hong Shuyun's** drama *Escape from the Tiger's Jaws/Foo hau yue sang/Hu kou yu sheng* (1951). In *Song of a Songstress*, Wang costarred with **Zhou Xuan** as the heartless playboy who not only exposes the doomed songstress's past, but ruins her future.

Wang acted in more than 30 films between 1955 and 1963 for Dianmao (forerunner of **Motion Pictures and General Investment, MP&GI**) and **Asia Film Company**, including **Tang Huang's** drama *Tradition/Chuen tung/Chuantong* (1955), **Wang Yin's action** movie *Time Is Running Short/Dip huet faan ma cheung/Die xie fan ma chang* (1960), and the thriller *Four Brave Ones/Dip hoi sei chong si/Die hai si zhuang shi* (1963). In *Tradition*, Wang starred as the leader of a revolutionary troop fighting the invading Japanese whose mistress betrays him.

In 1952, Wang founded Haiyan Film Company, directing many of its productions, among them the Mandarin musical family **melodrama** *Love Song/Luen goh/Lian ge* (1953). Wang played a musician whose marriage to **Chen Yanyan** is disturbed by the appearance of an old schoolmate (Lan Yingying) for whom he seems to have feelings. The movie was Haiyan's inaugural production. Wang's collaboration with **Huaqiao** Company (Taiwan) led to the anticommunist movie *14,000 Witnesses* (1962). He also acted in **Shaw Brothers** movies such as **Yang Gongliang's** drama *Good Faith* (1952) and **Tao Qin's** romantic epic drama *The Blue and the Black, Parts 1* and *2/ Laam yue hak/Lan yu hei* (1966). The latter, based on a popular novel by Wang Lan, was a big budget Shaw production, set in Tianjin during the Sino–Japanese War.

Wang's last film was *Prosperity Ahead/Chin ching chi gam/Qian cheng si jin* (1966), in which he acted and directed. Although he had established an acting school in the early 1960s, it did not succeed, and Wang entered the construction industry in Taiwan, occasionally returning to film, such as directing *Misgivings* (1969). Wang was once married to actress **Chen Yanyan**. Wang Tianli, a singer, is his daughter.

WANG, JIMMY YU (1943–). A former swimming champ during his school days in Shanghai, Wang Yu originally came to Hong Kong to attend college. His athletic prowess, however, led him to the newly expanded **Shaw Brothers** studio, where he won a leading role in the drama *Tiger Boy/Foo hap chin chau/Hu xia jian chou* (1966). While working at the studio, he trained in **martial arts** and displayed an aptitude for stunt work, which led to an impressive showing in the ***wuxia*** film *Temple of the Red Lotus/Kong woo kei hap/Jianghu qi xia*

(1965). But it was Wong's performance in the **Chang Cheh**–directed *One-Armed Swordsman/Duk bei diy/Du bidao* (1967) that resulted in the film breaking box office records in Hong Kong, and he was to become the top grossing martial arts star of the late 1960s, until the arrival of **Bruce Lee** changed the popular taste.

Chang Cheh had set himself the goal of "masculinizing" the *wuxia* genre as it had evolved through the early 1960s, with **women** frequently playing the male roles. Wang Yu embodied Chang's hypermasculine ideal of *yanggang* (staunch masculinity), as seen in the stoic hero who suffers without complaint. In films like *Golden Swallow/Gam yin ji/Jin yan zi* (1968) and *Return of the One-Armed Swordsman/Duk bei diy wong/Du bidao wang* (1969), Wang fought his enemies with ferocity and something like contempt, daring them to hack him into pieces before he can finish them off.

Wang prevailed on the Shaw studio to let him direct the feature *The Chinese Boxer/Lung foo moon/Long hu men* (1970), which has been hailed as the prototype of the modern **kung fu** movie with its attention to the training regimen and strategy of martial practice. He broke with Shaw Brothers the next year and relocated to Taiwan, where he continued to act and direct in both independent productions and under the aegis of the **Golden Harvest** studio. His most successful films were the *One-Armed Boxer/Duk bei kuen wong/Du bei quan wang* series (1971–1975), which pitted his trademarked disabled fighter against a wide variety of one-on-one opponents.

Wang Yu's private life has been dogged by legal and personal woes, but he remains a highly respected pioneer of the kung fu movie genre, having appeared in close to 75 films.

WANG, JOEY TSU-HSIEN (Wong Jo-Yin) (1967–). Born in Taiwan, singer and actress Joey Wang first garnered attention when she appeared in a **television** commercial for athletic shoes. After starring in a Taiwanese film, she was invited to Hong Kong by Mona Fong to star in *An Eternal Combat/Tian di xuan men* (1984). The next year, she appeared in the comedy *Let's Make Laugh 2/Joi gin chat yat ching/Zai jian qi ri qing* (1985) alongside **Derek Yee**, and the **Tsui Hark** comedy *Working Class (King of the Working Stiffs)/Da gung wong dai/Da gong huang di* (1985) with **Sam Hui**. She worked with **Chow Yun-fat** and **Andy Lau** in *A Hearty Response (Chivalry Over-*

shadows Clouds and Sky)/Yee gor wan tin/Yi gai yun tian (1986) and starred in the groundbreaking Tsui Hark–produced *A Chinese Ghost Story/Sin nui yau wan//Qiannu youhun* (1987). Starting in the late 1980s, Wang also gained a great deal of popularity in Japan and even starred in a Japanese TV series. Besides continuing to be cast alongside Chow Yun-fat in comedies such as *Fractured Follies (Love of Long and Short Legs)/Cheung duen geuk ji luen/Chang duan jiao zhi* and *Diary of a Big Man (Big Husband's Diary)/Daai jeung foo yat gei/Da zhang fu ri zi* (both 1988), Wang also appeared in the **Wong Jing** blockbuster *God of Gamblers/Do San/Du Shen* (1989) as Andy Lau's love interest and in *A Chinese Ghost Story 2/Ren jian dao Sin nui yau wan 2/Qiannu youhun 2* (1990).

In the early 1990s, Wang's popularity peaked. She appeared in *A Chinese Ghost Story 3/Sin nui yau wan 3: do do do/ Qian lui you hun 3: dao dao dao* (1991) and **Ching Siu-tung's** manic masterpiece *Swordsman 3: The East Is Red (Invincible Asia: Turbulence Rises Again)/Dung fong bat baai: Fung wan joi hei/Dong fang bu bai: Feng yun zai* (1992). She also costarred in Tsui Hark's *Green Snake/Ching se/Qing she* (1993) and **Jeff Lau's** wacky *The Eagle Shooting Heroes/Seh diu ying hung chuen ji dung shing sai jau/ Shediao yingxiong zhi dongcheng xijiu* (1993), a parody of the **Louis Cha** novel. After 1994, during which her only role was one that was cut from **Wong Kar-wai's** ***Ashes of Time*** *(Evil East, Malicious West)/Dung chea sai duk/Dong xie xi du* (1994), Wang retired to focus on a singing career and launched three albums. She returned to the screen in a Japanese film, *Peking Man/Pekin genjin* (1997), and has since appeared in **Yonfan's** *Peony Pavilion/Yau yuen geng mung/You yuan jing meng* (2001) and the Mainland Chinese film *Shanghai Story/Mei lai seung hoi* (2004).

WANG, JOHNNY LONG-WEI (Wong Lung-wai) (1949–). A favorite "bad guy" in Hong Kong **action** films from the 1970s and 1980s, Wang Long-wei was playing guitar in a nightclub band in Hong Kong when he heard that **kung fu** director **Chang Cheh** had opened a training program for actors in Taiwan. Chang had established his own production unit there, as a semiautonomous subsidiary of the **Shaw Brothers** studio. Wang, by his own admission, had been an indifferent student who loved to fight, and he had picked up some knowledge of **martial arts**. He applied to the program, and won a three-year contract with Chang's film company. His first film was *Shaolin Martial Arts/Hung kuen yue wing chun/Hong quan yu yong chun* (1974), and he went on to work nonstop for over 20 years at Hong Kong's top studios. He appeared, usually as a villain, in many of the most revered films of the genre. His extensive work for Chang included *New Shaolin Boxers/Choi lee fat siu ji/Cai li fo xiao zi* (1976), *Shaolin Temple/Siu lam chi/Shaolin si* (1976), and *Five Venoms/Ng duk/Wu du*(1978). In addition, he also was a favorite of martial director **Lau Kar-leung**, as in *Dirty Ho (Rotten Head Ho)/Laan tau Ho/Lan tou he* (1979), *Return to the 36th Chamber/Siu lam daap pang dai si/Shaolin da peng da shi* (1980), and *Martial Club/Miu goon/Wu guan* (1981). Wang can be an intimidating presence on film, looking very much the experienced brawler, right down to the scars on his knuckles. His fighting style incorporates both classic kung fu and Western-style boxing elements. A rare starring role that allowed him to triumph at the end is found in **Kirk Wong's** *Health Warning (Flash Future Kung Fu)/Da lui toi/Da lei tai* (1982), an exotic sci-fi fantasy with an extended smackdown that shows off Wang's combat technique. He also ventured behind the camera at times, directing the fast-paced Triad drama *Hong Kong Godfather/Chim dung hiu hung/Jian dong xiao xiong/Jian dong xiao xiong* (1985) in addition to a handful of other films.

WANG, LAI (Wong Loi) (1927–). Mandarin actress Wang Lai (real name Wang Delan), a native of Shandong province, grew up in Beijing and graduated from the Subsidiary Girls Middle School of the Beijing Teachers College. In 1943, she joined actor He Bin's Film Workers Drama Troupe and married him the following year, temporarily retiring from acting to raise a family. In 1949, she and her husband founded the Huaguang Troupe, and Wang returned to the stage. Her screen debut was *The Story of a Shrine* (1951).

The actress came to Hong Kong and starred in *The Handsome Man* (1953). By 1957, she had appeared in more than 20 films for **Shaw Brothers**, **Yonghua**, **Asia**, and **Xinhua** studios, in movies such as **Yan Jun's musical** comedy *Spring Is in the Air/Chun tin bat shut dau shu tin/Chuntian bushi dushu tian* (1954) and drama *Frosty Night/Yuet laai woo tai seung moon tin/Yue luo wu ti shuang man tian*

(1957), **Bu Wancang's** family drama *The Long Lane/Cheung hong/Chang xiang* (1956) and tragic romance *Fisherman's Delight (The Fisherman's Daughter)/Yue goh/Yu ge* (1956), and **Tao Qin's** drama *A Lonely Heart/Liang aan/Ling yan* (1956). In *Frosty Night*, she played the jealous sister of **Lucilla You Min**, who is in love with a reformed petty thief (Yan Jun, who also directed). She not only betrays her sister, who is almost raped as a consequence, but poisons her husband and fingers the former thief for the crime. *Fisherman's Delight* featured star-crossed lovers, a painter (Yan Jun) and a fisherman's daughter (**Linda Lin Dai**); she rescues him from drowning, but his father arranges a marriage between his son and Wang Lai, who instigates disagreements between the lovers. He escapes the marriage, but arrives too late to prevent his lover, driven insane, from drowning herself in the sea.

In 1957, Wang signed with Dianmao (**Motion Pictures and General Investment, MP&GI**), appearing in over 50 films as a supporting and character actor. Among those films are **Yue Feng's** historical drama *Golden Lotus/Gam lin dut/ Jin lianhua* (1957), **Tang Huang's** drama ***Her Tender Heart****/Yuk lui shut ching/ Yunu siqing* (1959) and *Fairy, Ghost, Vixen/Liu chai jeung yee/Liao zhai zhi yi* (1965), **Wang Tianlin's** comedy *All in the Family/Ga yau choi si/ Jia you xishi* (1959) and musical ***The Wild, Wild Rose****/Yau mooi gwai ji luen/Yemeigui zhi lian* (1960), **Evan Yang's** epic drama ***Sun, Moon and Star****/Sing sing yuet leung taai yeung/Xing xing yue liang tai yang* (in two parts, 1961), and **Chung Kai-man's** drama *Education of Love/Oi dik gaau yuk/Ai de jiao yu* (1961). In *Her Tender Heart*, Wang costarred as the mother who abandoned her husband and small daughter for a lover and returns years later, posing as the girl's aunt, with her new husband (actually natural father of the daughter) to claim her; Wang portrayed a complex **woman** with few choices, as sympathetically portrayed as the innocent daughter. Significantly, as a married woman, she left a loveless marriage in pursuit of love and a better material life.

In *The Wild, Wild Rose*, Wang portrayed **Ge Lan's** friend and confidant, but as a woman using men for money, she also served as a character foil to the good-hearted songstress. In 1964, she won Best Actress at the **Golden Horse Awards** for her portrayal in *Father and Son/Yan ji choh/Ren zhi chu* (1963). Wang worked throughout the

1970s and into the early 1980s, for various studios, including Shaw in Hong Kong and Central Motion Picture in Taiwan, appearing in movies like the historical dramas *Dream of the Red Chamber/Gam yuk leung yuen hung lau mung/Jin yu liang yuan hong lou meng* (1977) and *The Adventures of Emperor Chien Lung (Voyage of Emperor Chien Lung)/Gon lung gwong yeung chow/Qian long xia yang zhou* (1977), among others. She has appeared in more than 200 movies, and because of her versatility, was dubbed the "actress with a thousand faces."

When her husband passed away in 1980, Wang immigrated to Canada, but she continues to return to Hong Kong sporadically, appearing in films, such as **Taylor Wong's** crime-themed *Sentenced to Hang/Saam long kei ngon/San lang ji an* (1989), **Ann Hui's** cross-cultural drama *My American Grandson/Seung hoi ga gei/Shanghai jiaqi* (1991), and **Lawrence Lau's** youth movie *Arrest the Restless/Laam Gong juen ji faan fei jo fung wan/Lan Jiang zhuan zhi fan fei zu feng yun* (1992). She won three more Golden Horse Awards, one of them for Taiwanese director **Ang Lee's** *Pushing Hands/Tui shou* (1991).

WANG, LISA MING-QUAN (Wong Ming-chuen) (1947–). Actress and singer Lisa Wang was born in Shanghai. She has been on Hong Kong **television** since 1968, including Hong Kong television's golden age, and has starred in some of the most popular Hong Kong series including *A House Is Not a Home*, *Chor Lau Heung*, *The Shell Game 1* and *2*, and *Yesterday's Glitter*. She is still one of the most popular TV actresses today, despite a respite she took to fight off breast cancer. Wang's first film appearance was in *Singing Darlings/Mooi gwai cheuk ngok hoi tong hung/Mei gui shao yao hai tang gong* (1969). Due to a pro-China political position, Wang's films were banned in Taiwan, at the time a very important market. Consequently, she appeared in only four films in her career, sticking to television.

However, Wang, in addition to remaining a TV queen, also has a very successful singing career. Wang released her first album in 1969 and has gone on to record over 40 albums, in addition to giving concerts. She continues to perform live today, often to raise money for charity. She also performs in **Peking (Beijing) opera**s and was in **Roman Tam's** production of "The Legend of White Snake." She is the longtime girlfriend of Cantonese opera star and film actor **Law Kar-ying**.

While Wang's political statements may have hurt her film career, they have helped her political career. From 1988 until 1997 she was the Hong Kong/Macau delegate to the National People's Congress of the People's Republic of China (PRC). She then moved in 1998 to the Chinese People's Political Consultative Conference Committee; her term on that committee will expire in 2007. In addition, she is an ambassador for Oxfam Hong Kong, a group that works to help rural Chinese. She is a member of the executive committee of the Hong Kong Anti-Cancer Society, a board member of the Hong Kong Dance Company, and in 2004 became the chairman of the Hong Kong Television Association.

WANG, LIUZHAO (Wong Lau-chiu) (1926–1970). Writer and director Wang Liuzhao (real name Wang Zhaoyan), a native of Jiangsu province, graduated from Taiwan National Political University and was a film critic, translator, and author of several books on film. He joined Taiwan's Motion Picture Company as a script editor and began making Taiwanese-dialect films in 1957.

In 1958, Wang came to Hong Kong and worked as a director and writer at Dianmao, directing six films by 1970, although his reputation rested on his screenplays. His Mandarin comedy *All in the Family/Ga yau choi si/Jia you xishi* (1959) won the best screenplay award at the seventh **Asian Film Festival**. In the family **melodrama**, a rich businessman (**Lo Wei**) has pity for his young secretary (**Lucilla You Min**) whose mother is ill; he agrees to help in exchange for her being his mistress. His wife (**Wang Lai**) confronts her, but compassionately brings her home, shames the husband, and her son (**Kelly Lai Chen**) and the mistress fall in love. Wang wrote and codirected (with **Tang Huang**) the Mandarin thriller *Four Brave Ones/Dip hoi sei chong si/Die hai si zhuang shi* (1963), which won best screenplay at the third **Golden Horse** Awards.

Wang also wrote a number of screenplays for **Motion Pictures and General Investment (MP&GI)** and wrote and directed for **Shaw Brothers**. MP&GI films include Tang Huang's Mandarin drama *Between Tears and Laughter/Yuk lau saam fung/Yulou sanfeng* (1960) and Mandarin comedy *Beauty Parade/Tai yuk wong hau/Tiyu* *huangho* (1961). The former starred **Helen Li Mei**, **Kitty Ting Hao**, and Wang Lai as three **women** undergoing various relationships with men; their friendship holds them together. The latter starred Kitty Ting Hao as a country girl with the opportunity to attend school in the city; overcoming the prejudice of the city girls, she excels at sports but her grades suffer; Kelly Lai Chen tutors her and plays the sympathetic love interest. Wang's Shaw films include the ***huangmei diao*** *The Lotus Lamp (The Magic Lamp)/Bo lin dang/Baolian deng* (1964), Tang Huang's *Fairy, Ghost, Vixen/Liu chai jeung yee/Liao zhai zhi yi* (1965), the Mandarin comedy *Move over Darling/Fung lau cheung foo/Fengliu zhangfu* (1965), and Mandarin fantasy *The Goddess of Mercy/Goon sai yam/Guanshiyin* (1967). **Peter Chen Ho** starred in *Move over Darling*.

Wang suffered a nervous breakdown and committed suicide.

WANG, TIANLIN (Wong Tin-lam) (1928–). Born in Shanghai to a family from Zhejiang province, director Wang Tianlin studied at Hong Kong's Pui Ching Middle School. He entered the film industry in 1947, working on script continuity and as an assistant and deputy director. He took on technical positions including processing, sound, and editing. His directorial debut was the **martial arts** fantasy *The Flying Sword Hero from Emei Mountain (The Flying Sword Hero from Mount Emei), Parts One* and *Two/Ngo mei fei kim hap/Emei feijianxia, shang, xiaji* (1950), which was based on a folktale and starred **Sek Yin-ji (Chow Wan-chung)** as the hero (he became famous for playing **Fong Sai-yuk** in a series of films). His codirection (with **Zhang Shankun**) of the **musical** ***Songs of the Peach Blossom River****/Tou Fa Kong/Taohua jiang* (1956) elevated the quality of Mandarin musicals.

While shooting *Underground Sparks/Dei gwong feng dut/Di xia huo hua* (1958) in Thailand, he met **Stephen Soong** (Song Qi), who brought him into the fold at **Motion Pictures and General Investment** (MP&GI Cathay), where he remained until the early 1970s. He made his best films here, including *All in the Family/Ga yau choi si/Jia you xishi* (1959), ***The Wild, Wild Rose****/Yau mooi gwai ji luen/Yemeigui zhi lian* (1960), *The Greatest Civil War on Earth/Naam bak who/Nan bei he* (1961), and ***The Story of Three Loves****/Tai siu yan yuen/Ti xiao yin yuan* (1964). The former won him Best Director Award at the seventh

Asian Film Festival. His last film was *The Utmost Greatness/Daai dau daai/Da dou da* (1979). *The Wild, Wild Rose*, adapted from Georges Bizet's *Carmen* and Giacomo Puccini's *Madame Butterfly*, with a bit of Joseph von Sternberg's *Blue Angel* (1930, Germany) to boot, is a Mandarin musical noir transferred to a Hong Kong Wanchai setting with **Ge Lan** starring as a singsong girl. Both *The Wild, Wild Rose* and the **melodrama** *The Story of Three Loves* (1964), adapted from **Mandarin Duck and Butterfly** author Zhang Henshui's most famous romantic novel, showcase Wang's talent for showcasing strong **women** characters. The latter stars **Zhao Lei, Lin Cui**, **Wang Yin, Ge Lan**, and **Roy Chiao**. Zhao Lei plays the weak male who learns the true meaning of love and sacrifice from two women.

Wang's career covers 30 years and many genres, including musicals, swordplay, melodrama, and comedy. He recorded films in various dialects. In 1973, he joined Hong Kong Television Broadcasts (TVB) as a **television** producer, developing popular TV series. He has also made cameo appearances in recent **Johnnie To** movies, most memorable being an old-school Triad boss with a bad gambling habit in *The Mission/Cheong feng/Qiang ho* (1999). He is the father of producer-director-writer **Wong Jing**.

WANG, WAYNE (1949–). Hong Kong–born director Wayne Wang was named for Hollywood actor John Wayne, a favorite of his father. Educated in Catholic schools, Wang came to the United States for college, graduating from Foothill College and the California College of the Arts. He returned to Hong Kong and worked on Radio Television Hong Kong's (RTHK) **television** series *Under (Below) the Lion Rock*, which was shot on film and helped form **New Wave** filmmakers such as **Ann Hui** and **Yim Ho**, focusing on social issues, politics, idealism, and activism. He returned to the United States, and directed, cowrote, produced, and edited his first feature, for a little more than US$20,000. *Chan Is Missing* (1982) was shot in San Francisco, part mystery, part commentary on being Chinese in America. Wang has run the gamut from **independent** and interesting exploratory features such as *Dim Sum* (1985, starring Wang's wife Cora Miao), *Smoke*, and *Blue in the Face* (both 1995, written by novelist Paul Auster, with an ensemble cast including Harvey Keitel and William Hurt) and the unrated erotic *The Center of the World* (2001), to the mainstream crossovers *The Joy Luck Club* (1993, adapted from the Amy Tan novel, with an ensemble cast narrating numerous mother–daughter stories, a Chinese past and American present), *Anywhere but Here* (1999, based on the Mona Simpson novel and starring Susan Sarandon and Natalie Portman), *Maid in Manhattan* (2002, starring Jennifer Lopez and Ralph Fiennes), and *Because of Winn-Dixie* (2005, adapted from a children's book).

Wang returned to Hong Kong to address the return of the colony to the Mainland, making *Chinese Box* (1997), a political allegory with an international cast including Hong Kongers **Maggie Cheung** (as a realistic free spirit with a disfigured face) and **Michael Hui** (an entrepreneurial businessman afraid of romantic commitment to his Mainland immigrant girlfriend), British Jeremy Irons (as a dying and ineffectual English journalist who becomes obsessed with Cheung's character), Mainlander **Gong Li** (as an unpossessable exotic desired by Irons's character), and Latino Ruben Blades (a photojournalist and friend to Irons's character who provides a running commentary with a sardonic outlook, thus providing sympathy and much needed comic relief in tense times). Wang mixes personal stories of abandonment, loss, suffering, and survival with the larger political issues. Shot mostly handheld, with grainy footage, the film registers an urgency and rough texture that accurately reflects the moment.

WANG, WEIYI (Wong Wai-yat) (1912–). A native of Jiangsu, born in Shanghai, director Wang Weiyi graduated from art school in Shanghai and worked as a musician at a record company. He joined the Shanghai Experimental Troupe as an actor and director, and started in the film industry at Yihua Studio in 1934 as an actor and assistant director. He appeared in **Ma-Xu Weibang's** *Song of Midnight (Midnight Charm)* (1937) and served as assistant director on Shi Dongshan's *Eight Thousand Li of Cloud and Moon* (1947). He codirected *Spring Light Cannot Be Shut In (Spring in Its Charm)* (1948, with Xu Tao).

Most of his career was spent on the Mainland, but he is known in Hong Kong for ***Tears of the Pearl River*** *(Dawn Must Come)/Chu kong lui/Zhujiang lei* (1950) and *The House of 72 Tenants/Chat sap yee ga fong haak/Qi shi er gu fang ke* (1963). The former Cantonese film was produced by **Cai Chusheng** at Hong Kong's Nanguo Film

Company, and features Guangdong peasants exploited by a landlord, and, after much suffering, finding justice. The latter, in which a landlady plans to convert her dilapidated apartment building into a club for gambling and prostitution, displacing its residents, is a realist comedy, exposing the crowded living conditions of the working class; it was made largely by a Mainland Chinese crew. (A **Shaw Brothers** color remake appeared in 1973, directed by **Chor Yuen**.)

Wang was manager of the Pearl River Studio in Guangzhou in 1949, and later transferred to the Shanghai Film Studio, where he continued directing. He returned to Guangzhou in 1958 and collaborated on *Waves on the Southern Shore* (1959) with Cai. Wang's career was on hold during the Cultural Revolution; he began directing again in the 1980s; among the films was *The Story of a Murder/A gwan sat laai dik yat doi/A hun shi luo de yi dai* (1986). His film style and approach is similar to that of his mentor and collaborator, Cai Chusheng.

WANG, XINGLEI (Wong Sing-lui) (1931–). Director and writer Wang Xinglei was born in Shangdong province and studied literature at Zhen Hua Arts College. In 1949, he came to Hong Kong and joined the script department at Yonghua and worked as an assistant soundman briefly, leaving to become a screenwriter and writing more than 20 films for Cantonese and Amoy productions, including the popular **Wong Fei-hong** series.

Wang appeared as an actor in **Tao Qin's** *Followed Birds* (1954) and became assistant director on Tao's *My Four Precious Daughters* (1957) and **Yue Feng's** *Scarlet Doll* (1958). He worked as Yue's assistant at **Shaw Brothers** through 1961, and codirected *Between Tears and Laughter/San tai siu yan yuen/Xin ti xiao yin yuan* (1964, with Tao Qin and Luo Zhen).

Wang's directorial debut was *Romance in the Northern Country* (1967), for **Li Han-hsiang's** Guo Lian (Grand Motion Picture Company) in Taiwan. The film, adapted from Wu Mingshi's popular novel, concerned late Qing dynasty Chinese students' revolutionary actions in Japan against the Japanese. Wang's **swordplay** *Escorts over Tiger Hills/Foo saan hang/Hushan xing* (1969, Taiwan), for **Cathay**, was dubbed into English, French, and Portuguese. **Roy Chiao** played a hero uncertain of his role, a former fighter and present monk, required to take on one more mission, to deliver Tartar prisoners through enemy territory across the mountains, despite the imposition of an ex-wife (Hilda Zhou Xuan), a cunning Tartar warrior and daughter of an enemy agent. Han Yingjie's **action** direction and Hu Qiyuan's cinematography, including the anticipation of violent action as well as the freeze-frames, and moving camera, led to the success of Cathay's first attempt at a big-budget ***wuxia*** production.

With the rise of **kung fu** cinema, the director returned to Hong Kong. He wrote and directed *The Hero of Chiu Chow/Chiu chow liu hon/Chao zhou nu han* (1972), reminiscent of **Bruce Lee's** *The Big Boss* (1971). *Tornado of Chu Chiang (Tornado of Pearl River)/Chu kong daai fung biu/Zhu jiang da feng bao* (1974) followed, which Wang made for his own company, Dongfang. He returned to Taiwan, where he made *Devil Crows/Che moh/Xie mo* (1975), a cross between **Pu Songling's** Chinese classic of supernatural tales *Strange Tales from a Chinese Studio* and Alfred Hitchcock's *The Birds* (1963). His *Arhats in Fury* (1985) pits loyal Chinese harshly trained by austere monks at an Emei Mountain Buddhist monastery against Muslim invaders, with swordplay and **martial arts**.

WANG, YIN (1901–1988). Veteran actor-director Wang Yin (real name Wang Chunyuan), a native of Tianjin, was born in Shanghai. He joined Jinan Film Company and made his acting debut in *Scramble in the Sea* (1929) and starred in *The White Swan Hero* (1929). His directorial debut was *The Divine Monk of the Barren Hill* (1931). Between 1932 and 1940, he worked as an actor at Yihua, **Lianhua**, **Mingxing**, and **Xinhua** studios, becoming a star for his performance in *Escape* (1938). He was part of the **Orphan Island** group that remained in Shanghai during the Japanese occupation and acted in several pictures. After the war, he directed *Desire (Lust)/Yuk mong/Yuwang* (1946), a simple drama of a country girl who desires to move to the city but is eventually convinced of country virtues when a friend returns from city life with syphilis. Wang came to Hong Kong in 1947, founding Liangyou Film Company. Exile in Hong Kong became permanent and Wang participated in Mandarin films, both as actor and director, starting at **Shaw Brothers** in 1950, where he remained 10 years, directing numerous films. He directed the **musical** *Red Rose* (1952), starring **Li Lihua**, which was a box office hit.

Beginning in 1955, he acted in other studios' films, including **Tang Huang's** ***Her Tender Heart****/Yuk lui shut ching/Yunu siqing* (1959) at **Motion Pictures and General Investment (MP&GI)** and **Bu Wancang's** *Nobody's Child/Kuer liulang ji* (1960) at Guofeng. In the former, he played a single father who has raised a daughter (**Lucilla You Min**, in her first film at the studio); when her mother appears on the scene, the high-school girl is torn between her parents. In the latter, in one of his most memorable performances, Wang played an elderly street performer who adopts an orphan (the young **Josephine Siao Fong-fong**) and travels the country with her, a monkey, and three dogs; they are separated when he is put in jail, only to be reunited upon his release. Another touching role was the dedicated and humble ailing schoolteacher he played in **Chung Kai-man's** *The Education of Love/Oi dik gaau yuk/Ai de jiao yu* (1961), with **Lin Cui** as his caring daughter. Throughout his career, Wang brought a dignity and gentlemanly quality to his performances.

In 1959, Wang founded Tiannan Film Company, producing *Misty Rain* (1965). He won Best Actor **Golden Horse Award**s for performances in director **Li Han-hsiang's** *The Pistol/Sau cheong/shou qiang* (1961) and historical drama *The Story of Ti Ying/Tai Ying/Ti Ying* (1971), and the Best Supporting Actor Golden Horse Award for **Wang Tianlin's** historical drama ***The Story of Three Loves****/Tai siu yan yuen/Ti xiao yin yuan* (1964). The last film he directed was *The Old and the Young* (1974) and he last acted in *Born Rich/Daai foo yan ga/Da fu ren jia* (1976), thereafter retiring. In 1984, he developed paralysis and died in Shanghai at age 87.

WANG, YUANLONG (Wong Yuen-lung) (1903–1959). Director and actor Wang Yuanlong, a native of Sichuan province, attended the Baoding Military Academy and enrolled in the China Film Institute. He entered the film industry in 1922, and his film debut was *Conscience* (1924) at **Great China**. He starred in *The Young Factory Owner* (1925), based on his first screenplay, and continued acting in other productions.

Wang's directorial debut was *Visiting the In-Laws* (1926), and the detective thriller *The Silver Pistol Thief/Aau cheong diy/Yin qiang dao* (1928) followed. He created Yuan Long Film Company in 1929, producing three features, but bankruptcy led to a film hiatus. Meantime, he founded Ying Lian Studio and trained actors there, and starred in *The Hot Blooded Youth* (1934) and directed *The Dauntless Lady* (1934) for **Tianyi**. He starred in seven features for Yi Hua in the late 1930s–early 1940s; he appeared in *Heavenly Souls/Jinxu tiantang* (1949), starring **Butterfly Wu**, for Central M.P. Enterprise before immigrating to Hong Kong.

In Hong Kong, he directed and starred in five films for Great China, including *Revenge of the Great Swordsman (Assassin Zhang Wenxiang)/Daai hap fook chau gei/Daxia fuchou ji (Zhang Wenxiang cima)* (1949, codirector with Wen Yimin), in which he starred in the title role as the assassin Zhang Wenxiang, put on trial for killing a Qing dynasty provincial governor, and betrayed by one of his blood brothers. The story proceeds through a series of flashbacks. **Chang Che** would remake the film as *The Blood Brothers/Chi ma/Ci ma* (1973). In Gu Eryi's Mandarin drama *Floating Family/Shui seung yan ga/Shuishang renjia* (1949), he starred as Uncle Yu, one of a group of fisherman of Silver Dragon Bay oppressed by Great Grand Mai (played by the director), who monopolizes the fishing industry. Yu's nephew proposes starting a cooperative and all hell breaks loose, until the fishermen unite, defeat the exploiter, and set out for Tianmen Bay to start a new life. The film was partly shot on location in Cheung Chau, and the producers bought 6,000 catties of fish for Great Grand Mai's fish market set.

The actor joined **Great Wall** in 1950, and appeared in **Li Pingqian's** Mandarin drama *The Awful Truth/Suet fong sai gaai/Shuo huang shi jie* (1950) as a manager trying to save his company from bankruptcy through questionable means; **Li Lihua** played his mistress. From 1953 onward, Wang played character parts in films at Yi Hua, **Tai Shan**, and Xinghua. In the contemporary family tragedy *Do Not Forget Tonight/Mok mong gam siu/Mo wang jin xiao* (1953), he played a sleazy nightclub owner who lures the married Ouyang Shafei (Ouyang Feng) to leave her family; after seducing the mother, he attempts to seduce the daughter (also played by Ouyang Feng). He also played the widowed father of four very different daughters in **Tao Qin's musical melodrama** for **Motion Pictures and General Investment (MP&GI),** ***Our Sister Hedy*** *(Four Daughters)/Se chin gam/Si qianjin* (1957).

In 1956, Wang founded the China Film Institute, which trained actress Ding Hong and directors Yang Quan and Luo Ma. The actor died while shooting on location in Taiwan.

WANG, ZHIBO (1924–1964). Producer, manager, and writer Wang Zhibo was a Shanghai native who graduated with a BA from St. John's University and a law degree from Soochow University and was a famed Chinese calligrapher. He wrote several books on the art of calligraphy. He joined the film industry as a writer, and his first script was *A Scholar's Adventures* (1952). From 1952 to 1964, he wrote a dozen movies, for numerous studios, including **Yonghua**, Hsin Hwa, **Shaw Brothers**, and **Cathay** subsidiaries, including **Yan Jun's** Guotai. During the 1950s, he joined **Motion Pictures and General Investment's** (MP&GI) production department and became production supervisor.

Wang's productions include Yan Jun's **musical** comedy *Spring Is in the Air/Chun tin bat shut dau shu tin/Chutian bushi shi dushu tian* (1954), starring **Linda Lin Dai**, **Wang Lai**, and Yan Jun; *The 72 Martyrs of Canton* (1954, cowriter); Yan Jun's contemporary romance *Rainstorm in Chinatown/Fung yue ang che shui/Fengyu niucheshui* (1956), starring **Li Lihua** and Yan Jun; the contemporary musical comedy *Nonya and Baba/Malai niangre* (1956); the historical drama *Yang Kwei-fei, the Magnificent Concubine/Yeung gwai fei/Yang gui fei* (1962); *The Magic Lamp/Bo lin dang/Bao lian deng* (1964, cowriter); and *Fairy, Ghost, Vixen/Liu chai jeung yee/Liao zhai zhi yi* (1965, cowriter). His last film, posthumously, was the historical drama *Passion/Lui yan lui yan/Nu ren nu ren* (1967).

Wang was married to famous actress and painter Weng Mulan. He died in a plane crash with **Loke Wan Tho** and other MP&GI executives returning from the 11th **Asian Film Festival** in Taiwan.

WEI, WEI (1922–). Actress Wei Wei (real name Miao Mengying), a native of Guangdong province, was a typist before entering the film industry. She joined the Professional Drama Company of Shanghai in 1941, performing in many plays. Her film debut was in *Night Lodging* (1947), and she starred as the gentle Zhou Yuwen in Fei Mu's *Spring in a Small Town* (1948), shot in Songjiang. She came to Hong

Kong in 1949 at the request of Fei Mu. She was cast by Fei to appear in *The Show Must Go On (Sons of the Earth)/Jianghu ernu* (1952), for which he advised her to learn unicycle riding and plate spinning. Wei Wei played Lotus, a member of an acrobatic troupe run by her father that struggles to survive, from performing in a dance hall to in the streets. Fei died before the film's completion and **Zhu Shilin** and Qi Wenshao took over.

The actress worked for **Feng Huang** between 1955 and 1960, appearing in a number of films, including Zhu Shilin's family dramas *Year In, Year Out/Yat nin ji gai/Yi nian zhi ji* (1955) and *The Foolish Heart/Chik mok dik sam/Ji mo de xin* (1956), and his family comedy *They All Want a Baby/Siu laai laai ji mai/Shao nai nai zhi mi* (1956). In *Year In, Year Out*, she played one of the wives of two brothers at odds living under the same roof with their mother. In *The Foolish Heart*, she starred as a neglected wife ignored by her workaholic physician husband. She is persuaded by a swindler to seek a divorce. His scam is exposed in the nick of time and a remorseful wife returns to her husband. In *They All Want a Baby*, a patriarch announces that his first grandson will be heir to the family fortune, and his two childless sons and their wives scheme to get it. The actress played the eldest daughter-in-law. Both couples announce fake pregnancies and adopt babies; the old man dies with his grandsons and the couples discover an empty inheritance and responsibilities.

Wei Wei's last feature was *Alarm Conscious/Cho muk gaai bing/Cao mu jie bing* (1960), after which she retired and went into business. She reappeared on the big screen in Raymond Lee's Mandarin drama *I Want to Go on Living/Ngo yiu wood gwong hui/Wo yao huo xia qu* (1995) and **Peter Chan's** gentle drama *The Age of Miracles/Lut lut faan faan/Ma ma fan fan* (1996).

WENYI. The term *wenyi*, combining *wenxue* (literature) and *yishu* (art), is used to describe the approach of Mandarin movies, both **melodrama** and literary-based, predominantly in Hong Kong cinema of the 1950s, called *wenyi pian*. The term originated in, and the tradition can be traced back to, late 1920s Shanghai movies, when few film genres existed, and the term denoted movies emphasizing drama, plot, and character. The term was generally used to distinguish these films from another prevalent type, ***wuxia pian***, or martial chivalry movies, emphasizing action through **martial arts** and **swordplay**. As more genres developed, including horror, detective thrillers, and comedies, critics and intellectuals regarded *wenyi pian* as superior, with their deeper meanings and significance, while the other genres were thought of as simple entertainment.

In the 1950s, the Mandarin melodramas were viewed as more sophisticated than those of the Cantonese flavor, based on the historical traditions on the Mainland. Ironically, based on both literature and the arts, which were characterized by weak men in soft occupations, such elements led to the presence of weak scholars and weak men in the movies. *Wenyi pian*, however, were not limited to literary or stage adaptations; original stories were developed as well. Whatever the origins, *wenyi pian* were intended to evoke an emotional response from the audience and centered on the family, and romantic, often tragic, relationships.

***THE WILD, WILD ROSE* (1960).** Director **Wang Tianlin's** Mandarin musical *The Wild, Wild Rose/Yau mooi gwai ji luen/Yemeigui zhi lian* focuses on the figure of the doomed songstress (here played by **Ge Lan** in a memorable performance). The film is a musical *film noir*, with a femme fatale, tangible sexuality, and a cynical attitude. The music, by Japanese composer **Hattori Ryoichi**, combines popular songs with jazz, blues, and Western opera. Loosely based on Georges Bizet's *Carmen*, and also drawing on Giacomo Puccini's *Madame Butterfly*, since the singer-temptress also has a good heart, the movie also combines a little of Joseph von Sternberg's *Blue Angel* (1930, Germany). The story follows the singer as she sets her sights (through the eponymous cigarette smoke) on a music teacher turned piano-playing lounge lizard (**Chang Yang**), leading to his downward spiral and her inevitable suffering and death for love of him. The film oozes atmosphere and style and popularized several memorable songs.

WIN'S ENTERTAINMENT COMPANY LTD. In 1984, brothers Jimmy and Charles Heung founded Win's Movie Production & I/E Company, and its first film was **Eric Tsang's** *Double Trouble/Da xiao bu liang* (1984); they divided the company in 1995, with Jimmy's Win's Film Company no longer producing films but focusing on other aspects, while Charles's Win's Movie Entertainment

Limited continued producing them. Commercially successful movies in the 1980s–1990s include *God of Gamblers/Do san/Du shen* (1989), which revived a gambling-themed movie trend, including a sequel *God of Gamblers 2 (God of Gamblers' Return)/Do san 2/Du shen 2* (1994, coproduced with **Golden Harvest**), both of which starred **Chow Yun-fat**; and *Fight Back to School (Escape from School Mighty Dragon)/Tao xue wei long* (1991), which spawned two sequels, and *Flirting Scholar (Tong Pak-fu Chooses Chou-heung)/ Tong Pak-fu dim Chou-heung/Tang Bohu dian Qiuxiang* (1993), both star vehicles for **Stephen Chiau**. Now known as Win's Entertainment Company Ltd., the company has produced a number of Chiau's films, including *Forbidden City Cop (Big Inside Cop Ling Ling-fat)/Da nei mi tan 008* (1996) as well as actor and **Cantopop** king **Andy Lau's** *Full Throttle (Flaming Chariot)/Lieho zhanche* (1995). Win's Entertainment Organization is the main investor of Win's Entertainment Film and Television Production Service Center, opened in 1993 and located in Shenzhen, which occupies 200,000 square feet and has four sound stages. Director **Wong Jing** is most often associated with this studio.

WIREWORK. High-tech Hollywood relies on mechanically controlled wires and airbags or computer-enhanced touch-ups to erase wires and add special effects. But Hong Kong filmmakers, for practical reasons and because of limited budgets, still rely upon fine, almost invisible wires, all handheld; use apple or cardboard boxes; and include few computer-enhanced programming elements. Unable, like Hollywood, to afford machines to leverage a person, Hong Kong crews have used hand-controlled wires since the 1960s to pull people in wirework, and the method remains in favor to this day and the techniques are unique to Hong Kong. Using wire is time consuming and can be dangerous. How you wire a person is crucial for safety and delivery. The many different angles of movements include pulling straight up, swinging across, twists, turnings, and spinning a person around a couple of times. Sometimes wirework is used not to pull people, but simply to hold them when the stunt is dangerous. It is essential for the person being wired to understand how the wire works, and many stuntmen in Hong Kong specialize in the movements, training for many years. The experts holding and pulling the wire also work around gravity purely by experience and estimation. They have to have a practical knowledge of physics, and the timing and power of their pulling must be synchronized. They learn how to make it seem realistic, varying the strength and force they use in pulling.

Basic equipment for wirework includes a wire net harness (*wire mon*); a black belt similar to a seatbelt, used to set the wire wheel or pulley system used; and a wire wheel or pulley attached to a crossbar or beam firmly secured to a ceiling or an upper floor for interiors or from a crane if needed for exteriors, used to set the wire. The crossbar establishes three points of tension—the person(s) wired, the wire wheel, and the people pulling the wire. As many as six people can be used to pull a person.

Tsui Hark's *Zu: Warriors from the Magic Mountain/Suk san sun suk san geen hap/Zuo shan shen zuo shan jian xia* (1983) established wirework as a Hong Kong aesthetic, with **Corey Yuen** and **Yuen Biao** among its **action** directors. **Ching Siu-tung** is generally regarded as a master of the wire, known for having used 10 wires in one shot. He still uses old-fashioned wirework techniques and often serves as cameraman, using handheld cameras for the immediacy of the wirework action.

For some audiences, there is nothing more exciting on-screen than bodies hurtling through the air, spinning and soaring, defying gravity—mortal combat in space, if you will. Some audiences do not like wirework, and for them it just means unrealistic action and flying people. But, used sparingly and naturally, wirework can be used in realistic fighting to incorporate props or to emphasize power, as well as in fantasy action. And the popularity of such films as the Wachowski Brothers' action driven *Matrix* series (1999–2003) and **Ang Lee's** mythic *Crouching Tiger, Hidden Dragon* (2000), both with action direction by **Yuen Wo-ping**, underscores a new breed of filmmaking—wire-worked action vehicles, Hong Kong–style, with Hollywood budgets.

WOMEN AND FILMS. Examining women and Hong Kong cinema involves giving attention to three areas: the representation of women in its cinema, the woman's film, and films made by female directors. Women have always played a significant role in Hong Kong cinema, from the first appearance of a woman in a Hong Kong film, namely

Yan Shanzhan, wife of filmmaker **Li Minwei**, in a supporting role in *Zhuangzi Tests His Wife/Chong Ji shut chai/Zhuangzi shiqi* (1913); Li himself played the wife of the title, because the family and society disapproved of women appearing on-screen (while a ban remained on the theatrical stage, this was not so in film). Yan's image indicates the visual presence and power women would soon have. The stories of historical female generals Hua Mulan and Mu Guiying would be transferred to the screen, as well as tales of women masters of **swordplay** and **kung fu** (***nuxia***/*xianu*), first in the Chinese films *Red Heroine/Hong Xia* (1929) and *Swordswoman of Huangjiang/Huangjiang nuxia* (1930), and later in the films of **King Hu**, working with actresses like **Cheng Pei-pei** and **Hsu Feng** in films such as *Come Drink with Me/Daai chui hap/Da zui xia* (1966) and *A Touch of Zen (The Gallant Lady)/Hap lui/Xia nu* (begun 1968, released 1971), respectively. The tradition of confident heroines continues in the ***wuxia*** films of actresses like **Brigitte Lin** and **Michelle Yeoh**. Women also appeared in cross-dressing roles, particularly in **Chinese opera films**, especially seen in the careers of the duos of **Connie Chan Po-chu/Josephine Siao**, **Ivy Ling Bo/Le Di**, and **Yam Kim-fai/Pak Suet-sin**. The latter couple was greatly loved for the romantic aura they lent their performances together, and a good example is their star-crossed lovers in **Lee Tit's** ***The Purple Hairpin***/*Chi chaai gei/Zichai ji* (1959).

Women dominated in Hong Kong **melodramas** (***wenyi pian***) and **musicals** in the 1950s and 1960s, and they received top billing. The stories centered on extended families and featured dutiful daughters, virtuous wives, and caring mothers. Melodramas include movies such as *The Story of a Family/Tin Lun/Tianlun* (1961), starring **Pak Yin** as a virtuous wife faced with male weakness; *Mother's Heart Is Broken (Mother's Broken Heart)/Ngai sam sui miu sam/Er xin sui mu xin* (1958), starring **Fong Yim-fan** as a long-suffering mother; and *Education of Love/Oi dik gaan yuk/Ai de jiao yu* (1961), starring the "students' darling" **Jeannette Lin Cui** as a dutiful daughter substitute teaching for her ill father. A subgenre was the doomed songstress movie, such as ***Song of a Songstress***/*Goh lui ji goh/Genu zhi ge* (1948), starring **Zhou Xuan**; ***Blood in the Snow*** *(Red Bloom in the Snow)/Suet lee hung/Xue lihong* (1956), starring "sour beauty" (referring to an attractive but strong woman) **Li Lihua**; and ***The Wild,***

Wild Rose*/Yau mooi gwai ji luen/Yemeigui zhi lian* (1960), starring **Ge Lan**. As Hong Kong modernized, conflicts between career and traditional home life (**Wang Lai** in ***Her Tender Heart****/Yuk lui shut ching/ Yunu siqing* [1959]) became prominent, as well as stories of rebellious teens and disaffected youth torn between the Confucian values of their elders and a pleasure-seeking present (numerous films starring Josephine Siao, Connie Chan Po-chu, and **Lydia Shum**; an example would be *Teddy Girls/Fei liu jing chuen/Feinu zhengzhuan* [1969]). **Julie Ye Feng** and **Li Mei** added more blatant sex appeal to their characterizations.

When **Shaw Brothers**' and Cathay Studios' (**Motion Pictures and General Investment, MP&GI**) output declined, and Cantonese-language films became Hong Kong's dominant cinema by the 1980s, the "flower vase" role for women appeared and remained, as male protagonists superseded female roles in action cinema, as can be seen in **Maggie Cheung's** role in **Jackie Chan's** *Police Story* series or **Rosamund Kwan** in the *Once upon a Time in China (Wong Fei-hung)/Wong Fei-hung/Huang Feihong* series (1991–1997). As "flower vases," beautiful women are decorative, at best victimized by villains and protected by heroes, but generally uninformed and insignificant.

The musicals combined melodrama, lavish musical and dance numbers, and epic or extravaganza, with the music woven into the drama, and examples include ***Sun, Moon and Star****/Sing sing yuet leung taai yeung/Xing xing yue liang tai yang* (1961), directed by **Evan Yang**; ***The Story of Three Loves****/Tai siu yan yuen/Ti xiao yin yuan* (1964), directed by **Wang Tianlin;** and *Hong Kong Nocturne/Heung Kong fa yuet yeh/ Xiangjiang huayue ye* (1967), directed by **Inoue Umetsugu**. The films appealed to women, often presented fantasies of modernity, and women were the stars, with male characters appearing as love interests and weak, milquetoast men.

The so-called woman's film, depicting both failed romances and domestic stories, or the conflict between conformity and independence, or tradition and modernity, always involves emotional investment from the audience. Gendered space, and women conflicted by the "public man–private woman" conflict, has been updated in works by **Stanley Kwan**, **Jacob Cheung**, and **Yonfan**. Mainland director Xie Jin (1923–) observes in Kwan's *Yang and Yin: Gender in Chinese Cin-*

ema (1996) that male directors are better at making "women's films" because they closely observe women in detail in ways that other women do not. While arguable, it is an interesting proposition, and Kwan's oeuvre, including *Rouge/Yin chi kau/Yan zhi* (1988), *Full Moon in New York/ Yan joi nau yeuk/Ren zai niu yue* (1989), *Centre Stage* (aka *Actress)/Yuen Ling-yuk/Ruan Lingyu* (1992), *Red Rose, White Rose/Hung mooi gwai baak mooi gwai/Hong mei gui bai mei gui* (1994), and *Everlasting Regret/Chang hen ge* (2005); Cheung's *Intimates (Self-Combed)/ Ji soh/Zi shu* (1997) and *Midnight Fly/Fong sam ga gei/Huang xin jia ji* (2001); and Yonfan's *Peony Pavilion/Yau yuen geng mung/You yuan jing meng* (2001) are beautiful and sensitive portrayals of women's stories. Earlier, two directors, **Griffith Yue Feng** and **Bu Wancang**, developed sympathetic female characters. Yue worked with Hong Kong's most memorable female stars of the period, including Li Lihua, **Bai Guang**, **Lin Dai**, and Zhou Xuan, showcasing their talents and creating sensitive and feminist women's stories. Li Lihua and Lin Dai were his favored actresses. Outstanding films include *Three Women/Saam lui sing/San nuxing* (1947), *An Unfaithful Woman/Dong foo sam/Dang fu xin* (1949), *Flower Street/Dut gaai/Hua jie* (1950), and *Golden Lotus/Gam lin dut/Jin lianhua* (1957). Bu's realistic melodramas narrated women's stories (and he guided several actresses' careers), from his *Portrait of a Lady/Suk lui tiu/Diao jinqui* (1953), with Shi Hu, and *It Blossoms Again (The Moon That Breaks Free from the Clouds)/Jou chun fa/Zai chun hua* (1954), with Ge Lan, to *Nobody's Child (The Wanderings of a Poor Child)/ Kuer liulang ji* (1960), with Josephine Siao and **Butterfly Wu**. These directors, as well as the women directors mentioned below, have all overcome the typical "male gaze" that films have historically satisfied.

While Hong Kong's film industry has been dominated by men, women producers and directors have played a significant (albeit less represented) role. For example, in the 1930s, actress Tong Sing-to pioneered in producing and acting in Cantonese cinema. In 1952, Pak Yin established **Zhonglian** (Union) Film Company with **Ng Cho-fan** and others, and in 1954 founded Shanlian Film Company with director Wu Hui and actor **Cheung Wood-yau** (Zhang Huoyou). Nansun Shi, **Tsui Hark's** wife, is also his partner at **Film Workshop**. Among directors, **Tang Shuxuan** anticipated the Hong Kong **New Wave**, and her ***The Arch****/Dung foo yan/Dong fu ren* (1970), which she also wrote and produced, and which won numerous **Golden Horse Awards**, is a breakthrough film in gender relations and independent filmmaking. New Wave director **Ann Hui** has managed to make intimate political and gendered films for almost 30 years, and remains an icon for women filmmakers. Her semiautobiographical film ***Song of the Exile*** *(Exile and Autumn Sorrow)/Haak to chau han/Ketu qiuhen* (1990) explores one woman's journey of discovery, and in Hui's oeuvre characters undergo a revelatory experience. **Clara Law**, with her partner/husband **Eddie Fong**, also makes films outside the Hong Kong commercial mainstream, and open sexuality is often portrayed, honestly and in numerous permutations, from women's healthy sexuality and desire to abuse and prostitution. Director **Cheung Yuen-ting** likewise works with partner/husband **Alex Law**, and immigrant experiences have served as a common thread in their work. In Cheung's epic historical drama *The Soong Sisters (The Sung Family Dynasty)/Sung ga wong chiu/Song guhuang chao* (1997), three women are poised to create a new China. Similar to Law, Taiwanese director and actress **Sylvia Chang**, who works frequently in Hong Kong, deals honestly with women's sexual desire. Independent filmmakers **Carol Lai** and Mak Yuen-yan are among the new generation working. All of the filmmakers above have addressed the Chinese **diaspora**.

Many actresses have been popular, besides those named above, such as **Lisa Wang**, referred to as "Ah Jie" ("Big Sister"), in films since the 1960s and today at age 60 still popular on **television**. Stars who were also singers in the 1970s continue to perform onstage to sold-out audiences, such as Wang, **Frances Yip**, and **Jenny Tseng**. Other popular contemporary actresses include **Anita Mui**, **Michelle Reis**, **Carina Lau**, **Shu Qi**, and **Cecilia Cheung**. A typical pattern in recent years has been for actresses to start in the Miss Hong Kong contest, make films, marry, and retire. However, not all do so. Like others, Maggie Cheung has worked in all genres, and she has made more than 75 films to date. She has won numerous awards, including the Best Actress Award at the 2004 Cannes Film Festival for *Clean*, and she only gets better and better in nuanced performances.

WONG, ANNA MAY (Wong Liu-tsong, Huang Liushuang) (1907–1961). Actress Anna May Wong was the first Chinese American Hollywood star. Her grandparents were among the first wave of

Chinese immigrants following the gold rush, and she was born in Los Angeles' Chinatown and began as an extra in Hollywood at 12, introduced into the movies by her cousin, cinematographer **James Wong Howe**. By 16, she was a star, appearing opposite Douglas Fairbanks as a Mongol slave girl in the silent *The Thief of Baghdad* (1923), and she went on to make 30 silent films. After a stint in Europe to avoid stereotyping, she returned to Hollywood and was cast opposite Marlene Dietrich as a reformed prostitute and Dietrich's companion in Joseph von Sternberg's film noir *Shanghai Express* (1932). Overt racism prevented her from being cast in the lead of *The Good Earth* (1937) as O-lan, in the film adaptation of Pearl Buck's novel (the part went to Austrian actress Luise Rainer); when offered a supporting role, Wong declined. Among her roles was the heroine and titular character in William Nigh's *The Lady from Chungking* (1942), as the Chinese rebel Madame Kwan Mei who fights against the Japanese occupiers, Mata Hari style, and sacrifices herself for the cause. Although she was not used to her full potential, Wong is a true pioneer, blazing a trail on-screen for Asian actors; her career spanned 40 years and she made another 25 talking pictures before her death, caused by cirrhosis of the liver. In 2004, retrospectives were held at New York's Museum of Modern Art and the University of California at Los Angeles (UCLA) Film and Television Archive.

WONG, ANTHONY CHAU-SANG (1961–). Born in Hong Kong to a Chinese mother and British father, Wong began formal acting training at 21 at Asia Television Limited (ATV); when he graduated from Hong Kong's Academy of Performing Arts, he spent the 1980s working in **television**. He gained attention with his performance as the villain Johnny Wong in **John Woo's** *Hard-Boiled (Hot-Handed God of Cops)/Lat sau san taam/Lashou shentan* (1992) and as **Chow Yun-fat's** sidekick in **Cheung Yuen-ting's** *Now You See Love . . . Now You Don't (I Love Nau Man-chai [Rogue Meets Warrior])/Ngoh oi Nau Man-chai (lau man yue do bing)/Wo ai Nu Wen Chai (liu mang yu dao bing)* (both 1992). He received a Hong Kong Best Supporting Actor nomination for the latter, and won Best Actor at the **Hong Kong Film Awards** for his lead performance as Wong Chi-hang, a real-life serial killer who used his victim's remains to serve human pork buns in his restaurant in **Herman Yau's** *The Untold Story (The Eight Immortals Restaurant's BBQ Hu-*

man Pork Buns, aka *Bunman)/Baat sin faan dim chi yan yuk cha siu baau/Ba xian fan dian zhi ren rou cha shao bao* (1993), a true crime story. Diagnosed with thyroid disorder in the mid-1990s, Wong overcame his illness and won the Best Actor award for his police detective traversing the line between good and evil in **Gordon Chan's** *Beast Cops/Yau sau ying ging/Ye shou xing jing* (1998). In 2001, he was a triple nominee for *Princess D (Want to Fly)/Seung fei/Xiang fei*, *Just One Look/Yat luk che/Yi lu zhe*, and **Andrew Lau's** *Infernal Affairs/Mou gaan dou/Wu jian dao*; he won Best Actor from the **Hong Kong Film Critics Society** for *Infernal Affairs* and a Best Supporting Actor Award for *Princess D* at the Taiwan **Golden Horse Awards**.

Wong is a versatile and prolific actor, having appeared in over 100 films and television dramas. His film debut was in 1985, as the James Dean bad boy in *My Name Ain't Suzie/Dut gaai shut doi/Hua jie shi dai*, obviously a Chinese response to *The World of Suzie Wong*. He has directed two films, *The New Tenant (New Neighbor)/San fong haak/Xin fang ke* (1995) and *Top Banana Club (Golden Banana Club)/Gam jong heung ji kui lik bo/Jin zhuang xiang jiao ju le bu* (1996), the former a creepy, mood-saturated horror film with a terrific sense of place. Wong plays guitar and has recorded self-penned releases, "Underdog Rock" and "Useless Is Useful," both of which have been censored on the Mainland. He is a practicing **martial artist** in the style called Tai Shing Pek Kwar and is a student of Grandmaster Chau Sau-chung. He has appeared in Category 3 pictures (CAT 3), among them *The Underground Banker (Hong Kong Strange Case: The Bloodsucking Wealthy King)/Heung Gong on ji kap huet gwai lei wong/Xiang Gang qi an zhi xi xue gui li wang* (1993), a role among his favorites because of its humanized character.

Wong has frequently created memorable characters and collaborated with directors Herman Yau, **Kirk Wong**, and Johnnie To. He played real-life Italian activist priest Franco Mella in **Ann Hui's** *Ordinary Heroes/Chin yin maan yue/Qianyan wanyu* (1999) that won Best Film at the 19th Hong Kong Film Awards, and also won Taiwan's Golden Horse Award for Best Supporting Actor for his role in *Initial D/Tau man chi D/Tou wen zi D* (2005). He has also performed on the theatrical stage when he is not making films. Wong is not one to mince words, candid, irreverent, and holding strong opinions on numerous topics.

WONG, ARTHUR NGOK-TAI (1956–). Cinematographer Arthur Wong began shooting movies with **Lau Kar-leung's** ***36th Chamber of Shaolin****/Lam qui luk fong/Shaolin sa liu fang* (1978). To date he has shot close to 60 films, including many for **Tsui Hark**, as in the seminal *Once upon a Time in China/Wong Fei-hung/Huang feihong* series (1991–1993). He has won numerous Best Cinematography awards at the **Hong Kong Film Awards**, for films as varied as **Cheung Yuen-ting's** drama *Soong Sisters/Sung ga wong chiu/Song gu huang chao* (1997), **Lee Chi-ngai's** moody **action** film *Sleepless Town/Bat yau shing/Bu ye cheng* (1998), Teddy Chen's intense actioner *Purple Storm/Chi yue fung biu/Zi yu feng bao* (1999), **Ann Hui's** horror story *Visible Secret/Yau leng yan gaan/ Youling renjian* (2001), and **Carol Lai's independent** *Floating Landscape/Luen ji fung ging/Lian zhi feng jing* (2003).

WONG, BARRY PING-YIU (1946–1990). Screenwriter Barry Wong was born in Wuzhou, Guangxi province, and graduated from Hong Kong's Chinese University. Before he began writing screenplays in 1981, he was a secondary school teacher. He wrote more than 30 movies, including **Samo Hung's** *Prodigal Son/ Bai ga jai/Baijia zi* 1981 (1981) and *Heart of the Dragon/Lung dik sam/Long de xin* (1985), *Mr. Vampire 1* and *2/ Geung shi sin sang/ Jiangshi xiansheng* (1985, 1986), and John Woo's *Hard-Boiled/Kwong sau san taam/ Lashou shentan* (1992). He also acted in 17 films, including Woo's *The Killer/Dip huet seung hung/Die xie shuang xiong* (1989) and **Peter Chan's** *Alan and Eric: Between Hello and Goodbye/Seung shing goo si/Shuang cheng gu shi* (1991). Sadly, Wong died prematurely of a cerebral hemorrhage.

WONG, BILL CHUNG-PIU (1946–). Born in Guangdong province, cinematographer Bill Wong started as a still photographer before working as a **television** cameraman at Radio Television Hong Kong (RTHK), beginning in 1971, on the series *Under (Below) the Lion Rock.* He moved to Hong Kong Television Broadcasts Limited (TVB) in 1979, working with both **Ann Hui** and **Patrick Tam**, directors who would become part of Hong Kong's **New Wave**. He shot both Hui's *The Story of Woo Viet/Woo Yuet dik goo si/Hu Yue de gu shi* (1980), *Romance of Book and Sword/Shu kim yan chau luk/Shu* *jian en chou lu*, and *Princess Fragrance/Heung heung cung chu/Xiang xiang gong zhu* (both 1987) and Tam's *Nomad/Lit foh ching chun/Lie huo qing chun* (1982). He lensed close to 50 films in the 1980s and 1990s, working several times with directors like **John Woo**, **Tsui Hark**, **Corey Yuen**, **Lee Chi-ngai**, **Stanley Kwan**, and **Shu Kei**, a testament to his talent. He has won Best Cinematography at the **Golden Horse Awards** for four films, namely Tsui's *All the Wrong Clues (for the Right Solution)/Gwai ma ji doh sing/Gui ma zhi duo xing* (1980), **Tony Au's** *The Last Affair/Dut shing/Hua cheng* (1983) and *Dream Lovers/Mung chung yan/Meng zhong ren* (1986), and Kwan's *Full Moon in New York/Yan joi nau yeuk/Ren zai niu yue* (1989).

WONG, CHO-SAN (Huang Chushan) (1911–). Actor Wong Cho-san, a native of Guangdong province, was a **Chinese opera** actor whose stage name was Huang Jianbo, and he performed in the United States. With the assistance of Xie Yizhi, he joined **Tianyi** in 1935 and became a film actor. His screen debut was *The Fire of E Fang Palace* (1935). He also appeared in *The Boat Girl* (1936) under his stage name. Prewar films include *Hero of Dragon City/Lung shing fei cheung/Long cheng fei jiang* (1938) and *The Luminous (Luminescent) Cup/Yau gwong booi/Ye guang bei* (1939). During the Sino–Japanese War, Huang performed with the Mingxing Drama Group across Southeast Asia, playing the lead in *Sunrise* and *Thunderstorm*.

Wong was referred to as one of the "Licorice Root Actors," that is, a seasoned performer; he was one of the fine supporting actors whose subtle characterizations contributed to the lead on-screen. He appeared in hundreds of films before retiring in 1967, was cast in a wide variety of roles, but is most memorable for kindhearted and righteous or downtrodden characters. His best roles include parts in Lau Fong's *Laughter and Tears (Some Are Happy, Some Are Sad)/Jijia huanxiao jijia chou* (1950), *In the Face of Demolition/Aau lau chun hiu/ Weilou chunxiao* (1953), and **Ng Wui's** *Father and Son/Foo yue ji/Fu yu zi* (1954). In *Laughter and Tears*, Wong played a simple silkworm farmer with dignity; he is besieged by a city syndicate scheming to monopolize the silk business and is beaten to death by debtors; one of his sons jumps from a cliff when the silk farm is burned, and the other, a reformed profligate, leads a peasant rebellion. The story was based on the real lives of silk farmers in Shunde, and **Grandview** brought silkworms and cocoons from there for the Hong Kong shoot.

In 1966, Wong founded and managed the Hong Kong Actors' Company. He immigrated to the United States in 1967.

WONG, FAYE FEI (1969–). Born in Beijing, singer and actress Faye Wong has made only half a dozen films, but she is recognized internationally for her work with **Wong Kar-wai**. Faye Wong came to Hong Kong as a teenager to pursue a singing career; by the early 1990s she had established herself as an alternative pop diva, not unlike Bjork, singing primarily in Mandarin. Early on she appeared in several Hong Kong **television** soap operas, and her film debut was in *Beyond's Diary/Beyond yat gei mok hei siu nin kung/Beyond ri ji mo qi shao nian qiong* (1991) as the girlfriend of one of the members of a boy band (played by the real boy band Beyond). But it was in Wong's *Chungking Express/Chunghing sam lam/Zong qing sen lin* (1994), as a gamine slacker, that she captured hearts and minds; she recently appeared in Wong's sequel to *In the Mood for Love/Fa yeung nin wa/Hua yang nian hua* (2000), *2046* (2004), in two roles, one as a robot. She also appeared in **Gordon Chan's** bittersweet romantic comedy *Okinawa(n) Rendezvous/Luen chin chung sing/Lian zhan chong sheng* (2000), with **Leslie Cheung** and **Leung Ka-fai**, **Wilson Yip's independent-**spirited relationship movie *Leaving Me, Loving You/Dai shing siiu si/Da cheng xiao shi* (2004), opposite **Leon Lai**, and again opposite **Tony Leung Chiu-wai** in Wong Kar-wai's *2046.*

WONG FEI-HUNG SERIES. Wong Fei-hung (1847–1924) is a Chinese folk hero and **martial arts** legend. He was born in Nanhoi in China's southern province of Guangdong. His famous father, Wong Kei-ying, was a Chinese herbalist and master of Shaolin martial arts as handed down from the Southern Jiulianshan Monastery in Fujian (founded by renegade monks who fled the destruction of the Northern Songshan Monastery in Henan Province by Imperial forces in the 1700s). Although his father wanted his son to be a scholar, Wong Kei-ying eventually relented and he and his master Luk Ah-choy taught Fei-hung the Hung Gar style of martial arts. As a young man Wong Fei-hung made his living from martial arts street performances and was one of the province's best lion dancers. He also became a practitioner of herbal medicine at Po Chi Lam, the herbal medicine clinic passed on by his father, located in Fu Shan, where he practiced medicine and taught Hung Gar to select students, including his favorite Lam Sai-wing, as well as instructing the Cantonese Black Flag militia in basic martial arts. He married several times, and was survived by his last wife, Mo Kwei-lan, who moved to Hong Kong after his death and taught martial arts. No surviving portraits of the real Wong Fei-hung exist, and most of the accepted facts of his life are taken from the biography *The Extraordinary Martial Hero of Lingnan*, by Zhu Yuzhai. To the Chinese, Wong Fei-hung represents the values of true martial arts, including practicing for health and self-defense, protecting the oppressed and weak, championing truth and justice, and favoring nonviolent solutions.

In 1949 director **Wu Pang** (Hu Peng) was taking the ferry across Victoria Harbor with friend and **Cantonese opera** composer Wu Yi-xiao and read an installment of a Wong Fei-hung novel in the newspaper *Kung Sheung Daily News* that stated Wu had been a student of Wong Fei-hung; despite Wu Yi-xiao's denial, Wu Pang was intrigued and directed the first Wong Fei-hung film, *The True Story of Wong Fei-hung: Whiplash Snuffs the Candle Flame/Wong Fei Hung chuen/ Huang Fei Hong chuan*, that began a voluminous series. Wu scripted the first four films. Between 1949 and 1970, Wong Fei-hung served as subject for almost 100 films, and actor **Kwan Tak-hing**, an opera performer and martial arts practitioner, starred in 78 of them as the stern yet fair patriarch, creating an indelible screen presence that would forever link him to the character.

The golden age of the films was the 1950s, during which 62 were made, mostly directed by Wu Pang, with titles including *Wong Fei-hung Tries His Shadowless Kick/Wong Fei-hung choh shut mo ying geuk/Huang Feihong chu shi wu ying jiao* (1954), *Wong Fei-hung Wins the Dragon Boat Race/Wong Fei-hung lung jau duet gam/ Huang Feihong long zhou duo jin* (1956), and *How Wong Fei-hung Defeated the Tiger on the Opera Stage* (*Wong Fei-hung fai pang fook foo/Huang Feihong hu peng fu hu* (1959). **Shek Kin** became established as the villain and Yam Yin played the female lead; supporting casts included **Walter Tso Tat-wah**, **Sai Gua-pau**, and Lau Charn (father of **Lau Kar-leung**.) In the 1960s, 13 films were produced, with Wong Fung as major director, such as *Wong Fei-hung: The*

Invincible Lion Dancer/Wong Fei-hung seng shut duk ba mooi dut chong/Huang Feihong xing shi du ba mei hua zhuang (1968) and *Wong Fei-hung: The Duel for the "Sha Yu Ching"/Wong Fei-hung haau duet "qui yue ching"/Huang Feihong qiao duo "sha yu qing"* (1969). Supporting casts included **Kenneth Tsang Kong**, Cheung Ying-choi, and Lee Hung, while Kwan Tak-hing and Shek Kin remained, parlaying Kwan's Southern-style fighting (solid stances and power techniques) against Shek's Northern style (quick movements and fast, high kicks).

The best of the films were innovative by portraying realistic martial arts practices and weaponry (as opposed to the fantasy martial arts of palm power and flying swords then popular) as well as the styles favored in Guangdong. The authentic folk culture, traditions, and music of Guangdong and Hong Kong were brought to life, and the Cantonese dialect was spoken. Wong's traditional Confucian values made him heroic. In *The Invincible Lion Dancer*, for example, the simple plot highlights his stature. Wong demonstrates his skill, his students get in trouble with the villain, Wong reluctantly fights the villain, succeeds, but shows mercy. As a whole, the films were immensely popular.

After 1970, Kwan Tak-hing appeared in only three Wong Fei-hung movies, *The Sky Hawk/Wong Fei-hung siu lam kuen/Huang Feihong* (1974), *The Magnificent Butcher/Lam Sai-wing/Lin Shirong* (1979), and *Dreadnaught/Yung je mo gui/Yong zhe wu ju* (1981); the former and latter were directed by **Yuen Wo-ping**, who, as many other martial arts filmmakers (including **Lau Kar-leung**), got his start as a child working in small parts on earlier Wong Fei-hung films. (Yuen Wo-ping's father, **Simon Yuen Siu-tin**, had worked as action choreographer on many of them.) The legacy of the Wong films of the 1950s and 1960s includes the impact on many martial arts filmmakers currently working, whether they made Wong Fei-hung movies or not.

Yuen Wo-ping took the legend in a new direction, with a martial arts action comedy, *Drunken Master/Chui kuen/Zui quan* (1978), starring **Jackie Chan** and Yuen Siu-tin, and Chan and Lau Kar-leung directed another, *Drunken Master 2/Chui kuen 2/Zui quan 2* (1994), also starring Chan as Wong Fei-hung. In both films, Wong Fei-hung had a good heart but got into trouble on countless occasions. In the former, he underwent severe training by the master played by Yuen Siu-tin. In the latter film, Chan's Wong's mischievousness is encouraged by his mother (**Anita Mui**) and tempered by his father (**Ti Lung**). The disregarded closeness of age between these three characters, and Lau Kar-leung and Ti Lung's presence as **Shaw Brothers**' martial arts stars, were also part of the joke. Yuen Wo-ping is also largely credited with inventing Jackie Chan's comedic martial arts persona in period pieces, heading martial arts action in a new direction. Wong Fei-hung was parodied in *Once upon a Time a Hero in China/Wong Fei-hung siu chuen/Huang Feihong xiao chuan* (1992), starring Alan Tam as a Wong unversed in martial arts, and its sequel *Master Wong vs. Master Wong/Wong Fei-hung dui Wong Fei-hung/Huang Feihong dui Huang Feihong* (1993). Real life *wushu* champion and actor **Jet Li** also spoofed the legend in *The Last Hero in China/Wong Fei-hung ji tit gai dau ng gung/Huang Feihong zhi tie ji dou we gong* (1993). Even Kwan Tak-hing appeared in the **Lunar New Year's comedy** *It's a Wonderful Life*, as a benign grandfather who sets his mixed-up family aright, basically reprising and gently ribbing the recognizable Wong Fei-hung image.

Wong Fei-hung movies were reinvented in the 1990s. With 1997 on the horizon, **Tsui Hark** created a politically subtexted Wong Fei-hung for the 1990s, with his series ***Once upon a Time in China***, that essentially (but on a smaller scale) defined Jet Li as the new Wong Fei-hung (although Li appeared in only four of the six films). The series included *Once upon a Time in China/Wong Fei-hung/Huang Feihong* (1991); *Once upon a Time in China 2 (Wong Fei-hung 2: A Man Should Be Self-Sufficient)/Wong Fei-hung ji yi naam yi dong ji keung/Huang Feihong zhi er nan er dang zi qiang* (1992); *Once upon a Time in China 3 (Wong Fei-hung 3: The Lion King Struggles for Supremacy)/Wong Fei-hung ji saam si wong jaang ba/Huang Feihong zhi san shi wang zheng ba* (1993); *Once upon a Time in China 4 (Wong Fei-hung 4: Royal Demeanor)/Wong Fei-hung ji 4 wong je ji fung/Huang Feihong zhi 4 wang zhe zhi feng* (1993); *Once upon a Time in China 5 (Wong Fei-hung 5: Dragon City's Murderous Tyrant)/Wong Fei-hung chi neung lung shing chim bat/Huang Feihong zhi wu long cheng jian ba* (1994); and *Once upon a Time in China and America (Wong Fei-hung: West Territory Mighty Lion)/Wong Fei-hung chi sai wik hung shut/Wong Feihong zhi xi yu xiong shi* (1997).

Tsui Hark produced all of them, directing episodes 1, 2, 3, and 5. The films are epic in scale, featuring artful camerawork and impressive action sequences. They celebrate Chinese culture but establish an Eastern–Western and traditional–modern dynamic. Tsui's revisionist history also reimagines China to comment upon Hong Kong and Mainland relations. Tsui used Yuen Wo-ping as action director for the second film in the series, and collaborated with him again (as producer) on the Yuen-directed *Iron Monkey/Siu nin Wong Fei-hung ji tit ma lau/Shao nian Huang Feihong zhi tie ma liu* (1993), which serves as a prequel to Tsui's series (as well as the other traditional Wong Fei-hung movies). In this version, Wong is a young boy (played in the film by a young girl, martial artist Tsang Sze-man) learning from his Confucian father (**Donnie Yen**), with the father Wong Kei-ying usurping the characterization usually reserved for Wong Fei-hung. The character Wong Fei-hung remains a popular and enduring cinematic folk hero.

WONG, HOK-SING (Huang Hesheng) (1913–1994). Cantonese opera actor and director Wong Hok-sing was born in Guangdong province and was one of the first graduates of the Ba He Opera Training Institute. He joined famous opera actor **Sit Kok-sin's** Juexiansheng Opera Troupe, playing supporting roles. In the Wannianqing (Forever Green) Opera Troupe, he began playing leads in 1937. After performing in Vietnam, he came to Hong Kong and joined **Ma Sze-tsang's** Tai Ping Opera Troupe.

Wong's film debut was *General Di Qing* (1940), and over a 30-year film career he starred in more than 30 features and directed more than 160, produced both in Hong Kong and the United States. Among his title roles are *Massacre of the Innocents (One Hundred Thousand Children's Corpses)/Sap maan tung shut/Shiwan tongshi* (1940), an opera adaptation concerning a tyrannical emperor who sets out to eliminate an entire family of loyal officials, including the first-born child, at the advice of his favorite concubine; a brave knight sacrifices his own child. Another is *The Story of Mu Guiying, 1* and *2 (Legend of Wang Zhaojun)/Wong Chiu Wan/Wang Zhao Yin* (1940), mixing opera and comedy.

Wong's directorial debut was Hong Kong's first color film, *White Powder and Neon Lights/Gam fan aau seung/Jinfen nichang* (1947), shot in the United States. The director's opera films include *Seven Phoenixes/Gam fung cham gaau lung/Jin feng zhang jiao long* (1961), *Romance of the Phoenix Chamber/Fung gok yan chau ching mei liu/Feng ge en chou qing wei le* (1962), *Battling Sound/Lui ming gam goo chin fung sing/Lei ming jin gu zhan jia sheng* (1963), and *Who Should Be the Commander-in-Chief?/Lung fung chang gwa sui/Long feng zheng gua shuai* (1967). The opera comedy *Romance of the Phoenix Chamber*, starring **Mak Bing-wing**, **Fung Wong-nui**, **Leung Sing-po**, and **Tan Lanqing**, features a convoluted plot and humorous performances by the *chou* players (clowns, Shakespearean-style fools), especially Cantonese opera's prominent *chou*, Leung Sing-po, supported by his female counterpart, Tan Lanqing. Wong also made a **documentary** celebrating opera entitled *The Goddess of Mercy Celebrates Her Birthday at Xiangshan/Goon yam dak diy heung dut saan daai hoh sau/Guan yin de dao xiang hua shan da he shou* (1966). He directed modern films such as the comedies *Half a Bed/Boon cheung luk fung chong/Ban zhang lu jia chuang* (1964) and *All Packed in a Small House/Muk nguk qui din yue/Mu wu sha dian yu* (1965).

In 1971, Wong immigrated to the United States and worked in San Francisco's Chinatown Theater. He died in the United States.

WONG, JAMES JUM-SUM (1940–2004). Actor, composer, director, and lyricist, James Wong came to Hong Kong with his family in 1949 migrating from Guangzhou. Wong graduated from the University of Hong Kong in 1963. While working in advertising, Wong teamed with composer **Joseph Koo** at Hong Kong Television Broadcasts Limited (TVB). Koo composed the songs and Wong wrote the lyrics for some of the most famous **Cantopop** hits. Some of their most famous **television** collaborations include *Shanghai Beach* and *Under (Below) the Lion Rock*. Sometimes called "the devilish genius" Wong was a jack-of-all-trades. While working with Koo, Wong also began to branch out. His first film role was in *The Country Bumpkin/Daai heung lee/Da xiang li* (1974). Wong would continue to appear in many films, mostly comedies, all the way up until his death. Other memorable films include *Iron Monkey/Siu nin Wong Fei-h ung ji tit ma lau/Shao nian Huang Feihong zhi tie ma liu* (1993), *All's Well End's Well, Too/Dut tin hei si/Hua tian xi shi* (1993), *Flirting*

Scholar/Tong Pak-fu dim Chou-heung/Tang Bohu dian Qiuxiang (1993), and *It's A Wonderful Life/Daai foo ji ga/da fu zhi jia* (1994). He also provided the voice for the Taoist ghostbuster in *A Chinese Ghost Story: The Tsui Hark Animation/Siu sin/Xiao qian* (1997). Wong's voice is well known to people in Hong Kong for its distinctive deep, rich laugh.

However, Wong's music is his biggest contribution. Many of the biggest Cantopop stars including **Roman Tam**, **Frances Yip**, Johnny Ip, **Kenny Bee**, **Leslie Cheung**, and **Jenny Tseng** have attributed a great deal of their success to the songs written by Koo and Wong, or by Wong as a solo composer and lyricist. Wong composed the soundtracks to many of the most important Hong Kong films including *Shanghai Blues/Seung hoi ji yau/Shanghai zhiye* (1984), *Peking (Beijing) Opera Blues/Diy ma dan/Dao ma dan* (1986), *A Chinese Ghost Story/Sin nui yau wan/ /Qiannu youhun* (1987), *Swordsman/Siu ngo gong wu/Xiao ao jianghu*(1990), *Bullet in the Head/Dip huet gaai tau/Die xue jie tou* (1990), *Once upon a Time in China/Wong Fei Hung/Hwang Feihong* (1991), *Fong Sai Yuk/Fọng Sai Yuk/Fang Shiyu* (1993), and *Green Snake/Ching se/Qing she*. Wong also wrote the song "Dong Nin Ching" and gave it to **John Woo** to use for free in ***A Better Tomorrow*** *(True Colors of a Hero)/Ying hung boon sik/ Yingxiong bense* (1986).

Besides his film and music careers, Wong also wrote a series of bawdy books full of adult jokes. Wong was known as an uninhibited man during the 1970s, and he helped to break down some of the conservative barriers of traditional Chinese society. He also hosted several talk shows, somewhat similar in format to David Letterman's *The Late Show* in the United States. In 2003, Wong received his doctorate in music from the University of Hong Kong shortly before he died from lung cancer. In all, Wong wrote the lyrics for more than 2,000 Cantopop songs.

WONG, JING (1956–). Born in Hong Kong, the son of director **Wang Tianlin,** director, screenwriter, and producer Wong Jing graduated from Chinese University and began work as a scriptwriter for **television**, working on numerous series such as *The Good, the Bad and the Ugly* and *CID*. He began writing screenplays for film with *Cunning Tendency/Gwai ma kwong chiu/Gui ma kuang chao* (1978), and his directorial debut was *Challenge of the Gamesters/Chin wong dau chin ba/Qian wang dou qian ba* (1981), which he also wrote. Notable films as director and writer include *Winner Takes All/Chaak wong ji wong/Ze wang zhi wang* (1982) and *God of Gamblers/Do san/Du shen* (1989). Notable films as director are *God of Gamblers' Return (God of Gamblers 2)/Do san 2/Du shen 2* (1994); *Royal Tramp 1* and *2/Luk ting kei/Lu ding ji* (1992); *Casino Tycoon 1* and *2/Diy shing daai hang/Du cheng da heng* (1992); and *Boys Are Easy (Chasing Boys)/Chui lam chai/Zhui nan zai* (1993).

The most commercial filmmaker in Hong Kong (and Hong Kong film, for the most part, is commercial), Wong's primary goals are to entertain average and working-class people, providing them with a brief (90-minute) escape from reality, and to make money. He has succeeded at both. He is credited with a hand in over 120 movies since the 1980s. His movies share broad humor and the lowest common denominator in regards to taste; still Wong has borrowed shamelessly from Hollywood and recognizes and capitalizes on trends. Indeed, he restarted the gambling craze in Hong Kong movies with *God of Gamblers* after the genre had remained dormant since the 1960s. He is responsible for producing numerous **Stephen Chiau** and **Anthony Wong** films as well as for discovering **Chingmy Yau**. Wong also kept actors working during the aftermath of the Asian economic crisis, reverting, for a time, to the "eight-day wonders" of the past. He also occasionally acts or appears in cameos in films.

Wong set up **BOB & Partners** (Best of the Best) in the late 1990s, along with director **Andrew Lau** and writer Manfred Wong, and is credited with production of the *Young and Dangerous* series (1996–2000) as well as *Storm Riders* (1998).

WONG, KAR-WAI (1958–). Born in Shanghai, Wong Kar-wai immigrated to Hong Kong with his parents when he was five years old. His brother and sisters remained behind, planning to follow but unable to do so during the Cultural Revolution, and Wong's correspondence with his brother led to their sharing thoughts about the literature they read, including Leo Tolstoy, Honoré Balzac, and Fyodor Dostoyevsky. This experience, as well as seeing movies with his mother and growing up in the Shanghainese enclave in Hong Kong, with a language and sophisticated culture of its own, led to Wong's creative bent.

Graduating from Hong Kong Polytechnic in graphic design in 1980, he worked as a production assistant for Hong Kong Television Broadcasts Ltd. (TVB) and later became a scriptwriter for **Cinema City**. Credited with 10 scripts, including **Patrick Tam's** *Final Victory/Chui hau sing lei/Zui hou sheng li* (1987), Wong claims he wrote as many as 50, in collaboration with others for several companies.

Wong's directorial debut was *As Tears Go By (Mongkok Carmen, Carmen of the Streets)/Wong kok Ka Moon/Wang jiao Ka Men* (1988), an homage to Martin Scorsese's *Mean Streets*, starring **Andy Lau** as a gangster wanting to change his life, torn between the troublesome friend he is loyal to (**Jacky Cheung**) and the woman he loves (**Maggie Cheung**). The film garnered 10 **Hong Kong Film Award** nominations. His next film, *Days of Being Wild (The True Story of Ah Fei)/Ah Fei ching chuen/ Ah Fei zhengzhuan* (1990), was his first homage to the 1960s Hong Kong of his youth, starring **Leslie Cheung** as an emotionally needy wild and wounded bad boy charmer. The film won five Hong Kong Film Awards, including Best Film and Director. The Eastern–Western ***Ashes of Time*** *(Evil East, Malicious West)/Dung chea sai duk/Dong xie xi du* (1994) took two years to film in the desert and mountains of China, and during a respite of two months, Wong knocked off *Chungking Express (Chungking Forest)/Chung Hing sam lam/ Zong qing sen lin* (1994); both films were recognized at the 1995 Hong Kong Film Awards, the former winning three and the latter winning four, including Best Film and Director. *Fallen Angels/Doh lok tin si/Duoluo tianshi* (1995) was Wong's riff on **John Woo's** hit man from *The Killer* (1989) and **Allen Fong's** relationship movie *Father and Son/Foo ji ching/Fuzi qing* (1981), starring **Leon Lai**, **Michelle Reis**, **Kaneshiro Takeshi**, and **Karen Mok**. *Happy Together (A Sudden Leak of Spring Light)/Chun gwong ja sit/Chun guang zha xie* (1997), an ostensibly gay love story of two Hong Kong men lost in Argentina (Wong himself denies the love story is limited to gay characters, and sexual orientation is irrelevant to the story), and costarring Leslie Cheung and **Tony Leung Chiu-wai**, won Best Director and Actor awards (for Wong and Leung) at the 1997 Cannes Film Festival and shocked Hong Kong audiences by casting two stars in gay roles (albeit one of them, Cheung, was gay). *In the Mood for Love/Fa yeung nin wa/Hua yang nian hua* (2000) also costarred Leung and Maggie Cheung, and serves as

Wong's love letter to the Shanghainese community in 1960s Hong Kong. The film won Best Actor for Leung at the Cannes International Film Festival, Screen International Award, Best Non-European Film at the European Film Academy Awards, and Best Actress (Maggie Cheung), Best Cinematography, and Best Costume Design Awards at the Taiwanese **Golden Horse Awards**.

Wong has created his own production company, Block 2 Pictures/ Jet Tone. He goes against the grain of Hong Kong cinema, choosing art house projects over mainstream commercial films. His films are more popular internationally, screening at influential film festivals and in **independent** art house cinemas. Quentin Tarantino's Rolling Thunder, a subsidiary of Miramax, distributed *Chungking Express* nationwide in the United States. Others distributed include *Fallen Angels*, *Happy Together*, and *In the Mood for Love*.

Wong frequently collaborates with a handful of actors (Maggie Cheung, Tony Leung Chiu-wai, Leslie Cheung), cinematographer **Christopher Doyle**, and art director and editor **William Chang**. Music serves as an impetus for his films, and Wong and Doyle spend a great deal of time listening for mood. Ironically, since he began, after all, as a screenwriter, Wong makes it a practice of working without scripts and writing scenes and dialogue as he is filming, drawing his inspiration from place and characters situated in the location.

A distinctive look, varied film speeds, edgy and unusual camera angles, handheld and steadicam camerawork, nonlinear plots, voice-over (more accurately voice off, as narration does not necessarily match a character or place), and guerilla shooting (working without permits on location, Wong by necessity works fast) all demarcate Wong's films. He explains that he finds the film in the editing process. Evocative recurrent themes of love and loss, loneliness and alienation, chance and fate are meditated upon and mediated by visual style. In *Days of Being Wild*, alienated youth miss connecting with each other. In *Ashes of Time*, a deconstructed narrative of flashbacks and forwards relates the lives of two swordsmen (and those who love them) unraveling across an existential landscape. **Samo Hung** choreographed the action as cinematographer Chris Doyle and editor William Chang were remaking it, with slow motion, jump cuts, and freeze-frames. (Most **martial arts action** aficionados hated the movie.) With *In the Mood for Love,* Wong comes close to expressing the inexpressible, a love affair without the affair. *Happy Together* ends on an upbeat note, with Danny Chung's cover song of the Turtles' "Happy Together" playing as Tony Leung's character, riding the Taipei train, rushes to meet his future. Still, the lovers in this film can only be happy together apart. *Chungking Express*, Wong's most popular film, defines a new way of uniting for lovers of a particular place and time—Hong Kong on the verge of its return to the Mainland. Wong's current project, and first widescreen production, *2046*, which played the Cannes Film Festival, addresses Hong Kong and Mainland relations 50 years later.

Locally criticized as pretentious (he always wears reflective sunglasses for interviews and appearances), Wong belies the appellation by his sense of humor. He produced director **Eric Kot's** *First Love: The Litter on the Breeze* (1997), a parody of Wong's style and persona, as well as **Jeff Lau's** *Eagle Shooting Heroes* (1993), another parody, this one of **Louis Cha's** novel *The Eagle Shooting Hero*, which also served as the basis for Wong's serious film ***Ashes of Time***. Wong thinks of all his films as an ongoing story, all contributing to one in-progress movie.

WONG, KIRK CHE-KEUNG (1949–). Born in Hong Kong, director Kirk Wong is synonymous with hard-hitting, in-your-face **action**. In his youth, he studied fashion design at Jacob Kramer College in Leeds, and after graduating he entered Croydon College of Art to study stage design and film production, taking on **television** and theater work for Anglia Television and Covent Garden. In 1978, he returned to Hong Kong and immersed himself in television production. His first feature, *The Club (Dance Hall)/Miu teng/Wu ting* (1981), established him as a director and mapped out a territory he would continue to traverse—criminal stories based on true events. *Health Warning (Fighting for the Top Spot,* aka *Flash Future Kung Fu)/Dai lui toi/Da lei tai* (1983) charted new territory as a mixture of science fiction and **kung fu**, an apocalyptic vision of kung fu cults as constructive and destructive. *Crime Story (Serious Crime Unit)/Chung ngon cho/ Zhonganzu* (1993), *Organized Crime and Triad Bureau (True Record of Important Case: Department O)/Chung ngon sat luk O gei/Chong an shi lu O ji* (1994), and *Rock 'n' Roll Cop (South China's Public Enemy #1)/Saang Gong yat ho tung chap faan/Sheng*

Gang yi hao tong ji fan (also 1994) followed the direction of *The Club*, returning to true-life crime. In the first, **Jackie Chan** played a vulnerable and uncertain cop who often falls short in the performance of his duties, an uncharacteristic part for the prolific action comedy actor. In the second, **Danny Lee** and **Anthony Wong** costarred as cop and criminal nemeses. Wong reappeared as title character in the latter, and all three films were inspired by the life and writings of former Hong Kong cop Winky Wong.

These films, among others, set the tone for Kirk Wong's unrelenting action and visual stylishness. His signature tracking shots and unusual camera angles navigate a dark underworld and provide a parallel dark vision in which action emerges from characters' conflicts. Other films, like *True Colors/Ying hung jing chuen/Ying xiong zheng chuan* (1986, which costarred **Ti Lung** and **Raymond Wong**) and *Gunmen (Dragnet)/Tin law dei mong/Tian lun di wang* (1988, starring **Tony Leung Ka-fai**) cemented a code of honor for both sides of the law. The director joined fellow Hong Kongers in Hollywood and made *The Big Hit* (1998), which scored number one in the box office in its opening week. Starring Mark Wahlberg, Lou Diamond Phillips, and China Chow, the movie was budgeted at US$13 million and grossed double its production cost in its first year in the United States alone.

Besides directing, Wong has acted in almost 20 films, including numerous cameos and parts in movies such as *Legacy of Rage* (1986), *Casino Raiders* (1989), *God of Gamblers 2* (1991), and *The Mad Monk* (1993).

WONG, MAN-LEI (Huang Manli) (1913–1998). Actress Wong Manlei (real name Huang Wensu) was born in Hong Kong, her family came from Guangdong province, and she was educated in a convent school and Belilios Teachers' College for Women. In 1930, in Shanghai, she joined Ji Nan Film Company and appeared in the silent film *Twenty-Four Fighters* and the partially dubbed *Burning of the White Bird Monastery*. In the latter, she adopted the name Wong Man-lei.

When **Lianhua** opened a Hong Kong branch, Wong returned, appearing in three silent films, including the historical drama *The Sound of the Cuckoo in the Old Temple (Cry of the Cuckoo in the Temple)/Goo chi guen sing/Gu si juan sheng* (1932); she starred in the drama *Song of Yesterday (Yesterday's Song, Voice of the Broken Hearted)/Chok yat yau goh (Duen cheung yan yik duen cheung yee)/Zuo ri ye ge (Duan chang ren yi duan chang er)* (1935), the first Cantonese sound film. Between 1933 and 1966, Wong appeared in over 300 films, including **Lee Tit's** dramas *Melody of Life (Song of Life, A Lost Woman)/Yan sang kuk/Ren sheng qu* (1937) and *In the Face of Demolition/Aau lau chun hiu/Weilou chunxiao* (1953); **Ng Wui's** drama *Prodigal Son/ Baijia zia* (1952) and historical drama *Wilderness/Yuen yau/Yuan ye* (1956); **Chun Kim's** contemporary romance *Like the Cloud's Swift Passage/Liushui xingyun* (1954) and dramas *Following the Gentle Light (The Guiding Light)/Foo hoi ming dang/Ku hai ming deng* (1953) and *Neighbor's All/Ga ga woo woo/Gu gu hu hu* (1954); **Lee Sung-fung's** dramas *Cold Nights (It Was a Cold Winter Night)/Han ye* (1955) and *Broken Spring Dreams/ Chun chaan mung duen/Chun chan meng duan* (1955) and comedy *The Nouveau Riche/Faat data ji yan/Fa da zhi ren* (1956); **Tso Kea's** comedy *The Chair/Jinshan dashao* (1959) and dramas *Salvation/Tsz miu sam/Ci mu xin* (1960), *Many Aspects of Love/Laai ha goo miu/ Luo xia gu mu* (1961), and *Sunset on the River/Moon kong hung/Man jiang hong* (1962); and **Chor Yuen's** Cantonese horror historical drama *A Mad Woman/Fung foo/Feng fu* (1964).

In the tragic *Cold Nights*, a plea for peace, Wong played a matriarch who disapproves of her daughter-in-law; it takes war and her son's (**Ng Cho-fan**) death for the mother to gain understanding, and mother and daughter-in-law are reunited over the son's grave. The film was Hualian's inaugural production, the company having been founded by actor **Ng Cho-fan** and director Lee Sung-fung. In *Salvation*, adapted from dramatist Henrik Ibsen's *Ghosts*, she starred as a mother attempting to keep up her family's reputation after her philandering and decadent husband's death, but the sins of the father are visited upon the son. In the contemporary family comedy *The Chair*, Wong played mother to dissolute son **Cheung Ying**; she hides a diamond bracelet in a chair in case of emergency, and when she is hospitalized, she tells him to recover it; he learns his mistress has sold the chair. In *Many Aspects of Love*, a Zhang Henshui adaptation, she played a revolutionary. She was usually a supporting actress in Cantonese dramas, and most of the films had a social conscience.

Wong was one of the founders of **Zhonglian** Film Company, and she retired after the studio closed. She began appearing in **television** soap operas in 1970, including *The Dawn of Spring* (1972) and *Passenger* (1979). One of her last films was an appearance with **Chow Yun-fat** and **Brigitte Lin** in **Tony Au's** *Dream Lovers/Mung chung yan/Meng zhong ren* (1986).

WONG, MICHAEL MAN-TAK (1965–). A native of Shangdong province, Michael Wong grew up in the United States; he came to Hong Kong in 1983 and made his film debut in *City Hero/Fei foo kei bing/Fei hu ju bing* (1985). His brothers Declan (*God of Gamblers Back to Shanghai/Do hap seunghoi taan diy sing/Du xia shanghai tan du sheng*, 1991) and Russell (*The Vanishing Son,* U.S. TV series) are also actors. He has appeared in close to 65 movies. His breakthrough film was **Gordon Chan's** *Final Option/Fei foo hung sam/Fei hu xiong xin* (1994), and he has stood out since in Chan's yuppie dramedy *The Long and Winding Road (Bright Future)/Gam sau chin ching/Jin xiu qian cheng* (1994), **Lee Chi-ngai's** bittersweet romance *Lost and Found (Edge of the World)/Tin aai hoi gok/Tian ya hai jiao* (1996), the cop drama *The Log (3 Injured Policemen)/3 goh sau seung dik ging chaat/3 go shou shang de jing cha*, and Chan and Dante Lam's gangster–cop drama *Beast Cops/Yau sau ying ging/Ye shou xing jing* (1998), in which Wong held his own against **Anthony Wong**. Michael Wong generally plays very masculine men, although sometimes he is cast against type as an outer tough with a soft and sensitive underbelly.

WONG, RAYMOND PAK-MING (1948–). Actor, writer, and producer Raymond Wong was born in Hong Kong. After a brief stint as a radio announcer in Macau, he began writing for **television** drama series, with his first film credit being for writing and assistant directing on *For Whom to Be Murdered/Suen gwoh/Xuan wo* (1978). Wong is known, both on-screen and off, for his contributions to Hong Kong comedy. He was one of the cofounders (with **Dean Shek** and **Karl Maka**) of **Cinema City** in 1980s, and throughout the decade, Wong was responsible for many of the studio's classic scripts, such as **Tsui Hark's** *All the Wrong Clues (for the Right Solution)/Gwai ma ji doh* *sing/Gui ma zhi duo xing* (1981), *Aces Go Places 2/Chui gai pak dong daai hin sau tung/Zui jia pai dang da xian shen tong* (1983), the *Happy Ghost/Hoi sam gwai/Kai xin gui* series (1984–1991), and *Eighth Happiness (Eight Stars Greetings)/Bat sing bo hei/Ba xing bao xi* (1988), costarring Wong with **Chow Yun-fat** and **Jacky Cheung**.

In 1989, Wong founded his own company, **Mandarin Films**, and produced numerous comedies as well as dramas. Among the former are **Lunar New Year's comedies** (in which he also acted) such as *All's Well, End's Well (Family Has Happy Affairs)/Ga yau bei si/Jia you xi shi* series (1992, 1993, 1997), *It's a Wonderful Life/Big Rich Family/Daai foo ji ga/Da fu zhi jia* (1994), and *Ninth Happiness/Gau sing biu choi/Jiu xing bao xi* (1998). The dramas include **Ronny Yu's** extravagant *Phantom Lover/Ye boon goh sing/Ye ban ge sheng* (1995) and the passionate *Bride with White Hair/Baak faat moh nui Bai fa mo nu chuan* (1993, which Mandarin distributed) and **Ann Hui's** *Eighteen Springs/Boon sang yuen/Ban seng yuan* (1997).

Wong's performance in *It's a Wonderful Life* is characteristic of his comedy. An overworked husband trying to satisfy his boss, wife, parents, and siblings, he fails at everything, becoming an alcoholic and losing his family. He wins them back by cross-dressing as a nanny named Sharon Stone. The ensemble cast of this Chinese New year comedy is first rate, including **Leung Ka-fai**, **Teresa Mo**, **Fung Bo-bo**, **Kwan Tak-hing**, **Tso Tat-wah**, **Anita Yuen**, Lee Hung-kam, **Carol Cheng**, and **Lau Ching-wan**.

WONG, RUBY CHEUK-LING. Actress Ruby Wong began in advertising and debuted in **Johnnie To's** *Loving You/Mo mei san taam/Wuwei shentan* (1995) as the bartender; To cast her in a half dozen more films and became her agent. She has appeared in 20 films, usually cast as a serious, no-nonsense, strong **woman**, and she is notable for realistic parts but equally good in comedy. In To's *Lifeline/Sap maan feng gap/Shi wan huo ji* (1997), she played a firefighter and, like the other actors, performed almost all her stunts (with the danger of fire); in *Too Many Ways to Be No. 1/Yat kuo chi tau dik daan sang/Yi ge zi tou de dan sheng* (1997), she was a needy widow; in *Expect the Unexpected/Fai seung dat yin/Fei chang tu ran* (1998), a conflicted female cop; in *Where a Good Man Goes/Joi gin a long/Zai jian a lang* (1999), a Macau innkeeper; in *Running Out of Time 1* and

2/Aau chin/An zhan (1999, 2001), a believable authority figure, and in *PTU* (2003), a CID agent. She costarred opposite **Leslie Cheung** in *Double Tap/Cheong wong/Qiang wang* (2000), as his loyal girlfriend, despite the evidence weighing against him.

WONG, SAN (1926–1999). Character actor Wong San appeared in close to 80 movies in a career spanning 30 years, usually playing a comic role, and he can be seen in comedies such as **Michael Hui**'s *Games Gamblers Play/Gwai ma seung sing/Gui ma shuang xing* (1974) and **Johnnie To's** *Eighth Happiness/Bat sing bo hei/Ba xing bao xi* (1988). In To's *The Fun, the Luck, and the Tycoon/Gat sing gung chiu/Ji xing gong zhao* (1990) he played **Chow Yun-fat's** wise and supportive butler. He was affectionately called "Uncle Mao."

WONG, VICTOR CHI-KEUNG (1927–2001). Born in San Francisco, a fourth-generation Chinese American, character actor Victor Wong was founding member of Chicago's Second City improv comedy troupe. He attended the University of California, Berkeley and the University of Chicago and earned a master's degree from the Art Institute of San Francisco. Wong was also an artist and a member of San Francisco's Beat scene in the 1950s–early 1960s; City Lights Bookstore owner and poet Lawrence Ferlinghetti hosted his first art exhibit and author Jack Kerouac mentions him in *Big Sur*. Wong was also one of **television's** first Chinese American reporters, working at San Francisco's public television station KQED, from 1968 to 1974. He worked with the Asian American Theater Group in San Francisco, and made his screen debut in **Wayne Wang's** *Chan Is Missing* (1982), and he appeared in three more Wang films, including *The Joy Luck Club* (1993). He acted in close to 30 films, often cast as the wise elder, but with a sense of humor. Other Hollywood films include John Carpenter's cult favorite *Big Trouble in Little China* (1986), Bernardo Bertolucci's epic *The Last Emperor* (1987), and the *Three Ninjas* series (1992–1998). He also was cast in four Hong Kong movies, outstanding as Sissy, who cares for an elderly fellow cage dweller, in **Jacob Cheung's** *Cageman/Lung man/Long min* (1992). After two strokes, Wong retired from acting in 1998, but the **independent** filmmaker Renee Tajima focused on the actor in her documentary on the Asian American experience, *My America (. . . or honk if you love Buddha)* (1999). Wong died peacefully in his sleep.

WONG, YIU (Huang Yao) (1928–). Director and producer Wong Yiu was born in Hong Kong and graduated from Ying Wah College. His father owned a cinema, and during the Sino–Japanese War Wong worked in the family business that distributed foreign films in China. In the early 1950s, Huang learned editing, writing, and producing from director Li Yingyuan. He codirected the Cantonese horror film *Bloody Gloves/Huet sau tiu/Xie shou tao* (1961) with **Mok Hong-si**; he had a run with comedies starring **Tang Pak-wan** and **Sun Ma Sze-tsang**.

Wong's popular **musical** *Girl at Eighteen (Girls Are Flowers/Goo leung sap baat yat deu dut/Gu niang shi ba yi duo hua* (1966), along with Yu He's *Colorful Youth/Choi sik ching chun/Cai se qing chun* (1966), started the Cantonese youth musical trend and launched **Connie Chan Po-chu's** career distinctive from her **martial arts** movies. *Girl at Eighteen* incorporated flashbacks, zooms, and counterpoint between image and music. Chan played a bubbly and independent singing teen orphan with a can-do attitude. At the time, the film made half a million Hong Kong dollars, which set a new record for black-and-white Cantonese features and spawned many imitators.

Wong's more than 40 features include *The Strange Girl/Yan hoi kei dut/Ren hai qi hua* (1967), *Unforgettable First Love/Laan mong choh luen/Nan wang chu lian* (1968), and *Youth in Bloom* (1969). In *The Strange Girl*, **Patsy Ka Ling** starred as a psychologically disturbed young woman, and Wong's visual effects and the narration mirrored her confusions. Wong also made half a dozen films in Thaïland. He began working as a producer for **Shaw Brothers** in 1970 and retired completely in the mid-1980s. His son, Taylor Wong, is also a director/producer.

WOO, JOHN (Ng Yu-sum, Wu Yusen) (1946–). Film director John Woo represents the quintessential American immigrant success story. Woo is among a handful of directors responsible for the prominence, both artistically and commercially, of the Hong Kong film industry in the 1980s; he is one of a few Hong Kong directors who have successfully made the transition to Hollywood. He remains an authentic talent and sublime voice in filmmaking, internationally regarded.

Born in Guangzhou, Woo came to Hong Kong at five when his family emigrated, living in Shek Kip Mei, a shantytown of wooden huts that burned down in an immense fire in the early 1950s, and then in government tenements. An anonymous American Lutheran family from the United States helped support them. Movies and the church became Woo's escapes; early experiences would have an effect on his future filmmaking. Woo taught himself filmmaking by devouring film books and watching movies. He was greatly influenced by the current French New Wave and a mixed bag of films and filmmakers would exert a presence in his movies to come, including Hollywood **musicals** like *Singing in the Rain*, Westerns like *High Noon*, and especially the films of Jean-Pierre Melville. Woo determined, at 20, to become a director. His early works were experimental **independent** shorts.

In 1969, Woo began his first job in the film industry as a script supervisor and production assistant at **Cathay Studios**; by 1971 he was working as an assistant director at **Shaw Brothers** studios where he discovered his acknowledged mentor in **Chang Cheh**, a pioneer of **martial arts films** that celebrated masculinity. Woo directed his first film for an independent company; it was sold to **Golden Harvest** studios as *The Young Dragons (Young Dragons Farewell Buddy)/Tit hon yau ching/Tie han rou qing* (1973), and the studio soon contracted him to make another martial arts movie, *The Hand of Death* (*Shaolin Gate,* aka *Countdown in Kungfu)/Siu lam moon/Shaolin Men*, with **Samo Hung** and **Jackie Chan**, and a **Cantonese opera** film, *Princess Chang Ping (Princess Flower)/Dai Nui Fa/Dinu Hua* (both 1976). A string of comedies followed, including *Money Crazy/Faat chin hon/Fa qian han* (1977), *From Riches to Rags (Money Make Strange)/Chin jok gwaai Qian zuo guai* (1979), and *Plain Jane to the Rescue (Eight Variety Lam Ah Chun)/Baat choi Lam A Jan/Ba cai Lin Ya Zhen* (1982), the latter starring **Josephine Siao**. Woo left Golden Harvest in 1983 and joined a new company, **Cinema City**. There he made a gangster film, ***A Better Tomorrow*** *(True Colors of a Hero)/ Ying hung boon sik/Yingxiong bense* (1986) costarring **Ti Lung**, **Chow Yun-fat**, and **Leslie Cheung**, that not only revolutionized the Hong Kong film industry, but would have an effect on Hollywood **action** films. The rapport between Chow and Woo grew out of their similar situations at the time. Woo did not want to return to comedies and wanted to make a film from his heart; Chow, a famous **television** star, had not been as successful making the transition to the big screen; both felt this film gave them a second chance to be true to themselves and retain their dignity, feelings mirrored by characters in the film. Woo and Chow would become the Scorsese–DeNiro of Hong Kong, making five movies together, including a sequel *A Better Tomorrow 2 (True Colors of a Hero 2)/Ying hung boon sik 2/Yingxiong bense 2* (1987), a comedy caper *Once a Thief (Criss Cross over Four Seas)/ Jung waang sei hoi/Zong heng si hai* (1991), and the cop movie *Hard-Boiled (Hot-Handed God of Cops, Supercop)/Laat sau san taam/ Lashou shentan* (1992), one of which, *The Killer (A Pair of Blood-Splattering Heroes)/Dip huet seung hung/Die xie shuang xiong* (1989), the most stylish of the lot, became the darling of critics internationally. With *Bullet in the Head (Blood-Splattered Streets)/Dip huet gaai tau/Die xue jie tou* (1990), Woo not only addressed the Vietnam War (as Michael Cimino did in *The Deer Hunter* [1978]), but with veiled references to Tiananmen Square, alluded to the approaching return of Hong Kong to the mainland in 1997.

In *The Killer*, Chow's character inadvertently wounds an innocent young woman (**Sally Yeh**) in a shootout and consequently accepts responsibility for her well-being. He is mirrored by a loose cannon cop (**Danny Lee**) who is on his trail. Woo's romantic gangster dramas broke box office records in Hong Kong, and Chow's gangster look was imitated by Hong Kong teens, who took to the streets dressed like his characters in dusters and shades, despite Hong Kong's heat and humidity. Woo was uncomfortable with the way in which young people were glorifying gangsters, so he intentionally made Chow a cop in the subsequent *Hard-Boiled*, his cop Tequila mirrored by a little brother undercover cop (**Tony Leung Chiu-wai**) under deep cover in a gang. *Hard-Boiled* proved to be Woo's Hong Kong swan song; at film's end Leung's character sails away from the former colony just as Woo left for the United States in 1992.

To get at the heart of Woo's filmmaking, one need look no farther than his heroes, who value morality, friendship, honor, and love, like the ancient Chinese heroes of legend. Woo's hero, albeit an antihero, abides by a code of honor, and by selflessly sacrificing himself for a good cause, is ultimately redeemed. Woo's themes have translated into a visual style nonpareil. He uses close-ups and close-up freeze-frames when he wants to make a point by emphasizing an emotion or important value a character acts on. Action sequences are operatic and orchestral, with heroes rarely running out of bullets, outnumbered by countless villains coming at them, and body counts in the hundreds. There is either nonstop cutting during a shoot-out that establishes an action and emotional rhythm or extravagant slow-motion action. With Chow, Woo introduced his hero shooting with two pistols, as well as a revitalized Mexican standoff where characters point pistols at each other. Always his action is tied to emotion, motivation, and drama. Woo thinks of action and violence in terms of dance, and his character-driven stories are often described as balletic choreographed action of beauty and grace. Furthermore, Woo has always used religious iconography and symbolism, ranging from images of the Virgin Mary, white doves, and crosses, to settings in churches with votive candles and quiet refuge.

By early 1990, Hollywood had shown interest in Woo, and he eventually became the trailblazer for other Hong Kong filmmakers to follow, guided by partner **Terence Chang**, known in film circles for his business savvy and artistic acumen. Woo's first Hollywood movie, the Jean-Claude Van Damme actioner *Hard Target* (budgeted at $20 million), was a commercial success, grossing $33 million domestically and even more internationally. In 1994, Woo and Chang formed WCG Entertainment, and made *Broken Arrow*, with Christian Slater and John Travolta. He followed that up with Travolta and Nicolas Cage in *Face/Off* (1997). The film earned both critical and commercial success, leading to *Mission Impossible 2* (2000). The same year Woo and Chang formed Lion Rock Productions, and produced the epic World War II drama *Windtalkers*. Inspired by historical events, *Windtalkers* starred Nicolas Cage, Christian Slater, and Adam Beach, relating the story of Navajo code talkers whose unwritten language was adapted, coded, and used to relay important information in the Pacific theater. Rather than stylized action, *Windtalkers*'s action is more documentary style. Woo's next movie, *Paycheck* (2003), based on a Philip K. Dick short story and paying homage to Alfred Hitchcock, starred Ben Affleck, Uma Thurman, and Aaron Eckhart. Again Woo explored the themes closest to his heart—an unlikely hero with a moral code who chooses sacrifice for the well-being of others over monetary success at the price of corruption.

Woo currently has several projects in development, including a remake of Melville's *Le Cercle Rouge (Red Circle)* and a remake of *The Third Man*, but perhaps the forthcoming *The Divide*, which will reunite him with Chow Yun-fat for their first Hollywood movie, is the movie most anticipated by aficionados. The 19th-century story concerns the Chinese and Irish immigrants who built the railroad across this country. Woo is returning to Chinese-language film with a period epic, *Red Cliff*, shooting on the Mainland in 2006.

Ironically, Woo has been identified as a master-blaster with his aestheticized violence. Some academics have gone so far as to seriously discuss the homoerotic male bonding of his characters. His stylistic influence can be seen in Hollywood today in filmmakers' work as disparate as that of Quentin Tarantino, Oliver Stone, Luc Besson, Gore Verbinski, Lance Mungia, Robert Rodriguez, and the Wachowski Brothers. Woo's heart sets him apart. He says, "Movies are my way of having a conversation or writing a letter and the audience becomes my friend. For me, it's like talking to a friend. . . . I always feel the whole world is like a big family. We should care about each other. I know it sounds like an old theme but that's really what we need nowadays. People have hate because they have no understanding, no caring. I appreciate old traditions, old values. We should carry these on: loyalty, family and friendship. They have to keep these things dear. I want to remind people through my movies about the noble things in the world. People are not bad, we just need more patience in understanding each other" (personal interview, January 7, 2002).

In addition to directing, Woo and Chang have produced numerous films, including *The Replacement Killers* (1998, Chow Yun-fat's U.S. film debut), **Kirk Wong's** *The Big Hit* (1998), and *Bulletproof Monk* (also starring Chow Yun-fat, 2003). He has directed two TV pilots, **John Woo's** *Once a Thief* (1996) and *Blackjack* (starring Dolph Lundgren, 1998); the former became a Canadian series Woo and Chang executive produced. Woo and Chang have also expanded into other entertainment properties with their Tiger Hill game studio, currently developing three video games. Woo's *Song Song and Little Cat* (2005) is part of the anthology film *All The Invisible Children* (which also includes directors Ridley Scott, Emir Kusturica, and Spike Lee, among others) and premiered at the Venice International

Film Festival; film proceeds go to the United Nations Children's Fund (UNICEF).

WOODS, MICHAEL. With a strong screen presence and musculature to match, African American **martial arts action** actor Michael Woods entered the industry through his connection with **Donnie Yen**; Woods was a *wushu* student of Yen's mother, Master Bow Sim Mark, in Boston, and took the young Yen under his wing. Woods has appeared in edgy hand-to-hand combat with Yen in **Yuen Wo-ping's** urban contemporary action movies *Tiger Cage 1* and *2/Dak ging tiu lung/Te jing tu long* and *Sai hak chin/Xi hei qian* (1988, 1990), and *In the Line of Duty 4/Wong ga bye che 4/Huang gu shi jie 4* (1989), among others, that competed with current **Jackie Chan**, **Samo Hung**, and **Tsui Hark** actioners. Woods also appeared in Yen's *Ballistic Kiss/Saat saat yan tiu tiu mo/Sha sha ren tiao tiao wu* (1998), a low-budget, lots of bang for the buck homage to **John Woo's** *The Killer*. He has also worked with Yen on the German television series *The Puma*.

WU, BUTTERFLY (Hu Die) (1908–1989). Actress Butterfly Wu (Hu Die), a native of Jiangmen, was born in Shanghai to a Cantonese family and raised in Northern China. Her film debut was in silent pictures in 1924; in 1928, she signed with **Mingxing** (Star) Studio, where she first costarred in *The White Tower* (1928) with **Ruan Lingyu**. Subsequently she made *The Songstress* and then *Red Peony* (1941), China's first talkie. She became Mingxing's foremost star during its heyday (1921–1937), when Shanghai boasted 38 studios and made 1,100 movies. She was incredibly expressive emotionally in silent films, and unlike some actors, made the transition into sound film smoothly. Fluent in Mandarin and Cantonese, she made films in both languages.

Wu came to Hong Kong in 1937, starring in some of the first Hong Kong Mandarin-language films made. She remade Ruan Lingyu's silent film *The Goddess* as *Rouge Tears (Tears for the Society)/Yin chi lui/Yan zhi lei* (1938). She returned to Shanghai in the early 1940s, only to come back to Hong Kong after the war. Wu's strength was in drama, and she suffered. She starred in **Zhu Shilin's** *A Dream of Spring/Chun ji mung/Chun zhi meng* (1947), playing a young woman from a poor family who suffers for love, first for her rich husband, whose prejudiced father abuses her, and then for the sake of her stepdaughter, ending up alone. She starred as the title character in He Feiguang's *Madame X/Mau foo yan/Mou furen* (1947), playing a former actress married to a warlord. Her former lover, once a petty criminal, now a big timer, shows up to blackmail her. The warlord's second in command, secretly in love with her, assists, only to betray her when rejected. Banished by her husband, wearied of ill-gained luxury, she vows to start over, alone. In **Cheng Bugao's** *Heavenly Souls/Gam sau tin tong/Jinxu tiantang* (1949), she played a daughter from a rich family. Underway to her husband's home in the wedding procession, she gives a bejeweled dowry bag to a poor woman also on her way to her future husband. After a happy marriage and child, her family undergoes misfortune and she ends up as a servant in the other woman's household, now wealthy from investments; the other woman helps her find her husband and child she has been separated from, and restores the dowry.

Wu began appearing in more matronly roles, including *Nobody's Child/Kuer liulang ji* (1960), *Street Boys/Gaai tung/Jie tong* (1960), and **Chu Kei's** *Mother Love/Miu qi/Mui ai* (1961). In the first, she played a barge owner who takes in an orphan girl (the young **Josephine Siao**) as a companion to her bedridden daughter; in the second, she played elder to **David Chiang**; and, in the third, she was again paired with Josephine Siao, who portrayed her youngest daughter. Abandoned by her older children, the mother suffers, facing degradation after degradation, all painfully experienced by the young daughter so attached to her. At film's end, the absentee eldest son miraculously reappears to save his mother and affirm values of filial piety, loyalty, and love. Wu also starred in **Li Han-hsiang's** drama *Rear Entrance/Hau moon/Hou men* (1960) opposite **Wang Yin**.

Wu retired in 1967 and moved to Canada.

WU, JACQUELYN QIANLIAN (Ng Sien-lin) (1968–). Born in Taiwan, actress and singer Jacquelyn Wu graduated from the National College of Art. Wu's first film was the **Johnnie To**–produced *A Moment of Romance/Tin yuek yau ching/Tian re you qing* (1990), in which she co-starred with **Andy Lau**. She was nominated for a Hong Kong film award for her performance. Wu was recommended to To by fellow Taiwan native **Sylvia Chang**. Wu's next appearance was in the To-directed *Casino Raiders 2/Chi juen miu seung 2 wing ba tin gwong/Zhi zun wu shang 2 yong ba tian xia* (1991), again with Lau. Though occasionally making more comedic fare, Wu usually does not accept less serious roles. Wu cemented her career in Hong Kong by starring alongside **Chow Yun-fat** in *Treasure Hunt/Dut kei siu lam/Hua qi shaolin* (1994) and the critically acclaimed *To Live, Love, and Die in Tsimtsatsui/San bin yuen yan/xin bian yuan ren* (1994). She gained international recognition by starring in **Ang Lee's** *Eat Drink Man Woman/Yam jeung laam lui/Yin shi nan nu* (1994). Other significant films include *The Phantom Lover/Ye boon goh sing/Ye ban ge sheng* (1995), opposite **Leslie Cheung**, and **Ann Hui's** *Eighteen Springs/Boon sang yuen/Ban seng yuan* (1997) opposite **Leon Lai**. Wu also has a successful singing career in Taiwan and Mainland China.

WU, JIAXIANG (1919–1993). Actor and director Wu Jiaxiang, a native of Anhui province born in Beijing, acted in more than 100 stage plays during the war. In 1945, he came to Hong Kong. His film debut there was He Feiguang's contemporary romance *Gone Were the Swallows When the Willow Flowers Wilted/Liu dut faan baak yin ji fen/Luhua fanbai yanzi fei* (1946), **Great China's** first Mandarin production following the war. He later worked for **Yonghua** and 50th Year Motion Pictures. He was assistant director for **Tu Guangqi** on *Rose, Rose I Love You/Mooi gwai Mooi gwai ngo oi lei/Meigui Meigui wo ai ni* (1954), a Mandarin contemporary romance starring **Li Lihua** and **Lo Wei**.

In 1957, Wu joined **Motion Pictures and General Investment (MP&GI)** and appeared in more than 30 productions as a character actor, among them **Tao Qin's** crime genre *Murder in the Night/Miu tau ngon/Wu tou an* (1957), **Yue Feng's** comedy *Wayward Husband/Tiu dut wan/Tao hua yun* (1959), **Evan Yang's** family **melodrama** *My Darling Sister/Che mooi dut/Jie mei hua* (1959), and **Wang Tianlin's** contemporary romantic comedy *Lady on the Roof/Leung seung gaai yan/Liang shang jia ren* (1959), written by Evan Yang. He played uncles in both of the epic dramas ***Sun, Moon and Star****/Sing sing yuet leung taai yeung/Xing xing yue liang tai yang* (1961), directed by Evan Yang, and ***The Story of Three Loves****/Tai siu yan yuen/Ti xiao yin yuan* (1964), directed by Wang

Tianlin. During this same period, he collaborated with these directors as assistant on their productions.

Wu's directorial debut was *Father and Son/Yan ji choh/Ren zhi chu* (1963), in which **Kelly Lai Chen** plays a thief headed in the wrong direction. Other films include *Cosmopolitan (City) Fantasy/Diy shut kwong seung kuk/Dou shi kuang xiang qu* (1964) and *Passion/Lui yan! Lui yan!/Nu ren! Nu ren!* (1967). In 1965, he joined **Shaw Brothers** as an actor and a director. He appeared in **King Hu's** *The Fate of Lee Khan/Ying chun gok ji fung boh/Ying chun ge zhi feng bo* (1973), *The Valiant Ones/Chung lit tiu/Zhong lie tu* (1975), and *Raining in the Mountain/Hung saan leng yue/Kongshan lingyu* (1979). After leaving Shaw, he directed a single film, *Springtime in Pattaya* (1967). In 1980, he joined China **Television** Company in Taiwan as an actor. He died in Hong Kong.

WU, JUNLI (Ng Kwan-lai) (1930–). Actress Wu Junli (real name Wu Yanyun), a native of Guangdong province, was educated in Shanghai and came to Hong Kong after the war. She studied **Cantonese opera** in her early twenties, studying at Yinzizhong Music Conservatoire and at the Xiangjiang Cantonese Opera Institute, as well as under renowned opera actor Chen Feinong, composer Lu Wencheng, and Cantonese opera instructor Xiao Lanfang. She founded the Xinlisheng Opera Group. She was described as the "Beautiful *Dan* with a Jade Voice."

Wu made her screen debut with *The Model and the Car (The Model with a Car)/Yuk lui heung che/Yu nu xiang che* (1955); her first lead role was the Cantonese opera *A King's Revenge/Ngo san seung daam/Wo xin chang dan* (1955). In *The Model and the Car*, she sang "Butterflies Caress Not Scented Flowers." In *A King's Revenge*, set during the Warring States period, Wu played the Queen of Yue, who attempts to distract the King of Wu, who has invaded her kingdom. The film was Dongfang's inaugural production and was adapted from the Cantonese opera made famous by Sun Ma Sze-tsang.

In a career spanning a dozen years, Wu starred in over 120 features, mostly film adaptations of Chinese opera. Her films include the Cantonese operas *Two Immortals at the Pavilion of the Moon/Seung sin baai yuet ting/Shuangxian baiyue ting* (1958) and *The Unroyal Prince/Gaau ji ngaak gwan wong/Jiao zi ni jun huang* (1960), *A*

Couple in the Cold War/Laang chin foo chai/Leng zhan fu qi (1962), *Lust Is the Worst Possible Vice/Maan nyn yam wai sau/Wan e yin wei shou* (1963), and Wong Toi's Cantonese romance *Factory Rose/Gung chong mooi gwai/Gong chang mei gui* (1964). In the romantic *Two Immortals at the Pavilion of the Moon*, Wu played one of two lovers who are separated and mistake each other for dead; they are finally reunited at each other's grave. The film was loosely based on Guan Hanqing's *Moon Worship Pavilion/Bai yue ting* and the Hunan opera *Paying Tribute to the Moon/Bai yue ji*.

Wu set up Xinlisheng and produced three features, including the Cantonese opera *It's Sweet to Die for One's Love/Wai long tau duen wun sam tim/Wei lang tou duan ye xin tian* (1963) in which she also acted. Her last film was the Cantonese drama *The Full Moon/Yuet heung kwong fong yuen/Yue xiang na fang yuan* (1967). A popular opera singer, Wu made a number of recordings and performed for radio stations. She retired in 1967.

WU, LIZHU (Woo Lai-chu) (1910–). Actress Wu Lizhu was born in Zhejiang province and started in the movies with her first screen role, *Lover's Tragedy* (1925) for Shanghai's Commercial Press' Film Department, followed by *Mother's Heart* (1926) and *Portraits of the Eight Beauties in the Jia Xing Era* (1927). Her first lead was for Fu Dan with *River to Heaven* (1928). Many of her movies were Yue Ming productions, such as *The Hero of Guangdong* (in 13 parts), *The Woman Security Guard (Woman Security Escort)/Lui biu bye/Nu biao shi* (in six parts), and *Frenzy* (1935). She earned the title of China's first "queen of ***wuxia pian***" in the 1920s and starred in many films of her husband, director **Ren Pengnian** (who established Yue Ming in Shanghai and later in Hong Kong).

With the outbreak of the Sino–Japanese War, the actress immigrated to Hong Kong, and appeared in Cantonese productions; she joined Xing Guang Film Company, starring in a remake of *The Woman Security Guard* (1941) and *The Lady in Combat (Third Madam of Yongchun)/Wing chun saam leung/Yong chun san niang* (1941). In Ren Pengnian's spy thriller *Bloodshed in a Besieged Citadel (United as One)/Huet yim goo shing/Xieran gucheng* (1948), she played the owner of a village inn whose husband has been killed by the Japanese; she assists a teacher and his students to fight against them and liberate the territory.

The actress starred in many **martial arts** films throughout the 1940s–1950s, including *Third Madame Wing-chun and Hung Hei-kwun (Third Madam of Yongchun and Hong Xiguan)/Wing Chun saam leung yue Hung Hei Goon/Yong chun san niang yu Hong Xi guan* (1956). Wu costarred as Wing-chun, whose father is killed by a local tyrant wanting his lands; she trains herself in martial arts and joins forces with fellow disciple Hung Hei-kwun (**Walter Tso Tat-wah**) and her long lost sister (Chun Siu-lei) to destroy the villain. Wu's last film before retiring was Ren's *Three Swordswomen from Guangdong (Three Gallant Ladies of Guangdong)/Gwaan dung saam lui hap/Guangdong san nuxia* (1961). She died in Thailand.

WU, MA (Ng Ma) (1942–). Immigrating to Hong Kong in 1960 after having worked as a machinist in Tianjin, actor and director Wu Ma started working at **Shaw Brothers** in 1963. Wu made his acting debut in *The Lady General Hua Mu Lan/Fa Muk Lan/Hua Mu Lan* (1964), playing the brother of **Ivy Ling Bo**, the eponymous protagonist. Wu continued acting in films at Shaw Brothers, eventually coming into the orbit of legendary director **Chang Cheh**. Their first collaboration was *The Golden Swallow/Gam yan ji/Jin yan zi* (1968). He also worked as an assistant to Chang on the film. Wu continued collaborating with Chang both as an actor and director, gaining much experience behind the camera. Soon enough, Wu broke out on his own as a director with *Wrath of Sword/Lim kim kwong diy/Nu jian kuang dao* (1970). He followed that up with the acclaimed *Deaf and Mute Heroine/Lung a kim/Long ya jian* (1971).

Wu reunited with Chang to make *All Men Are Brothers/Dong kau jeung/Dang kou zhi* (1975). After that, Wu left and worked for the company that Chang formed in Taiwan, Chang's Film Company. Wu returned to Hong Kong with the wave of Cantonese films in the 1980s and appeared in every genre ranging from comedy to drama to horror. He began the decade working with **Samo Hung** and directed *The Dead and the Deadly/Yan haak yan/Ren he ren* (1982), which Hung wrote. Wu was nominated for Best Director at the **Hong Kong Film Awards** for the effort. Wu continued his collaborations with Hung and also began branching out as a character actor. He appeared as **Sally Yeh's** father in **Tsui Hark's** *Peking (Beijing) Opera Blues/Diy ma dan/Dao ma dan* (1986). He also memorably played the ghost-buster Swordsman Yin in *A Chinese Ghost Story/Sin nui yau wan/ Qiannu youhun* (1987). Wu starred in **Ann Hui's** *My American Grandson/Seung hoi ga gai/Shanghai jiaji* (1991). He also directed the **martial arts** film *Kickboxer/Wong Fei Hung ji Gwai Geuk Chut/ Hwang Fei Hong zhi Gui Jiao Chi* (1993). Wu has appeared in over 180 films and remains active in the film and television industry today. His most recent appearance was in **Stephen Fung's** *House of Fury/Cheng miu ga ting/Jing wu gu ting* (2005).

WUXIA, WUXIA PIAN. Literally meaning "martial chivalry" (*wu* meaning martial, but as a combination of *zhi* and *gi*, literally, stop fight, so that it takes fighting to stop fighting), *wuxia* refers to heroes who were a part of the ***jianghu***, the martial arts world. The *xia* or knight-errant, the chivalrous hero, followed a code of honor *(yiqi)* that forced the knight to keep his word and to help free righteous people from oppression, similarly for the ***nuxia/xianu***, his female counterpart. The knights value friendship, national duty, righteousness, and the taking of vengeance above their own lives. *Wuxia pian* are the stories of the *xia* and *nuxia*, whether told through literature, oral tradition, or film.

Zhang Huichong was Chinese cinema's first **martial arts** star, and he embodied the characters of the *xia*. He starred in the movies *Strange Story of the Xia* and *Boxer from Shandong* (both 1927, directed by Zhang Shichuan and written by Zhang Zhengqiu). *Legend of the Strange Hero* (1928), a *wuxia* novel of over 100 chapters by Xiang Kairan, was transformed into numerous screen adaptations of certain episodes, notably the swordsman Gui Wu's and his wife Gan Lianzhu's escape from her evil family. The first film was entitled *The Burning of the Red Lotus Monastery* (1928, directed by Zhang Shichuan); it was so popular, there were 18 subsequent episodes filmed, ushering in the golden age of fantastique *wuxia* movies. To mention but a few, others include *The Chivalrous Swordsmen of Sichuan Mountain* (1935), based on a *wuxia* novel by Huanzhu Louzhu. Also, *The Story of the Book and the Sword/Shu jian en chou lu* (1960) was the first adaptation of **Louis Cha's** *wuxia* novel of the same name. It depicts the conflict between Ming loyalists (the first real Triads), as represented by Chen Jialuo, and the imperial court; **Cheung Ying** plays two parts, as the Emperor Qian Long and the leader of the Red Flower Clan.

– X –

XIANHE GANGLIAN FILM COMPANY. Director **Chen Liepin**, publisher Lo Ban, and producer/director Miu Hong-yi founded Xianhe Ganglian (the Hong Kong Film Company) in 1961. Its first film was the three-part *The Secret Book* (1961). Over nine years, the company produced 39 films, the majority of which were **martial arts action** serials using special effects. Productions included Chen Liepin's four-part *The Golden Hairpin/Bixie jinchai* (1963), four-part *The Snowflake Sword/Xue hua shen jian* (1964), and three-part *The Six-Fingered Lord of the Lute/Liu zhi qin mo* (1965). Among the company's non-martial arts movies are Chen's *One Queen and Three Kings/Yi hou san wang* (1963), *Master Cute/Lao fu zi* (1965), and *Hotel Lavender/Lan se jiu dian* (1968).

XIAO, SHENG (1930–2004). Director and writer Xiao Sheng was born in Guangdong province and worked as a scriptwriter for Radio Macau before entering the film industry. He began as a continuity assistant for an Amoy-dialect film in 1955, and worked as assistant director on a Swatowese-dialect production, *The Jade Hairpin/Biyu zan* (1956), and as assistant director on director-actor **Cheung Ying** and Cai Chang's *Story of the Sword and Saber, 1* and *2/Yitian tulong ji* (1963). The film was based on **Louis Cha's** serial. Cheung played a prominent swordsman of one clan who marries **Bai Ying**, daughter of a father who heads a sinister cult; both groups persecute the couple, resulting in their dual suicide.

Xiao's directorial debut was the **martial arts** fantasy *Moslem Sacred Fire Decree 1* and *2/Miu lam sing feng ling/Wu lin sheng huo ling* (1965), and most of his 20 directorial features are in the martial arts genre. *Beautiful Queen of Hell, 1* and *2/Yuk min ming law/Yu mian yan luo* (1965) was the first Cantonese Cinemascope martial arts film in Hong Kong. *Sacred Fire, Heroic Winds/Sing feng hung fung/Sheng huo xiong feng* (1966) was a two-part sequel to the former. A mysterious weapon, the yin-yang sacred fire decree, is fought over by many, including its owners (**Josephine Siao Fong-fong** and **Connie Chan Po-chu**), fighters from the Sacred Fire Sect, and 36 Red Lotus Society disciples. The special effects of the movie are typical of the time; sounds, such as the music of the pipa and laughter, are used in combat.

In the 1970s, the director made coproductions with Thailand and South Korea. From 1974 to 1976, he worked as a producer for **television** series at Rediffusion Television as well as screenwriter for its *Ten Sensational Cases* and drama coach for its series *The Star, the Sun and the Moon*. In 1976, he moved to Commercial Television as executive producer of several martial arts series, and when the studio closed in 1978, he returned to Rediffusion, supervising martial arts series and later worked for Hong Kong Television Broadcasts Limited (TVB). He helped bring the martial arts style of 1960s film into the television of the 1970s and 1980s. He retired in the mid-1990s, and he died in Hong Kong.

XINHUA FILM COMPANY. Producer **Zhang Shankun** established Shanghai's Xinhua (Hsin Hwa) Film Company in 1934, adapting stage plays and making big budget films. Its first production was *The Story of the Red Lamb Knight* (1935). The film was what Zhang referred to as "opera with moving images," and he is often credited with combining **Peking (Beijing) opera** with film. Its second was *The New Peach Blossom Fan* (1935). As other studios closed during the **Orphan Island period**, Zhang's Xinhua branched out into Huaxin, Huacheng, and Xinhua to supply films to theater chains, and all three were incorporated into the Japanese company China United Film Company. After moving to Hong Kong and working with and leaving **Yonghua** and **Great Wall**, Zhang reestablished Xinhua there in 1952 and signed **Li Lihua**, who made *General Chai and Lady Balsam/Xiao bai cai* (1953). The company revived with the addition of **Tu Guangqi's** *Qiu Jin, the Revolutionary Heroine/Chau Gan/Qiu Jin* (1953) and *The 72 Martyrs of Canton* (1954). Directors **Evan Yang** and **Wang Tianlin** both worked for the studio. Over 10 years, the company made 47 films.

Zhang codirected several of the films, including the movie that helped launch the contemporary Mandarin **musical**, ***Songs of the Peach Blossom River****/Tou Fa Kong/Taohua jiang* (1956, with Wang Tianlin). Other codirections are the historical films *Blood-Stained Flowers (The Dawn of China's Revolution)/Bixue hua* (1953, with Tu Guangqi and others) and *Lady Balsam's Conquest/Xiao fengxian* (1955, with Wang Tianlin and Evan Yang).

Zhang was married to Tong Yuejuan, first an actress and later his business partner, who continued making films after Zhang's death in

1957, shifting the company's base of operations to Taiwan after 1962 and running the company until the mid-1980s.

XINLIAN FILM COMPANY. Xinlian Film Company, the largest of the four major Cantonese production companies, was established through investment of overseas Chinese and cofounded in 1952 by **Lo Dun** and Liu Yat-yuen. The company had close relations with **Great Wall** and **Feng Huang**, all labeled as leftist companies. Following liberation, China was shut off from the Western world, so Hong Kong was used as a conduit for Mainland film exposure, and the director of the company, Liu Yat-yuen, built the South China Theater and the Silver Theater in Hong Kong to screen the films of the three companies as well as films from Mainland China. The company was known for its family **melodramas**, including its inaugural production, **Ng Wui's** *The Prodigal Son/Baijia zai* (1952). **Lee Tit's** *In the Face of Demolition/Weilou chunxiao* (1953), **Chun Kim's** *Neighbor's All/Gu gu hu hu* (1954), Lo Dun's *Typhoon Signal No. 10/Shi hao fengbo* (1959), **Lee Sung-fung's** *So Siu Siu/Su Xiao Xiao* (1962), and **Wong Weiyi's** *The House of 72 Tenants/Qi shi er gu fang ke* (1963) are examples of the company's classic productions. The company also produced the *Silver Bus* series (1965–1966) and *Overflowing River*, the first Hong Kong **documentary** to earn over HK$1 million, and the Chaozhou-dialect film *So Luk Neung* (1960), popular in Thailand. In 1982, the company was absorbed by **Sil-Metropole**.

XU, ZHENGHONG (Sui Jang-hung, Chui Chang-wang) (1935–). Director and cinematographer Xu Zhenghong was born in Shanghai, where his father worked as a sound technician for **Great China**. In 1949, he came to Hong Kong, working for two years at Nan Guo Studio as assistant cameraman to Luo Junxiong, and then at **Xinhua** as a cinematographer. His first film credit is Jiang Nan's **musical** comedy *Fair Maidens among the Melons (Sweet as a Melon)/Choi sai gwa dik goo leung/Cai xi gua de gu niang* (1956). He shot the director's *You Are the Winds of Spring/Long yue chun yat fung/Lang ru chun ri feng* (1958) and **Wang Tianlin's** *Flight of the Phoenix/Fung wong yue fei/Feng huang yu fei* (1958), both musical romances among the company's first color productions and starring **Zhong**

Qing and Jin Feng. He also shot **Tu Guangqi's martial arts** movie *19 Swordsmen of Ching City/Ching sing sap gau hap/Ding cheng shi jiu xia* (1960), which won a **Golden Horse Award** for Best Cinematography.

Xu directed and photographed the period musical *Dragon Phoenix Romance* (1958), featuring Zhong Qing. He joined **Shaw Brothers** as a cinematographer, writer, and assistant director in 1964, and the next year began directing for the studio, including *Temple of the Red Lotus* (1965) and *The Twin Swords/Tut yeung kim hap/Yuan yang jian xia* (1965), both starring **Jimmy Wang Yu**. The former was a remake of the 1928 ***wuxia*** film and the latter a sequel. These movies helped lead to the rise of a new martial arts filmmaking style, bloody and gory, with realistic **swordplay**, and establish Xu as one of the key players in the Mandarin style *wuxia* initiated by Shaw Brothers by the mid-1960s. In Xu's version of *Temple of the Red Lotus*, Jimmy Wang Yu sides with the Guan family to defeat vicious monks.

In 1971, Xu left Shaw Brothers and joined **Golden Harvest**. He made the coproduction (with actor Katsu Shintaro) Chinese version of *Zatoichi and the One-Armed Swordsman* (1971), also costarring Wang Yu. With the support of Golden Harvest, the director founded Ku Gan Film Company in Taiwan and filmed two swordplay movies there, *Swordsman at Large/Siu sap yat long/Xia shi yi lang* and *Invincible Sword/Yat foo goon man/Yi fu dang guan* (both 1971).

– Y –

YAM, BING-YI (Ren Bing'er) (1931–). Cantonese opera actress Yam Bing-yi was born in Guangzhou, a native of Guangdong province. She is the sister of prolific Cantonese opera actress **Yam Kim-fai**, who discouraged her from pursuing an acting career. Xiao Manxia, fiancée of Cantonese opera actor **Ho Fei-fan**, brought her onto the opera stage, where she was performing supporting roles at age 11. Although she never received formal training, the actress's career, playing second leads, lasted 40 years. During the 1940s, Yam performed in the Xinsheng Opera Troupe in Macau, organized by her sister and another *huadan* (maiden or young woman, either vivacious or shrewish in nature) Chen Yannong. Following the war, she moved with the troupe to Hong Kong and continued performing as second *huadan*. In 1956, when her sister and **Pak Suet-sin** started the Xianfengming troupe, Ren followed. Her career is indelibly linked with her sister's.

Yam's film debut was Chan Pei's **melodrama** *Good Girl Covers for Both Sides/Hiu lui leung tau moon/Haonu liangtou man* (1948), one of only two contemporary films in which she appeared. Screen opera roles include *The Thirteenth Girl's Adventure in Nengren Temple* (1948), **Lee Tit's *The Purple Hairpin*/***Chi chaai gei/Zichai ji* (1959), **Mok Hong-si's** *The Fairy of Ninth Heaven/Gau tin yuen lui/Jiu tian xuannu* (1959), **Tso Kea's** *Princess Cheung Ping (Tragedy of the Emperor's Daughter)/Dai lui dut/ Dinu hua* (1959), **Wong Hok-sing's** *The Pitiless Sword/Miu ching bo kim yau ching tin/Wu qing bao jian you qing tian* (1964), and **Lee Sung-fung's** *Tragedy of a Poet King/Lee hau chu/Li hou zhu* (1968). Typically, the actress played maids, characters that help move the plot along; her role as a puritan girl in *The Pitiless Sword* is one of her unusually complex characterizations.

Yam was married to the late opera performer **Sek Yin-ji**. After leaving film, she continued performing onstage.

YAM, KIM-FAI (Ren Jianhui) (1912–1989). Cantonese opera actress Yam Kim-fai (real name Ren Licu) was born in Guangdong province, completed her primary studies, and began studying Cantonese opera under renowned performer Xiao Jiaotian, her aunt. She also studied, at age 14, under renowned actress Huang Luxia, known as the "female **Ma Sze-tsang**." Acting onstage in Guangzhou early in her career, she mostly performed in plays the actor had made famous. As she developed her style, she emulated famous stage actor Gui Mingyang. Her interpretation of male parts became her trademark, and she possessed a large female following as a result.

Yam performed with various opera groups in Macau from the mid-1930s, including the troupe she founded, Xinsheng. Following the war, her troupe moved to Hong Kong, where she again performed in many groups. In 1956, Yam and her partner, **Pak Suet-sin**, founded Xianfengming, for which they also performed. The famous Pak–Yam duo, with Yam playing the male roles and Pak the female roles, was regarded as the ideal couple, which spilled over into their offscreen relationship as well; their onstage performances are perceived as classics of Cantonese opera.

Yam's film debut was in a supporting role in the prewar film *A Mysterious Night/San bei ji yau/Shen mi zhi ye* (1937). Her first title role was *The Handsome Hero Perplexed by Love/Ching kwan miu poon on/Qing kun wu pan an* (1951). Over a film career spanning more than 30 years, the actress appeared in more than 300 movies, most of them screen adaptations of operas she made famous. Among them are Fung Chi-kong's *A King Speaks His Heart/Dai yuen chun sam dut do guen/Di-yuan chunxin hua dujuan* (1951), Chan Pei's *Wife in the Morning, Sister-in-Law at Night* (1952), **Mok Hong-si's** *Romance of Mount Fuji (Fuji Mountain)/Foo si saan ji luen/Fushi-shan zhi lian* (1954), Law Chi-hung's *The Nymph of the River Lo/Lok san/Luo shen* (1957), Cheung Wai-gwong's *A Buddhist Recluse of 14 Years* (1958) and *Girl of Pitiable Fate/Hoh lin lui/Ke lian nu* (1959), **Lee Tit's** ***The Purple Hairpin****/Chi chaai gei/Zichai ji* (1959), **Wong Hok-sing's** *Seven Phoenixes/Gam fung cham gaau lung/Jin feng zhang jiao long* (1961), **Lung To's** *Mysterious Murder/Hung ling huet/Gong ling xie* (1964), and Wong's Cantonese opera *The Red Robe/Daai hung piu/Da gong pao* (1965). *Romance of Mount Fuji* (1954), filmed in Japan, was Hongyun's inaugural production and its five stars (Yam, Pak Suet-sin, **Fung Wong-ni**, Chan Kam-tong, and **Leung Sing-po**) were all members of the Hung Wan Opera Troupe. In a story of star-crossed lovers, Yam cross-dressed as the male protagonist, who falls in love with a Japanese girl (Pak); she is forced to marry her family's benefactor, and he returns home to submit to an arranged engagement with his cousin. On a trip to Japan with his intended, he encounters his old love, and both couples break off their engagements for true love. Lee Tit's classic *The Purple Hairpin* featured the duo as star-crossed lovers, with a tangible romantic aura that defined their work together.

Yam's final film, **Lee Sun-fung's** Cantonese opera *Tragedy of a Poet King/Lee hau chu/Li hou zhu* (1968), enjoyed a long run and broke box office records at the time. When Yam retired from the film industry due to health-related problems, she continued her involvement with opera with partner Pak by training the next generation of actors at the Chufengming Opera Troupe. She died of illness. *See also* CHINESE OPERA FILMS.

YAM, SAI-KOON (1947–). Yam Sai-koon (Yen Shi-kwan, sometimes credited as Yang Yee-kwan) is the youngest son of director Yam Yu-tin. Yam began his career with **Lau Kar-leung's Shaw Brothers** stunt team and appeared in numerous **martial arts films** of the 1960s and 1970s as henchmen and extras. Some of the films he can be seen in include **Chang Cheh's** *The One-Armed Swordsman/Duk bei diy/Du bi dao* (1967) and *The Boxer from Shangtung (Killer from Shantung)/Ma wing ching/Ma yong zhen* (1972). Yam's break came in *The Monk* (1978), playing the protagonist, a character drawn from David Carradine's Kwai-chang Caine in the American television series *Kung Fu*. Though the film was not great, Yam's performance in it gained the attention of **Jackie Chan**, who cast him as the villainous Qing general in his directorial debut *Fearless Hyena/Siu kuen gwaai chiu/Xiao quan guai zhao* (1979). The ending fight scene between Chan and Yam is a **kung fu** classic, with Chan using humor and psychological attacks to outwit the eagle claw master. With the phasing out of the martial arts genre, Yam Sai-kuen also ceased to work much in film. However, he was at the forefront of the rebirth of the martial arts film playing the misguided Master Yim in **Tsui Hark's** *Once upon a Time in China (Wong Fei-hung)/Wong Fei-hung/Huang Fei-hong* (1991). He was also the villain in two other martial arts classics, ***Swordsman*** *2 (Smiling Proud Warrior: Invincible Asia)/Siu ngo gong woo ji Dung Fong Bat Baai/Xiao ao jianhu zhi Dongfang Bubai* (1992) and *Iron Monkey (The Young Wong Fei-hung: Iron Monkey/Siu nin Wong Fei-hung ji tit ma lau/Shao nian Huang Feihong zhi tie ma liu* (1993). Yam also parodied himself in **Stephen Chiau's** *Royal Tramp 2/Luk ting kei 2 san lung gaau/Lu ding ji 2 shen long jiao* (1992) and played the villain in **Johnnie To's** violent femme classic *The Heroic Trio (The Three Asian Heroines)/Dung fong saam hap/Dong fang san xia* (1993). More recent film appearances include To's *A Hero Never Dies (True Heart Hero)/Chan sam ying hung/Zhen xin ying xiong* (1998) with **Leon Lai** and *Gold Fingers/Yee ng chuen suet/Er wu chuan shuo* (2002).

YAM, SIMON TAT-WAH (1955–). Simon Yam worked as a model to pay his way through school (more than 80 advertisements) after his father's death (his father was a Hong Kong police chief) before joining the Television Broadcasts Limited's (TVB) actors' training program in the 1970s, and by 1974 he was playing swordsmen and policemen, and costarring with **Chow Yun-fat** in numerous **television** series. Acting in between 30 and 50 television series, with 60 episodes each, he began making films in 1989. Although more infamously known for his Category 3 films and for posing seminude in 1996, he has worked with talented directors and established memorable characters. Four outstanding roles include his ex-CIA agent in **John Woo's** Vietnam-set/*Dip huet gaai tau/Die xue jie tou* (1990), his gay psycho-killer in **Ringo Lam's** *Full Contact (Chivalrous Thief Ko Fei)/Haap dou Ko Fei/Xia dao Gao Fei* (1992), his Triad second-in-command in **Johnnie To's** ensemble mood piece *The Mission (Gunfire)/Cheong feng/Qiang ho* (1999), and his wise Triad in the first three films of the *Young and Dangerous/Goo wak jai/Gu huo zi* series (1996). Still, his titular serial killer in **Danny Lee's** *Dr. Lamb (Lamb Doctor)/Go yeung yi sang/Gao yang yi sheng* (1992) and numerous gigolos get attention as well as his work as an impotent cop with **Chingmy Yau** in *Naked Killer (Bare Naked Lamb Cake)/Chik loh go yeung/Chi luo gao yang* (1992). Yam was nominated for the 2001 **Hong Kong Film Awards** for Best Supporting Actor for his performance as a weary and aging gang boss in **Wilson Yip's** *Juliet in Love/Jue lai yip yue leung saan ang/Zhu li she yu liang shan ba* (2000). He crossed over to Hollywood films by appearing in Jan De Bont's actioner *Lara Croft Tomb Raider: The Cradle of Life* (2003), starring Angelina Jolie.

YAN, JUN (1917–1980). A native of Nanjing, actor and director Yan Jun studied at Beijing's Furen University and Shanghai's Da Xia University. After becoming famous as a stage actor, he made his film debut acting in *New Hell* (1939). He was called "the leading man with a thousand faces." He acted in over 100 movies, among them classics like *Modern Red Chamber Dream/San hung lau mung/Xin honglou meng* (1952). Based on the original story *Dream of the Red Chamber*, the contemporary melodrama shifted to 1949 and more vividly stressed antifeudal themes. Yan starred opposite **Li Lihua**, and he played the loving but weak son who could not oppose his father.

Yan made his directorial debut with *Love Eternal/Mo saan mang/Wushan meng* (1953), a family melodrama, in which he starred opposite Li Lihua as an adopted son opposed by his adopted brother

(Lo Wei). In *Singing under the Moon/Chui chui/Cuicui* (1953), he starred opposite the actress and **Bao Fang**, caught in a village love triangle involving two brothers who fall for the same woman but care deeply about each other. His *Laughter and Tears/Siu sing lui ying/Xiaosheng Leihen* (1958), with a screenplay by **Li Han-hsiang**, provoked both laughter and tears. He played a down-and-out salaryman who keeps up the pretense of success with his family by lavishing them with gifts. He is reduced to playing a clown in a strong man act to make ends meet. **Lin Dai** played his daughter and **King Hu** his son. The film includes fantasy sequences, subjective dream scenes, and **musical** interludes. Yan Jun directed more than 50 features, including *Liang Shanbo and Zhu Yingtai/Leung Saan Ang yue Chuk Ying Toi/Liang Shanbo yu Zhu Yingtai* (1964) and ***The Grand Substitution****/Maan goo lau fong/ liufang* (1965), both ***huangmei diao***. The former is based on the well-known story of the Butterfly Lovers, and the latter won Best Film at the 12th **Asian Film Festival**.

Yan was the brains behind Guotai (supported by International Films, forerunner of **Motion Pictures and General Investment**, MP&GI Cathay), Golden Dragon, and Hehe Films. Guotai produced *Merry-Go-Round/Foon lok nin/Huanle niannian* (1956) and *The Valley of the Lost Soul/Miu wan guk/Wanghun gu* (1957). He was married to actress Li Lihua, and they appeared opposite each other in numerous films. When he announced his retirement in 1972, he immigrated to New York with his wife and died there seven years later.

YANG, EVAN (Yi Wen) (1920–1978). Born in Jiangshu, director and writer Evan Yang (real name Yang Yanqi) graduated from St. John's University of Shanghai. At first he worked as a journalist, editor, and author, but he turned to screenwriting in 1949. Beginning in 1952, he wrote nine scripts in five years. His directorial debut was *Always in My Heart/Gui yuan* (1952); his forté was Mandarin **musicals**, whether comedy or **melodrama**, and his later films included musical numbers even if technically not musicals. Yang directed over 40 films, the famous ones including ***Mambo Girl****/Maan boh lui long/Manbo nulang* (1957), *Our Dream Car/Heung che mei yan/Xiang che mei ren* (1959), *Air Hostess/Hung chung siu che/Kongzhong xiaojie* (1959), and ***Sun, Moon, and Star****/Sing sing yuet leung taai yeung/Xingxing, Yueliang, Taiyang* (1961). *Mambo Girl* is one of the classic Mandarin musicals, combining dance and music as a part of the characterization of the "Mambo girl," portrayed by **Ge Lan** (Grace Chang).

Yang often wrote and directed with Ge Lan in mind. In the comedy *Our Dream Car*, she starred as part of a couple who begin squabbling as soon as they purchase an automobile, and in Yang's romantic melodrama ***Forever Yours****/Ching sam chi hoi/Qing shen si hai* (1960), she starred with **Kelly Lai Chen** as part of a loving couple whose happiness is cut short by his death, although he will live forever in her heart. *Air Hostess* was **Motion Pictures and General Investment's** (MP&GI, Cathay) first color film, drawing on the glamour of stewardesses air-hopping the globe and finding husbands, singing and dancing along the way.

The melodrama *Sun, Moon, and Star* (in two parts) was adapted from a popular novel, set during the Sino–Japanese War and depicting three roles for **women**, based on the title. Sun (**Ye Feng**) is an overseas Chinese, strong-willed, with a vivacious personality and representing the new generation of women. Moon (Ge Lan) is an educated city woman, but the embodiment of a wise but submissive traditional Chinese woman, and Star (**You Min**) is a wronged village girl. **Chang Yang** starred as the male lead, a gentle and honest, traditional, old-style son. The movie spoke to audiences, especially women, in its strong portrayal of women.

Yang worked as manager of the publicity department at **Shaw Brothers** starting in 1970. He wrote 60 scripts and published 8 novels and short story collections as well as translated a book about Hollywood.

YANG, GONGLIANG (Yeung Kung-leung, Yeung Gung-leung) (1911–). Director Yang Gongliang (also known as Yang Yutao), a native of Guangdong province, was born in Shanghai, where he grew up and was educated. Yang became an actor at **Mingxing** before becoming a director. His directorial debut was *Brotherhood* (1933), produced by Shanghai's Anwen Studio. He also directed the **Chinese opera** *Shinlin Offers Sacrifice to the Lefeng Pagoda* (1936), produced by Hong Kong's Nanyue and at the request of its manager Zhu Qingxian.

Yang directed more than 100 Cantonese features and seven Mandarin films for a variety of studios. Although he preferred thrillers, most consider his comedies outstanding. Best known among his Cantonese movies are the family **melodrama** *Red and White Peonies/Hung baak maau daan dut/Hongbai mudan hua* (1952); the ***wuxia pian*** *Eight Sword Heroes from Jiangnan (Eight Swordsman of Jiangnan)/Kung naam baat daai kim hap/Jiang nan ba da jian xia* (1950); the melodrama *Lady Red Leaf/Hung yip foo yan/Hong ye fu ren* (1954); the Chinese opera *A Patriot's Sword/Yat ang chuen chung kim/Yi ba cun zhong jian* (1958); the comedies the "Two Fools" series, including *Two Fools in Hell/Leung soh yau dei yuk/Liang sha you di yu, Two Fools in Paradise/Leung soh yau tin tong/Liang sha you tian tang*, and *Two Fools Capture the Criminal/Leung soh kam hung gei/Liang sha qin xiong ji* (1958 and 1959); and *The Apartment of 14 Families/Yat lau sap sei feng/Yi lou shi si huo* (1964). In *Red and White Peonies*, two sisters (**Hong Sin-nui** and **Pak Suet-sin**) both fall for their father's assistant (**Cheung Wood-yau**); the younger sister discovers her older sister was adopted and that her father (**Ma Sze-tsang**) was a smuggler. She uses this against her sister to cause trouble. The real father has a conscience, and the film ends as he witnesses his daughter's wedding at a distance.

The Apartment of 14 Families resembles much of Yang's other work in its loosely structured comedy, an ensemble cast of outstanding comedians, and numerous gags and punch lines. **Tang Pak-wan** plays a rich girl fleeing her family that has arranged a marriage for her to another rich man's idiotic son; she encounters **Hu Feng**, **Zheng Junmian**, and Mei Fei, who befriend her and take her into the apartment they share with 13 other families. There she learns what life is like for the poor, and also shares in the families' joys and sorrows.

Yang's thrillers included *The Music Hall Apparition* (1940) and *The Phantom of the Opera Boat* (1954). In the latter, a local tyrant (Cheng Wai-sum) covets the wife (Tang Pak-wan) of an opera singer (played by the director), but unable to woo her, sets their dwelling on fire. Husband and wife are badly burned and live as recluses, waiting for revenge. Twenty years later, the opera singer and his daughter (also played by Tang Pak-wan) prevent the tyrant from breaking up a relationship between another opera star and his lover (Law Kim-long and Zheng Biying).

Yang's Mandarin films included *Peach Blossoms Still Titter in the Spring Breeze* (1947), among others. He died in Hong Kong while filming *Secret Agent No. 101* (1965).

YAO, KE (1905–1991). Writer Yao Ke (real name Yao Chenglong, also known as Shen Nong), was a native of Anhui who graduated from Soochow University and studied at Yale University. He became an integral member of the Kugan Theater Troupe and was a renowned playwright. Yao wrote over 20 screenplays, his film debut being *The Qing Ming Season* (1936).

The writer excelled at drama and wrote some classic screenplays, including **Zhu Shilin's** historical drama ***Sorrows of the Forbidden City****/Ching gung bei shut/Qinggong mishi* (1948); **Li Pingqian's** Mandarin drama *A Strange Woman/Yat doi yiu gei/Yi dai yao ji* (1950); the drama *The Secret Life of Lady So Lee (Notorious Woman)/Ming lui yan bit chuen/ Ming Nuren Biezhuan* (1953), codirected by **Evan Yang** and **Tang Huang**; and **Tu Guangqi's** Mandarin **musical** *Rose, Rose I Love You/Mooi gwai Mooi gwai ngo oi lei/Meigui Meigui wo ai ni* (1954). *A Strange Woman* was a contemporary spy romance set during the last days of the warlords with the revolutionary nationalist army preparing for the Northern Expedition. A **Chinese opera** star (**Bai Guang**) sacrifices herself to other men in order to protect a revolutionary (**Huang He**); both of them are ordinary people acting extraordinarily to overcome oppression, and the film suggests revolution stems from oppression.

In 1955, Yao joined the scriptwriting committee at International Film (later **Motion Pictures and General Investment, MP&GI**), and with its other members, **Sun Jinsan**, **Stephen Soong**, and **Eileen Chang**, this intellectual, creative quartet developed a signature style for the studio.

In the 1960s, Yao taught at the Chinese University of Hong Kong. In 1969, he immigrated to the United States, teaching at the University of Hawaii and the University of California. In 1976, he briefly returned to Hong Kong and served as drama advisor to Rediffusion Television and instructor of its **television** acting classes.

YAO, MIN (1917–1967). Musician and composer Yao Min (real name Yao Zhenmin) had an interest in **Chinese opera** since early childhood, and as a sailor he became curious about and was exposed to Western pop music. At the close of the 1930s in Shanghai, he started a musical group, the Datong Troupe, with his sisters Yao Ying and Yao Li, and they performed and became popular on radio. Yao was self-taught, but learned music composition from renowned Japanese composer **Hattori Ryoichi**. He was adept at Shanghainese style as well as adapting Western modes and integrating them into movies.

Yao worked as both a water-meter reader and cinema usher before signing, in 1938, with Pathé Records, when he began composing songs for movies, starting with *The Flower That Understands* (1941), starring **Zhou Xuan**. Following the war, he became a popular and prolific songwriter. In 1950, he came to Hong Kong, joined Rediffusion, and, in 1952, when Pathé was founded, became head of its composition department. His first film score was for Wang Long's *Eighteen Circles of Hell* (1954).

Yao began writing songs for movies with "A Drifting Existence" for **Wang Yin's** historical drama *Chin Ping Mei/Gam Ping Mooi/Jin Ping Mei* (1955), for **Shaw Brothers**, starring Li Xianglan. He wrote music for many films, including many at **Motion Pictures and General Investment (MP&GI)**, among them "I Love Cha Cha" and "Tonight's Pleasure" for **Evan Yang's musical** vehicle for **Ge Lan**, ***Mambo Girl*/*Maan boh lui long/Manbo nulang*** (1957); 12 popular songs he rearranged for **Tao Qin's** Hollywood-style musical *Calendar Girl/Lung cheung fung mo/ Longxiang fengwu* (1959), including "Rose, Rose I Love You," which won best musical score at the **Asian Film Festival**; and others for **Wang Tianlin's *The Wild, Wild Rose*/*Yau mooi gwai ji luen/Yemeigui zhi lian*** (1960) and Evan Yang's *It's Always Spring/Tiu lee chang chun/Tao li zheng chun* (1962).

The composer wrote the song "Second Spring" for Evan Yang's *Flesh and Flame/Lian zhi huo* (1956) for Shaw Brothers, starring **Li Lihua**, which was later rearranged by Hollywood as the "Ding Dong Song" for Richard Quine's *The World of Suzie Wong* (1960), starring William Holden and Nancy Kwan. For another Shaw Brothers production, Tao Qin's musical *Les Belles* (1961), he won best musical score at both the **Asian Film Festival** and the **Golden Horse Awards**.

When ***huangmei diao*** (yellow plum opera) dominated Mandarin films in the mid-1960s, Yao wrote the music for MP&GI productions, exploring and experimenting with Chinese folk songs and operatic traditions to innovate film music. He wrote "The Irresistible Tease" for *Love in Bloom/Dut hiu yuet yuen/Hua hao yue yuan* (1962), using Northern Chinese *ping ju* melodies, he adapted drum songs for ***The Story of Three Loves****/Tai siu yan yuen/Ti xuao yin yuan* (1964); he composed "Nine Young Men" from folk songs for *Forget Me Not/Hung guk laan/Kong gu lan* (1966); and arranged folk songs for *Gunfight at Lo Ma Lake* (1969), including the Guangxi folk song "Do You Know?" The latter, one of his best songs, is written in the style of a Chinese folk ballad.

Between composers **Qi Xiangtang** and Yao, the style of the songs and music in most of the Mandarin musicals, as well as Mandarin movies generally (operating under the belief there must be a song in every movie) of the 1950s–1960s, was established.

YAU, CHINGMY SUK-CHING (1968–). Actress Chingmy Yau was a contestant in the Miss Hong Kong contest before entering the film industry; she began in comedies and her relationship with director/producer **Wong Jing** led to her becoming a prolific actress in the 1990s, making more than 50 films before she retired and married. She was known as a sex kitten (although she left nudity to others) and is famous for her portrayal of Kitty in **Clarence Ford's** male fantasy *Naked Killer/ Chik loh go yeung Chi luo gao yang* (1992) and **Andrew Lau's** rape revenge *Raped by an Angel/Heung gong kei ngon ji keung gaan/Xiang gang ji an zhi jiang jian* (1993), in both of which she costarred with **Simon Yam**; she also appeared opposite **Jackie Chan** in Wong Jing's *City Hunter/Shing shut lip yan/Cheng shi llie ren* (1993) and in Jing's ensemble comedy *Boys Are Easy (Chasing Boys)/Chui lam chai/Zhui nan zai* (1993). In lighter fare, she was often paired with **Ekin Cheng**. For her last film, *Hold You Tight/Yue faai lok yue doh laai/Yu kuai le yu duo la* (1998), **Stanley Kwan** chose her for a dual role for which she was nominated for Best Actress at the **Hong Kong Film Awards**.

YAU, HERMAN LAI-TO (1961–). Born in Hong Kong, cinematographer and director Yau studied communications, completing courses for a film degree from Hong Kong's Baptist University in 1984. A man of many interests, he began as a freelance writer for film magazines, expressing his feelings on film, also making **independent** shorts and working as a cinematographer. His credited film work began in 1987 as co-cinematographer on Taylor Wong's *Tragic Hero*, starring **Chow Yun-fat**. His feature directorial debut was with *No Regret/Ching mooi jing chuen/Jing mei zheng chuan* that same year, and he has directed almost 40 features, including the *Troublesome Night* horror franchise, *Troublesome Night 1–6 (Yin Yang Road)/Yam yeung lo/Yin yang lu* (1997–1999), and served as cinematographer on almost 25 others, including **Tsui Hark's** *Time and Tide* (2000) and *The Legend of Zu* (2001).

Yau gained notoriety for the true-crime horror feature *The Untold Story (The Eight Immortals Restaurant's BBQ Human Pork Buns,* aka *Bunman)/Baat sin faan dim chi yan yuk cha siu baau/Ba xian fan dian zhi ren rou cha shao bao* (1993) that won **Anthony Wong** a Best Actor Award at the **Hong Kong Film Awards** for the serial killer who serves his victims in human pork buns. **Danny Lee** played the cop in hot pursuit. Yau also directed *Master Q 2001/Low foo ji 2001/Lao fu zi 2001* (2001), produced by Tsui, the first Greater China film to combine live action with 3-D animation. Besides working in film, Yau has always been interested in music and during charity events jammed with friends also in the film business, Anthony Wong and **Teddy Robin Kwan**. (He has directed music videos for Wong, **Jacky Cheung**, Chang Kuan, Jie Chieng-jian, Andy Hui, and American jazz musician Eric Marienthal.) His career includes stints as actor, composer, editor, producer, and screenwriter. Although he has made comedies and **action movies**, he has also made a number of Category 3 movies, rated for their violence and sexuality, the Hong Kong classification associated with prurient fare. However, Yau's social satire and artistic creativity set these movies apart from others in the category. In 1999, he was honored to be chosen as Hong Kong Polytechnic University's first artist-in-residence.

He founded Step Forward Publications in 1997 and has published three of his four books (the fourth coauthored) and Elsa Chan's *From the Queen to the Chief Executive/Dang hau dung gin wa faat laai/Denghou dong jianhua faluo* (2001), about human rights violations among incarcerated youth, Yau's film version being the opening film of the panorama at the 51st Berlin International Film Festival, for which he was nominated Best Director at the **Golden Bauhinia**, and which won the Golden Torch Award presented by the International Catholic Organization for Cinema and Audiovisual. Yau adapted the book to the screen, and it was acknowledged among the 10 Best Movies of the Year and awarded Film of Merit by the **Hong Kong Film Critics Society** and Hong Kong Film Critics Association.

YE, FENG (Julie Yeh Feng) (1937–). Actress Ye Feng (real name Wang Jiuling), a native of Hubei province, moved at 11 to Taiwan with her family. In 1954, she was chosen to appear in a Universal Studios production to be shot in Taiwan, yet the film was never made. She was recommended by directors **Li Han-hsiang** and Li Zuyong to Yonghua in Hong Kong, so when the studio closed, **Stephen Soong** signed her to **Motion Pictures and General Investment (MP&GI**, Cathay).

Ye's first film was **Tao Qin's** ***Our Sister Hedy*** *(Four Sisters)/Se chin gam/Si qianjin* (1957), a musical **melodrama** of sibling rivalry and boyfriends among four very different sisters in which Ye played the selfish and impatient second sister. Although she received no training in singing, she sang in this one (and also later recorded with Pathé), a seductive and fun cha-cha number in order to steal her eldest sister's boyfriend. She also appeared in **Evan Yang's** Mandarin **musical** *Air Hostess/Hung chung siu che/Kongzhong xiaojie* (1959), supporting **Ge Lan**. Tall and slender, with a husky voice, Ye was the ideal star for **Tang Huang's** *Sister Long Legs/Cheung tui che che/Chang tui jie jie* (1960). In this Western-influenced Mandarin comedy, she played older sister to **Lin Cui**. As the aloof older sister, she and a supposed car mechanic, actually a rich man (**Roy Chiao**), fall in love while her former admirer falls for her little sister. A love triangle, good writing, and fast-paced comic scenes made this a delightful romp. Ye also costarred with Ge Lan and **You Min** in Evan Yang's epic drama ***Sun, Moon, and Star****, 1* and *2/Sing sing yuet leung taai yeung/Xingxing, Yueliang, Taiyang* (1961) as the strong and radiant Sun. All three women love the same, weak man (**Chang Yang**) who makes bad choices; in the second film, the setting is wartime, with the women bonding to make their lives meaningful.

After leaving MP&GI (Cathay) in 1962, Ye signed with **Shaw Brothers** and made numerous films, including the **Chinese opera** *The Shepherd Girl/Saan goh luen/Shan ge lian* (1964, with **Kwan**

Shan) and the historical drama *The Warlord and the Actress/Huet chin maau daan hung/Xie jian mu dan hong* (1964, with Chin Han). She retired after making *Farewell, My Love/Chun chaam/Chun can* (1969, also with Kwan Shan) but made a cameo in the Lin Cui–produced mahjong comedy *Sup Sap Bup Dup/Sap saam bat daap/Shisan bu da* (1975). She was married to actor Chang Yang from 1961 to 1965, but they divorced. She is currently a businesswoman traveling between Hong Kong, the Mainland, and the United States.

YEE, DEREK TUNG-SHING (1957–). Director Derek Yee appeared in more than 40 **Shaw Brothers martial arts** and **action** movies from the late 1970s before turning to directing; his directorial debut was *The Lunatics (Lunatics: True Story)/Din lo jing juen/Dian lao zheng zhuan* (1986), with a strong ensemble cast including **Chow Yun-fat**, **Tony Leung Chiu-wai**, **John Shum**, and **Paul Chun Pui** (his real-life brother; another famous brother is former Shaw star **David Chiang**). He also acted in films through the 1990s. Yee's specialty appears to be **melodrama**. His *C'est la Vie, Mon Cheri (New Endless Love)/San bat liu ching/Xin bu liao qing* (1993) won six of its 13 nominations at the 13th **Hong Kong Film Awards**, including Best Director and Best Picture and played for two months in Hong Kong, earning HK$30 million. Strong writing, genuine emotions, and good acting made this story popular among audiences and critics, and helped reinvigorate a genre much neglected since the 1960s. Yee's follow-up *Full Throttle (Flaming Chariot)/Lit foh jin che/Lieho zhanche* (1995) shifted the melodrama to the race track and starred **Andy Lau** and **Gigi Leung**. Yee collaborates with writer Lo Chi-leung on most of his projects.

Yee can be equally good at comedy, and his satirical *Viva Erotica (Sex Man Woman)/Sik ching nam nui/Se qing nan nu* (1996) was an insider's look at the operations behind the scenes in the film industry; the film starred **Leslie Cheung** and **Karen Mok**, and numerous filmmakers and actors had cameos.

YEH, SALLY TSE-MAN (1961–). Born in Taiwan, **Cantopop** singer and actress Sally Yeh has appeared in more than 20 films, although she is most remembered for her roles as a country girl come to the city in **Tsui Hark's** *Shanghai Blues/Seung hoi ji yau/Shanghai zhiye*

(1984) and as a frustrated wannabe **Chinese opera** performer in his pastiche musical, comedy, adventure, and **woman's film** *Peking (Beijing) Opera Blues (Fighting Dan* [name of a female fighting opera character]*]/Diy ma dan/Dao ma dan* (1986), alongside **Brigitte Lin** and **Cherie Chung**, and as **Chow Yun-fat's** love interest in **John Woo's** *The Killer (A Pair of Blood-Splattering Heroes)/Dip huet seung hung/Die xie shuang xiong* (1989). Yeh sang in the latter and was chosen by Woo for her wholesomeness and love of life for the characterization, a club singer inadvertently blinded by the hit man with heart. Yeh is married to actor and singer **George Lam**.

YEN, CHRIS CHI-CHING. The younger sister of **kung fu** star **Donnie Yen**, Chris Yen was born in Canton, China, but grew up in Boston, Massachusetts. She was introduced to **martial arts** at a very young age by her mother, tai chi master Bow Sim Mark, and was winning tournaments in China while still a preteen. This early success led to a featured role in a kung fu comedy directed by **Yuen Woping**, *Close Encounter of a Vampire/Jin ling bao bao* (1986). Yen then returned to Boston to complete her schooling. After graduating from Boston College, she worked as a production assistant on a number of films, including *Princess Blade/Shurayuki hime* (2001) and *Shanghai Knights* (2003). She stepped before the camera again for *Protégé de la Rose Noire/Gin chap hak mooi gwai/Jian xi hei mei gui* (2004), a slapstick comedy directed by her brother. Her role as a nunchuk-wielding schoolgirl landed her a spot on the *Today* show, and the lead role in a Hollywood kung fu film, *Adventures of Johnny Tao* (2006).

YEN, DONNIE CHI-TAN (1963–). Born in the Chinese province of Canton, Yen lived in Hong Kong before settling with his family in Boston, Massachusetts, where his mother, Bow Sim-Mark, a world famous *wushu* and tai chi master, ran the internationally known Chinese Wushu Research Institute. **Martial arts** became a major influence in his life as his mother began teaching him almost as soon as he walked. As a teenager, he was sent to Beijing, where he trained with the famed Beijing Wushu Team, studying with the same master as **Jet Li**. En route back to the United States, he met director **Yuen Wo-ping**, who cast him as lead in *Drunken Tai Chi/Siu taai gik/Xiao* *tai ji* (1984). Yen's physical versatility and improvisational skills led to collaborations with Yuen through the 1980s and 1990s, using kickboxing in the *Tiger Cage* series, and Western boxing à la Sugar Ray Leonard in *In the Line of Duty 4 (Royal Hong Kong Policewoman 4: Attacking the Witness Head-on/Wong ga si je ji 4 jik gik jing yan/ Huang jia shi jie zhi 4 zhi ji zheng ren* (1989). For Yuen's period piece *Iron Monkey (The Young Wong Fei-hung: Iron Monkey)/Siu nin Wong Fei-hung ji tit ma lau/Shaonian Huang Feihong zhi tie ma liu* (1993), showcasing traditional **kung fu** style, Yen performed *hung gar* style martial arts and the "shadowless kick" as Wong Kei-ying, father of **Wong Fei-hung** (appearing as a child and played by a girl). Although Yen doesn't know Hung Gar style, he credits his martial arts philosophy, influenced by **Bruce Lee**, with his success.

Period martial arts movies had returned to Hong Kong **action** cinema with director **Tsui Hark's** hit *Once upon a Time in China*, and Tsui chose Yen to play nemesis to Jet Li's Wong Fei-hung in the sequel, *Once upon a Time in China 2 (Wong Fei-hung 2: A Man Should Be Self-Sufficient)/Wong Fei-hung ji yi naam yi dong ji keung/Huang Feihong zhi er nan er dang zi qiang* (1992). Their fights have become classic action sequences, in one of which Yen used a rolled wet cloth as a weapon. Yen was also nominated for Best Supporting Actor at the 1992 **Hong Kong Film Awards** for his performance as a conflicted military officer. Yen went on to appear in martial arts period pieces such as *The Butterfly Sword (New Comet, Butterfly Sword)/ San lau sing woo dip gim/Xin liu xing hu die jian* (1993) and *Wing Chun/Wing Chun/Yong Chun* (1994) with **Michelle Yeoh**, and *New Dragon Gate Inn (Dragon Inn)/San lung moon haak chan/Xin longmen kezhan* (1992) with **Maggie Cheung** and **Brigitte Lin** (a remake of **King Hu's** classic).

After the **New Wave** of traditional kung fu films came to an end, Yen turned to Hong Kong **television** to develop his directing skills. He starred in and directed the action for two series, *Kung Fu Master* (1992) and *Fist of Fury* (1996). The former follows the story of a righteous martial artist, Hung Hei-kwun, during the subjugation of the Han people in the late Qing dynasty. The latter was inspired by Bruce Lee's classic *The Chinese Connection* (1971, directed by **Lo Wei**). Set in 1930s Shanghai in the international concession during the Japanese occupation, the 30-episode series for Hong Kong's Asia

Television Limited (ATV) fleshed out a backstory for featured characters and narrated events leading up to those depicted in the earlier movie. The series also quoted all the scenes and images audiences knew well from Lee's original, such as Chen Zhen (Yen), dressed in a white suit, mourning at his master's grave, or the hero taking on the Japanese dojo, encircled by Japanese fighters. The series was extremely popular and to this day, when Yen is on the streets, Asian audiences recognize him and still call him "Chen Zhen."

Yen's big-screen directorial debut was with the period piece *Legend of the Wolf (War Wolf Legend,* aka *New Big Boss)/Jin long chuen suet/Zhan lang chuan shuo* (1997). Part *Twilight Zone*, part gang tale, and all martial arts, *Legend* serves as an elegy for a time when kung fu movies reigned supreme. Yen stars as Man-hing, also known as Wolf, an aged former hit man who tries to dissuade potential clients from killing. Events are glimpsed in a series of flashbacks as a young man who has lost his memory and knows only to wait for his lost love. Yen used experimental camerawork and energetic rhythm and shot the movie in what remains of the Hong Kong countryside. Because of its unique style, the film earned critical acclaim across Asia and was particularly well received in Japan, where Yen became a cult icon among young film fans.

Yen's next film, *Ballistic Kiss (Kill a Little, Dance a Little)/ Saat saat yan tiu tiu mo/Sha sha ren tiao tiao wu* (1998), was shot on the 24-hour streets of Hong Kong itself, featuring imaginative gunplay sequences, accompanied by his signature kicks and hyperkinetic editing. Yen stars as the hit man Cat, who loves from afar. The film was shot for less than US$500,000 and under enormously difficult circumstances, considering that the Asian economic crisis hit halfway through filming and Yen's financial sources disappeared. Yen was nominated for the Best Young Director Award at the 1998 Yubari Fantastic Film Festival in Japan and *Kiss* has screened at many other international festivals.

Yen codirected a German TV action series in Berlin, called *Puma* (1999), and was courted by Miramax's Harvey Weinstein and signed to Dimension Films (a division of Miramax). He has appeared in the U.S. releases *Highlander: Endgame*, *Blade 2*, and *Shanghai Knights* (with **Jackie Chan**), and worked as martial arts action choreographer on the former two films. He appeared again as nemesis to Jet Li in

Mainland filmmaker **Zhang Yimou's** first action period piece, *Hero/Ying xiong* (2002). Yen has made a name for himself as a martial arts actor and action choreographer, as well as a director of several films of his own. He worked as action choreographer on *Twins Effect/Chin gei bin/Qian ji bian* (2003), which swept the 23rd Hong Kong Film Awards, winning Best Action Choreography for Yen, as well as Best Editing, Art Direction, Costume and Makeup, Art Direction, Sound Effects, and Special Effects. More recently, he directed the **Twins** (Gillian Chung and Charlene Choi) in *Protégé de la Rose Noire/Gin chap hak mooi gwai/Jian xi hei mei gui* (2004). Yen stars as the villainous swordsman general who wants to conquer the world in the movie's fantasy-action sequel, *Huadu Chronicles: The Blade of the Rose (Twins Effect 2)/Chin gei bin 2: Dut diy daai chin/Qian ji bian 2: Hua dou da zhan* (2004, directed by **Patrick Leung**), and he must overcome the Lord of Armor (Jackie Chan). The actor also costars in Tsui Hark's period martial arts *Seven Swords/Chat kim/Qi jian* (2005) and he stars and action directs in **Samo Hung's** *SPL/Sha Po Lang*. Yen splits his time between the United States and Asia, continuing to work on Hong Kong, Japanese, and U.S. productions both as actor and action director.

YEOH, MICHELLE (Yeung Chi-king, Michelle Khan) (1962–). Born in Malaysia, actress Michelle Yeoh studied dance and drama in England. Returning home, she won the title of Miss Malaysia in 1983. She shot a commercial with **Jackie Chan** in 1984. Her film debut was the same year, with *The Owl and the Flying Elephant (Owl vs. Dumbo)/Maau tau ying yue siu fei cheung/Mao tou ying yu xiao fei xiang* (1984). With *Yes, Madam (Royal Police Woman)/Wong ga si chea/Huang jia shi jie* (1985), she became known as the best **woman action** star; in *Police Story 3: Supercop* (known as *Supercop* in the United States)*/Ging chat goo si 3 chiu kap ging chat/Jing cha gu shi 3 chao ji jing cha* (1992), she out-stunted Jackie Chan with her motorcycle ride onto a moving train (she had to learn to ride a motorcycle to create the stunt); its director, **Stanley Tong**, promised her an action movie of her own, and in her next venture, *Project S (Super Plan,* aka *Supercop 2)/Chiu kap gai waak/Chao ji ji hua* (1993), she replaced Jackie Chan as the "supercop." She costarred with **Samo Hung** in **Ann Hui's** *Ah Kam (The Stunt Woman)/Ah Gam dik koo si/A*

Jin de gu shi (1996), which showed the difficult lives led by movie stunt people. She made the leap to Hollywood in the James Bond flick *Tomorrow Never Dies* (1997), matching, if not outfighting, Bond. She also starred in Taiwanese director's **Ang Lee's** tribute to the Chinese **martial arts** movies with which he grew up, *Crouching Tiger, Hidden Dragon/Ngo foo chong lung/Wo hu cang long* (2000), winner of four Academy Awards at the 2000 Oscars.

Yeoh set up her own production company, Mythical Films, with a five-year partnership with **Media Asia**, in 2000. Their first film, *The Touch/Tin mak chuen kei/Tian mai chuan ji* (2002), in which she also starred, was directed by cinematographer **Peter Pau**. Her next project, *Silverhawk/Fei ying nu xia* (2004) was directed by Jingle Ma, shot in Beijing, and stars Yeoh, who also produces with partner Thomas Chung. Yeoh is known for bringing strength and femininity to her film characterizations. Not trained in the martial arts, she claims her rigorous dance training made possible her convincing martial arts performances on-screen. Her latest film is the Hollywood production *Memoirs of a Geisha* (2005), directed by Rob Marshall.

YI, CHOW-SHUI (Yi Qiushui) (1904–1955). Actor Yi Chow-shui (real name Yi Jingrong), a native of Guangdong province, graduated from Queen's College in Hong Kong and worked as an English secretary in a law firm while nurturing his interest in acting by performing with one of Hong Kong's earliest drama troupes. He later joined Daluotian, a famous **Cantonese opera** group, taking the stage name Yi Xiaonong until changing it to Yi Chow-shui. An accomplished opera singer before he turned to film, Yi discovered a gift for comedy. Yi's film debut was *The New Generation (New Youth)/San chin nin/Xin qing nian* (1936), with his first starring role being *Her Majesty, My Wife (Wife, Emperor!)/liu poh wong dai/Lao po huang di* (1937).

Yi was called "the Oriental Charlie Chaplin" and "the Oriental Laurel" due to his facility at impersonation in movies such as **Yang Gongliang's** *Charlie and the Soul-Hunting Ghost (Charlie Meets the Specters)/Cha lei yue lip ching gwai/Cha li yu she qing gui* (1939) and Liu Fang's *Song of the Exile/Lau miu ji goh/Liu wang zhi ge* (1941). Yi was adept at speaking nonstop and using nervous hand gestures to comic effect. A film career of almost 20 years, cut short by his death, resulted in hundreds of films. Yi was known for playing the average person caught in embarrassing situations; he often portrayed the oppressed poor, optimistic, generous, and selfless, as in **Zhou Shilu's** *Daddy and Sonny/Leung chai yau/Liang zai ye* (1951), in which he played a vendor working with his baby on his back. There are only a few exceptions in which he played villains against type. Yi's last film was **Wu Pang's** *On the Hill of the Waiting Wife She Awaits Her Husband's Return/Mong foo saan seung mong foo foo/Wang fu shan shang wang fu gui* (1955).

Other Yi postwar films include **Ng Wui's** *The End of the Year Means Money* (1950); *The Kid/Sai lo Cheung/Xi lu Xiang* (1950); three "Broker La" films, including *The Adventures of Broker La and the Smart Fei Tiannan/Ging gei Laai yue fei tin naam/Jing ji La yu Feitian Nan* (1950); and **Chun Kim's** *A Melancholy Melody* (1952). In **Mok Hong-si's** *Broker La and the Smart Fei Tiannan* and *Mis-arranged Love Trap*, Yi played Fei Tiannan, a rival broker and boyfriend to the wife of Broker La (**Cheung Ying**), and the numerous comedic scenes in both, with impeccable timing and acting, provided a laugh for people living in crowded conditions and sharply contrasted the rich and the poor.

When Yi died of cancer of the larynx, the entire Cantonese cinema community attended his funeral and people lined the streets to glimpse the hearse escorted by police. Radio coverage lasted 15 minutes. A film, *Rear Window* (1951), was made collectively by Cantonese filmmakers to commemorate the actor and raise funds for his family.

YIM, HO (1952–). Born in Hong Kong, director Yim Ho grew up in a patriotic family. He was educated in a leftist school, took part in the 1967 riots in Hong Kong, and experienced despair, he claims, upon learning that the Cultural Revolution was a mistake. He had an early interest in music, but became interested in film through his association with director **Leong Po-chih**. Yim studied filmmaking at the London International Film School. He returned to Hong Kong in 1975, worked as a cameraman for **Yonfan** on a Commercial Television (CTV) project, and eventually joined Television Broadcasts Limited (TVB), writing a script for the **television** series *Kung Fu Crazy*. Six months later, he transferred to the camera unit, and was invited by director **Ann Hui** to direct an episode for the series *Wonderfun*. He moved on to a children's show, *Jumping Jet Plane*, and worked nonstop for the next three years at TVB. Yim is one of the leading directors of Hong Kong's **New Wave** that broke in the late 1970s; along with Ann Hui and **Allen Fong**, his social commitment remains strongest.

Yim's directorial feature debut, *The Extras/Ke lei fe/Jia li fei* (1978), a comedy about extras working in the movies, was a hit. His second feature, *The Happenings/Ye Che* (1980), was a youth problem movie from the point of view of disaffected youth, portraying Hong Kong society as disdainful. He turned to a "you can't go home again" drama with *Homecoming (The Years Flow* by *Like Water)/Chi shui lau nin/Si shui liu nian* (1984), which won six of the 14 awards at the **Hong Kong Film Awards** (including Best Picture, Best Director, and Best Screenplay). Josephine Koo played a Hong Kong woman who returns to her native Guangdong village to escape the materialism of Hong Kong life. **Siqin Gaowa** played Koo's sensitive childhood friend who remained behind. Yim personalized the details of simple country life, making this more than a political thesis. The movie was produced with Mainland money.

Most of Yim's films focus on interpersonal relationships with people whose lives are determined by destiny or are caught in an environment they cannot escape. Six of the 10 films he has directed focus on China. *Red Dust (Swirling Red Dust)/Gwan gwan hung chan/Gun gun hong chen* (1990), starring **Brigitte Lin**, **Maggie Cheung**, and **Chin Han**, follows four lives through the Sino–Japanese War and the rise of Communism, winning eight awards at the 1990 **Golden Horse Awards**. *The Day the Sun Turned Cold (Traitorous Prince)/Tin gwok ngaak ji/Tianguo nizi* (1995) is based on a true story of a son turning in his mother for murdering his father 10 years earlier. The film won Best Picture and Best Director Awards at the 1994 Tokyo International Film Festival. In *The Sun Has Ears/Taiyang you er* (1995), a man learns to control his destiny. This film won the Best Director Award at the Berlin Film Festival and the International Film Critics Federation (FIPRESCI) Jury Prize at the Berlin Film Festival in 1996. *Kitchen (I Love Kitchen)/Ngoh oi chui fong/Wo ai chufang* (1997), his favorite and most hopeful film, is an adaptation of Banana Yoshimoto's novel of the same title, with the setting shifted to Hong

Kong. Yim collaborated with director-producer **Tsui Hark** on *King of Chess* (starring **Leung Ka-fai**), an experiment based on combining two novels, contemporary Taiwanese novelist Zhang Xi-guo's *Chess King* with Mainland author Zhang A-cheng's *King of Chess (Chess King)/Kei wong/Qi wang* (1992), counterpointing a story set in present-day Taipei with one set in the Mainland countryside during the Cultural Revolution. Yim directed his first English-language film, *Pavilion of Women* (2001), starring Luo Yan, John Cho, and Willem Dafoe, and based on a Pearl Buck novel adapted by Luo.

YIP, AMY JI-MIE (1965–). Born in Hong Kong, actress Amy Yip appeared in films for a short period, from the late-1980s to the mid-1990s. She was born in Hong Kong and attended Kau Kam English College, graduated from Asia Television Limited (ATV) acting classes, and joined **Golden Harvest** in 1987, finding small roles in a variety of movies. The Category 3 *Sex and Zen/ Yuk po tuen chi tau ching biu gaam/Yu pui tsuan zhi tou qing bao jian* (1991) is her most infamous movie, and she became well-known for being well-endowed but never taking off all her clothes on-screen. *Erotic Ghost Story/Liu chai yim taam/Liao zhai yan tan* (1990) and *Robotrix/Lui gei haai yan/Nu ji xie ren* (1991) are other teasers. She appeared in 35 movies, played in some comedies poking fun at her image, and acted in a few dramas such as **Poon Man-kit's** *To Be Number One/Bai ho/Bo hao* (1991) as the mistress. She retired after marriage, common among Hong Kong actresses.

YIP, CECILIA TUNG (1962–). Born in Hong Kong, actress Cecilia Yip debuted in **Terry Tong's** *Coolie Killer/Saai chut sai ying poon/Shachu xiying pan* (1982), as the woman who helps the professional killer of the title (Charlie Chin) and whom he later shoots on the beach in a powerful scene. Yip won the **Golden Horse Award** for New Talent for her portrayal. She has been teamed with **Chow Yun-fat** in **Leong Po-chih's** *Hong Kong 1941 (Waiting for Dawn)/Dang doi lai ming/Deng gai li ming* (1984) and **Wai Ka-fai's** *Peace Hotel/Wing ping fan dim/Han ping fan dian* (1995), and with **Simon Yam** in Triad **action** dramas *Love among the Triads (Love in the Underworld Days)/Oi joi hak se wooi dik yat ji/Ai zai heishehui de rizi* (1993) and *Love, Guns and Glass (Glass Gun's Love)/Boh lee cheung* *dik oi/Bo li qiang de ai* (1995). In **Kirk Wong's** *Organized Crime and Triad Bureau/Chung ngon sat luk O gei/Chong an shi lu o ji* (1994), she gave a moving performance opposite **Anthony Wong** as his loyal girlfriend.

Yip won Best Actress at the **Hong Kong Film Awards** for her portrayal of a betrayed wife in **Lee Chi-ngai's** relationship drama *This Thing Called Love/Fan yan mat yue/Hun yin wu yu* (1991). She also recreated the real-life silent screen actress Lam Chuchu in **Stanley Kwan's** *Centre Stage (Actress)/Yuen Ling-yuk/Ruan Lingyu* (1992). Known primarily as a serious dramatic actress, she has appeared in close to 50 films, including action and comedy.

YIP, FRANCES LAI-YI (1947–). Born in Hong Kong, singer and actress Frances Yip, who is known as "Asia's leading lady of song," burst on the scene when she and a group of friends planned to audition for a record company. Yip was the only one who showed. After singing one line, she was told to stop, not to call the record company, and they would call her. Thinking this to be a rejection, Yip was surprised when they did call and she was put on Hong Kong **television** singing a cover of Dusty Springfield's "You Don't Have to Say You Love Me." That was in 1969, and Yip began recording English records, as was the trend at the time. During the 1970s, she began recording songs for Television Broadcasts Limited (TVB) series.

Yip is most famous for being the voice behind **James Wong** and **Joseph Koo's** "Shanghai Beach," the theme song of the eponymous TVB series that rocketed **Chow Yun-fat** to superstardom in the early 1980s. Yip has released over 80 albums, and has had hits in Cantonese, Mandarin, English, Japanese, Thai, and Polynesian. She has appeared in several films, including a starring role in *It Takes Two/Laan fonf laan dai/Nan xiong nan di* (1982), and a supporting part in **Michael Hui's** *Teppanyaki/Tit baan shiu/Tie ban shao* (1984). She has also acted on Hong Kong television. Yip continues to perform to this day, often for charity, with venues ranging from the Hong Kong Coliseum, to the Savoy in London, and the cruise ship *QE2*. She often speaks out about cancer since she herself is a breast cancer survivor; she created an inspirational program on the topic with Hong Kong Renaissance man James Wong. After a concert she performed in San Francisco in 2002, San Francisco declared May 28th Frances

Yip day. In 2004, she once again performed with the Hong Kong Philharmonic Orchestra, and she toured the world in early 2005.

YIP, VERONICA YUK-HING (1966–). Born in Hong Kong, actress Veronica Yip was second runner-up in the Miss Asia Beauty pageant, and became a popular **Cantopop** singer before entering the film industry, joining Television Broadcasts Limited (TVB) acting classes, and then making Category 3 (soft core) movies, such as *Pretty Woman/Hing boon gaai yan/Qing ben jia ren* (1991). However, she also appeared in some more substantive roles, such as *Rose/Baak mooi gwai/Bai mei gui* (1992), as **Maggie Cheung's** best friend and confidant, and as the Black Rose in Jacky Pang's spoof of the 1960s female superhero movies *Rose, Rose I Love You/Mooi gwai mooi gwai ngoh oi nei/Mei gui mei gui wo ai ni* (1993). One of her most captivating roles is as a single mother in **Tony Au's** *Roof with a View (The Moonlight from Heaven's Windowsill,* aka *Love on the Roof)/Tin toi dik yuet gwong/Tian tai de yue guang*, opposite **Leung Ka-fai**. Considering her reputation, it is ironic that she more than believably played the frigid White Rose in art house director **Stanley Kwan's** *Red Rose, White Rose/Hung mooi gwai baak mooi gwai/Hong mei gui bai mei gui* (1994).

Yip has appeared in 26 movies. When she was singing in Atlantic City in 1995, she met a New York supermarket magnate, married, retired, and raised several children, typical of Hong Kong actresses.

YIP, WILSON WAI-SHUN (1964–). Director Wilson Yip started working for **Cinema City** in 1985. He was assistant director for **Kent Cheng's** *United We Stand/Fei yeuk ling cheung/Fei yue ling yang* (1986) and Andy Chin's *Maidens of Heavenly Mountains/San tin lung baat biu ji tin saan tung liu/Xin tian long ba bu zhi tian shan tong lao* (1994). He directed the Triad drama *Mongkok Story/Wong gok fung wan/Wang jiao feng yun* (1996), starring **Roy Cheung** as a sympathetic boss, as well as *Juliet in Love (Butterfly Lovers)/Jue lai yip yue leung saan ang/Zhu li she yu liang shan ba* (2000), costarring **Francis Ng** and **Sandra Ng** in a contemporary version of the story of the Butterfly Lovers. To date, he has directed 14 films, including *Leaving Me, Loving You/Daai shing siu si/Da cheng xiao shi* (2004), an **independent**-style relationship movie costarring **Leon Lai** and

Faye Wong, and the detective **martial arts action**er *Sha Po Lang* (2005), starring **Samo Hung** and **Donnie Yen**, which played at the 2005 Toronto International Film Festival.

YONFAN (Yeung Fan) (1947–). Director Yonfan was born in Hankou, taken to Hong Kong at three by his family, and educated there and in Taiwan. In 1969, he traveled to the United States to study advertising and participated in choreography, theater, and performance arts. In 1973, he returned to Hong Kong, where he founded the Far Sun Film Company, which distributed French films in Hong Kong.

Yonfan maintains a dual career as a still photographer and filmmaker. He has published several collections of his photography in book form, among them *Ten Years by Yonfan* (1983) and *A Chinese Portrait* (1991). In 1978, Yonfan became a **television** writer and director. His directorial debut was *A Certain Romance/Siu lui yat gei/Shao nu ri ji* (1984), which earned him the title of the "aesthete director" due to its romantic vision and enlivening camerawork. Fyodor Dostoyevsky wrote, "beauty will save the world," which is the ethos by which Yonfan abides, believing in beauty, truthfulness, and kindness.

Yonfan's films have primarily been romances, although he has run the gamut from **martial arts** to **musicals**. *Bugis Street/Yiu gaai wong hau/Yao jie huang hou* (1995), cowritten with **Fruit Chan**, ventures into gay territory, which became much more explicit with *Bishonen (Love of a Beautiful Boy)/Mei siu nin ji luen/Mei shao nian zhi lian* (1998), exploring both gay and straight relationships, costarring Stephen Fung, Daniel Wu, **Shu Qi**, and Terence Yin. *Peony Pavilion/Yau yuen geng mung/You yuan jing meng* (2001) looked back to *kunqu* opera, a style originating in Kunshan, Jiangsu province, and it includes Rie Miyazawa's rendition of "Bu Bu Jiao." Set in the Suzhou Gardens in 1930, the story explores the emotional costs to a relationship between two **women** (Miyazawa and **Joey Wang**) when a male (Daniel Wu) intervenes. The film earned Miyazawa the best actress award at the Moscow International Film Festival and was selected by *Time Asia* as "Best of 2001." The director's continued interest in Chinese opera resulted in the documentary *Breaking the Willow* (2003), an official selection of the Venice Film Festival. His latest film is *Color Blossoms/Tiu sik/Tao se* (2004), starring Matsuzaka Keiko,

Teresa Cheung, and Harisu. Overall, Yonfan tackles the spectrum of what it means to be alive and relate to others intimately, as well as to dream and wish for a more beautiful experience. *See also* GAY FILMS.

YONGHUA FILM COMPANY (Yung Hwa). Yonghua was founded in 1947 by Li Zuyong with assistance from **Zhang Shankun** to make Mandarin films in Hong Kong and was its first large-scale private enterprise film company; after creative differences about running the company, Zhang left in 1948; that same year, the company organized an artistic committee. The studio, first located at Kowloon Tsai, was managed by Lu Yuanliang, and was the largest and most modernized, state-of-the-art, in the late 1940s and early 1950s. Lu remembers them renting a vegetable field from a Portuguese woman, with an area of 200,000 square feet, on which two sound stages were constructed. The studio made the epic films *Soul of China*, directed by **Bu Wancang** and adapted from Wu Zuguang's play *Song of Righteousness*, and ***Sorrows of the Forbidden City***, directed by **Zhu Shilin** and adapted by **Yao Ke** from his own play (both 1948), the latter one of the first Hong Kong films to gain international recognition. Other outstanding productions include Yuan Jun's *Hearts Aflame/Huozang* (1947), Wu Zuguang's *A Peasant's Tragedy (Hearts Aflame)/Shan he lei* and *Kinship Marriage/Chun feng qiu yu* (both 1949), and **Yan Jun's** *Singing under the Moon/Cuicui* (1953).

The main market for the company was China, but political change affected audience and finance. More than 20 films were produced between 1947 and 1954. A fire that broke out in a storage vault in 1954 destroyed the negatives of some films. Furthermore, the company owed a large debt to **Cathay** Organization in Singapore, so it was inevitable that its assets were surrendered.

Loke Wan Tho took over in 1955, and reorganized the studio as International Films and later **Motion Pictures and General Investment (MP&GI)** in 1957, creating a modern movie empire, Hong Kong–old Hollywood style, with integrated production, distribution, and exhibition. MP&GI productions were renowned in the Southeast Asian and Hong Kong markets throughout the late 1950s and early 1960s, and the company was a major force in Hong Kong cinema.

YOU, MIN (Lucilla Yu Ming) (1935–1996). Actress You Min (real name Bi Yuyi), a native of Guangdong province, was born in Hong Kong and brought up by her grandmother there. Her father, Pak Yuk-tong (Bai Yutang), was a famous **Cantonese opera** singer. **Runde Shaw** discovered her in 1952, and cast her in the never-released *Anything Can Happen/Yuk lui waai chun/Yu nu huai chun* (1952). She starred in 20 **Shaw Brothers** film, including **Tao Qin's** *A Thread of Life/Chaan sang/Can shang* (1953) and *Tragedy of Vendetta (The Feud)/Tung lam diu/Tong lin niao* (1955, costarring **Kenneth Tsang Kong**), and **Tang Huang's** *Love and War/Hung fan gon gwoh/Hong fen gan gei* (1959). In 1958, she signed with **Motion Pictures and General Investment (MP&GI,** Cathay**)**, for which she made ***Her Tender Heart****/Yuk lui shut ching/ Yunu siqing* (1959) and **Wang Tianlin's** comedy *All in the Family/Ga yau choi si/ Jia you xishi* 1959), winning Best Actress at the sixth and seventh **Asian Film Festivals**, respectively.

Tang Huang's *Her Tender Heart* (1959), adapted from a Du Ning novel, was You's first film at MP&GI. Although 25, she played the high-school daughter of a single father who has raised her, only to discover that the woman who suddenly appears, her "auntie," is her mother, and she is torn between them. The drama *A Night in Hong Kong/Heung gong ji yau/Xiang gang zhi ye* (1961), in which she starred opposite Japanese actor Takarada Akira, was extremely successful in Japan, making You a star with a non-Chinese-speaking audience.

You also costarred (with **Ye Feng** and **Ge Lan**) in **Evan Yang's** ***Sun, Moon, and Star****, 1* and *2/Sing sing yuet leung taai yeung/Xingxing, Yueliang, Taiyang* (1961) as the gentle and self-sacrificing Star, for which she won Best Actress at the **Golden Horse Awards** in the first film.

You's last film was Wang Tianlin's drama *Romance of the Forbidden City/Sam gung yuen/Shen gong yuan* (1964). She retired and married Hong Kong businessman Gao Fuqiu. She died of a heart attack in Hong Kong.

YOUNG, ALBERT (Yang Jun) (1915–). Cinematographer Albert Young was born in Beijing, majored in Economics at Nankai University of Tianjin, and became a newsman. His first experience as a cameraman was during the Songhu Campaign, during which he assisted United States' Paramount and Universal in shooting Shanghai newsreels.

Young joined director **Bu Wancang's Taishan** in 1951 as a production manager, cinematographer, and assistant director. That same year, the Macau government invited him to assist a foreign director on a project and he remained to make six **documentaries**.

In 1956, Young joined **Shaw Brothers** as the company's only cinematographer at that time. Eventually, he was made head of cinematography and trained at least 10 other cameramen. In 1959, he began shooting in Cinemascope. In 1961, Young became the senior cinematographer for the Hong Kong Government Information Services (HKGIS), but left in 1965 to join **Cathay** as the head of cinematography and technical advisor. He thereafter returned to the Information Services to direct films, and he remained there until his retirement in 1972, after which he set up his own film company, Sea Dragon Film Services.

Young, known for his vigorous but precise camerawork, photographed more than 100 Mandarin feature films, among them the award-winning ***The Kingdom and the Beauty****/Kong saan mei yan/Jiangshan meiren* (1959, directed by **Li Han-hsiang**) and *The Deformed/Gei yan yim foo/Jiren yanfu* (1960, directed by **Yue Feng**), both winning Best Cinematography Awards at **Asian Film Festival**s.

YU, LAI-JAN (Yu Lizhen) (1923–). Cantonese opera actress and producer Yu Lai-jan, a native of Guangdong province, was raised overseas but developed an interest in **Chinese opera** at a young age, performing onstage at 16 and becoming well known in overseas Chinese communities in the United States and Southeast Asia. Prior to wartime, Yu came to Hong Kong with Luo Pinchao, and they founded the Guanghua Opera Troupe; she also founded several other prewar opera troupes.

The actress was trained in the *zihou* (child's voice) singing mode and performed in numerous operas, including *The Sparrow's Pavilion*, *The Cuckoo's Spirit in March*, and *The Crab Beauty*. She was called the "Queen of Performers" and was known as one of the "Eight Peonies," including opera stars **Fung Wong-nui**, **Law Yim-hing**, **Tang Pik-wan**, and four others. Yu performed both **melodramatic** and **martial arts** roles.

Yu's film debut was **Hong Shuyun's** opera adaptation *The Cuckoo's Spirit in March/Saam yuet do guen wan/San yue du juan hun* (1947). In 1959, she cofounded the Lishi Film Production Company with her husband, librettist **Lee Siu-wan**, turning her attention away from the stage and on filmmaking; their productions were mostly opera films, and over the next 18 years, the company produced more than 70 features. Among their productions are **Fung Chi-kong's** *Riot in the Temple/Sap saam mooi daai laau lang yan chi/Shi san mei da nao neng ren si* (1960); **Wong Hok-sing's** *Seven Phoenixes/Gam fung chaam gaau lung/Jin feng zhan jiao long* (1961), *Uproar in the Palace/Gam gaan liu sui aau on din/Jin jian nu sui yin an dian* (1962), and *Half a Bed/Boon cheung luk fung chong/Ban zhang lu jia chuang* (1964); and **Wong Toi's** *A Girl Named Leng Qiwei, 1* and *2/Laang Chau Mei/Leng Qiuwei* (1964).

The actress's screen appearances include Fung Chi-kong's *A King Speaks His Heart/Dai yuen chun sam dut do guen/Diyuan chunxin hua dujuan* (1951) and *The Impeachment of Yim Sung (Yan Song)/Sap chau Yim Sung/Shizou Yansong* (1952), and *The Emperor's Nocturnal Sacrifice/Gwon Sui Wong yau Chai Jan Fei/Guang Xu Wang ye Jizhen Fei* (1952). *The Impeachment of Yim Sung* (1952) was written by Lee Siu-wan and adapted from the Tai Fung Wong Opera Troupe's performance; Yu played one of two concubines, taken by Ming emperor Ka Ching (**Sit Kok-sin**), who twice disguises himself as a commoner to venture among the people. Yu's concubine becomes mother of the crown prince. The second concubine (Siu Yin-fei) has a fortune teller father, Yim Sung (**Ma Sze-tsang**), whom the emperor makes minister. He crushes the people and conspires against the palace, and the crown prince and his mother encourage a righteous scholar to impeach him. Yu's duets included "Teasing My Lover with False Displeasure" and "Mourning over the Grave" (with Sit), and the song "Winning for Affection" with Sit and Siu Yin-fei.

However, Yu will always be remembered for her performances as the "Headless Queen" in a series of supernatural Cantonese opera films, including *The Headless Queen Bears a Son, 1* and *2/Miu tau dung gung sang taai ji/Wutou donggong sheng taizi* and *The Headless Queen (Empress) Rescues the Prince/Wutou donggong jiu taizi* (all 1957). Lee Siu-wan created (writing and producing) the series, which spawned many imitators, and the subgenre as a whole demonstrates the flexibility of Cantonese opera and the imaginative elements of film. Basically, the stories dramatize the conflict between good and evil of the benevolent East palace (and first wife) empress and the malevolent West palace (and second wife) in a struggle for dynastic succession. Yu starred as the good queen while Fung Wong-nui played her nemesis. All those close to the East palace empress are threatened or destroyed by the West palace empress and her cohorts; when the Eastern queen is beheaded, an immortal saves her spirit and she gives birth to her son while entombed. She is also given special powers that allow her to separate her head from her body, fly through the air, and fight her enemy head on.

The actress starred in over 100 films. She retired in 1968 and immigrated to Canada.

YU, MING (Yue Ming) (1924–). Actor Yu Ming (real name Ruan Yaolin), a native of Guangdong, was born in Guangzhou and participated in amateur dramatics beginning in primary school. Yu joined the film industry in 1947, through his brother, director Yu Liang, debuting in *P.O.W. 1* (1947). Yu appeared in hundreds of films in a career spanning 1947–1984. Early in his career, he was typecast as bandits or teddy boys, but later he became famous for comic roles.

Some of Yu's memorable Cantonese films include **Chan Lit-bun's** comedy *How Master Cute Thrice Saved the Idiot Ming/Liu foo ji saam gau soh chai ming/Lao fu zi san jiu sha zai ming* (1966), **Chan Wan's** romance **melodrama** *The Young Love/Qingchun zhi lian* (1967), and the **musical** comedy *Red Lips of May/Ng yuet dik hung sun/Wu yue de hong chun* (1968). *The Young Love* was a star vehicle for **Josephine Siao**, whose ballerina falls for a writer (Wu Fung); the writer is dying and jilts her, so she takes up with a cad (Yu), and the film includes two bizarre set pieces—a black wedding ceremony and a funeral march set in a hospital corridor.

In the early 1970s, Yu joined Television Broadcasts Limited's (TVB) program *Enjoy Yourself Tonight* as an actor and host. He turned to **television** drama in 1978, and has appeared in many series, including *The Young Detective* and *The Duke of Mount Deer* (both 1984).

YU, NELSON LIK-WAI. Hong Kong director, writer, and cinematographer Nelson Yu directed the **independent** short *Neon Goddesses*

(1996), a **documentary** about three young women from the provinces attracted to the neon of Beijing and its nightlife. The film won the Hong Kong Independent Short Film and Video award that year. Yu also worked as cinematographer on Sixth Generation Mainland director Jia Zhangke's *Xiao Wu* (1997), and **Ann Hui's** *Ordinary Heroes/Chin yin maan yue/Qian yan wan yu* (1999).

Yu's feature directorial debut was *Love Will Tear Us Apart (Ah Ying)/Tin seung yan gaan/Tian shang ren jian* (1999), which began as a project funded by Hong Kong Art's Development project, but director **Stanley Kwan** and actor **Tony Leung Ka-fai** came on as producers. The low budget film ($HK4 million) won the International Federation of Film Critics Award (FIPRESCI) and screened at Cannes. A deconstructed narrative structure, the story examines impermanent relationships between four alienated Mainlanders in Hong Kong, cross-cutting between their chance interactions and repeating visual imagery and dialogue that connects them. A study of their despairing psychology, torn between wanting to fit in and rebel, nostalgic for a home that no longer exists, the film breaks new ground for identity politics in recent Hong Kong cinema.

Yu's next project, the postapocalyptic *All Tomorrow's Parties/Mingri tianya* (2003), borrows from Jean-Luc Godard's *Alphaville* in setting a futuristic story here and now. Like *Love Will Tear Us Apart*, relationships between four characters are explored, yet here they are simply trying to survive the aftermath of a totalitarian regime. Similarly, the fragmentary narrative is original and audacious. Ironically, the film was fined by the Chinese government's Film Bureau, although the film is more a response to September 11th with its allusions relating more to the Taliban than anything Chinese. The film played at the 2003 Cannes Film Festival.

YU, RONGGUANG (Yu Wing-gong) (1958–). Mainland actor Yu Rong-guang trained in a traditional **Peking (Beijing) opera** school and began acting in Mainland **martial arts** movies. His breakthrough came in **Ching Siu-tung's** *Terracotta Warrior (Chin's Terracotta, Fight and Love with a Terracotta Warrior)/Chin yung/Qing yong* (1989, also starring **Gong Li** and Mainland director **Zhang Yimou**). He has worked with some of the best Hong Kong **action** stars, including **Jackie Chan**, **Michelle Yeoh**, **Jet Li**, and **Donnie Yen**, as well as some of the best martial arts action directors, including **Corey Yuen**, **Yuen Wo-ping**, Ching Siu-tung, Donnie Yen, and **Stanley Tong**. He is often cast as a villain, but Yuen Wo-ping chose him as the title heroic character in *Iron Monkey (The Young Wong Fei-hung: Iron Monkey/Siu nin Wong Fei-hung ji tit ma lau/Shaonian Huang Feihong zhi tie ma liu* (1993), and **Herman Yau** set him against **Anthony Wong's** psycho in *Taxi Hunter (Taxi Judge)/Dik si poon goon/Di shi pan guan* (1993). A villain of note is the gang leader of a smuggling ring in which he holds his own against Jet Li in *My Father Is a Hero/Kap ang ang dik san/Gei ba ba de xin* (1995).

Yu also appeared in Jackie Chan's comical United States release *Shanghai Noon* (2000) and new installment in the *Police Story* series (*New Police Story*, 2004) as well as playing a Mongol general in the Korean period piece epic *Musa the Warrior* (2001). He has acted in 50 films to date.

YU, RONNY YAN-TAI. Born in Hong Kong, director Ronny Yu has always been a man who enjoys challenges. He was born into a family of girls and contracted polio when very young; he fantasized stories while bedridden and was routinely taken to the movie theaters, where he would spend the day while his father worked. At 16, he attended boarding school in London. To please his businessman father, he studied marketing and graduated from college in Ohio. Returning to Hong Kong in 1975, he learned filmmaking on the job, as production manager of **Leong Po-chih's** *Jumping Ash/Tiu fooi/Tiao hui* (1976) and **Yim Ho's** *The Extras/Ke lei fe /Jia li fei* (1978); his directorial debut was *The Servant/Cheung laap cheing ngoi/Qiang nei qiang wai* (1979).

The Savior/Gau sai chea/Jiu shi zhe (1980) introduces a Clint Eastwood–style cop set against a psychotic serial killer (**Bai Ying**) with father issues (because of his mother's suicide) murdering prostitutes. Yu recreates the thriller by combining the standard tough cop (**Kent Cheng**), who also has a soft spot for an orphan, with the horror slasher flicks of Tobe Hooper (*Texas Chainsaw Massacre*, 1974), and the film walks the tightrope between sensational gasps and morality tale. Yu directed Brandon Lee in his film debut, *Legacy of Rage (Dragon All Over the Country)/Lung joi gong woo/Long zai jiang hu* (1986), long before *The Crow*, and showcased **Chow Yun-**

fat in his only **martial arts action**er, *The Postman Strikes Back (City Patrol Horse)/Chun sing ma/Xun cheng ma* (1982), until the actor starred in **Ang Lee's** *Crouching Tiger, Hidden Dragon* 20 years later.

Yu's masterpieces to date would be his two collaborations with the late actor **Leslie Cheung**, first in *The Bride with White Hair (The Evil White-Haired Lady)/Baak faat moh nui/Bai fa mo nu* (1993), and then in *Phantom Lover (Midnight Song)/Ye boon goh sing/Ye ban ge sheng* (1995). Bittersweet love stories, mesmerizing performances, and stunning visual style combined with lyrical **musical** themes characterize each. Using Cheung, Yu reinvented the martial arts fantasy genre with a sensitive hero in the former, and woozy romance in the latter via a Chinese version of *Phantom of the Opera* and *Romeo and Juliet*. The former won best screenplay and film song at the 30th **Golden Horse Awards** in Taiwan in 1993; the latter won Best Cinematography, Art Direction, and Costume and Makeup at the 13th **Hong Kong Film Awards** in 1994. The latter featured the cinematography of **Peter Pau**, the editing of David Wu, and the costumes of Emi Wada; filmed at the Beijing Film Studio on the Mainland, it was recorded with synch sound and it was the first Hong Kong film to incorporate Digital Theater System sound (DTS).

Yu would eventually leave Hong Kong for Australia and turn his eyes westward. With *Warriors of Virtue* (1996) he created a magical children's story with a message about developing one's own inner strength and learning cooperation. Next, he would pass on the chance to work with Wesley Snipes on *Blade* and tackle the *Child's Play* franchise with a campy and dark humored *Bride of Chucky* (1998) that satisfied both fans of the earlier flicks and those new to the character. After that, Samuel L. Jackson approached him for what would become *Formula 51* (aka *51st State*, 2001), a film over which Yu lost control because of the dozen producers involved. His next Hollywood project would be turning two of the longest running horror franchises, Freddy Kruger's *Nightmare on Elm Street* and Jason Vorhees's *Friday the 13th* series, into something besides cheap slasher flicks. *Freddy vs. Jason* (2003) earned $82,217,464, and was deemed by a right-wing religious group in the United States as the most violent Hollywood movie (despite its comedic take). Yu's strengths include creating an atmospheric sense of place where location is almost a character and incorporating lots of visual style to enhance the story. His latest film, *Fearless* (2006), stars **Jet Li**, with action direction by **Yuen Wo-ping**. Yu credits his wife's support and encouragement with his success on wide-ranging projects.

YU, SO-CHAU (Yu Suqui) (1930–). Actress Yu So-chau was born in Beijing. Her father, Yu Zhanyuan, was a famous **Peking (Beijing) opera** actor, and she began training in opera at eight years of age; her métier was as the *daomadan*, a traditional female character, martial in nature; her accomplishments in this type of performance, as well as her specialty in Northern Tou Shou technique, led to amazing stage performances in *Legend of the White Snake* and *Amazon at Sea* (both 1951), in which she used the technique of one foot to fend off a dozen consecutively thrown tasseled spears.

Yu started in the film industry in the Mandarin **martial arts** movie *Encounter at Hongbi/Wang bik yuen/Hong bi yuan* (1948) for **Great Wall**. In Shanghai, she starred in *The Heroine with the Double Spear/Fong kong lui hap/Huang jiang nu xia* (1949), and *The Heroine of the Deserted River/Fong kong lui hap/Huang jiang nu xia* (1950) was her first Cantonese martial arts picture. Over the next 15 years, she starred in over 170 martial arts movies.

Of the 200 films the actress made, the majority of them are in the martial arts genre, but she also made **Cantonese opera** films and detective thrillers. Among her martial arts films are *Revenge of the Great Swordsman/Daai hap fook chau gei/Daxia fuchou ji* (1949, codirected by and starring **Wang Yuanlong**), Ling Yung's *Burning of the Red Lotus Monastery* (1950), *Three Swordswomen from Guangdong (Three Gallant Ladies of Guangdong)/Gwaan dung saam lui hap/Guangdong san nuxia* (1961), and *The Golden Hairpin, 1–4/Bik huet gam chaai/Bixie jinchai* (1963, 1964), among others. In *Burning of the Red Lotus Monastery*, she played one of the martial heroes, alongside **Tso Tatwah**, who defeat the corrupt denizens of the Red Lotus Monastery, where a debauched monk has created a secret harem. In *The Golden Hairpin*, adapted by *wuxia* novelist Louis Chaf Jin Yong, Yu played one of the four **women** who assist a knight-errant avenger (**Cheung Ying**) who has acquired supernatural martial arts skills at the Shaolin Monastery before searching for his father's assassin.

Among Yu's Cantonese opera films is *Legend of the White Snake (The Snake Girl and the Flying Monster)/San lui fei moh/She nu fei mo* (1962) and among her detective thrillers is *House No. 13* (1960). In 1966, she became vice president of the Chinese Theatrical Institute, originally started by her father, whose pupils have included **Jackie Chan** and **Samo Hung**. She retired from the film industry after her marriage in 1966 to Cantonese opera star **Mak Bing-wing** (Mai Bingrong).

YUE, GRIFFIN FENG (1909–1999). Born in Shanghai and graduating from secondary school at the Chinese Public School in Shanghai at 18, Yue Feng (real name Da Zichun) entered the film industry as a continuity person and worked his way up to screenwriter and director. Yue's first script was *Daybreak* (1933) and his directorial debut was *Angry Tide of China's Seas* (1933) when he was only 23. He came to Hong Kong in 1948, worked 50 years in the film industry and made 80 films, retiring in 1972 and staying in Hong Kong. He remains one of the most underappreciated of the postwar Hong Kong directors. His career traverses left- and apolitical right-wing cinema, the former in his films for **Great Wall**, the latter at **Motion Pictures and General Investment (MP&GI)** and **Shaw Brothers**. A meticulous craftsman in his direction, Yue was sympathetic toward his characters (especially **women**), and he worked with Hong Kong's most memorable female stars of the period, including **Li Lihua**, **Bai Guang**, **Lin Dai**, and **Zhou Xuan**, both highlighting their talents and developing sensitive women's stories in the feminist vein, with the women searching for understanding and an equal footing with men. Li Lihua and Lin Dai were his favored actresses. After retiring, Yue lived in Hong Kong until his death.

In *Three Women/Saam lui sing/San nuxing* (1947), Yue's film uses the paths of three women's lives to examine the effects of circumstance and environment. One is forced to become a dancehall girl and commits suicide in shame; another becomes a wealthy man's ornament; and a third overcomes obstacles to make her own contributions to a better society. Li Lihua stars as the third character, an independent woman who brings up the daughter of a prostitute. In *An Unfaithful Woman/Dong foo sam/Dang fu xin* (1949), Great Wall's first production, Bai Guang starred as a downtrodden prostitute charged with the murder of her pimp; told in flashback, the story follows her from her beginnings as a carefree country girl sold into a rich household by her poor father. *Modern Red Chamber Dream/San hung lau mung/Xin honglou meng* (1952), which he directed and also wrote, is a contemporary version of the classic novel *Dream of the Red Chamber*.

An example of Yue's early left-wing phase work, the story serves as a contemporary allegory about the civil war waged between Communists and Nationalists, or the battle between feudalism and capitalism, and class struggle. Li Lihua (a discovery of Yue in 1940 Shanghai) stars as a lonely orphan, Lin Daiyu, adopted and abandoned by the powerful Jia family, with a kindly grandmother and a financial speculator patriarch. Although set in Shanghai, the movie creates an ambience that feels like Hong Kong. In *Flower Street/Dut gaai/Hua jie* (1950), Zhou Xuan stars as a street performer's daughter. Her father disappears at the start of the Sino–Japanese War and reappears onstage forced to sing pro-Japanese songs, but cleverly subverting them. In *Golden Lotus/Gam lin dut/Jin lianhua* (1957), Lin Dai plays a songstress, and both films reinforce Chinese patriotism and folk culture. His *Streetboys/Gaai tung/Jie tong* (1959) was an important work of Hong Kong's 1950s Mandarin cinema.

Yue's influences include **Bu Wancang**, Shi Dongshan, Tian Han, and Yang Hansheng. Family, human relationships, and romantic involvements are among his themes, with strong moral principles in play.

YUEH, HUA (Ngok Wah) (1942–). From 1966 to 1978, Yueh Hua was arguably the most prolific and versatile leading man among the **Shaw Brothers** team of actors. With his soft, babyish features, which he learned to use effectively in playing against type as a villain, Yueh was in demand for roles ranging from scholarly **swordsmen** to foolish drunks to romantic swains, and in the prime of his career he made five to 10 films a year.

Originally from Shanghai, Yueh was recruited by the Shaw studio in 1963, and, although he was first introduced to **martial arts** during a brief training period at the studio, he was immediately cast in a series of ***wuxia*** films. One of his first films for Shaw Brothers was the enormously successful *Come Drink with Me/Da zui xia* (1966), where he was paired with another Shanghai native, the lovely young actress **Cheng Pei-pei**. His sweetly nuanced portrayal of the melancholy beggar Drunken Cat contributed greatly to the film's popularity. He went on to costar with Cheng six more times.

But it was his long-standing collaboration with the Shaw studio director **Chor Yuen** that would provide Yueh with many of his most memorable roles. Unlike the savage combat presented by fellow Shaw director **Chang Cheh**, Chor's vision of *wuxia* chivalry was refined and poetic, which suited Yueh's style. When called on to play the villain, as in ***Killer Clans****/Liu xing hu die jian/Lau sing wu dip kim* (1976), Yueh rejected the stylized mannerisms familiar from Chinese opera, and played the character with cold reserve, almost as if he were the hero. His ability to maintain a dignified image despite the most lurid circumstances is documented in the notorious camp hit *Intimate Confessions of a Chinese Courtesan/Oi No/Ai Nu* (1972), where he plays the official investigating a series of murders.

In 1975, Yueh married Tanny Tien Ni, a young actress under contract to Shaw Brothers. The couple made several films together, but the era of Shaw dominance of the Asian market was coming to an end, and Yueh was working on films in Taiwan and on Hong Kong **television** by the end of the decade. He remained active through the 1980s, but then moved to Canada, where he continues to work in broadcasting. One of his last appearances in a Hong Kong film was a cameo in **Jackie Chan's** *Rumble in the Bronx/Hung faan kui/Hong fan qu* (1995).

YUEN, ANITA WING-YEE (1971–). Like others of her generation, Anita Yuen entered the entertainment industry after she won the Miss Hong Kong contest in 1990, starting at Hong Kong Television Broadcasts Limited (TVB) hosting **television** shows and debuting on film in the comedy *Days of Being Dumb (Ah Fei and Ah Kei) /Ah fei yue Ah Kei/Ya Fei yu Ya Ji* (1992), for which she won the Best Newcomer of the Year at the **Hong Kong Film Awards**. She followed this up the next year by winning the Best Actress award for her portrayal as an enthusiastic but dying young woman opposite **Lau Ching-wan** in **Derek Yee's melodrama** *C'est la Vie, Mon Cheri (New Endless Love)/San bat liu ching/Xin bu liao qing* (1993), which played for two months in Hong Kong and earned HK$30 million, praised by audiences and critics. Yuen became very popular for her effervescent characters, lively, innocent, a bit wacky, but always life-affirming and loveable. She played equally well in comedy as melodrama.

Yuen again won Best Actress at the **Hong Kong Film Awards** for her portrayal of an androgynous ordinary person enthralled by Hong Kong stars in **Peter Chan's** ***He's a Woman, She's a Man*** *(Golden Branch, Jade Leaf)/Gam chi yuk yip/Jin qi yu ye* (1994), in which she costarred with **Leslie Cheung** and **Carina Lau**. Although set in the music business, the gender-bending comedy allowed Chan to wryly comment on Hong Kong's movie industry's creation of product and its fanatical fan culture. Yuen was also paired with Cheung in several other films, including Chan's sequel, *Who's the Woman, Who's the Man? (Golden Branch, Jade Leaf 2)/Gam chi yuk sip 2/Jin qi yu ye 2* (1996) and **Tsui Hark's** *The Chinese Feast* (1995) and *Tri-Star* (1996).

In recent years she has done more television work than film.

YUEN, BIAO (1957–). The youngest of the **Seven Little Fortunes**, Yuen got his start by making a cameo in **Bruce Lee's** *Fist of Fury/Jing mou moon/Jing wu men* (1972) and the **martial arts** film *Hap-Ki-Do/Gap hei diy/He qi dao* (1972). Continuing to work as a stuntman, Yuen's first break came when he was cast as the lead by **Samo Hung** in *Knockabout/Chap ga siu ji/Za gu xiao zi* (1979). What made Yuen truly recognizable to Hong Kong audiences, though, was his role in Hung's *Prodigal Son (Son Ruining the Family,* aka *Pull No Punches) Bai ga jai/Baijia zi* (1981). Yuen would also star as the lead in **Tsui Hark's** *Zu: Warriors from the Magic Mountain/Suk san sun suk san geen hap/Zuo shan shen zuo shan jian xia* (1983). Throughout the next decade, Yuen would team up with his two **Chinese opera** brothers, **Jackie Chan** and Samo Hung, as well as other members of the Seven Little Fortunes, to make numerous classic films such as *Project A/A Gai waak/A Ji hua* (1983), *Wheels on Meals/Faai chaan che/Kuai can che* (1984), and *Dragons Forever/Fei lung maang cheung/Fei long meng jiang* (1988). Yuen is commonly considered to be one of the most acrobatic martial artists in the Hong Kong industry. He also made the ***wuxia*** fantasy *Iceman Cometh/Gap dung kei hap/Ji dong ji xia* (1989) with **Yuen Wah** and **Maggie Cheung**.

In the 1990s, Yuen cut back his workload. He appeared in Tsui's ***Once upon a Time in China****/Wong Fei-hung/Huang Feihong* (1991),

Corey Yuen Kwai's *Hero/Ma wing ching/Ma yong zhang* (1997), and the **Ekin Cheng** special effects–loaded *A Man Called Hero/ Chung wa ying hung/Zhong hua ying xiong* (1999). Yuen continued to gain more and more popularity in Japan, where he has appeared in several domestic films. Yuen has to his credit more than 100 films, but makes them infrequently now, citing a lack of availability of good scripts.

YUEN, CHAU-FUNG (Yuan Qiufeng) (1924–). Director Yuen Chau-fung, a native of Anhui, was born in Ha'erbin and graduated from Beijing's China University, specializing in economics and politics. Briefly working as a war journalist, he became involved in the film industry by apprenticing to **Ma-Xu Weibang**. Yuen's directorial debut was *Heroine of the Lone River* (1954), an Amoy-dialect film, and his first Mandarin film was *Mid-Nightmare/Yau boon goh sing/Ye ban ge sheng* (1962), written by Ma-Xu Weibang. The film starred **Le Di** and **Zhao Lei**, who appeared in many of Yuen's films.

In 1965, the director joined **Motion Pictures and General Investment (MP&GI)**, later Cathay, making the fantasy *Lady on (in) the Moon/Seung ngo ban yuet/Chang e ben yue* (1962), starring Le and Zhao; the war-themed *A Debt of Blood/Luen sai ngai lui/Luan shi er nu* (1966); and the **musical** comedy *Teenagers' Holidays/Ching chun dik suen lut/Qing chun de xuan lu* (1968). In 1968, Yuen established Golden Eagle Film Company with Le Di and **Kelly Lai Chen**; their first film was the **martial arts** *The Vagabond Swordsman/Fung chan haak/Feng chen ke* (1968), starring Le Zhao and **Shek Kin**.

In 1970, Yuen succeeded **Raymond Chow** as production manager at **Shaw Brothers**. In 1973, he retired from the film industry and pursued publishing interests.

YUEN, COREY KWAI (Ying Gang-ming). Director and **action** director Corey Yuen has the distinction of being one of the **Seven Little Fortunes**, hired out from his **Peking (Beijing) Opera** School as stuntman and extra in his early film days, appearing in both **Bruce Lee's** *Fist of Fury* (1972) and **Chor Yuen's** *Intimate Confessions of a Chinese Courtesan/Oi No/Ai Nu* (1972). Born in Hong Kong, Yuen joined Master Yu Zhan-yuen's (Yu Jim Yuen) Beijing Opera School at age nine, when his parents signed him up for a 10-year stint. He has since acted in 85 films, action-directed 45, and directed 24 to date. He was a member of **Jackie Chan**'s Stuntmen Club (recognized as gathering the world's best stuntmen).

When living in Seattle in 1985, Yuen contacted producer **Ng See-yuen** after seeing *The Karate Kid*, which led to his directing Jean-Claude Van Damme (as a villain) in *No Retreat, No Surrender* (1985). He has been instrumental in developing **Jet Li's** on-screen action persona, in movies like *Fong Sai-yuk 1* and *2/Fong Sai Yuk/Fang Shiyu* (1993) and *My Father Is a Hero (A Letter to Father)/Kap ba ba dik sun/Gei ba ba de xin* (1995); he has also collaborated with Li in numerous Hollywood productions. Yuen served as action choreographer on *The Transporter 1* and *2* (2002, 2005), starring Jason Stratham, directed by Louis Leterrier, and produced by Luc Besson.

Yuen has worked closely with director and writer **Jeff Lau** (including *Savior of the Soul ('91: The Mystical Condor Hero and His Companion)/'91 san diu hap liu/'91 shen diao xia lu* [1991] and *Mahjong Dragon (Mahjong Flying Dragon)/Lut cheuk fei lung/Ma que fei long* [1997]). He has begun combining **martial arts** action with computer graphics, as seen in *So Close/Chik yeung tin sai/Xiyang tianshi* (2002), his first action movie featuring all **women** fighters, and starring **Karen Mok**, **Shu Qi**, and Zhao Wei (Vicki Zhao), a coproduction of Columbia Pictures and Columbia Pictures Film Production Asia. More recently, he has worked as action director on **Patrick Leung's** follow-up to *The Twins Effect* (2003), *Huadu Chronicles: The Blade of the Rose(Twins Effect 2)/Chin gei bin 2: Dut diy daai chin/Qian ji bian 2: Hua dou da zhan* (2004), an action fantasy period piece starring **The Twins**, Charlene Choi and Gillian Chung, and **Leung Ka-fai**, **Donnie Yen**, and **Jackie Chan**.

YUEN, SIMON SIU-TIN (Yuan Xiaotian) (1912–1980). Best known as the father of action director **Yuen Wo-ping**, Yuen Siu-tin trained in **Chinese opera** from childhood and worked in the Shanghai film industry as a stuntman and choreographer. His early credits include the early ***wuxia*** series *Northeast Hero* (1928–1931), which starred the **martial arts** actress **Wu Lizhu**. After World War II, Yuen joined the exodus of Shanghai talent in emigrating to Hong Kong, where he was soon working with Wu and her husband, director **Ren Pengnian**, on films like *Lady Robin Hood/Nu luo bin han* (1947) and a remake of *Northeast Hero/Xin Guan Dong da xia* (1949). He was tapped by director Wu Pang to appear in a supporting role in the seminal kung fu hit *The True Story of Wong Fei-hung: Whiplash Snuffs the Candle Flame/Wong Fei Hung chuen/Huang Fei Hong chuan* (1949), and went on to work as actor, stuntman, and choreographer on the long-running **Wong Fei-hung series**. He acted in hundreds of films. Yuen's sons Wo-ping, Cheung-yan, Chun-yeung, Sun-yi, and Yat-choh all followed their father into careers in the Hong Kong film industry. In 1978, when Yuen Wo-ping was offered the opportunity to direct a young **Jackie Chan** in two highly successful **kung fu** comedies, *Snake in the Eagle's Shadow (Snake Form Trick Hand)/Sau ying diu san/She xing diao shou* (1978), and *Drunken Master (Drunken Fist)/Chui kuen/Zui quan* (1979), for producer **Ng See-yuen**, he cast his father as the wily older master opposite Chan. The older Yuen found himself in demand as a result, and recreated his iconic "Drunken Master" character in a number of kung fu films made over the next two years. He died in 1980, as he was prepping for a role in a Yuen Wo-ping movie, *The Magnificent Butcher.*

YUEN, TOE KIN-TO. Animation director Yuen Toe graduated from Hong Kong Baptist College as a film major and became a comics magazine editor, screenwriter, and special effects and computer animation specialist. For **television**, he directed the *McMug* cartoon (1997). *My Life as McDull/ Mak dau goosi/Maidou gushi* (2001) was his animation directorial debut on film, based on a successful comic series by Alice Mak and Brian Tse, followed by *McDull, Prince de la Bun/Mak dau boh loh yau wong ji/Mai dou bo luo you wang zi* (2004). Both films feature the piglike McDull as a Hong Kong everyman; details in location situate the Hong Kong characteristics of the story, along with Cantonese slang, puns, and cultural in-jokes. **Andy Lau** voiced McDull in the sequel.

YUEN, WAH (1950–). Actor Yuen Wah, born Yueng Kai-chi (Rong Jizhi), is a graduate of the China Drama Academy, a **Chinese opera** school set up in Hong Kong by Yu Jim-yuen (Yu Zhanyuan). Yu was a master of opera technique who also taught **martial arts** and stagecraft to **Jackie Chan**, **Samo Hung**, **Yuen Biao**, and **Corey Yuen**. By all accounts, life at the China Drama Academy was hard, and the training was brutal. Discipline was strictly enforced, with beatings as punishment. The physical movement in Chinese opera is grounded, to a large extent, in martial arts. But opera performers are also expected to be elegant or comic while fighting. To stay in character while executing combat moves, and singing too, requires years of training. Only the best students were chosen for the school's performance troupe, the **Seven Little Fortunes**.

Yuen Wah (many former students of Yu Jim-yuen continue to use their school names professionally, having adopted the surname "Yuen" to honor their teacher) was a star pupil at the school, and when the Seven Little Fortunes performed, his acrobatic technique was a standout. Several of Master Yu's students found work in the Hong Kong film industry as stuntmen and **action** directors in the early 1970s, and Yuen was no exception. He worked with Samo Hung at **Golden Harvest** for a few years, and was **Bruce Lee's** stunt double on *Fist of Fury/Jing wu men* (1972) and ***Enter the Dragon****/Lung chang foo dau/Loong zheng hu dou* (1973). In the mid-1970s, he put in a long stretch of stunt work and minor roles at the **Shaw Brothers** studio, working with directors **Sun Zhong**, **Tang Chia**, and **Chor Yuen**. Eventually Yuen saw his own fortunes rise with the growing industry power of his fellow Fortunes. He has been regularly tapped by Chan, Hung, and Yuen Biao as stunt choreographer, action director, and supporting actor in their classic **kung fu** films, frequently playing the villain.

The former stuntman also has a flair for physical comedy, making him a natural choice to play the lecherous, drunken, and most unlikely hero of **Stephen Chiau's** *Kung Fu Hustle/Kung fu/Gong fu* (2004). His on-screen chemistry with costar (and former opera school classmate) Yuen Qiao delighted audiences worldwide. In 2005, Yuen Wah took the Best Supporting Actor prize at the 24th **Hong Kong Film Awards** for his work in *Kung Fu Hustle*.

YUEN, WO-PING (1945–). Director Yuen Wo-ping was born in Guangzhou and trained by his father, **Yuen Siu-tin**, who brought his son to the attention of the producers of the **Wong Fei-hung** film series starring **Kwan Tak-hing**. The young Wo-ping worked on some of these films in the 1960s and also attended Master Yu Zhangyuan's (Yu Jim Yuen) Chinese Drama Academy, a traditional **Beijing Opera**

School in Hong Kong, along with **Samo Hung**. He worked as a stuntman at **Shaw Brothers**, appearing in movies including **Wang Yu's** *Chinese Boxer/Lung foo moon/Long hu men* (1970). His first credit as **action** choreographer was in **Ng See-yuen's** *Mad Killer/Fung kwong saai sau/Feng kuang sha shou* (1971), beginning a long-term relationship between the two. Yuen choreographed Ng's early **martial arts** films, including *Bloody Fists/Dong kau taan/Dang kou tan* (1972) and *Secret Rivals 2/Naam kuen bak tui dau gam woo/Nan quan bei tui dou jin hu* (1977). For Shaw Brothers, he choreographed the fights for **Chor Yuen's** *The Lizard/Bek foo/Bi hu* (1972) and *The Bastard/Siu chap chung/Xiao za zhong* (1973). When Ng See-Yuen created **Seasonal Films**, Yuen made his directorial debut with the influential *Snake in the Eagle's Shadow (Snake Form Trick Hand)/Sau ying diu san/She xing diao shou* (1978), starring a young **Jackie Chan**, followed by two sequels, *Drunken Master (Drunken Fist)/Chui kuen/Zui quan* (also starring Chan, 1978), and *Dance of the Drunken Mantis/Naam bak chui kuen/Nan bei zui quan* (1979, and starring brother Sunny Yuen Hsin-yee). To a great extent, Yuen created the martial arts comedy of Jackie Chan, incorporating the gimmicks of at-hand objects as a part of the action comedy. Yuen also worked for **Golden Harvest**, directing the Wong Fei-hung movies *Magnificent Butcher (Lam Sai Wing Benevolent No Enemies)/Lam Sai-wing yan je mo dik/Lin Shirong* (1979, starring Samo Hung) and *Dreadnaught (Brave, No Fear)/Yung je mo gui/Yong zhe wu ju* (1981, starring an aging **Kwan Tak-hing**). Yuen formed his own film company, producing and choreographing its first movie, Tsui Siu-ming's *The Buddhist Fist/For chung law hon kuen/Fo zhang luo han quan* (1979).

Yuen discovered **Donnie Yen** and directed him in his first starring role in *Drunken Tai Chi/Siu taai gik/Xiao tai ji* (1984). They went on to make a series of contemporary urban action movies featuring hand-to-hand combat, including *Tiger Cage (Special Cop Slaughter Dragon)/Dak ging tiu lung/Te jing tu long* (1988) and *In the Line of Duty 4 (Royal Hong Kong Policewoman 4: Attacking the Witness Head-on)/Wong ga si je ji 4 jik gik jing yan/Huang jia shi jie zhi 4 zhi ji zheng ren* (1989). Yuen choreographed the fight sequences for **Tsui Hark's *Once upon a Time in China 2*** *(Wong Fei-hung 2: A Man Should Be Self-Sufficient)/Wong Fei-hung ji yi naam yi dong ji* *keung/Huang Feihong zhi er nan er dang zi qiang* (1992, starring **Jet Li** and Yen) and directed *Iron Monkey (The Young Wong Fei-hung: Iron Monkey)/Siu nin Wong Fei-hung ji tit ma lau/Shaonian Huang Feihong zhi tie ma liu* (1993), starring Yen as Wong Key-yi, father of Wong Fei-hung (here played by a young girl). *Tai Chi Master (Tai Chi: Cheung Sam-fung)/Taai gik Cheung Sam-fung/Tai ji Zhang Sanfeng* (1993, starring Jet Li) and *Wing Chun/Wing Chun/Yong Chun* (1994, starring **Michelle Yeoh** and Donnie Yen) are other martial arts epics with Yuen's signature.

Yuen crossed over to Hollywood with the Wachowski Brother's blockbuster spectacle events *The Matrix* (1999), *The Matrix Reloaded* (2003), and *The Matrix Revolutions* (2003), making him a name in the United States. Yuen required the stars (Keanu Reeves, Hugo Weaving, Laurence Fishburne, and Carrie-Anne Moss) to undergo rigorous martial arts movie training for several months prior to filming. Wedding Hong Kong action style to Hollywood money, the film achieved a distinctive look defining the current cool. Yuen gained international attention for his lyrical choreography in **Ang Lee's** *Crouching Tiger, Hidden Dragon/Ngo foo chong lung/Wo hu cang long* (2000), which won four Oscars, including Best Foreign Film at the 73rd Academy Awards. Yuen also supervised stunt choreography on Quentin Tarantino's *Kill Bill* (2003 and 2004, in two parts). He has directed over 20 films, action directed over 30, and acted in over 20 to date.

YUEN, YANG-AN (1904–1994). Born in Zhejiang province, producer and director Yuen Yang-an graduated from law school at Soochow University and was a famous Shanghai lawyer. When he came to Hong Kong in 1947, he founded **Great Wall** Movie Enterprises with **Zhang Shankun**. Lu Jiankang came in after Zhang departed, as major shareholder. Yuen was general manager in charge of production and administration. Yuen's wife, Su Yansheng, became a costume designer for Great Wall. She had frequented a famous Shanghai boutique called Madam Greenhouse; when she came to Hong Kong, she brought over the tailor and opened her own boutique, but recognizing a need for better clothing at the studios, she became a costumer.

Yuen specialized in drama, and his directorial debut was the period romantic tragedy *A Torn Lily/Yip hoi dut/Niehai hua* (1953). His last

Great Wall film was the satirical **melodrama** ***The True Story of Ah Q*****/*A Q jing chuen/A Q Zhengzhuan*** (1958), which he also wrote. *A Torn Lily* starred **Hsia Moon** as the doomed daughter of a father murdered by a corrupt official; reduced to prostitution, she meets and marries a poor scholar who betrays her and aids her father's murderer. *The True Story of Ah Q* starred **Kwan Shan** in the title role as a township resident who can not make a go of it in the country or the city; the actor, at that time a newcomer, won Best Actor at the 12th Locarno Film Festival for his sympathetic portrayal of a character neither a clown nor a degenerate.

Yuen left Great Wall and began his own production company, Sun Sun, and he functioned as producer, administrator, director, and writer there. His first production, which he also directed, was *Teenagers' Holiday/Mai yan dik ga gei/Miren de jiaqi* (1959), starring Mao Mei (also Yuen's second daughter). Yuen retired from film in 1962 but returned to make *Boys in Love/Yau laam waai chun/You nan huai chun* (1970) in Taiwan.

YUI, PAUL (Yu Puqing) (1904–1970). Producer and manager Paul Yui was born in Shanghai and earned a BA from Soochow University. In 1940, he became manager of Paramount Picture's branch in Tianjin and was soon promoted as general manager in Shanghai to oversee distribution in Malaysia.

In 1957, **Cathay** appointed him manager of International Film Distribution Agency, and in 1964 he became manager of **Motion Pictures and General Investment (MP&GI)**, responsible for overseeing production operations. Over 100 films were produced during his tenure, including the ***huangmei diao*** *Liang San Bo and Zhu Zing Tai/Leung Saan Ang yue Chuk Ying Toi/Liang Shanbo yu Zhu Yingtai* (1964), starring **Lucilla You Min** and **Li Lihua**; **Wang Xinglei's** ***wuxia pian*** *Escorts over Tiger Hills* (1969); and **Zhang Zengze's** epic saga *From the Highway* (1970).

Yui died in Hong Kong.

YULE FILM COMPANY. Founded by Lo Kau and Cheang Wong in 1968, Yule specialized in the 1960s **Wong Fei-hung** series, beginning with its inaugural production *Wong Fei Hung: The Incredible Success in Canton/Huang Feihong wei zhen wu yang cheng* (1968), and including others like *Wong Fei Hung: The Incredible Lion Dancer/Huang Feihong xing shi du ba mei hua zhuang* (1969) and *Wong Fei Hung: The Duel for the Shayuqing/Huang Feihung qiao duo sha yu qing* (1969). Other productions besides the series include **Wong Yiu's** *Won't You Give Me a Kiss?/Gei wo yi ge wen* (1968), **Chan Wan's** *Social Characters/Fei nan fei nu* (1969), *Modern School Life/Xiao fu xin chao* (1970), and *My Lover/Nan wang chu lian qing ren* (1972).

YUNG, SIU-YI (Rong Xiaoyi) (1919–1974). Actress Yung Siu-yi, a native of Guangdong province, was brought up in Shanghai with her sister Rong Yu-yi, who also became an actress. Together they joined the Meihua Song and Dance Troupe. Yung was the dancing star of the group and was called the "Dainty Queen." When the troupe disbanded in 1938, Yung joined the film industry, debuting in *The Shining Purple Goblet/Chi ha booi/Zi xia bei* (1938). Her first leading role was in *Shattering the Copper Net Array (Breaking through the Bronze Net)/Daai poh tung mong chan/Da po tong wang zhen* (1939), and her outstanding performances in director **Cai Chusheng's** *Orphan Island Paradise/Goo do tin tong/Gudao tiantang* (1939) and ***Ten Thousand Li Ahead*** *(Bright Future, Boundless Future)/Chin ching maan lee/Qian cheng wan li* (1941) gained public attention.

The actress appeared and starred in numerous films, often as the idealistic, passionate **woman** who fights against oppression. In her later films, she sometimes played the villainess. She appeared in numerous films by directors **Lee Sun-fung**, **Chun Kim**, and **Ng Wui**. Her films include Ng Wui's *Family/Ga/Jia* (1953), Lee Sun-fung's *Spring/Chun/Chun* (1953), and Chun Kim's *Autumn/Chau/Qiu* (1954), the first, second, and third episodes of the Ba Jin *Torrent Trilogy*; the Cantonese dramas Ng Wui's *Father and Son/Foo yue ji/Fu yu zi* (1954), Chun Kim's *The More the Merrier (We Owe It to Our Children)/Ngai lui chai/Er nu zhai* (1955); and the Cantonese comedy Ng Wui's *Money/Chin/Qian* (1959). In *Father and Son*, Yung played the mother unnamed in the title; in *The More the Merrier*, she played a pregnant wife whose husband (**Lee Ching**) has been laid off. Yung's last leading part was in Ng Wui's comedy *The Wonderful Partner/Gai ming gau diy/Ji ming gou dao* (1960).

– Z –

ZHANG, SHANKUN (S. K. Chang) (1905–1957). Producer Zhang Shankun was a native of Zhejiang province, and worked in theater, running Stage-Cinema Troupe, after he graduated from university in Shanghai. He established **Xinhua** (Hsin Hwa) Film Company in 1932, adapting stage plays and making big-budget films. Its first production was *The Story of the Red Lamb Knight* (1935). The film was what Zhang referred to as "opera with moving images," and he is often credited with combining **Peking (Beijing) opera** with film. Its second was *The New Peach Blossom Fan* (1935). As other studios closed, Zhang took on Diantong and produced **Ma-Xu Weibang's** *Song of Midnight* (1937). He also signed on stars, including **Li Lihua**. During the **Orphan Island period**, Xinhua branched out into Huaxin, Huacheng, and Xinhua to supply films to theater chains, and all three were incorporated into China United Film Company (Huaying). Zhang worked closely with Japanese China expert Kawakita Nagamasa (1903–1981), also director of Japan's Toho. After the war, Zhang would be criticized by some as a collaborator and traitor to the cause, but he produced many films during the period to entertain local audiences, including *Universal Love* (1942).

At war's end, Zhang's holdings were confiscated. On a trip to the United States, he met Li Zuyong and upon return to Hong Kong and in 1947 he helped establish **Yonghua** to make Mandarin films in Hong Kong; after creative differences over running the company, Zhang left in 1948 and set up **Great Wall** Film Company (the only other company at the time producing Mandarin films in Hong Kong) with Yuen Yang-an; its first production was **Yue Feng's** *A Forgotten Woman/Dangfu xinn* (1949, starring **Bai Guang**). After Yue Feng's *Blood Will Tell/Hoi tong hung/Hai tang gong* (1949) and **Li Pingqian's** *A Strange Woman/Yat doi yiu gei/Yi dai yao ji* (1950), the studio had established itself. Around 1950, Great Wall had turned more pronouncedly left politically; Zhang himself left the company and formed the Far East Company, producing *Songs on a Rainy Night/Yuye gesheng* (1952, starring Bai Guang), and *24 Hours of Marriage/Git fan 24 siu shut/Jiehun ershisi xiaoshi* (1950). He reestablished Xinhua in 1952 and signed Li Lihua, who made *Little*

Phoenix/Siu fung sin/Xiao fengxian (1953), and the company revived with the addition of **Tu Guangqi's** *Qiu Jin, the Revolutionary Heroine/Chau Gan/Qiu Jin* (1953) and *The 72 Martyrs of Canton* (1954). Directors **Evan Yang** and **Wang Tianlin** both worked for the studio. In 1956, Zhang and others cofounded a union for Mandarin film workers, the Hong Kong and Kowloon Filmmakers Free General Association Limited, later called the Hong Kong and Kowloon Cinema and Theatrical Enterprise General Association Limited (1957), and then the Hong Kong Cinema and Theatrical Association Limited (1997). All required film companies to obtain a certificate before their films could be screened in Taiwan.

Zhang codirected several films, including the contemporary musical ***Songs of the Peach Blossom River****/Tou Fa Kong/Taohua jiang* (1956, with Wang Tianlin) and the historical film *Blood-Stained Flowers (The Dawn of China's Revolution)/Bik huet wong dut/Bixue hua* (1953, with Tu Guangqi and others). Zhang was married to Tong Yuejuan, first an actress and later his business partner, who continued making films until the mid-1980s. Together they were responsible for some 600 films, including classics like *Maiden in Armor (Mulan Joins the Army)/Muk laan chung gwan/Mulan cong jun* (1939, starring Nancy Chan) and *Dream of the Red Chamber* (1944, starring **Zhou Xuan** and Yuan Meiyun).

ZHANG, XINYAN (Cheung Yam-yin) (1934–). Director and editor Zhang Xinyan, a Ningbo native, was born in Shanghai and left school before finishing his secondary education. A relative introduced him to film work in Guangzhou, and he studied editing in Hong Kong until he was dismissed for political activities. Undaunted, and with the support of his family, he resumed editing under director **Zhu Shilin**. In late 1956, he studied editing in Japan, returning to Hong Kong to work at **Great Wall**. Zhang edited most post-1956 films at Great Wall. He also edited later **Wong Fei-hong** serial films, with the rhythm of their action and drama mirrored by a clear, rapid cutting style.

Zhang turned to directing with *Adventure of the Talents/Sam seung yan/Xin shang ren* (1960), codirected with Li Qiming (Lee Kaiming). Since the 1960s, he and **Hu Xiaofeng** became the two leading directors at Great Wall. Zhang's *The Jade Bow/Wan hoi yuk gung* *yuen/Yun hai yu gong yuan* (1966, written by **Fu Che**) helped redefine the **swordplay** film. Fu and **Chen Sisi** costarred in the film, which was adapted from a popular **martial arts** novel by Liang Yusheng. Fu played a righteous knight who comes to the aid of the Minshan school to fight a palm power villain, and the action steered away from fantasy and clumsy special effects courtesy of martial arts directors **Lau Kar-leung** and **Tang Chia**.

The director's Cantonese romance *Romance on the Bus/Ang si kei yue git leung yuen/Ba shi ji yu jie liang yuan* (1978) set a new record at the box office for Hong Kong leftist films. It was also the first post–Cultural Revolution production from the Great Wall/**Feng Huang**/Sun Luen complex with a powerful and enduring impact.

Zhang is also credited with introducing *wushu* champion **Jet Li** to a film audience. Li's film debut was in Zhang's ***Shaolin Temple/Siu*** *lam chi/Shaolin si* (1982), which featured impressive training sequences in the story of 13 monks taking on corrupt government forces. It was also the first film in Zhang's Shaolin trilogy, which also included *Kids from Shaolin (Shaolin Temple 2)/Siu lam siu ji/Shaolin xiao zi* (1984) and *Yellow River Fighter/Wong hiu daai hap/Huang he da xia* (1988).

ZHANG, YIMOU (1950–). Mainland director and cinematographer Zhang Yimou was born in Xian, Shaanxi province, and spent time in the countryside and working in a factory as a result of Cultural Revolution policies. Based on his photography, he was admitted to Beijing Film Academy in 1978 and became one of the leading directors of the Fifth Generation. At Guangxi Film Studio, he worked as cinematographer alongside director **Chen Kaige**, and directed his first feature, *Red Sorghum* (1987). Subsequent films gained international attention. Zhang became known for the aesthetic beauty of a sumptuous sensual style, his identification with the downtrodden, political symbolism and subtext, and the depiction of the sweep of history in China. Although internationally esteemed, the director has battled a love–hate relationship with Mainland censors, although he continues to work within the system. *To Live* (1994) remains banned.

Among Zhang's more than dozen films, he has recently turned to the **martial arts** stories of his childhood, using Hong Kong actors and action choreographers to make gravity-defying art house **action** films, in *Hero/Ying xiong* and *House of Flying Daggers/Shimian maifu* (2004). The former, a *Rashomon*-like epic narrative set during the Warring States period, focused on the rise of China's first emperor, Qin Shihuang, the first to unify the country, and starred **Jet Li**, **Maggie Cheung**, **Tony Leung Chi-wai**, Zhang Ziyi, **Donnie Yen**, and Chen Daoming, with cinematographer **Chris Doyle** and action directors **Ching Siu-tung** and Stephen Tung Wai. The film was well-received on the Mainland. Zhang's follow-up, *House of Flying Daggers*, set during the Tang dynasty (859 C.E.), concerns an antigovernment rebel group, conflicting allegiances, and a love story. Pop stars and actors **Andy Lau** and **Kaneshiro Takeshi** are cast as policemen in search of the group, with Zhang Ziyi as a blind dancer they suspect is the daughter of a murdered rebel. The director's use of dance, music, color, and visual design, as well as Ching Siu-tung's action choreography, make the film visually ravishing, with memorable sequences such as an echo game between Lau and Zhang Ziyi involving beans bouncing off drums as her garment sleeves flow across the screen when she dances and a bamboo forest scene recalling **King Hu's** *Xia nu* (1971).

ZHAO, LEI (Chao Lei) (1928–1996). Actor Zhao Lei (real name Wang Yumin) was born in Beijing and came to Hong Kong in 1947, He worked as a bank clerk before starting at **Shaw Brothers** in 1953, debuting in *The Little Couple/Xiao fuqi*. There, he frequently collaborated with actress **Lucilla You Min**, on such films as *The Third Life/Can sheng* (1953). Zhao joined **MP&GI** in the early 1960s, where he developed his most important collaborations with **Linda Lin Dai**; he had played opposite her as the first emperor in *Diau Charn/Diao Chan* (1958), followed by emperor roles in *The Kingdom and the Beauty/Kong saan mei yan/Jiangshan meiren* (1959), *Beyond the Great Wall* (1964), and *Romance of the Forbidden City/Shenggong yuan* (1964), opposite Lucilla You Min, earning him the title "Emperor of Actors." In the latter, he played the Qing emperor who becomes a monk because of love. He was generally regarded as elegant in his acting; he specialized in period dramas. His performance with **Li Di** (Betty Loh Ti) on *The Enchanting Shadow/Qiannu youhun* (1960) led to a 1987 remake in *A Chinese Ghost Story,* with **Leslie Cheung** taking on his part, but on a more personal level, he connected with Julie Shih Ying on *Meet Me after Spring (A Mellow Spring)/Chunguang wuxian hao* (1956), whom he married. Zhao also co-starred as a man torn between three women in ***The Story of Three Loves/Tai siu yan yuen/Ti xiao yin yuan*** (1964), based on the Zhang Henshui novel; he played and was accepted as both heroes and villains throughout his career.

Zhao made more than 50 films with Shaw Brothers and more than 20 with **MP&GI** (which he joined in 1964), appearing in numerous costume pictures, playing effete scholars and emperors, and becoming Cathay's ***wuxia*** hero for the period. He turned to business interests when Cathay closed shop, but his final film appearance was in **John Woo**'s *Just Heroes (Righteous Courageous Group of Heroes,* a.k.a. *Tragic Heroes)/Yi daam kwan ying/Yi dan qun ying* (1989). He died of pneumonia.

ZHENG, JUNMIAN (Cheng Kwun-min, Jeng Gwan-min) (1917–). Actor Zheng Junmian, a native of Guangdong province, attended Wah Yan College in Hong Kong, and began a long acting career in 1935 by performing with several stage groups. Zheng's screen debut was *Three Day Massacre in Guangzhou (Two Emperors Invade Guangzhou)/Gong chow saam yat tiu shing gei (Leung wong yap yuet daai saai Gong chow)* (1937). Since then, he has appeared in more than 200 movies.

Zheng's leading roles include *The Return of the Swallow* (1959), *The Fool Captures a Thief* (1960), and *To Catch a Cat/Cha lei chuk cho maau/Cha li zhuo cuo mao* (1969). Other popular Cantonese films he appeared in are *Queen of the Devil's Palace/Moh gung yiu hau/Mo gong yao hou* (1951); the "Two Fools" series (1958–1959), including *Two Fools Capture the Criminal (Two Fools Capture the Murderer)/ Leung soh kam hung gei/Liang sha qin xiong ji* (1959); the "Mr. Wang" series (1959), with *Mr. Wang Is in His Wife's Dress by Mistake (Mr. Wang Is in His Wife's Shoes by Mistake)/Wong sin sang chue cho liu poh huai/Wang xian sheng zhao cuo lao po xie* (1959); and the "King of Blunders" series, including *Siu Po-po Pokes Fun at the King of Blunders/Siu bo bo chat fai woo lung wong/Xiao bao bao qi xi wu long wang* (1960). He also appeared in some Mandarin films, such as *The Greatest Civil War on Earth* (1961). In *Two Fools in Paradise* (1958), Zheng played the "Oriental Elvis Presley" alongside the "two fools" **Sun Ma Sze-tsang** and **Deng Jichen**, and this film, as the others, featured improvisational slapstick and pantomime. In *Mr. Wang Is in His Wife's Dress by Mistake* (1959), Zheng played the tough who forces a singer to swindle Mr. Wang (Sun Ma Sze-tsang) out of money, because he erroneously believes him to be a millionaire.

Zheng was nicknamed "the Oriental Elvis Presley" because of his Westernized appearance; he wore an Elvis Presley hairstyle, checkered shirt, and blue jeans, and Fred Astaire white shoes. He was most often cast as teddy boys, playboys, prodigal sons, layabouts, and spendthrifts, often making a fool of himself while attempting to take advantage of others. Typically, toward film's end, he repented. In comedy, Zheng used exaggerated hand gestures and especially his singing and dancing skills toward humorous ends, which distinguished him from other comics. Often, when he was caught in embarrassing situations, he was temporarily speechless and his delayed response evoked laughter.

Zheng became involved in the broadcast industry early, starting in 1941 in Macau, continuing in the 1950s in many radio plays for Rediffusion Broadcasting, Hong Kong. He hosted the **television** variety show *Enjoy Yourself Tonight* for many years and was recognized for 10 years of service at Hong Kong Television Broadcasts Limited (TVB).

ZHILIAN FILM COMPANY. Filmmakers Kwan Chi-kong, Kwan Chi-kin, and others founded Zhilian in 1964, and its first film was *Love and Passion* (1964). Within five years, the company produced 38 feature films, capitalizing on youth films. Youth **musicals** include **Wong Yiu's** ***Girls Are Flowers***/*Gu niang shi ba yi duo hua* (1966), *Colorful Youth/Cai se qing chun* (1966), and Wong Yiu's *The Charming Little Bird/Mi ren xiao niao* (1967). Other films included **Chor Yuen's** *The Sinner/Zui ren* (1965), **Chan Wan's** *Romance of a Teenage Girl/Shaonu xin* (1967), and **Chan Wan's** *The Dutiful Daughter Zhu Zhu/Xiaonu Zhuzhu* (1966). Zhilian's last production was Wong Yiu's *Singing Darlings/Mooi gwai shao cheuk ngok hoi tong hung* (1969).

ZHONG, QING (Chung Ching) (1932–). Mandarin actress Zhong Qing (real name Zhang Linglin), of Hunan descent, was born in

Changsha and educated in an English school in Hong Kong, permanently settling there in 1949. In 1952, she joined an acting school organized by Taishan Film Studio, and she signed with the company upon graduating. Her screen debut was **Bu Wancang's** drama *Seven Sisters/Chat che mooi/Qi zimei* (1953) and her first leading role was in the same director's contemporary romance *It Blossoms Again/Jou chun dat/Zhai chun hua* (1954). She joined **Asia Film Company** and appeared in **Hong Shuyun's** historical drama *Yang E/Yeung Ngo/Yang E* (1955) and **Tang Huang's** family comedy *Life with Grandma/Moon ting fong/Man ting fang* (1957).

Zhong made the Mandarin **musical** ***Songs of the Peach Blossom River****/Tou Fa Kong/Taohua jiang* (1956) for **Xinhua**, which made her a star, leading to **Evan Yang's** musical *Holiday Express/Dak bit faai che/Te bie kuai che*, the romantic comedy (with opera) *You Are the Winds of Spring/Long yue chun yat fung/Lang ru chun ri feng*, and **Wang Tianlin's Chinese opera** comedy *The Storm Tossed Village/Fung leung tiu dut chuen/Feng yu tao hua cun* (all 1957). She made more than 24 films for Xinhua over 10 years. *Songs of the Peach Blossom River*, codirected by Wang Tianlin and **Zhang Shankun**, started a trend in which music integrated into story played an important role. Zhong played a singer, called "Wild Kitten," and **Lo Wei**, collecting songs along the Peach Blossom River, is attracted by her singing. When war erupts, she flees with him to Hong Kong and becomes a singing star. Zhong's popularity through the film earned her the nickname "Wild Kitten" and she was known for movies with song.

During the 1950s, the actress made films for **Yonghua** as well as for Taiwanese companies. Her movies in Taiwan included *Xi Shi/Ngo san seung daam/Wo xin chang dan*, *Over the Rolling Hills*, and *General Soaring Tiger* (all 1956). In 1958, she founded the production company Qilin, producing and starring in the Mandarin opera *A Perfect Match/Lung fung yan yuen/Longfeng yinyuan* (1958) and **Tu Guangqi's martial arts** movie *The Witch Girl (He Yueer)/Yiu lui hoh yuet ngai/Yao nu he yue er* (1961). *A Perfect Match* was adapted from the Hunan opera *The Story of the Jade Locket*. Zhong played an orphan girl saved by a fisherman; she later marries his son. But the son, after being crowned the number one scholar, not only denies his wife but attempts her murder, in order to marry the prime minister's daughter. Zhong finds her natural father, who is the inspector general, the husband regrets his actions, and the couple reunites.

After a screen hiatus in the early 1960s, Zhong returned in **Motion Pictures and General Investment (MP&GI)** movies *The Better Halves*, Wang Tianlin's *The Greatest Love Affair on Earth*, and *The Magic Lamp* (all 1964). *The Better Halves (The Halves)/Aau fung who ming/Luan feng he ming* and *The Magic Lamp/Bo lin dang/Bao lian deng* were operas; *The Greatest Love Affair on Earth/Naam bak hei seung fung/Nan bei xi xiang feng*, a comedy, was the third installment in a **North–South trilogy** and written by **Eileen Chang**. Zhong played a Mandarin-speaking cousin (opposite her Cantonese counterpart, **Christine Pak Lu-ming**); the cousins fall in love with two poor teachers, and their marriages are opposed by their Northern guardian (**Liu Enjia**), prejudiced against the Cantonese and the poor.

Zhong's last film was *New Peach Blossom River (New Version of Peach Blossom River)/San tiu dut kong/Xin tao hua jiang* (1967), after which she retired, married a businessman, and became involved in business. Well-known for her traditional Chinese paintings, she has exhibited in Hong Kong, Beijing, and Taiwan.

ZHONGLIAN FILM COMPANY LTD. Zhonglian (Union Film Enterprises Ltd.) was established by a group of 19 filmmakers in 1952 when Cantonese cinema flourished and several hundred films were being made a year. In 1949, a clean-up campaign had occurred to improve quality, and in 1952, **Chinese opera films** dominated, with factionalism among actors and singers. Director **Ng Wui** and producer Chen Wen originated the idea of a film collective, and actor **Ng Cho-fan** embraced the idea, along with actresses **Pak Yin** and **Wong Man-lei** and a handful of others, including producers Liu Fang and Zhu Zigui; directors **Lee Sun-fung**, **Lee Tit**, Wang Keng, **Chu Kei**, and **Chun Kim**; actors **Cheung Ying**, **Cheung Wood-yau**, and Lee Ching; and actresses Xiao Yanfei, Yung Siu-yi, Mui Yee, and **Tsi Lo-lin**.

The company wanted to make films that were socially responsible and both educated and entertaining. There were seven company directors elected by members and five departments (scriptwriting, business, production, executive production, and promotion). Salaries were decided by consensus. By adhering to high artistic standards and ethical content, the company provided entertainment that did not cater to popular trends or tastes. Its immediate effect on the industry was more respect for Cantonese-language films and a rapid increase in their production, at both **Shaw Brothers** and **Motion Pictures and General Investment** (MP&GI, Cathay). Its organization and mission would influence the industry long term by demonstrating an **independent** company relying on teamwork could produce a number of quality films.

During its 15 years of operation, 44 films were produced, the first being Ng Wui's *Family/Ga/Jia* (1953), an adaptation of Ba Jin's novel. Many of its films were adapted from literature and other art forms, such as Ng Wui's *Taking the Birthday Gifts Caravan by Strategy/Shui hui chuen chi chui sang san gong/Shui hu chuan zhi qu sheng chen gang* (1957, inspired by the classical Chinese novel *The Water Margin*) and *A Romantic Story of the West Chamber/Sai seung gei/Xi xiang ji* (1956, based on Chinese opera), Wang Keng's *Adultery/Gaan ching/Jian qing* (1958, from Shi De's contemporary novel) and *The Cruel Hand/Duk sau/Du shou* (1960, adapted from a contemporary novel by Gao Xiong), and Lee Sun-fung's *Broken Spring Dreams/Chun chaan mung duen/Chun can meng duans* (1955, reworked from Leo Tolstoy's *Anna Karenina*). Many of its films are Cantonese classics, including Lee Tit's *In the Face of Demolition* (1953) and *Everlasting Love (**Eternal Love**)/Tin cheung dei gau/ Tianchang dijiu* (1955) and Chun Kim's ***Parents' Hearts**/Foo miu sam/Fumu Xin* (1955).

The company dissolved in 1967 as a result of members having left to create other companies or work elsewhere or due to external political pressure. Labeled a leftist organization, the company was blacklisted by the Hong Kong & Kowloon Film and Drama Filmmakers Free General Association Limited and its movies banned, disastrous for its overseas markets. Still, Zhonglian's films were idealistic, artistically creative, educational, and entertaining.

ZHOU, KUNLING (Chow Kwun-ling). Actress Zhou Kunling was born and raised in the United States but learned **Cantonese opera** at an early age, performing in San Francisco and across the United States onstage. She joined **Grandview** Studio in the United States when Joseph Chiu Shu-sun moved back to make film in San Francisco in

1939, and her first leading role was in the color feature *Lovers at the Far End of the World* (released in Hong Kong in 1946), for which she was named "Queen of the Color Films." Other Grandview features included the Cantonese comedy *The Entangling Ones/Kwong fung long dip/Kuangfeng langdie* (1946), in which Zhou played a young woman eager for love entangled with a handsome rogue.

Zhou began working in Hong Kong in 1947, starring in the Cantonese drama *Reluctant to Meet My Old Love (Never Want to See the Past Love)/Ong gin gau ching long/Pa jian jiu qing lang* (1947). Within 10 years, she had made almost 200 films. Among them are the Cantonese dramas *A Brief Affair* (1948), **Chun Kim's** contemporary **melodrama** *Weep for the Fallen Petals/Yap chaan hung/Qi can hong* (1951), and *Pearly Tears/Ming chu lui han/Ming zhu lei hen* (1952), **Zhou Shilu's** Cantonese comedy *A Star of Mischief Is Born/Faan dau/Fan dou* (1951), and the Cantonese historical drama *Filial Piety/Haau diy/ Xiaodao*(1956). In *Weep for the Fallen Petals*, Zhou was chosen for the part by newspaper readers. She played the part of a woman torn between two men, the one she loved, from whom she is separated and who is killed, and the son of a high official, who rejects her and later regrets his decision. Set against the background of the Sino–Japanese War, Zhou's character survives, moving through several men and searching for her lost son. The story ends with Zhou's character jailed and a sad reunion with her son and his repenting father.

Other films include **Tso Kea's** two-part Cantonese drama *The Splendid Years of Youth/Gam Sau nin wa/Jin xiu nian hua* (1951) and Chun Kim's *Five Sisters/Ng che mooi/Wu jie mei* (1951). In *The Splendid Years of Youth*, Zhou played one of three high school girls who are like sisters and undergo numerous ordeals starting with their high school prom; Zhou's character is jilted and attempts suicide, but failing, blinds herself, only to be healed by the boy who truly loves her. Tso Kea's drama *Her Tragic Death (Love Lingers On)/Wan gwai lee han tin/Hun gui li hen tian* (1957) was Zhou's last film. She retired and returned to the United States in the late 1950s.

ZHOU, SHILU (Chow See-luk) (1914–1964). Director and cinematographer Zhou Shilu, a native of Guangdong province, joined Shanghai's **Tianyi** as an apprentice at the tender age of 13, and was soon promoted to assistant cameraman, becoming a cameraman at only 17. He assisted on *Spring in the Music Hall* (1931), Tianyi's first sound picture. His debut as cinematographer was *Between Husband and Wife* (1931). Between 1931 and 1941, he worked for Tianyi in Shanghai and Hong Kong, shooting *A Girl Named Yunlan* (1932) and *The Fallen Girl* (1933), among others.

Zhou's directorial debut was *The Third Master Sha and His Maid (Third Master Sha and Lady Ngan)/Sha Sanshao yu Yinjie* (1947). Based on a true incident, the story relates how a third master, attracted to a servant girl, kills her husband and is later put on trial by his own father. Zhou directed over 70 features for numerous studios, most of them comedies and **Chinese operas**. His films include the Cantonese comedies *The Great Idler/Sau wong/She wang* (1950) and *The Conmen/Chi tin duk dei/Zhi tian du di* (1951), the Cantonese drama *A Buddhist Recluses for 14 Years during the War/Feng mong faan gung sap sei nin/Huowang fangong shisi nian* (1953), the ghost story *The Ghostly Wife/Gwai chai/Gui qi* (1953), and the Cantonese **martial arts** movie *The Nocturnal Mourning of (for) the White Lotus/Yau diu baak foo yung/Ye diao bai fu rong* (1956). *The Great Idler* followed two idlers' adventures, including masquerading as corpses and reincarnated Buddhas. *The Conmen* featured a Mainland country couple who come to Hong Kong, are bilked of their money, and scheme by posing as wealthy people. *Nocturnal Mourning of White Lotus* was adapted from the **Cantonese opera** of the same title, and traces the love between a rich heir (Law Kim-long) and a tea peddler named White Lotus (**Law Yim-hing**), and the obstacles between them because of class differences.

Beginning in 1957, Zhou was the head of the Cantonese film division of **Shaw Brothers**, training actresses like **Patricia Lam Fung** and writers and directors like **Patrick Lung Gong** and Wu Dan. Zhou directed more than 20 films at Shaw, including *Sweet Girl in Terror/Yuk lui geng wan/Yu nu jing hun* (1958), the romance *The Love Knot/Chi sam git/Chi xin jie* (1960), and the comedy *When the Poles Meet/Naam bak yan yuen/Nan bei yin yuan* (1961). In *Sweet Girl in Terror*, a sociological thriller with song, the girl of the title (Patricia Lam Fung) is exploited by avaricious foster parents and elopes with her lover; the parents and a teddy boy devise his imprisonment, and the teddy boy abducts and attempts to rape the girl, who is rescued by her sister and wet nurse.

All told, Zhou directed more than 120 films, among them the Cantonese realist tragedy *Life/Yue chi yan sang/Ru ci rensheng* (1954), the Cantonese **musical** *A Pretty Girl's Love Affair/Yuk lui chun ching/Yu nu chun qing* (1958), and the drama *Mother's Heart Is Broken (Mother's Broken Heart)/Ngai sam sui miu sam/Er xin sui mu xin* (1958). *Life*, adapted from a literary work by Maxim Gorky, follows the decline of a **woman** (Lam Ye) who takes refuge at the "Inn of No Sorrow," but remains so troubled she commits suicide. Zhou's last film was *The Female Prince/Seung fung kei yuen/Shuang feng qi yuan* (1964). He died of liver cancer.

ZHOU, XUAN (1918–1957). The actress made famous by the Shanghai classic *Street Angel/Ma lu tin sai/Ma lu tian shi* (1937, in which she sang the song "Four Seasons" and the ballad "Tianya Songstress"/"Songstress of the World"), Zhou Xuan was known for her sweet singing voice and called "Jin Sangzi" (the Golden Throat, the Golden Voice). She starred in Hong Kong Mandarin **musicals** such as ***An All-Consuming Love***/*Cheung seung si/Chang xiangsi* (1947), directed by **He Zhaoshang**; ***Song of a Songstress***/*Goh lui ji goh/Genu zhi ge* (1948), a semiautobiographical film, and ***Orioles Banished from the Flowers***/*Dut ngoi lau aau/Huawai liuying* (1948), both directed by **Fang Peilin**; and *Waste Not Our Youth/Mok foo ching chun Mofu qingchun* (1949), directed by playwright **Wu Zuguang**. All were Shanghai- or Mainland-set **melodrama**s. She became the quintessential suffering nightclub songstress of Mandarin musicals.

Song of a Songstress is a semibiographical depiction of the singing actress. Filmmakers (with or without Zhou's consent) exploited events from her own life in this particular story, which the audience read as hers. Zhou suffered personal tragedy and depression; a difficult childhood with foster parents, an ended marriage, and subsequent affairs with men who used her; she spent her last years in a Mainland mental hospital. She died at 39 of an inflammatory condition that affected the brain. Art imitated life, because beneath the optimism and sweetness in her voice and acting, is a sense of suffering and tragedy.

ZHU, GUOLIANG (Choo Kok-leong) (1910–1996). Producer and manager Zhu Guoliang, a Malaysian Chinese born in Kuala Lumpur, studied at Oxford and worked for the Malaysian government and Serdang Agricultural College. In 1959, he joined the board of directors of Singapore's **Cathay** Organization, in order to assist **Loke Wan Tho**. Also in 1959, he was appointed to Malaysia's House of Lords. In 1964, when Loke was killed in a plane crash, Zhu became managing director of the company in Singapore. In 1965, he restructured **Motion Pictures and General Investment (MP&GI)** as Cathay Organization (Hong Kong).

Under Zhu's six years' leadership, Cathay continued distribution and produced over 90 films, including **Yuen Chau-fung's** war-themed *A Debt of Blood/Luen sai ngai lui/Luan shi er nu* (1966) and the Mandarin drama *The Homemaker/Ga yau yin chai/Gu you xian qi* (1970).

In 1985, Zhu retired and his daughter, Meileen Choo, took over the business.

ZHU, SHILIN (1899–1967). Director and writer Zhu Shilin, one of the Mainland pioneers in the Hong Kong film industry, was a native of Jiangsu born in Guangdong. His father was a bureaucrat and the son received his primary education in a village school and graduated from Shanghai Technical College. He worked at several jobs, as a trainee in the China Bank in Hankou in 1919, a staffer for the Longhai Railway Company in Beijing, and in 1922 as a translator for Beijing's True Light (Zhenguang) Theater, writing film synopses for the theater's flyers. This job led to Zhu becoming chief translator for Beijing's Huabei (North China) Film Company, headed by Luo Mingyou. Like many others at this time, Zhu's entry into film was through translation work.

Zhu suffered from arthritis for most of his life. Mistreatment by an incompetent physician almost left him completely paralyzed in 1926, and he suffered from depression; fortunately, he recovered over a three-year period (during which he began writing scripts), but his backbone was affected and he was never again able to bend over. After working for Huabei in Beijing (his close friend Fei Mu took over when illness forced him to resign), Zhu moved to Shanghai in 1930, working for **Lianhua** Studios (newly founded by Luo), where he made 10 films and wrote nine scripts for others. He made several silent films with actress **Ruan Lingyu**, including the short *Suicide Pact* (1930), and features *Homecoming* (1934) and *Song of the Nation* (1934, codirected with Luo). In 1934, when Lianhua was operating with three studios, Luo appointed Zhu its manager. Zhu worked for other companies during the **Orphan Island period** (1939–1944), including Chunming, Hezhong, and **Zhonglian**, and ironically, during this tense period Zhu forged his mastery of film aesthetics.

In Shanghai, Zhu made realist films that focused on family relationships and emphasized morality, subtly exposing society's ills. Films of this period included *Song of a Mother/Cimu Qu* (1937), *Old and New Times (Good Daughters)/Xinjiu shidai* (1937), *Romance of the Night/Dongfang huazhu ye* (1942), and *Rendezvous in the Late Afternoon/Ren yue huanghun hou* (1942), and in each, Zhu's mastery of film language and use of it to express content and emotion is obvious. In *Song of a Mother* and *Old and New Times*, scenery and architecture are used symbolically in relation to characters, and Zhu's films of this period have been compared to Chinese painting; with the camerawork of Huang Shaofen in the former and Chen Chen in the latter, the shots of each scene in each film reinforce the thematics and emotions. *Old and New Times* follows the disintegration of a feudal family through the lives of its son and four daughters; Zhu used family relations to critique the costs of feudalism. The youngest daughter, who runs a day care center for working mothers, criticizes her father's extravagance, believing their money should be spent on aiding the poor. The film ends with the collapse of the family mansion, captured in wideshot, and the camera registers the movement, from inside out, background to foreground; another shot, extremely wide, enlarges the world for the entire family group, emphasizing a new future and perception of society and the world.

After the Japanese took the foreign concessions, Zhu worked for Hua Ying (the Zhonghua United Film Production Company established by the Japanese) and the Japanese-controlled Zhonglian (a conglomerate of 12 Shanghai companies), all following guidelines issued by the Japanese; this would lead to criticism of him following the war. Some perceived these movies as collaboration films, others as a way to continue making Chinese films under adverse conditions. Of the films Zhu made during this period, some were comedies, such as *Independence* (1943), made for Hua Ying, a slapstick affair in which an *amah* goes on vacation and a bourgeois household falls into disarray. Others were portmanteau films made with numerous directors, such as *Love for Humanity* (1943), with Zhu's contribution *Marital Love*, focusing on love in a marriage.

Zhu came to Hong Kong in 1946 and remained. He first worked for **Great China** (Dazhonghua), where he directed *You're Smart in One Way, I in Another/Gok yau chin chau/Ge you qian qiu* (1947), which follows the female lead Bihua (**Zhou Xuan**), who believes in equality between the sexes and suffers for it, a serious examination of **gender** equality. Zhu was invited to join **Yonghua**, where he continued making films for the Mainland audience, such as the classic ***Sorrows of the Forbidden City****/Ching gung bei shut/Qinggong mishi* (1948). This allegorical film, which uses family dynamics as representative of larger national and ethical concerns, was a late-19th-century epic centering on the reform-minded last emperor under the control of the Empress Dowager Cixi and can be seen as a commentary on contemporary problems between the Nationalists and Communists. Not only was the film attacked upon its release for its politics, despite its superior aesthetics, but in 1967 it was severely criticized by Mao Zedong during the Cultural Revolution. In 1950, the Locarno Film Festival (Switzerland) deemed it one of the most important films of the year.

By the 1950s the director was making films set in Hong Kong and addressing everyday problems that Hong Kong audiences related to, such as *Spoiling the Wedding Day (The Little Trumpeter and A Cui)/Neung gaai gei/ Wu jiaqi* (1951, codirected with Bai Chen). This comedy follows the trials of a young couple, an honest and naïve trumpeter, and his fiancée A Cui (**Li Lihua**), a strong-willed factory worker. Both work hard saving for their wedding, but each time they are ready to marry, unforeseen circumstances prevent them.

In Hong Kong, Zhu also made his mark by nurturing two leftist studios. He took over at the newly founded **Longma** in 1952 and he founded **Feng Huang** in 1953; his film *Festival Moon/Chung chau yuet/Zhong qiu yue* (1953) was the latter's first release. *His Fabulous Wife/Taitai quanqi* (1956) humorously shows what happens when the wife of the title (**Wei Wei**) abandons her housekeeping and enjoys life while her children's home tutor is forced to take over the traditional woman's role. Zhu's last film, a **melodrama**, ***Garden of Repose****/Goo* *yuen mung/Guyuan meng* (1964), was adapted from a Ba Jin novel concerning decadent families in war-torn China, and was shot in vivid Eastmancolor in the classic studio style.

Zhu made films for both studios and guided emerging talent, training the first postwar generation of filmmakers, including **Hu Xiaofeng**, **Cen Fan**, **Ren Yizhi**, and **Chen Jingbo**. Zhu's career spanned 38 years and 77 films; he wrote 50 screenplays.

ZHU, XUHUA (1906–1988). Producer and manager Zhu Xuhua, a native of Zhejiang province, graduated from Shanghai's Daxia University. He wrote his first script for *Brother's Romantic Fortune* (1927). He managed the newspaper *Guangxi Daily* and represented Chengdu movie theaters during World War II.

With Li Zuoyong, he cofounded **Yonghua**, becoming publicity manager and studio head, continuing after **Motion Pictures and General Investment (MP&GI)** took over. Through MP&GI, he began his own company, Guofeng. The studio produced **Yan Jun's** contemporary romance *Golden Phoenix/Gam fung/Jin feng* (1956), starring **Linda Lin Dai**, Yan Jun, and **King Hu**, and the Mandarin drama *Nobody's Child (The Wanderings of a Poor Child/Kuer liulang ji* (1960), starring **Josephine Siao Fong-fong**, **Butterfly Wu**, and **Wang Yin**. In *Golden Phoenix*, Lin Dai starred as the title character, a country girl romanced by a country boy (Yan Jun); **Li Han-hsiang** wrote the script.

Zhu joined **Shaw Brothers** to found and publish the movie magazine *Hong Kong Movie News*, and he also supervised its actor training classes. In 1980, Zhu retired and immigrated to the United States, where he lived for some years, before returning to Hong Kong, where he lived until his death.

Bibliography

Of the resources listed below, the best are the publications of the Hong Kong Film Archive and the Hong Kong International Film Festival. The latter published retrospectives in tandem with the film festival through 1997; in 1998 the panorama replaced the retrospectives. The retrospectives were themed studies with essays by scholars and critics and provided detailed information regarding films not often widely seen in the West. The panorama relates more specifically to the current festival and year of film production. The Hong Kong Film Archive publications replace the approach of the retrospectives and have taken on the challenge of building a complete Hong Kong film history. These include specific themed studies as well as a currently five-volume Hong Kong filmography (the fifth volume currently in Chinese only; the first two volumes published by the Urban Council and the Provisional Urban Council, respectively). The archive also publishes a newsletter. Its website, at sc.lcsd.gov.hk/gb/www.csd.gov.hk/CE/CulturalService/HKFA/english/archivefct.html, provides excellent information. Furthermore, the Hong Kong Film Critics Society website can be found at www.filmcritics.org.hk/index1.php?ver=en. It includes current film reviews by local critics, an archive, and links.

In recent years, many interesting and intellectually challenging academic book-length studies on the general subject of Chinese and Hong Kong cinema have appeared. Specifically mentioned below are invaluable resources available in English (listed alphabetically).

Book-length studies: Ackbar Abbas's *Hong Kong: Culture and the Politics of Disappearance* (1997) addresses film, architecture, photography, and writing, but uses Wong Kar-wai to analyze Hong Kong cinema in a space of disappearance; David Bordwell's *Planet Hong Kong: Popular*

Cinema and the Art of Entertainment (2000) analyzes the aesthetics of Hong Kong cinema from the 1970s through the 1990s; Rey Chow's *Primitive Passions: Visuality, Sexuality, Ethnography, and Contemporary Chinese Cinema* (1995) focuses on Fifth Generation Mainland films but makes references to Hong Kong, and her approach provides food for thought regarding Hong Kong cinema; Yingchi Chu's *Hong Kong Cinema: Coloniser, Motherland, and Self* (2003) covers Hong Kong cinema from 1913 to post-1997 by examining different political formations of Hong Kong culture based on its status as a quasi nation with motherland (China) and colonizer (Britain); Poshek Fu's *Between Shanghai and Hong Kong: The Politics of Chinese Cinemas* (2003) is a pioneering work examining the complex interconnections between the film worlds of Hong Kong and Shanghai, 1935–1950, including information on films widely unseen in the West; Law Kar and Frank Bren's *Hong Kong Cinema: A Cross-Cultural View* (2004) is an excellent examination of cross-cultural Eastern and Western influences on Hong Kong cinema from its beginnings through the 1970s, providing a foundation for examination of films since; John Lent's work on Asian cinema is monumental, including years of research and interviews. His *The Asian Film Industry* (1990) provides a succinct and informative chapter on the Hong Kong film industry; likewise his *Asian Popular Culture* (1995) does the same with film; and, as editor, his *Animation in Asia and the Pacific* (2001) offers much needed information on Hong Kong animation. Gina Marchetti's *From Tian'anmen to Times Square: Transnational China and the Chinese Diaspora on Global Screens, 1989–1997* (2006) explores the impact of globalism and the contradictions between race, ethnicity, class, nationality, and gender as visualized on-screen in various Chinese cinemas, including Hong Kong. Lisa Odham Stokes and Michael Hoover's *City on Fire: Hong Kong Cinema* (1999) situates Hong Kong cinema in a social, economic, political, and cultural context, with succinct chapters on Hong Kong and film history, but focusing on films from the 1980s and 1990s; Kwok-kan Tam and Wilmal Dissanayake's *New Chinese Cinema* (1998), in the Images of Asia series, analyzes the work of six Chinese directors as innovators of form and style, including Hong Kong's Stanley Kwan; and, last, but certainly not least, is Stephen Teo's *Hong Kong Cinema: The Extra Dimensions* (1997), which narrates the whole of Hong Kong film history from 1909 to the end of the 1990s, provides brief analyses of innumerable films, and anticipates the "end of Hong Kong cinema" as the former colony returned to the Mainland.

Edited collections: Nick Browne et al.'s *New Chinese Cinemas: Forms, Identities, Politics* (1994) covers 1980s filmmaking trends as social documentation of Chinese cinemas; Poshek Fu and David Desser's *The Cinema of Hong Kong: History, Arts, Identity* (2000) provides transnational, cultural, and political context for Hong Kong films pre–World War II through the 1990s. Esther C. M. Yau's *At Full Speed: Hong Kong Cinema in a Borderless World* (2001) explores the repercussions of rapid circulation of Hong Kong films in a global culture by examining Hong Kong's New Wave, action cinema, and the resultant nostalgia, nonsense, and dislocation, is rigorously laid out, and offers provocative imaginings for the global future; and *Hong Kong Connections: Transnational Imagination in Action Cinema* (2005), edited by Meaghan Morris, Siu-leung Li, and Stephen Chan Ching-kiu, although limited to the action genre, examines various cultural contexts and the problematics of transnational study.

Several books have so far addressed individual directors, including Kenneth E. Hall's *John Woo the Films* (1999); Jean-Marc Lalanne's et al., *Wong Kar-Wai* (1997); Lisa Morton's *The Cinema of Tsui Hark* (2001); and Stephen Teo's *Wong Kar-Wai* (2005), in BFI's World Directors series. Furthermore, book-length studies of individual films are beginning to appear. A New Hong Kong Cinema Series began in 2003, published by Hong Kong University Press and providing in-depth analysis of individual contemporary Hong Kong films. Also Chris Berry edited a collection of close Chinese film reads, *Chinese Films in Focus: 25 New Takes* (2003).

The most comprehensive and focused scholarly journal is *Asian Cinema*, the publication of the Asian Cinema Studies Society. For many years, *Cinemaya: The Asian Film Quarterly* (India) published; in early 2005, it merged with Osian's Connoisseurs of Art, becoming *Osian's Cinemaya: The Asian Film Quarterly*; the current format includes shorter articles but numerous color photos and provides extensive Asian film festival coverage. Other English-language film periodicals that regularly address Hong Kong cinema include *Cineaction* (Canada);

Film Comment: *Film Quarterly*; and *Sight and Sound* (UK). David Chute's special section in *Film Comment*, "Made in Hong Kong" (1998), serves as a good introduction to contemporary Hong Kong cinema since the New Wave began. Chute is currently writing a book on Hong Kong martial arts movies. At *Sight and Sound,* Tony Rayns specializes in Asian cinema, especially Hong Kong. At *The Nation,* Stuart Klawans regularly reviews Hong Kong films playing in New York.

Books of interviews with directors and actors available include Fredric Dannen and Barry Long's *Hong Kong Babylon: An Insider's Guide to the Hollywood of the East* (1997), Miles Wood's *Cine East: Hong Kong Cinema through the Looking Glass* (1998), and Michael Berry's *Speaking in Images: Interviews with Contemporary Chinese Filmmakers* (2005). The latter includes Hong Kong directors Evans Chan, Fruit Chan, Peter Chan, Ann Hui, and Stanley Kwan. Jackie Chan has written an autobiography with Jeff Yang, *I Am Jackie Chan: My Life in Action* (1998), and cinematographer Chris Doyle has published collections of his on-set photography as well as an enlightening journal of the shooting of Wong Kar-wai's *Happy Together*, "Don't Try for Me, Argentina" in Faber and Faber's Projection series (1998). Expatriate film critic Paul Fonoroff's *At the Hong Kong Movies* (1998) conveniently collects 600 of his Hong Kong film reviews from 1988 to the return.

To date, a single encyclopedia of Chinese film exists, which covers all the Chinas, namely editor Yingjin Zhing's *Encyclopedia of Chinese Film* (1998). Bill Palmer, Karen Palmer, and Ric Meyer's *The Encyclopedia of Martial Arts Movies* (2003) includes entries on hundreds of martial arts movies.

Hong Kong movies have large fan bases internationally and there are numerous popular books available. To mention only a few useful ones: Bey Logan's *Hong Kong Action Cinema* (1995) was one of the first, which zeroes in on action, discussing martial arts and gangster films, with numerous black-and-white and color photos. Rick Baker and Toby Russell's *The Essential Guide to Hong Kong Movies* (1994) and Thomas Weisser's *Asian Cult Cinema* (1997) both provide brief reviews and ratings of hundreds of Hong Kong movies, primarily action from the 1960s to the 1990s. Also available is Brian Thomas's *Videohound's*

Dragon: Asian Action and Cult Flicks (2003) along the same lines. John Charles's *The Hong Kong Filmography, 1977–1997: A Complete Reference to 1,100 Films Produced by British Hong Kong Studios* (2003) includes complete credits and lengthier reviews, also rating the movies. Jeff Yang's *Once upon a Time in China: A Guide to Hong Kong, Taiwanese, and Mainland Chinese Cinema* (2003) follows the history of Chinese cinemas, including more than 300 movies in the narration. Among the magazines, Thomas Weisser's *Asian Cult Cinema* most consistently covers Hong Kong movies. *Impact: The Ultimate Action Magazine* (UK) regularly includes a "China Beat" segment.

Information, certainly not all of the same quality, abounds on the Web. Some recommended sources: The Hong Kong Movie Database maintained by Ryan Law out of Hong Kong at www.hkmdb.com contains one of the most complete databases for searching Hong Kong movies. The other is Lu Pin's Chinese Movie Database, which covers all Chinese film, at www.dianying.com/. Other sites contain articles and numerous reviews of Hong Kong movies. For example, Kungfu Cinema at www.kungfucinema.com includes reviews, interviews, and current news of everything martial arts action. Love Hong Kong Film at www.lovehkfilm.com provides reviews and some news. Several online journals pay special attention to Hong Kong cinema. The Illuminated Lantern at www.illuminatedlantern.com/cinema offers some lengthy articles and reviews, as does Senses of Cinema at www.sensesofcinema.com, which provides numerous thoughtful and lengthy essays and is devoted to "serious and eclectic discussion of film." The Bright Lights Film Journal, at www.brightlights.com, likewise has lengthier essays and devotes a special section to Hong Kong cinema. Hong Kong Entertainment News in Review at www.hkentreview.com presents current Hong Kong entertainment news both local and international, with numerous links to sources, as well as reviews. Likewise Jerry's SAR Hong Kong Film Top 10 at www.geocities.com/Tokyo/Towers/2038/. Shelly Kraicer's Chinese Cinema Page at chinesecinemas.org is highly recommended for its insightful analyses of Hong Kong and other Chinese film.

Abbas, Ackbar. *Hong Kong: Culture and the Politics of Disappearance*. Minneapolis: University of Minnesota Press, 1997.

Atkinson, Michael. "Songs of Crushed Love: The Cinema of Stanley Kwan." *Film Comment* 32, no. 3 (May–June 1996): 42–49.

Baker, Rick, and Toby Russell. *The Essential Guide to Hong Kong Movies*. London: Eastern Heroes Publications, 1994.

———. *The Essential Guide to the Best of Eastern Heroes*. London: Eastern Heroes Publications, 1995.

Berry, Chris, ed. *Chinese Films in Focus: 25 New Takes*. London: BFI Publishing, 2003.

———. *Perspectives on Chinese Cinema*. London: BFI Publishing, 1991.

Berry, Michael. *Speaking in Images: Interviews with Contemporary Chinese Filmmakers*. New York: Columbia University Press, 2005.

Bliss, Michael. *Between the Bullets: The Spiritual Cinema of John Woo*. Lanham, Md.: Scarecrow Press, 2002.

Bordwell, David. *Planet Hong Kong: Popular Cinema and the Art of Entertainment*. Cambridge, Mass.: Harvard University Press, 2000.

Braester, Yomi. "Modern Identity and Karmic Retribution in Clara Law's *Reincarnation of the Golden Lotus*." *Asian Cinema* 10, no. 1 (Fall 1998): 58–61.

Brown, Judith, and Rosemary Foot, eds. *Hong Kong's Transitions*. New York: St. Martin's, 1997.

Browne, Nick, et al., eds. *New Chinese Cinemas: Forms, Identities, Politics*. New York: Cambridge University Press, 1994.

Chan, Jackie (with Jeff Yang). *I Am Jackie Chan: My Life in Action*. New York: Ballantine, 1998.

Charles, John. *The Hong Kong Filmography, 1977–1997: A Complete Reference to 1,100 Films Produced by British Hong Kong Studios*. Jefferson, N.C.: McFarland, 2003.

Chow, Rey. "Between Colonizers: Hong Kong's Post-Colonial Self-Writing in the 1990s." *Diaspora* 2 (1992): 151–70.

———. *Primitive Passions: Visuality, Sexuality, Ethnography, and Contemporary Chinese Cinema*. New York: Columbia University Press, 1995.

———. "A Souvenir of Love." *Modern Chinese Literature* 7, no. 2 (Fall 1993): 59–78.

Chu, Yingchi. *Hong Kong Cinema: Coloniser, Motherland and Self*. London: Routledge Curzon, 2003.

Chua, Siew Keng. "The Politics of 'Home': *Song of the Exile*." *Jump Cut* 42: 90–93.

Chute, David. "Made in Hong Kong." *Film Comment* 24, no. 3 (1998): 33–56.

———, and Cheng-Sim Ling, eds. *Heroic Grace: The Chinese Martial Arts Film*. Los Angeles: UCLA Film and Television Archive, 2003.

Clouse, Robert. *The Making of "Enter the Dragon."* Burbank, Calif.: Unique Publications, 1987.

Collier, Joelle. "A Repetition Compulsion: Discontinuity Editing, Classical Chinese Aesthetics, and Hong Kong's Culture of Disappearance." *Asian Cinema* 10, no. 2 (Spring/Summer 1999): 67–79.

Dancer, Greg. "Film Style and Performance: Comedy and Kung Fu from Hong Kong." *Asian Cinema* 10, no. 1 (Fall 1998): 42–50.

Dannen, Fredric, and Barry Long. *Hong Kong Babylon: An Insider's Guide to the Hollywood of the East*. London: Faber and Faber, 1997.

Davis, Darrell W., and Yeh Yueh-yu. "Warning! Category III." *Film Quarterly* 54 (2001): 12–26.

Dissanayke, Wilmal, ed. *Melodrama and Asian Cinema*. Cambridge: Cambridge University Press, 1993.

———. *Wong Kar-Wai's Ashes of Time*. Hong Kong: Hong Kong University Press, 2003.

Doyle, Christopher. *Backlit by the Moon*. Tokyo: Little More, 1996.

———. *A Cloud in Trousers*. Santa Monica, Calif.: Smart Art Press, 1998.

———. "Don't Try for Me, Argentina." In *Projections 8: Filmmakers on Filmmaking*. Ed. John Boorman and Walter Donohue. London: Faber and Faber, 1998, 155–82.

———. "Hong Kong Dreaming [Interviewed by Ben Walters about Wong Karwai's *2046*]." *Sight and Sound* (April 2005): 86.

Fang, Karen. *John Woo's* A Better Tomorrow. Hong Kong: Hong Kong University Press, 2004.

Fonoroff, Paul. *At the Hong Kong Movies: 600 Reviews from 1988 till the Handover*. New York: Norton, 1998.

———. "Orientation." *Film Comment* (May–June 1988): 52–56.

———. *Silver Light: A Pictorial History of Hong Kong Cinema 1920–1970*. Hong Kong: Joint Publishing, 1997.

Fore, Steve. "Golden Harvest Films and the Hong Kong Movie Industry in the Realm of Globalization." *The Velvet Light Trap*, no. 34 (Fall 1994): 40–58.

Fu, Poshek. *Between Shanghai and Hong Kong: The Politics of Chinese Cinemas*. Stanford, Calif.: Stanford University Press, 2003.

———. "Eileen Chang, Woman's Film, and Domestic Shanghai in the 1940s." *Asian Cinema* 11, no. 1 (Spring/Summer 2000): 97–113.

———, and David Desser, eds. *The Cinema of Hong Kong: History, Arts, Identity*. Cambridge: Cambridge University Press, 2000.

Fu, Winnie, ed. *Fame Flame Frame: Jupiter Wong Foto Exhibition Catalogue*. Hong Kong: Hong Kong Film Archive, 2005.

———. *Hong Kong Filmography Vol. 1 1913–1941*. Hong Kong: Hong Kong Film Archive, 1997.

———. *Hong Kong Filmography Vol. 2 1942–1949*. Hong Kong: Hong Kong Film Archive, 1998.

——. *Hong Kong Filmography Vol. 3 1950–1952*. Hong Kong: Hong Kong Film Archive, 2000.

——. *Hong Kong Filmography Vol. 4 1953–1959*. Hong Kong: Hong Kong Film Archive, 2001.

Gentry, Clyde, III. *Jackie Chan: Inside the Dragon*. Dallas, Tex.: Taylor Publishing Company, 1997.

Glaessner, Verina. *Kung Fu: Cinema of Vengeance*. New York: Crown, 1974.

Hall, Kenneth E. *John Woo: The Films*. Jefferson, N.C.: McFarland, 1999.

——. "Hong Kong 1997: Mexico, 1917. Motifs and Historical Perspective." *Asian Cinema* 10, no. 1 (Fall 1998): 51–57.

Hammond, Stefan. *Hollywood East: Hong Kong Movies and the People Who Make Them*. Chicago: Lincolnwood Books, 2000.

——, and Mike Wilkins. Sex and Zen *and* A Bullet in the Head. New York: Simon & Schuster, 1996.

Hampton, Howard. "Venus, Armed: Brigitte Lin's Shanghai Gesture." *Film Comment* 32, no. 5 (1996): 42–48.

Hitchcock, Lori. "Transnational Film and the Politics of Becoming: Negotiating East Asian Identity in *Hong Kong Night Club* and *Moonlight Express*." *Asian Cinema* 13, no. 1 (Spring/Summer 2002): 67–86.

Ho, Sam, ed. *The Cathay Story*. Hong Kong: Hong Kong Film Archive, 2002.

——, ed. *The Swordsman and His Jiang Hu: Tsui Hark and Hong Kong Film*. Hong Kong: Hong Kong Film Archive, 2002.

Hong Kong Film Archive. *@Location.* Hong Kong: Hong Kong Film Archive, 2006.

——. *A Century of Chinese Cinema: Look Back in Glory*. Hong Kong: Hong Kong Film Archive, 2001.

——. *The Diary of Lai Man-wai.* Hong Kong: Hong Kong Film Archive, 2003.

——. *Director Chor Yuen.* Hong Kong: Hong Kong Film Archive, 2006.

——. *The Glorious Modernity of Kong Ngee.* Hong Kong: Hong Kong Film Archive, 2006.

——. *Hong Kong Cinema from Handicraft to High Tech*. Hong Kong: Hong Kong Film Archive, 2001.

——. *Hong Kong Film Archive Treasures: An Exhibition*. Hong Kong: Provisional Urban Council, 1998.

——. *Hong Kong on the Silver Screen*. Hong Kong: Hong Kong Film Archive, 2001.

——. *I-Generations: Independent, Experimental and Alternative Creations from the 60s to Now*. Hong Kong: Hong Kong Film Archive, 2001.

——. *The Making of Martial Arts Films—As Told by Filmmakers and Stars*. Hong Kong: Provisional Urban Council, 1999.

Hong Kong International Film Festival (HKIFF). *Border Crossings in Hong Kong Cinema.* Provisional Urban Council, 2000.
———. *Cantonese Cinema Retrospective, 1950–1959*. Hong Kong: Urban Council, 1978.
———. *Cantonese Cinema Retrospective, 1960–1969*. Hong Kong: Urban Council, 1982.
———. *Cantonese Melodrama, 1950–1969*. Hong Kong: Urban Council, 1986.
———. *Cantonese Opera Film Retrospective*. Hong Kong: Urban Council, 1987.
———. *Changes in Hong Kong Society through Cinema*. Hong Kong: Urban Council, 1988.
———. *The China Factor in Hong Kong Cinema*. Hong Kong: Urban Council, 1990.
———. *Cinema of Two Cities: Hong Kong–Shanghai*. Hong Kong: Urban Council, 1994.
———. *A Comparative Study of Post-War Mandarin and Cantonese Cinema: The Films of Zhu Shilin, Qin Jian and Other Directors*. Hong Kong: Urban Council, 1983.
———. *Early Images of Hong Kong & China*. Hong Kong: Urban Council, 1995.
———. *Fifty Years of Electric Shadows*. Hong Kong: Urban Council, 1997.
———. *Hong Kong Cinema in the Eighties*. Hong Kong: Urban Council, 1991.
———. *Hong Kong Cinema Survey, 1946–1968*. Hong Kong: Urban Council, 1979.
———. *Hong Kong Contemporary Cinema*. Hong Kong: Urban Council, 1982.
———. *Hong Kong New Wave—Twenty Years After*. Hong Kong: Provisional Urban Council, 1999.
———. *Hong Kong Panorama 96–97.* Hong Kong: Urban Council, 1997.
———. *Hong Kong Panorama 97–98*. Hong Kong: Provisional Urban Council, 1998.
———. *Hong Kong Panorama 98–99*. Hong Kong: Provisional Urban Council, 1999.
———. *Hong Kong Panorama 1999–2000*. Hong Kong: Provisional Urban Council, 2000.
———. *Hong Kong Panorama 2000–2001*. Hong Kong: Provisional Urban Council, 2001.
———. *Hong Kong Panorama 2001–2002*. Hong Kong: Provisional Urban Council, 2002.
———. *Mandarin Films and Popular Songs: '40s–'60s*. Hong Kong: Urban Council, 1993.
———. *Overseas Chinese Figures in Cinema.* Hong Kong: Urban Council, 1992.

——. *Phantoms of the Hong Kong Cinema*. Hong Kong: Urban Council, 1989.

——. *The Restless Breed: Cantonese Stars of the Sixties*. Hong Kong: Urban Council, 1996.

——. *A Study of Hong Kong Cinema in the Seventies*. Hong Kong: Urban Council, 1984.

——. *A Study of the Hong Kong Swordplay Film, 1940–1980*. Hong Kong: Urban Council, 1981.

——. *A Survey of the Hong Kong Martial Arts Film*. Hong Kong: Urban Council, 1980.

——. *Ten Years of Hong Kong Cinema*. Hong Kong: Urban Council, 1986.

——. *The Traditions of Hong Kong Comedy*. Hong Kong: Urban Council, 1985.

——. *Transcending the Times: King Hu and Eileen Chang*. Hong Kong: Provisional Urban Council, 1998.

——. *The 20th Anniversary of the Hong Kong International Film Festival, 1977–1996*. Hong Kong: Urban Council, 1996.

——. *William Chang, Art Director.* Hong Kong: Hong Kong International Film Festival Society, 2004.

Hu, Gigi Tze Yue. "Hong Kong Animation: My Life as McDull." *Asian Cinema* 14, no. 1 (Spring/Summer 2003): 80–89.

Hwang, Ange. "The Irresistible Hong Kong Movie *Once upon a Time in China* Series—An Extensive Interview with Direction/Producer Tsui Hark." *Asian Cinema* 10, no. 1 (Fall 1998): 10–24.

Jarvie, I[an] C. *Window on Hong Kong: A Sociological Study of the Hong Kong Film Industry and Its Audience.* Hong Kong: Hong Kong University, 1977.

Kaplan, E. Ann, and Ban Wang, eds. *Trauma and Cinema: Cross-Cultural Explorations.* Hong Kong: Hong Kong University Press, 2004.

Klawans, Stuart. "Gangs of Shanghai." *The Nation*, April 18, 2005: 35.

——. "Urban and Other Anomies." *The Nation*, March 4, 1996: 35.

Kwok, Ching-ling, ed. *Monographs of Hong Kong Film Veterans Hong Kong Here I Come*. Volume 1. Hong Kong: Hong Kong Film Archive, 2000.

Kwok, Jenny Wah-lau. "Besides Fists and Blood: Hong Kong Comedy and Its Master of the Eighties." *Cinema Journal* 37 (Winter 1998): 18–34.

LaDue, Gere. "A Look at Some Western Misconceptions and Misunderstandings about Hong Kong Film." *Cineraider* 2 (June 1994): 43–46.

Lalanne, Jean-Marc, et al. *Wong Kar-Wai*. Paris: Editions Dis Voir, 1997.

Lam, Michael, ed. *A Yam Kim-Fai Reader*. Hong Kong: Hong Kong Film Archive, 2005.

Law, Kar, and Frank Bren. *Hong Kong Cinema: A Cross-Cultural View*. Lanham, Md.: Scarecrow Press, 2004.

Law, Kar, and Stephanie Ng. *Shaws Galaxy of Stars*. Hong Kong: Hong Kong Film Archive, 2003.

Lee, Bono, and Li Cheuk-to, eds. *William Chang, Art Director*. Hong Kong: Hong Kong International Film Festival Society, 2004.

Lee, Nathan. "Elusive Objects of Desire [Wong Kar-wai's *2046*]." *Film Comment* July/August 2005: 31–32.

Lee, Vivian. "Cinematic Remembrances: The Search for Local Histories in Post-1997 Films by Ann Hui and Fruit Chan." *Asian Cinema* 16, no. 1 (Spring/Summer 2005): 263–85.

Lent, John A., ed. *Animation in Asia and the Pacific*. Bloomington: Indiana University Press, 2001.

———. *The Asian Film Industry*. Austin: University of Texas Press, 1990.

———, ed. *Asian Popular Culture*. Boulder, Colo.: Westview, 1995.

Leyda, Jay. *Dianying: An Account of Films and the Film Audience in China*. Cambridge: Cambridge University Press, 1972.

Li, Cheuk-to. "Political Censorship: The Fatal Blow." *Cinemaya* 4 (1989): 42–45.

———. "Tsui Hark and Western Interest in Hong Kong Cinema." *Cinemaya* 21 (1993): 50–51.

Little, John R., and Curtis F. Wong, ed. *Jackie Chan: The Best of Inside Kung-Fu*. Chicago: Contemporary Books, 1999.

Lo, Kwai-cheung. *Chinese Face/Off: The Transnational Popular Culture of Hong Kong*. Urbana: Univeristy of Illinois Press, 2005.

Logan, Bey. *Hong Kong Action Cinema*. Woodstock, N.Y.: Overlook Press, 1995.

Lu, Sheldon Hsiao-peng, ed. *Transnational Chinese Cinemas: Identity, Nationhood, Gender.* Honolulu: University of Hawaii Press, 1997.

Magal, Uma. "At One with the Other: An Examination of John Woo's Vision Climaxing in *Face/Off*." *Asian Cinema* 10, no. 2 (Spring/Summer 1999): 80–86.

Marchetti, Gina. *From Tian'anmen to Times Square: Transnational China and the Chinese Diaspora on Global Screens, 1989-1997.* Philadelphia: Temple Univeristy Press, 2006.

———. *Romance and the "Yellow Peril": Race, Sex, and Discursive Strategies in Hollywood Fiction*. Berkeley: University of California Press, 1993.

McDonagh, Maitland. "Action Painter: John Woo." *Film Comment* 29, no. 5 (1993): 46–49.

———. "Things I Felt Were Being Lost." *Film Comment* 29, no. 5 (1993): 50–52.

Meyers, Richard. *Great Martial Arts Movies: From Bruce Lee to Jackie Chan and More*. New York: Citadel Press, 2001.

Morris, Meaghan, Siu-leung Li, and Stephen Chan Ching-kiu, eds. *Hong Kong Connections: Transnational Imagination in Action Cinema*. Hong Kong: Hong Kong University Press, 2005.

Morrison, Susan. "John Woo, Wong Kar-wai, and Me: An Ethnographic Mediation." *Cineaction* 36 (Feb. 1995): 37–41.

Morton, Lisa. *The Cinema of Tsui Hark*. Jefferson, N.C.: McFarland, 2001.

Palmer, Bill, Karen Palmer, and Ric Meyers. *The Encyclopedia of Martial Arts Movies*. Lanham, Md.: Scarecrow Press, 2003.

Pang, Laikwan, and Day Wong, eds. *Masculinities and Hong Kong Cinema.* Hong Kong: Hong Kong University Press, 2005.

Rayns, Tony. "Hard-Boiled." *Sight and Sound*, August 1992, 20–23.

———. "The Long Goodbye [Wong Kar-wai's *2046*]." *Sight and Sound*, January 2005, 22–25.

———. "Poet of Time [Wong Kar-wai]." *Sight and Sound*, September 1995, 12–16.

Reid, Craig D. "Interview with Tsui Hark." *Film Quarterly* 48 (1995): 34–41.

Rist, Peter. "Neglected 'Classical' Periods: Hong Kong and Korean Cinemas of the 1960s." *Asian Cinema* 12, no. 1 (Spring/Summer 2001): 49–66.

Schneider, Steven Jay, ed. *Fear without Frontiers: Horror Cinema across the Globe*. Surrey, England: FAB Press, 2003.

Schroeder, Andrew. *Tsui Hark's* Zu: Warriors from the Magic Mountain. Hong Kong: Hong Kong University Press, 2004.

Sharrett, Christopher, ed. *Mythologies of Violence in Postmodern Media*. Detroit, Mich.: Wayne State University Press, 1998.

Stevens, Chuck. "Time Pieces: Wong Kar-wai and the Persistence of Memory." *Film Comment* 32, no. 1 (1996): 12–18.

Stokes, Lisa Odham. "An Interview with Tony Leung Ka-fai." *Asian Cult Cinema* 46: 52–61.

———. "Spending Time with Yu: A Special Interview with Ronny Yu." *Asian Cult Cinema* 41: 47–62.

———. "Wong Kar-wai's *In the Mood for Love* as Pure Mood Poem." *Tamkang Review* 32, no. 2 (Winter 2002): 127–49.

———, and Michael Hoover. "At the Hong Kong Hop: *Mr. Vampire* Spawns Bloodsucking Genre." *Paradoxa* no. 17 (2002): 68–76.

———. *City on Fire: Hong Kong Cinema*. New York: Verso Press, 1999.

———. "A *City on Fire*: Hong Kong Cinema as Cultural Logic of Late Capitalism." *Asian Cinema* 10, no. 1 (Fall 1998): 25–41.

———. "Donnie Yen: An Exclusive Interview." *Asian Cult Cinema* 29: 48–62.

———. "Food Fight, Food Fight: Culture and Economy in *Chicken and Duck Talk*." *Asian Cinema* 14, no. 2 (Fall/Winter 2003): 170–79.

———. "Hong Kong in New York." *New Political Science* 25, no. 4 (December 2003): 509–32.

———. "Hong Kong to Hollywood." *Cinemaya* (Winter 1999): 30–39.

———. "An Interview with Anthony Wong." *Asian Cult Cinema* 30 (2001): 4–14.

——. "An Interview with Herman Yau." *Asian Cult Cinema* 35 (2002): 33–45.

——. "Kirk Wong's Hong Kong Crimes." *Asian Cinema* 13, no. 2 (Fall/Winter 2002): 76–84.

——. "Like Father, Like Son: Yuen Wo-ping's *Iron Monkey* and the Evolution of Wong Fei-hung." *Asian Cinema* 12, no. 2 (Fall/Winter 2001): 110–18.

——. "Resisting the Stage: Imaging/Imagining Ruan Lingyu in Stanley Kwan's *Actress*." *Asian Cinema* 11, no. 2 (Fall/Winter 2000): 92–98.

Stokes, Tyler. "Rapacious Raptors and Global Technocrats in [Tsui Hark's] *The Wicked City*." *Asian Cinema* 16, no. 1 (Spring/Summer 2005): 339–45.

Stringer, Julian. "*Centre Stage*: Reconstructing the Bio-Pic." *Cineaction* 42 (1997): 28–39.

——. "Problems with the Treatment of Hong Kong Cinema as Camp." *Asian Cinema* 8, no. 2 (1996/1997): 44–65.

Sun, Shirley. "A Hong Kong Formula for Hollywood Success." *Asia* (November–December 1982): 38–43.

Tam, Kwok-kan, and Wimal Dissanayake. *New Chinese Cinema*. Oxford: Oxford University Press, 1998.

Tambling, Jeremy. *Wong Kar-Wai's Happy Together*. Hong Kong: Hong Kong University Press, 2003.

Tan, See-kam. "The Hong Kong Cantonese Vernacular as Cultural Resistance." *Cinemaya* 20 (July–September 1993): 12–15.

Tateishi, Ramie. "Jackie Chan and the Re-invention of Tradition." *Asian Cinema* 10, no. 1 (Fall 1998): 78–85.

Taubin, Amy. "The Long Goodbye [Wong Kar-wai's *2046*]." *Film Comment* July/August 2005: 26–29.

Teo, Stephen. *Hong Kong Cinema: The Extra Dimensions*. London: BFI Publishing, 1997.

——. "The Hong Kong New Wave Before and After." *Cinemaya* 23 (1994): 28–32.

——. *Wong Kar-wai*. London: BFI Publishing, 2005.

Thomas, Brian. *Videohound's Dragon: Asian Action and Cult Flicks*. Detroit, Mich.: Visible Ink Press, 2003.

Tilden, N. A. *Early Images of Hong Kong and China*. Hong Kong: 1995.

Tsui, Curtis K. "Subjective Culture and History: The Ethnographic Cinema of Wong Kar-wai." *Asian Cinema* 7, no. 2 (1995): 93–124.

Wang, Shujen. "*Big Shot's Funeral*: China, Sony, and the WTO." *Asian Cinema* 14, no. 2 (Fall/Winter 2003): 145–54.

Webster, Andy. "Duel Nature." *Premiere*, July 1997, 62–65, 99.

Weisser, Thomas. *Asian Cult Cinema*. New York: Boulevard Books, 1997.

Williams, Tony. "Apocalyptic Chaos in *Tiger Cage*." *Asian Cinema* 9, no. 2 (Spring 1998): 29–37.

——. "Border-Crossing Melodrama: *Song of the Exile*." *Jump Cut* 42 (December 1998): 94–100.

——. "*Crossings*: A Transnational Cinematic Text." *Asian Cinema* 11, no. 2 (Fall/Winter 2000): 67–75.

——. "From Hong Kong to Hollywood: John Woo and His Discontents." *Cineaction* 42 (1997): 40–46.

——. "Hong Kong Cinema, the Boat People, and *To Liv(e)*." *Asian Cinema* 11, no. 1 (Spring/Summer 2000): 131–43.

——. "Hong Kong Social Horror: Tragedy and Farce in Category 3." *Post Script* 21 (June 2002): 61–71.

——. "Kwan Tak-Hing and the New Generation." *Asian Cinema* 10, no. 1 (Fall 1998): 71–77.

——. "Michelle Yeoh: Under Eastern Eyes." *Asian Cinema* 12, no. 2 (Fall/Winter 2001): 119–31.

——. "Space, Place and Spectacle: The Crisis Cinema of John Woo." *Cinema Journal* 36, no. 2 (1997): 67–84.

——. "To Live and Die in Hong Kong: The Crisis Cinema of John Woo." *Cineaction* 36 (1995): 42–52.

——. "Tony Leung Ka-Fai: The Other Tony Leung." *Asian Cinema* 16, no. 1 (Spring/Summer 2005): 239–62.

——. "Transnational Stardom: The Case of Maggie Cheung Man-yuk." *Asian Cinema* 14, no. 2 (Fall/Winter 2003): 180–96.

Wong, Ain-ling, ed. *The Cinema of Lee Sun-fung*. Hong Kong: Hong Kong Film Archive, 2004.

——. *The Hong Kong–Guangdong Film Connection*. Hong Kong: Hong Kong Film Archive, 2005.

——. *Monographs of Hong Kong Film Veterans. An Age of Idealism: Great Wall and Feng Huang Days: Volume 2*. Hong Kong: Hong Kong Film Archive, 2001.

——. *The Shaw Screen: A Preliminary Study*. Hong Kong: Hong Kong Film Archive, 2003.

Wong, Ain-ling, et al., eds. *Chang Cheh: A Memoir*. Hong Kong: Hong Kong Film Archive, 2004.

Wood, Miles. *Cine East: Hong Kong through the Looking Glass*. Guilford, Surrey: FAB Press, 1998.

Yang, Jeff, et al. *Eastern Standard Time: A Guide to Asian Influence on American Culture*. Boston: Houghton Mifflin, 1997.

Yang, Jeff. *Once Upon a Time in China: A Guide to Hong Kong, Taiwanese, and Mainland Chinese Cinema.* New York: Atria Books, 2003.

Yau, Esther C. M., ed. *At Full Speed: Hong Kong Cinema in a Borderless World*. Minneapolis: University of Minnesota Press, 2001.

Zhang, Yingjin. *The City in Modern Chinese Literature and Film: Configurations of Space, Time, and Gender.* Stanford, Calif.: Stanford University Press, 1996.

——, ed. *Encyclopedia of Chinese Film*. London: Routledge, 1998.

Zhou, Juanita Huan. "*Ashes of Time*: The Tragedy and Salvation of the Chinese Intelligentsia." *Asian Cinema* 10, no. 1 (Fall 1998): 62–70.

About the Author and Contributors

Lisa Odham Stokes teaches Humanities and Film at Seminole Community College in Central Florida, where she sees the classroom as a site of contested terrain. She earned a BA, summa cum laude, from Emory University; an MA from the University of North Carolina at Chapel Hill; and a Ph.D. from the University of Florida, all literature degrees. She is coauthor (with Michael Hoover) of *City on Fire: Hong Kong Cinema* (Verso Press), and has authored numerous articles on film, music, and literature in various journals such as *Asian Cinema*, *Journal of American Culture*, *Journal of Third World Studies*, *Popular Music and Society*, and *Nature, Society, and Thought*. Her forthcoming book is *Peter Chan's He's a Woman, She's a Man* for the New Hong Kong Cinema series from Hong Kong University Press. She has been programming for the Florida Film Festival for many years.

Jean Lukitsh has studied Chinese martial arts with Master Bow Sim Mark for nearly three decades, and she worked as a projectionist in Boston's Chinatown from 1979 to 1986. She has contributed articles and reviews to *Inside Kung Fu* magazine and www.kungfucinema.com.

Michael Hoover is a professor of political science at Seminole Community College in Sanford, Florida. His writings have appeared in various academic journals, including *Asian Cinema*, *The Historian*, *Journal of Third World Studies*, *New Political Science*, *Popular Music and Society*, and *Nature, Society, and Thought*. He is coauthor (with Lisa Odham Stokes) of *City on Fire: Hong Kong Cinema* (1999) and serves on the editorial board of the journal *New Political Science*.

Tyler Stokes is majoring in Chinese Studies with a minor in Film Studies at Duke University. He has been watching Hong Kong films and television series since childhood and shares a vast knowledge of Hong Kong cinema. His first published article appeared in *Asian Cinema* in 2004.